Clement V led the Church during nine critical years, 1305–14. Elected two years after the outrage committed upon Boniface VIII at Anagni, Clement saw as his main goal the restoration of harmonious relations with the leading monarchs of Christendom. In achieving this aim, he paved the way for the Church in the modern period, when its authority was challenged less by the Holy Roman Empire than by the emerging national state. The notorious trial of the Templars was part of this difficult process of adaptation.

This book offers a complete analysis of Clement's pontificate from the two complementary viewpoints provided by diplomatic documentation and by narrative sources. Their point of convergence validates a re-evaluation of the Avignon period as the 'Babylonian captivity' of the papacy. As a result, Clement's pontificate no longer appears as a shameful surrender to Capetian interests. Rather, it demonstrates a consistent scale of priorities, among which the recovery of the Holy Land was accorded pre-eminence.

Cambridge Studies in Medieval Life and Thought

CLEMENT V

Cambridge Studies in Medieval Life and Thought
Fourth Series

General Editor:

D. E. LUSCOMBE

Leverhulme Personal Research Professor of Medieval History, University of Sheffield

Advisory Editors:

R. B. DOBSON

Professor of Medieval History, University of Cambridge, and Fellow of Christ's College

ROSAMOND McKITTERICK

Professor of Early Medieval European History, University of Cambridge, and Fellow of Newnham College

The series Cambridge Studies in Medieval Life and Thought was inaugurated by G. G. Coulton in 1921; Professor D. E. Luscombe now acts as General Editor of the Fourth Series, with Professors R. B. Dobson and Rosamond McKitterick as Advisory Editors. The series brings together outstanding work by medieval scholars over a wide range of human endeavour extending from political economy to the history of ideas.

For a list of titles in the series, see end of book.

CLEMENT V

SOPHIA MENACHE

CAMBRIDGE
UNIVERSITY PRESS

PUBLISHED BY THE PRESS SYNDICATE OF THE UNIVERSITY OF CAMBRIDGE
The Pitt Building, Trumpington Street, Cambridge CB2 1RP, United Kingdom

CAMBRIDGE UNIVERSITY PRESS
The Edinburgh Building, Cambridge CB2 2RU, United Kingdom
40 West 20th Street, New York, NY 10011-4211, USA
10 Stamford Road, Oakleigh, Melbourne 3166, Australia

First published 1998

Printed in the United Kingdom at the University Press, Cambridge

Typeset in 11/12 Monotype Bembo   [SE]

A catalogue record for this book is available from the British Library

Library of Congress Cataloguing in Publication data

Menache, Sophia.
Clement V / Sophia Menache.
p.   cm. – (Cambridge studies in medieval life and thought)
Includes bibliographical references and index.
ISBN 0 521 59219 4 hardback
1. Clement V, Pope, ca. 1260–1314.   2. Popes – Biography.
3. Papacy – History – 1309–1378.   I. Title.   II. Series.
BX1275.M46   1988
282′.092–dc21   97-27894 CIP

To Rami

CONTENTS

List of maps	*page* xi	
Foreword	xii	
List of abbreviations	xiv	
Introduction	1	
1 Clement V	6	
Bertrand de Got's early ecclesiastical career	6	
The election to the papacy	13	
Rome or Avignon?	23	
A personal portrait	30	
2 Church policy	35	
The papal curia	40	
The Church of England	54	
The Church of France	81	
3 Crusade and mission	101	
De recuperatione Terrae Sanctae	101	
The crusade at the Council of Vienne	112	
Charles de Valois and the crusade against Constantinople	119	
The *Reconquista*	121	
The borders of Christendom and mission	125	
4 Italy	129	
The Papal State	132	
Clement V and Henry VII	152	

Contents

5   France   174
    Flanders   180
    The trial of Boniface   191
    The canonisation of Pietro da Morrone   199
    The trial of the Templars   205

6   England   247
    Papal support in domestic affairs   249
    The Gaveston affair   256
    Relations with France   267
    Scotland   269
    The canonisation of Thomas de Cantilupe   275

7   The Council of Vienne and the *Clementinae*   279
    The Council of Vienne   281
    Church reform   284
    The *Clementinae*   288

    Afterword   306

    Bibliography   309
    Index   344

MAPS

1 Clement's sojourn in Languedoc   *page* 24
2 Dioceses of England and Wales   57
3 Dioceses of France   94
4 Italy in the fourteenth century   131

xi

FOREWORD

My first 'meeting' with Pope Clement V took place about thirty years ago, when as a young student I was studying the arrest of the Templars. My initial impression was that of a greedy, immoral pope, who fell easy prey to the endless ambition of Philip the Fair. As years went by and the excitement of my undergraduate years led to more meticulous research, I discovered that, notwithstanding the many studies on Clement V, uncertainty and ambiguity about his pontificate were still great and much work remained to be done. The present study was undertaken to meet the need for a reconsideration of prevailing premises in order to draw a more coherent picture of the pope and his pontificate.

The final version of this book was written during a sabbatical leave at Clare Hall, Cambridge. I would like to thank the College authorities for their kind hospitality, Gillian Beer, the president, in particular. Special thanks are also due to my colleagues, who invested precious time to improve and clarify obscure passages in the manuscript: Malcolm Barber, for his careful reading of the whole manuscript and for sharing with me his knowledge of 'our Templars'; Norman Housley and Tony Luttrell, for clarifying complex issues regarding the crusade and papal policy in Italy; Miri Rubin, for her constant support and providing an example of boundless energy; and Patrick Zutshi, whose wide knowledge of the Avignon papacy and whose careful use of terms served me as a guide. To all of them my deepest gratitude. My appreciation extends to David Abulafia, Marjorie Chibnall, Barry Dobson, Antonia Gransden, Jane Martindale, Rosamond McKitterick, and Gabrielle Spiegel, who supported me and generously offered their judicious advice. Special thanks to the general editor of this series, David Luscombe, whose comments have greatly improved the final version of this book, and to William Davies for his expeditious management of the publishing process.

It also gives me special pleasure to acknowledge the immense help I received from the staff of Cambridge University Library, whose scholarly advice, friendly attitude, and immense knowledge turned my many hours in the library into a stimulating intellectual experience. Finally, I am indebted to the University of Haifa Research Authority for research funds, to Daphna Benjamin for designing the maps, and to A. M. Goldstein, whose trained eye provided me, as always, with the most valuable editorial criticism.

This book is dedicated to my husband, Rami, whose constant support and encouragement helped make a dream become reality.

ABBREVIATIONS

CIC	*Corpus Iuris Canonici*
Concilia	*Sacrorum Conciliorum Nova et Amplissima Collectio*
FRG	*Fontes Rerum Germanicarum*
MGH	*Monumenta Germaniae Historica*
MGH, SS	*Monumenta Germaniae Historica: Scriptores*
PL	*Patrologiae cursus completus Series Latina*
PRO	Public Record Office
RHGF	*Recueil des historiens des Gaules et de la France*
RIS	*Rerum Italicarum Scriptores*
RS	*Rerum Britannicarum Medii Aevi Scriptores (Rolls Series)*
TRHS	*Transactions of the Royal Historical Society*

INTRODUCTION

The meeting point between past and new patterns of political behaviour makes the pontificate of Clement V (1305–14) an ideal case-study for research concerning the papacy and attitudes towards it in an era of transition. Of the many changes characteristic of the early fourteenth century, it is worth noting the consolidation of the western monarchies and the consistent involvement of the bourgeoisie in the political process. This evolution called for a re-assessment of past norms, first and foremost of the priorities of contemporaries as Christians and as members of the body politic. The choice was no longer between two universal factors, papacy and empire, but between apparently harmonious but actually conflicting loyalties; between a pope with universal claims journeying in southern France and national monarchs who, especially in France and England, were attempting to strengthen their respective standing as *advocatus ecclesiae*. Such a designation, especially for Philip the Fair and Edward I, hints at their status as equals, if not superiors, to the pope in the ecclesiastical affairs of their respective kingdoms. The expansion of the political arena to embrace the emerging bourgeoisie and the changing balance of power between *regnum* and *sacerdotium* turned appeal to propaganda into an integral part of the political process. From the perspective of papal leadership, it created new challenges with which to contend.

Notwithstanding the many studies devoted to Clement's pontificate, much remains to be done in order to find a suitable basis for analysing papal policy and the reactions to it. Generations of historians have fallen easy prey to some of the difficulties faced by fourteenth-century chroniclers in perceiving, let alone supporting papal policy. Many of the available studies actually echo a biased approach to Clement V and his policy. The trials of the Templars and of Boniface VIII, coupled with the pope's absence from Rome and what appeared to be a growing reliance on France and its king, often acquired the weight of unquestionable proof in turning Clement's pontificate into a main factor in the collapse of the medieval papacy. In contrast to Gregory VII and his proud successors, Clement V is often accused by historians of having submitted the papacy – whether willingly or not – to the boundless ambition of Philip the Fair. The criticism of papal policy, though most acute with regard to Clement V, touched his successors to the pontifical throne, as well. Thus, any historian who attempts to study the popes and the papal court during the so-called 'Avignon period' must deal frequently with their scandalous reputation, a characterisation that Petrarch encapsulated in his well-known expression 'Babylonian captivity of the papacy'.[1] Jean Christophe pointed to the national factor as the main catalyst for the prevailing negative, stereotyped attitudes towards the Avignon popes – French historians usually apologetic and Italians critical.[2] Historical research of the past 150 years, however, shows that a critical attitude towards Clement V goes beyond national boundaries. In this regard, James Muldoon represents a new, more moderate approach that has developed in recent years:

As research into the Avignon papacy continues, this era appears less and less as an aberration in the history of the papacy. More and more, the popes of Avignon can be seen as fitting within the mainstream of papal development during the Middle Ages. By continuing to employ and develop the institutional structure inherited from the thirteenth-century pontiffs, the Avignon popes automatically cast themselves in the same role that their predecessors had assumed. As a result, although it is common to view these popes as the antithesis of the reforming popes of the Gregorian era, it is important to realise that they saw themselves as continuing in that tradition.[3]

It is the thesis of this book that the papacy, though relying in the main on divine will and canonical exegesis for its justification, actually depended on the attitudes of its contemporaries and their acceptance of papal guidance. By the fourteenth century, the papacy was largely recognised as a vital institution, but any attempt to assert papal supremacy was regarded as a sign of greed and worldly ambition. What most contemporaries wanted from the pope – a vague spiritual leadership in most cases – appeared to be lacking in the gigantic bureaucracy characterising the papal curia. The growing gap between the papacy and the expectations that its contemporaries had of it provides a new viewpoint, and even a challenge, for a reconsideration of Clement V. This book thus attempts to re-evaluate the pontificate of Clement V in order to offer a more bal-

---

[1] D. Williman, 'Summary Justice in the Avignonese Camera', p. 437. On the factors behind Petrarch's adverse view of the Avignon papacy, see M. Bishop, *Petrarch and His World*, pp. 304–19.

[2] J. Christophe, *Histoire de la papauté pendant le XIVe siècle*, vol. I, pp. iv–v. Cf. B. Guillemain, 'Punti di vista sul papato avignonese', pp. 181–206. See also the excellent historiographical survey provided by D. Waley, 'Opinions of the Avignon Papacy', pp. 175–80.

[3] J. Muldoon, 'The Avignon Papacy and the Frontiers of Christendom', pp. 126–9.

anced picture of papal policy. Analysis has been carried out from complementary but not always congruent viewpoints, namely, those offered by official documentation (both ecclesiastical and secular) and by narrative sources. A third perspective has been provided by modern research, which has been considerable for the last two centuries. Special emphasis was placed on the different sources of inspiration for the pope's image, while an attempt was made to be most attentive to the attitudes of contemporaries and the different factors behind their views. This integrated approach raises some methodological problems that call for clarification.

An initial question focused on the prevailing approach to Clement V as inaugurating the Avignon period. Bernard Guillemain has rightly pointed out that neither in his intentions nor in his behaviour should Clement be considered the first pope of Avignon.[4] Yet Guillemain's own detailed analysis of Clement V in a book concerning the papal curia in Avignon reflects a rather ambiguous approach or, perhaps, the reluctance to change a historiographical trend that had reached the status of tradition. This book follows the example of fourteenth-century authors, who refer to Clement's absence from Rome without characterising it in terms of a permanent exile, much less such an exile in Avignon.

The attempt to analyse contemporary reactions to papal policy encountered not a few problems. Rather obviously, the common religious background left its mark on fourteenth-century chroniclers and the vocabulary they used. Reference to the same thesaurus of beliefs, idioms, and symbols made it extremely difficult to pinpoint significant ideological differences among the various sources. An attempt was made to identify contemporary authors and their political affiliation in order to determine the groups they represented and the popularity of their ideas. It soon became evident, however, that conventional categories, such as papalists and anti-papalists or Guelphs and Ghibellines, are rather problematic. The papalists and the so-called anti-papalists had more in common than not; such differentiation, moreover, was quite irrelevant to the pragmatic attitudes evinced towards papal policy on a particular issue. The classical categories of Guelphs and Ghibellines also proved to be quite obscure. Clement's policy in Italy weakened party differences and brought about a constant pendulum in the attitudes of the city-states and the chroniclers reporting them. The attempt to differentiate between *culture savante* and *culture populaire* also demanded much caution. The political tracts and a large proportion of the chronicles in one way or another expressed the ideas of the intellectual elite, and there is no clear indication as to the prevalence of their arguments in the lower social

---

[4] Guillemain, *La cour pontificale d'Avignon*, p. 77.

strata. The use of geographical criteria was of some help in overcoming certain of these problems. In many cases, the various reactions to papal policy could be classified according to location, making it possible to speak of prevailing attitudes in some areas of France, England, Aragon, and Germany. Here too, however, most generalisations were found wanting. The prevalent local patriotism, which in Italy assumed significant political weight, presented serious obstacles to any attempt at a prosopographical classification of the sources according to 'national' criteria. I have attempted to balance such impediments by constant reference to and comparison between theory and practice; that is, between reactions to the papal policy as reported in contemporary sources and developments in the political arena.

Reliance on narrative sources created further problems as to the originality of the authors, the extent of imitation, and even direct copying.[5] The monasteries of St Albans and St Denis still enjoyed historiographical pre-eminence, but their inherently monarchist attitude increases uncertainty about the prevalence of the opinions they voiced.[6] The 'Merton' *Flores* and the 1307–26 continuation, for example, were actually official histories, the latter covering the reign of Edward II to whom the original manuscript was presented.[7] It is highly doubtful whether the quantitative solution offered by Bernard Guenée – i.e., the number of manuscripts of each chronicle – can provide a satisfactory answer about the diffusion of ideas or the climate of opinion on specific issues.[8] Furthermore, the use of traditional idioms raises questions about the validity of paraphrases that were borrowed from the historiographical vocabulary of the past. In regard to England, for instance, it was rather easy to trace the influence of Matthew Paris, especially when the pope and his detrimental policy towards the Church of England were concerned.

Other methodological considerations related to the use of specific terms. During Clement's pontificate, the legatine system followed the tripartite classification defined by Guillaume Durant, namely, *legati a latere* (cardinals), *legati nati* (primates, with less authority than the former), and *nuncii* (all other categories, inclusive of papal collectors).[9] The officials of the papal curia were consistent in their different use of these terms. A

[5] On the extent of imitation in medieval chronicles, see R. Southern, 'Aspects of the European Tradition of Historical Writing', pp. 77–82. For the Avignon period, the most important contribution is that of Guillaume Mollat, *Etude critique sur les Vitae*; for Clement's pontificate, see pp. 1–30. Cf. W. Otte, 'Der historische Wert der alten Biographieen des Papstes Clemens V', pp. 3–73. [6] G. Spiegel, 'Political Utility in Medieval Historiography', p. 314.
[7] A. Gransden, 'The Continuations of the *Flores Historiarum*', pp. 487–9.
[8] B. Guenée, *Histoire et culture historique dans l'Occident médiéval*, pp. 248–58.
[9] G. Durandi Episc. Mimatensis, *Speculum juris* or *judiciale*, bk 1, pt 1, 'de legato', vol. 1, pp. 28–30.

cardinal who was dispatched as a vicarial representative of the pope – i.e., as a *legatus a latere* – was addressed as a *legatus sedis apostolice*. As such, he was not allowed to receive a portion of the cardinals' revenue, though a *nuntius* was. Most of Clement's envoys were actually nuncios, while legates were used for very important missions, such as the imperial coronation or the Hospitaller crusade. On the other hand, Johannes Andreae used the designation of *legatus* to refer to any kind of papal representative, while *nuntius* meant envoys or messengers. Chroniclers very often did not differentiate among the different categories, making indiscriminate use of the terms *legatus* and *nuntius*.[10] This book follows the nomenclature of the papal registers, which distinguishes between legates and nuncios. The term 'envoys' is used only in those cases in which no clear indication of their status appears in the text. Similar considerations concern the appellation of papal documents. Although outside the papal curia the term 'bull' was frequently used to describe papal documents, this form was not in use in the records of the chamber and in the chancery registers before the second half of the fourteenth century. It did gain in popularity in the fourteenth century as a description of documents issued under the leaden seal (for the leaden seal is what the word *bulla* means) as opposed to those issued under a wax seal.[11] The term *littere apostolice* remained the official term in the curia and the one most frequently used, thus justifying reference to 'papal letters' throughout this book. The attempt to follow coetaneous nomenclature also dictated reference to 'Assemblies', instead of 'Estates', during the reign of Philip the Fair. Contemporary chroniclers referred to the Assemblies as either *parlamentum* or *consilium* and did not use the term *Etats* until 1316. Thomas N. Bisson has noted that it is preferable to speak in terms of 'men of estates', whose traditional number, three, also appears to be inaccurate. Sometimes both theologians and lawyers were summoned, and contemporaries referred to them as separate groups.[12]

Throughout the text, the Christian names of kings and popes have been anglicised while other names kept in their vernacular forms. For coinage, the *librae*, *solidi*, and *denarii* or their French equivalents, the abbreviations *l.*, *s.*, and *d.* have been used. Where there was a question of a particular kind of currency, the vernacular term was used.

---

[10] C. I. Kyer, '*Legatus* and *Nuntius* as Used to Denote Papal Envoys', pp. 474–7.

[11] *Original Papal Letters in England*, p. xlvi.

[12] T. N. Bisson, 'The General Assemblies of Philip the Fair', pp. 558–64. Sicard's approach maintaining the continuity of the Etats Généraux since 1302 seems, therefore, questionable. See G. Sicard, 'Les Etats Généraux de la France capétienne', p. 59.

Chapter 1

CLEMENT V

Bertrand de Got was elected to the papacy on 5 June 1305, eleven months after the death of Benedict XI. The biography of the new pope up to this stage shows a successful ecclesiastical career in a supportive framework. Bertrand, the third son of Béraud de Got, lord of Villandraut, Grayan, Livran, and Uzeste, and of Ida de Blanquefort, was born in Villandraut (Gironde) in the middle of the thirteenth century.[1] Theirs was a large family of knightly rank, comprising eleven children, four sons and seven daughters, who in time provided Bertrand with more than twenty nephews.[2] The de Got family was related to the lineages of Mauléon, Fargues, Savignac, and Preyssac, all of whom had strong links with both the ecclesiastical and the political establishment in the area.[3] Bertrand's grandfather was the brother of Garcias de Benquet, bishop of Bazas (1166–79). His uncle, who had the same name, was bishop of Agen (1292–1305). His older brother, Béraud, received the archdeaconry of Montaut in Agen in 1279; ten years later, he was appointed archbishop of Lyons (23 July 1289),[4] the last stage before his nomination as cardinal-

---

[1] J. Duffour, 'Le lieu de naissance de Clément V', p. 371. The exact date of Clement's birth is unknown. He was in his fifties when elected to the papacy and died in his sixties. The best contemporary biography of the pope's early years appears in the *Chronicon fratris Francisci Pipini*, col. 747.

[2] Bernard Gui, in *Tertia Vita*, p. 54; Bernard Gui, in *Quarta Vita*, pp. 59–60; Amalric Auger, *Sexta Vita*, p. 89; *Notae ad vitas*, pp. 94–101. For biographical data on the authors of the *Vitae* and a critical evaluation of their writings, see G. Mollat, *Etude critique sur les Vitae*. On Clement's lineage, see the detailed table produced by F. Ehrle, 'Der Nachlass Clemens V', pp. 148–9, and by Guillemain, *La cour pontificale d'Avignon*, chart 3.

[3] *Rôles gascons*, nos. 2073, 2082, 2123, 2187, 2193, 3396, 4590, 4594; *Collectio actorum veterum*, pp. 8–9; *Actes du Parlement de Paris*, vol. II, no. 3226.

[4] On 29 October 1280, Béraud, at the time archdeacon of Montaut in Agen, was one of the two contestants for the see of Bordeaux, but the clergy elected Raimond des Cours. Raimond died shortly afterwards, and Béraud left his case for papal arbitration. Upon Béraud's appointment as archbishop of Lyons, Henry, the former archdeacon of Tonnerre, was sent to Bordeaux. See *Notae ad vitas*, p. 31, n. 1; Guillemain, 'L'essor religieux', pp. 135–6.

bishop of Albano (18 September 1294).[5] Another brother, Guillaume Seguin de Got, was papal chaplain and canon of Agen, and by 1297 enjoyed at least seven ecclesiastical benefices.[6]

Bertrand de Got began his education at the Grandmontine priory of Deffez in St Férreol (Lot-et-Garonne) in the diocese of Agen.[7] He studied canon and Roman law at the Universities of Orléans and Bologna,[8] thereafter returning to his native environment, which supported and facilitated his ecclesiastical career. He was successively canon and sacristan in the churches of Bordeaux, St Caprais at Agen, Tours, and Lyons. In 1289 (or perhaps at an earlier date), his meagre revenues from the canonry in Agen encouraged his appeal to Edward I for a more remunerative benefice.[9] By the summer or autumn of 1289, the king of England indeed granted him a substantial annual payment until a more suitable benefice was found. Edward empowered the royal receiver in the Agenais and the constable of Bordeaux to assign Bertrand an annual pension of 100 *Turonensium nigrorum* and 200 *currentis monete Burdegale* 'from our property'.[10]

---

[5] J. A. Kicklighter, 'La carrière de Béraud de Got', pp. 327–34.

[6] *Les registres de Nicolas IV*, nos. 1993–4. On the development of honorary papal chaplains, see C. Burns, 'Vatican Sources and the Honorary Papal Chaplains', p. 65; Kicklighter, 'An Unknown Brother of Pope Clement V', pp. 492–5.   [7] *Notae ad vitas*, p. 102, n. 2.

[8] *Regestum Clementis Papae V*, nos. 332, 360. The pope did not forget his debt to Orléans 'quod nos olim essentiam minoris status habentes legendi et docendi in legibus scientia decoravit'. At Orléans, Clement probably studied under the supervision of Pierre de la Chapelle, whom he nominated cardinal in 1305. Favier attributes to Clement's years in Orléans his transformation into a supporter of the Capetian monarchy; however, his claim that 'Bertrand de Got se sent français comme il se sent gascon' is not supported by papal documentation. See J. Favier, *Philippe le Bel*, p. 400. For papal privileges to Orléans, see n. 128 below. With regard to Bologna, as well, Clement showed special affection: 'Meritur igitur civitatem ipsam conscriptam gerimus in tabulis cordis nostri, digne in universitatis predicte radiis delectamur' (*Regestum Clementis Papae V*, no. 5274). On the many papal privileges to the university, especially concerning the teaching of Roman and canon law, see *Regestum Clementis Papae V*, nos. 5272, 5274–5, and n. 131 below. Cardinal Guilhelm Ruffat gave testimony of the pope's love for the University of Bologna.

[9] In his appeal to the king of England, Bertrand called himself 'canonicus Agenensis, devotus cum omni promptitudine serviendi'. He reminded the king of his past promise, when visiting his continental possessions, 'quia me pauperem sciebatis, non meis exigentibus meritis, mihi de vestra benignitate solita concessistis quod quam cito vobis facultas se offeret, personam meam aliquo bono beneficio ditaretis' (PRO, SC 1/14/144, printed by C. V. Langlois, 'Documents relatifs à Bertrand de Got', p. 49, n. 4; and by J. J. Champollion-Figeac, in *Lettres de rois, reines, et autres personnages*, no. 328, pp. 434–5). Langlois dated Bertrand's appeal to 1279, but he was not sure of the writer's identification: either it was the uncle or the future pope of the same name, both canons of Agen. Denton identifies the writer as the future Clement, but dates the letter ten years later, a logical solution in the light of the royal response in 1289. See J. H. Denton, 'Pope Clement V's Early Career as a Royal Clerk', pp. 307–8.

[10] *Rôles gascons*, nos. 1065, 1086. In 1284, the king bestowed special royal grace on Bertrand while referring to him as 'dilectum clericum nostrum, Bertrandum, archidiaconum Agenensem' (*ibid.*, no. 435). In 1290, as well, Edward I specifically mentioned the advice 'dilecti clerici nostri magistri Bertrandi, archidiaconi Agenensis' (*ibid.*, no. 1818). On the monetary systems of England and France, see H. A. Miskimin, *Money, Prices, and Foreign Exchange*, pp. 30–52, 132, 137, 143, 148–9, 158, 161–5, 202.

Edward's positive response to Bertrand's appeal was not fortuitous, since the de Got family maintained close relations with the king.[11] In 1279, Béraud, together with his father and uncle, served as witnesses in the transfer of the Agenais to England. By 1285, Bertrand, then canon of Agen, was acting as royal proctor in the Whitsun Parliament and managed the many litigations of Edward I at the Capetian court.[12] The king of England appreciated the de Got family's services and rewarded it most generously. In 1279, he recommended to Pope Martin IV the nomination of Béraud to the archbishopric of Bordeaux. The royal request, however, was not realised, probably because of the opposition of the local clergy. On 11 May 1296, Edward I granted royal protection to one of Bertrand's younger brothers, Guillaume, whom he referred to as canon of Wells and rector of the church of Manchester.[13] The de Gots' friendly relations with Edward I encouraged Pope Celestine V to send Bertrand on a diplomatic mission to England to foster the peace treaty with France (June 1294); at the same time, Béraud de Got participated in the papal delegation to France for the same purpose.[14]

Alongside royal support, Bertrand de Got's ecclesiastical career was crucially supported by his older brother, a fact mentioned in contemporary chronicles.[15] In his capacity as archbishop of Lyons, Béraud nominated Bertrand as his vicar-general. With his accession to the Sacred College, Béraud promoted the nomination of Bertrand to the rank of papal chaplain, and then raised his provision to a canonry and a sacristy in the cathedral of Bordeaux. On 28 March 1295, following an election *in discordia*, Bertrand was nominated bishop of St Bertrand-de-Comminges.[16] Four years later, on 23 December 1299, Pope Boniface VIII advanced him to the archbishopric of Bordeaux. The papal provision came in the wake of the resignation of Boson de Salignac, a former archdeacon of Médoc, who was transferred to St Bertrand-de-

---

[11] See Edward's letter to his seneschal in Gascony (22 November 1280): *Foedera*, I-4, p. 83. The friendly relations of the de Gots with the court of England were well known in Paris. When Béraud de Got was appointed archbishop of Lyons, Philip IV objected to his nomination on the grounds that he represented Edward's interests. During his pontificate, Archbishop Béraud obstinately defended the independence of his see against Philip's attempts at appropriation, which finally succeeded in 1310. Conversely, the Capetian court was very supportive of Bertrand, the future Clement V.

[12] PRO, Chancery Diplomatic Documents (C47), 29/1/16. According to Clement's own testimony in 1312, 'negotia progenitoris eiusdem in dicta curia praefati regis Franciae prosequendo' (PRO, SC 7/12/14; *Foedera*, II-1, p. 12); Kicklighter, 'English Gascony and the Parlement of Paris', pp. 121, 134.   [13] *Calendar of the Patent Rolls (1292–1301)*, pp. 189–90.

[14] Béraud died during this mission on 27 June 1297 (*Notae ad vitas*, pp. 31–2). See the anonymous letter written to Edward I on the occasion: Langlois, 'Documents relatifs à Bertrand de Got', p. 51.

[15] Adae Murimuth, *Continuatio chronicarum*, p. 8.

[16] Boniface VIII referred to Bertrand as 'canonicus Agensis, capellanus noster' (*Les registres de Boniface VIII*, no. 41).

Comminges. This promotion to the ecclesiastical metropolis of Gascony, which was at the core of the prolonged struggle between France and England, indicates Bertrand's good reputation in both ecclesiastical and political circles. Moreover, Bertrand's nomination, which came two years after his brother's death, suggests his personal merits and friendly contacts with the papal curia during the pontificate of Boniface VIII. These considerations found full expression less than six years later, during the difficult conclave that followed the death of Benedict XI.

Towards the end of the thirteenth century, Bordeaux was suffering one of the most difficult periods in its otherwise peaceful and prosperous existence. On 22 March 1294, Raoul de Clermont, sire of Nesle and constable of France, took over the city in the name of Philip IV the Fair, king of France.[17] This was an additional stage in the endless conflict between England and France, and paved the way for ten years of Capetian rule in the area.[18] The unfortunate results of the new regime soon became evident. Prominent families whose members were tortured or condemned to death by royal officers left the duchy to wait for more prosperous times.[19] The unavoidable outcome was economic deterioration and social unrest, while Edward's attempts to reinstate his power aggravated political instability in the whole area of Bordeaux. The brutality of Philip's rule, coupled with constant military repression, ultimately prompted an uprising, which succeeded in driving out Capetian rule (January 1303). The Bordelais thereby secured municipal autonomy until the peace treaty between England and France restored English hegemony over the area (20 May).[20]

Despite Renouard's assertion that 'the Bordelais pope owed his election in part to the prestige of his archbishopal see',[21] it is therefore rather

---

[17] *Livre des coutumes*, p. 456; *Lettres de rois, reines, et autres personnages*, no. 308, pp. 406–8.

[18] Between November 1295 and May 1297, Philip the Fair confirmed the many privileges that the citizens of Bordeaux had received from the kings of England. Royal generosity was justified on the grounds 'eorum majoris, juratorum et communie fide et devotione quam ad nos, progenitores nostros et coronam Francie, continuatis actibus, habuerunt' (*Livres des bouillons*, pp. 34–6, 29–31; *Livre des privilèges*, pp. 4–6). The royal claim regarding the good faith and devotion of the Bordelais to the Capetians, however, was rather wishful thinking, hardly corroborated in daily practice. As claimed by Boniface VIII, the Gascon nobles were, in fact, pursuing multiple loyalties to enhance their own independence and to provide opportunities for playing off one lord against another (J. G. Black, 'Edward I and Gascony in 1300', p. 521). On the pro-Angevin stand of the majority of Gascon nobles, see M. G. A. Vale, 'The Gascon Nobility and Crisis of Loyalty', pp. 207–16.

[19] For Edward's war efforts, see J. R. Strayer, 'The Costs and Profits of War', pp. 277–91; Vale, 'The Anglo-French Wars', pp. 15–19, 32–4.

[20] E. Lalou, 'Les négotiations diplomatiques avec l'Angleterre', pp. 342–3. The Capetian court treated the revolt of 1303 quite severely. Only on 17 July 1308, and after many papal requests, did Philip the Fair grant royal forgiveness to the Bordelais. See J. P. Trabut-Cussac, 'L'occupation française', pp. 199–211.

[21] Y. Renouard, 'Bordeaux dans le monde au XIVe siècle', p. 218. Contemporary sources did not identify Clement V as a Bordelais but as being 'natione vasco', more often than not in a

difficult to speak of Bordeaux in terms of prestige at the end of the thirteenth century. The prolonged war between England and France had brought the province to the verge of bankruptcy.[22] The critical lack of funds forced Bertrand, upon his nomination to the metropolis, to request a loan from the rich abbey of Ste Croix.[23] His poverty, however, did not cause the young archbishop to overlook his status. On the contrary, Bertrand was a jealous guardian of his prerogatives in regard to the nine dioceses entrusted to his governance – Agen, Condom, Saintes, Angoulême, Périgueux, Sarlat, Poitiers, Luçon, and Maillezais – and visited them regularly; he still maintained close contacts with the whole province after his election to the papacy. Bertrand also gave new impetus to the renovation work in the cathedral of St Andrew, which had begun in 1280.[24] It is a matter of controversy, however, whether the statue in the northern portal – built between 1361 and 1369 – contains a representation of Bertrand de Got/Clement V or of St Martial.[25] If the former, it seems that it was Bertrand de Got who left his mark on Bordeaux rather than vice versa, as claimed by Yves Renouard.

An important political trend during Bertrand's six-year pontificate in Bordeaux was his attempt to neutralise the influence of the archbishop of Bourges, with whom his predecessors had waged a long struggle over the primacy of Aquitaine.[26] Bertrand took upon himself the rank of primate, thereby incurring the risk of being excommunicated by his rival, Gilles Colonna. Gilles (also known as Gilles de Rome or by his Latin name, Aegidius Romanus) was a formidable opponent. A scion of the important family of Colonna, Gilles joined the Augustinian Order and became its first member to teach theology at the University of Paris. General of the Augustinians from 1291, he was appointed archbishop of Bourges by Boniface VIII.[27] After Boniface VIII confirmed Gilles'

---

pejorative context: *Marcha di Marco Battagli da Rimini*, p. 65; *Chronicon fratris Francisci Pipini*, col. 747; *Gesta archiepiscoporum Magdeburgensium*, p. 440; *Martini continuatio Brabantina*, p. 262; *Annales Genuenses*, p. 72.

22 On the economic-political friction in the city, especially among the leading families of Delsoler and Colomb, see Kicklighter, 'English Bordeaux in Conflict', pp. 1–3.

23 Clement did not forget the abbot's friendly attitude and nominated him cardinal in the first promotion of 1305. The abbey, as well, enjoyed papal gratitude through a long list of privileges: *Regestum Clementis Papae V*, nos. 3920–4, 4077.

24 J. Gardelles, 'La reconstruction de la cathédrale', pp. 326–9; *Regestum Clementis Papae V*, nos. 3694, 3696. The pope left 10,000 florins in his will to support the monumental work.

25 These opposing views have been presented by A. Leroux, 'Les portails commémoratifs de Bordeaux', pp. 413–24, 438, and R. Rey, 'L'énigme du portail nord de la cathédrale de Bordeaux', pp. 97–101.

26 G. Parisset argued that the primacy of Bourges had been recognised from the times of Dagobert, c. 630, and was corroborated by Pope Eugene III on 15 March 1142: Parisset, 'L'établissement de la primatie de Bourges', pp. 145–84, 289–328.

27 Gilles supported the pope unconditionally in the struggle with Philip the Fair; and it was his trea-

primacy in 1301, the latter appointed Gautier de Bourges, bishop of Poitiers, to proceed with a lawsuit against Bertrand de Got and even to excommunicate him should the archbishop of Bordeaux refuse to submit. According to some chroniclers, Clement took revenge on both prelates upon his election to the papacy. The pope brought about Gautier's degradation, compelling him to return to his Franciscan house. The bishop died soon afterwards, his last words calling for a second judgement either by a council or by God.[28]

Bertrand's obstinacy in relation with Gilles Colonna and Gautier de Bourges does not, however, suggest a brash character or a lack of diplomatic skills. Quite on the contrary. One of his most distinctive traits was to remain on friendly terms with the chief leaders of the time: Boniface VIII, Philip IV, and Edward I, who were in a state of continuous conflict or even open war with one another. One may further note that Bertrand's success did not rely on servile policy or on adopting a neutral stand on critical political events. On the contrary, he proved to be a zealous guardian of his prerogatives with regard to not only the archbishop of Bourges but also the Capetian court. Furthermore, his success in obtaining from Philip the Fair a large list of privileges indicates political skill. Four months after Bertrand was nominated to Bordeaux, indeed, Philip confirmed his metropolitan rights. The king forbade bailiffs and seneschals to interfere with the archbishop's income or to prevent his suffragans from appealing to ecclesiastical courts (3 March 1300).[29] Philip also graciously bequeathed to the metropolitan of Bordeaux the rich abbey of Guîtres, which had been confiscated by his officers (November 1302). These royal gestures of goodwill neither led to Bertrand's servility to the king nor limited his freedom of action. During the deliberations of the Assembly of Paris (1302), Bertrand demonstrated a resolute character and much courage when he declared himself exempt from any vassal allegiance to the king of France.[30] Philip accepted this claim and even granted Bertrand special protection against royal officers.[31]

---

tise, *De ecclesiastica potestate*, which served as the main source of inspiration for the constitution *Unam Sanctam*. None the less, Gilles also gained the esteem of Philip the Fair, who asked him to write a treatise on the suitable education of princes.

[28] *Continuationis chronici Guillelmi de Nangiaco*, p. 351. Callebant, however, denies the accuracy of this report: A. Callebant, 'Une soi-disant bulle de Clément V', pp. 670–2; Callebant, 'Une bulle du temps de Frédéric II', pp. 38–41, 47. On Clement's vindictive approach to Gilles Colonna and the reactions of contemporaries, see chapter 2.

[29] On the 1137 precedent of royal privileges, see *Ordonnances des roys de France de la troisième race*, pp. 7–8, 340–4.

[30] On the difference between homage, with vassal connotations and as such forbidden, and the fidelity that the clergy owed to rulers, see J. Brejon de Lavergnée, 'Le serment de fidélité des clercs au roi de France', pp. 127–33.

[31] The weight of the king's declarations in actual practice, however, was insignificant. Conversely,

Philip's generosity towards the archbishop of Bordeaux was undoubtedly calculated to win the support of a leading ecclesiastical figure in a
recently conquered area known for its political unrest. There were also
additional political considerations, such as Bertrand's position in the
English administration of Gascony. In his capacity as archbishop of
Bordeaux, Bertrand participated in the Gascon council and might have
been a member of the royal council during his visits to England.[32] Yet
the king's gestures of goodwill towards the archbishop did not secure
royal rule. The Bordelais rebelled against the Capetian representatives
while Bertrand was attending the Council of Rome. Following the
precedent of the Sicilian Vespers, they killed all royal officers and anyone
suspected of having co-operated with them (January 1303).[33] The timing
of the rebellion – surprisingly successful after Edward I's military failures
in the area – leaves unsettled the political stand of the archbishop on the
problematic option of choosing between England and France. Did
Bertrand possess any advance warning of the uprising? The documents
are silent in this regard. Still, both the many contacts of the de Gots in
the area and the fact that the family was not harmed during the vendetta
that followed the insurrection suggest that the archbishop of Bordeaux
maintained a friendly-neutral, though not openly favourable, attitude
towards the insurgents.[34]

Bertrand's political wisdom, which historians have evaluated at times
as opportunism, was further manifested during the conflict between
Philip IV and Boniface VIII.[35] Bertrand participated in both the
Assembly of Paris and the Council of Rome, the first summoned by
Philip IV against the pope and the second convened by Boniface VIII
against the king of France. The degree to which not only Bertrand but
his entire family succeeded in passing between opposing camps is evinced
by the strong affection expressed by Philip IV in 1305 towards 'the good
conduct, the great loyalty, and the firm constancy that we have found in
Arnaud Garsie de Got, brother of our holy father the pope, and in
Bertrand, son of the aforesaid knight, and in those of their lineage'.[36]

the reign of Philip the Fair was characterised by a continuous and deliberate encroachment of
ecclesiastical privileges: P. Fournier, 'Les conflits de juridiction entre l'Eglise et le pouvoir
séculier', p. 449.

[32] On the Gascon council, see Trabut-Cussac, *L'administration anglaise en Gascogne sous Henry III et
Edouard I*, pp. 191–4; Guillemain, *Le diocèse de Bordeaux*, p. 62.

[33] *Les grandes chroniques de France*, pp. 216–17; *Continuationis chronici Guillelmi de Nangiaco*, p. 334.

[34] Ernest Renan argued that, by 1295, Bertrand de Got was strongly supportive of English policy in
the area. This claim, which is not corroborated in contemporary documentation, seemingly
follows Villani's imaginary version of the pope's original hatred of the Capetians. See E. Renan,
'Bertrand de Got', p. 274.   [35] E. Caman, *Papes et antipapes à Avignon*, p. 6.

[36] *Notae ad vitas*, pp. 94–101. During the last war between France and England, Arnaud Garsie de
Got served in Guyenne on the Capetian side, under the leadership of the count of St Pol.

Similar or even more touching expressions of friendship and mutual respect are commonplace in the correspondence between Clement, when pope-elect, and the king of England.[37]

Up to 1305, then, Bertrand de Got appears as the scion of a well-known Gascon family, many of whose members reached high positions in ecclesiastical administration and which had excellent political connections with the Roman curia and the kings of England and France. Bertrand was an intellectual, a graduate in Roman and canon law of the leading universities of the day. His successful ecclesiastical and diplomatic career brought him into close contact with the leading rulers of Christendom, both secular and ecclesiastical. During his six-year pontificate in Bordeaux, Bertrand gave proof of administrative skills, showed high self-esteem for his status and prerogatives, and demonstrated personal refinement. There is no suggestion of a servile character or of any collaborationist policy with the royal or ecclesiastical powers of the time. Until ascending to the papacy, therefore, Bertrand de Got manifests clear signs of possessing both political acumen and diplomatic skills to pave the difficult way between opposing interests. The question thus remains whether, after he became the vicar of God on earth, Bertrand de Got turned into a characterless, pro-French pope, who allegedly dragged the papacy into its 'Babylonian captivity'.[38]

THE ELECTION TO THE PAPACY

The prolonged vacancy after the death of Pope Benedict XI (7 July 1304) reflected internal party conflicts in the College of Cardinals. Nineteen cardinals participated in the opening of the conclave in Perugia (18 July), the Italians and Romans in particular maintaining their ascendancy.[39] Until Christmas, the search focused on the Sacred College, but the cardinals' failure to agree on a suitable candidate from within their own ranks led them to look at the whole Church.[40] Matteo Rosso Orsini, the leader

---

[37] See chapter 6.

[38] Renan, 'Bertrand de Got', pp. 281ff.; Guillemain, *La cour pontificale d'Avignon*, pp. 129–30; N. Housley, *The Avignon Papacy and the Crusades*, p. 13.

[39] As against one cardinal from England, William Winterbun (Dominican), one from Castile, Peter Hispanus, and two from France, Jean le Moine and Robert de Pontiniac (Cistercian), there stood fifteen cardinals from Italy, the leading among them being Matteo Rosso Orsini, Giovanni Boccamazza, Napoleone Orsini, Francesco Caetani, Landolfo Brancaccio, Guglielmo Longo, Niccolò da Prato (Dominican), Riccardo da Siena (Cistercian), Leonardo Patrassi, Luca Fieschi, and Riccardo Petroni. Luca Fieschi and Riccardo Petroni replaced the two Colonnas, who had been excommunicated by Boniface. At the opening of the conclave, Giovanni Boccamazza was on a papal mission in the Empire. Four cardinals were eventually forced to leave the conclave because of illness. See the full list provided by Raynaldus, in *Annales ecclesiastici*, ad a. 1305, f. 6, vol. XXIII, pp. 393–4. [40] G. Fornaseri, 'Il conclave perugino del 1304–1305', p. 327.

of the majority group and an experienced member of the papal curia, constituted a main impediment to reaching a consensus. Being closely associated with the militant policy of Boniface VIII, Matteo saw himself as the most promising aspirant to the highest Church office.[41] Against his candidacy stood his nephew, Napoleone.[42] Besides perpetuating the familial feud, so characteristic of medieval Italy, the Orsinis represented the political dissension among the cardinals, ten of whom, mainly Italians, favoured the continuation of Boniface's policy and demanded satisfaction for the outrage at Anagni.[43] Against them stood the six-cardinal pro-French faction, Napoleone Orsini at its head, who pursued an immediate reconciliation with Philip the Fair.[44]

The dissension within the Sacred College did not go unnoticed in contemporary records. Among the Franciscan Spirituals, it acquired significance in terms of *historia sacra*, as the transition stage to the spiritual era. In the summer of 1304, Fra Angelo Clareno and Fra Liberato gathered with their followers in Perugia, where they probably wrote the *Vaticinia de summis pontificibus*, a set of prophecies about the popes.[45] More practical in their approach were the Capetians and their kin, who urged the cardinals to reach a decision in the shortest period of time and, if possible, to decide upon a candidate favourable to them. Charles II of Naples came to Perugia (8 March 1305)[46] to join a Capetian delegation that sojourned there or in Città della Pieve from 31 January until 29 April. Geffroy de Plessis, Itier de Nantevil, and Mouchet, who represented Philip the Fair, were received with much suspicion and even open hostility by the local inhabitants, who feared Capetian designs on their city.[47] In the meantime, Guillaume de Nogaret – chief counsellor, keeper of the seals of Philip the Fair, and main protagonist in Boniface's outrage at Anagni – did not desist from active participation in ecclesiastical matters.

---

[41] On 4 January 1305, Vidal de Villanova wrote to the king of Aragon about the 'mayor divisio et discordia ha entrels [cardenals]'. He further mentioned Matteo's oath that he would not allow the election of a new pope other than one who would revenge the assault on Boniface: H. Finke, *Aus den Tagen Bonifaz VIII, Quellen*, no. 14, p. lix. This report was corroborated by Garsias, prior of Ste Christine, who two weeks later wrote to James II, 'De papa non habetur magna spes quo ad presens, set potens est Deus ipsos dominos cardinales die unico concordare': *Acta Aragonensia*, vol. I, no. 11, p. 187. See also later reports on the constant dissension among the cardinals: *ibid.*, vol. I, nos. 124–5, pp. 186–94.

[42] A. Huyskens, 'Das Kapitel von St Peter in Rom', pp. 266–90; Matteo's biography in *Notae ad vitas*, pp. 70–2.   [43] R. Brentano, *Rome Before Avignon*, pp. 173–209.

[44] The most accurate report in contemporary chronicles appears in *Martini continuationes Anglicae Fratrum Minorum*, p. 257.   [45] M. Reeves, 'Some Popular Prophecies', pp. 107–16.

[46] *Acta Aragonensia*, vol. I, no. 123, p. 188.

[47] *Histoire du différend d'entre le pape Boniface VIII et Philippes le Bel*, pp. 277–8; Langlois, 'Notices et documents relatifs à l'histoire de France . . . Geffroy de Plessis', pp. 75–6. On Musciatto Franzesi or Mouchet and his impressive career in the Capetian court, see Langlois, 'Notices et documents relatifs à l'histoire de France au temps de Philippe le Bel: Documents italiens', pp. 322–5.

Playing the role of a 'devout' *miles ecclesiae*, he wrote to the cardinals in a rather suggestive tone:

> If some antichrist were to invade the Holy See, we must oppose him; there is no insult to the Church in such opposition. If order cannot be restored without violence, we must not relinquish our right. If, in the cause of right, violence is committed, we are not responsible.[48]

These words were meant, rather obviously, to justify Nogaret's deeds two years earlier at Anagni, while turning the legitimate pope, Boniface VIII, into the antichrist. They also hint at the challenge that faced the conclave, namely, finding the most suitable candidate, one who would free the papacy from the impasse with the king of France and his ministers, the zealous champions of the Catholic faith. Nogaret's message, coupled with the Capetian and Angevin delegations to Perugia, further indicates the delicate balance between Church and state, and the tendency of contemporary kings towards close intervention in delicate ecclesiastical affairs. This tendency was exercised in actual practice, though not legitimised, *before* Clement's accession to the papacy.

The cardinals' difficulties in reaching a consensus eventually facilitated the election of the archbishop of Bordeaux. His acceptability to, and good relations with, both Boniface VIII and Philip IV made it easier for the opposing factions at the conclave to look at Bertrand as a candidate of their own.[49] Besides, many cardinals knew him well from his services in the papal curia. The candidacy of Bertrand de Got was originally suggested by Francesco Caetani, Boniface's nephew, whom Bertrand had served as chaplain, and was at first accepted by Matteo's party. The election of Bertrand de Got, however, was not a decision carried out by the conclave without external interference. Napoleone Orsini had asked for, and eventually received, the Capetian blessing for Bertrand's candidacy. Only after obtaining a positive response from Philip the Fair did Napoleone Orsini procure the election of Bertrand de Got, who received ten of the fifteen votes (5 June 1305).[50]

Bertrand de Got received the news of his election two weeks later while visiting his province at Lusignan (Vienne).[51] The pope-elect returned at

---

[48] *Histoire du differend d'entre le pape Boniface VIII et Philippes le Bel*, p. 240. One should note that Nogaret was still excommunicated at that time, so it is improbable that his letter was in fact received by the cardinals.

[49] 'Chè ciascuno dicea che era amico di sua parte': Agnolo di Tura, *Cronaca Senese*, p. 288.

[50] *Notae ad vitas*, p. 31; *Registrum Roberti Winchelsey Cantuariensis archiepiscopi*, vol. II, pp. 673–5. Perhaps also Bertrand's once-bad relations with Gilles Colonna (see above, pp. 10–11) brought him the support of the Bonifacian party.

[51] The news of Clement's election spread incredibly fast. Edward I received the report after only twelve days: *Calendar of the Close Rolls (1302–1307)*, p. 337. On the notification to James II of Aragon, see *Acta Aragonensia*, vol. I, no. 126, pp. 194–5.

once to Bordeaux, where John of Havering, the seneschal of Gascony, offered him the lavish gifts of Edward I and led him in procession to the city.[52] On 24 July, after he had received the formal decree announcing his election, Bertrand held a formal meeting in the cathedral of St Andrew. He declared his consent to become the new spiritual leader of Christendom and took the name Clement V.[53] The pope-elect announced his intention to be crowned at Vienne (Dauphiné) on the feast of All Saints (1 November) and to proceed to Italy as soon as a final peace was concluded between France and England.[54] Following Philip's objections to Vienne, Clement transferred the ceremony to Lyons, which was also under imperial rule. The pope-elect departed from Bordeaux on 4 September and reached Lyons on 1 November.[55] Along the arduous journey, he resided in monastic houses in Béziers, Lézignan, Villalier, Montpellier, and Viviers, as well as in the abbey of Grandselve and the monastery of Prouille.[56] A new pattern of behaviour, which would come to characterise Clement's pontificate as a whole, thus began, namely, of ever-growing papal requests for hospitality in ecclesiastical institutions. This new pattern, with all its economic implications, soon had crucial weight in the deteriorating relationship between the pope and the clergy of France.[57]

Clement V was crowned in great splendour by the new dean of the Sacred College, Napoleone Orsini, in the church of St Just (14 November).[58] Yet not every stage of the coronation was festive. During

[52] J. Boucherie, 'Inventaire des titres', p. 340. Edward's gifts included a golden cross with precious stones, twenty barrels of wine, twenty oxen, and twenty pigs. See John of Havering's report to the king, in Langlois, 'Documents relatifs à Bertrand de Got', pp. 52–3. Clement recompensed the services of the seneschal with a long series of privileges to him and his relatives, and acknowledged his good services in a warm recommendation he wrote to Edward: *Original Papal Letters in England*, no. 41, pp. 21–2; *Foedera*, 1-4, pp. 68, 72; M. l'abbé Tauzin, 'Les sénéchaux anglais en Guyenne', pp. 149–66, 197–212.

[53] Bernard Gui, in *Quarta Vita*, p. 60; Bernard Gui, in *Tertia Vita*, p. 54. The earliest letters in Clement's register are dated 27 July 1305. There have been some reservations with regard to these letters, which were written before the coronation, since on 26 February 1307 Clement formally sanctioned them: *Regestum Clementis Papae V*, no. 2264; *Acta Clementis PP V*, no. 12; P. N. R. Zutshi, 'Some Early Letters of Pope Clement V', pp. 324–7.

[54] See Clement's letter to Edward I (25 August 1305): PRO, SC 7/11/33; K. Wenck, *Clemens V und Heinrich VII*, pp. 169–70. Fearing Capetian influence, Edward advised the pope to avoid unnecessary delays and to hasten his return to Rome: *Calendar of the Close Rolls (1302–1307)*, p. 348.

[55] M. Gouron, 'Le premier séjour de Clément V en Guyenne', pp. 257–65.

[56] Amalric Auger, *Sexta Vita*, p. 91.

[57] See chapter 2. According to the report of John of Havering, the expenditures for the first papal journey reached the considerable sum of 6,000 *livres tournois*. On his way back to Bordeaux, as well, Clement gave preference to monastic institutions; he halted at Cluny, and was hosted by the Dominicans in Bourges and by the Franciscans in Poitiers: Langlois, 'Documents relatifs à Bertrand de Got', pp. 52–4; C. de Vic and J. Vaissète, *Histoire du Languedoc*, vol. IX, pp. 285–6.

[58] The fact that the papal coronation was not performed in the cathedral but in the church of St Just may be attributed to the fact that this was the only area of the city under Capetian rule at this time: R. Fédou, *Les papes du moyen âge à Lyon*, p. 82.

the magnificent procession through the streets of Lyons, an old wall over-loaded with the crowd collapsed. Though the pope was not injured, twelve people, including Jean II, duke of Brittany, were killed. The description of the accident, which appears in many sources, was inter-preted by contemporary authors as an ill omen for the new pontificate.[59] On the other hand, the untimely accident did not mar the festivity of the occasion. Clement's coronation reflected all the components of a new era in the annals of the medieval papacy, characterised by renewed harmony between *regnum* and *sacerdotium*. Philip the Fair, Charles de Valois, Louis d'Evreux, Jean II, duke of Brittany, and Henry of Luxemburg (the future Henry VII) were present at the ceremony.[60] Although the war in Scotland prevented Edward I and the prince of Wales from coming to Lyons, the king of England sent an impressive delegation, which presented the pope with gifts valued at 1,343 *l.*, 3 *s.*, 5 *d.*[61] The presence of the leading mon-archs of Christendom at the papal coronation was not a simple matter of formal ceremony with little or no political meaning. They attempted, each in his own way, to gain Clement's positive response to the long list of requests they brought to Lyons. The question remains whether they were able to dictate the pope's political agenda; or, rather, was it Clement who used their needs and many requests to further his own priorities.

Some indication of papal plans at this early stage may be found in Clement's own testimony. Two days after his coronation, the new pope issued an encyclical asking all the faithful to pray for the success of his pontificate. He displayed due Christian humility as the 'unqualified' heir of St Peter, 'Nos indignum dicimus et nos inparem merito reputamus', and requested the believers to pray for the redemption of the souls of all Christians and for God's mercy to bestow on him the necessary means for the service of the Church and the faithful; most especially, the pope asked the faithful to pray for the recovery of the Holy Land.[62] Beyond the rhetorical humility required of St Peter's heir, this message hints at Clement's scheme of priorities, which gave precedence to the recovery of the Holy Land. Clement's devotion to the crusade eventually dictated

---

[59] See the papal report of the accident to Edward I (*Foedera*, 1-4, p. 46): 'Sicque dies ille, qui prima facie honoris exultationem praetendebat et gaudium, moeroris confusionem superinduxit et lamentum'. See also *Continuationis chronici Guillelmi de Nangiaco*, p. 350. Bernard Gui reports that 'mirati sunt universi et more vulgi multi plurima presagabant', while Tolomeo da Lucca refers to the accident as 'signum notabile': Bernard Gui, in *Quarta Vita*, p. 61; Tolomeo da Lucca, *Secunda Vita*, pp. 24–5. See also Jean de St Victor, *Prima Vita*, pp. 1–2; *Chronographia regum Francorum*, p. 176; *Continuatio chronici Girardi de Fracheto*, p. 26.

[60] *Chronique normande du XIVe siècle*, p. 28; Jean d'Hocsem, *Gesta Pontificum Leodiensium*, p. 344; B. Schimmelpfennig, 'Papal Coronations in Avignon', pp. 179–96.

[61] *Foedera*, 1-4, pp. 41, 42–3; *Annales Londonienses*, p. 143. The munificence of the royal presents was emphasised by contemporary chroniclers: *Flores historiarum*, p. 127; Rishanger, *Chronica*, p. 227.

[62] *Registrum Simonis de Gandavo*, vol. I, pp. 220–3.

not only his prolonged stay in the Comtat-Venaissin but also his unconditional support of a peace treaty between England and France, which he
regarded as critical for the implementation of a new Christian enterprise
overseas.

Contemporary chroniclers regarded the election of Bertrand de Got
as a compromise of sorts.[63] Still, they all recognised the canonical procedure and, ultimately, the unanimous election.[64] There is some evidence
of hopes being placed in the ability of the former archbishop of Bordeaux
to curb the extremism of Philip the Fair. An anonymous German chronicler expressed confidence that 'this pope will cause justice to be done
and wreak his revenge on those who had arrested Boniface'.[65] Flemish
sources showed a deeper awareness of the French efforts – by mediation
of the Colonnas – to bring about 'the nomination of a pope in accordance with the wishes of the king', who would transfer the apostolic see
to the kingdom of France.[66] Dino Compagni, as well, hints at the decisive role played by the alliance between Philip and the Cardinals Colonna
– who had been excommunicated by Pope Boniface in 10 May 1297 –
in the election of Bertrand de Got.[67] This pro-French tendency was
confirmed in time by Napoleone Orsini. Shortly after Clement's death,
Orsini confessed to Philip the Fair his aspiration, during the conclave in
Perugia, to see to the election of a pope who would be totally receptive
to the king of France and the interests of his kingdom.[68]

These pro-French considerations were known in the Italian peninsula
and, in the framework of the too-fresh memory of the outrage at Anagni,
incited extreme reactions. The 'French plot' had been immortalised in
the chronicles of Agnolo di Tura and Giovanni Villani. In spite of the
imaginary description, their review reflects the reaction to the choice of
a non-Italian pope who never crossed the Alps. They told how Bertrand

---

[63] Adae Murimuth, *Continuatio chronicarum*, p. 8; *Flores historiarum*, p. 123; *Continuationis chronici Guillelmi de Nangiaco*, pp. 348–9; *Continuatio chronici Girardi de Fracheto*, p. 25; Gilles li Muisis, 'Li estas des papes', p. 298; Bernard Gui, in *Tertia Vita*, p. 54; *Annales Parmenses Maiores*, p. 733.

[64] *Extraits d'une chronique . . . 1308*, p. 136; Jean de St Victor, *Prima Vita*, p. 1; John of Viktring, p. 349.

[65] *Annales Lubicenses*, p. 419.

[66] Before the election of Clement V, Philip had supposedly negotiated with the Colonnas and other cardinals the transfer of the papal curia to the kingdom of France: *Chronographia regum Francorum*, p. 170; *Anciennes chroniques de Flandre*, p. 396.

[67] Dino Compagni, *Cronica*, pp. 192–3. On the prolonged struggle between Boniface and the Colonnas and the latter's alliance with Philip the Fair, see S. Menache, 'Un peuple qui a sa demeure à part', pp. 196–7.

[68] 'Ut possem habere pontificem de regno, cupiens regi et regno esse provisum, et sperans quod quicumque regis sequeretur consilium, Urbem et orbem bene regeret et Ecclesiam reformaret. Et quoniam cum multis cautelis, quibus potuimus, hunc qui decessit elegimus, per quem crede-bamus regnum et regem magnifice exaltasse': written between May and 24 July 1314, the letter focused on the miserable status of the Church in general and of Italy in particular (*Collectio actorum veterum*, p. 237).

de Got's candidacy was promoted by Cardinal Niccolò Albertini da Prato, who was consistently depicted as a manipulative and rather sinister person.[69] At first, the cardinal's initiative seemed impracticable. Bertrand's animosity towards the Capetians, which stemmed from the damage inflicted by Charles of Anjou on his family property, had considerably lowered the archbishop's readiness to reach any compromise with the court of France. On the other hand, Cardinal da Prato thought the archbishop of Bordeaux to be a man 'lacking honour and nobility, since he was a Gascon, who are essentially rapacious'.[70] Niccolò da Prato thus encouraged the king of France to reach an early agreement with his candidate. The cardinal's advice supposedly led to a meeting between the king and the archbishop in St Jean d'Angély, where Philip the Fair's conditions were presented to Bertrand de Got. They included:

Re-acceptance of the king and his supporters, including the Cardinals Colonna, into the Church.

A formal denunciation of Boniface's memory.

A five-year tenth to finance the war in Flanders.

The nomination of cardinals friendly to France.

A secret clause, 'mysterious and great', which the king reserved in the meantime to himself but which would later be communicated to the archbishop.

Bertrand de Got's obsequious response satisfied the king and ensured Capetian support for the archbishop's election to the papacy: 'You [Philip] will command and I will obey, and it will always be settled in this way.'[71] Though this report long ago was proved to be purely imaginary, it reflects the background of Clement's election as perceived on the Italian peninsula.[72] It further suggests the critical reactions to be expected of Clement's close alliance with Philip the Fair.

The reticence and even opposition of contemporaries found ample

---

[69] R. Fei, 'Il Cardinale Niccolò da Prato', pp. 467–83.

[70] Rabanis demonstrated long ago the friendly relationship of Bertrand and all the de Got family with Philip the Fair, the adherence of Cardinal Niccolò da Prato to Boniface's policy, and the fact that Bertrand was elected, not by way of compromise, but by a majority, ten votes to five. See M. Rabanis, *Clément V et Philippe le Bel*, pp. 18ff.; C. J. Hefele and Dom H. Leclercq, *Histoire des conciles*, vol. VI-I, pp. 487–98.

[71] Villani, *Istorie fiorentine*, vol. IV, pp. 160–2; Villani, *Cronica*, pp. 109–11; Agnolo di Tura, *Cronaca Senese*, pp. 287–8.

[72] Odorico Rinaldi reproduced the whole report in his continuation of Baronius, though he expressed some doubts regarding its authenticity, 'si veritate nitantur'. Mansi was even more doubtful, relating to Villani's words as 'suspiciosam mihi ea reddant'. See Raynaldus, *Annales ecclesiastici*, vol. XV, pp. 1–2; *Annales ecclesiastici*, ed. G. D. Mansi, vol. IV, pp. 390n.–391n.; L. Andrat, 'L'entrevue de Bertrand de Got et de Philippe le Bel', pp. 230–2. See also Bertrand de Got's itinerary in the dioceses of Agen, Périgueux, and Poitiers, which proves beyond doubt the unlikelihood of a meeting between archbishop and king where and when assumed by Villani: Rabanis, *Clément V et Philippe le Bel*, pp. 152–9.

echo in the writings of Dante Alighieri, who depicted St Peter's anger at his see being usurped by a Gascon. In the poet's view, Clement had turned the apostle's sepulchre into a 'cloaca del sangue e de la puzza'.[73] The new pope's assiduousness in furthering the interests of his family, his instability, and his lust for power were responsible for the subjugation of the papal curia to the worship of avarice. Through his bad example, Clement had actually turned those expected to be shepherds into blood-thirsty wolves.[74] Comparing Clement to a 'new Jason', who had bought his appointment as high priest from Antiochus and thereupon introduced pagan and venal practices into the Temple of the Lord (2 Macc. 4:7–10), Dante also points to Clement's worst vice: his total submission to the king of France.[75] Thus extreme doubts arose in his mind concerning the ethical worthiness of papal leadership:

> Laws, indeed,
> there are, but who puts nations to their proof?
> No one. The shepherd who now leads mankind
> can chew the cud, but lacks the cloven hoof.[76]

Clement is capable of chewing his cud, a metaphor denoting wisdom and spiritual reflection, but is not cloven-footed, for he lacks the dimen-

---

[73] The usurper of the throne given to me,
to me, to me, there on the earth that now
before the Son of God stands vacant, he
has made a sewer of my sepulchre, a flow
of blood and stink at which the treacherous one
who fell from here may chuckle there below.
Dante Alighieri, *Divina Commedia, Paradiso*, c. XXVII, vv. 22–7.

[74] From here in every pasture, fold, and hill
we see wolves dressed as shepherds . . .
Gascons and Cahorsines are crouched to drink
our very blood.
Ibid., c. XXVII, vv. 55–9.

This section was probably written after Clement's death, since it also refers to the Cahorsins, a clear reference to the countrymen of John XXII: E. Gorra, 'Dante e Clemente V', p. 215. On the evolution of Dante's attitudes to the papacy and the main role of Clement V's last years in his anti-papal approach, see G. Holmes, 'Dante and the Popes', pp. 40–1.

[75] Before the west sends down a lawless Shepherd
of uglier deeds to cover him and me.
He will be a new Jason of the Maccabees;
and just as that king bent to his high priests' will,
so shall the French king do as this one please.
Dante Alighieri, *Divina Commedia, Inferno*, c. XIX, vv. 77–81.

The role of Antiochus is obviously bestowed on Philip the Fair. Dante was exiled from Florence in 1302, *inter alia*, on the grounds of his policy 'contra summum pontificem et d. Karolum pro resistentia sui adventus'. See *Codice diplomatico dantesco*, p. 106.

[76] Dante Alighieri, *Divina Commedia, Purgatorio*, c. XVI, vv. 96–9. See Lev. 9:1–4.

sion of virtue; he is unable to distinguish between good and evil. Dante's was not a lone cry in Italy. Some chroniclers accused the pope of simony, avarice, nepotism, and even intimate relations with Brunissende, the countess of Périgord, 'a most beautiful lady, daughter of the count of Foix'.[77] Villani went further, foretelling the destiny of the pope in the after-life, where he would share a palace with his nephew; the two, though, would lie on a bed of fire 'because of their simony'.[78]

The consensus regarding the legitimacy of Clement's election did not, therefore, carry any special sympathy for the new pope in Italy. On the other hand, the clear antagonism to what Italian sources regarded as a French or, rather, Philip the Fair's plot could suggest more positive attitudes in the kingdom of France. In contrast to the joy of the Bordelais at the election of their archbishop,[79] however, Clement's Gascon origin precluded any warm welcome for the pope in other areas of the Capetian kingdom. Geffroy de Paris found the prevailing scepticism reasonable in the light of the notorious reputation of Bertrand de Got, whom he depicted as rapacious and a tyrant.[80] In time, Clement's generosity towards his large family reinforced his reputation as a Gascon, with all the negative stereotypes that implied.[81] The animosity against the Gascons found violent expression in the riots attendant on the pope's coronation.[82] During a fight between Gascons and a retinue of Italian cardinals, Clement's brother was killed (23 November), an incident that heightened tension between the new pope and Louis de Villard, the archbishop of Lyons.[83] One of the pope's nephews, as well, was killed soon afterwards

---

[77] Agnolo di Tura, *Cronaca Senese*, p. 343; Villani, *Istorie fiorentini*, l. ix, c. 58, pp. 56–7. The Aragonese representatives who were so outspoken, however, did not mention even once her presence in the papal curia.

[78] Villani, *Istorie fiorentine*, l. ix, c. 58, p. 57. However, Raimond de Got died only in 1323.

[79] According to Bernard Gui, 'receptusque fuit Burdegalis processionaliter a toto clero et populo, cum ingenti gaudio et honore totius civitatis ac patrie, undique concurrentibus baronibus et prelatis': Bernard Gui, in *Quarta Vita*, p. 60; Bernard Gui, in *Tertia Vita*, p. 54; Amalric Auger, *Sexta Vita*, p. 90.

[80] Car l'esleü, cele jornee,
N'avoit pas bone renommee;
J'en atrai chascun a garant
Que l'en le tenoit a tyrant . . .
Plus est apert en la richece
Communement qu'en la prouece.
La chronique métrique attribuée à Geffroy de Paris, p. 136, vv. 2327–50.

[81] 'A seeker of honour and glory like a Gascon' or 'the avarice of the Gascons' became common clichés in contemporary sources. See *ibid.*, p. 175, vv. 4444–8.

[82] *Notae ad vitas*, p. 39.

[83] *La chronique métrique attribuée à Geffroy de Paris*, pp. 137–44, vv. 2379–2745; see also Thomas Jorz's letter to King Edward in January 1306: Langlois, 'Notices et documents relatifs à l'histoire du XIIIe et du XIVe siècles: Nova Curie', p. 71.

by a group of furious townsmen, who in this way punished the endless pursuit of their daughters by the pope's relative. Without possessing symptoms of local prejudice, Gervais du Bus vented his criticism by stressing Clement's greed and the resulting gap between the pope and St Peter, the fisherman, whose mission on earth Bertrand de Got was expected to fulfil.[84]

Clement's Gascon ancestry encountered a much more positive welcome in England, where most chroniclers refrained from painting a stereotyped portrait of the new pope.[85] The factors behind this sympathetic attitude were faithfully voiced, in retrospect, by Froissart: 'The pope . . . was a Gascon from Bordeaux and all his ancestors had been subject to the kings of England. In his status and actions he was an Englishman who would never harm the king of England.'[86] Without analysing in depth the political inclinations of the new pope, Murimuth attributed Bertrand de Got's successful ecclesiastical career to the pope's brother, the cardinal-bishop of Albano.[87] The hostile attitude of the chronicle of Malmesbury appears exceptional, especially in its extreme aversion to Clement's Gascon origin: 'For a long time back it has been unheard-of for a non-Italian to be elected pope; after this may it never happen that a man so near to us ascends the papal throne.'[88]

The sources cited above suggest an essential problem during Clement's pontificate: the election of a non-Italian pope who fixed his residence in the Comtat-Venaissin aroused suspicion and even anger.[89] Clement's

---

[84] Mès nostre pape d'orendroit
Si pesche en trop meillour endroit:
I a une roy grant et forte
Qui des flourins d'or li aporte
Tant que saint Peire et sa nacele
En tremble et ele chancele.
Gervais du Bus, *Le roman de Fauvel*, p. 23, vv. 553–8.

One should note that the king of France is depicted here as enriching the pope, in complete opposition to the actual relationship between Clement V and Philip the Fair (see chapter 2). The very fact that the king of France received the Church's money and the pope was left with the criticism suggests the detrimental consequences of papal policy. On *Le roman de Fauvel* and its place in medieval satire, see J. C. Mühlethler, *Fauvel au pouvoir*, pp. 17–29.

[85] Rishanger, *Chronica*, p. 227; *Chroniques de Sempringham*, p. 326.

[86] Jean Froissart, *Chroniques*, p. 52. This opinion was corroborated by Professor Tout, who claimed that 'Clement never forgot that he was a Gascon nobleman, a born subject of the Gascon duke, and a former archbishop of Bordeaux. From 1305 to 1308, it looked as if his only difficulty was whether he should rule the Church universal from Gascony or from Poitou': T. F. Tout, *The Place of the Reign of Edward II in English History*, p. 195.

[87] Adae Murimuth, *Continuatio chronicarum*, p. 8.

[88] These lines, however, were written at the end of Clement's pontificate and do not reflect the expectations of the early years: *Vita Edwardi Secundi*, p. 46.

[89] One should note that there had been four popes from France before Clement's pontificate: Urban II (1088–99), Urban IV (1261–4), Clement IV (1265–8), and Martin IV (1281–5). On their policy

Gascon origins made him less acceptable, since regional separatism was very strong. Just as authors from the Italian peninsula regarded him as French, chroniclers from the Ile-de-France treated him as Gascon. The only possible alternative remained England; but even there, Clement's unconditional support of Edward I and Edward II gradually weakened the original, positive approach.

ROME OR AVIGNON?

The criticism of Clement V by contemporary authors justifies further inquiry into the effect of the pope's absence from Rome in shaping his negative image. Papal absence from Rome was not unprecedented. During the two hundred years that preceded the pontificate of Clement V, popes had resided in Rome for only eighty-two years. To mention but a few examples: Benedict XI (1303–4) left Rome after some five months and departed for Perugia, where he died. Boniface VIII (1294–1303) spent much of his pontificate in Anagni, Orvieto, and Velletri. Celestine V (1294) did not come to Rome at all; elected in Perugia, he was crowned in Aquila and journeyed to Solmona, Capua, and Naples, where he resigned. Nicholas IV (1288–92) spent most of his pontificate in Rieti and Orvieto. Martin IV (1281–5), who was elected in Viterbo, did not leave Tuscany and Umbria. Nicholas III (1277–80) spent much time in Sutri, Vetralla, and Viterbo. John XXI (1276–7) did not leave Viterbo at all. After only two months in Rome, Gregory X (1271–6) travelled to Orvieto and Lyons and sojourned in Provence for a long period. Gregory IX (1227–41) spent more than eight years out of Rome.[90] With only a few exceptions, however, these papal wanderings before the Avignon period remained *within* the Italian peninsula and took place mostly inside the Papal State.[91] By contrast, Clement absented himself not only from Rome but from Italy as a whole. On the other hand, until 1309, when Clement fixed his residence in Avignon, the character of the papal curia was itinerant and hardly allowed reference to its absence from Rome as a permanent phenomenon.[92] On the whole, Clement did not reside in Avignon for more than 160 days, whereas he spent 133 days in Châteauneuf and 92 days in Monteux. Facts alone, thus, do not support reference to Clement V as the first pope of Avignon, whether in terms

and the reactions of contemporaries, see Menache, 'Réfléxions sur quelques papes français du bas moyen âge', pp. 117–30.

[90] For a more complete list, see G. Mollat, 'Papes d'Avignon', cols. 1535–6.

[91] A. Paravicini Bagliani, 'Der Papst auf Reisen im Mittelalter', pp. 501–14.

[92] G. Marchal, 'Autour du pape Clément V: Voyage de Poitiers' (1926), pp. 201–5; Marchal, 'Autour de Clément V, le pape en Toulousain', pp. 227–32; E. R. Labande, 'Clément V et le Poitou', pp. 11–33, 83–109.

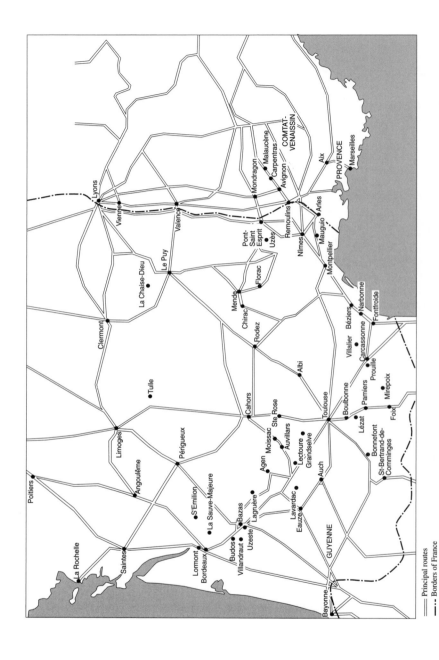

Map 1 Clement's sojourn in Languedoc

of 'captivity' or of free political choice. Yet, the pope's characterisation as a Gascon – an identification that Clement's nepotism made all the more acute – injected an additional factor into the contemporaries' view of papal wanderings in Languedoc.

The Italian cardinals were in the forefront of the opposition to the pope's absence from Rome.[93] In a letter to Bertrand de Got upon his election, they emphasised the bleak situation in Italy and the advantages that would follow the pope's immediate return to Rome:

The ship of Peter is in danger of sinking and the fisherman's net of breaking; instead of calm and peace, storm-clouds are piling up; disastrous wars are laying waste the lands of the Roman Church and the neighbouring regions.

After this touching description, they begged the pope to come, so that all Italy could enjoy the benefit of his presence.[94] But Clement was not moved by this appeal. At his death, Cardinal Napoleone Orsini summed up the effects of the pope's indifference:

The whole city [Rome] was destroyed by and because of him, and the See of St Peter and our lord Jesus Christ have been torn to tatters. Robbers lagged behind the magistrates in looting the Patrimony . . . *Nam nunc volens Ecclesiam reducere ad angulum Vasconiae.*[95]

Although Clement neither attempted 'to reduce the universal Church to a corner of Gascony' nor neglected the situation in the Papal State, it is also true that he did not assign first priority to Italy.[96] In the final analysis, it was the peace treaty between England and France, which the pope regarded as a precondition for the renewal of the crusade, coupled with his deteriorating health, that dictated Clement's protracted sojourn in the Comtat-Venaissin.

The Comtat-Venaissin had been an integral part of the Papal State since 1274 although Raymond VII, count of Toulouse, had awarded it to the papacy by 1229. Located on the left bank of the Rhône in the ancient kingdom of Arles, the Comtat-Venaissin comprised a number of fiefs held

---

[93] Finke, *Papsttum und Untergang des Templerordens*, vol. II, no. 16, p. 22.

[94] *Registrum Roberti Winchelsey Cantuariensis archiepiscopi*, vol. II, pp. 676–7; Raynaldus, in *Annales ecclesiastici*, ad a. 1305, f. 7, vol. XXIII, pp. 394–5.

[95] *Collectio actorum veterum*, p. 238. See n. 68 above. James II of Aragon used similar metaphors when he prayed for the help of Mary and the saints to save the ship of Peter, abandoned to the storms of the sea. Although it is not clear whether the king's criticism was directed particularly at Clement V, Jeanroy claims that it reflects a logical reaction to anti-Aragonese papal policy since the pontificate of Honorius IV. See A. Jeanroy, 'La poésie provençale dans le sud-ouest de la France', p. 16.

[96] Dante shared this critical approach of Cardinal Napoleone Orsini with regard to the harmful consequences of Clement's policy for Italy in general and Rome in particular. In his letter to the Italian cardinals after Clement's death, he begged them to prevent the ascendancy of the Gascons in the Church. See R. Morghen, *Dante, profeta tra la storia e l'eterno*, pp. 114, 137.

from the popes by homage and about sixty castles and villages held directly by the papacy. Clement's preference for Avignon, where he settled in the Dominican priory on 9 March 1309, probably resulted from its important position. The city was the first harbour up from the Mediterranean and, as such, a crucial intersection of river and land routes between Provence and Languedoc.[97] It was under the rule of the count of Provence and papal vassal, Charles of Anjou, whose protection was assured if need arose. In contrast to more prominent cities in the county – Carpentras, Cavaillon, Pernes, and Vaison – Avignon had only about 5,000 to 6,000 inhabitants. The new university, founded in 1303 by Boniface VIII, consisted of the faculties of arts and canon law.[98] There were eight parishes, including the cathedral, Notre Dame des Doms, three monasteries, and a Templar commandery. Besides the peaceful character of the inhabitants, the pope could also enjoy the climate and the nearby hills, which provided a refreshing retreat during the hot months of the summer.

Most chroniclers treated Clement's sojourn in Avignon as temporary and refrained from using the term 'exile'.[99] This attitude stemmed in part from the pope's declarations that fostered the illusion of an immediate return to Rome. In his encounter with Philip the Fair in Poitiers (April 1307), Clement did not hide his joy at the opportunity of a personal meeting with the king of France before his forthcoming journey to Rome.[100] According to a contemporary report, Clement's desire to return to Italy was also fostered by the many expenses involved in the lack of a permanent residence and the shortage of resources in Languedoc. Even Villani regarded the pope's decision to remain in the Comtat-Venaissin as provisional.[101] Henry of Rebdorf goes further, arguing that Clement's election *in absentia* was made possible because the cardinals had estimated that the archbishop of Bordeaux would immediately join them in Italy.[102] The very fact that the papal treasure was left in Perugia when the cardinals went to France and only later, after many expensive vicissitudes, transferred to Avignon shows the uncertainty that characterised the eventual home of the papacy at this stage.[103] As time went by and Clement did not fulfil the expectations of an immediate return, some German sources charged the Romans with responsibility for the pope's

[97] T. Sclafert, 'Les routes du Dauphiné', pp. 183–92.

[98] A. Gouron, 'Enseignement du droit', pp. 18–19.

[99] Some chroniclers were aware of the pope's wanderings between 'Lyons, Bordeaux, Poitiers, and Avignon', which excluded Rome: *Chronique normande du XIVe siècle*, p. 28. On the other hand, the perspective of 'Babylonian captivity' is completely absent in contemporary sources. Cf. Raynaldus, in *Annales ecclesiastici*, ad a. 1305, f. 1, vol. XXIII, p. 390.

[100] Finke, *Papsttum und Untergang des Templerordens*, vol. II, nos. 16, 86, pp. 21–2, 134–5.

[101] Villani, *Istorie fiorentine*, l. viii, c. 81, p. 165.   [102] *Heinrici Rebdorfensis Annales*, p. 552.

[103] Ehrle, 'Zur Geschichte des Schatzes', pp. 41–8.

exile: because of their continuous attacks on their bishop, the Romans actually forced Clement to live as a pilgrim in a foreign country. Conversely, the chroniclers refer to the many honours that the pope had received from Philip the Fair and his court.[104]

The chronicles of Tolomeo da Lucca and Marco Battaglia, on the other hand, claimed that upon his election, Clement had firmly decided to make his residence in the Viennois, a move that the pope had forced on the cardinals 'almost compulsorily'.[105] Dino Compagni, as well, emphasised the fact that Clement 'did never cross the Alps nor come to Rome, but he was consecrated in Lyons, on the Rhône'.[106] The chronicle of Bologna tells a more peculiar story, according to which there were persistent rumours of Bertrand de Got's imminent death and that these were what actually brought about his election to the papacy in Perugia. Accordingly, the choice of the archbishop of Bordeaux was just a subterfuge in order to achieve time and thus free the cardinals from external pressure to end the long interregnum. The deception of the cardinals was twofold, therefore, since Clement was to live for nine long years and eventually compelled them to join him in Languedoc.[107] Although at first reading illusory, this story does not appear so fantastic when evaluated in the light of both Clement's real illness from the very beginnings of his pontificate and the election, eleven years later, of Jacques Duèse, Pope John XXII. The latter's election was due in large measure to his old age and the rumours he himself had propagated about his precarious health. Whether the chronicle of Bologna was transferring later motivations to Clement's election or whether the reflections about Clement's approaching death already existed in 1305 is difficult to know. On the other hand, this story reflects the problematic relationship between a pope who, for whatever reasons, did not cross the Alps, and the Italian cardinals, who felt that they were losing their source of power by remaining in Languedoc.[108] These conflicting perspectives offer some explanation of Clement's curial policy, which some scholars have defined in terms of 'Gallicanisation'.[109]

The rumours about Clement's plans to remain in the Comtat-Venaissin acquired the weight of a threatening possibility among the inhabitants of Rome. Their concern for papal proximity resulted in the main from

---

[104] *Monachi Fürstenfeldensis Chronica*, pp. 42–3; John of Viktring, p. 349.

[105] Tolomeo da Lucca, *Secunda Vita*, p. 24; *Marcha di Marco Battagli da Rimini*, p. 65. In a report to James II of Aragon, mention was made of the papal summons to the cardinals to come to the Comtat-Venaissin and their assumption that the pope would stay there for the remainder of the year (16 September 1305): *Acta Aragonensia*, vol. I, no. 130, pp. 198–9.

[106] Dino Compagni, *Cronica*, p. 193; *Annales Forolivienses*, p. 63; *Annales Genuenses*, p. 72.

[107] *Corpus chronicorum Bononiensium*, pp. 270–1.

[108] Some chroniclers reported the continuous pressure of the cardinals to return to Rome, which encountered the pope's refusal: *Sifridi de Balnhusin Compendium*, p. 717.   [109] See chapter 2.

decreasing pilgrimage, coupled with the loss of resources normally provided by the papal entourage. Though the Romans had hardly done their
best to encourage their bishop's stay in their city, they called on the pope
'to go to Rome and establish his curia there, in the manner [that] his predecessors, high pontiffs, did'.[110] A delegation from Rome and Tuscany
presented Clement with an intimidating ultimatum, that 'the pope must
come to Rome, to his see, and hold his curia there; otherwise, the Romans
will chose themselves an emperor' (29 December 1305).[111] Agostino
Trionfo employed the convincing argument that there is no prophet in his
own city as a warning against both the bonds that could chain Clement to
France and a schism that could threaten the whole of Christendom. He
further encouraged the Italian cardinals to exercise collective pressure on
the pope in this matter.[112] In choosing between the principle of the uni-
versality of the papacy and that of loyalty to Rome, most Italian authors
thus clearly supported the concept of *pontifex Romanus*, who had the same
obligation of residence as any other member of the Church.

The antagonism to the pope's absence from Rome was not limited to
Italian writers. The monk of Osney refrained from stating whether the
wanderings of Clement V in Languedoc reflected the will of God or the
stubborn decision of flesh and blood.[113] Jean de St Victor solved the
riddle by asserting that the proximity to the Capetian court had actually
been forced on the pope and the cardinals, who 'almost violently were
caught' by Philip the Fair and his ministers; this version was echoed by
Dino Compagni.[114] In the 'Dispute between the church of Rome and
the church of France', Geffroy des Nés commiserated with the sorrows
of Rome while indicating the gap between the city's past glory and its
present desertion by both pope and emperor. Though he refrained from
judging the pope and left the whole matter to the verdict of God, he
referred to the universal duty of residence upon Catholic bishops. Still,
he recognised that in France Clement enjoyed 'good wine, good food,
and people who love him and are devoted to his service'.[115]

[110] *Flores historiarum*, ad a. 1305, app., p. 322.
[111] The source is a letter written by Dinus Silvestri to James II of Aragon: *Acta Aragonensia*, vol. II,
no. 341, pp. 111–12. Dupré-Theseider claims that this declaration lacked any real basis, but hints
at the Romans' awareness of their 'imperial rights', which had not been applied since the death
of Manfred: E. Dupré-Theseider, *Problemi del papato avignonese*, p. 92; Dupré-Theseider, *Roma
dal comune di popolo alla signoria pontificia*, p. 389.
[112] *Tractatus contra articulos inventos*, no. 18, pp. xci–xciii. Agostino also severely criticised Clement's
greed, love of riches, and nepotism: *ibid.*, III, 3, pp. lxxxviii–lxxxix.
[113] *Annales monasterii de Oseneia*, p. 341.
[114] Jean de St Victor, *Prima Vita*, pp. 5–6; 'tenendo il Papa quasi per forza': Dino Compagni, *Cronica*,
pp. 219–20.
[115] Geffroy des Nés, 'La desputaison de l'église de Romme et de l'église de France', p. 575, vv. 37–40;
p. 577, vv. 99–101; p. 579, vv. 158–60.

Beside the temporal advantages offered by Clement's transitory abode, there were some attempts to impart to Avignon a miraculous aura, such as the tradition ascribing to Jesus the building of the bridge over the Rhône, an enterprise that took eleven years and involved some miracles.[116] There were further attempts by canonists and Roman lawyers to provide the necessary legitimisation to papal residence out of Rome. Although the Franciscan Alvarez Pelayo recognised that the pope could not remove the apostolic see from Rome, he denied that the sanctity of the papacy depended on its location. The pope has ordinary jurisdiction over all churches in the world, since no place sanctifies men, nor does Rome the pope. Moreover, wherever the pope is, there is the Roman Church, he argued, since *Petrus* means Church. The pope is not obliged to stay in Rome since he is not called the Roman pope, but the pontiff of the universal Church.[117] Cardinal Jean le Moine and Jesselin de Cassagnes, as well, supported the claim that 'ubi est papa, ibi est Romana curia'.[118] On a theoretical level, the absence from Rome thus weakened the geographical component of the Petrine heritage. This development strengthened the universal conception of the papacy and helped to substantiate the identification of the pope with God, thereby further widening the gap between the papacy and all human institutions.[119]

French lawyers provided the papal move to Avignon with a messianic meaning. In developing this conception, Pierre Dubois talked much about the distortions inherent in the Roman tradition, which had carried the popes away from the Petrine heritage and the divine command, 'Render unto Caesar that which is Caesar's.' While recognising the connection between the first pope and the city of Rome, Dubois refused to consider the papal vicariate as an outcome of geographical considerations. Peter's ethical qualities had raised him above the other apostles, and these qualities obliged his heirs. In Dubois' mind, the move to France acquired the meaning of a papal act of contrition for the harm that

---

[116] M. Miserey, *A l'âge d'or d'Avignon*, pp. 48–9.

[117] '[Papa] habet iurisdictionem ordinariam in omnibus mundi ecclesiis . . . et universalis ecclesie presul est . . . et locus non sanctificat homines, nec Roma papam, que res inanimata est . . . quia ubicumque est papa, ibi est Ecclesia Romana . . . quia Petrus Ecclesiam significat . . . et quod papa non cogitur stare Roma . . . nec vocatur proprie Papa Romanus, sed universalis Ecclesie': N. Iung, *Un franciscain théologien du pouvoir pontifical*, p. 111. Alvarez Pelayo began his book, *De statu et planctu Ecclesiae*, in 1322, three years after his nomination to the apostolic penitentiary.

[118] On Jean le Moine's attitude to the papal monarchy, see J. Gaudemet, 'Aspects de la primauté romaine', pp. 126–9. Jesselin also wrote a commentary on the *Clementinae*, which he finished in 1323: Fournier, 'Jesselin de Cassagnes, canoniste', pp. 348–61.

[119] All these opinions, however, were voiced by clergymen who were close to the papacy and enjoyed curial benefices. Alvarez Pelayo worked in the penitentiary, Jean le Moine was cardinal, and Jesselin de Cassagnes was an auditor of causes. See Guillemain, *La cour pontificale d'Avignon*, pp. 90–1, 349–50.

Boniface VIII had caused to Philip the Fair. Furthermore, the stay in France would hasten the recovery of earthly Jerusalem, anticipating the celestial one.[120] Alongside the many advantages on the eschatological level, Dubois also stressed the climatic benefits of the Comtat-Venaissin to Clement's shaky health.[121]

Contemporary sources thus hint at the diversity of opinion that prevailed in regard to the papal absence from Rome, supporters and critics being found among both the ecclesiastical and political leading personages of the time. At least some of the sources, however, were actually projecting onto the pontificate of Clement V feelings and reactions that matured later, during the Avignon period, because of the continuing absence from Rome.[122] During Clement's pontificate it was difficult to speak in terms of exile; the papal wanderings in Languedoc, though, aroused conflicting attitudes among broad social strata, reflecting opposing interests. The protracted stay in the Comtat-Venaissin cannot, therefore, be regarded as a crucial factor in shaping Clement's image. It was, in fact, far less influential than the stereotyped description of the pope's Gascon origins or the behaviour attributed to him and his curia.

A PERSONAL PORTRAIT

Beyond the nepotistic, avaricious bias attributed to Clement, contemporary sources allow reference to more positive aspects of his character. Though the works of art undertaken under the pope's direction were not numerous, they are none the less remarkable.[123] The collegiate church at Uzeste and the impressive vaulting of St Bertrand-de-Comminges, which Clement saw as his personal effort 'to build a sumptuous building', evince his sophistication.[124] Following the fire at the Lateran (6 May 1308),[125] the pope brought about the construction of a new church that

---

[120] Pierre Dubois, *De recuperatione Terrae Sanctae*, LXX.111–12, pp. 190–2.

[121] *Ibid.*, p. 190; cf. Gilles li Muisis, 'Li estas des papes', p. 301.

[122] Guillemain, 'Punti di vista sul papato avignonese', pp. 185–90. On the implications of Clement's stay in France for the web of relations with the local clergy, see chapter 2.

[123] E. Renan – who is usually antagonistic to Clement's policy – gives a supportive evaluation of the pope's patronage of the arts. His view, however, was not backed by Lizerand: Renan, *Etudes sur la politique religieuse du règne de Philippe le Bel*, pp. 449–52; G. Lizerand, *Clément V et Philippe le Bel*, pp. 349–50.

[124] *Regestum Clementis Papae V*, no. 9909. On the many papal gifts to the cathedral, see also *ibid.*, no. 3994; Bernard Gui, in *Quarta Vita*, pp. 65–6; Amalric Auger, *Sexta Vita*, p. 97; O. Brel-Bordaz, 'Broderies d'*Opus Anglicanum* à Saint-Bertrand-de-Comminges', pp. 65–7.

[125] According to Bernard Gui, 'Unde in Urbe magna lamentatio facta fuit, quasi hoc super seipsos divinum judicium reputantes; feceruntque clerus et populus processiones ad Dei misericordiam et gratiam implorandam.' Tolomeo da Lucca further adds that in the general climate of penitence, 'multe facte paces, et multe sedate discordie': Bernard Gui, in *Quarta Vita*, p. 64; Tolomeo da Lucca, *Secunda Vita*, pp. 31–2; *Annales Urbevetani*, p. 272.

was 'more rich and more beautiful' than the original. This time, Clement's policy found strong support among Italian chroniclers.[126]

Being a man of letters, Clement developed the papal library, adding 100 manuscripts to the 600 mentioned in Boniface's time; there were about thirty liturgical books and one book of the Gospels in his treasury.[127] Clement also encouraged learning while increasing the papal patronage of young institutions. The pope encouraged the foundation of universities at Orléans,[128] Dublin,[129] and Perugia[130] and supported those of Bologna and Toulouse.[131] Papal support of these institutions was not just a matter of formalities but a true reflection of Clement's sincere interest in learning and in improving the intellectual skills of the clergy. In codifying the statutes of the faculty of medicine at Montpellier, the pope placed emphasis on the study of Greek and Arabic in its curriculum and established in detail administrative procedures and educational patterns to be followed.[132]

Clement had a pleasant character, which made personal contact with him easy and agreeable.[133] He was indeed affable by nature and tried to win men's hearts by skilful compliments; he was lavish in his praises, especially to monarchs.[134] In order to share some secrets with the Aragonese

---

[126] Villani, *Istorie fiorentine*, l. viii, c. 97, vol. IV, p. 195; Villani, *Cronica*, l. viii, c. 97, vol. II, pp. 131–2; Agnolo di Tura, *Cronaca Senese*, p. 302. Many relics were rescued from the blazing church by Jacopo Colonna, whose help was greatly appreciated by Clement; the pope entrusted to him supervision over the reparation: *Regestum Clementis Papae V*, nos. 3591–3603, 8764.

[127] Ehrle, 'Der Nachlass Clemens V', p. 80; Williman, *Bibliothèques ecclésiastiques au temps de la papauté d'Avignon*, pp. 20–1. During Clement's pontificate, the papal library was still in Italy. A proper library was built in Avignon only during the pontificate of John XXII: M.-H. Jullien de Pommerol and J. Monfrin, 'La bibliothèque pontificale à Avignon', pp. 147–8.

[128] The papal privilege elevated Orléans 'ad modum studii generalis Tolosani'. The pope conditioned his grant on Philip's sanction, which was denied. In protest, the students left the city, though according to some chronicles they returned the same year: *Regestum Clementis Papae V*, nos. 332–3, 360–3, 4056; *Les grandes chroniques de France*, pp. 284–5; *Continuationis chronici Guillelmi de Nangiaco*, p. 388; *Continuatio chronici Girardi de Fracheto*, p. 37; *Ordonnances des roys de France de la troisième race*, pp. 497–504. Philip reversed his policy in 1312: *Les olim ou registres des arrêts rendus par la cour du roi*, pp. 559–61, 582–6.

[129] *Regestum Clementis Papae V*, no. 8634; *Calendar of Entries in the Papal Registers*, p. 102. In 1312, John Leek, the archbishop of Dublin, obtained papal authorisation for founding a university in whatever science and faculty. The archbishop's petition, on which the statute is founded, stated that doctors and bachelors in theology and masters in grammar or arts had no university of scholars in Ireland, western Scotland, or Norway, so that there were few literate persons in these regions. Though there were a few masters and scholars in the 1320s, the establishment died out in the next generation, probably because of the lack of financial support. See H. Denifle, *Die Universitäten des Mittelalters*, pp. 639–43.

[130] *Regestum Clementis Papae V*, no. 3091; P. W. Knoll, 'The Papacy at Avignon and University Foundations', p. 192.

[131] *Regestum Clementis Papae V*, no. 1314; A. Gouron, 'Enseignement du droit', pp. 16–18.

[132] *Regestum Clementis Papae V*, nos. 1314–15, 1468, 6248–50, 6273; *Collectio actorum veterum*, pp. 136–8.   [133] *Chronicon fratris Francisci Pipini*, col. 752.

[134] Finke, *Papsttum und Untergang des Templerordens*, vol. II, nos. 126, 133, pp. 240–1, 264.

representative, Vidal de Villanova, the pope put his hands on Vidal's, thus creating an atmosphere of familiarity.[135] Clement was also endowed with a sense of humour and did not refrain from laughing in public.[136] Contemporary sources refer to the fact that the pope received Bucard III von Scrapelau, the archbishop-elect of Magdeburg, 'cum hilaritate'.[137] On the other hand, Clement zealously resisted any affront to his prerogatives. When the Aragonese representatives dared hint at their king's reprisals should the pope not endorse his financial requests, Clement brought about their immediate removal and later degradation.[138]

Yet Clement's character and, indeed, most of his pontificate were shadowed by a serious illness affecting his digestive system; this probably developed into a cancer of the bowel or the stomach, which affected the pope for long periods.[139] Under the effects of the disease, Clement became taciturn and lived as a recluse for months.[140] Edward I, early in Clement's pontificate, expressed his concern about the pope's health and sent a special messenger to the curia in order to receive reliable information (19 December 1305).[141] During an attack that lasted from August until the end of December 1306, Clement allowed no one near him, except four of his kinsmen.[142] The cardinals did not succeed in approaching him until Epiphany 1307, thus paralysing the normal operation of the curia for almost five months. Although papal correspondence suggests Clement's deep concern about his precarious health, it is still coloured by optimism and faith.[143] In a letter to Philip IV, the pope referred in a rather confident tone to his past illness, which had brought him to the verge of death but from which he hoped to have been cured by the joint efforts of divine providence and his physicians (5 November

---

[135] 'E puys pres les mies mans entre les sues' (February 1313): *Acta Aragonensia*, vol. III, no. 111, p. 233.

[136] *Ibid.*, vol. II, no. 354, p. 533.   [137] *Gesta archiepiscoporum Magdeburgensium*, p. 427.

[138] In a letter to the king (4 November 1309), Clement did not hide his exasperation: 'Sed nuntii memorati, nedum quod responsiones et concessiones nostras huiusmodi cum devotione susciperent, verum etiam satis irreverenter et in verba gravia temerarie prorumpentes a nostra presentia recesserunt. Super quo scire te volumus, quod, nisi ad honorem tuum habuisset consideratio nostra respectum, taliter correxissemus eosdem, quod fuisset ceteris in exemplum' (*Acta Aragonensia*, vol. III, no. 97, p. 210). Cf. the Dominicans' version: *ibid.*, vol. II, nos. 482, 566, pp. 771–3, 887–9.

[139] See the reports of the Aragonese representatives to their king (2 February 1313): *Acta Aragonensia*, vol. III, no. 110, pp. 232–3. Clement's illness gave rise to rumours about his imminent death throughout his whole pontificate: Langlois, 'Notices et documents relatifs à l'histoire du XIIIe et du XIVe siècles: Nova Curie', pp. 71–5; Finke, *Papsttum und Untergang des Templerordens*, vol. II, no. 14, p. 17.   [140] Finke, *Papsttum und Untergang des Templerordens*, vol. II, no. 112, p. 209.

[141] *Calendar of the Close Rolls (1302–1307)*, p. 424; *Foedera*, I-4, p. 45. See the papal letters to the king and the queen of England about his previous illness: *Foedera*, I-4, p. 67.

[142] Finke, *Papsttum und Untergang des Templerordens*, vol. II, nos. 16, 17, pp. 21, 23.

[143] His physical condition and his doctors' diagnosis ('Cum de consilio phisicorum, necessitate nostri corporis hoc admodum exigente') were constant elements in Clement's correspondence; see *Collectio actorum veterum*, pp. 73, 74, 77, and passim.

1306).[144] From 1309 onwards, the attacks occurred at increasingly shorter intervals. Tolomeo da Lucca, who claimed to have first-hand sources, referred to the pope's colics, vomiting, and loss of appetite.[145] Tolomeo regarded these symptoms as divine punishment for the papal policy towards the Friars, a rather peculiar judgement considering Clement's supportive policy in their regard.[146]

Worn out by suffering, Clement V died in Roquemaure (Gard), on his way to Gascony, on 20 April 1314.[147] In spite of his deep affection for his kinsmen and the people of Gascony, they do not appear to have reciprocated the pope's devotion during his last moments. Jean de St Victor reports – not without satisfaction – that the Gascons left the corpse without Christian burial for a full day in order to participate in the plunder of papal possessions.[148] This report was confirmed by Geffroy de Paris and Pepin, who emphasised the ruthlessness and greed of the pope's countrymen and relatives.[149] Clement's body was eventually transferred from Roquemaure to Uzeste in Gironde, the burial place chosen by the pope in his last will (9 April 1314).[150] Even then, Clement's mortal remains did not find peace. According to some chroniclers, a fire erupted

---

[144] 'Sed clementia favente divina nunc sumus, ut nobis videtur, et dicunt nostri medici, ab omni infirmitate liberati et restituti plenarie sanitati, tanta tamen debilitate depressi quod nostram debilitatem verbis vel litteris exprimere nequiremus': *ibid.*, p. 61.

[145] 'Fuerat autem multo tempore infirmus de torsionibus, ex quibus perdidit appetitum. Ymmo interdum patiebatur fluxum, et per ipsum mitigabantur torsiones. Interdum vero patiebatur vomitum. Et sic de talibus passionibus moritur; nec umquam fuit postea sanus postquam constitutionem contra religiosos mendicantes renovavit sicut audivi a suo confessore fidedigno': Tolomeo da Lucca, *Secunda Vita*, pp. 52–3.

[146] *De verborum significatione, Clementinarum*, l. v, tit. xi, c. 1, *CIC*, vol. II, col. 1193; *Conciliorum Oecumenicorum Decreta*, [38], p. 392. See also *Notae ad vitas*, pp. 93–4.

[147] *Les grandes chroniques de France*, p. 295.   [148] Jean de St Victor, *Prima Vita*, p. 23.

[149] Onques nul ne l'en secourust.
Por quoi? Por ce que Diex ne plost
Et que vivre plus il ne post.
Mains Gascoins espiciaument
Damage i orent grandement . . .
Se pristrent a piez et a poins
Et por le tresor s'entreprirent
Et de son cors force ne firent.
La chronique métrique attribuée à Geffroy de Paris, pp. 200–1, vv. 5785–5814.

Pepin gives a pitiful description: 'Et quamquam vivens torrentem possideret divitiarum, sic tamen a domesticis suis moriens etiam vestimentis nudatus est, ut unicum tantum palliolum repertum sit, quo posset contegi corpus ejus, ut Religiosi, qui tunc aderant, postmodum retulerunt' (*Chronicon fratris Francisci Pipini*, col. 750). G. Mollat negates the accuracy of this report. See *Notae ad vitas*, p. 69. On the *jus spolii*, i.e., the right to spoil the property of a bishop following his death, see C. Samaran and G. Mollat, *La fiscalité pontificale en France au XIVe siècle*, pp. 47–8. According to Elze, the pope's naked body was part of a Roman ritual that symbolised the triviality of earthly life: R. Elze, '*Sic transit gloria mundi*', pp. 23–41.

[150] L. Guérard, 'La succession de Clément V', p. 9.

in the funeral place, and since the pope's corpse had been left unattended, it engulfed half the body before the flames were extinguished.[151] Ultimately, Cardinal Gailhard de la Mothe erected a burial monument in Uzeste for Bertrand de Got, Clement V.[152]

---

[151] 'Fertur etiam, quod ea nocte, qua mortuus est, sic fuit desertus ab omnibus, ut ex cereorum igne supra eum delapso [sic] pars corporis sit adusta. In vita tamen multum dilexit propinquos, et divitiis ac honoribus illos auxit': *Chronicon fratris Francisci Pipini*, col. 751; Agnolo di Tura, *Cronaca Senese*, p. 343; *Notae ad vitas*, pp. 69, 170. On the other hand, this report may suggest a tendency to attest to the fulfilment of the curse of the last master of the Temple, Jacques de Molai, on account of the pope's policy against the Templars. See C. Beaune, 'Les rois maudits', pp. 13, 18–19.

[152] J. de Laurière and E. Muentz, 'Le tombeau de Clément V à Uzeste', pp. 275–92; J. Gardelles, 'Le tombeau de Clément V', pp. 81–6; cf. M.-M. Gauthier, 'Uzeste', pp. 305–24. In 1322, the parliament of Paris dealt with a suit brought by the pope's nephew, the viscount of Limoges, against those who were in charge of the papal monument, whom he accused of misapplication of considerable sums: *Actes du Parlement de Paris*, vol. II, nos. 6738, 6879.

Chapter 2

CHURCH POLICY

Criticism of the popes was hardly unique to the fourteenth century; rather, it accompanied the consolidation of the papal monarchy.[1] It also reflected, in a devious way, the gap between the popes' perception of the Church – as a perfectly established system, organised on monarchical lines, and unique in its supra-national character – and their contemporaries' expectations of a more spiritual Church, in harmony with the goals of early Christianity. The nepotistic bias that chroniclers ascribed to Clement V offers another aspect of the growing gap between the papacy and different sectors of Christian society, including the clergy itself. Whatever the goals and achievements of Clement's pontificate – and there were, indeed, important attainments on the legal, administrative, and financial levels – they were neglected by most contemporaries, whose accounts attest instead to the corrupt image associated with the pope and his curia.[2] In this regard, Clement's Church policy offers one of the most problematic meeting points between the pope and his flock because of its economic and political implications, which sometimes directly affected the authors of the sources at our disposal.

In his report to the Council of Vienne, Guillaume le Maire, bishop of Angers, criticised papal interference in ecclesiastical appointments, which very often did not take into consideration the skills of the nominees. He condemned the nomination of incompetent candidates who ignored the local language; conversely, if reliable and skilful persons were appointed to the highest Church positions, they would spend most of their time in the papal or the royal courts and would never be seen in

---

[1] J. A. Yunck, 'Economic Conservatism, Papal Finance, and the Medieval Satires on Rome', pp. 334–51; R. N. Swanson, *Church and Society in Late Medieval England*, p. 12.

[2] W. A. Pantin argues: 'Paradoxically, the period of the popes' apparent humiliation during the "Babylonish captivity" at Avignon was also the period when the papal curia, and the departments into which it was divided, came to be most highly organized': W. A. Pantin, 'The Fourteenth Century', p. 163.

their see.[3] This claim hints at a main problem during Clement's pontificate: the ambiguous demarcation between the political and ecclesiastical functions of the clergy in the framework of the emerging national state.[4] The many crises characteristic of Boniface VIII's pontificate had clearly demonstrated that the lack of clear boundaries affected the relationship between *regnum* and *sacerdotium* as a whole, on both the theoretical and the practical level.[5] Boniface VIII's assertion that 'it is altogether necessary for salvation for every human creature to be subject to the Roman Pontiff'[6] was in actual practice counterbalanced by the violent capture of the pope in Anagni. The emissaries of Philip the Fair then attempted to force Boniface's presence at a council, to be judged on charges of heresy. During Clement's pontificate, the status enjoyed by England and France as the pope's main partners in the renewal of the crusade acted to replace former conflicts with mutual co-operation.[7] Yet, it was very difficult, if not impossible, to find a *via media* between the interests of the universal Church and of the emerging state, on the one hand, and those of the papacy, the monarchy, and the 'national' Churches, on the other.

This chapter focuses on Clement's attempt to find a satisfactory solution to the main problems affecting the Church, at both the universal and local levels. The priorities of Clement V dictated the geographical scope and the different topics discussed below. Papal ecclesiastical policy is reviewed from its three main components, namely, curial policy, and

---

[3] Guillaume le Maire, in E. Bellone, 'Cultura e studi nei progetti di reforma presentati al concilio di Vienne', p. 108. The same complaint was also endorsed by Pierre Jame; see Fournier, 'Pierre Jame (Petrus Jacobi) d'Aurillac, jurisconsulte', p. 509.

[4] Ehrle, 'Ein Bruchstück der Akten des Konzils von Vienne', pp. 385–7.

[5] On the conflict over taxation of the clergy, see the general studies of T. Boase, *Boniface VIII*, pp. 297–351; F. M. Powicke, 'Pope Boniface VIII', pp. 48–73; the relevant documentation has been published by P. Dupuy, in *Histoire du differend entre le pape Boniface VIII et Philippes le Bel*; R. Scholz, *Die Publizistik zur Zeit Philipps des Schönen und Bonifaz VIII*; H. Wieruszowsky, *Vom Imperium zum nationalen Königtum*, pp. 89–108.

[6] *Unam Sanctam, De maioritate et obedientia, Extravag. Commun.*, l. i, tit. viii, c. i, *CIC*, vol. ii, col. 1246. Giacomo da Viterbo presents a no less extreme view of the papal monarchy: 'Hic est rex omnium spiritualium regum . . . Hic est dispensator summus et universalis ministrorum Dei . . . distributor dignitatum et officiorum beneficiorumque ecclesiasticorum. Hic est summus et universalis conditor canonum, et approbator legum sacrarumque omnium sanctionum, dispositor omnium ecclesiasticorum ordinum, confirmator institutionum et electionum': *De Regimine Christiano*, ii, 5, in H. X. Arquillière, *Le plus ancien traité de l'Eglise*, pp. 207–8.

[7] This is not, however, to say that papal policy in England and France, and the reactions to it, reflected a situation common to other areas of Christendom. In Hungary, for instance, papal provisions were far less numerous and the number of curialists (Italian and French) among those taking advantage of papal provisory rights was rather limited. See P. Bousquet, 'Papal Provisions in Hungary', pp. 104–7. Nor was papal primacy in the Church universally accepted. In Sicily, for example, the clergy, backed by Frederick III, often succeeded in impeding the implementation of papal provisions: C. R. Backman, 'The Papacy, the Sicilian Church, and King Frederick III', pp. 234–7; Backman, *The Decline and Fall of Medieval Sicily*, pp. 213–16.

nominations and taxation in the Church of England and of France, the two main monarchies of fourteenth-century Christendom and the closest allies of Clement V.

Papal policy in the Church was conducted along the lines laid down by Clement IV in *Licet ecclesiarum* (27 August 1265). This constitution established the right of the Roman pontiff to 'full control', by provision or reservation, of all churches, parsonages, dignities, and other ecclesiastical benefices vacated in the Roman curia.[8] According to Geoffrey Barraclough, the document represents a stage in the familiar process of the adjustment of law to fact, since the practice of papal provision – as an implementation of the pope's *plena potestas* – was already quite widespread.[9] Clement V improved existing practices and defined more clearly the charges and benefices reserved to the provision, collation, and disposal of the apostolic see. The constitution *Etsi in temporalium* included:

patriarchates, archbishoprics, bishoprics, monasteries, priories, parsonages, dignities, offices, canonries, prebends, churches with cure or without cure, and any other ecclesiastical benefices, by whatever name they are called, which are unknown at present to be vacant at the apostolic see, and which during the whole time of our pontificate may happen to be vacant in the future.

Clement's main innovation was specifically to involve patriarchates, archbishoprics, and bishoprics, which were not mentioned in the past. The document voiced the firm creed of the pope-elect concerning the need and justification for his close supervision of ecclesiastical nominations and, on the whole, his active intervention in all facets of Church life:

Though the caution of discretion should be had in the disposition of temporal goods, especially that they be disposed of worthily and in praiseworthy manner, nevertheless, in ecclesiastical matters it ought to be our intention to watch much more closely, so that for their utility and the praise of the divine name, according to the conditions and states of persons, there should be provided ecclesiastical persons of merit, since, according to canonical sanctions, there is nothing which hurts the Church of God more than that unworthy persons should be appointed to the rule of souls.[10]

Although Clement justified papal centralisation on spiritual grounds, his long expertise in ecclesiastical affairs would hardly have allowed him to ignore the economic and political implications of such a policy. The timing of this decree, 31 July 1305 – i.e., only one week after Bertrand de Got formally accepted his election to the papacy and before he met

---

[8] *De praebendis et dignitatibus, Liber Sextus*, lib. III, tit. iv, cap. 2, *CIC*, vol. II, col. 1021.
[9] G. Barraclough, *Papal Provisions*, pp. 148–55.
[10] *De praebendis et dignitatibus, Extravagantes communes*, lib. III, tit. ii, cap. 3, *CIC*, vol. II, col. 1258–9; W. Lunt, *Papal Revenues in the Middle Ages*, vol. II, no. 345, p. 221.

the cardinals – further suggests his independent character and clear vision of the prerogatives inherent in the highest Church office. Clement later amplified his decision to embrace cardinals, chaplains, and all those performing a service at the papal curia.[11]

The policy of centralisation was not an innovation of Clement V. It characterised the thirteenth and fourteenth centuries and has received wide support in modern research. Guillaume Mollat regarded papal centralisation as inevitable because of the failure of the electoral body and the internal conflicts that often called for papal arbitration.[12] Geoffrey Barraclough, too, saw in the increasing number of petitioners to the Holy See the main catalyst for papal centralisation. It was the clergy's, not the popes', initiative that gradually caused the papal curia to replace local structures. Accordingly, papal centralisation responded to real, urgent needs, and was vital for any effective reform of the Church.[13] Still, the implementation of papal centralisation was contingent on the degree of determination of individual popes to foster such a policy and on the balance of power among the pope, the clergy, and the Christian princes.[14]

It is difficult to speak in terms of resoluteness to the long term with regard to Clement V. Although the former archbishop of Bordeaux demonstrated a clear conception of the scope and intensity of ecclesiastical authority, he was very sensible, and perhaps too vulnerable, to personal requests, whether they came from his ever-unsatisfied relatives, the clergy, or Christian princes. The gap between the pope's rigid intentions and daily practice was rather clear from the beginning of the pontificate. During a period of illness that pushed him to the verge of death, Clement revoked all provisions to major benefices made *in commenda*, on the grounds that their cures were being neglected (20 February 1307).[15] This decision was in accord with the resolutions of the Second Council of Lyons, which had restricted the number of benefices carrying the cure of souls to be held by one prelate. The overall period of the *commenda* was limited to six months.[16] This, however, was a kind of policy that Clement found very difficult, if not impossible, to accomplish in the long run. As soon as he recovered from his illness, the pope could not withstand the many requests of his relatives, ecclesiastics, and princes, to the point that the number of benefices *in commenda* for the rest of his pontificate actually increased.

[11] *Regestum Clementis Papae V*, nos. 3708, 8254, 8932, 9799.
[12] G. Mollat, *La collation des bénéfices ecclésiastiques*, pp. 66, 80–1.
[13] Barraclough, *Papal Provisions*, pp. 153–77; Barraclough, *Public Notaries and the Papal Curia*, pp. 130–1; Guillemain, 'Punti di vista sul papato avignonese', pp. 190–4.
[14] On the earliest precedents of papal provisions, see G. Mollat, *La collation des bénéfices ecclésiastiques*, pp. 19–21. [15] *Regestum Clementis Papae V*, no. 2263.
[16] *De electione et electi potestate*, Liber Sextus, l. i, tit. vi, c. 15, *CIC*, vol. ii, col. 954.

Taxation, as well, presented a central issue in the papal policy of centralisation in the Church, the implementation of which was influenced, if not dictated, by the degree of co-operation between pope and kings. In the fourteenth century, this co-operation acquired new, crucial relevance. Elizabeth Brown has convincingly proved the traditional animosity towards taxation inherent in medieval society, with prelates appearing in the forefront of the opposition to royal levies.[17] The crusade had undermined the opposition to taxation to some extent, paving the way for regular taxes.[18] The prevailing readiness to pay crusade taxes, however, did not reflect a new economic conception but, rather, an identification with the goals served by the levy.[19] Such identification did not exist with regard to the king, the kingdom, or the growing needs of both, which were relegated to the private concern of monarchs. Moreover, the Roman axiom, 'What touches all must be approved by all', provided an additional impediment to royal taxation, since it subjected kings in matters of general concern to the consent of all their subjects.[20] On the other hand, the continuous state of war in Gascony, Scotland, and Flanders created a chronic economic deficit in both England and France.[21] Although the expulsion of the Jews from England and Aquitaine in 1290 and from France in 1306 provided the kings with a massive gain in the short term, such action brought to a halt a regular source of income.[22] Notwithstanding the pressing needs of the growing state, the community of the realm often expressed its reticence about royal taxation in the framework of parliaments or assemblies. The absence of the mystical aura of a *real* crusade – i.e., the lack of a well-accepted justification – coupled with the reluctance of their subjects to pay taxes provided the main incentive for the kings to appeal to the papal camera for financial assistance.

During the pontificate of Clement V, the collection of the tenth was still justified on the grounds of a forthcoming crusade. Whatever the appeal of crusading terminology among contemporaries, the fact remains that in England and France, for example, between 75 and 92 per cent of the amounts collected actually reached the royal treasury. Although the

---

[17] E. A. R. Brown, 'Taxation and Morality in the Thirteenth and Fourteenth Centuries', pp. 26–8.

[18] E. H. Kantorowicz, '*Pro patria mori* in Medieval Political Thought', pp. 478–9.

[19] Lunt, *Financial Relations of the Papacy with England*, pp. 200–2.

[20] 'Quod omnes tangit ab omnibus approbari debet', *Codex Iustinianus, De auctoritate praestanda*, 5, 59, 5 #2, in *Corpus Iuris Civilis*. On the development of the principle of consent in the fourteenth century, see A. Marongiù, 'Il principio della democrazia e del consenso', pp. 555–75; G. Post, 'A Romano-Canonical Maxim', pp. 197–251.

[21] E. B. Fryde, 'The Financial Policies of the Royal Governments', p. 831; E. Miller, 'War, Taxation, and the English Economy', p. 22.

[22] W. C. Jordan, *The French Monarchy and the Jews*, pp. 200–13; R. R. Mundill, 'Medieval Anglo-Jewry'; Menache, 'The King, the Church, and the Jews', pp. 223–36.

attempt to give the curia financial independence had made papal taxation inevitable, in the early fourteenth century its scope was therefore dictated by the needs of Edward I, Edward II, Philip the Fair, and other Christian monarchs who shared the papal income, though to a lesser degree.[23] From the kings' point of view, it was useful, if not imperative, to support papal taxation, the greatest allotment of which augmented the royal treasury. It was also expedient to support papal provisions, which facilitated the path of court protégés to central Church positions. In England, for instance, papal provisions increased the number of royal clerks at the highest levels of the Church hierarchy, thus encouraging a joint front of the king and his protégés – now enjoying leading ecclesiastical positions – against anti-monarchical factors, either barons or prelates. As a result, the latter gradually found a common language in their opposition to the king and to the pope who backed him.[24] The kings of France, too, found advantageous ways of co-operation with the papal curia, which became a regular source of power for royal protégés.[25] In this convergence of different goals and various, but not opposing, interests, the pontificate of Clement V heralds an era of close co-operation with the kings of England and France; royal protégés could be, and were indeed, promoted to the highest Church positions while the kings themselves were granted a large proportion of ecclesiastical resources. The question remains open with regard to the outcomes of papal policy in the light of the new political challenges.

THE PAPAL CURIA

Clement's first nomination to the Sacred College (15 December 1305) consisted of ten cardinals, nine of them from the kingdom of France (six from Gascony) and one from England.[26] Four of the new nominees were the pope's relatives: Raimond de Got,[27] Arnaud de

---

[23] Lunt, *Financial Relations of the Papacy with England*, p. 31; Lunt, *Papal Revenues in the Middle Ages*, vol. I, pp. 71–7; J. Michelet, *Histoire de France*, vol. v, pp. 93ff. C. Samaran and G. Mollat found Clement V responsible for the corrupt fiscal practices of the Avignon period: *La fiscalité pontificale en France*, p. 158.

[24] J. R. H. Moorman, *Church Life in England in the Thirteenth Century*, pp. 213ff.

[25] G. Campbell, 'The Attitude of Monarchy Toward the Use of Ecclesiastical Censures', pp. 535–55; see also the grievances presented by the clergy of France in 1247: A. Smith, *Church and State in the Middle Ages*, p. 145.   [26] Amalric Auger, *Sexta Vita*, p. 92.

[27] The son of Arnaud Garsie, viscount of Lomagne and brother of Clement, he was archdeacon of Sens when the pope nominated him cardinal-deacon of S. Maria Nuova. Philip the Fair, too, was very generous towards him and his sister, a fact that brought about the macabre story of Villani regarding his place in the afterlife (see chapter 1, n. 78): F. Duchesne, *Histoire de tous les cardinaux français*, vol. I, pp. 364–6; *Notae ad vitas*, pp. 132–4.

Pellegrue,[28] Arnaud de Canteloup,[29] and Guilhem Ruffat;[30] one was the pope's old friend, Pierre Arnaud de Poyanne.[31] Their nomination to the College was not just a papal gesture of goodwill to his relatives and friends but, first and foremost, a political move. These appointees, placed at the core of curial activities, provided Clement with a group of close advisors and trustworthy legates for important missions.[32] Arnaud de Canteloup received the post of chamberlain and, as such, was responsible for the management of the apostolic camera and its financial policy; he actually performed the functions of both a finance and a foreign minister.[33] Raimond de Got was the pope's closest confidant. Arnaud de Pellegrue was entrusted with crucial missions to Italy, and Pierre Arnaud de Poyanne became vice-chancellor.[34] The description *de Vasconia* further characterised Clement's choices for the household, the camera, the chancery, and the penitentiary.[35] The other cardinals nominated in 1305 were Pierre de la Chapelle,[36] Bérenger Frédol

---

[28] Son of the Mothe Pellegrue family of Perigord, he was archdeacon in Chartres when Clement nominated him cardinal-deacon of S. Maria in Portico. One of the closest papal advisors, Arnaud was nominated legate in Italy and accompanied Henry VII to Rome. Protector of the Franciscans and the sisters of Ste Clare, he died in Avignon in 1335: Duchesne, *Histoire de tous les cardinaux français*, vol. I, pp. 361–3; *Notae ad vitas*, pp. 125–32.

[29] Born in a village in the diocese of Bordeaux, he was nominated archbishop by his uncle, Clement V. Before he took charge, however, Arnaud was raised to the title of cardinal-priest of S. Marcello. He died in December 1313, leaving large parts of his fortune to Bordeaux: *Notae ad vitas*, pp. 116–17; Duchesne, *Histoire de tous les cardinaux français*, vol. I, pp. 348–9.

[30] Cardinal-deacon of SS. Cosma e Damiano, he participated in the trial of Boniface VIII and died in 1311: Duchesne, *Histoire de tous les cardinaux français*, vol. I, pp. 359–60; *Notae ad vitas*, pp. 123–5.

[31] A Benedictine and abbot of Ste Croix, he supported the former archbishop of Bordeaux during the latter's difficult years. Clement nominated him cardinal-priest of S. Prisca and vice-chancellor of the Roman Church; he died in 1306: Duchesne, *Histoire de tous les cardinaux français*, vol. I, pp. 356–8; *Notae ad vitas*, pp. 134–5.

[32] The Aragonese representative was aware of their influence and advised James II to pay them an annual pension to assure their co-operation: *Acta Aragonensia*, vol. II, nos. 355–6, pp. 538–40. The bishop of Winchester, too, requested his agent in the curia, James Simbaldi, archdeacon of Winchester, to determine how much he should grant to Raimond de Got. See *Registrum Henrici Woodlock*, vol. II, pp. 700–1.   [33] *Notae ad vitas*, pp. 116–17.

[34] Head of the chancery, which included all departments that dealt with papal correspondence. Once the request or supplication of a candidate for a benefice – generally brought by a proctor – had been approved and signed by the pope, it had to be registered by the Board of Supplications; the Board of Examinations had to assure its fitness; the Board of Inscriptions drew up the letter that conferred the benefice; the Board of Engrossment put it into form; the Board of the Collector collated the engrossment; the Board of Seals sealed it; finally, the Board of Registration registered it. This process occupied more than one hundred notaries and writing clerks.

[35] Guillemain, 'Les Français du Midi à la cour pontificale d'Avignon', pp. 29–38; Guillemain, 'Le personnel de la cour de Clément V', pp. 139–81.

[36] Son of a noble family of Haute Marche, he began his ecclesiastical career as canon in the church of Notre Dame in Paris; later, he became bishop of Agen, Carcassonne, and Toulouse. Master of Roman law, he taught at Orléans, where Clement probably met him. As cardinal-priest of S. Vitale, later cardinal-bishop of Palestrina, he participated in papal diplomatic missions to Philip

(the elder),[37] Nicolas de Fréauville,[38] Etienne de Suisy,[39] and Thomas Jorz.[40]

Some chroniclers argued that the nominations were formulated 'according to the merits of each candidate'.[41] Those from England emphasised the fact that Thomas Jorz was *natione Anglicus*.[42] Yet most records condemned the pope's concern for his family and his assiduity on

IV. Clement required his services both in the inquisition of the Templars and in the internal conflict among the Franciscans. He died in 1312: Duchesne, *Histoire de tous les cardinaux français*, vol. I, pp. 343–5; *Notae ad vitas*, pp. 106–11; *Regestum Clementis Papae V*, no. 532.

[37] Son of a noble family of Languedoc, he was born in the castle of Benne in the diocese of Maguelonne. He became chaplain of Boniface VIII and later bishop of Béziers. Because of his legal skills, Boniface entrusted him with the compilation of the *Sextus*. Clement V nominated Bérenger cardinal-priest of SS. Nereo ed Achilleo and afterwards cardinal-bishop of Tusculum. He was entrusted with managing secret negotiations with Philip the Fair (5 November 1306). Later, Bérenger was delegated to hear the allegations in the trial of Boniface and to investigate the Templar leaders. In 1310, the pope conferred on him special powers to deal with the conflict between Conventuals and Spirituals. He wrote many legal treatises and was considered a serious candidate for the papacy after Clement's death. He died in 1323: *Notae ad vitas*, pp. 111–16; *Collectio actorum veterum*, pp. 61, 71–2, 98–100, 109; Duchesne, *Histoire de tous les cardinaux français*, vol. I, pp. 345–7; J. P. Migne, *Dictionnaire des cardinaux*, col. 941.

[38] Son of a noble family in Normandy, he was probably a nephew of Enguerrand de Marigny, with whom he maintained close links. Nicolas joined the Dominicans and became master of theology at Paris. Confessor of Philip the Fair, he achieved a strong position in the Capetian court. He defended the king against Boniface VIII, who summoned him to the papal curia, but the pope died before taking any measures against him. Philip's strong support brought about his nomination to cardinal-priest of S. Eusebio. Notwithstanding his stand against Boniface, Clement entrusted him with hearing the allegations against the late pope. One of the best preachers of the time, Nicolas was sent in 1313 to preach the crusade in France and he conferred the Cross on Philip, his sons, and Edward II. He died in 1323: *Notae ad vitas*, pp. 117–19; Duchesne, *Histoire de tous les cardinaux français*, vol. I, pp. 350–2; G. Minois, *Le confesseur du roi*, pp. 191–5.

[39] Born in the village of Suisy, near Laon. Archdeacon of Tournai, he became close to the court and supported Philip the Fair in his struggle against Boniface. His good services brought him the title of chancellor. The king interceded on his behalf with the pope, who nominated him cardinal-priest of S. Cyriac. After Etienne joined the Sacred College, Philip compensated him with an annual grant of 1,000 *l.t.* He was delegated by Clement to conduct confidential negotiations with Philip (5 November 1306), to hear the allegations in the trial of Boniface, and to investigate the Templar leaders. He died in 1311: *Notae ad vitas*, pp. 120–3; *Collectio actorum veterum*, pp. 61, 71–2, 98–100, 109; Duchesne, *Histoire de tous les cardinaux français*, vol. I, pp. 353–5.

[40] Doctor in theology, Thomas taught at the University of Oxford, where he was prior of the Dominicans and afterwards general of the Order in England. During a mission to the pope on Edward I's behalf, he was appointed cardinal. Former confessor of Edward I, Thomas maintained a close correspondence with him. After joining the Sacred College, he participated in the trial of Boniface and in the papal inquiry of Pierre Jean Olieu's theories. Thomas wrote many theological treatises, most of which have not survived. He died on his way to Rome for the coronation of Henry VII: A. B. Emden, *A Biographical Register of the University of Oxford*, vol. II, p. 1023; *Foedera*, I-4, pp. 62–3; *Notae ad vitas*, pp. 43–4; Migne, *Dictionnaire des cardinaux*, cols. 1105–6. Upon his death, Edward II failed to convince the pope and the cardinals to bring about the nomination of another cardinal from England. See *Foedera*, I-4, pp. 184, 193.

[41] *Les grandes chroniques de France*, p. 248; *Continuationis chronici Guillelmi de Nangiaco*, pp. 351–2; *Continuatio chronici Girardi de Fracheto*, p. 26.

[42] Walsingham, *Historia Anglicana*, p. 108; Rishanger, *Chronica*, p. 227.

behalf of the interests of Philip the Fair.[43] Jean d'Hocsem suggested that many cardinals were, in fact, selected by the king of France in compensation for their services to the crown; he further indicated the simoniacal character of these nominations, an allegation that actually characterised Clement's pontificate as a whole.[44] Tolomeo da Lucca carefully pointed to the main considerations that dictated Clement's nominations; namely, to be a member of his family and/or of the royal inner circle.[45] Bernard Gui reported the return to the Sacred College of the Cardinals Colonna, 'who had been deposed by pope Boniface'. Further, the papal decision was 'due to the requests of the king of France',[46] a decision that Ferreto de' Ferreti did not venture to judge himself but left, instead, to divine discernment.[47] Other authors from the peninsula regarded Clement's nominations as a major means in the Gallicanisation of the papal curia and the relegation of the Italian cardinals to a marginal position.[48] Villani reports that all the new cardinals had one main virtue in common: '[they were] friends and officers of the king, among them, as he [Clement] had promised, Cardinals Giovanni and Piero Colonna'.[49] The subservience of Clement V to Capetian interests, coupled with his disregard of Boniface's policy, thus appeared a logical outcome of his previous commitments at St Jean d'Angély. Clement's curial policy met with disfavour out of Italy, as well. The crucial influence of Philip the Fair was confirmed by Johannes Burgundi, the Aragonese representative in the curia, who failed to bring about the nomination of a cardinal from Aragon.[50] The *Flores* also referred to the growing discontent among the cardinals because of the pope's devotion to the Capetian king.[51]

---

[43] On the king's links with Pierre de la Chapelle whom Philip nominated 'amicus noster carissimus', see *Collectio actorum veterum*, pp. 226–9, 233–4.

[44] Jean d'Hocsem, *Gesta Pontificum Leodiensium*, p. 344.

[45] Tolomeo da Lucca, *Secunda Vita*, p. 25.

[46] Bernard Gui, in *Tertia Vita*, p. 55; Bernard Gui, in *Quarta Vita*, p. 61; *Continuatio Pontificum Anglica Brevis*, p. 715. See the letter of Philip IV to the pope thanking him for having reinstated the Colonnas to their former position (December 1305–February 1306): *Collectio actorum veterum*, p. 49; *Notae ad vitas*, pp. 135–8.

[47] 'Si tamen id debuerit agere, cum potuerit, discernat Ille qui iustus est iudex, et nulla fallitur tergiversatione ledentium': Ferreto de' Ferreti, *Historia rerum in Italia gestarum*, p. 183; *Chronicon Parmense*, p. 93; *Annales Parmenses Maiores*, p. 735; *Annales Urbevetani*, p. 272.

[48] Paolo di Tommaso Montauri, *Cronaca Senese*, p. 232; Dino Compagni, *Cronica*, p. 192; Agnolo di Tura, *Cronaca Senese*, p. 288.   [49] Villani, *Cronica*, l. viii, c. 81, p. 113.

[50] The pope justified his refusal on the grounds 'quod tunc non erat locus'. In contrast to the papal neglect of the Aragonese requests, Johannes Burgundi emphasised Clement's special consideration of Philip the Fair: 'De rege Francie communis habet vox et credimus esse verum, quod faciet, quidquid vult. Et etiam ad eius instantiam fient aliqui de suis cardinales in proximis quatuor temporibus, [ut] dicitur. De quibus predictis est magna ad[mir]acio apud multos et apud aliquos turbacio' (Finke, *Papsttum und Untergang des Templerordens*, vol. ii, no. 7, pp. 8–9).

[51] 'Hinc aliqui e fratribus murmuraruntt': *Flores historiarum*, p. 126; T. Schmidt, 'Zwei neue Konstitutionen Papst Clemens V', pp. 335–45.

In the second nomination to the Sacred College (19 December 1310), five cardinals were appointed: Arnaud de Falguières,[52] Bertrand de Bordes,[53] Arnaud Nouvel,[54] Raimond-Guilhem de Fargues,[55] and Bernard de Garves.[56] All of them were from France; two were the pope's nephews. Once again, Tolomeo da Lucca did not hide his criticism in emphasising the main assets of the new cardinals: 'all of them were Gascons . . . and two of them his nephews'.[57] Bernard Gui acquainted his readers with familiar details: Raimond-Guilhem de Fargues was the son of Marquise de Got – the pope's sister, who had married Bérenger Guilhem de Fargues – while Bernard de Garves was related to the pope 'from the side of another sister'. These facts were obviously most relevant to their appointment to the College, since they had not yet been ordained sub-deacons.[58] Other authors, too, were aware of the pope's preference for his relatives and friends, even if young and illiterate, whose nominations were deemed detrimental to the Church.[59]

Nine cardinals were nominated on 23 December 1312, all of them from Languedoc:[60] Guillaume de Mandagout, 'a most erudite man',[61]

---

[52] Born in Gascony, he became archbishop of Arles thanks to the mediation of Robert of Sicily. Clement nominated him cardinal-bishop of Sabina. Arnaud participated in secret papal missions to the Capetian court in 1307, in the coronation of Henry VII, and in the inquisition of the Templar leaders: *Notae ad vitas*, pp. 141–3; Duchesne, *Histoire de tous les cardinaux français*, vol. 1, pp. 367–8.

[53] Chamberlain of Clement V. The pope provided him to Albi and later nominated him cardinal-priest of SS. Giovanni e Paolo, but Bertrand died shortly afterwards: Duchesne, *Histoire de tous les cardinaux français*, vol. 1, p. 369; *Notae ad vitas*, pp. 143–5; *Regestum Clementis Papae V*, no. 2887.

[54] Originally from Ariège, Arnaud became abbot of the Cistercian monastery of Fontfroide in Narbonne. He was master of Roman law at Toulouse; Clement nominated him cardinal-priest of S. Prisca and vice-chancellor of the Roman Church. In this capacity, the pope required him to redact the statutes of the Order of Grandmont. Sent to England to negotiate between Edward and his barons and to secure the transfer of Templar property to the Hospital, he did not succeed in fulfilling the pope's expectations. He, too, enjoyed Philip's grants. He died in 1317: Duchesne, *Histoire de tous les cardinaux français*, vol. 1, pp. 370–2; *Notae ad vitas*, pp. 145–6.

[55] Dean of the cathedral church of Bayeux, Raimond was nominated cardinal-priest of S. Pudenziana. He died shortly after Clement: Duchesne, *Histoire de tous les cardinaux français*, vol. 1, pp. 373–4; *Notae ad vitas*, pp. 147–9.

[56] He was studying at Orléans when his uncle nominated him cardinal-deacon of S. Eustachio. John XXII conferred on him the title of cardinal-priest: Duchesne, *Histoire de tous les cardinaux français*, vol. 1, pp. 375–6; *Notae ad vitas*, pp. 149–51.   [57] Tolomeo da Lucca, *Secunda Vita*, p. 38.

[58] Bernard Gui, in *Tertia Vita*, p. 56; Bernard Gui, in *Quarta Vita*, p. 69. See also *Notae ad vitas*, p. 151.

[59] 'Iste papa multos cardinales fecit tam cognatos suos quam extraneos, pueriles, iuvenes et illiteratos. Unde dicitur ecclesiam Dei multum dehonestasse ponendo tales personas': *Martini continuatio Brabantina*, p. 262.   [60] Amalric Auger, *Sexta Vita*, p. 103.

[61] Son of a noble family, Guillaume was sent by Boniface VIII on a diplomatic mission to Aragon together with Charles II of Provence. Doctor *utriusque iuris*, Guillaume was archbishop of Embrun before joining the Sacred College as cardinal-bishop of Palestrina. He was highly thought of by other cardinals, who seriously considered his candidacy for the papacy after the death of Clement V: Duchesne, *Histoire de tous les cardinaux français*, vol. 1, pp. 377–9; *Notae ad vitas*, pp. 152–4.

Bérenger Frédol (the younger),[62] Raimond de Saint-Séver,[63] Guillaume Testa,[64] Arnaud d'Aux,[65] Jacques Duèse,[66] Guillaume de Peyre de Godin,[67] Vidal du Four,[68] and Michel du Bec.[69] Tolomeo da Lucca refers in a positive vein to the intellectual skills of these cardinals, since four of them were doctors in canon and Roman law, two were masters in theology, and only two responded to the usual description of 'the pope's relatives'.[70] Dante Alighieri, however, found unsatisfactory the papal preference for legal skills, a tendency that confined evangelism to a secondary role:

> And so the Gospels and Great Doctors lie
> neglected, and the Decretals alone
> are studied, as their margins testify.

[62] Nephew of the cardinal of the same name, who was nominated in 1305; he became bishop of Béziers in 1309 and cardinal-priest of SS. Nereo ed Achilleo in 1312. He died in 1323: *Notae ad vitas*, pp. 154–5; Migne, *Dictionnaire des cardinaux*, col. 941.

[63] A Benedictine, Raimond was abbot of St Sever in Aire, which he directed for twenty years. Nominated cardinal-priest of S. Pudenziana, he did not take an active part in political life: Duchesne, *Histoire de tous les cardinaux français*, vol. I, pp. 394–5; *Notae ad vitas*, p. 166.

[64] Born to a poor family, he entered the pope's service in his youth. Though he participated in papal diplomatic delegations to England from 1305 onwards, it is not certain whether he was ordained as a priest before his nomination as cardinal-priest of S. Cyriac; he was later bestowed the title of cardinal-bishop of Albano: Duchesne, *Histoire de tous les cardinaux français*, vol. I, pp. 396–9; *Notae ad vitas*, pp. 167–8.

[65] Born in Laromiou, a small village in Gascony, he was only twelve years old when he entered the service of Bertrand de Got, at the time archbishop of Bordeaux, who supported his education. Following the deposition of Gauthier de Bourges, Clement nominated him bishop of Poitiers, and afterwards cardinal-bishop of Albano. He was sent to England with Arnaud Neveau in 1312: Duchesne, *Histoire de tous les cardinaux français*, vol. I, pp. 380–4; *Notae ad vitas*, pp. 155–7.

[66] Originally from Cahors, he became bishop of Fréjus and, in parallel, chancellor of the king of Sicily. He was forced to resign as chancellor in 1310, when he was transferred to Avignon. Jacques conducted the negotiations with the Capetian court in the Boniface affair and was active in the Council of Vienne. He was nominated cardinal-priest of S. Vitale, and only four months later cardinal-bishop of Porto, the final stage before his election to the papacy in 1316: *Regestum Clementis Papae V*, no. 5391; Duchesne, *Histoire de tous les cardinaux français*, vol. I, pp. 400–6.

[67] A Dominican, he excelled in intellectual skills and was successively master of theology in Paris, lector at the papal palace at Rome, and papal chaplain. Clement nominated him cardinal-priest of S. Cecilia and entrusted him with the trial of Boniface in 1309. He died in 1314: Duchesne, *Histoire de tous les cardinaux français*, vol. I, pp. 385–7; *Notae ad vitas*, pp. 157–62.

[68] Originally from Bazas, he was considered one of the most learned persons of his generation. After joining the Franciscan Order, Vidal became master of theology and wrote many treatises on Holy Scripture. Clement nominated him cardinal-priest of S. Silvestro, and entrusted him with investigating the doctrines of Pierre Jean Olieu. He also participated in the inquisition of Bernard Délicieux. He died in 1327: Duchesne, *Histoire de tous les cardinaux français*, vol. I, pp. 388–9; *Notae ad vitas*, pp. 162–6.

[69] Son of a noble family of Normandy, Michel was dean of St Quentin in Vermandois and canon of Notre Dame de Paris. Clement nominated him cardinal-priest of S. Stefano al Monte Celio. An outstanding intellectual, he possessed one of the richest libraries of the time. He died in 1318: Duchesne, *Histoire de tous les cardinaux français*, vol. I, pp. 390–3; *Notae ad vitas*, p. 166.

[70] Tolomeo da Lucca, *Secunda Vita*, p. 48; Bernard Gui, in *Tertia Vita*, p. 57; Bernard Gui, in *Quarta Vita*, pp. 74–5.

So pope and cardinal heed no other things.
Their thoughts do not go out to Nazareth
where the blessed Gabriel opened wide his wings.[71]

Dante's complaints reflect an anachronistic aspect of the criticism levelled against the curial policy of Clement V. The Gospels and Nazareth – that is, the spiritual longing for a mythical, egalitarian Christianity – furnished terms of reference for analysing papal policy at the beginning of the fourteenth century. Pierre Dubois, too, though pleased with the preference for French prelates – which he accepted as just compensation for the Italians' former monopoly – treated the predilection for jurists as a contradiction of the Gospels and an offence against the Christian faith.[72]

Avarice and simony were considered to typify not only Clement's policy, but also affected the cardinals as well; contemporary records often described them as 'wolves charged with guarding the sheep'. The cardinals were accused of successively serving God and the devil, their pursuit of profit causing the loss of souls and being a source of corruption for the whole of Christendom.[73] With the melancholic tone characteristic of his whole treatise, Gervais du Bus found it difficult to make any comparison between the apostles and the cardinals of his own day, who instead of living in poverty and charity made a cult of avarice and vainglory.[74] This criticism was undoubtedly influenced by the luxury and ostentation that typified the way of life of many cardinals, whose extravagance served as a source of inspiration to their retinues as well.[75]

The criticism levelled at Clement by his contemporaries has been reinforced by modern research. Ernest Renan described Clement's policy in the College of Cardinals as 'one of the most abrupt revolutions recorded in ecclesiastical history', one that hindered the Gregorian Reform and caused Philip the Fair to win an overwhelming victory, from which the papacy was never freed.[76] Neither was J. Bernard lenient in his criticism. He considered 'the Gascon invasion of the Church' to be a major source of the abuse of the canons and the increase in simony.[77] The criticism of Clement's curial policy thus included two complementary, though opposing, views. One trend referred to papal policy as nepotistic and, as

---

[71] Dante Alighieri, *Divina Commedia, Paradiso*, c. IX, vv. 133–8.

[72] Pierre Dubois, *De recuperatione Terrae Sanctae*, LXX.III–12, pp. 190, 192.

[73] 'Sed domina pecunia omne negotium consummat in curia': *Vita Edwardi Secundi*, p. 197; Finke, *Papsttum und Untergang des Templerordens*, vol. II, no. 102, p. 185.

[74] Gervais du Bus, *Le roman de Fauvel*, p. 25, vv. 593–606; Gervais' strong criticism of the cardinals and their behaviour covered 145 lines; see *ibid.*, pp. 25–30, vv. 593–738.

[75] P. Jugie, 'Les *familiae* cardinalices et leur organisation', pp. 41–59.

[76] Renan, *Etudes sur la politique religieuse de Philippe le Bel*, p. 100. Cf. Dupré-Theseider, *Problemi del papato avignonese*, p. 31; Guillemain, *La cour pontificale d'Avignon*, p. 178.

[77] J. Bernard, 'Le népotisme de Clément V', p. 410.

such, corrupt; this is the view of historians who look at the Church as a bureaucratic establishment, with a clear differentiation between the ruler and his domain, which could not be managed as private property.[78] On the other hand, the pope's policy of centralisation proved too modern for many of his contemporaries, especially the chroniclers, whose concepts and scheme of priorities were rooted in the feudal world. Conversely, Guillaume Mollat has justified Clement's curial policy on the grounds of his need to ensure the loyalty of the College of Cardinals, a policy that proved itself in actual practice.[79] Furthermore, the branching out of curial activities demanded the advice of lawyers, while attenuating the dominance of theologians.[80]

The need for a more professional organisation was hardly unique to the papal curia, nor was it new. The growth of cities, the increase of trade, the proliferation of universities, and the emergence of national monarchies had all elevated the status of jurists everywhere. Lawyers became predominant whenever people came into contact with the royal court or its agents.[81] This process of change, though, did not affect critical attitudes towards Clement V and the papacy in general. The contradiction between daily practice, on the one hand, and expectations of the papacy, on the other, embraced also active protagonists of the process of change. Notwithstanding the fact that Pierre Dubois had been educated in the Roman heritage, which he employed extensively in the service of Philip the Fair, he barricaded himself behind anachronistic concepts when it came to evaluating the curial policy of Clement V. Other authors accused the vicar of Christ of competing with the antichrist in drawing Christian society away from salvation, since – they charged – Clement did not have friends other than money.[82] The anachronism characteristic of contemporary authors does not centre in their expectations of the papacy's return to an apostolic role, which a few years earlier brought about the election of Celestine V. It focuses, rather, on their expectations of a non-bureaucratic papal system, in complete disregard of the jurisdictional and administrative exigencies of the times.

---

[78] On the distinction between the king and the crown, see Kantorowicz, *The King's Two Bodies*, pp. 364–8.

[79] G. Mollat, 'Contribution à l'histoire du Sacre Collège', pp. 23–31. Still, G. Mollat himself mentions the close links of Cardinal Bérenger Frédol with the king of Aragon, whom he advised on the most profitable procedures that were to be fostered in the papal curia, sometimes against Clement's policy. On Clement's authority in the Sacred College, see R. Gaignard, 'Le gouvernement pontifical au travail', p. 213.

[80] B. Barbiche, 'Les procureurs des rois de France à la cour pontificale d'Avignon', p. 82; F. Tamburini, 'La penitenzieria apostolica durante il papato avignonese', p. 268; B. Schwarz, *Die Organisation Kurialer Schreiberkollegien*, p. 40.

[81] A. Gouron, 'Enseignement du droit', pp. 1–33; C. R. Cheney, *Notaries Public in England*, pp. 41–7.

[82] 'Dou pape, dou roi et des monnoies', in Renan, 'De diverses pièces relatives aux différends de Philippe le Bel avec la papauté', p. 380.

The nostalgia for a more glorious past has been the lot of many generations, but it turned most poignant in times of crisis. Adversity, poverty,
and the political crises at the beginning of the fourteenth century
encouraged a fatalistic approach to current reality; emphasis was placed
on the growing gap between the Church's ideals and, in sharp contrast,
the pope's detour from evangelical principles.[83] On the other hand,
Clement's preference for his relatives – the outcome of which, in terms
of political expediency, has still to be reconsidered – could hardly be
overlooked. During his pontificate, seven members of the de Got family
joined the College of Cardinals, while many others were promoted to
leading positions in the ecclesiastical establishment.[84] To mention a few
examples: after Clement nominated his beloved nephew and successor in
Bordeaux, Arnaud de Canteloup, to the College, Arnaud was replaced
by another nephew of the same name, who governed the province for
twenty-seven years. Members of the pope's extended family, especially
his d'Aux and de Mothe relations, also received a large number of ecclesiastical benefices in Poitiers and Bazas.[85]

Though in many cases Clement's nominations were successful and his
relatives proved effective in advancing papal policy, the pope was forced
at times to retract his decision. Such was the case of his nephew, Bernard
de Fargues, whom Clement nominated bishop of Agen notwithstanding
his youth (25 February 1306).[86] After only three months, Bernard was
transferred to the archbishopric of Rouen (4 June), his many virtues,
according to the pope, amply justifying his promotion.[87] In order to free
him from the performance of pastoral duties, Clement allowed his relative to appoint suitable vicars in spiritualities and temporalities.[88] Still,
Bernard fell short of the pope's expectations. 'Because of his youth and
impertinence, he failed to deal with the Norman nobility.' The clash
between the parties eventually forced Clement to transfer his nephew to
the archbishopric of Narbonne (5 May 1311).[89] This turn of events was

---

[83] *La laie Bible*, pp. 26–7; Gervais du Bus, *Le roman de Fauvel*, pp. 14–15, vv. 311–40; cf. J. Huizinga,
The Waning of the Middle Ages, pp. 37–9; A. Sachs, 'Religious Despair in Medieval Literature and
Art', pp. 231–56.

[84] On their exemption from payment of wages to the curia, see J. Trenchs Odena, 'Las tasas apostólicas y el "gratis" papal', p. 328.   [85] Guillemain, 'L'apogée religieux', p. 302.

[86] *Regestum Clementis Papae V*, nos. 901, 1515.

[87] 'Virum experte probitatis claritate conspicuum te laudabila tue probitatis indicia representant. Sic
enim studiis virtutum insistis, sic laudabiliter dirigis actus tuos ad merita probitatum quod nos ad
tui honoris promotionem invitas, et ad exhibitionem animas gratiarum': *ibid.*, no. 1030; *Collectio
actorum veterum*, pp. 126, 127–30. The local record emphasises the fact that Bernard did not achieve
the see 'per electionem capituli, sed per provisionem summi pontificis', and further refers to his
main virtues; namely, his being 'nepos Clementis papae . . . de Vasconia natus': *Ex altera chronici
Rotomagensis continuatione*, p. 351.   [88] *Regestum Clementis Papae V*, no. 2070.

[89] *Ibid.*, nos. 6775, 6794, 7151. The transfer of prelates became a common practice during the
Avignon period, in contrast to the former reluctance of the Church to interfere in the mystical

reported in contemporary sources, not without satisfaction.[90] In 1309, Clement was also compelled to send back his old uncle, Bertrand de Got, to Agen after the pope had provided him to the bishopric of Langres, which embraced nobility.[91] Upon Bertrand's death (5 May 1313), another nephew, Amanieu de Fargues, canon of Reims and brother of Bernard, was provided to Agen (1313 to 1356 or 1357).[92]

The nepotistic bias that characterised many of Clement's nominations, however, did not remain an exceptional phenomenon. Contemporary rulers, as well, followed the pope's example in their display of 'Christian charity' towards the pope's relatives. Philip the Fair bestowed knighthood and the viscounty of Lomagne and Auvillars on Arnaud Garsie de Got, one of Clement's elder brothers.[93] Arnaud's heir also received the manor of Duras.[94] Edward I and Edward II were no less munificent, and awarded Arnaud Garsie's son the castles of Blanquefort, Puyguilhem, and Saint-Clair and the fortresses of Monségur, Dunes, and Donzac. Bertrand de Sauviac, too, received castles, royal benefices, and fortresses, while Raimond-Guilhem de Budos was given royal grace to build a stronghold, together with a confirmation of his jurisdictional rights in Budos.[95] The Angevins of Naples endowed the pope's family with the castle of Meyrargues and several manors in Pena Savordona and Pertuis.[96] Avoiding mention of the virtues of the recipients, which could have made them worthy of royal grace, the charters instead laid emphasis on their being nephews 'of Clement, by divine grace pope of the Holy Roman Church'. The concern of Christian princes towards the welfare of Clement's relatives, however, could hardly blur the problematic nature of the pope's nepotistic approach. Contemporary sources refer critically

marriage between prelates and their see. For the scope of this practice during Clement's pontificate, especially during his last years, see *ibid.*, nos. 295, 2887, 2893, 4554, 5391, 5426, 6474, 6865, 6961, 7001, 7417, 7434, 8014, 8018, 9271, 9551, 9578, 9718–20, 9888.

[90] *Continuationis chronici Guillelmi de Nangiaco*, p. 382; Jean de St Victor, *Vita prima*, p. 19; *Les grandes chroniques de France*, p. 280; *Continuatio chronici Girardi de Fracheto*, p. 35; Finke, *Papsttum und Untergang des Templerordens*, vol. II, no. 13, p. 15; *Registrum Clementis Papae V*, no. 1220. The local record emphasised the fact that Clement was 'avunculum suum': *Ex altera chronici Rotomagensis continuatione*, p. 351.

[91] *Regestum Clementis Papae V*, nos. 901, 1105, 1220, 1515. Although the pope justified this peculiar exchange on the grounds of Bertrand's nomination to Rouen, the old bishop's desire to return to his former see had actually forced Clement to reverse his former decision: *Collectio actorum veterum*, pp. 138–40.   [92] *Regestum Clementis Papae V*, no. 132.

[93] See the pope's letter in this regard (23 March 1308): *Regestum Clementis Papae V*, no. 3556; for papal privileges on behalf of Arnaud Garsie de Got, see *ibid.*, nos. 3766–73, 5374, 6373–5.

[94] Philip also sanctioned the grants of Edward II: *Registres du Trésor des Chartes*, nos. 225–30, 1513–14, 2012, 2022, 2033, 2238–9, 2241.

[95] *Notae ad vitas*, pp. 94–101; *Foedera*, I-4, pp. 45, 48, 123–4, 129, 140, 147–8; II-1, pp. 10, 24–5, 28; Renouard, 'Edouard II et Clément V d'après les Rôles gascons', pp. 129–33.

[96] J. Bernard, 'Le népotisme de Clément V', p. 385; Ehrle, 'Der Nachlass Clemens V', pp. 140–5.

to the pope's favouritism not only towards his relatives but also to all churches of his native area.[97]

Yet the prevalence of the de Got family in the Church, especially in Gascony, though reaching its peak during Clement's pontificate, had begun long before Bertrand ascended to the papal see. Furthermore, the involvement of the de Gots in ecclesiastical affairs was not an exceptional phenomenon; it continued, rather, a widespread tendency by thirteenth- and fourteenth-century popes to nominate local families to high ecclesiastical offices. Other lineages, too, were attached to the Church. Thus, after Bérenger Frédol (the elder) was nominated cardinal, he was replaced by his nephew of the same name at the see of Béziers (1309–12).[98] When Bérenger Frédol (the younger) was himself designated cardinal in 1312, he was succeeded in Béziers by his brother, Guillaume Frédol (1314–49). Another brother, André Frédol, served as bishop of Maguelonne.[99] This state of affairs was not considered nepotism by contemporary authors who reviewed nominations to the Church. On the contrary, after Clement's death, Bérenger (the elder) was proposed as a serious candidate for the papacy. One can point to other cases, as well. In 1299, Guillaume Durant (the younger) was provided to Mende after the death of his uncle, Guillaume Durant, 'the speculator', notwithstanding the fact that the former had not yet been ordained to priesthood.[100] Another example is provided by the Aycelin family, one of the most distinguished lineages in Auvergne. After Hugues Aycelin joined the Sacred College in 1288 and became cardinal-bishop of Ostia in 1294, he advanced the ecclesiastical career of two of his brothers and of his nephew. Jean Aycelin became secular abbot of Bourges and Clermont; he held prebends in the family church of Billom and in other churches in the dioceses of Clermont, Beauvais, Le Puy, and Narbonne.[101] His nephew, Albert, was prebendary in Langres, Chartres, Rouen, Narbonne, and in several churches in Clermont, including the family church of Billom. He amassed this considerable empire in spite of the fact that he was under age and deficient in orders.[102] The cardinal of Ostia

---

[97] 'Idem Clemens genus suum sublimavit, et plura castra idem construxit, decimas Leomaniae nobilibus concessit contemplatione vicecomitis nepotis sui, et collegium de Villendrau et Uzestae instituit, et jus patronatus generi suo concessit in perpetuum': *E chronico Aimerici de Peyraco*, p. 207; Agnolo di Tura, *Cronaca Senese*, p. 343.

[98] Clement confirmed his election, notwithstanding the fact that he had reserved the see. The pope justified this exceptional favour on the grounds of Bérenger's many skills and his familiar pedigree: *Regestum Clementis Papae V*, nos. 4055. In many other cases, as well, Clement was most generous to the cardinals' nephews and relatives whom he promoted to lucrative benefices. See, for example, *ibid.*, nos. 4420, 4666, 5346, 5986, 6601, 6785, 8088, 8117.

[99] Migne, *Dictionnaire des cardinaux*, col. 941.

[100] On the diocese of Mende and the relationship of the Durants with both king and pope, see C. Fasolt, *Council and Hierarchy*, pp. 64–111.   [101] *Les registres de Boniface VIII*, nos. 295, 2018.

[102] *Ibid.*, nos. 300, 2019.

further used his influence to favour Gilles Aycelin, whom Nicholas IV nominated papal chaplain. By 1289, Gilles held a provostship, an archdeaconry, and three priories in Clermont, pensions in various monasteries, and prebends in Bayeux, Rouen, Le Puy, and Billom. In 1290, Nicholas IV provided him to the metropolitan see of Narbonne.[103] For the twenty years that Aycelin held his see, he was rarely in residence and spent most of his time in the royal court. Clement later transferred him to Rouen and conferred on him a leading role in the trial of the Templars.

The nepotistic character ascribed to Clement's policy in the College of Cardinals, though corroborated by fact, was not therefore a peculiar innovation of his; rather, it was a practice rooted in the ecclesiastical establishment of the age. Furthermore, when Clement was crowned at Lyons, only sixteen cardinals were alive; none of them was from England, and only one was from France. The nominations of 1305 thus appear justifiable, since they balanced the College, with twenty-eight members, to include one cardinal from England, one from the Iberian peninsula, ten from France, and sixteen from Italy.[104] It was only towards the end of Clement's pontificate that the Italians were relegated to a secondary role, a fact that minimised their chances of appointing a new pope from their ranks. By 1314, there were only six Italians by comparison with twenty-four cardinals from France. Though this situation was unprecedented, it still reflected the leading place of France in fourteenth-century Christendom and the main role it was expected to play in Clement's crusading projects.

Clement, on the other hand, treated the curia, the treasury, and the Church as a whole as his personal domain, without leaving room for a 'public space'.[105] This attitude is clearly reflected in his last will, which considered the papal treasury as a personal fortune: 320,000 florins went to enrich the treasuries of France and England. The pope's nephew, the viscount of Lomagne, received 300,000 florins towards his future participation in the crusade and his engagement of 500 knights for up to two years.[106] Another 200,000 florins were shared by Clement's relatives – i.e., the families of Albret, Durfort, Pis, Salviac, and Espanha – his

---

[103] *Les registres de Nicolas IV*, nos. 980, 3709, 4963.

[104] Clement V's appreciative gesture towards England was not repeated by his successors. After Thomas Jorz's death, no cardinal from England was appointed until 1368, when Urban V designated the archbishop of Canterbury to the College. The absence of an English cardinal acquired all the perspectives of a political mistake because of the Hundred Years War and the pro-French bias that was attributed to the Avignon papacy.

[105] F. P. Caselli, 'L'espansione delle fonti finanziarie della Chiesa', p. 66.

[106] After a prolonged trial and many attempts to prevent the accomplishment of the penalties sanctioned, Bertrand de Got was forced to return half this amount to the papal treasury; he eventually did so only on 6 October 1322. The remaining 150,000 florins were to be invested in the forthcoming crusade.

friends, and the members of his household. Only 70,000 florins were bequeathed to his successor.[107] Pierre Jame complained, not without reason, that 'Our lord father the pope is saving treasures, and works very hard to improve the status of his family and relatives. But he does not care very much to eradicate the many abuses in the Church.'[108]

In addition to Clement's close family, whole areas of Aquitaine, where the pope was born, was educated, and had served in different stages of his ecclesiastical career, enjoyed papal generosity. Of some 10,500 letters in the papal registers, more than 2,500 concern Aquitaine,[109] namely, the dioceses of Cahors, Rodez, Albi, Toulouse, Maguelonne, Couserans, Pamiers, St Bertrand-de-Comminges,[110] Tarbes, Lescar, Auch, Aire, Condom, Lectoure, Dax, Bayonne, Agen, Bazas,[111] Bordeaux,[112] Saintes, Angoulême, Périgueux, Limoges, Carcassonne, Narbonne, Béziers, and Montpellier.[113] Clement's special concern for these areas is faithfully reflected in 337 papal letters that bestowed plenary indulgence, in some cases for fifteen years, to those who, 'truly penitent and having made confession', make pilgrimages to their shrines. Clement's generosity with regard to celestial forgiveness appears questionable, not only because of its clear favouritism but also because of its inflationary essence; this became most evident when compared with the average of c. 400 days conferred in former indulgences.[114] Clement further transformed the churches of Villandraut and Uzeste into collegiate churches; promoted restoration works at Villandraut, Uzeste, St Bertrand-de-Comminges, and Bordeaux; and favoured contributions on their behalf as well as on

---

[107] See the pope's wills of 29 June 1312 and 9 April 1314: Ehrle, 'Der Nachlass Clemens V', pp. 15–31. Cf. Guérard, 'La succession de Clément V', pp. 7–9. For the inventory of the papal treasury after Clement's death, see *Regestum Clementis Papae V*, no. 10552.

[108] Fournier, 'Pierre Jame (Petrus Jacobi) d'Aurillac, jurisconsulte', p. 509.

[109] One should note, however, that most of Clement's secret letters have been lost.

[110] Clement bestowed many privileges on the cathedral, and he himself delivered the relics of St Bertrand, thereby turning Comminges into a centre of pilgrimage: *Regestum Clementis Papae V*, no. 3994; Guillemain, 'Les papes d'Avignon, les indulgences, et les pèlerinages', pp. 257–8.

[111] Bordeaux, Bazas, and Comminges were the sees that benefited most from the pope's will. Some justification of Clement's generosity could be found in the expensive building of Gothic cathedrals at the time, which local prelates could hardly afford. A considerable number of papal privileges, indeed, emphasised the construction expenses of the local clergy: *Regestum Clementis Papae V*, nos. 4276, 4278, 5369, 5444, 5713, 7126, 7654, 8074, 8119, 8339; A. Clergeac, 'Les concessions d'indulgences de Clément V aux églises de Gascogne', p. 105.

[112] Clement did not conceal his appreciation of his former see: 'Hec est enim ecclesia, que a iuventutis nostre primordiis suis delitiis nos educavit ut filium more matris, huiusmodi quidem dulcedinis ubera suximus.' The pope translated his esteem into practice when he exempted the province from any subordination to Bourges (26 November 1306) and increased the privileges of its archbishop and local clergy: *Regestum Clementis Papae V*, nos. 1001–2, 2212, 3210, 3541, 3759, 4430–1, 4920–1, 4601, etc.; *Notae ad vitas*, pp. 101–2.

[113] Gaignard, 'Le gouvernement pontifical au travail', pp. 174–82.

[114] Guillemain, 'Les papes d'Avignon, les indulgences, et les pèlerinages', pp. 257–66.

behalf of the chapter at Agen, where he had begun his studies.[115] The pope's concern for his family and for Gascony led Bernard Guillemain to speak in terms of Clement's 'morbid feelings' for his *petite patrie*.[116]

Although the favouritism that coloured Clement's policy cannot, therefore, be neglected, there are still important reforms that the pope and his relatives introduced into the curia that indicate a modernisation process. These reforms were necessitated, at least partly, because of the semi-nomadic operation of the curia until 1310; but there are also some changes that testify to the pope's tendency to effect budget cuts.[117] In the chancery, for instance, Clement curtailed the number of writing-clerks from 110 to 96;[118] their number was reduced in the penitentiary from twenty-one to twelve.[119] Still, the number of clerks in the apostolic camera remained seven, although it later decreased to three or four for the rest of the century.[120] From 1310, the pope ordered that all payments in kind be stopped and that wage payments be made in cash. In parallel, the previous formula of 'according to the old tenth tax',[121] which appeared in curial documentation until the spring of 1308, was replaced by a new formulation, 'according to the common tax'.[122] This was not just a theoretical modification but a true reflection of the need to make taxes conform to economic developments, particularly because of the unstable monetary policy of Philip the Fair.[123] The pope's awareness of monetary developments was felt everywhere. In a letter to the bishops of London and Lincoln, whom he had appointed collectors of the tenth in Scotland, Clement urged his representatives to update the taxes, since their collection was adversely affected during the long conflicts that had affected the area.[124]

In the framework of administrative reorganisation, Clement also tried to weaken the curia's dependence on Italian bankers, such as the Bardis, the Spinis, the Riccardis, and the Cerchis.[125] The pope encouraged the

---

[115] Ehrle, 'Der Nachlass Clemens V', pp. 121–8.

[116] Guillemain, *La cour pontificale d'Avignon*, p. 151.

[117] See the accounts published by Guillemain for the years 1308–9: Guillemain, *Les recettes et les dépenses de la chambre apostolique*.

[118] P. Rabikauskas, 'La parte sostenuta dalla cancelleria nelle concessioni papali delle grazie', p. 234.

[119] See the papal letter to Cardinal Bérenger Frédol of 2 September 1311: *Regestum Clementis Papae V*, no. 7359.   [120] *Ibid.*, app., vol. I, p. 156.   [121] *Ibid.*, nos. 774, 958, 2451, 2669, 2673.

[122] *Ibid.*, nos. 2500, 2931, 3131, etc.

[123] J. D. Morerod, 'Taxation décimale et frontières politiques en France', pp. 338–9.

[124] 'Ne praedictam decimam secundum antiquam taxationem fructuum tempore . . . factam, sed secundum modernum valorem redituum exigant': *Regestum Clementis Papae V*, no. 2329.

[125] We have little knowledge of the financial dealings of Italian bankers with the papal court in the pontificate of Clement V. No doubt they were more restricted than they had been earlier, because more papal money was transferred by clerks between 1306 and 1316. Many payments to the papal chamber were still being made by Florentine bankers, like the Cerchis, Peruzzis, Bardis, and Spinis, as well as by the Bellardis of Lucca.

emergence of an independent accountancy, with the chamberlain, Bertrand de Bordes, at its head.[126] This step was probably fostered by the Italians' denial of loans at the beginning of the pontificate, because of the critical insolvency of the curia.[127] By means of the collection of annates, fruits during vacancies, tenths, census, and fees for common services, Clement increased the curial yearly income to about 200,000 florins, its current needs amounting to barely half this amount.[128] As a result, the apostolic camera stored the considerable sum of 1,040,000 florins at the end of the pontificate.[129] Because of Clement's endowments, however, the Church enjoyed very little of this treasury, a regrettable situation which John XXII tried hopelessly to change.[130]

THE CHURCH OF ENGLAND

The two main channels of papal influence in local churches were nominations and taxation. Because of their economic implications, these means were directly influenced by the degree of co-operation between *regnum* and *sacerdotium* which, at least with regard to England and France, was rather high during the pontificate of Clement V. Still, papal provisions put this co-operation to the test notwithstanding the fact that Clement consciously avoided the provision of foreigners to major benefices; these were provided to the subjects of Edward I and Edward II either in England or on the Continent. The pope emphasised the unprecedented nature of this policy,[131] which brought about the confirmation or nomination of the following prelates:

[126] *Regestum Clementis Papae V*, nos. 2294, 2296; Caselli, 'L'evoluzione della contabilità camerale nel periodo avignonese', pp. 414–15. On the parallel evolution in France, see Menache, 'The Templar Order', pp. 18–20.

[127] Clement referred to their refusal in a letter of 1 February 1306: 'And what is shameful to relate and is not free of astonishment, the merchants who offered themselves to the service of that Church failed it in a time of immediate necessity' (J. P. Kirsch, 'Die Annatenbulle Klemens V. für England, Schottland, und Irland', pp. 202–7).

[128] Ehrle, 'Der Nachlass Clemens V', pp. 123–8. Cf. Caselli, 'L'evoluzione della contabilità camerale nel periodo avignonese', p. 416; C. McCurry, '"*Utilia Metensia*"', pp. 311–23.

[129] Caselli, 'L'espansione delle fonti finanziarie della Chiesa', p. 65.

[130] See the terms of the pope's will, nn. 106–7 above.

[131] Clement argued before the king 'cum non recolamus unquam, neque credamus nos alicui, qui non sit de regno Angliae, seu ducatu Aquitaniae, vel aliis terris, tuae ditioni subjectis natus, in eodem regno Angliae providisse, licet praedecessores nostri, sicut in aliis terris et regnis, consueverint, sicut expedit providere': *Foedera*, I-4, p. 117. Nearly all fourteenth-century bishops and archbishops were from England, most of them royal nominees; the majority of provisors to lesser benefices were also natives, except in cathedral chapters, where the proportion of Italian and French to dignitaries and canons also declined in the second half of the century: R. L. Storey, 'Papal Provisions to English Monasteries', p. 91.

Henry Woodlok (Winchester, 1305–16);[132]
John Langton (Chichester, 1305–37);[133]
Ralph Baldock (London, 1306–13);[134]
William Greenfield (York, 1306–15);[135]
Walter Stapeldon (Exeter, 1308–26);[136]
Walter Reynolds (Worcester, 1308–13; Canterbury, 1313–27);[137]
John of Droxford (Bath and Wells, 1309–29);[138]
John Ketton (Ely, 1310–16);[139]
Richard de Kellaw (Durham, 1311–16);[140]

[132] Henry belonged to a family of landed gentry with many branches in the southern counties, especially in Hampshire. After he entered the Benedictine Order, he became prior of Winchester Cathedral priory. For the socio-economic origins of English bishops, see the excellent study by K. Edwards, 'The Social Origins and Provenance of the English Bishops', pp. 51–79.

[133] Upon his appointment as chancellor in 1292, he was described as a simple clerk in the chancery. Dismissed by Edward II, he still played an active role in the negotiations between king and barons.

[134] *Regestum Clementis Papae V*, no. 477; *Foedera*, I-4, pp. 46–7; Adae Murimuth, *Continuatio chronicarum*, p. 8. Formerly dean, he wrote a history of England and edited a rule for St Paul's chapter, which has not survived. Appointed chancellor by Edward I, Ralph was dismissed by Edward II, probably under Gaveston's influence.

[135] *Regestum Clementis Papae V*, nos. 475–6; *Calendar of Entries in the Papal Registers*, pp. 7–8; Adae Murimuth, *Continuatio chronicarum*, p. 8. He owed much of his career to his powerful kinsmen, Godfrey Giffard, bishop of Worcester, and Walter Giffard, archbishop of York, who paid for his education at Oxford and collated him to his first benefices in the South-West and Yorkshire. Edward I sent him on many diplomatic missions. William also won Edward II's patronage and was directly involved in the Scottish wars: *Chronica Pontificum Eboracensis*, p. 413.

[136] Master in arts and doctor in canon and Roman law, Walter had been a leading member of the cathedral chapter before his election. Though he was committed to the king from the start, he was often absent from the crucial political events during Edward II's reign. He was appointed royal treasurer between 1320 and 1325: M. Buck, *Politics, Finance and the Church in the Reign of Edward II*, pp. 38, 115, and passim.

[137] A simple priest with no formal education, son of Reginald, a baker in Windsor. Walter joined Edward I's court. Between 1301 and 1307, he was keeper of the wardrobe of the prince of Wales. Highly criticised for his luxurious lifestyle and waste of money, he owed his ecclesiastical appointments to Edward II: K. Edwards, 'The Political Importance of the English Bishops', pp. 314, 326–7.

[138] *Calendar of the Patent Rolls (1307–1313)*, p. 100; *Foedera*, I-4, p. 149. A wardrobe clerk from a distinguished family of the village of Droxford in Hampshire, he was collated by Bishop Woodlock to the rectory there. Possibly with legal training from Oxford, he became administrator of the wardrobe in 1291 and was promoted to keeper or treasurer in 1297. During the Scottish campaigns, he accompanied Edward I, who mentioned to the pope his long and faithful service to the crown and the heavy expenses that he had incurred (7 October 1306). Edward II appointed him chancellor of the treasury. By March 1308, John held five churches, canonries, and prebends in twelve dioceses, and other benefices. On that date, he was allowed dispensation, at the request of the king, to continue to hold all but two of these benefices, with a licence of non-residence for two years, during which time he did not have to be ordained a priest: *Foedera*, I-4, p. 63. Having quarrelled with the king in 1313, he was put on trial, the case being transferred to the papal court: *Calendar of the Patent Rolls (1307–1313)*, p. 72; *Calendar of Entries in the Papal Registers*, p. 39; N. G. Brett James, 'John of Drokensford, Bishop of Bath and Wells', pp. 281–301.

[139] An almoner of Ely whose name suggests that his family originated in the village of Ketton near Stamford, in the county of Rutland.

[140] A monk and sub-prior of Durham from a family of burgesses who also held land outside the city. A bitter enemy of Edward II, who had opposed his election, Richard became reconciled with

Gilbert Segrave (London, 1313–16);[141]
Walter Maidstone (Worcester, 1313–17).[142]

Some prelates – Stapeldon, Droxford, Ketton, Kellaw, and Segrave – had been canonically elected. Although the king's influence on the chapter was quite evident in most cases, Richard de Kellaw was elected to Durham against the royal candidate, Anthony Passagno.[143] Edward II had especially dispatched Gilbert of Clare, earl of Gloucester, to Durham, but the chapter remained adamant.[144] John Ketton, too, was elected to Ely against the king's candidate, the Lombard Boniface da Saluzzo.[145] Contemporary chroniclers referred to Edward II's influence on episcopal elections as a major factor in the deterioration of the Church, since '[the king] promoted to ecclesiastical offices inept and unfit people who afterwards harmed him with a stick in his eye and a lance in his side'.[146] This reference probably suggests the support by many prelates of Isabella's *coup d'état* in 1326, which led to the deposition and eventual murder of Edward II. Awareness of the king's detrimental influence on episcopal nominations characterised the reign of Edward II as a whole. Yet it was neither strong enough nor sufficiently independent of political considerations to give the pope the support necessary for restraining the king. The very fact that support of papal intervention was dependent on the precarious situation of Edward II and the unpopularity of his policy may have facilitated criticism of the king but did not imply any attempt to replace royal influence with that of the pope on an effective/continuous basis. On the contrary, although the prelates of England failed to present a united front *vis-à-vis* either Edward II or Clement V, especially after the death of Winchelsey, they eventually opted for supporting the king against the pope in parliament.[147]

Both Edward I and Edward II succeeded in guarding royal prerogatives, especially with regard to temporalities. The declaration by Walter Jorz, archbishop of Armagh on 29 September 1307, hints at the complete subservience of the prelates to the king of England: 'I acknowledge the reception of these temporalities – which I received from your royal grace

---

the king only in 1314 when he offered Edward 1,000 marks and a valuable war horse on his way to Bannockburn. His predecessor in Durham, Antony Bek (1283–1311), was a royal clerk and the son of Walter Bek, lord of Eresby in Lincolnshire. See C. M. Fraser, *A History of Antony Bek, Bishop of Durham*, pp. 50–78.

[141] A younger son of Nicholas Segrave, lord of Segrave, in Leicestershire.
[142] *Calendar of Entries in the Papal Registers*, p. 115. He was canon of York of obscure origins; his family is completely unknown.
[143] A Genoese active in the court of Edward II. On his involvement with royal finances, see chapter 6.   [144] Robert de Graystanes, in *Historiae Dunelmensis Scriptores Tres*, pp. 93–4.
[145] W. E. L. Smith, *Episcopal Appointments and Patronage in the Reign of Edward II*, p. 15.
[146] *Polychronicon Ranulphi Higden*, vol. VIII, pp. 298–300.
[147] K. Edwards, 'The Political Importance of the English Bishops', pp. 346–7.

Map 2 Dioceses of England and Wales

and not by virtue of apostolic letters – and I totally submit myself to you on their behalf.'[148]

During the reign of Edward I, the entente between pope and king was essentially based on the readiness of each side to solve the many crises that plagued the pontificate of Boniface VIII. Clement revoked *Clericis laicos* as a gesture of goodwill towards the king (1 February 1306).[149] There are contradictory testimonies regarding the degree to which the papal decision was carried out in England. The revocation of *Clericis laicos* was included in the register of Richard Swinfield, bishop of Hereford, and was quoted, almost verbatim, by Simon of Ghent, bishop of Salisbury.[150] On the other hand, the clergy of York relied on *Clericis laicos* as late as May 1311 to justify their refusal to advance a grant to the king.[151] These opposing attitudes leave open the question of the acceptance or rejection of Clement's reversal of his predecessor's policy. The lack of conclusive evidence also characterises the reactions to another papal gesture of goodwill towards Edward I, the suspension of Robert Winchelsey, the archbishop of Canterbury and primate of England.

In a letter to Clement, Edward referred in touching terms to the many perils and disturbances that the archbishop had brought upon him and the realm. Addressing the pope's devotion to the Holy Land and his own desire to depart overseas, Edward peremptorily concluded that the suspension of the archbishop was a condition *sine qua non* for his participation in the crusade.[152] Clement could not remain unresponsive to such an appeal. It seems that the pope's animosity towards the primate of England, which probably went back to the days of his pontificate in Bordeaux, did not need much encouragement. Winchelsey's unconditional struggle against royal centralisation represented the antipode of Clement's personal creed. When Winchelsey's proctors presented the pope with a gift upon his election, Clement uttered threats against the archbishop. Winchelsey, aware of Clement's hostile attitude, tried to enlist some cardinals to his side, but his appeal fell on deaf ears.[153] On 12 February 1306, Winchelsey was summoned to the papal curia. In a rather patronising tone, Clement endowed his decision with all the components

---

[148] *Foedera*, 1-4, p. 89. One month earlier, Clement had written to Edward requesting immediate restitution of the archbishop's temporalities: *Concilia Magnae Britanniae et Hiberniae*, pp. 289–90.

[149] Clement based his decision on the grounds that because of his predecessor's decision 'nonnulla scandala, magna pericula et incommoda gravia sunt secuta et ampliora sequi nisi celeri remedio succurratur': *De immunitate ecclesiarum*, *Clementinarum*, l. III, tit. xvii, *CIC*, vol. II, col. 1178.

[150] *Registrum Simonis de Gandavo*, vol. I, p. 472.   [151] *Councils and Synods*, pp. 1340–1.

[152] The king emphasised the fact that Winchelsey had caused the kingdom 'damna quamplurima . . . quodque per factores et procuratores suos regnum nostrum sic dudum commotum fuerat et turbatum': *Concilia Magna Britanniae et Hiberniae*, p. 284; *Calendar of the Close Rolls (1302–1307)*, pp. 430–1; *Foedera*, 1-4, pp. 49, 54.

[153] *Registrum Roberti Winchelsey Cantuariensis archiepiscopi*, vol. II, pp. 679–80, 1348–9.

of an apparently equitable verdict, while trying to teach a lesson to the ecclesiastical hierarchy as a whole:

The higher the place attained in the Church of God by our venerable brother the archbishop of Canterbury, if he merits to be called venerable, the more he should walk in the paths of pontifical modesty by taking the greatest possible care that he should not commit those things that will provoke against him divine majesty and the apostolic see.[154]

The temporary suspension of Winchelsey left no room for doubt concerning the conciliatory policy of the former archbishop of Bordeaux towards his feudal lord of earlier times. The pope, however, did not fulfil Edward's request to provide a Gascon prelate to Canterbury instead of Winchelsey.[155] Clement's reluctance to fulfil the royal request did not prevent the king from proceeding with his personal vendetta. Shortly before the archbishop's departure from England, Edward took pains to order the constable of Dover Castle and the warden of the Cinque Ports to apply to the primate of England and his retinue the ordinance that prohibited carrying any money and gold or silver vessels out of the country.[156]

The suspension of Winchelsey was widely reviewed in contemporary sources, though neither the pope's action nor the king's initiative was criticised. Murimuth emphasised that the archbishop's exile resulted from royal pressure, while the *Flores* refers to Edward's wrath at Winchelsey's flouting of royal prerogatives during the king's sojourn on the Continent.[157] The *Flores* further hints at the prophetical aura bestowed on the archbishop during his exile in Bordeaux, where the exact timing of Edward I's death was revealed to him.[158] The rather moderate reactions to Winchelsey's suspension appear surprising in light of the praise of the archbishop attendant upon his death a few years later. These

---

[154] *Annales Londonienses*, p. 145. The papal letter was submitted to Winchelsey only on 18 May, and he departed for Bordeaux on the following day. Winchelsey stayed near the papal court throughout his suspension, roughly ten months at Bordeaux and ten months at Poitiers. Although according to the London annalist Clement declared his intention to give a just hearing to the archbishop, the latter waited a long time before being granted an audience: *Annales Londonienses*, p. 150; *Registrum Roberti Winchelsey Cantuariensis archiepiscopi*, vol. II, p. 1350.

[155] See Clement's own testimony in a letter to Edward II, written between 16 and 30 June 1313, in which the pope refers to Edward I's request 'ut eundem archiepiscopum ad sedem apostolicam vocaremus'. This letter was not entered in Clement's surviving registers and exists only in a corrupt transcript in a register of Christ Church, Canterbury: British Mus. Additional MS 6159, fo. 150. H. G. Richardson published it in his paper, 'Clement V and the See of Canterbury', pp. 101–3.   [156] *Calendar of the Close Rolls (1302–1307)*, p. 375.

[157] Adae Murimuth, *Continuatio chronicarum*, p. 9; *Flores historiarum*, pp. 126, 130.

[158] *Flores historiarum*, ad a. 1307, app., p. 328. The vision of somebody else's death, confirmed in reality, was a common *topos* in medieval literature; see S. Menache and J. Horowitz, 'Rhetoric and Its Practice in Medieval Sermons', pp. 345–6.

changing attitudes in an interval of seven years hint not at different approaches to Robert Winchelsey, but at the changing balance of power between the king and the Church of England. Just as Edward I's relatively strong position in 1306 prevented any criticism of Winchelsey's suspension, so his son's weakness in 1313 encouraged vociferous applause of the archbishop and his political stand. When Clement died, the *Flores* dealt in detail with the pope's irresponsible behaviour towards Canterbury which, rather surprisingly, the chronicler related to the pope's continuous harassment of the monastic Orders as a whole.[159]

The coronation of Edward II did not affect the harmonious co-operation between king and pope, nor did it lessen royal intervention in ecclesiastical affairs. On the contrary, notwithstanding Edward's unstable position at home, he took a leading role in ecclesiastical affairs from the very beginning of his reign, and in certain issues he was more extreme than his predecessor. Only one month after his father's death (7 August 1307), Edward II ordered the arrest of Walter Langton – one of Edward I's closest advisors, bishop of Coventry and Lichfield, and treasurer of England – who had dared to criticise Edward II's favouritism towards Gaveston.[160] On 20 September, Langton's lands were seized and various inquiries into his wealth and debts initiated. The master of the Temple in London was ordered to surrender any treasure that Langton had deposited there (3 October), and four days later most of Langton's money was paid to the wardrobe.[161] Walter Reynolds, an intimate of Edward II, was appointed treasurer of England instead, thus beginning a successful career, which was to include the bishopric of Worcester later that year and the archbishopric of Canterbury in 1313.

Edward II's severe actions against the bishop of Coventry and Lichfield were not exceptional. In France, too, there were at least two well-known cases of bishops arrested for political reasons during the reign of Philip the Fair – Bernard Saisset, bishop of Pamiers, and Guichard, bishop of Troyes.[162] These punitive actions, with all their detrimental effects on ecclesiastical immunity, resulted from the involvement of prelates in royal administration, which exposed them to conflicts of interest. On the other hand, continuous royal infringement of ecclesiastical privileges created a vicious circle, which Clement V was unable to break. This is not to say that the pope conferred apostolic blessing on royal violations of ecclesiastical immunity. In actual practice, however, it was Clement V, not Edward II, who in most cases chose the way of compromise. The exam-

---

[159] *Flores historiarum*, ad a. 1314, p. 157.   [160] *Foedera*, I-4, p. 92.
[161] *Records of the Trial of Walter Langton*, pp. 1–5; *Concilia Magnae Britanniae et Hiberniae*, pp. 301–2.
[162] See nn. 292–302 below.

ples that follow indicate the delicate balance between pope and king where major benefices were concerned.

Shortly after the death of William of Geinsborough, bishop of Worcester, Clement reserved the appointment of his successor (5 October 1307).[163] In the meantime, the chapter received royal authorisation to proceed with the election, through which the king hoped to favour the new treasurer, Walter Reynolds. Edward sent Hugh Despenser to Worcester in order to influence the chapter on behalf of the royal clerk. By this time, however, report of the papal reservation reached England. The king reacted by instructing the convent to proceed with the election without further delay[164] and, according to the royal letter of recommendation, Walter Reynolds was unanimously elected.[165] In the meantime, Clement provided the see to Peter of Savoy, though taking into consideration the possibility of a new election, should Peter refuse the charge.[166] Thus, a typical case of conflicting interests between pope and king arose, with the chapter relegated at best to a secondary role.

In his many letters to the pope and the cardinals, Edward II depicted the papal provision to Worcester as a frontal attack on the chapter's right to hold a free election. The king took upon himself the convenient role of *advocatus ecclesiae*, who by force of circumstances was compelled to defend the Church of England against papal usurpation. In the process, Edward also voiced the royal version of the status and liberties of the 'national' Church. From the beginning of Christianity, the clergy had always enjoyed free elections; this right had been confirmed by both King John and Pope Innocent III. Still, a *congé d'élire* had to be sought of the king, and the bishop-elect was to be presented for royal approval. If the king considered the candidate to be an enemy, a foreigner, or otherwise unsatisfactory, he could quash the election. The appointment of bishops touched the crown's right of patronage and, for that reason, the apostolic see could neither reserve nor bestow bishoprics. Edward further expressed his fears that, should the pope succeed in Worcester, there would never be free elections in England, thus launching an attack on papal provisions and associated canonical exegesis, which had been so carefully elaborated throughout generations.[167] The implementation of

[163] William of Geinsborough was a Franciscan, lecturer in theology at Oxford and the papal court. He played an active role in diplomatic delegations to Rome and France during the reign of Edward I: *Regestum Clementis Papae V*, no. 2273; *Calendar of Entries in the Papal Registers*, p. 31; R. M. Haines, *The Church and Politics in Fourteenth-Century England*, p. 9.

[164] *Calendar of the Close Rolls (1307–1313)*, p. 4.   [165] *Foedera*, I-4, pp. 98–9.

[166] The provision was not registered in the papal records: W. Thomas, *A Survey of the Cathedral Church of Worcester*, pp. 158–9.

[167] See Edward's strong complaints to the cardinals on 20 January 1308: *Foedera*, I-4, pp. 98–9; W. E. L. Smith, *Episcopal Appointments and Patronage in the Reign of Edward II*, pp. 11–12. Edward

papal provisions, which reached its zenith during the Avignon period, does not therefore indicate royal recognition of the papal monarchy. Most papal provisions actually succeeded because of the popes' readiness to co-operate with the monarchs in advancing their protégés to leading Church positions.

As to the crisis in Worcester, the election proceeded on 13 November, and the prior, who was commissioned to make the choice, decided for Walter Reynolds. The latter was cautious, giving his consent only after some delay, with the excuse that no notice of a papal reservation had come by trustworthy channels either to the convent or to himself. On 21 November, Edward wrote to the pope and the cardinals to notify them of the election and ask for the appointment of a suitable substitute for Winchelsey – still in Bordeaux – to consecrate the bishop-elect.[168] Clement was therefore presented with a *fait accompli*, on which he soon bestowed apostolic blessing. In the provision of Walter Reynolds, the pope apologetically referred to the chain of events that had postponed the confirmation of the prelate. Since the pope had reserved the see, the bishop-elect had refused to give his consent, expecting to be formally notified of the reservation or its cancellation. As Walter Reynolds seemed a fit person and had been so vehemently recommended by the king, the pope finally provided him to Worcester (12 February 1308).[169] At the king's request and on account of his occupation with state affairs, Clement also permitted Reynolds to postpone his consecration until the feast of St Andrew (30 November).[170] Actually, Walter Reynolds was consecrated at Canterbury only on 13 October 1309, i.e., nearly one year after his election and eight months after his provision.[171] The indifference of the new bishop to his see did not weaken over the years. Treasurer of the Exchequer from 1307 to 1310, chancellor from that year until April 1314, and appointed the king's lieutenant during the wars in Scotland, Reynolds was also keeper of the great seal and remained a central figure in the royal council during the troubled reign of Edward II. Reynolds'

corresponded actively with members of the papal curia. In 1307, when he was pressing for the canonisation of Thomas de Cantilupe, he wrote to twenty-five cardinals. The same year, he wrote once to eleven and another time to six cardinals protesting the harm being done to royal prerogatives. See *Foedera*, I-4, pp. 102, 103, 109, 117. Wright calculates a total of 1,538 letters that Edward II wrote to the cardinals. His evaluation was based on the Roman Rolls in the Public Record Office, which by no means contained all correspondence of this type: J. R. Wright, *The Church and the English Crown*, pp. 309–12.   [168] *Foedera*, I-4, p. 98.

[169] *Regestum Clementis Papae V*, no. 2464; *Calendar of Entries in the Papal Registers*, p. 34. The royal grant to the bishop-elect of the issues and profits of the see from the date of vacancy was made on 5 April 1308: *Calendar of the Patent Rolls (1307–1313)*, p. 63.

[170] The pope justified the prorogation on the grounds that Walter was 'circa magna negotia in regno Angliae utiliter occupato': *Regestum Clementis Papae V*, no. 2890; *Calendar of Entries in the Papal Registers*, pp. 37, 41.   [171] Haines, *The Administration of the Diocese of Worcester*, pp. 77–8, 280.

leading role in English politics clearly suggests his priorities, among which spiritual duties towards his diocese were relegated to a secondary role, at best.

The name of Walter Reynolds appears again five years later in the contested elections to Canterbury. Upon his accession to the throne, Edward II wrote to the pope to seek the return of Robert Winchelsey, with full restitution of his prerogatives.[172] Weakened by a stroke of paralysis, which he suffered during his stay in the papal curia, Winchelsey died on 11 May 1313.[173] Some time before, Clement had reserved the right to appoint the new primate of England (27 April).[174] This decision was apparently transmitted to the papal nuncios in England, Cardinals Arnaud Nouvel and Arnaud d'Auch, with special instructions to postpone its delivery to the prior and monks of Christ Church until July.[175] In the meantime, being granted the license of free election by the king, the chapter speedily elected Thomas Cobham.[176] This result challenged the expectations of Edward II, who supported the candidacy of his chancellor and confidant, Walter Reynolds. Whatever Clement's original intentions had been, his former reservation annulled any argument that he might have put forth on the impropriety of setting aside a canonical election.[177] Neither legal

---

[172] Edward expressed his desire to bring about Winchelsey's restitution for two main reasons: to redeem his father's soul and to allow his proper coronation by the primate of England as had been common practice among his ancestors for generations: *Concilia Magnae Britanniae et Hiberniae*, pp. 290–1; *Regestum Clementis Papae V*, nos. 2372–3; *Calendar of the Patent Rolls (1313–1317)*, pp. 77, 87–8; *Calendar of Entries in the Papal Registers*, p. 33; *Foedera*, I-4, p. 105. The king postponed his coronation to allow Winchelsey to perform it (25 February 1308), but the archbishop was not able to return in time and delegated the bishop of Winchester to act in his place: *Gesta Regum Continuata*, p. 322. In a later letter to the king, Clement alluded to Edward's support of the archbishop: 'Nos vero tuis supplicacionibus inclinati archiepiscopum ipsum ad ecclesiam remisimus antedictam.' These words hint at the pope's reservations in regard to the extremist policies of the archbishop and his influence on English politics. A transcript of the original manuscript is in Richardson, 'Clement V and the See of Canterbury', p. 102.

[173] In his obituary of Winchelsey, the Malmesbury chronicler eulogised: 'of him especially it can be said: "None is found like unto him to preserve the law of the Highest" [Eccles. 44:20]' (*Vita Edwardi Secundi*, p. 40); Trokelowe, *Annales*, p. 81; Walsingham, *Historia Anglicana*, p. 136; *Flores historiarum*, pp. 154–5. Winchelsey's candidacy for canonisation was offered by petition to parliament in 1327: J. H. Denton, *Robert Winchelsey and the Crown*, pp. 17–18, 21–7; J. Cox Russell, 'The Canonization of Opposition to the King', pp. 279–90.

[174] *Regestum Clementis Papae V*, no. 9713; *Calendar of Entries in the Papal Registers*, p. 115.

[175] According to the *Annales Paulini*, the letter of reservation was read in St Paul's, London, on 5 July, the same day that the monks of Canterbury dispatched their proctors to Avignon. It was not until 7 July that the monks were informed by the papal nuncios in England of Clement's decision: *Annales Paulini*, p. 274; *Concilia Magnae Britanniae et Hibernia*, pp. 424–5.

[176] *Calendar of the Patent Rolls (1307–1313)*, p. 586; *Concilia Magnae Britanniae et Hiberniae*, pp. 427–8; Denton, 'Canterbury Archiepiscopal Appointments', pp. 320–1.

[177] Denton rejects Richardson's suggestion that the pope had Thomas Cobham in mind, since Clement's main concern was to find a suitable candidate for Canterbury 'who would be as conciliatory to the king and the king's ministers as he was inclined to be himself': Richardson, 'Clement V and the See of Canterbury', p. 98; Denton, 'Canterbury Archiepiscopal Appointments', p. 323.

considerations nor his own precedent in Worcester a few years earlier, moreover, prevented Edward from demanding the full implementation of papal prerogatives while displaying a careful deference towards the papal reservation.[178]

The papal reservation to Canterbury was mentioned by the annalist of St Paul's, John Trokelowe, the chronicler of Malmesbury, and Thomas Walsingham.[179] Most chroniclers, however, ignored Clement's reservation and described the chapter meeting where Thomas Cobham was unanimously elected.[180] Although the sources are unanimous in regard to Cobham's many virtues – his noble lineage, his learning in law (Oxford), theology (Cambridge), and arts (Paris) – they disagree on the causes of his deposition.[181] Most chroniclers point to the opposition of Edward II as the reason that the canonical nominee failed.[182] Trokelowe and Walsingham after him, however, attribute the initiative to Clement V, out of his desire to find a candidate 'who could greatly lessen the sufferings of the Church of England' in such a way that 'the Church and the kingdom will derive much benefit'.[183] Indeed, the papal provision on behalf of Walter Reynolds gives testimony to the pope's desire 'to provide a suitable person by the providence of the apostolic see' (1 October 1313). The suitability of Walter Reynolds was not based on his spiritual or intellectual skills. The archbishop represented the political stand of those royal clerks who maintained a close collaboration with the court, as opposed to the independent policies of Winchelsey, Pecham, and Kilwardby, his predecessors at Canterbury.[184] Walter Reynolds' strong political position and his excellent relations with Edward II made him, therefore, an ideal candidate to lead the clergy in the path chosen by Clement V – that of collaboration with the royal court.[185]

---

[178] *Foedera*, II-1, p. 55.

[179] *Annales Paulini*, p. 274. Trokelowe emphasises the monks' neglect of the papal reservation: 'monachi dicti loci, licentia a rege obtenta . . . ad electionem procedentes . . . non deferentes inhibitioni summi pontificis, qui ante mortem dicti Roberti ipsius honoris collationem sibi reservavit': Trokelowe, *Annales*, p. 81; *Vita Edwardi Secundi*, p. 45; Walsingham, *Historia Anglicana*, p. 136. [180] Adae Murimuth, *Continuatio chronicarum*, p. 19.

[181] Murimuth found it necessary to report that in the end justice was done, since John XXII compensated Thomas Cobham with the diocese of Worcester (1317): Adae Murimuth, *Continuatio chronicarum*, pp. 19–20.

[182] *Vita Edwardi Secundi*, p. 45; *Gesta Edwardi de Carnavan*, p. 45; *Chroniques de Sempringham*, p. 330; *Chronicon Angliae Petriburgense*, p. 160.

[183] Trokelowe, *Annales*, p. 82; Walsingham, *Historia Anglicana*, p. 136.

[184] Denton, 'Walter Reynolds and Ecclesiastical Politics', pp. 248, 271–3; Wright, *The Church and the English Crown*, pp. 243–74.

[185] In order to facilitate Reynolds' difficult work, the pope conferred on him a three-year privilege by which he could visit his diocese and province by deputy, and by this means receive his procuration (13 January 1314): *Regestum Clementis Papae V*, no. 10152; *Calendar of Entries in the Papal Registers*, p. 120; *Concilia Magnae Britanniae et Hiberniae*, p. 434. The last two sources wrongly point to January 1313 as the date of the papal privilege, for it antedates Reynolds' provision.

The *Realpolitik* of Clement did not prevent contemporary chroniclers from considering it simoniacal. The author of the *Flores* suggested that the pope was convinced 'by means of a large amount of gold and silver'.[186] The Malmesbury chronicler, too, stated that 'a large sum had passed' between king and pope.[187] Other authors were more precise in their assessments of the primacy of England. The chronicler of Maux evaluated the price of Clement's compliance at 32,000 marks,[188] a considerable sum, which was reduced to 'only' 1,000 marks by the priest of Bridlington.[189] The accuracy of such charges has been disputed by scholars. J. R. Wright argues that there is a lack of evidence to support the charges of simony; he lays emphasis, instead, on Reynolds' many services to the crown and the Church. Conversely, H. G. Richardson refers to the simoniacal charges as 'undoubtedly true'.[190] The lack of satisfactory evidence and the differences between assessments of the remuneration preclude a clear judgement of whether bribery was involved in the papal provision to Canterbury or not.[191] This question, however, seems rather irrelevant in the light of Clement's tendency to co-operate fully with Edward II in complete disregard of the opposition to Walter Reynolds in the Church of England. This opposition caused the charge of simony to become an integral part of the stereotyped image of both the archbishop and the pope.

The *Flores*, indeed, depicted Reynolds as 'a layman and boor who pronounced his own name with difficulty'.[192] As a *vir Belial et lubricus*, he 'publicly desecrated the holiness of the clergy and set an odious example in his province by displaying in his actions the doctrine of Balaam'.[193]

---

[186] *Flores historiarum*, pp. 155–6. The *Flores* exploited the occasion to connect the 'infernalis avaritia' of Clement to his Gascon ancestry: *ibid.*, p. 157.   [187] *Vita Edwardi Secundi*, pp. 45–6.

[188] *Chronica Monasterii de Melsa*, vol. ii, p. 329.   [189] *Gesta Edwardi de Carnavan*, p. 45.

[190] Wright, *The Church and the English Crown*, pp. 243–6; Richardson, 'Clement V and the See of Canterbury', p. 99.

[191] Since the second half of the thirteenth century, there were fees paid by patriarchs, archbishops, bishops, and abbots on the occasion of their appointment or confirmation in consistory by the pope. These fees were composed of two payments: the principal sum was for common services (*servitia communia*) and was divided between the pope and the college of cardinals, and the other for petty services (*servitia minuta*), which was shared by the officials and servants of both the pope and the college. When and how the services became required payments, fixed in amount, are questions still seeking answers. See some illustrations of these 'secret services' in Lunt, *Papal Revenues in the Middle Ages*, vol. ii, pp. 245–51.

[192] *Flores historiarum*, pp. 155–6. The illiteracy of the archbishop was further confirmed by the authors of the *Vita Edwardi Secundi*, p. 45, and the *Chronicon de Lanercost*, p. 222. Wright denies such charges, arguing that, though the new archbishop lacked a formal university education, his library and career point to his wide education. According to this interpretation, the *Flores'* version indicates Reynolds' inferiority with regard to Winchelsey, the former rector of the University of Paris and chancellor of Oxford, and Cobham, who also enjoyed high academic repute. See Wright, 'The Supposed Illiteracy of Archbishop Walter Reynolds', pp. 67–8.

[193] *Flores historiarum*, pp. 155–6; cf. *Vita Edwardi Secundi*, pp. 45–6. Belial is a Hebrew word of uncer-

The chronicle of Lanercost, as well, did not mince words in criticising the archbishop, whom it found unworthy of his high rank. It described Reynolds' promotion as another step taken by Edward II against his own people.[194] In an inspiring passage from a metrical chronicle written in the vernacular, the royal policy in Canterbury was reviewed in terms of *le monde à l'envers*, as a faithful reflection of the complete transmogrification of accepted social norms:

> Ke de enfaunt fet rey. e prelat
> de vileyn. e de clerc fet cunte.
> Dunke vet la tere a hunte.

> Wos maket of a clerc hurle.
> And prelat of a cheurle.
> And of a child maked king.
> Dann is pe londe vndirling.[195]

Though Trokelowe did not join the general antagonism to the nomination of Walter Reynolds, he pointed out that the archbishop received the pallium 'after long resistance'.[196] A papal letter requiring the clergy of Canterbury to show due obedience to Reynolds corroborates reports of the unrest in the province.[197] As years went by, the readiness of Walter Reynolds to enlist the Church of England in the war efforts of Edward II – in complete opposition to the hostile policy of Winchelsey – provided a substantial factor in strengthening the animosity towards him.[198]

The chroniclers' criticism of Reynolds' nomination evolved, therefore, not from their rejection of papal intervention, but from the candidate's dubious pedigree. Narrative sources imply that, when papal provisions encountered opposition, the objection focused on the particular circumstances of the nomination or on the skills of the candidate without challenging the pope's right to designate the leading prelates of the Church of England. On the other hand, electoral processes *per se* did not guarantee support. Gilbert Segrave, who was elected to London in 1313, was depicted as 'a man excelling in his nobility', but also as 'a pseudo-

---

tain etymology, probably meaning 'worthlessness' or 'destruction' (Deut. 13:13; 2 Cor. 13:7). Balaam was a heathen prophet invited by Balak, king of Moab, to curse the Israelites. Divinely inspired, Balaam uttered blessings in place of curses (Num. 22:5). The rabbis associated Balaam with Israel's lapse into immorality.

[194] 'Homini quasi illiterato, et, secundum judicium humanum, tam ratione vitae quam scientiae omni gradu dignitatis indigno. Ecce! praeter turbationem quam fecit rex in populo, quale damnum fecit in clero, dum procuravit quod unus talis homo totius Angliae foret primas!': *Chronicon de Lanercost*, p. 222.

[195] *An Anonymous Short English Metrical Chronicle*, p. 107, vv. 618–24.

[196] Trokelowe, *Annales*, p. 82.   [197] *Registrum Simonis de Gandavo*, vol. I, pp. 477–9.

[198] *Concilia Magnae Britanniae et Hiberniae*, p. 439; *Vita Edwardi Secundi*, pp. 76–7; *Flores historiarum*, pp. 170, 173.

archbishop, and odious to many'.[199] The prevailing approach to Clement's policy in contemporary chronicles thus focused on its motives and outcomes; the criticism, which appeared more often than not, did not question the plenitude of papal power or its actual implementation.[200] To what degree this principle was accepted by the clergy as a whole, however, is more difficult to establish since both the process of papal provisions and the alliance between pope and king considerably restricted the clergy's room for manoeuvre.

The election in Exeter illustrates an attempt to weaken the king's overriding influence on ecclesiastical elections. Walter Stapeldon was elected by scrutiny on 13 November 1307, and the king confirmed his election by the *maior et sanior pars* (3 December).[201] The election, however, was contended by Richard Plumstoke, who was in the papal curia at the time. Edward II took prompt measures to support the bishop-elect and wrote to the pope and several cardinals on his behalf.[202] His cause was also taken up by the dowager Queen Margaret, and her brother, Philip the Fair. Archbishop Winchelsey, recently restored to his see, was commissioned by Clement to investigate the case, and he finally confirmed Stapeldon on 13 March 1308, four months after his election.[203] Internal conflicts of this kind could hardly have affected the acceptability of papal monarchy or the implementation of its prerogatives. On the other hand, there is also indication of a lack of co-operation with the pope, even when minor benefices were concerned. At the beginning of 1312, Clement consented to the request of Robert de Lareye and John of Havering, whom he entrusted with the administration of Wynston and Gateshead churches in Durham. The age and education of the nominees failed to conform to canonical demands and made papal intervention imperative. Still, it is apparent from the pope's letter to the bishop of Durham in December that the papal decision was not carried out in spite of repeated requests.[204] Although further evidence is lacking, it may be concluded that it was the threat of an interdict that finally brought about the implementation of the nominations after a year. This delay calls for attention, for it concerns Durham, one of the poorest dioceses in England.[205]

---

[199] *Flores historiarum*, p. 156.

[200] Gaudemet, 'Aspects de la primauté romaine', p. 125. A. Hamilton Thompson emphasises the complete rule of the Avignon popes over English benefices until the middle of the fourteenth century: *The English Clergy and Their Organization*, p. 11.

[201] *Calendar of the Patent Rolls (1307–1313)*, p. 20.   [202] *Foedera*, 1-4, pp. 101–2.

[203] *Calendar of the Patent Rolls (1307–1313)*, pp. 28, 52.

[204] *Registrum Palatinum Dunelmense, the Register of Richard de Kellawe*, vol. 1, pp. 129–30, 140–2, 144–6.

[205] Though Wright comments that 'most provisions at this time can be said to have taken effect more or less automatically', only about 75 per cent of papal provisions to Lincoln and Salisbury were actually put into practice: Wright, *The Church and the English Crown*, pp. 31–4.

The fragmentary documentation at our disposal indicates a clear gap between the limited scope of papal intervention, on the one hand, and the vociferous criticism of contemporaries, on the other. Although Clement drew upon his power to provide all benefices that fell vacant with the death of their incumbents at the apostolic see, papal provisions affected only bishops appointed by the papacy who had been consecrated at the Holy See.[206] Yet, Murimuth overlooks the pope's moderation – at least when compared with the policy of his successors – and turns papal provisions into a main fault of Clement V:

The same Clement made reservations of bishoprics, and particularly in the kingdoms of France and England, in order that he might extort private and common service. And he reserved to the collation of the apostolic see all benefices vacant by his promotions and by the death of his nuncios and chaplains dying anywhere.[207]

Murimuth's description of Clement's policy seems rather exaggerated for major benefices; it accurately depicts, though, papal methods in regard to minor benefices, where the alliance between pope and king disappeared as if it had never been. The archdeaconry of Richmond (York) provides a case in point. Since 1301 at least, this post had been occupied by Francesco Caetani, the nephew of the cardinal of the same name, who had been recognised by Edward himself.[208] Yet Edward II attempted to confer the benefice on John de Sandale and prohibited Caetani from disputing the appointment (25 April 1309). The king also ordered his sheriffs to arrest any person who attempted to impede the presentation. John de Sandale himself was forbidden to respond to any summons outside the realm, and the constable of Dover was told to arrest him should he try to leave England.[209] The many appeals by the king against the nomination of a foreigner to Richmond, however, were of no avail, and Clement left Francesco Caetani in his post.[210] A similar conflict of interests between pope and king followed the nomination of Cardinal Arnaud de Canteloup to the deaconry of St Paul's in May 1309; Edward did not succeed in revoking the nomination.[211] The king also failed to contest papal designations successfully in cases that did not affect cardinals or their

---

[206] *Regestum Clementis Papae V*, nos. 2562, 2830, 4424, 4871, 5464, 6412, 7212, 7228, 7455. On the culmination of papal provisions during the pontificate of John XXII, see A. Deeley, 'Papal Provision and Royal Rights of Patronage', pp. 497–527.

[207] Adae Murimuth, *Continuatio chronicarum*, p. 174.

[208] *Calendar of the Patent Rolls (1307–1313)*, p. 111.

[209] *Calendar of the Close Rolls (1307–1313)*, pp. 173–4.

[210] *Foedera*, I-4, pp. 102, 136, 143–4; *Regestum Clementis Papae V*, nos. 1901–2.

[211] *Foedera*, I-4, p. 139. Edward claimed that the many duties embraced by this benefice obliged residence. Conversely, the pope regarded the benefice as a source of income, thus placing stress on the *beneficium* rather than on the *officium*.

relatives. Sometime prior to 1311, Edward II had conferred the prebend of Northenbald in the church of St Peter (York) on his relative, Richard de Cornouailles. Pandolfo Savelli, who had been provided to this benefice, appealed to the royal court and, after his plea was rejected, to the pope. All efforts by Edward to defend his relative were of no avail, and the case remained open until Clement's death.[212] These episodes were not fortuitous; it was precisely over cathedral dignities and prebends that the crown and the papacy were most likely to come into conflict. Such benefices were normally in the gift of the bishop and, therefore, seemed suitable for papal provision, particularly when vacated by those who had been promoted by the pope in the first place. Further, they provided the kind of income that the pope was always looking for in order to remunerate cardinals and clerks working at the curia.[213] On the other hand, being in the gift of bishops, cathedral dignities and prebends were constantly being claimed by the king during the vacancy of bishoprics, since Edward regarded them as his *regalia*. It was mainly the claim of his right to exercise episcopal patronage during vacancies that brought Edward into conflict with Clement V.[214]

The conflict between pope and king concerning minor benefices justifies further research into the extent to which foreigners held parochial benefices during Clement's pontificate. The extant documentation suggests that their number was rather small. Of nearly 3,000 incumbents in the diocese of Durham, there were about forty foreigners, i.e., about 1.4 per cent. On the other hand, the offices that did not oblige residence, such as dean, precentor, chancellor, treasurer, archdeacon, and ordinary prebend or canon in cathedral chapters and collegiate churches, were considerably more affected by papal provisions, especially in York, Lincoln, and Salisbury, which provided the most lucrative benefices.[215] After the suppression of the Temple, Clement also reserved all benefices in certain areas that had been this Order's to award. Of the sixty provisions made during Clement's pontificate, thirty-three were for dignities, canonries, and prebends of cathedrals and collegiate churches. The collegiate churches (five in all) were subject to considerably fewer provisions than were the cathedrals (twenty-eight in all).[216]

---

[212] A. H. Thompson, *The English Clergy and Their Organization*, p. 11. For other cases, see W. E. L. Smith, *Episcopal Appointments and Patronage in the Reign of Edward II*, pp. 61–70.

[213] Raimond de Got, for instance, was at various times dean in York, Lincoln, and London, and precentor in Lichfield.

[214] For a critical approach to the nomination of foreigners to English benefices, see 'When Rome Is Removed', in *Historical Poems of the Fourteenth and Fifteenth Centuries*, pp. 118–20.

[215] Pantin, *The English Church in the Fourteenth Century*, pp. 59–60.

[216] For the implementation of papal reservation for minor benefices, see Wright, *The Church and the English Crown*, pp. 28–49.

Paradoxically, it was the problematic issue of taxation that provided Clement V and the kings of England more feasible ground for co-operation. In early July 1305, Edward I sent an impressive delegation to the pope-elect to explain his urgent financial needs. Among the royal representatives were Bartholomew of Ferentino and Otto de Grandson, who had represented royal interests before Benedict XI. The fruits of their mission soon became evident: on 1 August 1305, Clement granted Edward the right to collect the tenth for seven consecutive years. The tenth was imposed as three separate taxes: for two years beginning on All Saints (1 November 1305),[217] and for two and three years, beginning on 1 November 1307 and 1309, respectively.[218] John Dalderby, bishop of Lincoln,[219] and Ralph Baldock, bishop of London, were appointed papal collectors, and they were joined three days later by Walter Langton, bishop of Coventry and Lichfield.[220]

According to the letters addressed to the clergy, the tenths were levied for the needs of the Holy Land, which Clement depicted in moving terms:

Because both before and after the fortune of our promotion to the highest apostolic office, we have often tasted the bitterness of the cup of oppression extended over the Holy Land, which the impious hand of the Saracens, always eager to be drenched in Christian blood, wounds and lacerates . . . For avenging her – or rather our Saviour's – injuries, we propose to hasten, we intend to devote ourselves . . . to labour . . . lest that land should be unsuitably destituted of the aid of Christ's faithful.[221]

Although Edward I already wore the Cross, he was not required to pledge himself to depart overseas at a definite date or to restore the money should he remain in England. Moreover, the papal collectors were care-

---

[217] *Calendar of the Close Rolls (1302–1307)*, pp. 382–4, 439.

[218] *Foedera*, I-4, pp. 56–7; *Calendar of the Close Rolls (1307–1313)*, pp. 227, 237; *Original Papal Letters in England*, nos. 1, 7–9, pp. 3, 6–7; Zutshi, 'Some Early Letters of Pope Clement V', pp. 324–7.

[219] An Oxford graduate from the village of Dalderby in Lincolnshire, where his family held the advowson of the church, he was resident chancellor of Lincoln cathedral at the time of his election to the bishopric. John was active in the trial of the Templars in England. After his death, he was considered a saint, but John XXII opposed his canonisation (1328).

[220] Langton's arrest soon afterwards prevented his active participation in the collection of the grant. Of modest origins, he became treasurer of England in September 1295, and was one of the most important and influential ministers during the reign of Edward I. His methods in the Exchequer were often fraudulent, however. Accused of simony and nicolaism, he was eventually exonerated by Boniface VIII. Arrested by order of Edward II a few weeks after his accession to the throne, Langton was later released thanks to Winchelsey's and the pope's intervention on his behalf: *Regestum Clementis Papae V*, nos. 3699, 4351; *Calendar of Entries in the Papal Registers*, p. 49; J. Hughes, 'Walter Langton, Bishop of Coventry and Lichfield', pp. 70–6; A. Beardwood, 'The Trial of Walter Langton, Bishop of Lichfield', pp. 5–42. On the proceedings of the Exchequer for the collection of Langton's debts and the complaints against the bishop, see *Records of the Trial of Walter Langton*, pp. 9–243, 247–351.   [221] *Foedera*, I-4, p. 56.

fully instructed to deliver 10,000 pounds in five annual payments to Queen Margaret in order to defray the cost of her charity.[222] The proceeds of the second year were designated for the prince of Wales, to be applied against his expenses;[223] the rest, including almost the whole yield for the next five years, was meant to satisfy the financial needs of Edward I.[224] On 16 January 1307, however, the pope reserved for 'the burdens and necessities of the Roman Church' a quarter of the tenth during four of the years in which the king was to receive all of the proceeds, a modification which Clement had sought and for which he obtained the consent of the king.[225] The sums reserved to the queen, however, were excepted.

There was a growing gap, therefore, between Clement's declarations about his personal commitment to the crusade, on the one hand, and the investment of the tenth in the ever-growing needs of the royal family and the papal curia, on the other. The justification of the tenth further substantiates the ambivalence of papal fiscal policy. In the sanction given in 1306, Clement mentioned the needs of the Holy Land as making such taxation obligatory, and described Edward I as a 'Catholic prince and jealous guardian of the true orthodox faith'.[226] As early as February 1307, however, the crusade goal disappeared, replaced by the needs of the papal curia and 'various necessities' of the royal court.[227] This reversal of the goals of the tenth did not go unnoticed by contemporary chroniclers. When Rishanger refers to the tenth, he states that papal sanction was given 'for the Holy Land . . . but it was dissipated for other [uses]'.[228]

The pope's attempt to replace crusader ideology with the needs of the state and the curia was obviously favourable to the king; further, it could deepen the 'national' conscience of those prelates who were involved in royal administration and who fostered royal interests.[229] This was, however, the stand of a narrow group, influential as it was, which did not echo prevailing attitudes. It is also doubtful whether papal policy was of benefit for the apostolic camera, which was left with only meagre revenues. Edward I's acceptance of the first papal levy of annates (4 April 1307),[230] his promise to pay the arrears of the annual census for fifteen years, and his formal commitment to allow papal administrators to take

---

[222] *Original Papal Letters in England*, nos. 3–6, 11, pp. 4–6, 8; *Foedera*, 1-4, pp. 56–7.

[223] *Calendar of the Patent Rolls (1307–1313)*, pp. 60, 107; *Foedera*, 1-4, pp. 56, 57.

[224] *Original Papal Letters in England*, nos. 2, 10, pp. 3–4, 7.   [225] *Foedera*, 1-4, pp. 56–7, 68.

[226] *Ibid.*, 1-4, p. 56.

[227] PRO, SC 7/11/13, SC 7/11/24; printed in *Foedera*, 1-4, p. 68; Zutshi, 'The Political and Administrative Correspondence of the Avignon Popes', p. 373.

[228] Rishanger, *Chronica*, p. 228.

[229] On this development, see the excellent analysis by Kantorowicz, '*Pro patria mori* in Medieval Political Thought', pp. 472–92.   [230] *Foedera*, 1-4, p. 72.

over the temporalities of Canterbury may be seen as a *quid pro quo* for Clement's compliance (7 and 11 September 1306).[231]

The suspension of Winchelsey undoubtedly facilitated the work of Edward I, inasmuch as it removed a main obstacle to the taxation of the clergy. Edward I's death on 7 July 1307 did not interrupt the collection of the tenth, since the income of the second year was granted to Edward II; but the death of the old king invalidated the remaining grants. Clement renewed the three-year tenth in favour of Edward II and conceded a new tenth, to begin on 1 November 1312, when the triennial expired (18 May 1309).[232] Three weeks later, however, the pope instructed the bishops of Lincoln and London to pay the king only three-quarters of the total amount, thus leaving one-quarter to the apostolic camera. Edward II confirmed that this arrangement was carried out 'with our assent and will'.[233] The tenth of 1312, like the previous tenths during the pontificate of Clement V, was also associated with the crusade, on the grounds that Edward II was directing his energies towards the Holy Land. This was a rather imaginary description of the king's set of priorities at the time, when the Gaveston crisis was at its peak. Moreover, Edward was required neither to specify a date for his departure overseas nor to return the money should he fail to comply.[234]

The decision of the Council of Vienne to collect a six-year tenth for the forthcoming crusade provided Edward with an additional source of income. In 1314, he received a loan of 1,300 marks from the money collected for the crusade in the province of York.[235] In the contribution of the diocese of Salisbury, special mention was made of the goals to be served by the tenth, namely,

the king's attack on Robert de Brus and his accomplices, the king's enemies and rebels, who have entered the march of England and traitorously attacked and laid waste the castles, towns, churches, and other sacred places therein and perpetrated homicides, plunderings, sacrileges, and other crimes, and hasten to perpetrate worse evils with a great multitude of armed men.

---

[231] *Registrum Simonis de Gandavo*, vol. I, pp. 213–18; *Foedera*, I-4, p. 61; *Calendar of the Patent Rolls (1301–1307)*, p. 512. The king emphasised the exceptional nature of this grace, which was not to be used in the future in detriment to royal prerogatives. The continuous collection of annates and the king's renunciation to enforce the statutes of Carlisle led Tout to speak in terms of 'a double triumph' of papalism during the pontificate of Clement V. See Tout, *The Place of the Reign of Edward II in English History*, p. 206.

[232] Lunt, 'William Testa and the Parliament of Carlisle', p. 337, no. 2.

[233] Lunt, *Papal Revenues in the Middle Ages*, vol. II, no. 278, p. 105.

[234] In a letter to the abbot and convent of Faversham, Edward II mentioned 'the Scotch wars and other things' that would shortly force him to face great expenses, and asked the monks to display as much diligence as possible in collecting the tenth (17 August 1309): *Calendar of the Close Rolls (1307–1313)*, p. 227. [235] *Calendar of the Patent Rolls (1313–1317)*, pp. 188, 197, 438, 548.

No wonder that after such a display of devotion to the king and his kingdom, Edward II offered the clergy of Salisbury royal defence 'against the pope, the Roman Church, and many others who could claim any [part] of the said sum'.[236] The royal statement indicates the fragile essence of the alliance between pope and king, on the one hand, and its serious implications on the relationship between the pope and the clergy, on the other.

The critical weight of Clement's compliance with the fiscal demands of Edward I and Edward II becomes most evident when viewed in the light of the clergy's reluctance to enlist in the war effort. On 14 April 1311, Edward II failed to obtain the grant of a shilling in the mark from the clergy to subsidise his wars in Scotland.[237] Only one year later, however, the clergy acquiesced in paying Winchelsey a subsidy of four pence in the mark to cover the archbishop's financial needs and to improve the situation of the poorest churches in the province.[238] Edward protested against the decision, and rightly so from his perspective.[239] The subsidy was ordered by Winchelsey without any attempt to conceal its compulsory nature. By so doing, the primate of England asserted his authority to levy a tax on the clergy's income, including that of the exempt Orders, with the consent of an ecclesiastical council.

Winchelsey's display of an independent fiscal policy, however, was of no avail in the light of the pope's graciousness towards the king of England. Of the total yield of tenths paid by the clergy on papal orders, Edward II received 92 per cent. Of about 255,000 pounds that Edward II secured from subsidies paid by the clergy, 75 per cent was levied on papal orders.[240] When analysed from the viewpoint of contemporaries, Clement's generosity towards the king of England acquired all the characteristics of a political error. The Malmesbury chronicler reflects the perspective of the lower clergy, the main victim of the close alliance between pope and king, when he claims: 'Amongst all the provinces of the world England alone feels the pope a burden.' He deemed Clement's fiscal policy as bordering on anarchy and, as such, justifying disobedience. He further mocked papal arrogance towards the Church of England – the pope himself having submitted to all royal demands. In his dealings with the clergy, Clement had abandoned all restraint; no reason or caution

---

[236] *Calendar of the Fine Rolls (1307–1319)*, p. 207; see also the similar letter to Durham, *ibid.*, pp. 211–12.   [237] *Councils and Synods*, pp. 1305–6.

[238] *Ibid.*, pp. 1356, 1378. The tax was being collected in the diocese of Exeter early in July 1312. The exempt abbey of Bury St Edmunds, however, appealed to the curia against it.

[239] *Concilia Magnae Britanniae et Hiberniae*, p. 426; *Councils and Synods*, pp. 1367–8.

[240] Lunt, 'Clerical Tenths Levied in England by Papal Authority', p. 182. From the twelve original letters extant in the Public Record Office from the pontificate of Clement V, eleven concern the tenth: Lunt, *Financial Relations of the Papacy with England*, p. 417.

guided his actions: 'All fat rents he reserves for himself, and at once excommunicates the rebellious; legates come and plunder the land, men armed with bulls come and claim prebends.' The pope's yoke on the prelates was heavier than that of the emperor on the laity. Against this background, the chronicler tried to teach the heir of St Peter a basic lesson in Christian ethics: 'perhaps the pope will say that he is above the laws and consequently cannot be bound by the laws. But he ought not to do what he must prohibit others from doing, lest wrongs arise whence rights should have proceeded.' Driven by a sense of helplessness, the chronicler finally turned to heaven: 'Lord Jesus! Either take away the pope from our midst or diminish the power that he presumes to exercise over the people, for he deserves to lose his privilege who abuses the power granted to him.'[241] In a more ironic manner, Murimuth also voiced similar charges:

Whence among the *curiales* of the apostolic see it has become a proverb that the English are good asses, ready to carry all the intolerable burdens that are put upon them. Against which no remedy can be ordered by the prelates and bishops, because, being almost all promoted by the apostolic see, they do not dare to utter a word that might offend that see.[242]

The chroniclers further pointed to two parties that shared the booty with the pope, the king and the prelates, thus indicating a growing awareness of the pro-royal stand of the ecclesiastical elite. Clement's decision on 1 February 1306 to keep the annates for three years was accordingly regarded as inspired by the avarice of the prelates, for 'What could be demanded by inferiors could undoubtedly be also demanded by superiors' – a fact of life that led the pope to conclude that 'charity begins at home'.[243] Though the annates were not an invention of Clement V, he was the first to ensure their regular collection. The pope justified the tax on the grounds of the special economic needs of the curia, the past looting of the papal treasury, and the many expenses engendered by his coronation:

Indeed, because that Roman mother Church . . . was recently, in times not long past, assailed by many troubles and shaken by storms . . . partly, also, because in the time of Pope Boniface VIII, our predecessor of celebrated memory, several sons of perdition . . . robbed the treasure of that Church, [and] its money was exhausted; partly because, after we were called to the height of the highest apostolic office by divine disposition, expenses greater than usually have to be made hung and hang over us, especially at this beginning of our election to office.

---

[241] *Vita Edwardi Secundi*, ad a. 1313, p. 47.
[242] Adae Murimuth, *Continuatio chronicarum*, pp. 173–6. Though this entry was enclosed at a later date, Lunt considers it relevant to Clement's time.
[243] Walsingham, *Ypodigma Neustriae*, ad a. 1305, p. 236; Rishanger, *Chronica*, p. 228; *Flores historiarum*, pp. 130–1.

It is rather doubtful whether the reasons detailed in the papal letter could have been favourably received or could have balanced the continuous harm inflicted on the clergy's income. Nevertheless, Clement appointed Guillaume Testa, archdeacon of Aran in Comminges,[244] and Guillaume Géraud de Sore, canon of Rouen, as papal collectors in England.[245] He carefully detailed the scope of their mission and the wide range of benefices assigned to their scrutiny:

the fruits, rents, and revenues of the first year of each and all of the ecclesiastical benefices, with cure and without cure, and also parsonages and dignities of all churches, monasteries, priories, and other ecclesiastical places, both secular and regular, exempt and non-exempt, which are at present vacant and which shall happen to be vacant within three years in the kingdoms of England and Scotland and the provinces or parts of Ireland and Wales, their cities and dioceses, only the fruits belonging to the mensal incomes of archbishops, bishops, and regular abbots excepted.[246]

Having learned from the difficult experience of his predecessor, Guillaume Testa made a declaration of goodwill before Edward I upon his arrival.[247] The papal collector professed his desire to conduct curial affairs without prejudice to the king and his kingdom. He further asked Edward I to be notified of any business that the king would consider prejudicial and to be endowed with royal goodwill for the accomplishment of his mission.[248] These gestures of goodwill, however, did not prevent the complaints of the Parliament of Carlisle soon afterwards (20 January 1307).[249] On the contrary, Guillaume Testa supplied a suitable target at which to direct the unrest of the clergy, which was prompted by papal taxation, while avoiding a hopeless conflict with the king, the main beneficiary of the taxes.

---

[244] Being also originally from Gascony, Testa probably met Bertrand de Got at Comminges when he was the bishop. Clement compensated him in 1312 by nomination to the Sacred College.

[245] *Foedera*, 1-4, p. 60; *The Chronicle of Walter of Guisborough*, p. 364. The growth of papal taxation brought about a new curial agent, the resident papal collector; he was appointed by the papal chamberlain and was accountable to him. The office first appeared in thirteenth-century England; during the next century, permanent collectorates were established all over the western Church.

[246] Lunt, 'The First Levy of Papal Annates', pp. 62–4; Lunt, *Papal Revenues in the Middle Ages*, nos. 421–2, pp. 318–24. See also his report for the year beginning 1 October 1310: Lunt, *Financial Relations of the Papacy with England*, pp. 682–5.

[247] Testa's predecessor was Gérard de Pecorara, canon of Reims and papal chaplain, who was appointed papal collector in England by Benedict XI (15 February 1304). When he tried to fulfil his assignment, however, Edward I forced him to leave the realm within seven days, and his goods and documents were sequestered by the constable. See his report to the pope in Lunt, 'The Account of a Papal Collector in England', pp. 318–21.

[248] Lunt, *Papal Revenues in the Middle Ages*, vol. 1, no. 56, pp. 208–9.

[249] There was a widespread belief that papal collectors were employed as spies in order to discover vacancies to which the pope could make a provision: Lunt, 'William Testa and the Parliament of Carlisle', p. 340.

The complaints drawn up at the Parliament of Carlisle were in some measure reiterations of the clergy's grievances to Boniface ten years earlier.[250] The parliament accused Clement V of having caused a two-fold blow to the church founders, for their property had been taken out of the country at the expense of the poor, for whom it had been intended. In their sharp criticism of the pope's expropriation of the annates, Peter's pence, and the sale of indulgences, the parliament not only voiced the harm caused to 'royal jurisdiction and dignity', but it also accused the pope of acting 'in detriment of divine cult and towards the pauperisation of the Church of England'. The words of the prophet, 'Therefore thus saith the lord, God of Israel against the pastor that feed my people: ye have scattered away my flock, and driven them away and have not visited them' (Jer. 23:2), suggested the fears of both prelates and nobles of the serious implications of papal policy. Indeed, '[the pope] had made a desert of your nest which like Sodom and Gomorrah is totally submerged'. The employment of biblical symbolism did not avoid reference to more mundane matters, such as Clement's harmful intervention in the affairs of the realm. While conveniently neglecting the close co-operation between pope and king, the parliament focused its charges against the main components of papal policy:

Papal provisions.

The collection of annates.

The demand of 1 *d.* a hearth for Peter's pence instead of a stipulated yearly sum.[251]

Taxation of the churches' temporalities and the appropriation of advowsons.

Demand for the payment of a fine pledged to the Holy Land or to the Roman Church as a penalty for a breach of contract; those who had incurred such penalties were cited by papal representatives in open contravention of royal jurisdiction.

The tendency to channel gifts and legacies meant for the Holy Land to other purposes.

The propensity to expropriate all chattels of a deceased testator that were not covered by the specific legacies enumerated in the will.

The demand for the whole of the debt from debtors when the creditor had promised half.[252]

---

[250] On the participation of the clergy in parliament, see Denton, 'The Clergy and Parliament in the Thirteenth and Fourteenth Centuries', pp. 104–6. Although some of the complaints voiced at Carlisle were exaggerated, they still represent what may be called the prevailing opinion against the pope and his policy: G. Mollat, *La collation des bénéfices ecclésiastiques*, p. 100.

[251] See the letters of William Testa in this regard: *Registrum Simonis de Gandavo*, vol. I, pp. 199–200.

[252] *Rotuli Parliamentorum*, vol. I, pp. 219–20; *Chronicle of Walter of Guisborough*, pp. 371–4. Walter of Guisborough had written sources of information that enabled him to include in his chronicle a

The parliament gave statutory sanction to former objections to payments made by English houses of Cistercians, Premonstratensians, and Cluniacs to their foreign abbots. It also forbade reimbursements of taxes, rents, or tallages of any kind outside the kingdom.[253] It did, though, safeguard the right of abbots to visit their dependencies in England.[254]

Walter of Guisborough enclosed with the parliamentary proceedings a letter signed by a knight Peter, son of Cassiodorus, that reached its members 'as if from heaven'. The anonymous author focused, not on the rights of the founders, but on the sufferings of the Church of England, 'daughter of Jerusalem', 'virgin of Zion', who in vain sought salvation in the papal curia. As against Clement's arrogance, the knight pointed out that at the Resurrection, St Peter would have reverted to his profession of fisherman. Further, God had not nominated a vicar for Himself 'for spoliation and vandalism, nor for imposing annual census, nor for restricting people', but to guide the bewildered back to the path of righteousness and to teach the faithful the path to eternity. In his approach to the Church of England, the author argued, Clement behaved like Nebuchadnezzar in the Temple, serving God and Mammon. The anonymous author questioned whether a shepherd who does not protect his flock when the lion is roaring was worthy of confidence. Finally, he expressed his despair in an emotional appeal to God to descend, to hear the tribulations of his people, and to release them with a high hand from their servitude to Pharaoh.[255]

The animosity aroused by the fiscal policy of 'Pharaoh' found a

---

fairly long account of the Carlisle proceedings. On a manuscript once belonging to Whalley Abbey (British Museum Add. MS 10374), the copyist added that the appropriated temporalities and advowsons were bestowed on cardinals and other foreigners: E. M. Thompson, 'The Petition of 1307 Against Papal Collectors', p. 420. H. G. Richardson and G. O. Sayles cite from the same manuscript the original 'petitions of the earls, barons, and community of the Land presented to the parliament', which they define as 'A Newsletter from Carlisle': 'The Parliament of Carlisle', pp. 433–7; Lunt, 'William Testa and the Parliament of Carlisle', p. 339.

[253] *The Statutes of the Realm*, pp. 150–2; *Councils and Synods*, pp. 1232–6. Both Edward I and his son accomplished the parliament's decision, the only exception being the annates, the collection of which continued. See Edward I's letter to Guillaume Testa on 26 June 1307: *Calendar of the Close Rolls (1302–1307)*, p. 538.

[254] See the pope's letter to the king of 13 December 1307 complaining about the many obstacles raised by royal officers to the abbots of Cîteaux when they attempted to travel to the chapters of their Order: *Original Papal Letters in England*, no. 49, pp. 25–6; *Calendar of Entries in the Papal Registers*, p. 19.

[255] 'Vide, Domine, et descende, quia cor dicti viri super cor Pharaonis est nimium induratum quia non dimittet populum tuum abire liberum nisi in fortitudine manus tue': *Chronicle of Walter of Guisborough*, pp. 373, 371–4; British Museum Add. MS 10374, fo. 15–16. Note the influence of Matthew Paris: 'Dixit enim Dominus Petro, Pasce oves meas, non tonde, non excoria, non eviscera vel devorando consume' (Matthew Paris, *Chronica Majora*, ad. a. 1258, p. 693). Heath sees in declarations like this the strengthening of anti-papal tendencies in England in the framework of parliament; see P. Heath, *Church and Realm*, p. 63.

concrete outlet in the measures taken against the pope's representatives. The Council of Canterbury decided to conduct a new investigation against Guillaume Testa to support the grievances to be presented at the Council of Vienne (9 December 1310).[256] Contemporary chroniclers were unanimous in assessing the harm caused to the Church of England by Testa and other papal representatives, who were described as rapacious, their main aim being to squeeze out money from the clergy in complete disregard of the customs of the realm.[257] Murimuth, himself an active ecclesiastical lawyer, did not mince words in reporting the greed of papal legates and nuncios.[258] Though the sources are divided with regard to the political results of papal missions – whose usual purpose was to settle the endless conflict between king and barons or to reach a truce in Scotland – there is wide consensus as to the economic burden that they imposed on local churches. Thus, the author of the *Flores* severely criticised the greed of Cardinal Peter of Sabina, who came to England to negotiate the marriage of the prince of Wales and Isabella of France, but at the expense of the churches of England. After the cardinal tried to extort excessive taxes, the clergy appealed to the king, and the papal nuncio was forced to satisfy himself with half the sum that he had originally demanded.[259] Later on, when the *Flores* referred to Arnaud of St Prisca and Arnaud of Albano, who had come to England to arrange a peace between Edward II and the barons, it called the papal nuncios 'most clever extirpators of money'.[260] In time, the prevailing discontent was accompanied by physical attacks on papal envoys and their retinues.[261]

Clement's liberal attitude and the broad powers he conferred on his representatives only aggravated the prevailing resentment against them. When Cardinal Peter of Sabina was sent as papal nuncio to England, Scotland, Ireland, and Wales (1306), apostolic authority was conferred on him to provide to any vacant benefices with or without cure, including dignities reserved to the collation of the apostolic see. He was also empowered to provide to benefices vacated by the death or resignation

---

[256] *Councils and Synods*, pp. 1297–8, 1353–6; Denton, 'Complaints to the Apostolic See', pp. 389–93, 400–1.

[257] *Chronicle of Walter of Guisborough*, pp. 376–7. In a 1305 memorandum, the author asked for greater papal control over those religious houses that escaped episcopal surveillance. He complained that papal authority existed only *de jure* but was not effectively exercised over exempt monasteries in England: *ibid.*, pp. 396–8.   [258] Adae Murimuth, *Continuatio chronicarum*, ad a. 1312, p. 16.

[259] *Flores historiarum*, p. 136.   [260] *Ibid.*, p. 154.

[261] On their way to Durham, Cardinals Gaucelin d'Eusa and Luca Fieschi were set upon by Gilbert de Middleton and his men, who stole their possessions but let the papal nuncios and their retinue go with no bodily harm. In this case, too, the *Flores* refers to their mission as one 'magis ad rei publicae detrimentum quam augmentum': *ibid.*, ad a. 1317, pp. 179–80; Adae Murimuth, *Continuatio chronicarum*, pp. 27–8; *Registrum Palatinum Dunelmense, the Register of Richard de Kellawe*, vol. I, pp. 396–9; vol. IV, pp. 394–5.

of any of his or the pope's chaplains who were in his retinue, to receive resignations, and to facilitate permutations of benefices.[262] Though the provisory powers of Arnaud of St Prisca and Arnaud of Albano were more limited, they still received competence to bestow benefices and dignities on their clerks, to release people from oaths, to enforce obedience by means of ecclesiastical censures, to grant necessary dispensations, and to revoke and annul any statutes and ordinances made by the nobles against the king.[263]

Against the considerable authority bestowed on the pope's representatives, there stood the community of the realm, manifested by its claims in parliament. On the other hand, Edward I and Edward II could rather easily manipulate prevailing anti-papal feelings in order to strengthen their position both on the internal front and in their dealings in the papal curia. Thus, Edward II utilised the strong criticism of the Parliament of Carlisle to justify his own policy against papal intervention. Upon his accession to the throne, he enforced most of the limitations placed by the parliament, going so far as to arrest one of the papal collectors. Conversely, Edward refused to arrest persons excommunicated by papal representatives and prohibited summoning Englishmen abroad to ecclesiastical courts.[264] Edward also forbade the free transmission of papal letters that had any concern with royal rights without receiving his formal authorisation (8 November 1307). Although Edward II declared his good intentions towards the Roman Church, inasmuch as it would not harm his prerogatives,[265] the Parliament of Stamford (6 August 1309) voiced anew the baronial perspective, which left little room for the papal monarchy.[266] The barons declared their Catholic faith in the pope, whom 'Jesus Christ had appointed His vicar on earth', but this creed did not prevent them from protesting against papal taxation and its regrettable implications for the kingdom and the faith. Here, too, they focused on the painful subject of advowson:

It was not their intention [i.e., of the church founders] that their contributions would fall to the use of foreigners, who do not know how to eradicate sins or

---

[262] *Regestum Clementis Papae V*, nos. 2246–54; *Calendar of Entries in the Papal Registers*, p. 31.

[263] *Regestum Clementis Papae V*, nos. 8177, 8786, 8825, 9568; *Calendar of Entries in the Papal Registers*, pp. 104–7, 117–18.

[264] *Foedera*, 1-4, pp. 94, 102. This policy caused A. Deeley to argue for a reconsideration of Edward II's reign. In spite of Edward's many weaknesses and his apparent anxiety to keep on good terms with the pope, she argues, there was no timid submission to the enlargement of ecclesiastical prerogatives. Long before the anti-papal statutes of 1351 and 1353, she envisaged methods of protection against papal claims: Deeley, 'Papal Provision and Royal Rights of Patronage', pp. 526–7. Cf. Tout, *The Place of the Reign of Edward II in English History*, p. 206.   [265] *Foedera*, 1-4, p. 139.

[266] Edward II took care that all earls and barons affixed their seals to the letters protesting against papal transgressions sent to the curia, in accordance with the agreements made in parliament (6 August 1309). See *Calendar of the Patent Rolls (1307–1313)*, p. 180; Adae Murimuth, *Continuatio chronicarum*, p. 14.

identify the intentions of the flock, who ignore the language and neglect the holy columns of the sacred edicts which they were supposed to fulfil.

Though the barons expressed their confidence in the pope's positive reply, they nevertheless took pains to declare that according to the 'laws of the land', Church property should be returned to the donors or their heirs if it had been exploited in contravention of original intentions.[267]

Clement did not remain indifferent to the constant attacks on the Church and its leader. In a series of letters *ad personam* to all prelates of England (October 1307–April 1308), the pope condemned the continuous infringement of the Church's liberties and gave the impression that he felt personally wounded by Edward II. Clement detailed the many transgressions perpetrated by royal officers against the Church: writs of caption following excommunications were ignored; ecclesiastical jurisdiction was impeded by royal writs of prohibition; bishops were not allowed to deal with criminal clerks; members of the clergy were compelled to appear in royal courts; and grave damage was inflicted upon episcopal lands, monasteries, priories, and churches. Besides these general claims, Clement exhorted the prelates to use their influence with the king to advance the release of the bishops of Coventry and Lichfield, St Andrews, and Glasgow. The pope also used the occasion to complain about Edward's negligent approach towards the Templars and cited Philip the Fair as an example to be followed. Finally, he announced the mission of Arnaud d'Aux, bishop of Poitiers (from 1312, cardinal-bishop of Albano), as his personal nuncio to the king.[268]

Some of the papal complaints were echoed by the provincial Council of London and Lambeth, held by Winchelsey in November 1309.[269] Gaveston's return to England, considered by the primate an open infringement of the king's previous commitments, encouraged Winchelsey to enlist his suffragans in his fight to preserve ecclesiastical liberties, an area in which he believed he could easily achieve papal support. Indeed, Clement had urged him to admonish the king on the serious grievances of the Church of England and to require the immediate payment of the 1,000 marks owed to the curia. Backed by eleven bishops, Winchelsey voiced the papal claims before Edward II (16

---

[267] *Foedera*, 1-4, p. 149; *Councils and Synods*, pp. 1236–40; *Registrum Ricardi de Swinfield*, pp. 472–5; *Annales Londonienses*, pp. 161–5; on the pope's complaints to the king, see *ibid.*, pp. 165–7. On the influence of Church's property on the relationship between the clergy and the laity, see B. Thompson, '*Habendum et tenendum*', pp. 197–238.

[268] *The Register of John de Halton*, vol. I, pp. 309–13; *Foedera*, 1-4, pp. 104, 116–17.

[269] *Concilia Magnae Britanniae et Hiberniae*, pp. 314–22; *Registrum Roberti Winchelsey Cantuariensis archiepiscopi*, vol. II, pp. 1013–31, also encloses the king's responses to the grievances presented by the clergy.

December).[270] The primate also demanded the immediate release of Walter Langton, the bishop of Coventry and Lichfield, whom Clement had summoned to the papal curia to answer charges 'against his character' (21 May).[271] Yet Robert Winchelsey's readiness to support papal policy within the framework of his own struggle with the king in the Gaveston affair does not characterise the political stand of most primates of England in those rare instances when the normally close alliance between pope and king was severed. The pro-royal stand of the ecclesiastical elite becomes even more evident in France during the reign of Philip the Fair.

THE CHURCH OF FRANCE

Analysis of both episcopal nominations and taxation in France during the pontificate of Clement V corroborates the existence of a strong alliance between pope and king, one which had very similar causes and outcomes to that found in England. Philip the Fair was very sensitive to ecclesiastical nominations and required that he be regularly informed of any vacant benefice, both to enjoy his regalian rights and to foster the election of his protégés.[272] The promotion of royal clerks to major benefices in the Church of France was facilitated by the fact that the chapter was not allowed to exercise its right to canonical elections except after receiving royal approval. About one hundred letters extant in the *Trésor des chartes* were written to Philip for this purpose. From the king's perspective, this was a convenient arrangement that facilitated harmonious co-operation with the clergy. It left open, however, the question of the *libertas ecclesiae* and the no less problematic division of labour between Philip the Fair, as *advocatus ecclesiae*, and the pope, as the indisputable leader of the universal Church. The examples that follow illustrate the close alliance between king and pope and its main victim: the clergy of France and ecclesiastical rights.

On 27 August 1306, Philip the Fair thanked the pope for the nomination of three royal candidates to key Church positions: Pierre de Belleperche to Auxerre, Guillaume Bonnet to Bayeux, and Nicolas de

---

[270] *Councils and Synods*, pp. 1269–74; *Registrum Roberti Winchelsey Cantuariensis archiepiscopi*, vol. II, pp. 1031–42. For Winchelsey's discouraging report to the pope (21 May 1309), see *ibid.*, pp. 1049–50; W. R. Jones, 'Relations of the Two Jurisdictions', pp. 95–101. The clearest representatives of a pro-royal stand at this time were Walter Reynolds, John of Droxford, John Salmon, and Henry of Woodlock. They were joined shortly afterwards by Walter Langton. See K. Edwards, 'The Political Importance of the English Bishops', pp. 322–3.

[271] *Registrum Roberti Winchelsey Cantuariensis archiepiscopi*, vol. II, pp. 1049–50. On the many papal letters on the subject, see also *Foedera*, I-4, pp. 198–9.

[272] E. Boutaric, *La France sous Philippe le Bel*, p. 65.

Lusarches to Avranches.[273] Two years later, Philip did not hide his horror at the possibility of ecclesiastical elections in Auxerre. He hastened to apprise the pope of such a risk, which could only 'create scandals while bringing about the total destruction of the benefices of the aforesaid church and should still engender big controversies'.[274] The royal position was echoed by Clement V in the resulting reservation (4 April 1308). The pope argued that elections 'often brought about serious scandals, not a few damages, and many dangers'.[275] Again, when the see of Laon became vacant, the king shared with the pope his great concern at finding the most suitable candidate 'who would jealously labour for the honour of the king and the kingdom'.[276] Clement also advanced royal protégés to key positions in the Empire. On 10 November 1306, the pope nominated Peter von Aichspalt to the archbishopric of Mainz and Otto de Grandson to the see of Basle. After an election *in discordia*, Gérard de Bonars, archdeacon of Autun, was provided to Constance (5 December 1307), and Baldwin to Trier (12 February 1308).[277]

Although papal intervention on behalf of Philip's protégés became commonplace in the Church of France, it did not arouse much of an echo in contemporary sources. Joseph R. Strayer offers a possible explanation, according to which a mutual dependence characterised the relationship between Philip the Fair and the Church – the pope and the clergy of France included. The clergy, especially the secular clergy, knew from experience that it could rely more on the king and his court than on the pope and his curia. The results were evident in actual practice. Notwithstanding the many threats to apply ecclesiastical measures against royal officers who had harmed ecclesiastical prerogatives, action was seldom taken.[278] The acceptance of royal interference thus reflects a compromise between *regnum* and *sacerdotium*, achieved first between the king and the prelates of France, on which Clement bestowed apostolic blessing. The question remains, however, as to the implications of the pope's benevolent attitude for the status of the papacy and the future of papal monarchy.

At first glance, Clement's acceptance of royal intervention in ecclesiastical nominations was in tune with prevailing opinion, a state of affairs corroborated in contemporary records. Jean de St Victor reports that

---

[273] *Regestum Clementis Papae V*, nos. 1156, 1651; *Collectio actorum veterum*, pp. 70–1.

[274] *Collectio actorum veterum*, p. 69.

[275] *Regestum Clementis Papae V*, no. 3552; *Collectio actorum veterum*, p. 94.

[276] *Collectio actorum veterum*, pp. 69–70.

[277] *Regestum Clementis Papae V*, nos. 1211, 1213, 2332, 2468; K. Rieder, *Römische Quellen*, p. 40; F. Gutsche, *Die Beziehungen zwischen Reich und Kurie*, pp. 25–42. For Clement's intervention in Münster against the archbishop of Cologne, see *Regestum Clementis Papae V*, nos. 3619, 5362.

[278] Strayer, *The Reign of Philip the Fair*, pp. 237–40.

Pierre de Grès was nominated to Auxerre (12 July 1308) only 'after a long vacancy'.[279] While describing the nominee as 'a man of a noble lineage and expert in Roman and canon law', Jean reports in a rather off-hand manner the fact that the new bishop had not yet been ordained to priesthood.[280] The skills of Pierre de Grès, indeed, were quite foreign to an ecclesiastical career. He had been in royal service at least since 1298, when he was charged with a diplomatic mission to Flanders. Appointed chancellor of Navarre, Champagne, and Brie, he was an active member in the commission that inquired into the charges levelled against Guichard, bishop of Troyes. One may point to other, similar cases as well. Following the death of Berthaud de Saint-Denis (1 August 1307), Jean de St Victor referred to the appointment of Raoul Grosparmi, 'a royal clerk, with considerable legal expertise', to Orléans without evincing much awareness of Philip's influence on this nomination (28 December).[281] Narrative sources thus remained indifferent to the motives and outcomes of the delicate division of labour between clergy and king, on the one hand, and king and pope, on the other. When a protest is encountered, one anonymous author was satisfied with deprecating the encroachment on episcopal rights, but expressed little concern about the king, the major promoter and beneficiary of the process.[282]

Only in very extreme instances do contemporary sources show some mindfulness to the political implications of the close alliance between pope and king. Such was the case with Enguerrand de Marigny, the king's senior counsellor, and his nepotistic policy in the Church. Enguerrand's brother, Philippe, was provided to Cambrai (12 January 1306)[283] and later promoted to Sens (22 December 1309), where he played a macabre role in the trial of the Templars; another brother, Jean, was provided to Beauvais; and Enguerrand de Marigny's nephew, Nicolas de Fréauville, who already enjoyed the status of the king's confessor, was appointed cardinal in the first nomination to the Sacred College by Clement V.[284] All these promotions were depicted in contemporary records as clear manifestations of Enguerrand's ability 'to demand [and receive] whatever comes to his mind from the king and the pope'.[285] The transfer of his brother, Philippe de Marigny, from Cambrai to the archbishopric of Sens was accordingly described in terms of a joint action 'by pope and king', a possibility supported by the active exchange of letters on the subject

---

[279] Jean de St Victor, *Prima Vita*, pp. 7, 14; *Regestum Clementis Papae V*, no. 2851.

[280] Jean de St Victor, *Prima Vita*, pp. 7, 14.

[281] *Ibid.*, p. 7; *Regestum Clementis Papae V*, no. 2383. For royal intervention in episcopal nominations, see also *Collectio actorum veterum*, p. 121.

[282] Langlois, 'Satire cléricale du temps de Philippe le Bel', pp. 146–8.

[283] *Regestum Clementis Papae V*, no. 269.   [284] See above, n. 38.

[285] *Regestum Clementis Papae V*, nos. 4554, 5170, 4455; *Fragment d'une chronique . . . 1328*, p. 149.

between the two.[286] The pope's argument that he had resolved to prevent elections in Sens in order to find the most suitable shepherd for the province after considering the whole matter with the cardinals appears, therefore, hardly convincing.[287]

On the other hand, Clement denied Philip's requests to provide Guillaume de Trie to Cambrai and Pierre de Laon to Orléans.[288] On 26 March 1310, the pope also demanded that all clergymen avoid further requests for the next two years, since too many expected benefices had already been granted.[289] These few instances of Clement's free will, however, did not challenge the continuous royal intervention in ecclesiastical matters, nor did they improve the pope's status. Notwithstanding the success of Philip's propaganda in strengthening his religious halo in his capacity of the 'Most Christian King',[290] Clement's collaborationist policy did not gain him the support of contemporaries. On the contrary, Gervais du Bus, for example, vehemently protested against the outcomes of papal policy, which actually left the prelates at the king's mercy. Gervais was particularly critical of the encroachment on ecclesiastical jurisdiction by royal clerks, who were constantly usurping the Church's prerogatives.[291]

The arrest of Guichard de Troyes hints at the dangers inherent in the lack of a clear distinction between *regnum* and *sacerdotium*, with the general balance of forces being clearly in favour of Philip the Fair. Guichard had been elected to Troyes in the second half of 1298 and confirmed to his see soon afterwards. He rose rapidly in the Church and royal administration thanks to the patronage of Blanche of Artois, the dowager queen of Navarre and countess of Champagne, and her daughter, Jeanne, queen of France. By 1300, though, he fell into disfavour with the dowager queen, who brought about his imprisonment. The death of Blanche of Artois in 1302 fostered rumours that Guichard had in fact poi-

---

[286] Jean de St Victor, *Prima Vita*, p. 16; *Collectio actorum veterum*, pp. 117–20.

[287] 'Imminente nobis ecclesiarum omnium sollicitudine generali, circa illas salutaris providentie studium adhibere nos convenit quas interdum carere conspicimus regimine prelatorum, ut assumantur ad illarum regimen, annuente Domino, pastores ydonei, quorum providentie studiis Deo propicio preserventur a noxiis, et salutaribus proficiant incrementis': *Collectio actorum veterum*, p. 116.

[288] Pierre de Mirepoix succeeded Philippe de Marigny in Cambrai: see *Notae ad vitas*, pp. 60–1; *Collectio actorum veterum*, p. 121.   [289] *Regestum Clementis Papae V*, no. 6281.

[290] Menache, 'Philippe le Bel', pp. 689–702.

[291] Le pape n'i met sa chape
Ne du clergié n'est pas tuteur,
Mès le roy fait executeur,
Si que par la laie justise
Est justisie sainte Yglise.
Gervais du Bus, *Le roman du Fauvel*, p. 24, vv. 582–6.

soned his former benefactor. The case, however, was closed two years later, when the main accusers, Jean de Calais and Noffo Dei, retracted their former imputations (17 April 1304).[292]

Guichard was arrested a second time and his temporalities were seized in August 1308. This time he was charged with having killed the queen, Jeanne of Navarre, by piercing a waxen image of her with a pin, and of having tried to poison Charles de Valois and Louis of Navarre.[293] The bishop was placed under the custody of the archbishop of Sens, but soon afterwards was transferred to the Louvre.[294] In clear contravention of ecclesiastical prerogatives, Guichard remained in royal prison for about a year and a half and was delivered to the pope only in 1311. This peculiar situation did not prevent Philip from presenting the case before the pope and even urging him to investigate the charges. The king also threatened to judge the bishop himself, a warning that was rather inauspicious, coming as it did from Philip the Fair. Clement ordered the archbishop of Sens, the bishop of Orléans, and the bishop-elect of Auxerre – the latter two, Raoul Grosparmi and Pierre de Grès, had participated in Guichard's first trial – to investigate the charges. According to the papal letter, Guichard was also suspected of 'having perpetrated many and enormous crimes against royal majesty, giving a pernicious example and causing many scandals' (9 August 1308).

Though contemporary chroniclers refer to Guichard's arrest, they were no more sensitive than was the pope to the king's gnawing away at the Church's immunity.[295] Guichard de Troyes was ultimately released in 1313[296] following a confession by Noffo Dei, who after admitting his perjury was hanged in Paris 'for his many crimes'.[297] During Guichard's five years of confinement, he had continued to exercise his episcopal functions; however, Philip the Fair was not inclined to allow the bishop's complete rehabilitation, let alone his return to Troyes. On the other

---

[292] On 3 June 1307, Clement released the bishop from his summons to the papal court by Benedict XI: *Regestum Clementis Papae V*, no. 1642. The best account of the bishop, his personality and trial appears in Strayer, 'The Case of Bishop Guichard of Troyes', pp. 248–60.

[293] *La chronique métrique attribuée à Geffroy de Paris*, p. 148, vv. 2971–98.

[294] *Collectio actorum veterum*, pp. 83–4; *Regestum Clementis Papae V*, no. 5509 (18 July 1310); E. Rigault, *Le procès de Guichard, évêque de Troyes*, pp. 37–9.

[295] *Les grandes chroniques de France*, pp. 263, 293–4; Jean de St Victor, *Prima Vita*, p. 13; *Continuationis chronici Guillelmi de Nangiaco*, pp. 369, 400. Though the bishop's temporalities were seized, he was allowed to administer his spiritualities: *La chronique métrique attribuée à Geffroy de Paris*, p. 148, vv. 2986–9. The continuation of the chronicle of Gérard de Frachet refers to the fact that Guichard was incarcerated owing to the testimony of 'false witnesses' and was kept under arrest 'by the pope': *Continuatio chronici Girardi de Fracheto*, p. 31; *Collectio actorum veterum*, pp. 83–4.

[296] See Clement's ultimatum to the archbishop of Sens and the bishops of Orléans and Auxerre to end Guichard's inquisition within three months (9 February 1311): *Regestum Clementis Papae V*, no. 6591. [297] *Les grandes chroniques de France*, pp. 293–4.

hand, Guichard remained adamant in his refusal to relinquish his see. In order to avoid further inconveniences and following the advice of Enguerrand de Marigny, the pope finally transferred Guichard to Diakovar in Bosnia, a very poor and distant diocese. It is doubtful whether Guichard ever took possession of this see, since he resigned early in the pontificate of John XXII and died shortly afterwards (22 January 1317).

The arrest of Guichard de Troyes was not an unprecedented act during the reign of Philip the Fair; there were the precedents of Bernard Saisset during Boniface's pontificate and of the Templars during Clement's own reign.[298] From the royal point of view, the arrest of Guichard was an ordinary penalty for crimes that the bishop had supposedly perpetrated against the queen and the Capetian family as a whole. The innovation, if any, did not focus on royal policy but, rather, on the papal response – more precisely, the lack of a papal response – to the king's move.[299] Conversely, the militant reaction of Boniface VIII to the arrest of Bernard Saisset in 1301 had accorded with the norms of the Church and was largely justified by canon law.[300] In actual practice, however, Boniface's move did not bring about either the release of the bishop of Pamiers or a new concordat between *rex* and *sacerdos*; on the contrary, it led to the outrage of Anagni. Clement's conciliatory policy, though not supported by canonical exegesis, thus appears to present a reasonable outcome of former developments. Moreover, the very fact that the pope's silence encountered no criticism in contemporary sources hints at the possibility that Clement's inaction represented a political trend approved by contemporaries. It also helps to corroborate Strayer's argument of a basic agreement between Philip the Fair and the Church of France.[301] This analysis is however at variance with the conclusions, though not the premises, advanced by Walter Ullmann:

Historically, the pontificates of Boniface VIII and of Clement V depict the two extremes to which the papal pendulum had swung. Ideologically they are a study in contrasts. For Clement's papacy was to all intents and purposes the very denial

---

[298] Bernard Saisset was arrested on 24 October 1301 and restored to royal favour in 1308. At the time of his arrest, 40,000 *l.t.* were taken from his see and deposited 'with his consent' in a monastery. It is not clear whether Saisset ever recovered the money. At least 15,000 *l.t.* of the deposit were used towards suppressing the rebellion in Bordeaux. For the accusations against the bishop of Pamiers, see *Histoire du différend d'entre le pape Boniface VIII et Philippes le Bel*, pp. 621–2.

[299] For the continuous interference of royal officers in ecclesiastical affairs, see the well-documented case of the diocese of Toulouse, in *Lettres inédites de Philippe le Bel*.

[300] Notwithstanding the prominent position of the see of Troyes, Boniface did not react at all to Guichard's early arrest, a few months before that of Saisset.

[301] Strayer, *The Reign of Philip the Fair*, pp. 237–40.

of the historically conditioned bases upon which Boniface's papacy had taken its stand. This is not to say that Boniface's policies had much chance of success, because the papacy in the anteceding decades had not come to terms with the new forces, but Boniface at least adhered to the traditional papal patterns, while in Clement's pontificate lack of statesmanship, experience, training, and vision accounted for the veritable volte-face of the papacy. What remained was little more than rearguard action which can hardly be called a programme. What was lost was the moral, spiritual, and authoritative leadership which the papacy had built up in Europe over the centuries of minute, consistent, detailed, dynamic, forward-looking work.[302]

If one neglects the political and economic framework of Clement's pontificate, then papal policy would seem to have turned into what Ullmann describes as a 'lack of statesmanship, experience, training, and vision'. One may perhaps agree with Ullmann in terms of the spiritual and moral grounds of the papacy; however, the conflict between *regnum* and *sacerdotium* was essentially political, though often translated into moral and spiritual terms for propaganda purposes. From a political perspective, Clement's policy appears the only feasible alternative within the limitations posed by the emerging national state. Moreover, collaboration with the king of France was also imperative for the realisation of Clement's dearest goal, the crusade.

Although Clement's collaborationist policy in the case of Guichard de Troyes did not encounter criticism, the location of the papal curia in Languedoc created new points of friction between the clergy and its spiritual leader. The closeness to the papal curia was an unprecedented situation in France, unique to the Avignon period; because of the itinerant character of Clement's curia, it became particularly crucial during his pontificate. Although Clement avoided travelling with the entire papal entourage – keeping only necessary personnel with him and ordering cardinals and clergymen to wait at the next station[303] – the expenses borne by papal visits became a serious burden on local churches. Most ecclesiastical establishments in Languedoc did not have the resources, let alone the motivation, to subsidise the ever-growing increasing papal requests. When referring to the many difficulties posed by the papal wanderings in the area, the chronicle attributed to Geffroy de Paris emphasises the financial onus imposed upon villages and towns. It goes further and alleges Clement's devotion to the cult of money, which supposedly had corrupted the pope to such a degree that he willingly sold indulgences to all customers, regardless of spiritual

---

[302] W. Ullmann, *A Short History of the Papacy*, p. 282.
[303] Guillemain, *Les recettes et les dépenses de la chambre apostolique*, p. xiii.

considerations.[304] These claims – extreme as they were – did not lack a certain foundation and reflect the many expenses and troubles caused by the pope's prolonged sojourn in southern France. The growing resentment was also influenced by the estimates, often exaggerated, of the wealth ascribed to the papal curia.[305]

A few examples will illustrate the problematic relationship between the pope and his flock. After the abbey of St Gilles provided lodgings for Clement, two cardinals, and their retinues in Veuvert, the abbot became so impoverished that he was forced to ask the priors of his Order for a double tenth. The bishop of Nevers, too, received special authorisation to raise 10,000 l.t. from the religious institutions nearby following a papal visit.[306] Subsequent to a long stay by the papal court in Bourges, Gilles Colonna became so ruined that 'he was forced to ask for daily contributions' like a simple priest.[307] The many chroniclers who reported this regrettable affair found it difficult to justify the pope's desire to make the archbishop of Bourges pay for their former rivalry over the primacy of Aquitaine. Gilles' bankruptcy was seen as a Job's warning against the disastrous economic consequences of papal visits.[308] The pernicious influence of the papal wanderings did not focus on Bourges alone; it was felt throughout the whole area 'where many damages and robberies to churches, both secular and regular, were perpetrated by the pope and his ministers'.[309] When Jean de St Victor reviewed the first year of Clement's pontificate, he concluded: 'Many damages he has done . . . made immoderate expenses . . . many were burdened.' Little wonder, therefore, that when the pope arrived in Bordeaux (10 May 1306), 'he was not favourably received'.[310] Less than a year after the Bordelais had welcomed the election of their archbishop to the See of St Peter with general exulta-

---

[304] Il n'i ot ville, ne cité
De quoy le pape eüst pité . . .
Et sus touz ama il argent,
Et por l'argent, par maintes foiz,
Donna il et croches et crois.
La chronique métrique attribuée à Geffroy de Paris, p. 144, vv. 2757–86.

[305] Renouard, *Les rélations des papes d'Avignon et des compagnies commerciales et bancaires*, pp. 20–38. Agostino Trionfo provides the cardinals' perspective and their complaints of the many expenses to which they were exposed because of the prolonged stay in France: 'Nam cardinales stando, ubi nunc curia stat, coguntur omnino magnas expenssas facere, tum quia non est consuetum ibi curia stare, tum quia patria communiter cara est, tum quia moneta est multum grossa, tum quia cardinales non habent adminicula de proventibus ecclesie, que haberent Rome, si ibi starent' (E. Kraack, *Rom oder Avignon?*, p. 21).

[306] L. de Flamere, 'Le pape Clément V à Nevers', pp. 13–22.

[307] *Continuationis chronici Guillelmi de Nangiaco*, pp. 352–3; *Notae ad vitas*, p. 36.

[308] *La chronique métrique attribuée à Geffroy de Paris*, p. 144, vv. 2773–83; *Continuatio chronici Girardi de Fracheto*, p. 26: Lizerand, *Clément V et Philippe IV, le Bel*, pp. 28–9.

[309] *Les grandes chroniques de France*, p. 248.   [310] Jean de St Victor, *Prima Vita*, p. 3.

tion, they became so hostile to the papal curia that Clement seriously considered the possibility of proceeding to Toulouse.[311] Although the deteriorating economic situation in Languedoc encouraged a critical approach and even reluctance to accept the proximity of the Vicar of God – with its negative financial consequences – it did not affect the basic acceptance of papal monarchy. The Cistercian abbot Jacques de Thérines recognised that 'whether [the popes] stay in Rome or in Bordeaux, they could do right or evil, and they could in a similar fashion proceed by proctors everywhere'.[312]

The alarming consequences of the papal burden drove the clergy to seek royal protection from the very beginning of Clement's pontificate. The archbishops of Rouen, Reims, Sens, and Tours were spokesmen for the protest. They were eagerly encouraged by the Capetian court, notwithstanding the fact that the wave of unrest had been aggravated by a papal grant to the king himself (7 January 1306).[313] An Aragonese report told of several other catalysts for the protest: Clement's nomination of his nephew, Bernard de Fargues, to Rouen and the papal reservation of the see of Auxerre. Furthermore, rumours of a papal summons of the archbishop of Lyons, Louis de Villars, supposedly had caused the prelate to urge the convocation of a council and the election of a new pope.[314] Such a move appeared logical in the light of the precedents set by the Colonnas and Philip the Fair against Boniface VIII.[315] Whether this report was accurate or not, it reflects the main catalysts of the growing tension between Clement V and the clergy of France: papal taxation, papal provisions, and the nepotistic character being attributed to them both.

Philip the Fair presented the clergy's reproaches to Clement, who realised the seriousness of the protest and assumed an apologetic tone.[316] Though his conscience was clear, the pope did not regard himself as any better than the inhabitants of Noah's ark, which was said to contain one sinner for every eight chosen passengers. Still, the former archbishop of Bordeaux did not hide his disappointment with the clergy's direct appeal to the king, which he regarded as an expression of mistrust, 'for we are descendants of the same kingdom and have maintained close and friendly

---

[311] According to B. de Biterris' report to James of Aragon, 'Item quod dominus papa est Burdegualis et speratur, quod veniat Tolosam ad tenendum ibi curiam suam, quia, secundum quod dicitur, non multum graciose recipiuntur Burdegualis cardinales nec alii curiam sequentes': Finke, *Papsttum und Untergang des Templerordens*, vol. II, no. 12, p. 14.

[312] 'Quodlibetum secundum', in N. Valois, 'Jacques de Thérines, cistercien', p. 191, no. 2.

[313] *Continuationis chronici Guillelmi de Nangiaco*, p. 354; Jean de St Victor, *Prima Vita*, p. 4; *Continuatio chronici Girardi de Fracheto*, p. 27.

[314] Finke, *Papsttum und Untergang des Templerordens*, vol. II, no. 13, pp. 15–16. Though the accuracy of this report is rather dubious, it still reflects the unpopularity of papal provisions to his relatives and the king's protégés.   [315] Menache, 'Un peuple qui a sa demeure à part', pp. 196–203.

[316] *Collectio actorum veterum*, p. 44.

ties with them . . . considering them our close friends, who desire our good'. Finally, Clement undertook to investigate the transgressions attributed to his emissaries and relatives, provided that he would be supplied with all the facts (Bordeaux, 27 July 1306).[317]

Clement aimed, first and foremost, to weaken resentment against the curia while avoiding the consolidation of a dangerous common front by Philip the Fair and the prelates of France. Looking for easy solutions – of the kind that hardly faced the real causes of the conflict – the pope exempted a large number of prelates from their duty of visitation.[318] Gilles Colonna, who had already been exempted provisionally from personal visitations in Bourges, was twice accorded confirmation of this privilege.[319] When Gilles died on 22 December 1316, the dioceses of Limoges, Clermont, Cahors, Albi, and even Bourges itself had not been visited at all.[320] On the other hand, Clement also urged the prelates to moderate their procurations and, thus, to alleviate the difficult situation of the clergy. These were, however, rather poor means of balancing the losses caused by the pope's own stay in Languedoc.[321]

Economic losses strengthened criticism of Clement and his curia to the point that some sources depicted the pope as the chief factor in the general decline of the Church of France.[322] An anonymous author mourned the prelates' loss of their former freedom of action; they were no longer able to recompense their servants and *familia* with ecclesiastical benefices, since everything was reserved by the pope in order to reward his own protégés. Lacking a regular source of income, the prelates of the Church were subjected to a daily struggle for survival. The conclusion was clear: the pope had to stop expropriating benefices.[323] The

[317] 'Sane, licet de gravaminibus per nuncios nostros ecclesiis et personis ecclesiasticis, ut dicti tui nuncii proponebant, illatis miremur plurimum et turbemur, miramur tamen amplius quod prelati, qui hec gravamina pertulisse dicuntur, quos, cum de regno oriundi simus eodem, et magnam habuerimus plerumque familiaritatem cum illis ante promotionem nostram ad apostolatus apicem dignitatis, nostros speciales amicos et benivolos credebamus, nunquam verbo vel scripto, nuncio seu epistola, vel alio quovis modo aliquid de predictis nobis significare vel per aliquem de fratribus nostris cardinalibus facere significari curarunt': *Collectio actorum veterum*, pp. 44–6. [318] *Regestum Clementis Papae V*, nos. 146, 239.

[319] The papal dispensation was given on 5 August 1306 for two years, and it was renewed for an additional two years on 3 March 1310: *ibid.*, nos. 1222, 5957.

[320] Samaran and Mollat, *La fiscalité pontificale en France*, p. 35.

[321] *Regestum Clementis Papae V*, nos. 471, 553, 767, 797, 1254, 1668, 1809, 2478, 3710, 3719, 4300, 4670, 8833, 9380, 9408, 9431.

[322] Jean de St Victor, *Prima Vita*, p. 22; *La chronique métrique attribuée à Geffroy de Paris*, pp. 144, 149, vv. 27–72, 3026–39; Langlois, 'Satire cléricale du temps de Philippe le Bel', pp. 147–8.

[323] Dare suos redditus solebant prelati,
Nunc sunt illis penitus per papam privati.
Fructum non dat servitus, servi sunt sufflati;
Premia sperata dant mala multa pati.

deep-rooted image of the king of France as *advocatus ecclesiae* did nothing, therefore, to improve the image of Clement V or to obscure the damaging results of the curial wanderings in Languedoc. The clergy was not ready to balance its fiscal losses with the future benefits that the papal presence purportedly would bring by hastening peace between England and France and/or the renewal of the crusade. On the contrary, the proximity to the papal curia bred contempt. The attitude of the population of the Midi approached the hostility displayed towards the popes and their retinue by Romans and Italians in former generations. In the process, Clement and the curia lost much of the mythical aura that had previously benefited the Holy See in the Capetian Kingdom.

A main factor in the growing tension between Clement V and the clergy of France was the pope's readiness to enlist the Church in support of the royal efforts to bring about economic recovery. This policy, however, did not represent an original initiative of Clement V. Pope Benedict XI had granted a tenth for two years in 1304, to be effective when good money was restored; this was actually collected in 1307 and 1308.[324] On the other hand, futile attempts by Boniface VIII to prevent royal taxation of the clergy, and ultimately his complete capitulation, convincingly testify to Philip the Fair's adamant fiscal stand. By responding to the king's pressing needs, both Benedict and Clement actually fulfilled the expectations of Philip the Fair, especially in regard to the division of labour between pope and king, on the one hand, and the royal court and all inhabitants of the realm, the clergy included, on the other.

From Philip's perspective, indeed, royal fiscal demands did not constitute a usurpation of ecclesiastical prerogatives; they were simply an equitable requisition in the light of the clergy's duty to support the defence of the realm by all means at its disposal.[325] In a letter to the bishop of Amiens, the king declared his determination to enlist the clergy 'for the necessary defence of the aforesaid kingdom'.[326] Following some attempts to evade payment of the double tenth, Philip urged all prelates and exempt monasteries to pay, and justified his demand on their being an integral part of the political body. As such, they were obliged to

. . .

Solita clementia, summe presul, gratis
Redde beneficia data a prelatis
De tua potencia privilegiatis,
Qui facis ut pateant celestia regna beatis.
Langlois, 'Satire cléricale du temps de Philippe le Bel', pp. 146–8.

[324] *Inventaire d'anciens comptes royaux dressés par Robert Mignon*, no. 796.
[325] On the chroniclers' contribution to the diffusion of this motto, see Spiegel, '"Defense of the Realm"', pp. 115–33; for Philip's early reign, see pp. 126–9.
[326] *Ordonnances des roys de France de la troisième race*, p. 382.

contribute their share to the defence of the realm (October 1305). The king did not rely on the patriotic feelings of the clergy, and hinted at his right to use force against all culprits.[327] In order to overcome the latent opposition and undermine its inner unity, Philip also summoned provincial councils at different times and places and tried to attain consent through large concessions.

Early in 1305, the king promised to reform the currency, a goal that had been supported enthusiastically by Benedict XI. Philip's promise, though, was not found satisfactory, and the clergy compelled him to deal with the payment of debts and to put an end to royal infringements of ecclesiastical jurisdiction. Not satisfied with general statements, the clergy further forced the king to give clear responses. After difficult bargaining, Philip guaranteed that, if the pope granted him a tenth, he would postpone its collection until the subsidy granted by the clergy was paid; moreover, the collection of the tenth would stop altogether if a truce or peace were achieved in Flanders. This was a clear case of 'cessante causa, cessat effectus', when the cause ceases (in this particular case the war in Flanders), the effect (namely, the royal tax) also ceases.[328] Special auditors would also be appointed to hear and remedy all grievances aired by the Church. The local assemblies, with their detailed demands, probably encouraged Philip to conclude an unsatisfactory peace with Flanders that would release him from his critical financial situation and from the clergy's fiscal and political pressure.[329] Having fulfilled most requests, Philip proceeded to take practical measures to assure the accomplishment of the clergy's own obligations. The archbishop of Narbonne, the bishop of Auxerre, and Pierre de Belleperche, a canon from Bourges, were empowered to collect the tenth and to nominate general collectors for every ecclesiastical province (1305). Still, the ecclesiastics of Rouen did not contribute their share until 1306, and even then they restricted their contribution to a single tenth.[330]

Philip's vulnerability *vis-à-vis* the prelates of France determined the crucial importance of papal fiscal support. As early as 1305, Clement had authorised Philip to collect the annates for three years.[331] Contemporary chroniclers echoed the formal justification mentioned in the papal letter, namely, the pressing need to improve the coinage and to revert to its value

---

[327] Strayer, 'Consent to Taxation Under Philip the Fair', p. 41.

[328] On the application of this clause during Philip's reign, see Brown, '*Cessante causa* and the Taxes of the Last Capetians', pp. 574–7.

[329] Strayer, 'Consent to Taxation Under Philip the Fair', p. 90.

[330] *Inventaire d'anciens comptes royaux dressés par Robert Mignon*, p. 110.

[331] *Ibid.*, pp. 110–13; Samaran and Mollat, *La fiscalité pontificale en France*, pp. 23–4. The papal letter was not entered in Clement's surviving registers.

in the reign of St Louis.[332] Between 1304 and 1307, the Church was not asked for additional grants, perhaps because of the confiscation of the wealth of the Jews and the Templars. Clement V granted the king of France two additional tenths in 1310 and 1312, both also justified on the grounds of the imperative need to improve royal finances.[333] The pope did not restrict himself to the purely fiscal needs of Philip the Fair and enlisted apostolic authority to comfort his conscience as well. First, Clement released the king of France from any remorse that the king might feel for his agents' infringements on Church property. Next, the pope threatened with excommunication anyone who dared propagate false coins, a possibility that, rather obviously, excluded the king himself.[334]

Apostolic generosity appears most surprising in light of the disastrous outcomes of Philip's fiscal policy, first and foremost, on the clergy itself. Resumption of royal fiscal pressure in 1310–12 brought ecclesiastical establishments to the verge of ruin. The powerful abbey of St Germain des Prés in Paris was forced to ask for loans in order to pay a subsidy to the king. When the archbishop of Tours and the abbot of St Martin objected to paying more than a single tenth, their refusal brought about the seizure of their temporalities. The bishop of Albi and the archbishop of Sens each suffered a similar fate.[335] Against this critical situation stood the alliance between pope and king, which acquired crucial importance for the Capetian treasury. During the reign of Philip the Fair, the value of the tenth was about 250,000 *l.t.*; this meant an ecclesiastical income of about 2,500,000 *l.t.* per year, which was five to six times greater than the royal revenue.[336] Clement's sanction of the tenth thus released Philip not only from his chronic financial deficit but, first and foremost, from pressure by the clergy, which could rather easily be translated into political dictates in the framework of local assemblies.[337] Papal policy thus adversely affected the clergy's room of manoeuvring *vis-à-vis* the emerging national state and the royal policy of centralisation.

The tenth regained its crusade essence at the Council of Vienne, where the prelates accorded a six-year tenth for the *passagium generale*. According to papal letters, the tenth was to be collected on Ste Madeleine (22 July) and on 2 February during the six following years. Only the

---

[332] *Continuationis chronici Guillelmi de Nangiaco*, pp. 350–1; *Les grandes chroniques de France*, p. 247.

[333] *Inventaire d'anciens comptes royaux dressés par Robert Mignon*, nos. 815, 828, 838, pp. 80–3.

[334] *Regestum Clementis Papae V*, no. 5010.

[335] *Gallia Christiana*, vol. I, p. 12. On the king's many infringements of the Church's privileges, see L. Bourgain, 'Contribution du clergé à l'impôt sous la monarchie française', pp. 65–77.

[336] B. Causse, *Eglise, finance, et royauté*, vol. I, p. 245.

[337] See, for instance, the king's concessions to the clergy of Toulouse in 1307: *Lettres inédites de Philippe le Bel*, no. 70.

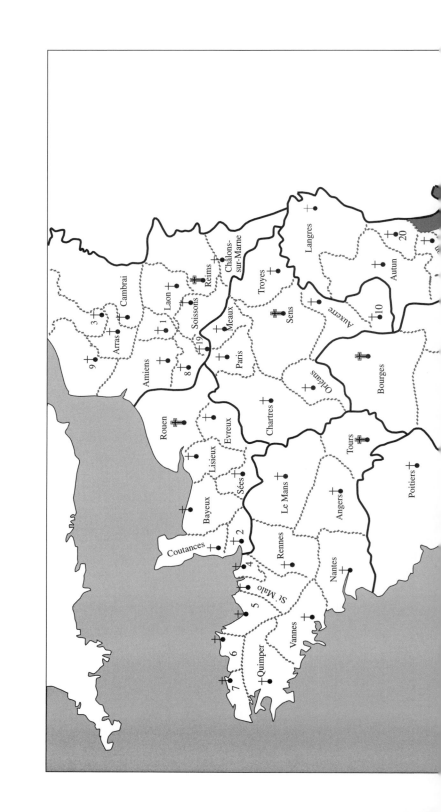

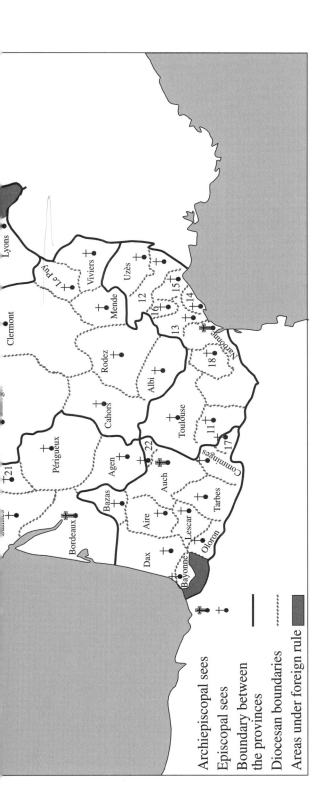

Map 3 Dioceses of France

1 Noyon; 2 Avranches; 3 Tournai; 4 Dol; 5 St Brieuc; 6 Tréguier; 7 St Pol de Léon; 8 Beauvais; 9 Thérouanne; 10 Nevers; 11 Pamiers; 12 Nîmes; 13 Béziers; 14 Agde; 15 Maguelonne; 16 Lodève; 17 Couserans; 18 Carcassonne; 19 Senlis; 20 Chalons-sur-Saône; 21 Angoulême; 22 Lectoure

revenue of the last year (1318) was to be reserved for the curia. Four administrators – Pierre de Grès, bishop of Auxerre; the archdeacon of Vaux-de-Vire in Coutances; the king's clerk, Geffroy du Plessis; and Gilles de Pontoise, abbot of St Denis – were appointed to collect the money and to deliver it to Philip, the captain of the forthcoming crusade.[338] Philip in the end never departed for the Holy Land nor did his son, Louis X; the crusade tax actually provided the necessary funds for the Capetian wars on the Continent.[339]

The unprecedented fiscal burden, coupled with the pope's complaisant policy towards Philip the Fair, eventually intensified criticism of Clement V. The chronicle attributed to Geffroy de Paris regards the pope's deference to the king as the main source of the suffering and poverty of the inhabitants of Paris.[340] It further argues that nobody knew how and where the large sums accumulated by papal collectors, supposedly for the crusade, were actually invested; though everyone was aware of the grave situation, nobody dared to react. It concluded, rather hopelessly, that the prelates remained silent, since they were aware that it was their own shepherd who was causing their suffering and, through them, the decline of the whole Church.[341] Gervais du Bus added his voice to this criticism, putting emphasis on the heavy papal burden that lay on the Church of France. Clement V, he bitterly complained, had reduced the Church to a state of continuous tribulation in complete disregard of divine plans.[342] God had raised men above beasts, the sun above the moon, the Church above the kingdom, Gervais went on, but now divine order was in fact being subverted by the pope when he allowed the king – who is supposed to personify the

---

[338] *Redemptor noster unigenitus* (19 December 1312): *Regestum Clementis Papae V*, nos. 8986–7; *Inventaire d'anciens comptes royaux dressés par Robert Mignon*, pp. 114–19. On the amounts collected in 1313, see Causse, *Eglise, finance, et royauté*, vol. I, pp. 205–18.

[339] On the costs of Philip's military campaigns, see Lalou, 'Les questions militaires sous le règne de Philippe le Bel', pp. 46–52.

[340] *La chronique métrique attribuée à Geffroy de Paris*, p. 195, vv. 5505.

[341] Mes je ne sai pas ou fu mise
La peccune qu'en fu levee . . .
Li prelaz n'en osent plus faire,
Car il regardent que du chief
Vient a l'Eglyse le meschief;
Le chief met les membres a mort.
Ibid., p. 149, vv. 3024–43.

[342] Le pape . . . devers le roy . . .
De ces diesiesmes li envoie
Et des prouvendes li otroie . . .
Que par ce voion sainte Eglise
Tributaire et au dessous mise.
Gervais du Bus, *Le roman de Fauvel*, p. 24, vv. 569–78.

moon and, consequently, its inferior status – to attain dominion over the Church.[343]

Clement's largesse towards Philip the Fair was not based on cosmological considerations, but on the pope's awareness of the critical financial situation of his main partner in the crusade. In a rather patronising tone, Clement shared with Capetian emissaries his political evaluation of the king and the kingdom of France. According to the pope, there had been three distinctive periods during the reign of Philip the Fair: first, the king had been at peace with his neighbours, his subjects had been obedient, and both the king and his kingdom had abounded in wealth. In the second stage, the king had conducted futile wars against England and Flanders, which had brought about the collapse of his treasury and the suffering of his subjects.[344] Now, in the third period, Philip enjoyed peace with his neighbours and the obedience of his subjects, but he had no money. Clement's conclusion was somewhat expected: the king would certainly become wealthy again if he preserved the peace and prevented his officials from usurping the rights of others.[345] Although one may doubt Clement's impartiality and the practical effects of his advice, the Aragonese ambassadors to Avignon reported to James II that there had never been a monarch in France as poor and as little respected as Philip the Fair.[346]

Analysis of Clement's policy in the Church of England and France shows a similarity of goals and outcomes. Clement V was well aware of the critical economic situation of both kingdoms and enlisted the resources of the Church on their behalf. This was not an outcome of royal coercion of the kind that had led a few years earlier to Boniface's retraction of *Clericis laicos*. It reflected, rather, Clement's political priorities and his genuine desire to strengthen royal authority in the leading monarchies of Christendom as a prerequisite to launching the crusade. At the beginning of the fourteenth century, such an alliance between *rex* and *sacerdos* seems inevitable. Yet, the papacy paid heavily for it. Clement's support of the kings was regarded as simoniacal or as a reflection of the pope's indifference to the sufferings of the Church, just

---

[343] La seignorie temporel,
  Qui deüst estre basse lune,
  Est par la roe de Fortune
  Souveraine de sainte Eglise.
  Ibid., p. 20, vv. 472–5. See also *ibid.*, p. 18, vv. 404–31.

[344] Note Clement's negative approach to the king's wars in Flanders and Gascony; a more detailed discussion of these issues appears in chapter 5.

[345] 24 December 1310: *Constitutiones et acta publica imperatorum et regum*, vol. IV-1, no. 514, pp. 469–70.

[346] *Acta Aragonensia*, vol. I, no. 179, p. 263.

as the pope's independent policy in the very few cases when he challenged royal policy was regarded as a manifestation of antagonism and even hostility to the clergy.

The reactions to taxation reveal further aspects of the problematic nature of papal policy. Royal requests, which during Clement's pontificate turned more pressing, damaged the bilateral relationship between the pope and the 'national' Churches. Though this situation was hardly new, the novelty of Clement's pontificate focused on the pope's readiness to legitimise royal intervention in ecclesiastical affairs and to facilitate its implementation. This was a surprising development, considering its implications on the political, economic, and ideological levels. The opposition to taxation was such that the king could hope for little co-operation from his own subjects, the clergy included. Clement V, though, released the western kings from the need to consult the clergy and to make concessions in order to obtain approval. By doing so, the pope became the focus of the odium provoked both by the continuous increase in taxes and by the kings' release from the principle of consent.

The disapproval of the close alliance between pope and king found clear reflection in English records, which continued the historiographical patterns of St Albans and, especially, of Matthew Paris in the previous century.[347] On the other hand, the criticism of papal policy, prevalent as it was, had no significant political weight. From the end of 1312, when Winchelsey retired from the political arena, the Church of England lacked leaders of his stature who could pursue an unconditional struggle in defence of ecclesiastical liberties. Even the parliaments of Carlisle and Stamford appear, in retrospect, to have been manipulated, respectively, by Edward I and Edward II to strengthen their position at home and to advance their interests in negotiations with the papal curia. Conversely, French contemporary records lack a similar political awareness. In many cases, chroniclers merely reported Philip's intervention in ecclesiastical affairs without criticising it. When critics are eventually found, as in the *Roman de Fauvel*, they acquire a melancholic, anachronistic tone, with longings for an egalitarian past that never was and could not exist. The coercive policy of Philip the Fair allowed only general references, with some cosmological allusions to the detrimental effects of the alliance between pope and king. On the other hand, criticism of the pope and his harmful influence on the Church and the clergy intensified to the point that it became a common motif in contemporary literature.

The results of the policy of Clement V were not limited to detri-

---

[347] Matthew Paris, *Chronica Majora*, ad a. 1240, pp. 31–2, 14–15, 73; ad a. 1244, pp. 362–74; ad a. 1246, pp. 528–36, 550, 559; ad a. 1252, pp. 316, 324–8; ad a. 1253, pp. 389–93; ad a. 1256, p. 584; ad a. 1257, p. 625.

mental effects on the papal image; they also had serious political and financial implications. Although Clement V seemingly continued the centralising policy of his predecessors, and papal provisions and taxation were carried out without encountering resistance, the papal monarchy lost much of its former independence. Clement more than mobilised the Church's income for the royal treasuries; he also diluted the most precious goal of the Gregorian Reform, the *libertas ecclesiae*, in the widest meaning of the term. Papal provisions became a sort of compensation for the king's protégés, and the tenth turned into a staple of royal revenue. One should further note that the close alliance between pope and king was independent of the king's status in his own realm and, especially, of the relationship between the king and the clergy. Clement did not make any effort to channel the resentment against royal exactions or to advance his own status among the clergy as defender of the universal Church.

By sacrificing the prelates to his alliance with the monarchs of England and France, Clement V eventually helped to strengthen the national character of the ecclesiastical hierarchy, which in turn appealed to the king against papal exactions.[348] Notwithstanding the fact that these same kings were the main beneficiaries of papal fiscal policy, they willingly played the role of *advocatus ecclesiae* – whether in the framework of parliament or by a direct appeal to the pope. In either case, Clement was left with the resentment aroused by his close alliance with the king.[349] The developments in England, especially the parliamentary decisions against Clement, his representatives, and papal policy in general, hint at the dangers implied in the pope's non-reciprocal devotion to the king. Clement's support of Edward I and Edward II encouraged an entente between the nobles and large sectors of the clergy, who found it more feasible to direct their frustrations against the papal curia than against the king, who was the main beneficiary of papal policy. A similar process occurred in France under Philip the Fair. The alliance among all victims of papal policy eventually created the first seeds of Anglican and Gallican parliamentarism, which found full expression in the second half of the fourteenth century.[350] By 1388, the collection of the tenth had so

---

[348] Despite the attempts by ecclesiastics to counterbalance papal centralisation, the papacy, in fact, neutralised the power of the chapter in ecclesiastical elections. See G. Mollat, *La collation des bénéfices ecclésiastiques*, pp. 64, 133.

[349] This peculiar division between pope and king had also operated during the pontificate of Boniface VIII. See Lunt, 'Papal Taxation in England in the Reign of Edward I', p. 417.

[350] Bernstein defines Gallicanism 'as the consciousness of a viable, particular, French church, united in defense of local rights, and protected by the king of France'. See A. E. Bernstein, '*Magisterium* and License', p. 306. On the outcomes of papal policy in the long run, see J. Favier, 'Temporels ecclésiastiques et taxation fiscale', p. 125.

essentially changed that when Pope Urban VI sought to collect a twentieth in England, he was met with a response in the form of a petition from the Commons that anyone who levied such a tax without the assent of the king should be adjudged a traitor.[351] This development weakens the weight ascribed by Walter Ullmann to Clement's pontificate and justifies making the focus of analysis into the political process characteristic of the fourteenth century as a whole. It was the emergence of the national monarchies that dictated not only the means but also the outcomes of Clement's policy in the Church.

---

[351] Keen argues that from the reign of Edward I onwards, the roles of king and pope in the taxation of the clergy underwent a complete reversal: M. H. Keen, *England in the Later Middle Ages*, p. 205.

Chapter 3

CRUSADE AND MISSION

DE RECUPERATIONE TERRAE SANCTAE

Clement V was elected to the papacy fourteen years after the fall of Crusader Acre (18 May 1291), a traumatic event that was still felt in Christendom.[1] Sylvia Schein argues that his pontificate marked the beginning of serious and intensive efforts to launch a crusade.[2] There is no doubt, indeed, about Clement's devotion to the recovery of the Holy Land, which was clearly reflected in the papal encyclical to the faithful only two days after his coronation.[3] This was not just a rhetorical proclamation. Throughout his entire pontificate, Clement devoted himself and curial resources to the implementation of the crusade.[4] The political circumstances in the west seemed to be most propitious for the success of the Christian enterprise *Outremer*. The peace process between England and France, which was strengthened in 1308 by the marriage of Edward II and Isabella, the daughter of Philip the Fair, and the close alliance between Clement V and the kings of England and France created the illusion of a united Christendom, ready to renew the 'Just War' against the 'Infidel'. On the other hand, the long and (one may say) also scandalous trial of the Templars (1307–12) required much papal energy and cast a heavy shadow over the negotiations between the curia and the different rulers of Christendom.

The political and security circumstances of the kingdoms of Armenia and Cyprus were no less problematic. The two kingdoms originated as by-products of the crusade, and their defence by western Catholics was an important goal of papal crusading policy in the fourteenth century.[5]

---

[1] A. Luttrell, 'The Crusades in the Fourteenth Century', p. 124.
[2] S. Schein, *Fideles Crucis*, pp. 181–2.
[3] *Registrum Simonis de Gandavo*, vol. I, pp. 220–3; see above, pp. 17–18.
[4] *Regestum Clementis Papae V*, nos. 750–3, 1247–8, 1250, 2148, 2987, 2988, 2992, 3010.
[5] The kingdom of Cilician or Lesser Armenia dated from January 1198, when Prince Leo II was crowned by Bishop Conrad of Hildesheim, chancellor and envoy of Emperor Henry VI. Cyprus'

By 1274 Cilician Armenia, a non-Frankish country, was economically debilitated, politically chaotic, and immensely vulnerable to Islamic attack. In 1304, the grand khan, Ghazan, declared Islam the official faith of his dominions. His successor, Kharbanda, ordered all Christians to wear a 'mark of opprobrium', a black linen stripe over the shoulder. Religious coercion was soon accompanied by military action. In 1303, Ouljaitou invaded Cilician Armenia and forced the king, Hetoum II, to retreat to Taurus. The Mongol intruders were followed by the Mamluks of Egypt, though Hetoum succeeded in overcoming them.[6] The critical situation, coupled with his own deep religious feelings, led Hetoum to seek rapprochement with the west while encouraging the unification of the Armenian and Catholic churches. His friendly approach to the west was also suggested by the marriage of his sister, Isabella, to Aimery of Cyprus, the nominal lord of Tyre and brother of Henry II of Lusignan.[7] In 1305, Hetoum retreated to a Franciscan house and left the crown to his nephew, Leo IV, who was eight years old. Two years later, when both were visiting the Mongol emir Bilarghu at Anavarza, they were murdered, along with all their attendants (17 November 1307).[8] Since neither uncle nor nephew had offspring, the throne passed to Hetoum's brother, Oshin (1307–20).[9] Besides, Marino Sanudo Torsello listed the Tartars, the Mamluks, the Turkish emirs of Anatolia, and Christian pirates among the formidable enemies with whom the Armenians had to contend.[10]

The fragile situation in the fight against Islam brought the Military Orders to invest much effort in Cilician Armenia. According to the Hospital Statutes, the brethren went fairly regularly to the area; between 1300 and 1305, the master, Fr Fulk of Villaret, led two considerable expeditions, and on each occasion stayed in Armenia for some time.[11] Yet, the position of the Military Orders in the kingdom was unsatisfactory. The brothers remained there at the mercy of the crown, and neither the Hospitallers nor the Templars enjoyed much support from the local population. In his report to the pope, the master of the Templars, Jacques de Molai, referred to the Armenians' suspicion of the Latins and the

status as a kingdom was also a gift of Henry VI. In 1197, the emperor brought about the coronation of Aimery of Lusignan at Nicosia. On crusading activity in both kingdoms, see Housley, *The Later Crusades*, pp. 178–203.   [6] H. Pasdermadjian, *Histoire de l'Arménie*, pp. 216–17.

[7] *Chronique d'Amadi*, p. 240.

[8] Modern historians consider this act a reprisal for Hetoum's pro-Catholic policy. The *Chronique d'Amadi*, however, points to Bilargou, the Mongol general, as responsible for the massacre: *Chronique d'Amadi*, pp. 269–70.

[9] T. S. R. Boase, 'The History of the Kingdom', pp. 29–30.

[10] Marino Sanudo Torsello, 'Liber secretorum fidelium crucis', pp. 7, 26, 37–8. On his crusading efforts, see C. J. Tyerman, 'Marino Sanudo Torsello and the Lost Crusade', pp. 57–73.

[11] *Cartulaire général de l'ordre des Hospitaliers*, vol. III, no. 4515; vol. IV, no. 4549; *Acta Aragonensia*, vol. III, p. 146.

probable lack of support that the crusade would encounter among them.[12] None the less, Clement tried to enlist the active support of western princes and the Italian communes on behalf of Cilician Armenia, but his early efforts to this end met with little or no success.[13]

In Cyprus, as well, a Saracen pirate raid in 1302 along with the dominant position of the Genoese brought the island to the verge of anarchy. On 26 April 1306, Henry II of Lusignan was forced to abdicate in favour of his brother, Aimery of Tyre, and to recognise him as 'governor and rector' of the kingdom.[14] Aimery gained the support of a large portion of the nobility, the Templars included, on the grounds of Henry's illness and his failure to protect the realm against the Genoese and the Egyptians.[15] Clement V did not allow this turn of events, which could affect his projects for a crusade, go unheeded. The pope appointed Nicholas, archbishop of Thebes, and Raimond de Piis, one of his chamberlains and canon of Bazas, as papal nuncios to manage the difficult situation (23 January 1308).[16] Raimond eventually reached Cyprus, but only on 4 March 1310, a considerable delay that caused Aimery to complain about the pace of papal diplomacy.[17]

The slowness of papal intervention – which could have been deliberate at a time when the pope's main concern was to launch a crusade – hardly affected tragic developments on the island. On 5 June 1310, Aimery was murdered by Simon de Montolif, an act that left Henry II – at the time, prisoner in Cilician Armenia – the sole aspirant for the throne. In the unrest that followed, the Hospitallers were accused of the murder because of their continuous attempt to interfere in the rule of the kingdom.[18] Whether this accusation was true or not, the Hospitallers succeeded in liberating Henry II in the midst of a military expedition (27 October 1310).[19] Although the Hospitallers' attack rendered the long negotiations conducted by Raimond de Piis with King Oshin null and

---

[12] A. S. Atiya, *The Crusade in the Later Middle Ages*, pp. 41–3, 55–6.

[13] *Regestum Clementis Papae V*, nos. 748, 750–1.

[14] For the Latin version of the deposition act of Henry and the election of Aimery, see C. Kohler, 'Documents chypriotes du début du XIVe siècle', pp. 444–52; M. L. de Mas Latrie, *Histoire de l'Ile de Chypre*, vol. II, p. 101; *Chronique d'Amadi*, pp. 248–62; *Chronique de Strambaldi*, pp. 18–22.

[15] *Chronique d'Amadi*, pp. 249–55. Amaury's claims were faithfully voiced in his letter to the king of Aragon, in which he restated the same arguments presented to the pope: *Acta Aragonensia*, vol. II, no. 463, pp. 745–6. Still, Clement was hesitant in his approach to the new regime: *Regestum Clementis Papae V*, nos. 2469–72; P. Edbury, *The Kingdom of Cyprus and the Crusades*, pp. 109–21.

[16] Ch. Perrat, 'Un diplomate gascon', pp. 35–90.

[17] *Regestum Clementis Papae V*, nos. 2824–8, 3543. Upon Raimond de Piis' arrival in Cyprus, Aimery declared 'che haveria gran piacer de la sua venuta, et li rincresseva et dispiaceva che l'ha tardato tanto': *Chronique d'Amadi*, pp. 326–7.

[18] These accusations were not completely imaginary. Fr Fulk of Villaret had been authorised by Henry of Lusignan to rule Cyprus until his liberation: *Chronique d'Amadi*, pp. 315–25, 368–71.

[19] *Chronique de Strambaldi*, p. 26.

void,[20] the resulting impasse made papal intervention imperative in order to obviate an open conflict between the king of Cyprus and his former captor, the king of Armenia.[21] By the end of the year, a peace treaty was signed between Henry II of Lusignan, Oshin, and Isabella, Aimery's widow, in the presence of Raimond de Piis and Bishop Pierre of Rodez – the papal legate in the Hospitaller passage.[22] The success of Clement's envoys in re-establishing peace in the eastern kingdoms created a relatively good basis for launching a crusade. The question still remained, however, whether the pope's devotion to the Holy Land was shared by his contemporaries or whether it was Clement's dearest dream, to which Christian rulers were ready to pay lip-service in order to advance their particular interests.

Clement's original scheme for the crusade was based on a double alliance with the kings of France and Naples. Following his coronation, the pope obtained a formal undertaking from Philip the Fair to depart on the crusade, with the proviso that the king decided the proper time; further, Philip's commitment would be invalidated should his departure overseas threaten the safety of his kingdom.[23] The pope also took advantage of the critical economic situation of the king of Naples and enlisted him, too, for the crusade. During the negotiations over the repayment of Charles II's debts to the papal camera, Clement outlined a plan in the form of Angevin aid to the east (20 July 1307). For two-thirds of the considerable sum of 360,000 gold ounces, Charles or one of his sons was to depart with 300 knights on the forthcoming crusade and remain in the Holy Land 'as long as the Church considers it useful, until the remainder of the above debt has been repaid'. Charles was also to keep twenty galleys afloat in the eastern Mediterranean for four months each year, during and after the general passage.[24] If one bears in mind the poor state of papal finances at the beginning of the pontificate, Clement's readiness to reach such an agreement suggests the overriding importance he attributed to the recovery of the Holy Land. On the other hand, we also have here a clear reflection of the western kings' manipulative approach in regard to the crusade. As in the case of the kings of England and France, the Angevins' theoretical readiness to depart overseas secured them, too, generous papal benefices.

---

[20] In order to close the gap between the parties, the nuncio had departed on another journey to Armenia on 18 July 1310: *Chronique d'Amadi*, p. 371.

[21] Raimond de Piis died in 1311 and was buried in the Dominican house in Nicosia: *ibid.*, p. 391.

[22] *Regestum Clementis Papae V*, nos. 7214, 10477; Mas Latrie, *Histoire de l'Ile de Chypre*, vol. II, pp. 113–16; Edbury, *The Kingdom of Cyprus and the Crusades*, pp. 125–33. To avoid any contestants to the throne of Armenia, Isabella and her two sons were murdered in 1320 by another Oshin, lord of Corycus, who claimed to be acting as regent for the young heir, Leo V.

[23] Wenck, 'Aus den Tagen der Zusammenkunft Papst Klemens V und König Philipps des Schönen zu Lyon', pp. 189–203.   [24] *Regestum Clementis Papae V*, no. 2269.

De recuperatione Terrae Sanctae

Clement also tried to enlist Edward I, Albert I, and James II in order to bestow a pan-Christian character on the Christian enterprise *Outremer*. The kings of England, Germany, and Aragon, each in his own particular way, were indeed ready to express their deep commitment to the recovery of the Holy Land and their devotion to the papal plans in most touching terms; but beyond their formal declarations, it was the war in Scotland, the imperial coronation and an unstable position at home, and the strengthening of the Christian frontier in the Iberian peninsula to which each of them gave first priority. The rather low crusading motivation of the Christian princes eventually facilitated Clement's appeal to the Military Orders, the traditional allies of the papacy in the crusade. On 6 June 1306, the pope summoned the masters of the Temple and the Hospital 'for a deliberation and consultation about the recovery of the Holy Land'.[25] Soon after, Fr Fulk of Villaret arrived at the curia; by this time, however, the trial of the Templars had begun, and the pope was forced to rely on the Hospital alone.[26]

On 11 August 1308, Clement issued a series of letters proclaiming a Hospitaller *passagium particulare*. In defining its main aims in *Exsurgat Deus*, the pope focused on the defence of Cyprus and Armenia against Mamluk and Turkish attacks and on the need to obstruct the illegal trade of Christians with the Muslims in the Mediterranean:

Our minds are terrified by the gravest apprehension lest the fortitude of the noble kingdoms of Cyprus and Armenia, which are oppressed by incursions of the enemies of the Cross, deeply wounded within, and afflicted by the growing, perfidious variety of multiple torture, as indicated by the cries of those faithful, oppressed kingdoms, may fall down under the madness of their persecution; and those kingdoms, having been placed in the ruin of desolation by the rage of their enemies, those faithful may be exposed to the possibility of a horrible death . . . O what serious confusion the whole Christian religion would receive if such fortune should arrive, which may God avert! O what opprobrious damage of deformity it would incur if, through the truculent rage of those enemies, it should happen, God forbid, that such noble members would be mutilated![27]

Clement also referred to his long-term plans for a general crusade under the leadership of Philip the Fair: 'through the zealous service of that king, that one aiding, whose business is done in this matter, the aid of a general passage may come to that [Holy] land and the light of recovery

---

[25] *Ibid.*, nos. 1033, 10368–9; *Acta Clementis PP V*, no. 8; Finke, *Papsttum und Untergang des Templerordens*, vol. II, no. 23, pp. 33–6; *Continuatio chronici Girardi de Fracheto*, p. 28. See Jacques de Molai's approach: *Collectio actorum veterum*, pp. 145–9.

[26] On Clement's concern about the Hospital and its rights, see my forthcoming article, 'The Hospitallers in the Pontificate of Clement V'.

[27] *Regestum Clementis Papae V*, nos. 2988–90; *The Register of John de Halton*, vol. II, pp. 41–50; L. Thier, *Kreuzzugsbemühungen unter Papst Clemens V*, pp. 79–82.

may dawn happily'.[28] This reference to the crusading plans of the king of France in the midst of the Hospitaller crusade was not fortuitous. It hinted, rather, at Clement's awareness of the hostility of Philip the Fair to the Hospitaller crusade, namely, to the independent papal enterprise. From the Capetian perspective, the Hospitaller crusade might harm the political status of Philip the Fair as the recognised secular leader of Christendom and, as such, the theoretical captain of the crusade. No less importantly, it might invalidate any justification the king might advance to collect the tenth.[29]

Philip's reluctance to support the Hospitaller crusade – significant as it was, coming from the pope's main ally – was not the only inconvenience encountered by Clement's crusading plans. The commercial blockade of the Mediterranean presented difficult challenges, as well. The need to halt all trade with the Muslims had already been voiced by the Third Lateran Council (1179);[30] it was echoed by the synod of Montpellier (1195),[31] and finally established in the Fourth Council of Lateran (1215). Led by the energetic policy of Innocent III, the council threatened with excommunication 'all those faithless and impious Christians, who against Christ Himself and the Christian people provide the Saracens with weapons, iron, and wood for their galleys'.[32] The fall of Crusader Acre brought about more severe regulations. Nicholas IV extended previous prohibitions and rigorously forbade the export of arms, horses, iron, wood, foodstuffs, 'and any other form of merchandise' to Egypt and Syria, with violators to be punished by excommunication and perpetual infamy (23 August 1291).[33]

Conciliar and papal prohibitions, however, were worthless in the face of commercial interests and the mutual rivalry among Catalans, Venetians, Pisans, and Genoese, to mention only the leading Christian parties involved in trade with the Muslims. The popes themselves at times weakened former bans and, for example, allowed merchants from Catalonia, Majorca, and Aragon to trade with the Infidel, albeit under some restrictions.[34] Lacking the prerogative of the *Reconquista*, the Venetians did not ask for papal authorisation at all, and actively traded in all kinds of merchandise with Egypt and the ports along

---

[28] *Regestum Clementis Papae V*, nos. 2987–8.

[29] Philip complained to the pope of not being properly informed of the preparations and of the lack of suitable representatives from France in the Hospitaller crusade: *Cartulaire général de l'ordre des Hospitaliers*, nos. 4831, 4841. See the apologetic response of the pope (27 October 1309): *Collectio actorum veterum*, pp. 105–8.   [30] *Conciliorum Oecumenicorum Decreta*, [24], p. 223.

[31] *Concilia*, ed. Mansi, vol. XXI, col. 1160.

[32] *Conciliorum Oecumenicorum Decreta*, [71], p. 270; O. R. Constable, *Trade and Traders in Muslim Spain*, pp. 64, 133, 233–40.   [33] *Les registres de Nicolas IV*, no. 6784.

[34] Trenchs Odena, '*De Alexandrinis*', pp. 246–52; D. Abulafia, *A Mediterranean Emporium*, pp. 159–64.

the Syrian coast.[35] In 1302, Venice signed a commercial treaty with Egypt that granted the city unusual exemptions from duties on imports and exports, and a permanent consul, Francesco da Canali, was formally admitted in Alexandria. In exchange for these gestures of goodwill, the Venetians further agreed to sell contraband articles of war.[36]

Clement V tried to stop this lucrative trade or, at least, to make some profit from it.[37] The pope threatened with excommunication all merchants implicated in handling contraband. Culprits would be absolved only by apostolic mandate, provided they handed over to the crusade a sum equal to the value of their illegal trade with Islam.[38] Clement also requested Philip IV to enforce the blockade on the southern ports of his kingdom and to punish all lawbreakers.[39] The pope wrote similar messages to the bishops of Pisa, Genoa, Ancona, Naples, Venice, and Brindisi,[40] trying to enlist the Italian prelates in the economic blockade and, through them, their insubordinate flock. In parallel, Clement made maximum effort to facilitate the Hospitallers' passage eastwards. The pope wrote to the always reluctant Italian maritime communes, which he urged to give priority to the fight against the Infidel over their income from wages and taxes on the Hospital.[41] In a letter to the bishops of Viviers and Valence, the count of Savoy, and the dauphin of Vienne – namely, prelates and lords who held fortresses along the Rhône – the pope ordered that all necessary precautions be taken so that the brothers would not be charged any tolls (20 March 1309).[42] Clement repeated his order two weeks later, threatening violators with excommunication.[43] The pope also tried to enlist the Teutonic Knights to join the Hospitaller passage (20 September 1308).[44]

Clement's crusade plan envisaged a force of 1,000 knights and 4,000 foot soldiers, who would remain in the east for five years. For the implementation of this plan, the pope committed the apostolic camera to the considerable sum of 300,000 florins, which in his opinion the critical situation justified:

[35] Mas Latrie, 'Traité des Vénitiens avec l'émir d'Acre', pp. 406–8.
[36] F. C. Hodgson, *Venice in the Thirteenth and Fourteenth Century*, p. 323.
[37] E. Ashtor, 'Investments in Levant Trade in the Period of the Crusades', pp. 427–41.
[38] *Regestum Clementis Papae V*, nos. 2994–5, 5090. The money collected in this way was used in Aragon to rescue Christian prisoners and to subsidise the royal campaign against Granada: Trenchs Odena, 'De Alexandrinis', pp. 276–9.   [39] *Regestum Clementis Papae V*, nos. 2986, 2994–5.
[40] *Ibid.*, nos. 3088, 7118–19.   [41] *Ibid.*, no. 3218.
[42] The pope clearly ordered that the brothers be allowed free passage 'sine pedagio, leude, portulagii seu exactionis alterius prestatione': *ibid.*, no. 3825.   [43] *Ibid.*, no. 3857.
[44] *Ibid.*, no. 3219; Thier, *Kreuzzugsbemühungen unter Papst Clemens V*, pp. 63–74; Housley, 'Pope Clement V and the Crusades of 1309–1310', pp. 30–1.

At the insistent urgency of the said kings of Cyprus and Armenia, for the defence and safe-keeping of that moderate reminder of the aforesaid faith . . . and for preparing suitable obstacles for perfidious Christians lest they carry victuals and prohibited wares to those Saracens . . . as should be possible, not from an imposition of a tenth or from any part of ecclesiastical incomes but from the treasure of our camera, the bountiful financial subsidy of the king of the Franks being added to this.[45]

More specifically, 100,000 florins were expected from the Capetian treasury, which was rather wishful thinking with regard to Philip the Fair and the critical situation of his treasury.[46] The bulk of the expenses otherwise depended on the laity, through their purchase of indulgences, which were carefully graduated according to the amount of the donation. Thus, those who contributed the total expenditure of one passage to the Holy Land or even half this amount were granted plenary indulgence, while those who contributed 24 *l.t.* received indulgence for twenty-four years. Clement outlined the conversion rates clearly:

Also to all regular and secular ecclesiastical persons as well as to any others of Christ's faithful . . . who shall pay to the said master and brothers [of the Hospital] as much from their goods as they would have spent in one year if they had gone personally to the aid of the aforesaid land, we grant full pardon of their sins for which they shall be of contrite heart and orally confessed; to those, moreover, who shall give to the aforesaid master and brothers a half of that which they would have expended during the period of the aforesaid year had they gone personally to the aid of the said land, we grant a pardon of half of their sins for which they shall be contrite in heart and orally confessed. Furthermore, we will bestow those who shall aid the aforesaid master and brothers in the said passage with a larger or smaller subsidy to be sharers of the aforesaid remission in proportion to the larger or smaller amount of the subsidy and the feeling of devotion.[47]

The pope also authorised the commutation 'of vows of any abstinence and of any pilgrimages, the pilgrimage beyond the sea [i.e., Jerusalem] alone excepted', in exchange for monetary aid during the next five years.[48] Following the example of his predecessors, Clement also tried to enlist the faithful in the pursuit of heavenly favour and ordered litanies to be prayed throughout Christendom:

---

[45] *Regestum Clementis Papae V*, no. 3753; *Registrum Simonis de Gandavo*, vol. I, pp. 305–6.
[46] *Regestum Clementis Papae V*, nos. 2986, 3218, 5384; Finke, *Papsttum und Untergang des Templerordens*, vol. II, no. 92, pp. 154–8. See also the pope's letters to Philip IV (6 June and 27 October 1309) requesting his financial help: *Collectio actorum veterum*, pp. 120–1, 105–8.
[47] *Regestum Clementis Papae V*, nos. 2987–90, 2996–7; *Continuationis chronici Guillelmi de Nangiaco*, p. 371; *Continuatio chronici Girardi de Fracheto*, p. 32. For the Hospitallers' campaign for funds in Italy, see Agnolo di Tura, *Cronaca Senese*, p. 304.
[48] *Regestum Clementis Papae V*, nos. 4773, 7227, 7716; *The Register of John de Halton*, vol. I, pp. 317–18; *Registrum Simonis de Gandavo*, vol. I, pp. 311–12.

Furthermore, by apostolic authority we strictly enjoin you that, whenever you happen to celebrate the offices of masses, you cause to be said in the offices of those masses, with minds utterly devout, and by ecclesiastical persons . . . in pious feeling of heart, the sermons ordered by the Church against the perfidy of the pagans, of which the first begins 'Omnipotent eternal God', the second, appointed especially for the secret, 'The sacrifice of God', and the third, accustomed to be said especially after communion, 'Protector'.[49]

The pope still refrained from encouraging the massive participation of the faithful in the *passagium*, which remained the sole enterprise of the Hospital.

Fr Fulk of Villaret, the master of the Hospital and, as such, the pope's main partner in the crusade, expressed a rather different approach to the *passagium* under his lead. Fulk primarily viewed the expedition overseas as a means of accomplishing the conquest of Rhodes.[50] From his perspective, the consolidation of Hospitaller rule on the island would create a propitious basis from which to launch an attack on Byzantium – then under the rule of Andronicus II, the son of Michael Palaeologus, who had been excommunicated in 1307 – and then to recapture Antioch or Jerusalem within five years.[51] Eventually, the Hospitaller crusade did lead to the conquest of Rhodes, Kos, and other islands, but it hardly achieved the ambitious aims suggested by both the pope and the master of the Hospital.

Clement's efforts to bring about the renewal of the crusade were reported in contemporary sources, which did not accord it any enthusiastic welcome. Having learned from previous futile attempts, the chroniclers found it sufficient to mention the main characteristics of the papal campaign and, especially, the unprecedented sale of indulgences. The chronicle of St Denis provides a typical version:

And in this year was proclaimed in the kingdom of France the great indulgence that the pope had awarded the last year, when he stayed in Poitiers, for all those who would contribute from their property on behalf of those departing overseas for the assistance of the Holy Land. The master of the Hospital was nominated receiver of the income. It was also provided that in all churches a chest or a special place would be provided, in which everyone would contribute from his [property] according to his faith. And this procedure continued for about five years, as long as the papal absolution lasted.[52]

---

[49] *Regestum Clementis Papae V*, nos. 2989–90, 4769, 4772.

[50] On 5 September 1307, the Hospitallers won papal confirmation for the territories in Rhodes which they had conquered from the Greeks and the Genoese: *Regestum Clementis Papae V*, no. 2148; *Acta Clementis PP V*, no. 19.

[51] B. Z. Kedar and S. Schein, 'Un projet de passage particulier proposé par l'Ordre de l'Hôpital', pp. 220–6.

[52] *Les grandes chroniques de France*, pp. 265–6; Jean de St Victor, *Prima Vita*, p. 15. For the chest placed in the cathedral of Bordeaux, see *Regestum Clementis Papae V*, no. 4923.

In other areas of Christendom, as well, the chroniclers pointed to the extensive papal propaganda, backed by a massive bestowal of indulgences 'the like of which we had never heard before'.[53] Only a few chroniclers welcomed the papal scheme and linked the Hospitaller Crusade with the defence of Armenia and Cyprus and the forthcoming *passagium generale*.[54]

Early in 1310, the Hospitaller Crusade departed from Brindisi eastwards, its squadron of twenty-six or twenty-seven galleys under the lead of Fr Fulk of Villaret.[55] It was the first expedition to leave for the east since 1291. The pope's support and leading role in the enterprise were indicated by the presence of his special legate, Pierre de Pleine Chassagne, bishop of Rodez.[56] In practice, however, the expedition was led by Fulk alone and intended for the achievement of the Hospitaller objectives as had been defined by the master. Once in the east, the army consolidated Hospital dominion in Rhodes – the conquest of which had begun in 1306 – and thus facilitated the transfer of the Order's headquarters, which remained on the island until 1522.[57] The unbalanced relationship between master and legate did not cause any mutual resentment, and Pierre eventually regarded the enterprise as an achievement. Clement himself shared this estimation, and in 1314 recompensed the bishop's services by appointing him patriarch of Jerusalem.

The military success of the *passagium* in Rhodes contributed a suitable basis for launching future crusades, in particular the general passage planned by Clement to be led by Philip the Fair. The blockade of the Mediterranean, however, still presented many obstacles. In the winter of 1311, the Hospitallers seized a Genoese ship sailing from Alexandria with a cargo of spices and refused to release it without papal authorisation. The Genoese ambassador, enraged at their refusal, began intensive nego-

---

53 'Et ad excitandum super hoc animos hominum concessit indulgentias culparum et poenarum quales a saeculo non erant auditae': *Annales Paulini*, p. 266; *Continuatio Mellicensis*, p. 511.

54 'Eodem anno [1309] idem dominus papa Armenie et Cipri regnis, que tunc Sarracenorum incursibus frequenter molestabantur, volens succurrere, quo facilius Terra sancta in futurum recuperari posset, per magistrum et fratres Ierosolimitanenses sancti Iohannis ad ipsa regna mandavit generale passagium instaurari, christicolis per orbem universum eos in hoc negocio promoventibus diversas gracias et indulgencias largiendo': *Continuatio Florianensis*, p. 752.

55 *Continuationis chronici Guillelmi de Nangiaco*, p. 376; Amalric Auger, *Sexta Vita*, p. 98; Bernard Gui, in *Quarta Vita*, p. 67.

56 The large list of privileges accorded the legate and the peremptory letters of Clement calling all prelates to provide him with help testify to the pope's concern for the success of the enterprise. See *Regestum Clementis Papae V*, nos. 3753, 3822, 3852–3, 4384, 4392, 4459, 4496–4516. See also the pope's letter to the kings of Cyprus (no. 4494) and Armenia (no. 4495); *Acta Clementis PP V*, nos. 36a–c; F. Heidelberger, *Kreuzzugsversuche um die Wende des 13. Jahrhunderts*, pp. 24–62.

57 Bernard Gui, in *Quarta Vita*, pp. 62, 68; Amalric Auger, *Sexta Vita*, p. 93; *Les grandes chroniques de France*, p. 271; *Continuatio chronici Girardi de Fracheto*, p. 33; Agnolo di Tura, *Cronaca Senese*, p. 304; Luttrell, 'Feudal Tenure and Latin Colonization at Rhodes', pp. 755–75; Luttrell, 'The Hospitallers of Rhodes', pp. 243–66.

tiations with the Muslims. He endeavoured to persuade a Muslim prince – whose name does not appear in the sources – to imprison the Rhodian merchants and other subjects of the Order who were in his territory. The Genoese ambassador accompanied his request with a large subsidy of 50,000 golden florins should the Muslims launch an expedition to drive the Hospitallers out of Rhodes. Furthermore, Genoese ships proceeded to take prisoner any knights they found sailing in the Mediterranean, and to keep them in prison until Clement ordered their release (26 November 1311).[58] Incidents of this kind reveal the opposing interests facing the pope's crusading plans and, especially, the lack of minimal co-operation among those expected to be leading participants in the crusade. Still, Clement was not discouraged by the lack of Christian zeal among the Genoese. He tried to enlist the services of Emperor Henry VII – a close ally of Genoa, where he had wintered before his coronation – to induce the insubordinate Genoese to give up their vendetta against the Hospital and, no less importantly, to reach an agreement with the king of Cyprus (28 April 1313).[59]

The Genoese were not alone in obstructing papal plans; examples of contraband trade with the Muslims, notwithstanding the severe ban, could be found everywhere. In the summer of 1310, Pons Huc III, count of Ampurias, seized a Venetian ship on its way from Rhodes to Italy with contraband merchandise from Alexandria. James II of Aragon, who feared a Venetian reprisal that could jeopardise his plans for the conquest of Corsica and Sardinia, tried to force his reluctant vassal to return the merchandise. Pons Huc, however, refused, thus creating an impasse in the otherwise good relations between Aragon and Venice. The threat of Venetian retaliation persuaded the *Cortes* to order Pons immediately to satisfy Venetian demands and to impose a punitive expedition against his land. The apologetic tone of the Aragonese towards the Venetians acquires further significance in the light of the excommunication and interdict to which the Venetians were subject at this stage. The energetic invective of Clement V against Venice did not prevent long negotiations between the commune and the king of Aragon, in which the Venetians took the lead.[60] Christian 'solidarity' was not any stronger where the pope was residing. On his way to receive a papal blessing prior to his departure on the crusade, Otto de Grandson was attacked on the Rhône and his property stolen by a local lord, Aymond de Palud.[61]

Similar conflicting interests also appeared in the duchy of Athens. In

---

[58] See the severe reaction of Clement: *Regestum Clementis Pope V*, no. 7631.
[59] *Ibid.*, nos. 9250, 9257.
[60] V. Salavert y Roca, 'Notas sobre la política italiana de Clemente V', pp. 258–64, docs. 2–11, pp. 274–88.   [61] *Regestum Clementis Pope V*, no. 8205.

1311, the duchy was conquered by the Catalan Grand Company, an army of veterans from the Sicilian war which had been called on to help the duke against the Byzantines.[62] Clement, probably influenced by Angevin pressure and the many atrocities attributed to the Catalans, outlawed the Company and supported the legitimate ruler, Duke Gaucher II, who was the grandson of Gaucher de Châtillon, the constable of France.[63] The pope further urged the Hospitallers to help Gaucher to expel the Catalan invaders and to contribute four of the Order's ships for the defence of Athens.[64] Clement's intervention, however, did not succeed in changing the turn of events. Looking for some kind of legitimisation, the Company asked Frederick III of Trinacria to become its lawful leader. After some hesitation, their request was granted in the form of the appointment of Frederick's five-year-old son, Manfred, who became duke of Athens. For the next quarter-century, Sicily held ultimate sovereignty over the province.[65] These incidents suggest the real obstacles that plagued the implementation of Clement's crusading plans and, especially, the lack of a Christian joint front that might have had any chance of defeating the Infidel.

THE CRUSADE AT THE COUNCIL OF VIENNE

The Council of Vienne presented a suitable framework for dealing effectively with the chronic lack of solidarity among the Christian powers; it could further bring about the emergence of a pan-Christian front that would advance the recovery of the Holy Land. After the trial of the Templars, the crusade indeed received the highest priority on the council agenda. According to the Aragonese representatives, the pope raised the matter of the crusade at the end of January 1312. Clement consulted the prelates, according to *nationes*, about the tenth, which was expected to provide the necessary funds.[66] The pope's primary concern for resources hints at the practical lessons he had learned from the Hospitaller Crusade, which had resulted in a serious financial deficit to both the Order and the apostolic camera.[67] The

---

[62] *Chronique de Ramon Muntaner*, p. 250. R. I. Burns regards the Company's advance as perhaps 'the most fantastic military adventure of the later Middle Ages': R. I. Burns, 'The Catalan Company and the European Powers', pp. 751–7.

[63] *Regestum Clementis Papae V*, nos. 8138, 7890–1, 8597, 9153.

[64] *Ibid.*, nos. 10166–8; Luttrell, 'The Latins of Argos and Nauplia', pp. 34–5.

[65] Backman, *The Decline and Fall of Medieval Sicily*, pp. 55–6.

[66] Finke, *Papsttum und Untergang des Templerordens*, vol. II, no. 135, p. 269; Thier, *Kreuzzugsbemühungen unter Papst Clemens V*, pp. 99–104.

[67] *Regestum Clementis Papae V*, nos. 5384, 8986; Thier, *Kreuzzugsbemühungen unter Papst Clemens V*, p. 83; Housley, *The Avignon Papacy and the Crusades*, pp. 159–68. The Hospitallers alone provided the considerable sum of 154,000 florins: Luttrell, 'Notes on Foulques de Villaret, Master of the Hospital', p. 76.

prelates from England, Germany, and Arles supported the papal request and, without further consideration, expressed their readiness to provide a six-year tenth.[68] Those from Italy and Aragon also acquiesced, but conditioned their support on a parallel military enterprise in the Iberian peninsula. More hesitant were the prelates of France, who asked to take up the matter with their king, 'without the advice of whom nothing is done'.[69] They acceded to papal demands in the end, but only after receiving Philip's explicit blessing. This appeal to royal approval in the framework of an ecumenical council indicates, again, the balance of forces not just between *rex* and *sacerdos* but, first and foremost, between Philip the Fair and the prelates of France in the emerging national state. It confirms the meagre chances of implementing any militant papal policy in tune with *Clericis laicos* fifteen years earlier. Clement was well aware of the delicate equilibrium between the king and the Church of France and, accordingly, acted in a way that would best earn the co-operation of Philip the Fair. The victim of this alliance was eventually the clergy itself, which paid the expenses and still supported the king.[70]

The extent to which the French prelates at Vienne were aware of the political implications of their reliance on the king is difficult to ascertain. On the other hand, not all kings were able to retain the proceeds of the tenth. The kings of Sweden, for example, were forced to reach a compromise with the papal curia. When the emperor-elect, Henry VII, asked for the collection of the tenth and the annates for one year – which he needed to finance his expedition to Italy, made under papal blessing – Clement refused the king's appeal on the grounds that such a concession would harm the crusade (June 1310).[71] Conversely, all or most of the tenth income ended up in the coffers of the kings of France and England, with explicit papal permission.[72]

The eventuality that the king would enjoy the revenues of the tenth

---

[68] Guillaume Durant had advised conditioning the collection of the tenth on the clergy's consent: 'quae debentur ex negotiatione, artificio, scientia, militia et venatione, et maxime in Italia et multis aliis partibus . . ., videretur esse propter animarum periculum super his per Ecclesiam providendum': 'Tractatus de modo celebrandi concilii', pt III, tit. 21, in P. Viollet, 'Guillaume Durant, le jeune, évêque de Mende', p. 104. On Guillaume's adherence to the Roman maxim of 'quod omnes tangit', and his refusal to acknowledge the pope as 'legibus solutus', see Fasolt, *Council and Hierarchy*, pp. 280–4.

[69] Finke, *Papsttum und Untergang des Templerordens*, vol. II, no. 135, pp. 269–71.

[70] This prevailing stand was clearly reflected during the long conflict between Philip and Boniface VIII: Menache, 'A Propaganda Campaign in the Reign of Philip the Fair', pp. 453–4.

[71] *Constitutiones et acta publica imperatorum et regum*, vol. IV-I, no. 391, pp. 340–2.

[72] For England, see *Calendar of the Patent Rolls (1313–1317)*, pp. 188, 197, 438, 548; *Calendar of Entries in the Papal Registers*, pp. 207, 211–12; Lunt, *Financial Relations of the Papacy with England*, pp. 395–404; Lunt, 'Clerical Tenths Levied in England by Papal Authority', pp. 166–82; and pp. 70–81 in this volume.

was taken into consideration and largely justified by Guillaume de Nogaret in the memorandum he presented to the Council of Vienne. Not surprisingly, Nogaret voiced support for the Capetian king and suggested the nomination of Philip the Fair as leader of the forthcoming enterprise *Outremer*. After finding in Philip the Fair the most suitable heir to St Louis, the crusader king, Nogaret advised investing in the crusade not only the wealth of the Templars but that of the whole ecclesiastical Order; the clergy would, therefore, be left only with those funds necessary for its daily subsistence.[73] Three additional reports were presented to the council by Guillaume le Maire, Ramon Lull, and Henry II of Lusignan.[74] Guillaume le Maire posited a rather long period of preparation of ten to twelve years, with the Templar wealth covering part of the expenses.[75] Ramon Lull strongly advocated the unification of all Military Orders in order to present a solid Christian front against Islam.[76] He recommended centring crusade efforts on Constantinople and proceeding from there against Syria and Egypt. At the same time, he envisaged a minor offensive in Granada and Morocco, a project that was very dear to the heart of the king of Aragon.[77] Ramon also took into consideration the auspicious possibility of conversion and dealt at length with its implementation.[78] The king of Cyprus, too, supported preparations on a grand scale, including a complete trade blockade of the Muslims. He further suggested Cyprus as the launching pad for any attack against Egypt, since the Mongol advance in Syria made Christian efforts in that region superfluous.[79] Viewed as a whole, the reports presented to the Council of Vienne thus envisaged long-term preparations. The authors' position resulted not only from the interests of the parties involved – quite obviously so in the case of Guillaume de Nogaret and Henry II of Lusignan – but also from the receipt of more reliable information about the political and military situation in the Levant.[80] Both factors had encouraged

[73] 'Quod dominus rex Francie, postpositis periculis omnibus, audacter sub Christi confidentia, viriliter et patenter assumat prosequcionem ipsius negocii cum Ecclesia Dei et ejus subsidio magno et valido, sine quo rex ipse commode complere onus ipsum non posset': Boutaric, 'Notices et extraits de documents inédits relatifs à l'histoire de France sous Philippe le Bel', no. 37, pp. 199–205.   [74] Schein, *Fideles Crucis*, pp. 181, 200–18.

[75] C. Port, 'Le livre de Guillaume le Maire', pp. 474–6.

[76] Jacques de Molai argued that the cessation of the rivalry between the Orders 'maximum dampnum esset Terre Sancte . . . et ex hoc proveniret magnum commodum Saracenis', since it would nullify a central catalyst in the growth and belligerency of both the Temple and the Hospital: Lizerand, *Le dossier de l'affaire des Templiers*, no. 1, pp. 2–14; *Collectio actorum veterum*, pp. 150–4.

[77] Finke, *Papsttum und Untergang des Templerordens*, vol. II, nos. 126, 128, 130, pp. 240–1, 249, 253–4.

[78] E. Müller, *Das Konzil von Vienne*, pp. 693–7.

[79] Mas Latrie, *Histoire de l'Ile de Chypre*, vol. II, pp. 118–25; Edbury, *The Kingdom of Cyprus and the Crusades*, pp. 133–5.

[80] Menache, 'Communication Changes in the Crusader Period', pp. 77–8, 89–90.

a reconsideration of previous assumptions while introducing a more real-istic assessment of the crusade.[81]

Basing his sermon on the biblical verse, 'the desire of the righteous shall be granted' (Prov. 10:24), Clement apprised Christendom of a new general passage overseas (3 April 1312). The pope announced the inten-tion of the ecclesiastical establishment to sustain all expenses, and of Philip the Fair to take the Cross.[82] According to his nephew, Bertrand de Got, Clement had by this time become thoroughly disillusioned with minor crusading expeditions and placed his hopes on a *passagium generale*, which the curia might more easily control.[83] In complete accord with the pope's expectations[84] and in the presence of the papal nuncio, Cardinal Nicolas de Fréauville,[85] Philip the Fair took the Cross in 1313; he was joined by his three sons, Edward II,[86] and many nobles in one of the most splendid ceremonies that Paris had ever witnessed. For an entire week, the whole city shared in the king's religious enthusiasm for the Holy War to the point that both sky and earth were covered with an unprecedented display of banners, music, and favours.[87] Yet the crusade did not materi-alise. Both Philip IV and Clement V died shortly afterwards, and Philip's

---

[81] Guillaume Durant's memoir – it is not clear whether it was actually presented at the council – still advocates the old concepts of Christian peace and universal participation as a requirement for the fulfillment of a successful crusade. See Viollet, 'Guillaume Durant, le jeune, évêque de Mende', pp. 129–34; Fasolt, *Council and Hierarchy*, pp. 305–6.

[82] *Regestum Clementis Pope V*, nos. 8781–3, 9983; *Calendar of Entries in the Papal Registers*, p. 118; *Registrum Simonis de Gandavo*, vol. I, pp. 523–8; Finke, *Papsttum und Untergang des Templerordens*, vol. II, no. 144, p. 293; *Continuationis chronici Guillelmi de Nangiaco*, pp. 391–2.

[83] Thier, *Kreuzzugsbemühungen unter Papst Clemens V*, p. 104. Norman Housley correctly claims that the pope's conclusion was hardly supported by past events: Housley, 'Pope Clement V and the Crusades of 1309–1310', p. 41.

[84] Clement allowed Philip to postpone until the knighthood ceremony of his sons (21 December 1312) the fulfilment of the vow made in Vienne to depart for the crusade within one year. The pope used the occasion to express his hopes for a large response from the French nobles to the crusade: *Regestum Clementis Papae V*, no. 8964.

[85] See the papal letters regarding his mission on behalf of the crusade (10 March 1313): *Regestum Clementis Pope V*, nos. 9649–50, 9941–63.

[86] On Edward's departure for France, 'at the request of the pope and the king of France', in the midst of difficult negotiations with the barons, see *Calendar of the Close Rolls (1307–1313)*, p. 583.

[87] Tel deduit, tel joie, tel feste
Onques ne fu fete de teste . . .
S'a Paris present ne feüst,
Car je vous di, de rue en rue
Ne veoit on ne ciel ne rue,
Car Paris estoit tout couvert,
Blanc, noir, jaune, rougë ou vert.
La chronique métrique attribuée à Geffroy de Paris, pp. 181–2, vv. 4741–4814.

'Non est memoria quod umquam fuerit in Francia tantum festum': Jean de St Victor, *Prima Vita*, p. 21; Tolomeo da Lucca, *Secunda Vita*, p. 50; *Chronographia regum Francorum*, pp. 210–11; Amalric Auger, *Sexta Vita*, pp. 103–4; *Les grandes chroniques de France*, pp. 287–9; *Acta Aragonensia*, vol. I, no. 308, pp. 459–60; *Annales Lubicenses*, p. 422; *Anciennes chroniques de Flandre*, p. 399.

heirs – Louis X, Philip V, and Charles IV – as well as Edward II, found themselves involved in internal crises, which made their participation in the crusade unfeasible. This state of affairs led the anonymous continuator of Guillaume de Nangis to conclude, rather pejoratively, that, after all the declarations and preparations for the crusade, '[the king] however did nothing'.[88]

Notwithstanding Clement's many efforts on the diplomatic and fiscal levels, coupled with the implementation of the Hospitaller crusade and its achievements in Rhodes, the pope's policy failed, again, to achieve the blessing of Christendom. Ironically, a significant number of writers criticised Clement's indifference to the Holy Land, manifested, as they saw it, by his diversion of crusade funds to other needs. Dante Alighieri reflects the view of many contemporaries when he refers sarcastically to 'the Holy Land / which seems to have slipped from the pope's memory'.[89] These suspicions emanated, perhaps with some justification, from Clement's own changing declarations concerning the use of crusade resources. When according to the decisions of the Council of Vienne the tenth was levied in 1312, Clement defined its aim simply as 'in aid of the Holy Land'. As early as March 1314, however, the papal declaration had significantly been modified to 'aid for the Holy Land or *elsewhere* against the unfaithful and the enemies of the Catholic Faith'.[90] This alteration did not go unnoticed. After emphasising the huge amount of money that had been contributed for the crusade, an anonymous chronicler dealt with the detrimental consequences of Clement's policy: 'But the pope guarded the money, and his cousin, the marquis, had his share; and the king and all who had accepted the Cross remained here; and the Saracens live in peace there, and I believe they can continue to sleep in security.'[91] This diatribe faithfully describes developments after Clement's death, when he left the considerable sum of 300,000 florins to his nephew, Bertrand de Got, the viscount of Lomagne, on account of his vow to depart for a crusade, which never materialised.[92] The Malmesbury chronicler was even less enthusiastic about the crusading policy of Clement V. In eulogising the pope, he mentioned the fact that

for eight years and more Pope Clement V has ruled the Church universal. But how it has profited anyone escapes my memory. He brought together a Council

---

[88] *Continuationis chronici Guillelmi de Nangiaco*, p. 396; Schein, 'Philip IV and the Crusade', pp. 121–6.

[89] Dante Alighieri, *Divina Commedia, Paradiso*, c. IX, vv. 125–6. '[Iste papa] diversis modis ecclesiam oppressit et sub pretextu Terre Sancte multum aurum extraxit, quod totum diabolus devoravit': *Martini continuatio Brabantina*, p. 262.

[90] Emphasis mine. 'In Terre sancte subsidium et alias contra infideles et inimicos catholice fidei convertendam': *Regestum Clementis Papae V*, nos. 7759, 10298.

[91] *Fragment d'une chronique . . . 1328*, ad a. 1313, p. 150.

[92] For the detailed instructions in the pope's will, see above, pp. 51–2.

at Vienne, disposed of the Templars, granted indulgences for the Holy Land, collected a vast amount of money, but it profited the Holy Land nothing at all. He granted tithes to kings, despoiled the churches of the poor. It would be better for rectors not to have a pope than to be subject to so many daily exactions.[93]

The failure to implement what contemporaries perceived to be a crusade – i.e., a general passage to the Holy Land – alongside the intensive collection of the tenth, put the very basis of Clement's probity into question.[94] On the other hand, there were also voices that questioned the very *raison d'être* of the crusade in its most traditional form. In an anonymous letter allegedly written by the sultan 'Balthasar' to Clement V, the pope was accused of being a stepfather to Christendom, since he was more concerned with the conquest of Jerusalem, Acre, and Tyre than with the well-being of his own sons. Accusing the pope of sending his flock to a certain death, the writer rather bitingly asked him, 'Are you forcing your sons to come to us and you yourself do not come?' The unavoidable conclusion was that 'because of you, the number of martyrs is fulfilled'.[95]

These opposing views of the crusade hint at the transformation of European society twenty years after the fall of Acre and the changing expectations of the indisputable leader of the crusade, Clement V. The gap between the papal perception of the crusade and the climate of opinion of the age is further indicated by the 'Crusade of the Poor':

In the summer [of 1309] innumerable hosts of simple folk from England, Picardy, Flanders, Brabant, and Germany, taking up the Cross without consulting the bishops, to conquer the Holy Land, set off to the Roman curia, which at that time was at Avignon, to seek the consent and aid of the pope and cardinals. But these were not granted them, as they had no strong, rich, or powerful leaders, and had set out without discretion. So they returned in confusion to their own homes.[96]

As with previous mass movements of this kind, contemporary chroniclers did not hide their criticism of popular enthusiasm. They referred to the *Crützebrödere* as 'parasites, in pursuit of idleness'. The chaotic mixture of peasants, craftsmen, and invalids was despised on the grounds of its being 'a crowd lacking a leader'. The chroniclers disapprovingly mentioned the impertinence of these bands and the harm they caused defenceless Jews whom they had encountered on their way. Following the precedents of the First Crusade, the crusaders had violently stolen Jews' property and

---

[93] *Vita Edwardi Secundi*, ad a. 1314, p. 46.   [94] *Continuatio Zwetlensis tertia*, pp. 664, 666.
[95] W. Wattenbach, 'Fausse correspondence du sultan avec Clément V', pp. 299–300.
[96] *Annales Gandenses*, p. 97. A similar emphasis on the absence of leadership characterised the report of Gilles le Muisit: 'Et dominus papa qui erat Avinioni, videns quod nullum habebant capitaneum aut ductorem, fecit eos reverti, et sano utens consilio, iter eorum impedivit; et ad propria sunt reversi' (*Chronique et annales de Gilles le Muisit*, p. 44).

massacred them.[97] When the mob eventually reached Avignon, Clement granted them partial indulgences and succeeded in dispersing them to their homes with an ambiguous promise that they would be reassembled when the large crusade materialised (25 July 1309).[98]

The Crusade of the Poor suggests the unrest that existed among the lower social strata in the light of a changing economy, the rules of which they could barely understand.[99] Their use of crusader terms of reference indicates their persistent adherence to former ideals, which Clement did not succeed in diverting to more constructive channels, namely, those that were more in accordance with the needs of the Church and his allies, the western kings. It is rather doubtful whether papal crusading projects in Cyprus, Armenia, and the Iberian peninsula or, less so, in Italy could have ameliorated the sense of frustration of the common folk. Referring to the crusade in the Council of Vienne, Paul, bishop of Pozzuoli, bitterly complains:

> Money, weapons, and many other things were collected by the faithful for the passage, men and women offered to the Hospitallers sent here their most precious property, which was sold at low prices. But concerning the passage nothing happened. Because of which a great scandal arose among the Christians.[100]

Similar to reactions to other aspects of papal policy, the criticism of Clement's crusade plans reflects archaic notions that disregarded the needs and limitations posed by fourteenth-century reality. One may charge Clement V with a failure to make his policy understandable, let alone acceptable, to his contemporaries. Still, this is a failure in propaganda, not in policy; it does not reduce the value of papal policy or obscure the political and economic pressure exerted on the curia by Christian kings, who were more successful in the field of propaganda. The criticism of Clement's policy in the narrative sources appears all the more anachronistic in the light of the growing financial needs of the national monarchies and the high costs of the crusade, two factors that ultimately dictated the scope and character of Clement V's policy. Conversely, the crusading fervour of the peasants sharply contrasted with the utilitarian approach of contemporary kings and of the Venetians, Catalans, Genoese, Pisans, and Aragonese, i.e., all those parties who were able to

---

[97] According to Tolomeo da Lucca, probably an eye-witness, about 30,000 'Anglicos et Theutonicos, sed de Theutonicis plures' reached Avignon and eventually returned to their homes 'cum scandalo multo': *Secunda Vita*, p. 34; *Continuatio Florianensis*, p. 752; *Chronicon Elwacense*, p. 39; *Gestorum abbatum monasterii Sancti Trudonis, pars 2*, p. 412; *Annales Lubicenses*, p. 421; *Annales Colbazienses*, p. 717; *Annales Tielenses*, p. 26; *Ex libro memoriarum S. Blasii Brunsuicensis*, p. 825; *Annales Cistercensium*, p. 545; Heidelberger, *Kreuzzugsversuche um die Wende*, pp. 44, 45.

[98] *Regestum Clementis Papae V*, no. 4400.   [99] J. Day, *The Medieval Market Economy*, pp. 90–102.

[100] Paulin, bishop of Pozzuoli, *Quinta Vita*, p. 82; *Annales Lubicenses*, p. 421.

launch a crusade in actual practice.[101] Yet, the religious fervour of the mobs that reached Avignon in 1309–10 could hardly have helped the pope to implement the crusade. In this regard, Clement's pontificate suggests not the beginning of a new era, but the continuation of futile attempts by the papacy to recover the Holy Land. The genuine devotion exhibited by Clement V in this regard cannot be questioned; yet, he did not succeed in convincing the commercial and political powers of his time to foster a crusade of a universal, pan-Christian nature. Clement's crusade gradually turned into a utopian enterprise, one that was manipulated by contemporary rulers to advance conflicting interests.[102]

CHARLES DE VALOIS AND THE CRUSADE AGAINST CONSTANTINOPLE

Clement was not more successful in his attempts to return his prodigal sons to the path of the 'one, holy, Catholic and apostolic Church'. At the beginning of the fourteenth century, the Byzantine Emperor remained the main target in the papal struggle against the Orthodox Church, on which Clement tried to endow all the means of a crusade. Andronicus II (1282–1328), the son of Michael Palaeologus (1260–82), had abruptly changed his father's conciliatory policy and renewed the schism. This development increased the Catholic zeal of Charles de Valois, who became a devout 'papal knight', ready to fight the Just War against a schismatic emperor. Backed, at least in theory, by his powerful brother, Philip the Fair, Charles also relied on the legitimate claims of his wife, Catherine de Courtenay, the granddaughter of Baldwin II and, as such, the titular empress of Constantinople.[103]

From the beginning of his pontificate, Clement urged all Catholic bishops to support the meritorious plans of Charles de Valois in the east on the grounds that Michael Palaeologus and Andronicus II had not only betrayed the true faith but had also miserably failed in the defence of their empire. The conquest of Constantinople by the Capetian scion would renew Church union while preventing the conquest of Christian territories by the Saracens.[104] On 3 June 1307, the pope formally excommunicated Andronicus and threatened with excommunication and forfeiture

---

[101] On the Catalans' reluctance to co-operate with the pope, see *Regestum Clementis Pope V*, nos. 7890–1; *Acta Clementis PP V*, nos. 47–47a. Marino Sanudo has argued, correctly, that no commercial blockade could succeed without the support of the maritime communes. See Marino Sanudo Torsello, 'Liber secretorum fidelium crucis', p. 31.

[102] On the manipulation of the crusade for advancing political aims, see Menache, 'Religious Symbols and Royal Propaganda in the Late Middle Ages', pp. 55–61.

[103] The papal privileges on her behalf emphasised her imperial status: *Regestum Clementis Papae V*, nos. 455–6, 518.   [104] *Ibid.*, nos. 243, 245.

of property any Christian who dared help him.[105] The excommunication of Andronicus II turned the expedition by Charles de Valois to Constantinople into a crusade, with the grant of indulgences traditionally accorded those who departed for the Holy Land. According to papal documentation, the goals of the crusade were the noble ones of returning wicked rulers who had been led astray to the right path and reinstating the lawful ruler of Constantinople. As schismatics, the eastern emperors were no longer capable of performing the basic function of the Christian Empire, mainly, the defence of the Church against its enemies. The pope, therefore, had the right to transfer the title to a ruler who would more properly perform this function. In the process, Clement bestowed on Charles de Valois all the attributes of a Christian knight who fought a Holy War. Charles was called an 'excellent warrior of the faith, audacious fighter for the Church, devout lover of peace, and dangerous enemy of those harming the unity of the faith'. These many virtues were rather expected, the pope argued, since by his acting against Constantinople, Charles de Valois was actually 'following the steps of his ancestors . . . who had always manifested a fraternal devotion to God and to the Apostolic See'.[106] Against the schismatic background of Andronicus II there stood the heroic image of the Capetians and their devotion not only to the Holy Land and the crusade but also, and primarily, to the Holy See. Clement did not rely on theoretical pronunciations alone; he translated his support into actual practice, granting Charles a two-year tenth in France[107] and a three-year tenth in the *Regno* (14 January 1306).[108] The pope also urged the Venetians to keep their promises and to offer Charles naval assistance.[109]

By 1310, however, the ambitious projects of Charles de Valois seemed to be condemned to complete failure. The lack of funds, primarily because of the reluctance of Philip IV to allow the collection of the tenth, led the Venetians to retract their original commitment to provide a fleet. The kings of Aragon, Sicily, Lesser Armenia, and Naples, as well as the Catalans, all of whom had formally guaranteed their participation in the holy enterprise, also found that their economic and political interests were actually opposed to a new expedition against Constantinople.[110] Clement V, who had done his best to support Charles de Valois, was at this stage

---

[105] *Ibid.*, no. 1759; *Acta Clementis PP V*, no. 15.

[106] *Regestum Clementis Papae V*, no. 1768. On the historical background, see A. E. Laiou, *Constantinople and the Latins*, pp. 200–42.

[107] *Regestum Clementis Papae V*, nos. 243, 245. The pope repeated his order on 3 June 1307, since the collection of the tenth had not yet begun: *ibid.*, nos. 1757–8.

[108] *Ibid.*, nos. 244, 246; *Acta Clementis PP V*, no. 1. The collection of the tenth in Sicily, as well, had not yet begun a year and a half after the papal mandate: *Regestum Clementis Papae V*, nos. 1755–6.

[109] *Regestum Clementis Papae V*, no. 248.   [110] Schein, *Fideles Crucis*, pp. 185–90.

already engaged in the Hospitaller Crusade. On the other hand, the brutal ravages of the Catalan Company in his territories convinced Andronicus of the need to improve his links with the west. On 7 June 1311, he dispatched a bishop to consult with Clement V, Philip the Fair, and Charles de Valois, with hints of submission to Rome and a union of the churches if a match could be arranged between Charles' daughter (the Latin heir to Constantinople) and one of Andronicus' sons. This scheme, however, did not find any welcome in either the papal or the royal court.[111]

THE *RECONQUISTA*

More successful was the marriage alliance between Castile and Aragon, on which Clement bestowed apostolic blessing. The pope did not neglect the situation on the Christian frontier and tried to strengthen the always fragile relationship between the Christian kingdoms of Aragon and Castile through the marriage of the son of James II of Aragon and the daughter of Ferdinand IV of Castile.[112] This alliance was most imperative in the light of the common effort to force the Moors out of the Iberian peninsula.[113] On the other hand, Clement's attitude towards both kingdoms was crucially influenced by his own plans for a crusade to the Holy Land and the readiness of the Iberian kings to support it.

James II of Aragon was well aware of Clement's order of priorities and acted accordingly. Although he maintained peaceful relations with the sultans of Egypt and coveted the crown of Jerusalem for his house,[114] he made an unconditional offer to the pope of his kingdom and all its treasure in order to advance the recovery of the Holy Land (Montpellier, 7–17 October 1305).[115] Though there is ample room to question the seriousness

---

[111] R. I. Burns, 'The Catalan Company and the European Powers', p. 757.

[112] *Chronique de Ramon Muntaner*, pp. 265–6.

[113] For a general review of the papal policy in Aragon during the Avignon Period, see E. Berger, 'Jacques II d'Aragon, le Saint-Siège, et la France', pp. 281–94, 348–59.

[114] J. N. Hillgarth, *The Problem of a Catalan Mediterranean Empire*, pp. 40–1. From 1309 to 1311, James II engaged Arnaud de Villanova to persuade Robert of Naples to renounce his title in favour of his brother, Frederick III of Trinacria. According to the Treaty of Caltabellota (1302), Frederick had received the rule of Sicily for life, but the island was to return to the Angevins after his death: R. Manselli, 'Arnaldo da Villanova e i papi del suo tempo', p. 155. On Frederick III and his reform-minded mysticism, see Backman, *The Decline and Fall of Medieval Sicily*, pp. 52–5, 204–5.

[115] On the meticulous preparations for the meeting, see *Acta Aragonensia*, vol. II, no. 551, pp. 873–4. James repeated his rhetorical devotion to the crusade in the Council of Vienne. His delegate declared to the pope: 'de part vostra a aquests affers la vostra persona . . . els vostres gens, e tot ço que vos hi poguesets metre, e demanans essert donat a vos tal loch en aquests affers, quey poguessets servir nostre senyor e la sancta esgleya e el senyor papa honradament e poderosament segons queus tany' (Finke, *Papsttum und Untergang des Templerordens*, vol. II, no. 126, p. 240). On James' manipulation of the crusade for fiscal purposes, see J. Fernández Conde and A. Oliver, 'La corte pontificia de Aviñón', p. 362.

of such a declaration, the king received a generous papal reply. Clement V gave apostolic blessing to Aragonese claims to rule in Sardinia and Corsica after James did liege homage and promised to conquer both islands within one year (28 May 1305).[116] In order to hasten the accomplishment of such commendable plans, the pope granted James a four-year tenth.[117] He also confirmed Boniface's grant of all revenues from fines imposed on the illegal trade with Egypt.[118] Clement did not conceal his hope that once the conquest of the Mediterranean islands had been achieved, the king of Aragon would indeed be able to devote himself and his kingdom to the recovery of the Holy Land.[119] The pope also granted James II of Majorca a tenth to subsidise his fight against the Muslims and pirates who plagued the Mediterranean, a goal that obviously served the interests of the blockade (10 November 1305).[120] Still, Clement never recognised Aragonese rule in Sicily, which he regarded as a usurpation of the legitimate rights of the Angevins of Naples. The pope meticulously addressed both Charles and Robert of Anjou as 'kings of Sicily', while Frederick of Aragon, who ruled over Sicily in actual practice, was addressed as 'king of Trinacria'. Following the death of Charles II (6 May 1309), Clement bestowed theoretical rule over the island on Charles' first born, Robert the Wise, who duly did homage to the pope (27 August).[121]

The most harmonious meeting point between Clement V, James of Aragon, and Ferdinand of Castile thus remained the *Reconquista* against the kingdom of Granada, where pope and kings could more easily join forces against the Infidel. The two countries made an important agreement at Alcalá de Henares (1308) which envisaged assaults on Almería by

---

[116] *Regestum Clementis Papae V*, nos. 1444, 10372. Since 1137, the king of Aragon was also count of Barcelona and king of Majorca, Valencia, Sicily, and Sardinia. After Peter III had conquered Sicily in 1282, he tried, in his will, to separate the island from Aragon. His son, James II (1291–1327), kept the island from 1291 to 1295, but in 1298 Boniface VIII forced him to withdraw from Sicily, which was then transferred to his younger brother, Frederick III, and to deliver Majorca to his uncle, James II, the younger son of James I, who had granted him the island in 1263. In 1323, James II of Aragon finally succeeded in launching a force of fifty-three galleys for the conquest of Sardinia, which remained the single Mediterranean island under Aragonese rule. See Marongiù, 'Le "corts" catalane e la conquista della Sardegna', pp. 871–3.

[117] *Regestum Clementis Papae V*, nos. 357, 1313.

[118] *Ibid.*, nos. 223, 225; Bernard Gui, in *Quarta Vita*, p. 62; Amalric Auger, *Sexta Vita*, p. 92. On the development of this trade and its crucial economic importance for the crown, see Trenchs Odena, '*De Alexandrinis*', pp. 237–320.

[119] The meagre resources of Aragon actually delayed the conquest of Sardinia for seventeen years, while the conquest of Corsica was completely abandoned. See Hillgarth, 'El problema del Imperio Catalano-Aragonés', pp. 147–51.

[120] *Regestum Clementis Papae V*, nos. 530–1. On the ambivalent economic policy of the Majorcan monarchy, see Abulafia, *A Mediterranean Emporium*, pp. 151–64.

[121] *Regestum Clementis Papae V*, no. 4782. For papal indulgences on behalf of those who would pray for the late king's soul, see *ibid.*, no. 5322. Still, Robert of Anjou ruled only half of his kingdom. The island itself and much of the province of Calabria were ruled by Frederick III.

James II of Aragon, and on Algeciras by Ferdinand IV of Castile. The agreement included the Marinid Sultan, who hoped to use the general attack to regain Ceuta, seized by Granada in 1306.[122] In 1309, a joint campaign by Castile and Aragon began promisingly with the siege of Almería and Algeciras and the capture of Gibraltar in the first days of September.[123] The Marinids, however, deserted the alliance as soon as they regained Ceuta. Clement's letter to the bishop of Valencia expressed satisfaction in light of the crusaders' achievements as well as the pope's intention to re-establish the bishopric in Almería immediately after the city reverted to Christian hands (11 September).[124] From April to November 1309, the pope bestowed on the Iberian crusaders a series of privileges, placing them on a par with the Hospitallers.[125] The kings of Castile and Aragon were granted a three-year tenth and placed under the special protection of the apostolic see.[126] In granting the tenth, the pope referred to James of Aragon as 'a warrior of Christ and magnificent defender of the Christian faith, fighting for the achievement of the kingdom of Granada'.[127] The bishop of Valencia was ordered to preach the crusade[128] and to remove ecclesiastical sentences, including excommunication, that might have been pronounced against those participating in the war against the Saracens.[129] Gundisalvo, the archbishop of Toledo, was nominated papal legate.[130]

The gradual increase in papal privileges indicates the close attention that Clement paid to developments on the Iberian peninsula. At the beginning of his pontificate, the pope had conferred only traditional privileges on those participating in the *Reconquista* out of a fear that the war against Granada would harm the crusade in the Holy Land; the promising developments of 1309 now brought about a radical change of attitude.[131] This was an important achievement for James II, since he had opposed the Hospitaller enterprise from the outset. The king, indeed, compelled the Aragonese Hospitallers to participate in the *Reconquista*; he forbade the Order to export its arms and horses, and prevented mercenaries from taking service with the Hospital.[132] In early 1310,

---

[122] Housley, *The Later Crusades*, p. 277.
[123] This achievement was considerably emphasised in contemporary records. See *Continuationis chronici Guillelmi de Nangiaco*, p. 372; Jean de St Victor, *Prima Vita*, p. 16; *Les grandes chroniques de France*, p. 266; *Chronique de Ramon Muntaner*, p. 266; *Notae ad vitas*, p. 61.
[124] The pope urged the bishop to look for suitable clergymen to be provided to the new see: *Regestum Clementis Papae V*, nos. 4555–6.   [125] *Ibid.*, no. 4031.
[126] *Ibid.*, nos. 3819, 3988–91, 4034, 4046–51, 4054, 4535, 5090–5.   [127] *Ibid.*, no. 4152.
[128] *Ibid.*, no. 3989.   [129] *Ibid.*, no. 4519.   [130] *Ibid.*, no. 4049.
[131] *Ibid.*, nos. 4519–24; Tolomeo da Lucca, *Secunda Vita*, pp. 32–3, 35; Thier, *Kreuzzugsbemühungen unter Papst Clemens V*, pp. 18–32, 89–93; Salavert y Roca, *Cerdeña y la expansión mediterranea de la corona de Aragón*, vol. II, nos. 323, 332, 340, 345.
[132] Luttrell, 'The Aragonese Crown and the Knights Hospitallers of Rhodes', pp. 1–19.

however, the Castilian army abandoned the siege of Algeciras – mostly because of internal problems demonstrated by the quarrelling of the Castilian magnates at the siege – and the Aragonese retreated from Almería.[133] Although James II still tried to keep papal privileges on the grounds of his fight to safeguard Christian shipping through the Straits of Gibraltar, Clement became more reluctant to fulfil his requests.[134] In August 1312, the pope still urged crusade preaching and granted concessions to Ferdinand IV of Castile; the following January, he gave way on the Aragonese share of the Vienne tenth.[135] The death of Ferdinand IV (17 September 1312) and the long minority of Alfonso XI (1312–25), however, brought about a new change in papal policy.[136] The Aragonese representative in the curia, Johannes Burgundi, reported to James that the pope was having second thoughts: 'Since you have remained alone in the enterprise, he [the pope] does not believe that you would be able to bring about its accomplishment by yourself' (16 February 1313).[137] This was not only a political evaluation but, primarily, a clear symptom of Clement's lack of faith in James II. There are additional symptoms of the deteriorating relationship between pope and king. In an authorisation to send a special ambassador to the 'sultan of the Turks' in order to obtain the release of Aragonese subjects who had been captured by the Muslims, the pope reminded the king of Aragon of the grave penalties that he would incur by any trade with the Infidel (22 August 1313).[138]

The doubts of Clement V regarding the good faith of James II were not without basis. The attacks by the Catalan Grand Company against Emperor Andronicus – after he had set up the murder of the Company's leader, Roger de Flor (4 April 1305) – could at first have benefited the papal offensive against Constantinople.[139] In the years to come, however, the Company invested much energy in the duchy of Athens, thus openly challenging papal interests. The pope was well aware that the Company had received the blessing of Frederick III of Trinacria, the younger brother of James II. Besides, the Mediterranean policy of the king of Aragon, especially his continuous dealings with Venice during the papal interdict, did little to improve relations between Clement V and James II. The pope soon translated his hesitations into actual practice by remaining adamant in his refusal to allow the king of Aragon a share in Templar

---

[133] *Chronique de Ramon Muntaner*, pp. 268–9; Tolomeo da Lucca, *Secunda Vita*, p. 36; Thier, *Kreuzzugsbemühungen unter Papst Clemens V*, pp. 89–93.

[134] The pope still renewed former privileges for both Aragon and Castile; see *Regestum Clementis Papae V*, nos. 5484, 6312, 6379–80, 6737, 6939–42.   [135] *Ibid.*, nos. 8459–64.

[136] *Ibid.*, nos. 5492, 5494.   [137] *Acta Aragonensia*, vol. II, no. 489, pp. 782–3.

[138] *Regestum Clementis Papae V*, no. 9893.

[139] This view was formally expressed by the papal vice-chancellor, Arnaud Novel, in the Council of Vienne.

property. It was left to Pope John XXII to convey the Templar wealth in the kingdom of Aragon to the Order of Montesa (10 June 1317).[140] The new Order received the rule of Calatrava and was subjected to its master, thus assuring close royal supervision of its policy and, no less important, its funds.[141]

THE BORDERS OF CHRISTENDOM AND MISSION

Clement V also directed attention to Catholic countries on the borders of Christendom, which were fighting a daily battle for existence. At the beginning of the fourteenth century, Poland was experiencing continual political crises. The death of Wenceslas II in 1305, followed one year later by that of his son, Wenceslas III, drove the country to the verge of anarchy. The inhabitants of Cracow, with the bishop at its head, opted for a union with the kingdom of Bohemia. The king, Wenceslas II, on whom Albert I of Habsburg had bestowed all lands previously conquered by the Czechs, crowned himself king of Poland. Prince Ladislas I Lokietek, who aspired to the throne, was forced to flee and, according to later tradition, arrived at the papal curia; other princes, however, surrendered to Wenceslas. Rather surprisingly, Clement recognised Wenceslas II and developed good relations with him, notwithstanding his complete disregard of papal rights.[142]

More successful was Clement's policy in Hungary, where his intervention in favour of Carobert (1310–42) brought to an end an anarchical situation that had lasted for fifteen years.[143] The pope sent a special legate, Cardinal Gentile da Montefiore,[144] who crowned Carobert, the nephew of Queen Maria of Sicily, in Bude (15 June 1309).[145] In February 1314, Clement bestowed upon the king a three-year tenth and plenary

---

[140] Amalric Auger, *Septima Vita*, p. 190; J. F. O'Callaghan, 'Las definiciones medievales de la Orden de Montesa', pp. 213–51.

[141] The centralisation policy of the Iberian kings reached its zenith in 1494, when Ferdinand the Catholic assumed the mastership of all Military Orders. On this process, see Menache, 'A Juridical Chapter in the History of the Order of Calatrava', p. 321.

[142] I. Sulkowska-Kuraś and S. Kuraś, 'La Pologne et la papauté d'Avignon', pp. 115–27.

[143] See the papal letter to Otto, duke of Bavaria, telling him to present his claims, if he had any, to the papal curia (10 August 1307): *Regestum Clementis Papae V*, no. 1797; *Continuatio Zwetlensis tertia*, p. 662.

[144] The legate left the curia on 19 October 1307 and remained in Hungary until 10 September 1311: *Regestum Clementis Papae V*, nos. 2274–90; *Acta Clementis PP V*, no. 18; *Notae ad vitas*, pp. 40–2; E. Horn, 'La mission diplomatique d'un franciscain', pp. 405–18; A. de Regibus, 'Le contese degli Angioini di Napoli per il trono di Ungheria', pp. 38–85, 264–305.

[145] *Vetera Monumenta Historica Hungariam Sacram Illustrantia*, nos. 664, 669, 1256, pp. 415–17, 423–5, 820–1. The legate enlisted the prelates of Hungary in support of the king: *ibid.*, no. 1257, pp. 821–2. See the formal papal recognition: *Regestum Clementis Papae V*, nos. 10597, 10601–3, 10628; Agnolo di Tura, *Cronaca Senese*, p. 315.

indulgence for his soldiers who had died fighting the Tartars and the Lithuanians.[146] Carobert recognised his duty to the pope and left him a completely free hand in Church nominations.

In the far east, Clement enthusiastically supported the Franciscans' missionary work, which paved the way for the establishment of the Church in the area, especially in China.[147] The pope appointed the Franciscan Giovanni da Montecorvino to the archbishopric of Kambalik (Peking) while giving him ecclesiastical authority over the whole Mongol Empire, from China to the Carpathians.[148] Giovanni was also given apostolic authority to establish the diocesan limits for his six suffragans, all of them Franciscans: Andrea da Perugia, Nicolas da Banzia, Gérard Albuini, Ulrich vom Seyfriestorf, Peregrino da Castello, and Guillaume de Villanova (23 July 1307).[149] Papal concern with the mission among the Mongols is further indicated by the appointment of three new bishops, to replace those who had died during the long trip eastwards (19 February 1311).[150] By 1314, there were some fifty Franciscan convents in China. The Aragonese representative refers to Mongol messengers who arrived at the papal curia in Poitiers and offered military assistance for the forthcoming crusade (26 June 1307).[151] On 1 March 1308, Clement wrote to Khan Olgetucan, encouraging his conversion to Christianity and trying to clarify the terms for Mongol financial assistance against the common enemy, the Saracens.[152]

Clement also tried to strengthen papal influence in areas that had recognised the Orthodox Church. On 1 April 1308, he sent messengers to the Serbian king, Uros II, Milutin, calling for closer links with the Roman Church.[153] The pope enlisted the Friars for this purpose and furnished the king with the Principles of the Faith while emphasising the complete supremacy of the Vicar of God on earth.[154] This was not the first contact between the pope and the king. On 25 February 1307,

---

[146] *Annales ecclesiastici*, ad a. 1314, no. 13, vol. XXIV, p. 23.

[147] L. Bréhier, *L'Eglise et l'Orient au moyen âge*, pp. 288–308.

[148] The archbishop's nomination was not registered; only those papal letters concerning his suffragans were. They established that the archbishop's jurisdiction comprised 'curam et sollici-tudinem animarum existentium in toto dominio Tartarorum'. See the text provided by Raynaldus, in *Annales ecclesiastici*, ad. a. 1305, f. 19, vol. XXIII, pp. 400–1. Giovanni had arrived in Kambalik at the end of 1292 and died there some time between 1328 and 1330. On his missionary efforts, see J. Richard, *La papauté et les missions d'Orient*, 146–52.

[149] *Regestum Clementis Papae V*, nos. 2216–21, 2300–1; *Acta Clementis PP V*, no. 17.

[150] *Regestum Clementis Papae V*, nos. 7480–2.

[151] Finke, *Papsttum und Untergang des Templerordens*, vol. II, no. 25, pp. 38–9.

[152] *Regestum Clementis Papae V*, no. 3549.

[153] The Serbian king, son of Urosio I and Anna Dandolo, both Catholics, had manifested his desire to strengthen links with the spiritual leader of Christendom.

[154] *Regestum Clementis Papae V*, nos. 3559–62; *Acta Clementis PP V*, nos. 25–9; *Vetera Monumenta Slavorum Meridionalicum Historiam Illustrantia*, nos. 181–2, pp. 127–30.

Clement had recommended the archbishop of Bar, Montenegro, to Uros II.[155] In these complementary ways, Clement hoped to weaken the influence of the Orthodox Church in the area while creating a stronger basis for Catholic mission.

The vicissitudes of the crusade and the Catholic mission during the pontificate of Clement V are illuminating with regard to the ecumenical essence of papal diplomacy and its weaknesses. Papal representatives were active everywhere, trying to strengthen the fragile coalition between Christian rulers and to motivate them to fight the Infidel. Clement achieved important successes in Cyprus, Armenia, Rhodes, and Hungary. Papal diplomacy also strengthened links with Mongol and Serbian rulers. On the other hand, Clement's mistrust of James II of Aragon reflects the practical lessons learned from the futile negotiations concerning the crusade that the pope and his representatives had conducted with the leaders of Christendom. The original good faith that accompanied Clement's dealings with Christian princes at the beginning of his pontificate was gradually replaced by mistrust and the pope's increasing reliance on *do ut des*.

Still, Clement's dearest dream remained the recovery of the Holy Land, which towards the end of his pontificate acquired all the characteristics of a *Gesta Dei per Francos*. This development was not due to the pope's surrender to Philip the Fair or his subjects; rather, it was dictated by the prevailing political situation in the different areas of Christendom, the suppression of the Temple, the trial of the Teutonic Order,[156] and the engagement of the Hospitallers in the recently conquered Rhodes. The Templar affair – which acquired all the characteristics of an oncoming storm rumbling away in the background – undoubtedly influenced papal policy and, especially, Clement's failure to launch a *passagium generale*. Besides, the complete lack of any sense of solidarity among the Christian powers, which became most evident with regard to the Italian communes, also favoured a papal alliance with a strong king, one who would be able to bring about the blockade in the Mediterranean while restricting the anarchic situation in Christendom. The events of 1313 seemingly indicate the consummation of papal policy when, in an unprecedented display of ceremony, Philip IV, Edward II, and the nobility of France and England took the Cross. They also mark the switch of papal policy, the Hospitallers being replaced by Philip the Fair as the pope's partner in the crusading enterprise. This development, with all its financial effects in the collection of the tenth, hints at the inability of the Hospital to advance

---

[155] *Vetera Monumenta Slavorum Meridionalicum Historiam Illustrantia*, no. 176, p. 124.
[156] See below, pp. 214–15.

the papal plan further. Having succeeded in the conquest of Rhodes and perhaps also in enforcing its rule over some Muslim princes inland, the Order could not face the challenge presented by Genoa and Venice or stop their lucrative trade with the Muslims in the Mediterranean. In other words, it was the maritime communes which actually pushed the pope into the hands of Philip the Fair. Clement V, however, died in 1314, before his dream for a *passagium generale* could materialise. That year can indeed be regarded as the end of a serious papal attempt to launch a crusade after the fall of Crusader Acre.

Chapter 4

ITALY

Ah Italy, thou slave of woe, vessel without pilot in a great storm, not the mistress of provinces, but a brothel.

Dante, Purgatorio, c. VI, vv. 76–8

The political fog in Italy had not yet cleared when Clement V was elected to the papacy. The struggle between Guelphs and Ghibellines, in so far as it was still being waged, lacked political principles or established beliefs as to the inherent superiority of pope or emperor. It served, rather, to obscure the real issues of controversy, such as the determination of regional hegemonies and of political, legal, and proprietary relations among opposing political factions. Between the Battle of Benevento, when Charles I of Anjou defeated and killed Manfred Hohenstaufen (26 February 1266), and the Sicilian Vespers, when the French garrison in Palermo was massacred and the crown of Sicily offered to Pedro of Aragon as Manfred's heir (30 March 1282), the Guelphs had enjoyed virtually unchallenged hegemony under the lead of the papacy, the Angevin monarchy, and Florence. Important communes in the Guelph *taglia* included Perugia, Siena, Bologna, Cremona, and Padua.[1] The Sicilian Vespers and the following peace treaty, however, substantially altered the political balance, undermining Angevin and papal power everywhere. Guelphism became a vague concept, easily manipulated to advance ever-changing, particularist interests.

The Florentines provide a case in point. On a theoretical level, they identified themselves as 'the faithful and devoted people of the Holy Church, lovers of the *popolo* and the commune, and supporters of the liberty of Florence and of the *parte guelpha*'. In everyday practice, however, Florence used Guelphism to gain economic and political

---

[1] W. M. Bowsky, *A Medieval Italian Commune*, pp. 162–63; G. Arnaldi, 'Le origini del Patrimonio di S. Pietro', pp. 105–47; P. Partner, 'Guelf and Ghibelline in Italy', p. 576.

hegemony over Tuscany without feeling bound to adhere to the mandates or the political interests of the Holy See, let alone of other Guelph cities.[2] This political opportunism eventually brought about five interdicts against the city between the years 1300 and 1307.[3] It became rather clear to papal envoys that *Florentina libertas*, if it had any meaning, was for the Florentines alone.

The clash of interests with the papacy was not unique to Florence; it affected cities in the Patrimony of St Peter in Tuscany as well, thus creating endless conflicts. In the autumn of 1303, Boniface VIII imposed an interdict on Orvieto for its onslaught against the Aldobrandeschine *contado*. Clement confirmed the interdict in 1307, notwithstanding serious attempts by the commune to obtain papal absolution. Only after a painful bargain, at a considerable cost of 16,000 lire, was Orvieto finally reinstated in the community of the faithful (1313).[4] Besides the chaotic situation inherent in the intricacies of Italian politics, the conflict between Boniface VIII and Philip the Fair deprived the Guelphs of French support, thus deepening their inner disruption. Boniface's tendency to involve the papacy in his family's vendetta against the Colonnas also did little to provide stability for the Guelph camp. At the pope's death, although the Caetanis had attained a place of prominence, with Catalan mercenaries fighting on their behalf, the conflict between the leading families of Rome was far from over. Neither the mediatory attempts by Roman magistrates in 1305 nor those by Clement V and Robert of Naples in 1312 were of any avail.[5] On the contrary, in order to strengthen their ranks against the Colonnas, the Caetanis revolted in Campagna against the Guelphs' traditional ally, the Angevins of Naples. The war between Bologna and Ferrara added more confusion to the Guelph ranks, while the situation in Romagna deteriorated further.

Ghibellism, as well, lacked coherence. It consisted of various locally based *signorie*, which were united in the main by their opposition to the pope and to the king of Naples.[6] This antagonism hardly provided a concrete basis for co-operation, and it did not obviate the conflicts for local hegemony that were so characteristic of the *trecento*. Important cities like Venice subordinated the communes of their *contado* to a status of colonial dependence and ruthlessly exploited them for their own economic interest. The bishop of Butrinto, one of the participants in Henry VII's

[2] Bowsky, 'Florence and Henry of Luxemburg', p. 178.

[3] Dino Compagni, *Cronica*, pp. 215–18; R. Davidsohn, *Geschichte von Florenz*, vol. III, pp. 130–2, 193–4, 307–25; Partner, 'Florence and the Papacy', pp. 76–7. Cf. E. Jordan, *Les origins de la domination angevine en Italie*, p. 194.   [4] Waley, *Mediaeval Orvieto*, pp. 75–8.

[5] Waley, 'Lo Stato Papale dal periodo feudale a Martino V', p. 282.

[6] G. Tabacco, *The Struggle for Power in Medieval Italy*, pp. 251–67; Partner, *The Lands of St Peter*, pp. 297–9; Housley, *The Italian Crusades*, pp. 23–4.

MARCH OF TREVISO

Milan

Brescia

Pavia   Lodi   Verona   Vicenza   Treviso   Aquileia   Grado

Crema   Cremona   Mantua   Padua   Venice

Piacenza   Po

Parma

LOMBARDY   Reggio   Ferrara

Genoa   Bologna   Modena   Ravenna

I

Lucca   Pistoia   Rimini

Pisa   Florence

Urbino

S. Gimignano   Osimo

Arezzo   Fabriano   Recanati

Siena   Macerata

TUSCANY   Perugia   Fermo

UMBRIA   II

Orvieto   III   Spoleto

Viterbo   Rieti

IV   Castello   Aquila

Sutri   Tagliacozzo

Tivoli   Alatri

Rome   V

CORSICA

SARDINIA

Ceprano

Lucera

Foggia

Gaeta   Capua   Benevento   Barletta   Trani   Bari

Naples   Monopoli

Salerno   APULIA

Sorrento   PRINCIPATO   Taranto   Brindisi

BASILICATA   Otranto

Cosenza

CALABRIA

Palermo

SICILY

0   50   100   150   200 km

0   50   100 miles

Map 4 Italy in the fourteenth century

journey to Rome, described Venice as 'a fifth essence, which wished to recognise neither God, nor the Church, nor emperor, nor sea, nor land, unless in so far as pleased their inhabitants'.[7] After the failure of the plot of Bajamonte Tiepolo and Mario Querini (15 June 1310), political power resided in a merchant oligarchy that ruled through the Council of Ten,

---

[7] *Nicolai episcopi Botrontinensis Relatio de itinere italico Henrici VII*, p. 503. Nicholas, bishop of Butrinto, was originally from a French-speaking region, probably in Flanders or Luxemburg. His report of Henry's journey was written between 24 August 1313 and 20 April 1314; though favourable to the emperor, his general approach seems quite accurate. On the source, see U. Chevalier, *Répertoire des sources historiques du moyen âge*, vol. II, col. 3325.

which was an effective instrument for discovering and suppressing conspiracies.[8]

Clement's policy in Italy aimed at advancing papal authority while maintaining the delicate political equilibrium among rival factions and preventing any of them from gaining pre-eminence. This was true with regard to the Caetanis and the Colonnas as well as to Guelphs and Ghibellines. In contrast to his predecessors, Clement was less devoted to the Guelphs, perhaps because of the opposing interests that plagued this camp, which made papal support of the Guelphs as a whole an impossible mission.[9] Still, such a neutral stand was very difficult, if not impossible, to follow in the political reality of the *trecento*. Whatever the means employed by papal policy – which ranged from alliances to the use of excommunication, interdict, and in most extreme cases a call for a crusade against political opponents – and no matter whether Italian cardinals, Clement's relatives, or the emperor represented papal policy, Clement V did not really dictate the rules of the game. Even when he won an irrefutable victory, as in the struggle against Venice in Ferrara, the ephemeral achievements of the pope were manipulated to serve the city-states that supported or opposed papal policy according to their narrow interests. Eventually, it was these same city-states that succeeded in causing the alliance between Clement V and Henry VII to collapse completely, a breakdown that constituted neither a personal failure of either pope or emperor nor a victory for the Guelphs. It was a short-lived stage in a process in which there was no further room for a central power with universal claims. The political scenario was prepared for the rule of despots and the *signorie*, which were going to determine the destiny of a disunited Italy for centuries to come.

THE PAPAL STATE

By the beginning of the fourteenth century, the Papal State comprised the Campagna-Marittima, the March of Ancona, the Duchy of Spoleto, the Patrimony of St Peter in Tuscany, and Romagna. The administration of the papal provinces, which was largely standardised, relied on the

---

[8] Bowsky, 'Dante's Italy', p. 84.

[9] G. Holmes assumes that the papal policy of pacification between the years 1305 and 1312 was dictated by Cardinals Napoleone Orsini and Niccolò da Prato, and it involved the support of the Ghibellines and Whites against the Black Guelph regimes in control of Florence, Siena, and Lucca. A close analysis of Clement's policy, however, suggests the complete absence of a party stand, whether Guelph or Ghibelline and, instead, a persistent attempt to safeguard the remnants of papal power (see below, pp. 161–73): Holmes, *Florence, Rome, and the Origins of the Renaissance*, pp. 188–9.

custody of two officials with plenipotentiary authority, the rectors. A *rector in temporalities* was expected to keep the peace and to protect the province, the property of its inhabitants, and the privileges of the Church. He also served as judge or arbiter when conflicts arose. The *rector in spiritualities* possessed a rather confusing title, since his main concern was also administrative, particularly fiscal. In theory, the Papal State presented the appearance of an ordered state, equipped with laws, bearing arms, and collecting revenue.[10] The situation revealed by local records, however, is one of constant anarchy, with papal rule requiring an incessant process of reconquest. The chaotic situation brought the cardinals, after Benedict XI's death, to question the chances of the survival of the papal monarchy. According to Aragonese sources, the princes of the Church had supposedly asked: 'How can we rule in other lands if we cannot dominate and pacify our own?'[11]

The authority of the bishop of Rome was neither secured nor widely recognised in any of the papal provinces. The resulting imperative to maintain a continuous state of alertness absorbed all the resources of the Papal State as well as a large portion of those of the apostolic camera.[12] Besides, papal income experienced great fluctuations; an account book of the Patrimony of St Peter in Tuscany reflected the fiscal repercussions of the political situation for the years 1304–6. Of thirty-three towns owing the *tallia militum* – i.e., the money commutation for military levies – fifteen completely evaded the obligation, leaving papal collectors with only 47 per cent of the expected amount. The hearth-tax was paid by only eighteen of the thirty-seven towns owing it. The prominent towns of Viterbo, Orvieto, Todi, and Narni completely evaded payment. Though the situation was less chaotic in the Duchy of Spoleto, it provided the papal treasury with only 378 florins for the whole year in 1304, instead of 2,611 florins for a period of about ten months between 1290 and 1291.[13] Powerful cities were also the least amenable against papal authority. Foreign influences – Angevin, French, Italian – periodically intruded, but the main threat to papal supremacy came from the communes and feudal lords. Bologna was ruled by oligarchs who, though opposing each other, were always ready to unite forces in opposition to

---

[10] On the administration and institutions of the Papal State, see Waley, *The Papal State in the Thirteenth Century*, pp. 91–124.

[11] 'Nostris terris non possumus dominari nec pacem dare, quomodo poterimus alienis?': *Acta Aragonensia*, vol. I, no. 116, p. 177.

[12] P. J. Jones, *The Malatesta of Rimini and the Papal State*, pp. 1–11.

[13] Waley, 'An Account Book of the Patrimony of St Peter in Tuscany', pp. 18–25. On the duchy's revenues, see C. Reydellet-Guttinger, *L'administration pontificale dans le Duché de Spolète*, pp. 69–78. On Clement's efforts to improve the collection of papal taxes in Italy, see *Regestum Clementis Papae V*, nos. 7461–2, 7591–4, 8762.

any papal interference. By 1300, most areas of the March of Ancona were also under despotic rule.[14]

The province of Romagna offers a typical case of the gradual deterioration of papal government. The geopolitical situation of the province, especially Bologna, substantially changed because of Clement's move to southern France. From being at the very limits of the Papal State, it became the nearest area to the Comtat-Venaissin by land routes, a fact that justified papal attention to the area.[15] The collapse of imperial power, however, coupled with the failure of Bologna to attain pre-eminence, meant that there was no central authority in Romagna capable of imposing some order. The majority of Ghibellines and White Guelphs had been banished from Bologna following a bloodthirsty civil war. At the end of 1305, the papal envoys, Guillaume Durant, bishop of Mende, and Pelfort de Rabastens, abbot of Lombez, reported that 'in this province there was no count during the time when we were there, but a vicar whom almost none obeyed'. They presented an apocalyptic report of the situation and asked for immediate papal intervention to restore peace and, thereby, pave the way for the return of the papacy to Rome.[16]

Their advice, however, expressed an overly simplified evaluation of the situation and, especially, of the pope's capacity to bring about a satisfactory solution. In many cases, inter-party struggles, which had originally been dictated by concepts of aristocratic honour, affected other social strata as well. The nobles, as land owners, were able to call upon their *fideles* as a military force to sustain them in the *contado*; as creditors of merchants and artisans, they could also ensure a body of dependants in the towns and dominate them through communal machinery. In this way, local nobles could draw all social strata into their internecine conflicts. Their rule was rooted in violence, which included the exile of opponents and any possible rivals, and had a composite character. They were at once despots, *signori*, ruling urban communes, and, in parallel, the temporal subjects of the pope. As leaders of their communes, they fought against papal oppression; in strange contrast, as allies of the papacy, they resisted other political forces in the province. As circumstances dictated, they successfully oscillated between opposing policies to secure their rule, which was to become permanent and legitimate. For the average citizen, indeed, the stable rule of one family was infinitely preferable to intermittent anarchy and heavy papal taxation. At a later stage, the *signori* received some kind of legitimacy from the commune, by obtaining

---

[14] P. J. Jones, 'Communes and Despots', p. 71.
[15] A. Vasina, 'Il papato avignonese e il governo dello Stato della Chiesa', p. 141.
[16] Davidsohn, *Forschungen zur Geschichte von Florenz*, vol. III, pp. 287–301; see also Langlois, 'Notices et documents relatifs à l'histoire de France au temps de Philippe le Bel', p. 325.

appointments as captains or defenders, and from the papacy, by their appointment as vicars. After the *signoria* was created, it tried and succeeded in seizing villages from the communes or from the papacy in the *contado*.[17] This development, characteristic as it was in the *trecento*, had fatal consequences for the Church, on both the jurisdictional and the territorial level. It furthered the pauperisation of the ecclesiastical establishment, especially in northern Italy. By the sixteenth century, only some 10 to 15 per cent of lands remained in Church hands, against 65 to 70 per cent in the south until the end of the eighteenth century.[18]

Rome, which at least in theory was not only an integral part of the Papal State but its capital as well, offers another example of the unstable political balance among the papacy, the commune, and its neighbouring territory. During the chaos that characterised Boniface's later years, Rome became more aggressive towards its adjacent territories; its expansionist policy eventually gave rise to the district, a protectorate under Roman control. Under the lead of Giovanni da Ignano, *capitano del popolo* between 1305 and 1306, the city secured control of Ninfa, Corneto, Toscanella, Amelia, and Vetralla. In 1308, Amelia tried to reject Roman authority, but the preparations for a punitive expedition and the lack of effective support from the papal rector in the Patrimony forced the Amelians to retract hastily.[19] The little town of Sutri, some 30 kms north of Rome, was more successful in evading Roman punishment. In 1310, the town elected Count Domenico d'Anguillara as its *podestà*, without consulting Rome. This move caused the acting senator of Rome, Louis of Savoy, to quash the election and to fine Sutri on the grounds that the lordship of the town belonged to the Roman people, the choice of the *podestà* being one of its prerogatives.[20] Early in 1311, Sutri appealed to Clement V in his capacity as 'senator of Rome, whose vicar in charge is Louis' to discipline his subordinate. Several years earlier, indeed, in 1307, Clement had been elected senator of Rome for life, a gesture that the pope regarded as a symbol of devotion and reverence towards him and the papacy.[21] Though Clement ordered Louis of Savoy to refrain from taking further steps against Sutri, pending the hearing of its appeal, the pope refused to take a clearer stand (1 March 1311).[22]

Clement's neutral attitude, surprising as it appears at first glance, resulted from the political situation, in particular the delicate balance of

---

[17] J. Larner, *The Lords of Romagna*, pp. 76–80. [18] C. M. Cipolla, 'Une crise ignorée', pp. 317–22.

[19] J. von Pflugk-Harttung, *Iter Italicum*, p. 598; *Acta Imperii Angliae et Franciae*, no. 195, pp. 130–1.

[20] C. M. Small, 'An Episode at Sutri in the Patrimony of St Peter', pp. 309–15.

[21] 'Sane prefatus populus gerens erga personam nostram devotionis et reverentie specialis affectum, et intendens nos specialiter honorare, dispositionem regiminis dicte Urbis ad vitam nostram nobis hactenus unanime voluntate commisit': *Regestum Clementis Papae V*, nos. 2257, 5056.

[22] *Ibid.*, no. 6678.

power at this time between Robert of Anjou and Henry VII.[23] Louis of
Savoy was one of the closest allies of the emperor-elect.[24] Sutri was also
a key point in the *Romfahrt*, since it dominated the route from Florence
to Rome via Viterbo. Papal support of Sutri in 1311 could, therefore,
have been evaluated as a measure against Henry VII and support of the
emerging Guelph league, which was challenging imperial authority in
Italy. Such a papal move could have adverse effects when Henry was
paving his difficult way to Rome with apostolic approval. The lack of
papal support, however, did not prevent the inhabitants of Sutri from following their own path. When Rome rose up against Louis of Savoy
during the anarchy that followed the imperial coronation (1312), Sutri
used the occasion to leave Count Domenico in charge while evading
payment of the fine. Still, the city remained an integral part of the district and, as such, subject to Roman hegemony. Conversely, the pope
failed to preserve apostolic rights in Rome and the adjacent territories.
Clement's continuous attempts to recover direct power over 'castles, territories, and areas in the Patrimony of St Peter in Tuscany which pertained to the Church by law and were wrongfully occupied' were
doomed to failure, nor did they lead to a new territorial division between
the Romans and their bishop.[25]

Besides opposing political interests that arose from time to time, the
prolonged stay in the Comtat-Venaissin did little to improve the relationship between Clement and the Romans, particularly the nobility.[26]
During the papal absence, pilgrimage to the city was severely damaged
and the inhabitants missed the rich income that the pope, the cardinals,
and hundreds of curial officers could otherwise provide. For the first time
in Church history, moreover, the Roman aristocracy became a 'foreign'
factor, one that was relegated to a secondary plane in papal diplomacy.
After Clement's death, Dante referred in macabre terms to the deplor-
able situation into which Rome had deteriorated because of papal
absence. Quoting the lamentation of Jeremiah, the Florentine poet
commiserated with the miserable fate of the city, which used to be ruler
of the world. The desertion of its spiritual leader, who had followed the
path of the Pharisees out of greed and cupidity, had condemned Rome
to ruin, Dante lamented.[27]

---

[23] On the relationship between Henry VII, the emperor-elect, and Robert of Anjou, the nominal
king of Sicily and head of the Guelph party, see below, pp. 160–73.

[24] Having been elected for the senatorial position in 1310, he established his headquarters in the
Lateran in clear usurpation of papal prerogatives. The move did not lead to papal censure, however.

[25] *Codex Diplomaticus Dominii Temporalis S. Sedis*, no. 631, pp. 468–9; Dupré-Theseider, *Roma dal
comune di popolo alla signoria pontificia*, pp. 395–7.

[26] See chapter 1, pp. 27–8; *Regestum Clementis Papae V*, nos. 2257, 2272, 5056.

[27] 'Quomodo sola sedet civitas plena populo facta est quasi vidua domina gentium. Principum

This sense of abandonment – which was shared by the Italian cardinals and large parts of the Roman aristocracy – should not be perceived in terms of geographical distance. On the contrary, available data suggest the existence of ongoing communication between the Papal State and other areas of Christendom, including Languedoc. For example, the news of the election of Bertrand de Got in Perugia reached the court of Edward I in only twelve days.[28] The protracted stay of the papacy in Avignon actually brought about a systematisation of the transmission of news while improving fluent contacts between different areas of Italy and the papal curia. In 1335, a messenger succeeded in covering the distance from Florence to Avignon by sea in ten days; by 1364, messages were delivered between Avignon and Perugia in fifteen to nineteen days. In terms of medieval communication, all these cases suggest a rather high speed.[29] The many problems encountered by Clement V in the Italian peninsula were not, therefore, an unavoidable result of territorial distance; rather, they were a consequence of the fragile political situation in Italy, the roots of which long antedated Clement's pontificate. On the other hand, according to Daniel Waley, the chaotic situation in the Papal State was not in itself sufficient to justify Clement's failure to cross the Alps. Yet, Avignon was not an obviously bad choice: proximity was not a solution and distance would not necessarily be a disadvantage.[30] Moreover, Clement's struggle for regaining control over the Papal State could more easily be conducted from a territorial base outside Italy.

These considerations, however attractive they may appear, were little appreciated during Clement's pontificate and did nothing to improve the pope's fragile position in Rome; this was especially true with regard to the local nobility, which was affected the most by the papal passage. In the early fourteenth century, the Roman nobility counted about thirty families, the leading names being Anguillara, Annibaldi, Capocci, Colonna, Conti, Frangipani, Orsini, S. Eustachio, Stefaneschi, Vico, Boccamazza, Normandi, and Savelli. It is rather doubtful whether Clement's declarations on behalf of their status as 'special disciples of the Roman Church' could have balanced the switch of political power from their city to the Comtat-Venaissin.[31] There is, in fact, proof of the pope's

---

quondam fariseorum cupiditas, qui sacerdotium vetus abominabile fecit, non modo levitice prolis ministerium transtulit, quin, et preelecte civitati David, ossidionem peperit et ruinam.' The text has been edited by R. Morghen, 'La lettera di Dante ai cardinali italiani' (1956), pp. 25–31.
[28] See chapter 1, n. 51.   [29] Menache, 'Communication in the Jewish Diaspora', pp. 50–1.
[30] Waley, *The Papal State in the Thirteenth Century*, pp. 251, 303.
[31] 'Nam etsi summus Pontifex Christi Vicarius totius sit Christianitatis Antistes, tamen specialis Episcopus fore dinoscitur Romanorum . . . [Romani] ipsi sunt Romane ecclesie speciales alumpni, quos sinceris complectimur brachiis et paterni favoris ubere confovemus': *Codex Diplomaticus Dominii Temporalis S. Sedis*, no. 588, pp. 407–8.

deliberate attempt to weaken their former privileged status. A new type of correspondence characterised the whole Avignon period by which the popes addressed the Roman nobility as a whole; many letters appealed only to the 'senators and the Roman people', in clear disregard of the former privileges enjoyed by some of the Roman families.[32] As the situation in the city deteriorated, Clement did not limit himself to diplomatic gestures. He accused the Roman aristocracy of being a main factor in the unrest in the city (15 January 1310).[33] The papal claim did not lack foundation, in particular with regard to the leading families. As part of their conflict with the Caetanis, the Colonnas, for example, opened a new front against the Orsinis in Rome (1309).

In order to prevent further deterioration, Clement invested Guglielmo da S. Marcello, a Franciscan from the papal penitentiary, with wide powers to re-establish order in the city (15 June 1310). Additionally, the pope made some gestures of goodwill. Two months later, Clement bestowed greater municipal authority on the Romans and allowed them to choose between two senators, one, or more *capitani del popolo* for six or twelve months, whichever would be more suitable to their needs.[34] The failure of this liberal policy, however, soon became evident. On 10 February 1313, Clement nominated Jacques Arlotti as senator of Rome in order to restrict the nobles' freedom of action.[35] Papal appointments of this kind were dictated by the chaotic situation in the city and, as such, were provisional; they were not intended to displace the regular institutions of government in the Papal State. Still, Clement's envoys, whether they originated from Italy or Languedoc, found it almost impossible to restore order, let alone advance papal interests. Some examples illustrate the problematic situation: on 16 June 1307, Clement nominated Guitto Farnese, bishop of Orvieto, as rector *in spiritualibus* in Rome.[36] Farnese's conflict with Stefano Colonna, however, soon brought about his replacement by Isnardo, archbishop of Thebes (12 August 1308).[37]

The appointment of local officials from both the secular and the ecclesiastical establishment (with which they were well acquainted) drove papal diplomacy into the intricacy of familiar feuds. On the other hand, the nomination of the pope's relatives, who were much less aware of local politics, advanced papal interests no better; on the contrary, it strengthened the nepotistic bias associated with Clement V. In 1305, Clement

[32] J. Coste, 'Les lettres collectives des papes d'Avignon à la noblesse romaine', pp. 152–5.
[33] In a letter to the Roman nobility, the pope argued that 'ad vos aliosque nobiles, a quibus principaliter huiusmodi turbationum causa dependet': *Regestum Clementis Papae V*, nos. 6275–6, 6297.
[34] *Codex Diplomaticus Dominii Temporalis S. Sedis*, no. 602, p. 429; Dupré-Theseider, *Roma dal comune di popolo alla signoria pontificia*, p. 398.
[35] *Codex Diplomaticus Dominii Temporalis S. Sedis*, no. 633, p. 469.
[36] *Regestum Clementis Papae V*, nos. 1645–7.   [37] *Ibid.*, nos. 1147, 3577.

nominated Amanieu d'Albret, *consanguineo suo*, rector in temporalities of the Patrimony in Tuscany. Amanieu received extraordinary powers to collect all taxes and to be exempt from periodic reports to the curia. The pope also cancelled former privileges that his predecessors had granted to local lords and cities on the grounds that his relative's 'many merits and virtues were well known to us through familiar experience'.[38] The Italian arena, however, proved to be more difficult than the positive familiar experiences to be obtained among members of the de Got family. Amanieu was forced to resign in 1311; his successor, Gailhard de Faugères, did not go to Italy at all. His vicar, Bernard de Coucy, was eventually sent to the March of Ancona to inquire into financial scandals (1312). This appointment also proved unfortunate, since Bernard brought the whole area to the verge of civil war.

The conflict in Pistoia exemplifies the intricacy of the Italian political arena and the inability of papal representatives to handle the situation, whether they were the pope's relatives or not. When Clement was elected to the papacy, his immediate intervention in support of Pistoia was requested. The Ghibellines and White Guelphs had been under siege for months and were at the end of their resources. Surrounding Pistoia's walls, the Black Guelphs, led by Lucca and Florence and reinforced by Robert of Anjou, were preparing a final assault.[39] The papal envoys, Guillaume Durant and Pelfort de Rabastens, declared a truce and summoned the belligerent parties to appear before them in person or by proxy to conclude a peace. The Black Guelphs, however, accused Pistoia of being a nest of Ghibellines and traitors and, seeing their final victory at hand, refused to submit to the peremptory demands of the pope's representatives.[40] Applying the power conferred on them, the papal envoys pronounced an excommunication against anyone who dared to disobey their order and threatened all transgressors with heavy fines.[41] These measures were of no avail. Lucca and Florence tightened the siege, and Pistoia was eventually forced to capitulate (10–11 April 1306). 'And in this way was abolished the pride and magnificence of the inhabitants

---

[38] *Ibid.*, nos. 364–72, 877, 880–1, 1463, 1655.

[39] See the report of Robert of Calabria to James II of Aragon (14 September 1305); *Acta Aragonensia*, vol. II, no. 340, p. 511; Holmes, *Florence, Rome, and the Origins of the Renaissance*, pp. 181, 188.

[40] Agnolo di Tura, *Cronaca Senese*, p. 295; *Cronaca Senese di autore anonimo*, p. 86; Dino Compagni, *Cronica*, p. 196; *Annales Urbevetani*, p. 272; *Annales Forolivienses*, p. 60; R. Caggese, *Roberto d'Angiò e i suoi tempi*, vol. I, pp. 31ff.; Davidsohn, *Geschichte von Florenz*, vol. III, pp. 292–318.

[41] According to Villani, Robert of Anjou was forced to withdraw the siege because his father, Charles II, was on his way to do homage to the pope. Still, he left behind an army of 300 knights, with Diego de la Rat at its head. See Villani, *Istorie fiorentine*, l. viii, c. 82, p. 168. Cf. Caggese, *Roberto d'Angiò e i suoi tempi*, vol. I, pp. 35–41. On the political stand of Italian chroniclers, see L. Green, 'The Image of Tyranny in Early Fourteenth-Century Italian Historical Writing', pp. 337–45.

of Pistoia, and purified from their sins they were led to such servitude.'[42]
What Villani defines in terms of 'purification' was the beginning of joint
rule by Lucca and Florence, who nominated in rotation the podestà and
capitano del popolo of Pistoia.[43]

The triumph of the Black Guelphs in Pistoia provided the catalyst for
the pope's conferment of legatine powers on Napoleone Orsini in
Tuscany and Emilia.[44] Aragonese sources refer to Clement's desire 'to
secure papal authority in the lands of the Church in Italy, for as long as
the pope stayed in France',[45] namely, to strengthen apostolic rule without
guaranteeing an immediate return to Rome. Although the nomination
of Orsini did not support the nepotistic nature ascribed to Clement's
policy, his appointment did little to blur the party conflicts that plagued
the peninsula. On the contrary, the Florentines suspected him of
Ghibelline/White associations that might favour their enemies; as a
result, they mistrusted his mission from the outset.[46] The prevailing suspicions about his neutrality had probably encouraged Orsini to declare
before the pope, 'You will never find a true Roman who is either Guelph
or Ghibelline.' The cardinal further contended that he did not really
understand what a Guelph or a Ghibelline was, and that his goal was to
bring about real peace and concord in Italy.[47]

Orsini's declarations of goodwill earned him papal support, but did
little to change the hostile attitudes of the papal allies. On the contrary –
his authority soon rejected in Florence, Orsini also failed to reach a compromise between the warring factions in Bologna. He was forced to leave
the city pursued by armed bands calling, 'Death, death to the traitor'
(22 May 1306).[48] The legate responded by preaching a crusade against

---

[42] Villani, *Cronica*, l. viii, c. 81, pp. 113–15; Villani, *Istorie fiorentine*, l. viii, c. 82, pp. 166–70.

[43] *Storia dal principio del secolo XIII*, p. 108; Petri Cantinelli, *Chronicon*, p. 96. Manselli, 'La Repubblica
di Lucca', pp. 660–1. P. Partner speaks in terms of 'pure political opportunism' with regard to the
relationship between Clement V and Florence: Partner, 'Florence and the Papacy', p. 82.

[44] *Regestum Clementis Papae V*, no. 3634.

[45] Finke, *Papsttum und Untergang des Templerordens*, vol. I, no. 13, p. 16.

[46] They argued that 'videntes quod ipse legatus sotiatus est Ghibellina familia et rebellibus nostris et
quod ipse eos favorat, dubitent de eodem et per licteras captas et inventas et per alias indictia man-
ifesta suspicionis materia creverit in eisdem et maxime, cum sine assensu sotiorum Guelforum
Tuscie veniat': A. Eitel, *Der Kirchenstaat unter Klemens V*, p. 26; *Corpus chronicorum Bononiensium*,
pp. 273, 276. On the other hand, Ferreto de' Ferreti describes Orsini in terms of 'virum pruden-
tem et e cetu cardinalium non mediocrem, ad Italicas partes pro tollendis bellorum excessibus et
paccandis discordie tumultibus, utque inobedientes meritis pene tormentis afficiat, studiose
legavit': Ferreto de' Ferreti, *Historia rerum in Italia gestarum*, p. 209. See Holmes, *Florence, Rome,
and the Origins of the Renaissance*, pp. 188–9.

[47] 'Vere pater sancte, nec sum Gebellinus nec Guelfus, nec bene intelligo, quid est dictum per
Guelfum et Gebellinum, set vellem bonam pacem et concordiam': *Acta Aragonensia*, vol. II,
no. 393, p. 615; Villani, *Cronica*, l. viii, c. 85, pp. 117–18.

[48] Petri Cantinelli, *Chronicon*, p. 97; Tolomeo da Lucca, *Secunda Vita*, pp. 25–6; *Notae ad vitas*,
pp. 70–2.

Bologna and Florence and placing the whole region under interdict.[49] The deteriorating situation obscured Orsini's original mission as an angel of peace who had come in search of universal concord and made it easier for him to join the White army in Arezzo, where

> he was received with great honour. And during his stay in Arezzo he gathered his friends and the faithful from Rome, the March [of Ancona], the Duchy [of Spoleto], and from Romagna, and all the White [Guelphs] and Ghibellines from Florence and other areas of Tuscany, to the amount of 1,700 knights and numerous people, in order to prompt a war against Florence.[50]

The use of interdict and the call for a crusade were integral components of the struggle for predominance between the bishop of Rome and his restless subjects. At the beginning of the fourteenth century, however, the increase in the use of ecclesiastical punishments, coupled with the pope's absence that gave his legates an almost completely free hand, strengthened the arbitrariness of ecclesiastical weapons while weakening their efficacy. In the present case, there is no evidence that Napoleone Orsini received authority to launch a crusade, in particular against communes that traditionally had been noted for their support of the papacy. Florence, in particular, which only recently had supplied 'athletes of Christ' for the struggle against the Sicilian rebels and the Colonna heretics, was now transformed by Orsini into a genuine enemy of the faith. Little wonder, therefore, that the crusade against Florence, Lucca, and Bologna soon turned against papal interests.

Even close adherents to the curia began to have doubts about the ethics – let alone the results – of papal policy. Dino Compagni, a merchant supporter of the White Guelphs in Florence who had retired from politics, acknowledged the discipline due the Church, 'mother of all Christians, when the shepherd king does not sway it from the path of righteousness . . . But the evil shepherds are sometimes nominated by God to [atone] for the sins of the people.'[51] It is highly doubtful whether this explanation 'for our sins' could advance papal authority among city-states so jealous of their political freedom. Dante Alighieri went further, questioning the validity of papal punishment:

> No man may be so cursed by priest or pope
> but what the eternal love may still return
> while any thread of green lives on in hope.[52]

---

[49] *Cronaca Senese di autore anonimo*, pp. 87–8; Tolomeo da Lucca, *Secunda Vita*, p. 28; *Annales Forolivienses*, pp. 60–1; C. A. Willemsen, *Kardinal Napoleon Orsini*, pp. 44, 174.
[50] Villani, *Cronica*, l. viii, c. 89, pp. 120–1; Villani, *Istorie fiorentine*, l. viii, pp. 172–3, 177–9.
[51] Dino Compagni, *Cronica*, ad a. 1308, pp. 215–17.
[52] Dante Alighieri, *Divina Commedia*, Purgatorio, c. III, vv. 133–5.

These verses reflect the hesitations that dimmed the pope's religious aura and went beyond a passing utilitarian attitude to his legates. True, the equation that identified hostile political tendencies with heresy was justified by the contemporary trend in canon law, which considered any attack on the Church and its privileges to be heresy. Heresy thus displayed itself as much in political hostility to the pope and the Church as in heterodox beliefs.[53] On the other hand, canonical developments could not shape political reality in Italy or change the balance of forces in favour of Clement V. The many vicissitudes encountered by the pope's representatives were noted by contemporaries, who, each from his own perspective, reached practical conclusions about the moral quality and, no less importantly, the political value of papal leadership.

Even in those rare cases when a city requested papal intervention, such an appeal expressed but short-term political interests. The developments in Ferrara provide a case in point. The city had been under papal suzerainty since 1077, when Countess Matilda presented Ferrara to Gregory VII. The citizens enjoyed wide political freedom under the Guelph marquises of Este, Obizzo, and Azzo. During the thirteenth century, although the popes developed cordial relations with the ruling oligarchy, they actually lost direct power over the city. In 1305, the otherwise powerful rule of Azzo VIII d'Este was put to the test because of his marriage to the daughter of Charles of Anjou, the unquestionable leader of the Guelphs. The marquis' political move fostered unrest in Ferrara and facilitated the emergence of a Ghibelline party,[54] which was supported not only by Ghibellines of neighbouring cities but also by the discontented members of the d'Este family, with Aldevrandino and Françesco d'Este, Azzo's brothers, at their head.[55] The already fragile equilibrium in the city came to an end on 31 January 1308, when Azzo VIII died. War immediately broke out over the succession, which the late marquis had bequeathed to Folco, his grandchild from his natural son, Fresco.[56] In order to oppose his uncles' challenge, Fresco, as the legal representative of his son's rights, called on the Venetians for help, an appeal that followed a long tradition of alliances between the two cities.[57] Pursuant to Fresco's call for help, the Venetian Great Council

---

[53] G. Volpi, *Movimenti religiosi e sette ereticali nella società medievale italiana secoli XI–XIV*, pp. 135–54.

[54] *Chronicon Estense*, col. 351.   [55] T. Dean, *Land and Power in Late Medieval Ferrara*, pp. 10–18.

[56] *Chronicon Mutinense*, cols. 568–9; *Historia Gulielmi et Albrigeti Cortusiorum*, cols. 776–7. The local record, however, refers rather apologetically to the late marquis' abrogation of former wills as well as his last desire to have his brother Françesco succeed him: *Chronicon Estense*, p. 360; L. Chiappini, *Gli Estensi*, pp. 59–60; on the will's terms, see Eitel, *Der Kirchenstaat unter Klemens V*, pp. 170–3.

[57] As early as 1240, Azzo VII d'Este besieged Ferrara with the support of Venetian and papal troops. This joint enterprise responded to the different, though not opposing, interests of each side. Pope Gregory IX wished to see the Ghibelline Salinguerra deposed; the Venetians expected to receive

announced the dispatch of troops (8 July).[58] To counterbalance this threat, Aldevrandino and Françesco d'Este appealed to the papal court against Fresco and his Venetian allies.[59] Their request gave Clement the chance to regain control over Ferrara while displaying papal authority against an external threat.

Françesco d'Este appeared to be the most suitable candidate to receive full papal support. The nuncios, Arnaud de St Astier and Onofrio de Trevi, supported his rights and started an offensive against the usurpation by his nephew and the Venetians.[60] On 23 September, Fresco received a warning to resign his lordship over Ferrara within five days under threat of spiritual and temporal penalties. The papal nuncios did not wait for long and issued the excommunication on 25 October. They specifically mentioned Venice, its *doge*, counsellors, and captains – Giovanni Soranzo and Vitale Michiel, who had fought against papal troops – and the *podestà* of Chioggia, whose boats had operated against those of the Church on the Po. The nuncios voided all treaties and agreements made with the Venetians, and prohibited the export of provisions to Venice or Chioggia. In addition, all apostolic privileges that had been granted to the two cities were revoked.

A few days after the nuncios' threat against Fresco, the Ferrarese opened the city gates to the papal army (5 October). Françesco d'Este entered the city in triumph, accompanied by the papal nuncio, Arnaud de St Astier. According to the local record, the citizens supported their returning leader with cries of 'Long live the Marquis of Este!', but Françesco required them to be more grateful to the Church, which had paved the way for his return. In contrast to his reverent attitude, the anonymous chronicler described the infamous behaviour of the papal nuncio:

Against the wish of his people and all his friends, Master Françesco brought the rule of the papal legate to the town; and put him in and conferred upon him his ancient castle; unfortunately accepting the legate's promise that he would restore the city to him; however, the ways of churchmen often being suited to rapacious

---

substantial commercial concessions, in particular to secure exclusive rights to transport merchandise along the Po. In the years to come, Venice also helped Azzo VIII against his enemies from Bologna, Verona, and Mantua: J. K. Laurent, 'The Signory and Its Supporters', pp. 40–1.

[58] Villani, *Istorie fiorentine*, l. viii, c. 103, pp. 202–3; Hodgson, *Venice in the Thirteenth and Fourteenth Century*, pp. 205–8.   [59] *Regestum Clementis Papae V*, nos. 6316, 10442.

[60] *Ibid.*, nos. 3570, 3572–4, 5087–8. The pope specifically granted them power to invalidate any pacts, sermons, or contracts that the citizens of Ferrara had made that could jeopardise their return to apostolic obedience. In parallel, Clement wrote to the Ferrarese encouraging their support of Françesco: *ibid.*, no. 3171. See the supportive report of papal policy at this stage by the local record: *Chronicon Estense*, col. 364. Cf. Paolo di Tommaso Montauri, *Cronaca Senese*, p. 233; *Corpus chronicorum Bononiensium*, p. 303.

wolves, the legate kept his power over the city and the whole district, to nobody's surprise, while Master Françesco was left empty handed.[61]

Just one year of papal rule in Ferrara was, therefore, sufficient to make the nuncio and his retinue synonymous with *lupi rapaces*.

Outside Ferrara there were more favourable reactions to the papal policy against Venice, which provided a unique chance to conclude old feuds while advancing particularist interests. The chronicle of Parma mentions the enthusiastic response to the nuncios' call for a crusade, further seeing an expression of God's blessing in the achievements of the papal army on the battlefield.[62] Not so Bernard Gui, who was more realistic about the celestial inspiration of this crusade. Setting God's will aside, Bernard stressed the heavy toll among both the Ferrarese and the Venetians taken by the bloodthirsty conflict among Christians.[63] Indeed, it was rather ironic that the first crusade waged in fourteenth-century Italy, for which documentary evidence survives, was declared against Venice, which like Florence a few years earlier had been a faithful daughter of the Church. A deep sense of frustration thus characterised its ambassadors' appeal to the curia in 1309. Protesting about the sanctions against their city, they alleged that Venice 'had been always a faithful and constant defender of the honour and glory of the Roman Church, whether in the Holy Land against the Saracens and other barbarians, or in Italy against Frederick II, Ezzelino da Romano, or the many other persecutors of the Church'.[64] Rhetorical declarations aside, Clement's policy in Ferrara, especially his declaration of a total war against Venice, shadowed the traditional political stance of the papacy and blurred even more the already ambiguous dividing line between Guelphs and Ghibellines. It also demonstrated that *Realpolitik*, which very often bordered on political opportunism, was not monopolised by the pope's adversaries.

The first papal successes in Ferrara, however, proved to be transitory. Using their naval advantages, the Venetians cut off river communications and starved the inhabitants, whom they exposed to heavy fire.[65] The attempts by the nuncio to negotiate were greeted by the Venetians with abuse. To make matters worse still, wherever Arnaud de St Astier went

---

[61] *Chronicon Estense*, ad a. 1308, col. 364. I have followed here the original version, which did not differentiate between 'legate' and 'nuncio' and used both terms indiscriminately.

[62] *Chronicon Parmense*, ad a. 1309, p. 113.

[63] Bernard Gui, in *Quarta Vita*, p. 66. When the Venetians tried to break through enemy lines on the night of 27–8 August, they suffered a bloody defeat that took 2,000–3,000 lives. See the accounts of papal victories by Arnaud de Pellegrue (July–September 1309): *Acta Aragonensia*, vol. II, nos. 407, 415, pp. 643–4, 656–7.

[64] G. Soranzo, *La guerra fra Venezia e la Santa Sede per il dominio di Ferrara*, pp. 133–4.

[65] *Chronicon Estense*, col. 365.

into the city, he was greeted with cries of 'death to the legate' and a hail of stones. Under growing internal and external pressure, Arnaud concluded a peace treaty with the Venetians on 1 December that left the papacy only a nominal power in Ferrara. Clement, however, refused to bestow apostolic blessing on the shameful capitulation of his representative. Instead, on 27 March 1309, the pope enforced the excommunication against the *doge*, all citizens of Venice, and anyone who aided or abetted them. Clement further ordered the prelates and communes throughout Italy, as well as the kings of Naples, Aragon, Portugal, and Trinacria, to confiscate all Venetian property, wherever it was located, to annul all treaties or contracts with the Venetians, and to ban the supply of provisions or merchandise to the city.[66] The *doge*'s subjects were given apostolic absolution from their oath of fidelity, while all the faithful received papal blessing to deprive the Venetians of their liberty. Finally, Clement ordered ecclesiastical persons to depart from Venetian territory within ten days.[67] Additionally, he nominated his favourite nephew, Cardinal Arnaud de Pellegrue, as legate and reinforced him with two thousand men (22 May).[68]

Clement's policy in Ferrara shows the pope's resolute character and his complete dedication to the defence of the Papal State, even against the readiness of his nuncios *in situ* to reach a compromise. True, the *doge* was not Philip the Fair and the pope's firm stand against Venice cannot illustrate Clement's policy with regard to the Most Christian King or his country. Still, both the goals and the outcome of papal policy in Ferrara show some facets of Clement's character that were found during his prelacy in Bordeaux and that have been neglected in historical research. Some years later, the papal rector in the Romagna, Raimond d'Aspello, wrote to Cardinal Raimond de Got that the papal victory over the Venetians had raised the prestige of the Church in the region to unprecedented heights.[69] Little wonder that when Arnaud de Pellegrue returned to the curia, he was magnificently received by Clement.[70]

Soldiers from Ferrara, Bologna, Romagna, Padua, Vicenza, Florence, Lucca, and Siena joined Cardinal de Pellegrue in his merciless war against

---

[66] The papal order was not universally fulfilled. James II of Aragon, for instance, stated that obedience to the papal interdict would harm his subjects in Venetian territory. Only in July 1312 did he change this policy: Salavert y Roca, 'Notas sobre la política italiana de Clemente V', pp. 257–8, docs. 1, 12, 16–17, pp. 273–4, 288–9, 293–5.
[67] *Clementis Papae V, Monitorum, et declaratio excommunicationis*, pp. 3–12; *Regestum Clementis Papae V*, nos. 10425, 5081–2, 5084; *Codex Diplomaticus Dominii Temporalis S. Sedis*, nos. 594–5, pp. 412–15; *Historia Gulielmi et Albrigeti Cortusiorum*, col. 777.
[68] *Regestum Clementis Papae V*, nos. 5024–54, 6290; *Chronicon Estense*, col. 366.
[69] 'Nam tota Christianitas scire potest, quod nunquam ecclesia Dei tantum quantum nunc in istis partibus honoris et glorie acquisivit!': *Acta Aragonensia*, vol. II, no. 413, p. 654.
[70] Ferreto de' Ferreti, *Historia rerum in Italia gestarum*, p. 263.

Venice.[71] Villani reports that the Florentines were ready to help Cardinal de Pellegrue as long as the 'Holy War' was directed against Venice. The legate obtained knights and foot soldiers from the city; further, Arnaud was received with 'great honour, and processions were made upon his arrival, and he was bestowed with 2,000 golden florins by the commune'.[72] The 'holiness' of the common goal against Venice thus completely eradicated the former disagreement over Pistoia, an unpleasant memory of the near past that both the Florentines and the papal curia willingly forgot. Clement annulled all bans that had been pronounced against the city and its inhabitants by Cardinal Napoleone Orsini (11 September 1309). The complete metamorphosis of the relationship between the curia and Florence did not remain unique, being soon followed by new papal alliances with Bologna, Lucca, Cesena, and Rimini.[73] On 24 August, Clement thanked his beloved sons, the *podestà*, and other officers of Padua for sending to Ferrara 200 knights and 1,000 foot soldiers to assist him against 'the detestable barbarity' of the Venetians and for preventing the delivery of provisions to Venice through their territory. The crusader fervour of the Guelphs was soon imitated by some Ghibelline centres. Mantua, Verona, and Milan, as well, joined the apostolic offensive. Support of the papal cause was manifested by the presence in the papal army of the oldest son and heir of the Viscontis, the leading Ghibelline family in Milan.[74]

The powerful alliance under the apostolic banner finally brought about a crucial change in the balance of forces, and the Venetians were defeated both economically and militarily. The harsh papal measures against the city severely harmed its trade and, indeed, its supremacy in northern Italy.[75] By September, the Venetians began to negotiate a compromise with the pope through the mediation of Philip the Fair.[76] Clement, however, did not receive their appeal favourably and opposed any arrangement that would allow the Venetians 'to glorify themselves in their malicious insanity' (18 October).[77] It was only on 17 February 1313 that Clement solemnly announced to Christendom the Venetians' return to the congregation of

---

[71] *Annales Parmenses Maiores*, p. 751; *Corpus chronicorum Bononiensium*, pp. 305–8. Because of the interests of its merchants, industrialists, and bankers, however, Sienese support of papal policy was of short duration. See Bowsky, *A Medieval Italian Commune*, pp. 217–18.

[72] Villani, *Istorie fiorentine*, l. viii, c. 115, p. 210.

[73] *Regestum Clementis Papae V*, nos. 4245, 4401–2, 4600, 4735–6, 5271–7, 5285–6.

[74] F. Cognasso, 'L'unificazione della Lombardia sotto Milano', p. 366.

[75] *Chronicon Estense*, col. 367; Tolomeo da Lucca, *Secunda Vita*, pp. 32–3; Amalric Augerii, *Sexta Vita*, p. 97; *Notae ad vitas*, pp. 79–80.

[76] *Codex Diplomaticus Dominii Temporalis S. Sedis*, no. 604, pp. 430–2; *Clementis Papae V, Monitorum, et declaratio excommunicationis*, pp. 13–16.

[77] *Collectio actorum veterum*, pp. 103–5. On the future relationship between Ferrara and Venice, see the papal letter of 25 November 1311: *Regestum Clementis Pope V*, no. 8748.

the faithful. This act was not the result of papal benevolence but, rather, of the Venetians' renunciation of all privileges that they had 'unjustly' received from Fresco d'Este and of their readiness to pay the costs of the war, amounting to the considerable sum of 50,000 gold florins.[78] Clement testified to the importance of this achievement at the Council of Vienne, where he claimed that the intervention of Venice in Ferrara had been the greatest blow to the Roman Church in the last twenty years, thus making an implicit comparison with the Sicilian Vespers.[79]

The defeat of Venice and, no less importantly, the unification of the Guelph camp under papal leadership undoubtedly improved the status of Clement V in Italy, but it did not consolidate papal hegemony in the long term, especially in the Papal State. Conversely, the developments in Ferrara are symptomatic of the chronic fragility characterising Italian politics. Between 5 and 12 March 1310, some 3,500 inhabitants of Ferrara, of a total population of about 20,000, swore fidelity to the pope.[80] As a first stage, all Ferrarese, including those who had relatives in the city, were excluded from political affairs, which were monopolised by papal delegates.[81] On 21 May 1310, Guillaume, viscount of Bruniquel, was appointed vicar-general, but after only two months his malpractices and opportunism caused the citizens 'to revolt against him and the Church'. The insurrection was harshly repressed by Cardinal de Pellegrue, who condemned thirty-six leading citizens to death.[82] Worse still, on 24 August 1312, the cardinal's former partner and most active supporter, Françesco d'Este, was murdered by Dalmasio da Banoli, captain of the papal troops. This event was the final catalyst in dragging Ferrara to the verge of anarchy. On the one hand, with the Venetian threat gone, the chief motive for accepting papal rule disappeared. On the other hand, the suspicions harboured by papal officials concerning the subversive mood of the Ferrarese and, in consequence, the attempt to compel obedience by brute force only fortified hostility to papal rule. The nomination of Robert of Anjou as papal vicar did not halt further deterioration, since the Ferrarese remained adamant in their refusal to welcome papal representatives, whether Angevins or Gascons.[83] The tense political situation

---

[78] *Codex Diplomaticus Dominii Temporalis S. Sedis*, no. 629, pp. 459–68; *Regestum Clementis Papae V*, nos. 10650–1; *Clementis Papae V, Monitorum, et declaratio excommunicationis*, pp. 17–23. Some sources mention twice this amount; see Tolomeo da Lucca, *Secunda Vita*, pp. 39, 48; *Historia Gulielmi et Albrigeti Cortusiorum*, col. 778.

[79] 'Que la major onta, que la esgleya de Roma agues presa, XX ans ha, li havien feta Venecians en lo fet de Ferrara': Finke, *Papsttum und Untergang des Templerordens*, vol. II, no. 133, p. 263.

[80] *Regestum Clementis Papae V*, nos. 6316, 10461.   [81] *Ibid.*, nos. 10457–9.

[82] *Ibid.*, nos. 6313–14, 6317; *Chronicon Estense*, col. 370; Villani, *Istorie fiorentine*, l. ix, ch. 4, vol. v, p. 5.

[83] Albertino Mussato, *Heinrici VII Caesaris Historia Augusta*, cols. 499–501, 524. Robert of Anjou did not play an active role in the crusade against Venice. He limited himself to arresting Venetians in

came to an end on 4 August 1317, when a violent insurrection dismembered the remnants of papal rule.[84]

In other areas of the Papal State, as well, Clement's representatives encountered little or no success. Raymond Athon d'Aspet, Bertrand de Got, and Arnaud Bernard de Pressac, who had been nominated rectors in temporalities in Massa Trabarea, Città di Castello, Urbino, Romagna, the March of Ancona, and Campagna-Marittima were absent most of the time.[85] In the nomination of Bertrand de Got to the March of Ancona, Clement expressed a genuine desire that his nephew 'serve the cult of justice, the purity of the faith, and the opulence of peace in those areas'. Still, papal correspondence indicates that this was rather wishful thinking, at least in so far as peace was concerned. Clement's envoys were forced to fight a hopeless war against the 'rebels of the Holy Church', whose number only increased.[86] In the March of Ancona, for example, peace was restored between the Holy See and the local citizens only on 20 March 1311.[87]

The situation was hardly better in the Duchy of Spoleto. With the election of Clement to the papacy, the rector in temporalities was an Italian, Deoticlerio da Loiano. Early in 1306, the pope replaced him with his brother, Arnaud Garsie de Got, 'whose prudence is well known to us'.[88] Arnaud did not arrive in the duchy at all, and Anger de Baslada was appointed his vicar (18 March). Anger was later replaced by Pierre de Doliva, whose place in turn was taken by Arnaud's son, Sanche Garsie de Manas (1311).[89] When Arnaud Garsie died in early 1312, he was succeeded by another nephew of the pope, Bertrand de Sauviac.[90] It is uncertain whether Bertrand himself ever came to the duchy, but his son was active in the parliament of 1313, together with the rector in spiritualities, Robert d'Auberives.[91] Clement also appointed still another nephew, Raimond-Guilhem de Budos, to Benevento. On this occasion, the pope granted the new rector in temporalities unprecedented prerogatives while annulling former privileges conferred on other officials in the area that might harm his nephew's freedom of action.[92]

The nominations in the Papal State demonstrate Clement's tendency to appoint his relatives for the management of temporal affairs, and

---

his land, confiscating their goods, and placing an embargo on trade with their city. The 'neutrality' of the undisputed leader of the Guelph party was due to the fact that he had no personal interest in the conflict, which could seriously damage the thriving commercial links between Venice and Apulia. See G. Yver, *Le commerce et les marchands dans l'Italie méridionale*, pp. 254–65. On the pope's efforts to use Robert's services to consolidate the peace treaty between Ferrara and Venice (24 January 1313), see *Regestum Clementis Papae V*, nos. 9283–4, 9006–11; *Chronicon Estense*, col. 375.   [84] Dean, *Land and Power in Late Medieval Ferrara*, pp. 18ff.

[85] *Regestum Clementis Papae V*, nos. 380, 386, 883–4, 886–9, 2599–2602.

[86] *Ibid.*, nos. 3622–4, 4395, 5002, 5537–40.   [87] *Ibid.*, nos. 6626, 6680–6.   [88] *Ibid.*, nos. 374–5.

[89] *Ibid.*, nos. 6331, 7613.   [90] *Ibid.*, nos. 9974–8.   [91] *Ibid.*, no. 9139.   [92] *Ibid.*, nos. 312–13.

clergymen from the kingdom of France for the spiritualities.[93] This tendency, which had been later followed by the Avignon popes, has been evaluated in terms of nepotism and favouritism and, therefore, as harmful to the papal monarchy. According to P. J. Jones, 'If the Avignon papacy succeeded in resisting the wider Italian ambitions of France and Anjou, within its own territories the French invasion was universal, and French officials entered everywhere to aggravate the inherited deficiencies of papal administration.'[94] This conclusion was echoed by Daniel Waley, though he found a noticeable difference between Clement V and the popes of the Avignon period, to the former's detriment.[95] The question remains whether, beyond the pope's approach to Italian offices as a kind of recompense to his *nepoti* and favourites, there was also a genuine effort to nominate foreign administrators who, at least in principle, were not involved in the intricacy of Italian politics. Such a tendency could have found ample justification in daily practice. The nomination of Cardinal Napoleone Orsini as legate at the beginning of Clement's pontificate brought large sectors of the Guelph camp into open conflict with the papacy. It clearly exposed the difficulties faced by Italian envoys in extricating themselves and their families from party conflicts.

Although Clement's nominations could be justified from a political perspective, it was actually the behaviour of his nominees or, more accurately, their misbehaviour that condemned papal policy to complete failure. Often appointed for a short period of time in a foreign country, most administrators of the Papal State were concerned with making their office a lucrative source of income, an attitude also shared by their subordinates. Contemporary criticism of papal representatives referred to the sale of ecclesiastical rights, misappropriations, extortions and forced gifts, biased administration of justice, bribery, local nepotism, and even adulterate coin. That such accusations were not without foundation is revealed by Clement's decision to start an inquiry into his own representatives whom he accused of causing severe damage to the image and status of the Holy See (1 July 1311).[96] A few months later, the pope commissioned the abbot of Obterre in Etampes to investigate the serious charges against his envoys in Ferrara, who were accused of extortion and illegal dealings.[97] The growing resentment against apostolic officials did

---

[93] *Ibid.*, nos. 381, 385, 1653, 2578, 3544–7, 3576, 6331.

[94] P. J. Jones, *The Malatesta of Rimini and the Papal State*, p. 42.

[95] Waley, 'Lo Stato Papale dal periodo feudale a Martino V', p. 303.

[96] *Regestum Clementis Papae V*, nos. 7582–3; L. Guérard, 'La succession de Clément V', p. 18.

[97] 'Extendentes ad illicita manus suas, varias et diversas pecuniarum summas a nonnullis de civitate et districtu predictis indebite et contra iustitiam extorserunt, et alia multa illicita commiserunt ibidem per que nostris et apostolice sedis honoribus derogatur': *Regestum Clementis Pope V*, no. 8749.

not limit itself to accusations. When Raimond Athon d'Aspet – the pope's nephew, who had been nominated rector in temporalities in Romagna, Bologna, and Bertinoro on 24 May 1309[98] – transported the considerable sum of 100,000 gold florins (200,000 according to the report by Cardinal Bérenger Frédol), his escort was suddenly attacked between Bologna and Modena by the people of Reggio. Raimond himself was taken captive, tortured, and put to death, his mutilated corpse displayed through the streets of Modena to the exultation of the crowd.[99] This barbaric behaviour led to an interdict on the city, which lasted until 1327.[100]

The vicissitudes of Clement's policy in the Papal State reflected a deteriorating situation, in which the status and authority of the pope was undermined by local circumstances. The dividing line between Guelphs and Ghibellines, which remained rather theoretical, was of little relevance, since disregard of the pope and his envoys had become the prevailing attitude. The incontestable victory of the papal forces over Venice was not a Guelph victory over a Ghibelline threat, but the victory of an opportunist, heterogeneous coalition, which included the leading Guelph and Ghibelline powers, all united in their rivalry with the Queen of the Adriatic. Moreover, Clement's victory against Venice could hardly be regarded as the opening of a new era; it was, in the long term, an ephemeral episode in the unstable papal rule in its own state. This instability was the result not of the papal absence from Italy, but of the chaotic situation in the peninsula, which Clement's predecessors had also failed to resolve. In 1273, the representatives of Philip III had suggested to Gregory X the appointment of a secular ruler, obviously from the kingdom of France, for better administration of the temporalities of the Papal State. This secular arm of the papacy, the French argued, would release the pope from the need to conduct a continuous battle for political survival. Rather surprisingly, Gregory replied that he himself would welcome such an arrangement and that the Capetian monarch would undoubtedly fulfil the challenging task satisfactorily.[101]

During Clement's pontificate, the idea of a Capetian protectorate of the Papal State received new life in the writings of Pierre Dubois, whose work was dominated by two profound convictions: the indispensable nature of universal Capetian domination and the utter destruction of the

---

[98] *Ibid.*, no. 5057.
[99] The papal letters speak in terms of 'post cruente mortis supplicium' and point to Rolando da' Carboni and Francesco da Menabò as the main perpetrators of the crime: *Regestum Clementis Papae V*, nos. 10027, 10355; Tolomeo da Lucca, *Secunda Vita*, p. 52; *Notae ad vitas*, p. 93; *Acta Aragonensia*, vol. I, no. 220, p. 329; vol. III, no. 113, p. 237.
[100] M. Vaini, *Dal comune alla signoria*, p. 259.
[101] *Documents historiques inédits tirés des collections manuscrites de la bibliothèque royale*, vol. I, pp. 653–4.

temporal power of the Church.[102] Although Philip the Fair contented himself with alliances with the princes of the Rhine and, after fruitless intrigues on behalf of his brother and son, was satisfied with the annexation of Lyons,[103] the lawyer of Coutances sketched more ambitious plans for the king of France.[104] In his treatise *De recuperatione Terrae Sanctae*, Dubois suggested that 'it would be a source of much profit and honour to the king if the empire could be procured for his brother and nephews in perpetuity'.[105] From a practical perspective, Dubois called attention to the fact that most popes were old and lacked necessary military skills; being forced to fight a daily struggle for political survival, they were condemned to failure. Conversely, the king of France was the most suitable *miles papae*, who would free the popes from their unpleasant duties. Any other selection would cause 'the most grave detriment to the Roman Church, the Empire, the Holy Land, and all the Christian Republic'. Philip's rule, either directly or as suzerain, had to extend eastwards and westwards alike, and include both Muslims and Christians. Should the pope confer on the Capetians the temporal rights he himself had been accorded by the Donation of Constantine, together with the title of senator of Rome, the king of France would receive suzerainty over Naples, Sicily, Aragon, Hungary, and England, the kings of which were vassals of the pope.[106] Not satisfied with this arrangement, Dubois further extended his plans to the whole of Christendom. Thus, Lombardy should be obtained from the emperor or the electors by treaty. French influence in Spain had to be secured by armed intervention on behalf of the *infantes* de la Cerda, the grandsons of St Louis, who had been unjustly despoiled of their rights; they would be given the kingdoms of Granada and Portugal to hold as vassals of France. In this general scheme, the whole Papal State would be transferred to the custody of the king of France, who would appoint a senator of Rome and receive the homage

---

[102] E. E. Power, 'Pierre Du Bois and the Domination of France', pp. 146–50.

[103] *La chronique métrique attribuée à Geffroy de Paris*, p. 174, vv. 4359–98; *Continuatio chronici Girardi de Fracheto*, pp. 34–5. The town straddled the Saône, but extended to the Rhône, the two rivers popularly thought to mark the limits of France. In May 1271, Philip III, responding to an appeal of the inhabitants, took the city under his 'protection and special custody'. Philip IV renewed the Capetian pledge in 1290, and was welcomed by the archbishop of the city, Louis de Beaujeu. After a failed attempt at rebellion in 1312, Philip actually annexed the city, and his officials enforced royal legislation: *Ordonnances des roys de France de la troisième race*, pp. 348, 509–10; C. T. Wood, '*Regnum Francie*', pp. 139–40. On Henry's opposition (1309–10), see *Acta Imperii Angliae et Franciae*, nos. 182, 193, pp. 122, 130. Clement supported Henry's position and asked Philip to control his officers and avoid any harm to the prerogatives of the king of Germany (24 December 1310): *Constitutiones et acta publica imperatorum et regum*, vol. IV-1, no. 514, p. 469.

[104] L. Gatto, 'I problemi della guerra e della pace nel pensiero politico di Pierre Dubois', p. 177.

[105] Pierre Dubois, *De recuperatione Terre Sancte*, LXXI.116, p. 193.

[106] *Ibid.*, p. 194. Rather obviously, this part was not included in the copy of the *De recuperatione* sent to Edward I.

of those who held their territories from the pope. The Capetian prince was to deliver to the apostolic camera all revenues after deducting administrative expenses.[107]

CLEMENT V AND HENRY VII

The many challenges presented by the Papal State justified Clement's readiness to look for a suitable political partner who would advance apostolic interests more successfully. Still, Clement rejected the appeal by Albert of Habsburg to be crowned emperor. A first request in this regard had been made in February 1306 by the chancellor John, bishop of Eichstadt, and by Philip von Rathsamshausen, abbot of Päris (Basle).[108] The murder of the king of Germany on 1 May 1308, however, opened up new alternatives, while allowing Clement's more active intervention in the election of an appropriate candidate. Yet the pope had to overcome Capetian pressure for the nomination of Charles de Valois, Philip the Fair's brother and, from the perspective of the Capetian court, the most suitable candidate to fulfil the highest temporal office in Christendom.[109]

The candidacy of Charles de Valois, the pope's nominal partner in the crusade against Andronicus II Palaeologus, met with some support in the curia itself. Early in July, Cardinal Raimond de Got strongly recommended Charles de Valois to the archbishop of Cologne, pointing to the many advantages that would accompany his election in terms of justice and peace for the whole of Christendom.[110] No scholarly consensus exists as to whether this was a completely independent move, as has been argued by E. E. Stengel and G. Mollat, or whether it was a concession by Clement to Philip the Fair, as was maintained by K. Wenck and G. Lizerand.[111] If Clement wished to advance the candidacy of Charles de Valois, however, a direct address to the electors was more appropriate.

---

[107] Pierre Dubois, *Summaria brevis et compendiosa doctrina*, pp. 12–13; Pierre Dubois, *De recuperatione Terrae Sanctae*, XVII.33, p. 135; LXXI. 116, pp. 192–4; Boutaric, 'Notices et extraits de documents inédits relatifs à l'histoire de France sous Philippe le Bel', no. 30, pp. 186–9; W. I. Brandt, 'Pierre Dubois, Modern or Medieval?', p. 514. F. M. Powicke further emphasises Dubois' scorn for the Italian cities, their independence and pride, and his desire to see them defeated: F. M. Powicke, 'Pierre Dubois', p. 177. [108] Gutsche, *Die Beziehungen zwischen Reich und Kurie*, p. 18.

[109] *Acta Imperii Angliae et Franciae*, nos. 179–80, p. 119. On Philip's great concern for his brother, see Brown, 'The Prince Is Father of the King', p. 301.

[110] The cardinal solemnly declared that 'si, De[o] volente, ad hujusmodi electionem procedi contingeret, sub felici suo regimine salubriter gubernari, quietis et pacis habundare delitiis, et in suis deperditis juribus restaurationem recipere salutarem': *Collectio actorum veterum*, pp. 97–8. On the political inclinations of the electors, see Bowsky, *Henry VII in Italy*, pp. 17–22.

[111] E. E. Stengel, *Avignon und Rhens*, pp. 13–15; G. Mollat, 'Clément V', col. 1121; Wenck, *Clemens V und Heinrich VII*, p. 106; Lizerand, *Clément V et Philippe le Bel*, pp. 174–5.

The pope eventually did this, but only in October; that is, five months after the assassination of Albert of Habsburg.[112] The possibility that the cardinal acted independently may indicate the lack of papal authority in the curia, with Clement's own relatives representing party interests.[113] On the other hand, the pope's neutral attitude by itself indicates that Clement had his own scale of political priorities, which was not always identical to, nor even congruent with, that of Philip the Fair. Furthermore, Clement's future alliance with both Henry of Luxemburg and Robert of Anjou meant the construction of a new political balance in Italy, from which the Capetians were excluded; at best, they would be represented by their Angevin branch, but at the same time considerably restricted by the emperor.

The election of Henry of Luxemburg on 27 November 1308 put an end to all conjectures.[114] Both because of his family background and the high esteem that he enjoyed among contemporaries, Henry appeared to be an ideal candidate to curb Capetian ambitions and to advance papal authority in Italy. The chronicle attributed to Geffroy de Paris pointed out that Clement's main reason for supporting Henry was the latter's formal oath that he would safeguard the rights and privileges of Rome.[115] This possibility is supported by R. Davidsohn, who suggests that Clement V indeed had hoped to use imperial power to re-establish papal authority in Italy, a goal corroborated by later developments. R. Caggese's claim that the pope's main concern was 'to restore imperial power under the protection of the Church'[116] seems rather impracticable in the light of the many difficulties encountered by the pope and his envoys in maintaining, let alone restoring, apostolic authority in Italy.

Whatever the priorities of the pope, contemporary authors, especially in Italy and the Empire, referred to Henry's election as a reflection of the will of Providence to save the Roman Church from being totally subjugated to the Capetian dynasty. According to Dino Compagni, the main reason for Henry's election was the desire of the pope and the cardinals to enlist 'a [secular] hand or defender'.[117] More unambiguously, Villani informed his readers of the pope's reluctance to support the candidacy of

---

[112] See the full authority entrusted by Philip the Fair to Gérard de Landry, Pierre Barrière, and Hugues de la Celle to advance the candidacy of his brother (11 June 1308): Boutaric, 'Notices et extraits de documents inédits relatifs à l'histoire de France sous Philippe le Bel', no. 31, p. 189.

[113] G. Mollat refers to this state of affairs not only with regard to the pontificate of Clement V but also with regard to the whole Avignon period: 'La diplomatie pontificale au XIVe siècle', p. 512.

[114] *Cronica S. Petri Erfordensis Moderna*, p. 441; Matthew of Nüwenburg, *Cronica*, p. 180.

[115] *La chronique métrique attribuée à Geffroy de Paris*, p. 162, vv. 3711–12.

[116] Davidsohn, *Geschichte von Florenz*, vol. III, p. 414; Caggese, *Roberto d'Angiò e i suoi tempi*, vol. I, p. 118. For Clement, the papal curia, and the election of Henry VII, see Stengel, *Avignon und Rhens*, pp. 298–314. [117] Dino Compagni, *Cronica*, pp. 219–21.

Charles de Valois, notwithstanding the pressure exerted by the Capetian court, 'since the pope recognised that its requests were in complete opposition to ecclesiastical liberty'. Accordingly, after secret deliberations with Cardinal da Prato, the prelate wrote to the German electors to encourage them 'to act as quickly as possible, without further delays, in order to prevent the rule and jurisdiction of the empire falling into French hands'.[118] In contrast with Villani's own report of the early alliance between Bertrand de Got and Philip the Fair in St Jean d'Angély, his description of Clement's support of Henry of Luxemburg included all the components of an independent papal policy, which opposed Capetian interests. Villani's view is supported by some German chroniclers, who regarded Clement as the main party in hastening the electors to reach a decision on behalf of Henry of Luxemburg.[119]

Whether the election of Henry of Luxemburg was the pope's intention or not is still open to analysis. What is clear, however, is that Clement gave a very cordial welcome to the German ambassadors, who requested papal blessing for their king (2 June 1309). On the occasion, the bishops of Basle and Chur, the counts of Savoy, Flanders, and Charpont, and the dauphin of Vienne reported to the pope on Henry's devotion to the Holy Land, the recovery of which should take precedence over all other concerns.[120] In a solemn consistory held in the convent of the Dominicans at Avignon (26 July), Clement confirmed the election of Henry of Luxemburg and announced that the imperial coronation would take place in St Peter's Cathedral after the Council of Vienne, that is, on 2 February 1312. If Clement were prevented from consecrating the emperor, the pope reserved for himself the right to postpone the date.[121] Couched in terms of the Gelasian tradition, the encyclical issued at this stage manifested a complete harmony between *sacerdotium* and *regnum*. Clement stressed the desirable co-operation between the two superior authorities of Christendom, whom he identified with the two main stars

---

[118] Villani, *Cronica*, l. viii, c. 101, p. 135; Villani, *Istorie fiorentine*, l. viii, c. 101, pp. 197–201. This version was echoed by other sources, as well; see *Pisaner Chronik*, pp. 248–9.

[119] *Monachi Fürstenfeldensis Chronica*, pp. 29–30.

[120] Henry's representatives did not mince words in depicting their king's devotion to both the Holy Land and the Roman Church: 'non ociose, non perfuntorie set seriose ad negocium intendens et, cum dictus dominus noster Romanorum rex negocium Terre sancte pre omnibus aliis negociis mundi in intentione cordis sui gerat et amplectetur prosequendum, ut cum maiori potentia et effectu pleniori eidem negotio intendere possit, ac defensioni sacrosancte Romane Ecclesie supradicte' (*Acta Henrici VII*, no. 1, pp. 1–3); *Notae ad vitas*, p. 81. Norman Housley considers the emperor-elect's promise to go on a crusade as 'a powerful bribe': Housley, *The Italian Crusades*, p. 80.

[121] *Regestum Clementis Papae V*, nos. 4302–3, 4305; Jean de St Victor, *Prima Vita*, p. 16; Tolomeo da Lucca, *Secunda Vita*, p. 34; *Chronicon fratris Francisci Pipini*, p. 748; Wenck, *Clemens V und Heinrich VII*, pp. 132–40.

fixed by God to rule over inferior worlds. Clement further expressed his confidence in the mutual respect and complete concord that would prevail in the relationship between pope and emperor.[122]

Nevertheless, Clement took certain precautions. The pope displayed a series of gestures of goodwill towards Robert of Anjou, king of Naples, including his release from payment of the census.[123] He also appointed Robert rector of Romagna and the county of Bertinoro for an indefinite period of time, with the exception of Bologna, Ferrara, and their surrounding districts (19 August 1310).[124] Both pope and king thus conveniently ignored Robert's former oath – taken less than a year earlier, when as the nominal king of Sicily he had paid liege homage to Clement – that he would never accept any other papal office or dignity. [125] The pope's confidence in Robert of Anjou was substantiated by past experience since from the time that Charles of Anjou defeated Manfred at Benevento, the Angevins had been faithful and effective papal vassals. Clement thus tried to create a new political balance in Italy by the joint rule of the Angevins and the house of Luxemburg, who were expected to replace the chaotic rule of the *signorie*. To complete his political scheme, Clement renewed an old project of Pope Nicholas III, that of a marriage alliance between the daughter of Henry of Luxemburg and the son of Robert of Anjou, to be cemented by granting the kingdom of Arles as a dowry.[126] The papal scheme was also meant to prevent Henry's imperial coronation from deteriorating into a Ghibelline defiance of papal authority.

Clement also made gestures of goodwill towards the emperor-elect. He approved the election of Louis of Savoy as senator of Rome and

---

[122] *Divine sapientie, Clementinarum,* l. ii, tit. ix, c. un., *CIC,* vol. ii, col. 1149; *Collectio actorum veterum,* pp. 217–25; *Regestum Clementis Papae V,* no. 4304; *Acta Henrici VII,* no. 2, pp. 3–6.

[123] *Regestum Clementis Papae V,* nos. 4345, 4589. Some chroniclers criticised papal policy as manipulative and contrary to Clement's former alliance with Henry: *Annales Forolivienses,* p. 59; *Gesta archiepiscoporum Magdeburgensium,* p. 428.

[124] *Regestum Clementis Papae V,* nos. 10347, 7246–7; *Codex Diplomaticus Dominii Temporalis S. Sedis,* no. 608, pp. 435–6.

[125] Bitter experience with the successors of Frederick Barbarossa caused Clement to include in Robert's homage solemn promises that the kingdom of Sicily would never be united with the Empire and that Robert and his heirs would never become emperors, kings of the Romans, rulers of Tuscany or Lombardy, or even accept an office in other papal lands: *Regestum Clementis Papae V,* no. 4782.

[126] *Constitutiones et acta publica imperatorum et regum,* vol. iv-1, no. 514, p. 473, fol. 15. For the nomination of Henry's proctors to negotiate the marriage (10 March 1312), see *Acta Henrici VII,* no. 139, pp. 218–19; *Acta Aragonensia,* vol. i, no. 196, p. 281. Clement's policy, however, was quite ambivalent in this regard. Notwithstanding his own declaration that 'he would sin mortally should he impede that matrimony from which might come peace between Ghibellines and Guelphs', the pope later wrote to Philip the Fair that he would not consent to the granting of the Arelate to any person or entity except the Holy Roman Church (1 May 1311). See *Constitutiones et acta publica imperatorum et regum,* vol. iv-1, no. 612, pp. 575–6.

granted Henry the right to nominate fifteen ecclesiastics in Germany. Still, the pope refused to allocate to the emperor-elect the collection of the tenth and the annates for one year on the grounds that such a concession would harm the projects for a crusade.[127] Without showing any awareness of his distinct approach to the kings of France and England, Clement accorded himself the right of *do ut des*. He urged Henry to behave like the King of Peace in Italy and to take a formal oath concerning his complete devotion to the Church at all times; this expected vow included a formal commitment not to harm the Church or its interests in any way and a confirmation of all privileges granted on its behalf by the previous kings of the Romans and emperors. To these requests for goodwill, the pope enclosed a detailed list of territorial and political claims that was more far-reaching than ever. Henry was asked to give up imperial rule over Perugia and Castello, to acknowledge papal rule over each of the key communes and areas of the entire Romagna and the Patrimony of St Peter in Tuscany, and specifically to grant the pope all rights and jurisdiction pertaining to all the territories listed.[128]

At this stage, prior to the imperial coronation, all advantages were on Clement's side. Henry endorsed most of the papal requests at Hagenau (17 August 1310); he expressed his readiness to go on a crusade, to defend the Church, and to honour its privileges in Rome and the Papal State.[129] Yet, in his territorial concessions, he did not specifically mention the cities of Bologna and Orvieto, the county of Bertinoro, and Arce Cesarum, a fortress near Terni. Nor did he retain the clause 'integrally with all the cities, lands, limits, boundaries, and confines, and with all the rights and jurisdictions of the same', which Clement had carefully inserted after each of the major cities and regions for which he claimed papal supremacy.[130] The pope was not ready to bargain and called the attention of the emperor-elect to these 'few, light omissions', which he charitably ascribed to the carelessness of the scribe.[131] In Lausanne,

---

[127] *Regestum Clementis Papae V*, no. 7500; *Constitutiones et acta publica imperatorum et regum*, vol. IV-I, nos. 390, 449, pp. 338–9, 392; *Acta Henrici VII*, no. 19, pp. 24–6.

[128] *Constitutiones et acta publica imperatorum et regum*, vol. IV-I, no. 391, pp. 340–2; *Acta Henrici VII*, no. 26, pp. 42–5. See the papal letters of the same day calling on the prelates of Italy to bring their flock back to the obedience of the Holy See: *Regestum Clementis Papae V*, no. 6332; *Acta Henrici VII*, nos. 27–37, pp. 45–8.

[129] Henry's representatives claimed in his name 'quod tanquam princeps catholicus advocatus, et defensor sancte Romane Ecclesie iuvabimus ipsam, sibique assistemus contra quoscumque occupantes, invadentes vel turbantes provincias ipsas vel terras, vel aliquam ipsarum partem'. The contemporary record emphasised the fact that the king swore to respect the obligations he had contracted towards the Church 'viva voce', with his hands on the Gospels: *Acta Henrici VII*, no. 25, pp. 38–42; *Constitutiones et acta publica imperatorum et regum*, vol. IV-I, nos. 294–9, 513, pp. 255–65, 467–8.

[130] *Constitutiones et acta publica imperatorum et regum*, vol. IV-I, no. 393, pp. 343–6.

[131] *Ibid.*, vol. IV-I, no. 438, pp. 382–4; *Acta Henrici VII*, no. 38, pp. 48–50.

Henry finally removed all the apprehensions of the papal curia (11 October). The emperor-elect recognised his obligations towards the Church and, with unprecedented generosity, acknowledged the papal areas of influence. He also declared his intention 'to favour the devoted and pious sons of the Church', a statement of his somewhat optimistic hopes of avoiding any confrontation with the Guelphs.[132] According to Villani, Henry further declared that he would 'regard the Florentines as a whole, without distinction of parties among them, as his faithful subjects and turn their city into his capital and core of the empire'.[133] Other chroniclers praised Henry's pursuit of peace and his genuine attempt to end the perpetually chaotic situation in Italy.[134] True, the concessions of Henry VII were meant to pave the way for his journey to Rome by neutralising the pope's hesitancy and, no less importantly, the Guelphs' latent opposition.[135] Nevertheless, as William Bowsky has argued, 'Never before had an emperor bound himself in this way.'[136] Henry's concessions created, if only for a short time, the illusion of peaceful coexistence between the two swords, a concept that had not yet lost its magic in the early *trecento*.[137]

Henry received his reward on 1 September 1310 in the form of a long series of papal gestures of goodwill. In an encyclical to all cities and prelates in Italy, Clement ordered that Henry be received peacefully and obediently as their temporal lord.[138] Two months earlier, the pope had assured the representatives of Guelph cities in Lombardy that Henry would cherish and love them in their present condition and rights as suits a just king and a pacific lord. To guarantee the accomplishment of such commendable purposes, Clement wrote to Henry along the same lines, referring to his journey to Rome as one taken 'for the honour of the Church and its protection, for bringing peace to the warring factions in Italy, a land comprising a third of Christendom'.[139] In parallel, the pope

---

[132] *Constitutiones et acta publica imperatorum et regum*, vol. IV-I, nos. 391, 441, 454–5, pp. 340–2, 387–8, 395–401. Matthew of Nüwenburg refers to Henry's good intentions towards the Guelphs and his early attempts to foster a peace between them and the Ghibellines. Still, the emperor soon realised that his hopes were too optimistic and abandoned his original plan: Matthew of Nüwenburg, *Cronica*, p. 182.   [133] Villani, *Istorie fiorentine*, l. ix, c. 7, p. 7.

[134] Thus, the chronicle of Parma described Henry's main goal in terms of 'faciendo fieri pacem ubique inter omnes': *Chronicon Parmense* (de Rubeis), p. 254.

[135] On Henry's delegations to the Italian city-states and to the Capetian court to encourage support of his journey, see F. Vercauteren, 'Henri de Jodoigne, légiste, clerc, et conseiller des princes', pp. 461–7.   [136] Bowsky, 'Clement V and the Emperor-elect', p. 57.

[137] E. R. Labande, 'Les idées politiques de Dante', pp. 23–35.

[138] *Regestum Clementis Papae V*, nos. 6336–40.

[139] *Ibid.*, no. 6334; *Constitutiones et acta publica imperatorum et regum*, vol. IV-I, nos. 435–6, 441, pp. 375–81, 387–8; *Acta Aragonensia*, vol. I, no. 185, pp. 265–6. This view was echoed by the Fürstenfeld chronicler, who refers to Clement's hopes that Henry's journey would bring peace to Italy and return its population to apostolic authority, especially the Romans, 'qui contra fas

nominated Cardinal Arnaud de Pellegrue as his legate *a latere* during Henry's journey and Cardinal Arnaud de Falguières as his legate in Lombardy and Tuscany to help the emperor-elect to re-establish peace there.[140] These nominations, made in response to Henry's specific request, were regarded by contemporary authors as additional proof of the alliance between emperor and pope and their cordial relationship at this stage.[141]

Papal support of Henry VII won wide approval, including that of some Guelphs, who were well aware of the hazards inherent in the Capetian alternative.[142] Dante Alighieri went further, depicting Henry's approach to Rome in eschatological dimensions. All Italy must rejoice, wipe its tears, and prepare for the great moment, he wrote; Henry's mercy, generosity, and piety should pave the way for a new era that would rebuild Italy from its ruins.[143] Following the pope's request to the cities of Lombardy and Tuscany to support the emperor-elect, Dante referred to the new alliance between *regnum* and *sacerdotium* in very supportive terms, borrowed from papalist tradition. The Florentine poet urged his country-men to follow the papal call and contribute their share to the harmonious coexistence between the two stars.[144] Dante did not remain alone. Chroniclers from the empire heaped praise upon Henry VII, whose devotion, love of peace, and moral qualities, they said, justified the pope's confidence in him.[145] Henry's affinity to French culture and his proficiency in the French language greatly enhanced his popularity in the Capetian Kingdom, even if his candidacy could have appeared as a

---

de sua malitia successorem beati Apostolici pulsum de Sede propria sicut peregrinum in terra coëgerunt [sic] degere aliena': *Monachi Fürstenfeldensis Chronica*, pp. 42–3.

[140] *Regestum Clementis Papae V*, nos. 6338, 6341–69, 7548–81; *Constitutiones et acta publica imperatorum et regum*, vol. IV-1, nos. 390, 435, 437, pp. 338–40, 375–8, 381–2; *Acta Henrici VII*, no. 19, p. 24.

[141] *Storie Pistoresi*, pp. 50–1; Tolomeo da Lucca, *Secunda Vita*, p. 37; Albertino Mussato, *Heinrici VII Caesaris Historia Augusta*, cols. 330–1; *Pisaner Chronik*, p. 249; *La chronique métrique attribuée à Geffroy de Paris*, p. 163, vv. 3799–3801. The double stand of Arnaud de Pellegrue, however, led Henry to ask the pope to recall him in 1313: *Constitutiones et acta publica imperatorum et regem*, vol. IV-2, no. 1006, pp. 1048–51; Dino Compagni, *Cronica*, p. 248. Arnaud de Falguières was appointed rector of Sabina: *Regestum Clementis Pope V*, nos. 8750–61.

[142] Agnolo di Tura supposedly voiced God's will that the election of Henry of Luxemburg was meant to avoid the risk 'che la Chiesa di Roma fusse al tutto sottoposta a la casa di Francia': Agnolo di Tura, *Cronaca Senese*, pp. 303–4.

[143] For Dante, the renewal of the Empire meant peace, a reflection of the heavenly harmony that passes all understanding: E. Sharwood Smith, 'Dante and the World Empire', pp. 107–38.

[144] 'Hic est quem Petrus, Dei vicarius, honorificare nos monet; quem Clemens nunc Petri successor luce Apostolicae benedictionis illuminat; ut ubi radius spiritualis non sufficit, ibi splendor minoris luminaris illustret': Dante Alighieri, 'Letter to the Princes and Peoples of Italy' (Letter V), *Dantis Alagherii Epistolae*, p. 58. Paget Toynbee pointed out (*ibid.*, n. 6): 'Dante here accepts the symbolism against which he argues in the *De Monarchia* (III.4) and which he rejects in the *Commedia* (*Purg.* xvi. 107–108).'

[145] *Cronica Reinhardsbrunnensis*, p. 651; *Cronica S. Petri Erfordensis Moderna*, p. 445; *Excerpta ex expositione Hugonis de Rutlingen*, p. 132; John of Viktring, p. 377.

counter-measure to Charles de Valois. In England, as well, contemporary authors described Henry as 'an honest man, valorous in military exercises, devoted to God and to the Church, and just to the people'.[146] Henry's many virtues justified, in their view, Clement's haste in confirming his election and undertaking to hold the imperial coronation in two years.[147]

Up to the end of 1310, therefore, Clement's policy towards the emperor-elect acquired all the characteristics of a well-founded alliance that could assure papal interests in Italy and solve the difficulties formerly encountered by papal envoys in the troubled peninsula. Moreover, what seemed to be an independent papal policy was welcomed by most contemporaries, who were well aware of Philip's pressure to promote his own candidate for the Empire. From its very beginning, however, Henry's journey to Rome hinted at the problems that eventually caused the alliance between pope and emperor to collapse completely, notwithstanding the good intentions displayed by both sides. Clement saw the journey to Rome as a means of crushing those who rebelled against apostolic authority while restoring usurped lands to the Papal State. He was not interested in any plans that Henry might have for the restitution of imperial rights in Italy. Although the emperor-elect was ready to protect ecclesiastical rights, it is rather difficult to see how he might have seen his journey to Rome in the narrow terms dictated by papal interests. On the contrary, Henry had made clear his intention to bring about a *renovatio imperii* and the restoration of imperial rights. These clashing perspectives created a fragile basis for a long-term alliance between *regnum* and *sacerdotium*. In less than two years, Dante was accusing the pope of having betrayed the confidence of the emperor-elect, thereby harming the chances for peace and renewal for the whole peninsula.[148] Henry's journey to Rome further destroyed any illusions regarding harmonious

---

[146] *Flores historiarum*, p. 144; *La chronique métrique attribuée à Geffroy de Paris*, p. 161, vv. 3685–98.

[147] *Continuatio chronici Girardi de Fracheto*, p. 32; *Continuationis chronici Guillelmi de Nangiaco*, pp. 370, 372–3; *Annales Osterhovenses*, p. 555.

[148] Before the Gascon sets his low intrigue
to snare high Henry, men will start to speak
of his disregard of money and fatigue . . .
The prefect of the holy court will be
a man who will profess his cause in public
while working to defeat it secretly.
But after that God will not long permit
his simony, he shall be stuffed away
where Simon Magus, headfirst in the pit,
pays for his guilt.
Dante Alighieri, *Divina Commedia*, Paradiso, c. XVII, v. 82, c. XXX, vv. 142–8.

See D. Mancusi-Ungaro, *Dante and the Empire*, pp. 46–50.

coexistence, whether between emperor and pope or between them both and the city-states. The tortuous ways of the *Romfahrt* clearly indicated the consolidation of the city-states, which became independent of any wheeling and dealing between emperor and pope.[149] Henry's presence in Italy further hastened the transition from communes to *signorie* while sharpening old feuds between Guelphs and Ghibellines.[150]

On 6 January 1311, Henry of Luxemburg was crowned with the iron crown by the archbishop of Milan in the presence of representatives of most Italian cities.[151] The elaborate ceremonials, however, did not lessen the political tension created by the emperor-elect's journey to Rome 'with a numerous army'.[152] Although Venice was represented by a splendid embassy and allowed Henry to enlist 1,400 crossbowmen in its territory, its representatives refused to swear him fealty. Worse still, the absence of Florence and its allies hinted at latent opposition, which soon crystallised in the League of Tuscany.[153] Henry's journey thus gradually served as a catalyst for the unification of the Guelphs, who joined ranks against what they saw as a German threat.[154] The renewed solidarity of the Guelph camp was not based on disdain towards Henry VII, who might have appeared, at least at first, as an ideal candidate for the Empire; he certainly appeared as such to the pope. The opposition to the emperor-elect was dictated by the unique political situation of large areas of the peninsula. In Piedmont, Lombardy, Veneto, Emilia, Liguria, and Tuscany, many territories were, at least in theory, still subject to the direct jurisdiction of the Holy Roman Empire. Even communes which dated their legitimate existence as semi-autonomous political entities to the Peace of Constance (1183) had to bow to supervisory imperial rights. On

---

[149] Kraack, *Rom oder Avignon?*, pp. 23–34.

[150] Bowsky, 'Dante's Italy', p. 94; J. K. Hyde, 'Contemporary Views on Faction and Civil Strife in Thirteenth- and Fourteenth-Century Italy', p. 296.

[151] *Constitutiones et acta publica imperatorum et regum*, vol. IV-1, nos. 518–19, pp. 479–80; Villani, *Istorie fiorentine*, l. ix, c. 9, pp. 9–10. The event was widely reported in contemporary records; see *Chronicon Mutinense*, col. 569; Albertino Mussato, *Heinrici VII Caesaris Historia Augusta*, cols. 338–9; *Historia Gulielmi et Albrigeti Cortusiorum*, col. 779. Clement V reported this development to Philip the Fair in a secret letter (19 January 1311) only a few days later. The original is in the Archives nationales de Paris (L294, no. 33) and has been described by B. Barbiche, *Les actes pontificaux originaux des Archives nationales de Paris*, p. 73. On the category of secret letters, see P. Gasnault, 'L'élaboration des lettres secrètes des papes d'Avignon', pp. 209–22.

[152] *Continuationis chronici Guillelmi de Nangiaco*, p. 381.

[153] *Constitutiones et acta publica imperatorum et regum*, vol. IV-1, no. 597, pp. 558–9; *Acta Henrici VII*, pt 2, nos. 13, 16, pp. 10–11, 13–15; Villani, *Cronica*, l. ix, c. 9, p. 152; *Cronaca Senese di autore anonimo*, p. 90; *Luccheser Fortsetzung derselben Chronik*, p. 250. Some records point to Robert of Anjou as the sinister conspirator behind this development: Petri Azarii, *Liber Gestorum in Lombardia*, p. 14.

[154] Orvieto offers a case in point. Following the entry of Henry's army into Italy, the city joined the Guelph league. Though the local Ghibellines, hoping to enjoy imperial support, used the occasion to rebel, they were eventually crushed by the Guelphs, who were reinforced by an army from Perugia (August 1313). See Waley, *Medieval Orvieto*, pp. 86–92.

the other hand, since the death of Frederick II (13 December 1250), most areas of Italy had enjoyed relative freedom from imperial control.[155] The fragile dividing line between historical rights and usurpation determined the tortuous path of Henry's journey and suggests the reactions that were to be expected from most communes.

Guelph opinion was divided between those who took the papal support of Henry seriously and those who ignored it on the grounds that any emperor would be bound to favour the Ghibellines and could not bring any good to the Guelphs. The first point of view was represented by Padua and its spokesman, Albertino Mussato; the second was voiced by Florence, whose White Guelphs might well have swung the decision the other way had they not been excluded from political influence. The attitudes to Henry VII thus acquired much significance not only with regard to the emperor-elect but also, and perhaps first and foremost, with regard to Clement V, since his support of Henry was a matter of general knowledge by the beginning of 1311. Florence, at the time ruled by Black Guelphs, provides a good indication of the climate of opinion among the 'most faithful allies of the Church and the pope'. In the summer of 1309, the Florentines had made diplomatic efforts at the courts of Naples, Paris, and Avignon to prevent the emperor's journey out of fear that Henry would harm their *contado*, large areas of which were directly dependent upon the Empire and had been subjected to Florence by force.[156] One year later, the city directed a league army of 4,000 cavalry, with the active participation of Bologna, Lucca, and Siena, that was expected to act 'in honour of Christ, the Church, the pope, the cardinals, and the king, Robert of Anjou' (1 May 1310).[157] At this stage, the Florentines, like other members of the league, still recognised the imperial status of Henry, which had been formally recognised by the pope.[158] Neither this recognition nor their declared devotion to the Church and the pope at its head, however, carried much weight later on in Florentine politics.[159]

Soon after Henry entered Italy, it became clear that the emperor-elect was unable to bridge old feuds and that expectations of the renovation of the Empire by peaceful means were premature.[160] In a general

---

[155] This state of affairs was emphasised in contemporary chronicles; see *Gesta archiepiscoporum Magdeburgensium*, p. 428; *Annales Halesbrunnenses Maiores*, p. 48.

[156] *Constitutiones et acta publica imperatorum et regum*, vol. IV-1, no. 597, pp. 558–9; *Acta Henrici VII*, pt 2, nos. 3, 12, pp. 3, 9–10.

[157] *Italienische Analekten zur Reichsgeschichte des XIV. Jahrhunderts*, nos. 1–6, pp. 21–4, nos. 9–10, p. 25.

[158] Bowsky, 'Florence and Henry of Luxemburg', pp. 184–6.

[159] G. Holmes found these circumstances reminiscent of the period following the collapse of the Hohenstaufen forty years earlier. Facing an external threat throughout Tuscany, the Blacks, like their ancestors confronting the Ghibellines, decided that they could survive only by invoking Neapolitan help: Holmes, *Florence, Rome, and the Origins of the Renaissance*, pp. 181–2.

[160] Vaini, *Dal comune alla signoria*, pp. 254–7.

assembly held in Milan, Henry announced his intention to remove the rulers of Lombardy and to nominate 'competent *podestà*, rectors, vicars, and prefects at the royal pleasure' instead. A vicar-general would also be appointed to administer the region during the monarch's absence (10 January 1311).[161] Within four days, Henry designated his brother-in-law, Count Amadeus de Savoy, to this post. The economic and political results of Henry's administrative reform became evident before long: 300,000 gold florins a year was the sum that fifty Lombard cities and lords were required to pay in order to bear the expenses of imperial administration. This considerable fiscal burden was not accompanied by political concessions that would have made the new regime more palatable. On the contrary, from the list of twenty-four imperial vicars – half of whom cannot be identified – five were well-known Tuscan Ghibelline or White Guelphs exiles and one was a leading Pisan Ghibelline. None of the great tyrants in power or the aspiring *signori* of Lombardy received an imperial vicarship.[162] These decisions provided a clear indication of Henry's attempt to renew imperial rule in Italy in a very direct way. Such a policy, accompanied by a display of force, could hardly have favoured a welcoming of the emperor-elect among the already reluctant Guelphs.[163]

Support of the emperor-elect was not much stronger among Ghibelline bastions. One month after Henry's coronation in Milan, blood flowed in the streets of the city and cries of 'death to all Germans' rang out (12 February 1311).[164] The downfall of the powerful family of della Torre[165] and the threatening presence of the imperial army acted as catalysts for the

---

[161] *Constitutiones et acta publica imperatorum et regum*, vol. IV-I, no. 517, pp. 478–9.

[162] Petri Azarii, *Liber Gestorum in Lombardia*, p. 13; Bowsky, *Henry VII in Italy*, pp. 91–2, 236–7.

[163] The monk of Fürstenfeld refers to the fact that after Henry achieved peace and stability in Germany, his journey to Italy was meant 'rempublicam augmentare', namely, to return the cities of Lombardy to imperial rule: *Monachi Fürstenfeldensis Chronica*, p. 32.

[164] Villani, *Istorie fiorentine*, l. ix, c. 11, pp. 11–13; Paulin, bishop of Pozzuoli, *Quinta Vita*, p. 83; *Nicolai episcopi Botrontinensis Relatio de itinere italico Henrici VII*, p. 506; *Annales Genuenses*, p. 77.

[165] Villani, *Cronica*, l. ix, c. 11, pp. 152–3; Petri Azarii, *Liber Gestorum in Lombardia*, pp. 15, 17; *Chronicon Estense*, col. 372; John of Viktring, pp. 368–9; Matthew of Nüwenburg, *Cronica*, p. 182. Since 1302, this noble Guelph family had ruled the city with allies from Cremona, Lodi, and Vercelli. It seems, however, that its links with the papal curia were quite problematic, since on 21 October 1309 Clement asked the bishops of Padua and Turin to arrest Guido della Torre and to deliver him to the archbishop of Milan. On 11 December 1311, Henry sent an imperial force to occupy the fortress of Vigevano, which was controlled by Guido. Afterwards, the Torrini were deprived of their *signoria* and replaced by an imperial vicar; they were further forced to exchange the kiss of peace with the Viscontis, their Ghibelline rivals: *Constitutiones et acta publica imperatorum et regum*, vol. IV-I, nos. 509, 660–660a, pp. 461–3, 628–31; *Acta Henrici VII*, no. 121, pp. 189–91. After della Torre's plot against Henry was discovered, the family was forced to flee into exile (12 February 1312). On 20 September 1313, Matteo Visconti was proclaimed lord and rector-general of Milan: *Regestum Clementis Papae V*, nos. 4832–3.

eruption of violent riots in the city.[166] Milan did not remain alone, its example soon followed by the Guelph cities of Lombardy. Cremona, Crema, Brescia, and Reggio expelled the Ghibellines along with the imperial vicars.[167] Parma and Lodi ostracised the Ghibellines but allowed the imperial vicars to remain.[168] Though Florence obviously supported this development, the rebellion in Lombardy was not its initiative and the movement lacked internal unity.[169] One after another, the insurgent communes submitted to a mere show of force by the emperor-elect. In May, Cremona capitulated peacefully and its leader, who had led the rebellion, fled into exile.[170] After a cruel four-month siege, Brescia was forced to surrender (18 September).[171] All the city defenders were members of the Guelph party, with Theobald Brusati at their head. Though they had received military help from Florence, they did not succeed in challenging the imperial army.[172] Well aware of his achievement, Henry sent one of the city gates to Rome as a trophy.[173] In the light of these dramatic events, Clement assumed a paternalistic approach towards his defeated sons. He wrote to Henry and asked forgiveness for the inhabitants of Brescia on the grounds that 'it is befitting the clemency of royal benignity that you shower an abundance of mercy upon your subjects, whom the blindness of error is leading away from royal fealty'.[174] Although Clement recognised that the rebellion in Brescia was a 'blind error', the pope's intervention suggests the difficult alternatives that faced him in the clash between his declared ally, Henry VII, and the traditional allies of the papacy, the Guelphs.

The events in Lombardy put an end to Henry's mission as an 'angel of peace' and gradually dragged both pope and emperor-elect into the

---

[166] During the riots in the city, an interdict was pronounced, but Clement annulled it soon afterwards (28 August 1311): *Regestum Clementis Papae V*, no. 7274.

[167] Albertino Mussato, *Heinrici VII Caesaris Historia Augusta*, cols. 342–5, 364–5; *Chronicon Mutinense*, col. 570; Matthew of Nüwenburg, *Cronica*, p. 183; *Chronicon Parmense* (de Rubeis), pp. 256–7.

[168] *Nicolai episcopi Botrontinensis Relatio de itinere italico Henrici VII*, pp. 506–11; *Continuatio Mellicensis*, p. 511.

[169] The chronicles of Parma include in this league Robert of Anjou 'et multi de Romagna': *Chronicon Parmense* (de Rubeis), p. 259; *Annales Parmenses Maiores*, p. 752.

[170] Villani, *Cronica*, l. ix, c. xiv–xv, p. 155; Villani, *Istorie fiorentine*, l. ix, c. 16, p. 16; A. Cavalcabò, *Le ultime lotte del comune di Cremona*, pp. 41ff.

[171] Villani, *Cronica*, l. ix, c. xx, pp. 157–8; Villani, *Istorie fiorentine*, l. ix, c. 16, pp. 16–17, c. 19, pp. 19–21; *Heinrici Rebdorfensis Annales*, p. 511; John of Viktring, pp. 370–1; *Continuationis chronici Guillelmi de Nangiaco*, p. 385; *La chronique métrique attribuée à Geffroy de Paris*, pp. 166–8, vv. 3939–4036.   [172] *Acta Henrici VII*, pt 2, no. 46, pp. 37–8.

[173] Dino Compagni, *Cronica*, p. 239; *Cronaca Senese di autore anonimo*, p. 91; Albertino Mussato, *Heinrici VII Caesaris Historia Augusta*, cols. 393–5.

[174] *Constitutiones et acta publica imperatorum et regum*, vol. IV-1, no. 648, pp. 617–18; *Acta Henrici VII*, no. 117, pp. 183–4. For the previous intervention of papal legates, see Albertino Mussato, *Heinrici VII Caesaris Historia Augusta*, cols. 383–8; for Henry's response to the legates' intervention (7 December 1311), see *Acta Imperii Angliae et Franciae*, no. 223, pp. 147–8.

dead-end of Italian politics. On 1 April 1311, the Tuscan communes begged the pope to prevent Henry VII from entering Tuscany.[175] At the same time, Florence drastically changed its approach, referring to the emperor-elect as 'king of Germany' or as 'emperor of the Germans', thus excluding itself and perhaps also other Italian city-states from his rule.[176] By the end of the year, a new Guelph league came into existence in Bologna, the members of which pledged themselves 'to return the province of Lombardy entirely to the party of the Holy Mother Church and the Guelphs'. Immediately following Jesus, the Virgin Mary, and all saints and angels in heaven, the league ranked the Holy Mother Church, Pope Clement V, the cardinals, Robert of Anjou, his brothers and descendants, and all the royal house of France.[177] What began as a spontaneous resistance to imperial power thus gradually turned into a holy alliance of an international nature, embracing both the Angevins and the Capetians. Beyond the new alliance stood Florence, which succeeded in using Guelphism to resist imperial power. Less clear at this stage was the stand of Clement V, though there are clear signs of his hesitation. The pope indeed faced difficult alternatives: on the one hand, a renewed Guelph party was calling for his leadership, although it had demonstrated a dubious devotion to the pope and his policy in the past and had strong Capetian–Angevin inclinations in the present. On the other hand, Henry VII demonstrated aspirations to restore imperial rights, a goal that could only present new challenges to the already problematic situation of the bishop of Rome on the peninsula. On 22 June 1311, Clement asked Henry to affirm his oath of fealty to the Church after his coronation and to transmit four copies of it to the papal legates.[178] This was, however, a rather weak panacea for the growing gap between pope and emperor.

On 21 October, Henry came to Genoa to spend the winter. By this time, his army was critically diminished by increasing defections among both Germans and Ghibellines. The city received the emperor-elect with great honour 'as its lord . . . and they acknowledged his lordship over the whole area; and this was greatly evaluated because of the freedom and strength of the Genoese, who were so powerful that no Christian city could equal them'.[179] The warm welcome of Henry VII in Genoa,

---

[175] See the pope's letter to Perugia (18 May 1311): *Regestum Clementis Papae V*, no. 7516.

[176] *Constitutiones et acta publica imperatorum et regum*, vol. IV-1, nos. 582–4, 597, pp. 538–40, 558–9; *Acta Henrici VII*, pt 2, nos. 20, 22–4, pp. 17–22.

[177] Cavalcabò, *Le ultime lotte del comune di Cremona*, pp. 209–10. It is clear that Philip the Fair aimed at keeping Italy in a continuous state of turmoil and at perpetuating Italian dislike for imperial rule. He also translated the advantages of Henry's difficulties in Italy into the annexation of Lyons.

[178] *Regestum Clementis Papae V*, nos. 7179–80.

[179] Villani, *Istorie fiorentine*, l. ix, c. 23, p. 25; *Nicolai episcopi Botrontinensis Relatio de itinere italico Henrici VII*, pp. 519–20; Agnolo di Tura, *Cronaca Senese*, p. 315; *Annales Genuenses*, p. 77.

however, did not reflect the situation in other areas of Italy. Parma and Reggio successfully rebelled against the imperial forces on 4 and 6 December, respectively. To improve his deteriorating situation, Henry signed an alliance with Frederick III of Trinacria (March–April 1312). The main target of the alliance with the Aragonese branch of Sicily was obviously the king of Naples, Robert of Anjou, whom Henry suspected of backing the Guelph offensive. Frederick undertook to supply the imperial army with 700 horsemen and thirty galleys for the period of one year. In return, he was to be given imperial help against all of his enemies, a rather convenient definition for the nominal king of Sicily, Robert of Anjou.[180] The alliance between Henry and Frederick probably played a major role in alienating Clement from the emperor-elect at this difficult stage. The king of Trinacria, indeed, appeared to the pope to be a key obstacle to the Angevin–imperial alliance, which he warmly supported and on which he had placed his hopes for the pacification of Italy. Even worse, in the light of the negotiations concerning a marriage between the Aragonese and Luxemburg dynasties, it was feared that the treaty between Henry and Frederick could foster the unification of Sicily with the Empire, a threat which the popes had tried to obviate by all means since the pontificate of Innocent III.[181]

The imperial army left Genoa, landed at Pisa, and on 23 April 1312 set out for Rome.[182] The situation in the city was extremely chaotic at this point. Gentile and Poncello Orsini had led a successful attack on the Colonnas (November 1311).[183] To fortify their position, they asked for the assistance of Robert of Anjou, who sent his brother, Jean de Gravina. The Angevin presence in Rome was formally justified on the grounds that the king of Naples had to pay the emperor homage upon his coronation.[184] The feudal devotion of Robert of Anjou, however, was suspected by Sciarra Colonna and Louis of Savoy, who asked for the immediate arrival of Henry of Luxemburg. The suspicions of the emperor's allies

---

[180] *Constitutiones et acta publica imperatorum et regum*, vol. IV-2, nos. 765–6, pp. 754–6; *Nicolai episcopi Botrontinensis Relatio de itinere italico Henrici VII*, p. 530.

[181] Bowsky, 'Clement V and the Emperor-elect', p. 68. On the pope's apprehension over these developments, see his letter to James II and the king's reply (20 March–13 May 1312): *Acta Aragonensia*, vol. I, nos. 196, 206, pp. 281, 303.

[182] Villani, *Cronica*, l. ix, c. 37, pp. 165–6; c. 40, pp. 167–8; Villani, *Istorie fiorentine*, l. ix, c. 36, pp. 31–2.

[183] On the allotment of the city among the leading families and their fortifications, see Brentano, *Rome Before Avignon*, pp. 202–3.

[184] Jean d'Hocsem, *Gesta Pontificum Leodiensium*, p. 353; Matthew of Nüwenburg, *Cronica*, p. 184. Robert of Anjou had formerly received papal exemption from performing the act in person on the grounds that the latent tension between Guelphs and Ghibellines would only deteriorate into civil war because of the presence of both the emperor and the king in Rome (8 January 1312): *Constitutiones et acta publica imperatorum et regum*, vol. IV-2, no. 726, pp. 715–16; *Acta Henrici VII*, no. 137, pp. 216–17.

soon proved well founded. In mid-February 1312, a formal meeting of the Roman senate dismissed Louis of Savoy as senator on the grounds that 'his policy and deeds had brought the city to the verge of a civil war'.[185] At the same time, the Angevin troops barred the approaches to Ponte Molle, thus controlling access to the city via the Tiber.[186] Florence, Lucca, Siena, Perugia, and Bologna sent additional troops to strengthen the ranks of what could be defined as a Guelph army, the character of which was clearly anti-imperial.[187] At this point, the alliance between Clement V and Henry VII suffered its most crucial test. Henry asked for papal assistance against the Angevin troops, which were preventing his peaceful entry into Rome. Bound by his former undertakings, Clement was at first ready to comply, and he wrote the appropriate letters. According to the Aragonese representatives in the curia, however, a Capetian delegation convinced the pope to refrain from any interference. The request was based on the contention that papal intervention in Rome would harm the Angevins and turn them into easy prey for German aspirations.[188] Through his neutral attitude, Clement actually left Henry to his own devices (28 March 1312), a decision that Robert Davidsohn, the eminent historian of Florence, saw as the turning point in the alliance between the pope and the emperor-elect.[189]

Nicholas de Ligny, bishop of Butrinto, described the prevailing mood in Rome upon the arrival of Henry VII. The bishop had much to say about the chaotic situation, with orders and counter-orders spreading from the opposing sides. It seems that at this stage only the Colonnas stood fast for Henry of Luxemburg. The general confusion did not spare the cardinals who had been sent by the pope to perform the coronation.[190] Though the imperial army succeeded in entering Rome by 6 May, the Guelph troops occupied more than half the city while barring the way to St Peter's.[191] After futile negotiations and a fierce battle near Ponte Sant' Angelo (26 May), the legates agreed to accomplish the coronation in a new place instead of conducting the traditional ceremony in St Peter's.[192] On 29 June, the cardinal-bishop of Ostia, Niccolò

---

[185] Dupré-Theseider, *Roma dal comune di popolo alla signoria pontificia*, pp. 403–4.
[186] *Nicolai episcopi Botrontinensis Relatio de itinere italico Heinrici VII*, p. 533; Tolomeo da Lucca, *Secunda Vita*, p. 43.
[187] *Acta Henrici VII*, pt 2, no. 127, p. 102; *Cronica S. Petri Erfordensis Moderna*, p. 444; *Chronicon Mutinense*, p. 572; Albertino Mussato, *Heinrici VII Caesaris Historia Augusta*, pp. 449–60.
[188] *Acta Aragonensia*, vol. I, no. 201, pp. 291–2; Tolomeo da Lucca, *Secunda Vita*, p. 44.
[189] Davidsohn, *Geschichte von Florenz*, vol. III, p. 469.
[190] *Regestum Clementis Papae V*, nos. 7180–1.
[191] Agnolo di Tura, *Cronaca Senese*, pp. 319–21; Bowsky, *A Medieval Italian Commune*, pp. 151–7.
[192] *Nicolai episcopi Botrontinensis Relatio de itinere italico Heinrici VII*, p. 539. See also the detailed papal instructions regarding the ceremony: *Regestum Clementis Papae V*, no. 7181; *Codex Diplomaticus Dominii Temporalis S. Sedis*, no. 617, pp. 442–7.

Albertini da Patro, anointed Henry VII with holy oil in the Church of St John Lateran before a large assembly of archbishops, bishops, abbots, clergy, nobles, and citizens of Rome. Following the hymns, the cardinal, assisted by Arnaud de Falguières and Luca Fieschi, invested Henry VII of Luxemburg with the mitre, the diadem, the orb, the sceptre, and the sword.[193]

The imperial coronation, with its manifestations of violence, doomed all hope of the start of a peaceful era. Instead, a renewed conflict between pope and emperor became just as extreme and uncompromising as in the old days.[194] The chronicle of Siena, reflecting the climate of opinion in the Guelph camp, considered the papal legates to be tools of the Ghibellines. It further argues that the coronation had been carried out 'by force, according to the wishes of the Ghibellines, and the dictates of the Colonnas'.[195] Against this background, the attempt by several chroniclers to stress the continuing alliance between pope and emperor appears rather spurious.[196] The bishop of Butrinto reports the intention of Henry VII to leave Rome at once, after the coronation, in spite of the Ghibellines' efforts to persuade him to lengthen his stay. Yet, before Henry's plan materialised, he was astonished by the papal mandate to sign an armistice with Robert of Anjou (19 June).[197] In a rather approving manner, the bishop quoted the arguments of the imperial lawyers, who denied any justification of papal intervention in a conflict between the emperor and his vassal, who was accused of *lèse-majesté*. They contended that the emperor and the king of Naples were not subservient in equal measure to the temporalities of the Church; for, though Henry was a 'defender and advocate' of the Church, he was completely independent in his temporalities. Conversely, Robert was a subject vassal who had received his kingdom from the Church. If the emperor allowed Clement V to command him in his temporalities, as suited a vassal, 'he would be harming the imperial privileges which he had sworn to augment but not to diminish'.[198] This legal reasoning effectively made a mockery of Clement's

---

[193] *Constitutiones et acta publica imperatorum et regum*, vol. IV-I, nos. 644–7, pp. 606–17; *Annales Lubicenses*, p. 422; *Chronicon fratris Francisci Pipini*, p. 748; Albertino Mussato, *Heinrici VII Caesaris Historia Augusta*, pp. 460–3; Petri Azarii, *Liber Gestorum in Lombardia*, p. 15; *Cronica Reinhardsbrunnensis*, pp. 650–1; *Luccheser Fortsetzung derselben Chronik*, p. 251.

[194] See Clement's letter to Henry from July 1312: *Constitutiones et acta publica imperatorum et regum*, vol. IV-2, no. 810, pp. 811–12. [195] *Cronaca Senese di autore anonimo*, p. 94.

[196] Dino Compagni, *Cronica*, p. 258; *Les grandes chroniques de France*, p. 197; *Pisaner Chronik*, p. 249; *Chronographia regum Francorum*, pp. 193–4. In this particular passage, the *Chronographia* is actually quoting the last lines of Clement's decretal, *Romani principes*. Cf. *CIC*, vol. II, col. 1150.

[197] *Acta Imperii Angliae et Franciae*, no. 227, pp. 150–1; *Regestum Clementis Papae V*, nos. 10516, 10521.

[198] *Nicolai episcopi Botrontinensis Relatio de itinere italico Heinrici VII*, p. 542; cf. *Constitutiones et acta publica imperatorum et regum*, vol. IV-2, nos. 839–40, pp. 841–4. Contemporary chroniclers do not agree about whether the emperor did homage to the pope or not. Though Henry of Rebdorf

demands. The duty of *augere*, by which the emperor's hands were tied, cancelled any prior pledge to the pope – a powerful argument that was to be used against the legitimacy of the Donation of Constantine.[199]

The emperor formally sanctioned these concepts in the *Constitutio contra hereticos et sacrilegos*. Henry VII stressed the divine source of his office, openly ignoring the intervention of the pope, whose role was relegated to the spiritual sphere.[200] The tendency to abolish papal mediation turned the emperor's oath during his coronation into a matter of conscience and, as such, one that was lacking any binding legal validity.[201] The imperial camp, not content with restricting its claims to an ephemeral political situation, assumed the authority of the Roman heritage. Before becoming the See of St Peter, Rome had been the capital of the Caesars. This historical fact determined Henry's predominance over Clement and subsequently justified the subservience of all Christian kings to the emperor.[202] Of particular interest was the emperor's claim that the pope could not force on him any truce with Robert of Anjou, since a war that began under an emperor's order becomes a Just War. Through the *lex regia*, the Roman heritage thus bestowed on the emperor *potestas* and *imperium*.[203]

In all these claims, it is doubtful whether Henry VII of Luxemburg added any of his own to the declarations made in the past by Frederick II and his supporters.[204] The importance of Henry's claims relied, rather, on their circulation among the Ghibellines and the White Guelphs, who placed their hopes for the rebuilding of Italy on the emperor. Indeed, Henry of Luxemburg widely projected the image of the Christian ruler at the peak of his glory. A contemporary Sicilian lawyer stated, 'The emperor is the ruler of the world.' In the same treatise, which was probably written as a response to the papal attempt to force on Henry a truce

---

claims that the emperor did, and supports this claim with reference to the *Clementinae*, John of Viktring points to the same source as an indication of Clement's reaction to the emperor's refusal: *Heinrici Rebdorfensis Annales*, p. 512; John of Viktring, p. 374.

[199] Dante Alighieri, *De Monarchia*, c. III, v. 10, pp. 80–3.

[200] *Acta Imperii Angliae et Franciae*, no. 295, pp. 244–7; *Constitutiones et acta publica imperatorum et regum*, vol. IV-2, nos. 799–800, pp. 799–801; Albertino Mussato, *Heinrici VII Caesaris Historia Augusta*, pp. 524–35. On the document's influence on late medieval political philosophy, see D. Quaglioni, '*Fidelitas habet duas habenas*', pp. 381–96. R. Folz regards Henry's claims as a renewal of extreme imperial ideology, which brought about Henry's downfall: *L'idée d'Empire en Occident*, pp. 162–5.

[201] *Constitutiones et acta publica imperatorum et regum*, vol. IV-2, nos. 1248, 840, pp. 1312, 843.

[202] *Ibid.*, vol. IV-2, no. 801, pp. 802–4; on Philip the Fair's disagreement with the emperor's claims, see *ibid.*, vol. IV-2, no. 811, pp. 812–14.

[203] *Ibid.*, vol. IV-2, no. 1250, pp. 1327–31. Though the pope acknowledged the emperor's right to declare a *justum bellum*, he limited it to cases in which there was no specific papal prohibition, since imperial authority depended on the pope *ratione peccati*: *ibid.*, vol. IV-2, no. 1251, pp. 1342–3.

[204] *Historia diplomatica Friderici Secundi*, vol. III, p. 73; vol. IV, p. 910; vol. VI, pp. 359–61.

with Robert of Anjou, the author negates any papal rule in temporal affairs. Further, he finds that the emperor's oath during the coronation had no implications of vassality, since the emperor received his power from his election, not from the ceremony of coronation, which lacked any political meaning.[205] Similarly, Dante Alighieri called Henry VII the 'ordinary judge' for the whole human race.[206]

Henry's advantages on the theoretical level were soon translated into political practice by his declaration of war against the Angevins of Naples, a further challenge to papal suzerainty in the region (26 April–12 May 1313).[207] On the other hand, the imperial threat served to strengthen the devotion shown by Robert of Anjou to the papal curia. Robert agreed to act as a devout *miles papae* and, as such, became the spokesman for papalist concepts. Not satisfied with disqualifying the imperial coronation of Henry VII on procedural grounds, the king demanded the total dissolution of the Empire. He presented such an action as a measure for the protection of Italy, especially of 'the faithful sons of the pope' – namely, the Guelphs, the Angevins, and indirectly also the French – against their northern enemies, the barbarian Germans.[208] Though it is doubtful whether this policy was acceptable to many, it indicates the radical positions with which the pope was faced during 1312. Similar claims circulated in both the Capetian and the papal spheres of influence. Pierre Dubois, for instance, supported the elimination of the German Empire and urged the pope to put an end to the electoral functions of imperial magnates. In order to prevent any opposition, Dubois suggested bribing the lay electors, a policy that had demonstrated its effectiveness in the past, and applying papal pressure on the imperial prelates. After being freed from the German threat, the Empire, Dubois advocated, should be transferred to the Capetians.[209] Agostino Trionfo, as well,

---

[205] 'Temporalia omnia sub ipsius Romani principis protectione . . . divina quadam providentia ac institutione gencium constituta . . . Non sacramentum subiectionis seu vassallagii . . . sed . . . obsequium christianitatis et fidei . . . Non ideo sequitur quod sola electio Romani principis ei ius non tribuat imperandi': *Constitutiones et acta publica imperatorum et regum*, vol. IV-2, app. 7, no. 1248, pp. 1308–17. This view was shared by many antipapalists; see W. D. McCready, 'Papalists and Antipapalists', pp. 244–5.

[206] Dante Alighieri, *Il Convito*, c. IV, v. 4, pp. 128–9; *De Monarchia*, c. II, v. 11, p. 61.

[207] *Constitutiones et acta publica imperatorum et regum*, vol. IV-2, no. 946, pp. 985–90; *Nicolai episcopi Botrontinensis Relatio de itinere italico Heinrici VII*, pp. 546–7; Tolomeo da Lucca, *Secunda Vita*, pp. 49–50. The chronicle of St Denis emphasises the pope's immediate revocation of this decision: *Les grandes chroniques de France*, pp. 290–1; Bowsky, *Henry VII in Italy*, pp. 169–84.

[208] See the fourteen issues developed by the king's representatives in the curia (6 August 1313): *Constitutiones et acta publica imperatorum et regum*, vol. IV-2, nos. 947, 1253, pp. 991–3, 1369–73; *Acta Henrici VII*, no. 147, pp. 233–46; Lizerand, 'Les constitutions *Romani principes* et *Pastoralis cura*', pp. 730–1; E. Jordan, *Les origines de la domination angevine en Italie*, pp. 613–14.

[209] Pierre Dubois, *De recuperatione Terrae Sanctae*, LXX.111, LXXI.115–16, pp. 189–93; Brandt, 'Pierre Dubois, Modern or Medieval?', pp. 512–13.

completely denied that the German electors possessed any inherent independent rights. He maintained that the seven electors were the ministers of the pope, indeed his representatives, in the elections to the Empire; there was no doubt, he claimed, that the pope, if he wished, could deprive them of this privilege. According to Agostino, the pope was entitled to confer the right of election on others, to elect the emperor by himself, or to make the Empire hereditary.[210]

These principles received the force of law in the constitutions *Romani principes* and *Pastoralis cura*, which reflected the papal response to the political developments and to the radical declarations of Henry VII and his lawyers.[211] Both documents immortalised in canon law Henry's status as 'subditus homoque ligius et vasallus', a claim supported by the oath given by Henry of Luxemburg to Jean de Molhans, the canon of Toul and papal chaplain, which was appended to the document.[212] *Romani principes* called attention to the fact that it was the pope who had transferred the Empire from the Greeks to the Germans. Besides the historical background, the document clarified the nature of the oath that Henry VII had sworn to the papal representatives. It accused the emperor of bad faith, since his own ambassadors had taken oaths of fealty, which 'by virtue of our apostolic authority and having consulted our brethren, we declare . . . are oaths of fealty and must be considered as such'.[213] *Pastoralis cura* proclaimed the superiority of the Holy See over the Empire and decreed Henry's policy against Robert of Anjou null and void. Henry's summons to the king of Naples (12 September 1312) was declared invalid because it had been announced outside the Empire, in the kingdom of Sicily. As judge in ordinary of its vassal, only the Holy See could have summoned the king. Hence the pope's unavoidable verdict:

We annul it by virtue of the incontestable supremacy of the Holy See over the Empire and of the right of the head of the Church to administer that Empire during a vacancy, and by that fullness of power that Peter received from Jesus Christ, King of kings and Lord of lords.[214]

---

[210] 'Ius eligendi imperatorem non est concessum aliquibus in favorem ipsorum sed in favorem ecclesie et populi Christiani cuius caput est ipse papa. Unde quando sibi videretur hoc esse in favorem ecclesie et pacem Christiani populi, potest tale ius eis subtrahere sicut propter talem causam eis concessit': Agostino Trionfo, *Summa*, qu. 35.1 ad 1; qu. 35. 3 ad 2; qu. 35. 1; qu. 35. 6.

[211] Published on 14 March 1314, the same day on which Robert of Anjou was appointed imperial vicar for Italy. See *Regestum Clementis Papae V*, no. 10321; Tolomeo da Lucca, *Secunda Vita*, pp. 51–2; *Heinrici Rebdorfensis Annales*, p. 512; M. Della Piana, 'Intorno ad una bolla papale', pp. 23–50.

[212] See the two memoranda that preceded the papal constitutions in Lizerand, 'Les constitutions *Romani principes* et *Pastoralis cura*', pp. 734–43.

[213] *De iure iurando*, *Clementinarum*, l. ii, tit. ix, cap. un., *CIC*, vol. ii, cols. 1147–50.

[214] *De sententia et re iudicata*, *Clementinarum*, l. ii, tit. xi, cap. 2, *CIC*, vol. ii, cols. 1151–4; Matthew of Nüwenburg, *Cronica*, pp. 185–6. Before the decretal was published, Clement had applied these

The papal constitutions came too late to encounter any response from Henry VII, since the emperor was dead by the time of their publication.[215] Victim of a fever that had attacked him in Buonconvento, in Sienese territory, Henry died on 24 August 1313, when he was moving southward against Robert of Anjou.[216] Only fourteen months had passed since his coronation in Rome and thirty months since his arrival in Italy as 'an angel of peace'.[217] On the political level, the sudden death of the emperor obviously cleared the way for Clement V, Robert of Anjou, and the Black Guelphs, who were now free of their most powerful rival. In the last month of his life (14 March 1314), Clement, in his capacity as senator of Rome for life, prepared, but did not issue, a letter appointing Robert of Anjou imperial vicar in all the lands of the Empire in Italy, with the single exception of Genoa. The papal document specified that the charge was limited to the vacancy of the Empire and would end two months after the confirmation of a new king of the Romans.[218] For twenty years and more, the Papal State became an Angevin protectorate, however inefficiently this was exercised.[219] In Romagna, for example, John XXII brought about Robert's dismissal in 1317 because of the poor achievements of his seven-year rectorship.[220] On the psychological level, the death of Henry VII aroused conflicting reactions, ranging from rejoicing in Florence, Padua, and Parma[221] to genuine mourning in Pisa, which had been destroyed on both the political and the economic level.[222] According to Dante Alighieri, the failure of the emperor was the failure of justice. The 'blind cupidity' of Clement, he charged, was the main factor delaying redemption and the rebuilding of Italy, the

principles by appointing Robert vicar-general of the Empire in Italy: *Constitutiones et acta publica imperatorum et regum*, vol. IV-2, no. 1164, pp. 1205–6; *Continuationis chronici Guillelmi de Nangiaco*, p. 397. On Dante's extreme reaction to the papal legislation, see A. P. d'Entrèves, *Dante as a Political Thinker*, pp. 60–75.

[215] An anonymous memorandum written in the papal curia raised the question of whether it was possible to annul imperial sentences after the emperor's death; see Lizerand, 'Les constitutions *Romani principes* et *Pastoralis cura*', pp. 746–1.

[216] *Notae ad vitas*, pp. 90–1. See also Nicholas of Butrinto's touching description of the emperor's last hours: *Nicolai episcopi Botrontinensis Relatio de itinere italico Heinrici VII*, pp. 549–52.

[217] Villani, *Cronica*, l. ix, c. li–liii, pp. 177–9; Villani, *Istorie fiorentine*, l. ix, c. 51–2, pp. 50–2.

[218] *Regestum Clementis Papae V*, no. 10321. The pope's decision was received in Parma with such joy that all church bells rang to celebrate it: *Chronicon Parmense*, p. 134.

[219] Partner, *The Lands of St Peter*, p. 309.

[220] Caggese, *Roberto d'Angiò e i suoi tempi*, vol. I, pp. 129, 346; vol. II, pp. 24–6.

[221] With transports of joy the Florentines announced the 'felicissimos rumores' of the departure from this world of the 'tirannus ille sevissimus'. See their letter of 27 August 1313: *Constitutiones et acta publica imperatorum et regum*, vol. IV-2, no. 1240, pp. 1300–1. For Padua, see *Historia Gulielmi et Albrigeti Cortusiorum*, col. 786.

[222] 'Morto lo 'mperadore Arrigo, la sua oste, e'Pisani, e tutti i suoi amici ne menarono grande dolore, e'Fiorentini, Sanesi, e Lucchesi, e quegli di loro lega ne feciono grande allegrezza': Villani, *Cronica*, l. ix, c. liii, p. 179. Cf. *Chronicon Parmense*, p. 130.

consummation of which the Florentine poet had envisaged just two years previously. Clement's antagonism towards the Empire, he expounded, was not to be tolerated by God any longer; it had caused enough damage by bringing about the failure of the emperor. Henry VII had been the anointed and the minister of justice for Dante; and whatever failure the emperor had encountered on earth, the poet now enthroned him at the heart of the city of God.[223]

Strong feelings towards the late emperor were not restricted to Italy. Henry's sudden death encouraged the glorification of his memory, enshrining it with an aura of martyrdom. The chronicle attributed to Geffroy de Paris described Henry as a tortured saint, sacrificed on the altar of Empire – a concept echoed in the chronicles of St Denis.[224] Jean de St Victor voiced rumours that the emperor had actually been poisoned by his confessor, the Dominican Bernard de Montepulciano, a suspicion that led to serious retaliations against the Order.[225] The sorrow over the premature demise of Henry of Luxemburg assumed tragic dimensions in German sources, which mourned his death deeply.[226] The archbishop of Mainz supposedly declared that in the last five hundred years there had not lived a man whose death might have caused more harm to the whole of Christendom.[227] Other chroniclers could not understand how God had allowed such an unjust event.[228] Hugh of Rutlingen found it necessary to mention the split between the late emperor and Clement V, and the threat of excommunication that had been avoided by Henry's sudden death.[229] There was, in fact, a strong tendency to implicate Clement V in the emperor's death. Moved by the Florentines' call for help – which they had properly accompanied by vast amounts of gold – Clement supposedly had conspired with a certain Dominican to cause the emperor's death when Henry was absorbed by the war against the Guelph–Angevin league outside Florence. The chroniclers who reported this plot did not forget to mention the terrible remorse that his criminal

---

[223] Dante Alighieri, *Divina Commedia, Paradiso*, c. xxx, vv. 133–48; E. Peters, 'The Failure of Church and Empire', pp. 334–5; Holmes, *Florence, Rome, and the Origins of the Renaissance*, pp. 245–52.

[224] *La chronique métrique attribuée à Geffroy de Paris*, p. 161, vv. 3697–8. The chronicles of St Denis, however, absolved the Dominicans of any plot against the emperor, 'whom they loved': *Les grandes chroniques de France*, pp. 291–2.

[225] Jean de St Victor, *Prima Vita*, p. 22; *Annales Colbazienses*, p. 717; *Chronicon Mutinense*, cols. 573–4; *Luccheser Fortsetzung derselben Chronik*, pp. 252–3; Jean d'Hocsem, *Gesta Pontificum Leodiensium*, p. 354. The *Chronographia* further reports that the perpetrator of the crime found shelter in the court of Robert of Anjou: *Chronographia regum Francorum*, p. 197. Tolomeo da Lucca, on the other hand, emphasised that the emperor died a natural death, 'quicquid aliqui malivoli dicant': *Secunda Vita*, p. 51. This version was corroborated by Albertino Mussato, *Henrici VII Caesaris Historia Augusta*, col. 568. See also *Notae ad vitas*, pp. 90–1.

[226] *Monachi Fürstenfeldensis Chronica*, pp. 44–5; *Annales Lubicenses*, p. 423; *Nicolai episcopi Botrontinensis Relatio de itinere italico Heinrici VII*, pp. 549–52.   [227] *Annales Halesbrunnenses Maiores*, p. 48.

[228] *Continuatio Zwetlensis tertia*, p. 665.   [229] *Excerpta ex expositione Hugonis de Rutlingen*, p. 132.

act caused the pope when on his deathbed.[230] The accusation was obviously baseless, but it indicates the positive image projected by the late emperor that could easily have assumed eschatological dimensions.[231] Other sources, more careful in their report, suggest that the accusations against the Dominicans were in fact unfounded rumours.[232] Still, Clement V was tainted with the possibility of having committed a cowardly murder, which did not enhance his image as the spiritual leader of Christendom.

The death of Henry VII did little to advance papal interests on the peninsula. On the contrary, it marked the collapse of Clement's political scheme of an Angevin–imperial alliance that was to restore peace to Italy while protecting papal interests, especially in the Papal State. Conversely, the emperor's death actually cleared the way for the particularistic forces that eventually brought about the downfall of Angevin aspirations as well. From the perspective of papal authority, especially Clement's status in Italy, it is clear that his early support of the emperor-elect did not clear the way for Henry among the pope's presumed allies, the Guelphs. Conversely, the pope's latent opposition from 1312 onwards did not obstruct the emperor's advance. The *Romfahrt* failed both to ensure Clement's rule in the Papal State and to strengthen apostolic authority among the Guelphs, let alone the Ghibellines. The touching declarations about devotion to the Church and the pope clearly constituted manipulative manifestos, with very little political meaning. Beyond a circumstantial co-ordination of interests between Clement V and the city-states, in the long term an attitude of reserve prevailed towards the pope and his legates. The sudden demise of Henry VII did not prevent the pope's political downfall in Italy, but accelerated it. With the imperial threat removed, particularistic forces increasingly predominated. Once again, the complexity of Italian politics defeated both emperor and pope, though this failure could hardly be charged only against Clement's account.

---

[230] *Cronica Reinhardsbrunnensis*, p. 651; *Chronica S. Petri Erfordensis Moderna*, p. 444. There were also rumours about a Lombard plot to poison all wells in order to prevent the advance of the emperor's army, which they had failed to challenge on the battlefield: *Continuatio Zwetlensis tertia*, p. 664.

[231] Reeves, 'History and Prophecy in Medieval Thought', pp. 51–75.

[232] *Heinrici Rebdorfensis Annales*, p. 512; *Excerpta ex expositione Hugonis de Rutlingen*, p. 132; Matthew of Nüwenburg, *Cronica*, p. 186. John of Viktring went even further in indicating his serious doubts: 'Tam etiam nefarium scelus per religiosum tam famosum etiam imperatori tam karissimum fieri, difficile vel nullatenus est credendum': John of Viktring, p. 376.

Chapter 5

FRANCE

Historians have often considered Clement V subservient to Philip the Fair. In this regard, Edgard Boutaric reflects a common view when he claims that 'the pontificate of Clement V was . . . a continuous chain of concessions to the endless exigencies of the king'.[1] Heinrich Finke echoes this premise when he argues that no pope of the later middle ages was more subservient to a king, a conclusion shared by Joseph R. Strayer.[2] Such evaluations reflect the views of fourteenth-century chroniclers and their criticism of the alliance between pope and king, which they considered detrimental to the Church. A close analysis of contemporary documentation, however, offers a more complex picture: the pope may have given vociferous support to the king, but he implemented an independent policy based on his own scale of priorities. In the most crucial events of Philip's reign, such as the crisis in Flanders and the trials of Pope Boniface and the Templars, Clement succeeded in sabotaging the original plans of Philip the Fair, while, if not advancing, at least protecting papal aims. By trying to find a middle course between his own and the king's interests, Clement prevented an open conflict with Philip the Fair that might have put an end to the dearest goal of his pontificate: the crusade.

Clement's belief in the *Gesta Dei per Francos* turned the achievement of a durable peace between France and England into a primary objective of curial diplomacy. Further, it justified papal assistance to Philip the Fair on all fronts. Clement enlisted Church resources on behalf of the Capetian treasury and fostered the nomination of royal protégés to leading ecclesiastical positions. Beyond the domain of papal finances, Clement supported Capetian policy against dissident forces that could threaten the interests of the monarchy. From the pope's perspective, the

---

[1] Boutaric, *La France sous Philippe le Bel*, p. 124.
[2] Finke, *Aus den Tagen Bonifaz VIII*, p. 289; Strayer, *The Reign of Philip the Fair*, p. 284.

peace treaty between the leading monarchies of Christendom, the improvement of royal finances, and the strengthening of the king's position at home all constituted an imperative, as they would facilitate Philip's departure overseas and thus hasten the recovery of the Holy Land.

Papal commitment to the king of France demanded consensus on the division of labour between *regnum* and *sacerdotium*. In contrast to the belligerent policy of his predecessor, Clement made considerable efforts to achieve close co-operation with Philip the Fair. In his letter, *Rex gloriae virtutum*, which was generously studded with biblical idioms, the pope bestowed apostolic legitimacy on what Fawtier calls 'the cult of the French monarchy'.[3] Acknowledgement of the 'fact' that the *natio Gallicana* had been chosen by God caused His Vicar to recognise that the kingdom of France enjoyed special divine grace.[4] Thus, papal policy on behalf of the Most Christian King – according to Clement's reasoning – reflected the will of providence in actual practice. Papal declarations on behalf of the kingdom of France and its king created a convenient background for concord between pope and king; they also brought Clement V closer to the political trends supported by Capetian propaganda. The reign of Philip the Fair was indeed characterised by a deliberate attempt to enlist all vital political forces, especially the bourgeoisie, in support of royal policy. The *tiers état* formally received political acknowledgement in 1302, when it was allowed to join the ranks of the traditional elites, both ecclesiastical and lay, in the Assembly. Lacking political traditions of its own, the bourgeoisie was more exposed to royal propaganda and, therefore, more ready to welcome its tenet that Philip the Fair was 'emperor in his realm'.[5]

The cult of monarchy was a determining factor in the complex relationship between Clement V and Philip the Fair, the latter at times posing a challenge to papal authority.[6] Being the scion of Charles Martel,

---

[3] See below, n. 11.

[4] 'Sicut israeliticus populus in sortem hereditatis dominice . . . assumptus fuisse dignoscitur, sic regnum Francie in peculiarem populum electus a Domino in executione mandatorum celestium specialis honoris et gratie titulis insignitur': *Regestum Clementis Papae V*, no. 7501. Cf. Dupuy's version, which is the one that appears in the French archives: *Histoire du differend d'entre le pape Boniface VIII et Philippes le Bel*, p. 592.

[5] Wieruszowski, *Vom Imperium zum nationalen Königtum*, pp. 89–121; Strayer, 'Defense of the Realm and Royal Power in France', pp. 291–9; R. Fawtier, 'Comment le roi de France au début du XIVe siècle pouvait-il se représenter son royaume?', p. 71; Guenée, 'Espace et état dans la France du bas moyen âge', p. 758; Guenée, 'Etat et nation en France au moyen âge', pp. 26–9; Menache, 'Philippe le Bel', pp. 689–702. For the concept of *Rex Christianissimus*, see H. Leclerq, 'Roi très chrétien', cols. 2462–4.

[6] Wilks contends that the dualism propounded by Philip the Fair effectively deprived the pope of spiritual jurisdiction within the kingdom of France. It actually gave rise to a concept of kingship in which the ruler was not only *imperator in regno suo* but pope as well. Although the pope was theoretically permitted full spiritual jurisdiction over all Christians, the ultimate objective of royal

Charlemagne, and St Louis, Philip the Fair rather naturally assumed the function of *defensor ecclesiae*, in terms borrowed from the thesaurus of political Augustinianism. The complete identification of the king of France with the Church and the most sublime goals of Christendom found full expression in a sermon preached during the Capetian campaign in Flanders (c. 1302). Its anonymous author equated the peace of the king with that of the kingdom and the Church, since the peace of the king embodied wisdom, virtue, and justice and, as such, also advanced the recovery of the Holy Land. 'Therefore, whoever acts against the king is actually acting against the Church, against Catholic doctrine, against the holiness [of the crown], justice, and the Holy Land.' Conversely, 'those who died for the justice of the king and the kingdom are undoubtedly crowned as martyrs by God'.[7] Galvano da Levanto, a Genoese serving in the papal curia, described Philip as 'a very dedicated warrior of Jesus Christ . . . defender and promoter of the true faith, and protector of the Roman Catholic Church'.[8] These qualities invested the king of France with ethical authority of a universal scope, a belief held in common by Jean de Jandun and Pierre Dubois.[9] Ramon Lull, too, was outspoken in regard to Philip's commitment to the Christian faith and the Church.[10] These principles were internalised by Philip the Fair, who became the most devout apostle in the cult of monarchy. Being charged with a sacred mission, the king of France believed himself to be accountable for its proper management only before Almighty God.[11]

Particularly during the trials of Boniface VIII and the Templars, doubts arose about the genuineness of Philip's Catholic faith, whether it was an

---

policy was to deprive him of all coercive authority. See M. Wilks, *The Problem of Sovereignty in the Later Middle Ages*, pp. 78–83.

[7] D. J. Leclercq, 'Un sermon prononcé pendant la guerre de Flandre sous Philippe le Bel', p. 170.

[8] 'Archipugil Jhesus Christi . . . prothopugnator et promotor fidei ortodoxe necnon et protector catholice ac romane ecclesie': Galvano da Levanto, 'Liber sancti passagii Christicolarum', p. 231. On the treatise, see Gatto, 'I problemi della guerra e della pace nel pensiero politico di Pierre Dubois', pp. 162–3.

[9] Jean de Jandun, 'Tractatus de laudibus Parisius', p. 60; Pierre Dubois, *Summaria brevis et compendiosa doctrina*, pp. 1–2. Powicke sees in Dubois' adherence to the king as a source of stability, growth, and comfort, the popular tendencies of the time as they appear in the *Chansons de geste*. See Powicke, 'Pierre Dubois', p. 174. It is rather dubious, however, whether Dubois' ideas were indeed so popular beyond the direct sphere of Capetian influence.

[10] Hillgarth, *Ramon Lull and Lullism in Fourteenth-Century France*, p. 117; Strayer, 'France', pp. 304–5; Menache, 'Un peuple qui a sa demeure à part', pp. 193–208; Menache, 'A Propaganda Campaign in the Reign of Philip the Fair', pp. 427–54.

[11] Fawtier, *L'Europe occidentale de 1270 à 1328*, p. 301. Much less complimentary in his approach was Robert-Henri Bautier, who delineates the personality of a vulnerable king lacking the minimal skills of expression. He further claims that Philip was completely devoted to hunting until 1302, and, after his wife's death in 1305, to a mystical religion: R.-H. Bautier, 'Diplomatique et histoire politique', p. 27. On the difficult dividing line between religious duties and politico-economic considerations, see Brown, 'Royal Salvation and Needs of State', pp. 372–5.

efficient tool manipulated by royal counsellors, or whether it reflected a true aspect of the king's character. Such scepticism, although expressed in different ways, is common to fourteenth-century sources and historical research. Yet a close examination of available documentation indicates the consistency of the king's faith. It was Philip's religious devotion, which sometimes bordered on mysticism, that often dictated his policy, even in clear antagonism to royal interests. One clear example is provided by the prosecution of the lovers of Philip's daughters-in-law for treason against the blood of France (1314). The publicity given to the sinful behaviour imputed to members of the royal family could easily have endangered the legitimacy of the Capetian progeny while jeopardising the image of monarchy.[12] Still, Philip did not limit himself to the severe punishment of the culprits; he also made their penalty a moral lesson for the inhabitants of the realm as a whole. Contemporaries then had the chance to witness the personal example of a king whose sense of justice 'shall not respect persons in judgement' (Deut. 1:17). Without renewing the old question of the balance of forces between Philip the Fair and his lawyers, the religious zeal of the king – inasmuch as it could have been manipulated for political purposes by Guillaume de Nogaret, Guillaume de Plaisians, or Enguerrand de Marigny – appears genuine.[13] As such, it played an important role in the problematic interplay of Clement V and Philip the Fair.

From the very beginning of Clement's pontificate, Philip the Fair developed strong contacts with the papal curia, trying to make the former archbishop of Bordeaux a main supporter, if not an active partner, of royal policy.[14] French chroniclers referred to Clement's diligence in complying with royal demands before the royal entourage left Lyons.[15] In addition to economic benefits, Philip received papal gestures of goodwill, such as the transfer of St Louis' relics – the larger part of his head, considered the most important member of the body – to the royal chapel.[16] The Cardinals Colonna, whom Philip considered 'our very dear

---

[12] On the religious character of the king and his problematic stand in this case, see Brown, 'The Prince Is Father of the King', pp. 289–90.

[13] Favier emphasised the influence of lawyers, a view shared by Bautier; conversely, Strayer and Pegues saw in Philip a real authority. See Favier, 'Les légistes et le gouvernement de Philippe le Bel', pp. 104–8; Strayer, 'Philip the Fair', pp. 18–32.

[14] During the pontificate of Clement V, at least ten royal proctors appear in papal documentation; see Barbiche, 'Les procureurs des rois de France à la cour pontificale d'Avignon', pp. 82–90.

[15] *Continuatio chronici Girardi de Fracheto*, p. 26; *Continuationis chronici Guillelmi de Nangiaco*, pp. 350–1; *Les grandes chroniques de France*, pp. 246–7; Wenck, 'Aus den Tagen der Zusammenkunft Papst Klemens V und König Philipps des Schonen zu Lyon', pp. 189–202.

[16] *Collectio actorum veterum*, pp. 63–4; *Continuationis chronici Guillelmi de Nangiaco*, pp. 353–4; *Continuatio chronici Girardi de Fracheto*, p. 26; Jean de St Victor, *Prima Vita*, p. 3; *Branche des royaux lignages*, pp. 481–2, vv. 12511–21. On the admiration of St Louis, see Brown, 'The Prince Is Father

friends', were returned to the College of Cardinals, and nine of the ten cardinals listed in the first nomination to the Sacred College came from the kingdom of France.[17] Some chroniclers were sensitive to the ostentatious presence of Philip the Fair in Lyons and the gratuitous generosity of the new pope towards the king.[18] Authors from the Italian peninsula, in particular, regarded Clement's close ties with France as a complete surrender to the Capetian dynasty.[19] The support that some Flemish chroniclers gave to the mutual understanding and affection between pope and king appears quite exceptional, though they also referred to the fact that the new entente was based on the pope's positive response to most of the king's many requests.[20]

Between 1305 and 1307, a long list of papal privileges was added to the Lyons bequests.[21] Chroniclers from the Ile-de-France spoke of Clement's generosity without a hint of criticism; instead, they emphasised the reciprocity between pope and king.[22] The reaction in the papal curia, however, was rather different, especially among the Italian cardinals. They feared a total submission to Philip the Fair that would undo Boniface's policy and undermine their status. At the meeting between the pope and the king in Poitiers (April 1307),[23] Tolomeo da Lucca reported

---

of the King', pp. 326–7, 332. The pope conferred indulgences on those who visited the chapel, especially during the transfer of St Louis' relics: *Regestum Clementis Papae V*, nos. 1191, 7878.

[17] See above, pp. 40–3.

[18] Jean de St Victor recognised that 'rex Francie et fratres ejus baronesque Francorum ipsum [papam] invenerunt propitium ac benignum': Jean de St Victor, *Prima Vita*, p. 3; *Flores historiarum*, p. 127.

[19] Dante Alighieri, *Divina Commedia*, *Inferno*, c. xix, vv. 79–81. After referring to Clement's grant of the tenth and his nomination of French prelates to the Sacred College, Dino Compagni emphasised the fact that the pope did not surrender to Philip in the trial of Boniface: Dino Compagni, *Cronica*, p. 193.

[20] 'Et quant le roy eust très bien fait ses besoignes par devers le saint père, il s'en retourna en son pays à grant joye': *Anciennes chroniques de Flandre*, pp. 396–7; *Chronographia regum Francorum*, pp. 175–6.   [21] *Privilèges accordés à la couronne de France par le Saint Siège*, pp. 108–27.

[22] 'Multam aliam munificentiam in civitatibus et castellis suis contulit Papae Rex Francorum, per quod in omnibus negotiis suis expediendis gratiam multam promeruit et favorem': Raynaldus, in *Annales ecclesiastici*, ad a. 1305, f. 13, vol. xxiii, p. 398; Boutaric, *La France sous Philippe le Bel*, p. 124.

[23] The very selection of the meeting place was a matter of long deliberations between the papal and royal courts. Against Philip's proposal of Tours, Clement supported Toulouse; eventually both sides accepted Poitiers: *Collectio actorum veterum*, pp. 72–5, 77–8. Clement was in Poitiers twice, sixteen months in total, between 21 April 1306 and 15 May 1307, and between 26 May and 18 August 1308. In Poitiers, he met Charles II of Naples and his son, Philip of Taranto; the kings of Navarre and Majorca; the count of Flanders; and Charles de Valois. The transformation of the city into the centre of European diplomacy created many practical problems. On the emergency measures of the seneschal, Pierre de Villeblouain, see L. Levillain, 'A propos d'un texte inédit relatif au séjour du pape Clément V à Poitiers', pp. 73–86. On the papal itinerary to and from Poitiers, see Marchal, 'Autour du pape Clément V' (1926), pp. 201–5, and Marchal, 'Autour de Clément V, le pape en Toulousain', pp. 227–37; E. R. Labande, 'Clément V et le Poitou', pp. 11–33, 83–109. On the struggles in the city between servants of the Capetians and those of the cardinals, see *Collectio actorum veterum*, pp. 98–100.

the unrest in the papal curia that was prompted by Philip's extraordinary demands, which 'were far beyond royal prerogatives'.[24] The cardinals' unease was hardly caused by the attempts to foster a peace treaty between France and England through the marriage of Edward II and Isabella of France.[25] It reflected, rather, their opposition to the Capetian demands, which included opening a trial of Pope Boniface, granting an indulgence to Nogaret, and possibly bringing about the dissolution of the Order of the Temple.[26]

The Italian cardinals and, especially the Bonifacian party, did react unduly in expressing their reservation over what might have seemed a biased, pro-Capetian papal policy. Clement's readiness to uproot the core of Boniface's ecclesiastical creed while abrogating the constitutions *Clericis laicos* and *Unam Sanctam* in France, in effect questioned the justification of his predecessor's agenda.[27] Clement's policy acquired crucial significance in the light of the debate over papal infallibility, which reached its zenith shortly afterwards, during the pontificate of John XXII.[28] James Muldoon observes that Clement was careful not to reject the principles on which Boniface had acted, only some of the conclusions: Clement's constitution, *Meruit*, simply stated that *Unam Sanctam* had in no way changed the relationship that should exist between the papacy and the kingdom of France. On the other hand, Boniface's claims and formulations with regard to papal responsibility for all human souls continued to inspire Clement and his successors during the whole Avignon period.[29] These subtle considerations, however relevant they might have been in the long run, were not shared by most contemporaries. On the contrary, Clement's concessions, estimated to be unprecedented in the annals of the medieval papacy, were largely criticised. Moreover, the pope's benevolent attitude towards the king of France reinforced rumours regarding Clement's prior commitments to Philip the Fair, which had facilitated the way of Bertrand de Got to the See of St Peter.[30] Villani, the main source for the imaginary meeting at St Jean d'Angély, also reported the difficult alternatives with which the pope had been faced at Poitiers:

---

[24] Tolomeo da Lucca, *Secunda Vita*, pp. 27–8.

[25] *Foedera*, II-I, pp. 1, 3, 4, 18, 25; *Lettres des rois, reines, et autres personnages*, pp. 34–7, 39–45.

[26] See the report of Johannes Burgundi to the king of Aragon (Poitiers, 11 July 1308): *Acta Aragonensia*, vol. III, no. 86, pp. 188–9.

[27] *Regestum Clementis Papae V*, no. 906; *Histoire du differend d'entre le pape Boniface VIII et Philippes le Bel*, p. 288.   [28] B. Tierney, *Origins of Papal Infallibility*, pp. 15–50.

[29] Muldoon, 'The Avignon Papacy and the Frontiers of Christendom', pp. 136–42.

[30] Tolomeo da Lucca, *Secunda Vita*, p. 26; Bernard Gui, in *Quarta Vita*, pp. 61–2; Amalric Auger, *Sexta Vita*, p. 92; Agnolo di Tura, *Cronaca Senese*, ad a. 1307, p. 298. Renan accepts the 'Italian' version and looks upon Clement's policy until 1311 as an expression of the accord reached in St Jean d'Angély: Renan, 'Guillaume de Nogaret', p. 286.

And seeing that the Church was under the pressure and persecution engendered by the king [of France], the pope did not decide how to react, since he found it reprehensible to violate his own oath and promise, which he had given to the king, but he thought it even worse to cause further damage to the Roman Church.[31]

Without considering the long-range causes of papal policy, but well aware of its immediate consequences, Agostino Trionfo found it difficult to justify, let alone abide, the essential weakness of Clement *vis-à-vis* the perpetrators of the outrage at Anagni.[32] Rather different was the prevailing approach among the chroniclers of France, who deliberately refrained from criticising the strengthening alliance between pope and king.[33] Folk-songs went further, praising the renewed harmony between *regnum* and *sacerdotium* and emphasising the sorrows of the former separation during Boniface's pontificate.[34] Resumption of the 'marriage' between pope and king, however, did not guarantee papal acquiescence with Capetian demands in Flanders or during the trial of Boniface VIII, the canonisation process of Celestine V, or the trial of the Templars.

FLANDERS

An integral part of the alliance between pope and king, when translated into political terms, was the attempt by Philip the Fair to transform Clement V into the mainstay of royal interests in Flanders. The critical years of the Flemish crisis had passed when Clement was elected to the papacy, but a satisfactory agreement was still wanting. The Matins of Bruges (18 May 1302) and the shameful French defeat at Courtrai (11 July 1302) were seemingly reversed by Philip's victory at Mons-en-Pévèle (18 August 1304). Still, the long conflict had exhausted the resources of both sides without advancing negotiations for a long-term peace.[35] The chronicle of the counts of Flanders points to the conflict as a main factor in Philip's constant pursuit of additional resources, which resulted in a continuous collection of the tenth and an increase in taxes. When these

---

[31] Villani, *Cronica*, l. viii, c. 91, p. 123; Villani, *Istorie fiorentine*, l. viii, c. 91, pp. 181–3.

[32] *Tractatus contra articulos inventos*, II, 5, pp. lxxxiii–lxxxiv.

[33] Bernard Gui, in *Quarta Vita*, pp. 61–2; Amalric Auger, *Sexta Vita*, p. 92.

[34] Mariage est de bon devis
de l'Eglise et des fleurs de lis,
quand l'un de l'autre partira,
chacun d'eux si s'en sentira.
Boutaric, *La France sous Philippe le Bel*, p. 120.

[35] On the developments in Flanders during the reign of Philip the Fair, see the views of the opposing sides in *Chronique artésienne*, pp. 35–51, 81–93; *Chronique et annales de Gilles le Muisit*, pp. 62–8, 76–8; Favier, *Philippe le Bel*, pp. 206–46.

proved insufficient, the king expelled the Jews in order to confiscate their money and brought about the arrest of the Templars for similar reasons.[36]

Jean de Cuyk, Jean de Schoorisse, Gérard de Moor, and Gérard de Sotteghem represented the county in the difficult negotiations with the court of France.[37] All were knights, thus leaving the towns – the most radical factor during the struggle against Capetian rule – without representation. The king was represented by his half-brother, Louis d'Evreux, and by Jean de Dreux, Robert de Bourgogne, and Amadeus de Savoy, all of them personages of high nobility with little understanding of, let alone sympathy for, the climate of opinion prevailing in Flemish towns.[38] They were later joined by two leading Capetian officers, Gilles Aycelin, archbishop of Narbonne, and Pierre de Mornay, bishop of Auxerre.[39] On 23 June 1305, Philip the Fair and the count, Robert de Béthune, signed a peace treaty at Athis-sur-Orge. The treaty of Athis-sur-Orge acquired all the characteristics of a French vendetta against Flanders, especially its towns, led by Bruges. The count was to establish a rent for the king amounting to 20,000 *l.t.* a year on the district of Rethel, near Reims. Until this clause was executed, Philip was to hold Lille, Douai, and Béthune, towns that he had already seized and that were largely French-speaking. The Flemings were also expected to pay an indemnity of 400,000 *l.t.* within four years for the damages they had caused.[40] To expiate the Matins, 3,000 inhabitants of Bruges were to go on pilgrimage, one-third of them to the Holy Land. The fortifications of Ghent, Bruges, Ypres, Lille, and Douai were to be destroyed.[41] The count, the nobles, and all members of town councils were to swear to observe these terms.[42] Philip further included a clause stipulating that non-compliance with the treaty would be punished by excommunication and interdict, a

---

[36] 'Nota, quod Philippo regi a nobilibus regni, qui parentes suos in Curtraco perdiderant et amicos, persuasum erat . . . ut Flandriam destruant et illos nobiles Curtraci peremptos vindicent. Consiliis pluribus super his tentis, eo quod thesaurus regis erat evacuatus . . . non poterant habere stipendiarios ad invadendam Flandriam. Idcirco adinvenerunt novam practicam de decimis, de vestigalibus, assisiis, praestariis civium et burgensium, talliis, et diversis aliis exactionibus, et de quarta assisia vini, de confiscatione bonorum Templariorum in regno Franciae, ac etiam similiter de destructione Judaeorum in regno Franciae, qui pro tunc ditissimi erant': *Chronicon comitum Flandrensium*, p. 177.

[37] See their report of the negotiations (16 January 1305): *Codex Diplomaticus Flandriae*, vol. I, no. 144, pp. 335–6.

[38] The *Annales Gandenses* emphasise the gap between the French delegation, composed of 'great and noble counts', and the representatives of the county, 'for the Flemish were knights, not of such high standing': *Annales Gandenses*, p. 85.   [39] G. Bordonove, *Philippe le Bel*, p. 167.

[40] H. van Werveke, 'Les charges financières issues du traité d'Athis', pp. 81–93.

[41] This clause was widened to include all Flemish cities; see *Codex Diplomaticus Flandriae*, vol. I, no. 155, pp. 365–6.

[42] *Codex Diplomaticus Flandriae*, vol. I, no. 158, pp. 368–70; *Annales Gandenses*, pp. 85–6; F. Funck-Brentano, *Philippe le Bel en Flandre*, pp. 492–4.

rather clear expression of his expectations from the Church and of the pope at its head.

The pathetic request for a collective penitence in Bruges, though it corroborates the religious approach of the king, puts into question the political skills of Philip the Fair and those who acted on his behalf. On the other hand, Philip's genuine religious zeal did not preclude the use of ecclesiastical means, such as excommunication and interdict, to advance political goals. Besides, two main factors made Athis-sur-Orge an ill-founded treaty: the doubtful possibility that the count could fulfil his financial obligations and the even more doubtful acquiescence of the towns in demolishing their fortifications in order to implement the Capetian vendetta.[43] This situation was clear to the chronicler of St Denis, who suggested that the Flemings were rather reluctant to fulfil the treaty, 'in which, in any case, they have little faith'.[44] The annalist of Ghent emphasised the aversion of townsmen towards the Flemish negotiators, who were suspected of treason by endorsing such a miserable surrender to the Capetians.[45] Moreover, suspicion arose that the common goal of both the count and the nobles was actually to support Capetian policy in order to weaken the popular party. The townsmen, therefore, expressed their wish to die rather than live in servitude:

When the letter [of Athis-sur-Orge] was shown to the communes they were highly indignant with their arbiters and proctors, saying they would rather die than bind themselves to such slavery. So the said arbiters and proctors, and some of the nobles, who had gladly agreed to the decree in order that the communes might be trampled upon (for they had been much enriched and strengthened by the preceding wars and had become bold and powerful), were at times in great danger of their lives. It was often thought that the communes would have slain them, and so it would have been, undoubtedly, if anyone in France or Flanders had been daring enough to ask that the said letter should be put into execution.[46]

In the aftermath of Athis-sur-Orge, Clement avoided taking a clear stand on the long conflict in Flanders. On the other hand, he displayed a generous attitude towards Robert de Béthune and his son, whom he granted a large list of privileges.[47] Count Robert received special apostolic protection from any excommunication that would be pronounced against him, even by papal legates, without special papal authorisation.[48] This was an important concession that Clement usually granted to his

---

[43] Besides the political tension between king and count, and between both of them and the Flemings, the unrest in the towns was also due to the socio-economic tensions between the patriciate and the artisans. See Lalou, 'Les révoltes contre le pouvoir à la fin du XIIIe et au début du XIVe siècle', pp. 171–80.   [44] *Les grandes chroniques de France*, pp. 244–5.

[45] The opposition of interests acquired 'national' significance in the political songs of the time; see Menache, 'Vers une conscience nationale', pp. 85–97.   [46] *Annales Gandenses*, p. 86.

[47] *Regestum Clementis Papae V*, nos. 449–53, 1004, 1122–31, 1136–7.   [48] *Ibid.*, no. 1121.

closest allies, such as Philip the Fair, Edward I, and Edward II. The inclusion of the count with the leading monarchs of Christendom could hardly have advanced Capetian interests when Philip was threatening with excommunication those who disobeyed the peace treaty. The pope went further and, in a touching gesture of goodwill, allowed the secular and regular clergy of Flanders to advance loans to the count on account of the large sums that he owed the Capetian court (17 January 1306).[49] Moreover, on 1 June 1310, Clement conferred indulgences on all faithful who visited the church of St Basil at Bruges following the miraculous change in the blood of Christ, its most precious relic.[50] True, concessions of this kind appear rather regularly in the papal registers; in most cases, though, they concern churches in Languedoc and, mainly, those in the province of Bordeaux. Papal generosity towards both the count of Flanders and Bruges implied a challenge to Philip the Fair, especially to his attempts to eradicate all remnants of independence in the county.

In his meeting with the pope in Poitiers, Philip tried to change Clement's benevolent policy towards the Flemings and to enlist apostolic support for Capetian interests (May 1307). The king summoned Robert de Béthune and his brother Guillaume, together with the nobility and proctors of the Flemish towns, to Poitiers, and requested them to renew their oath before the pope to obey all clauses of Athis-sur-Orge. Philip's position was then presented by Guillaume de Plaisians, Gilles Aycelin, Gilles Colonna, one noble, and two bourgeois from Paris and Toulouse, respectively.[51] In his response, Clement V praised the royal policy, which he described as tolerant and Christian. Bearing in mind the painful experiences of previous crises and wishing to avoid further bloodshed among Christians, the pope declared that Robert and his subjects should be excommunicated if they transgressed any article of the treaty. In such an event, all lands, towns, and territories of Flanders would be subject to interdict. In an unprecedented manner, Clement further added that this pronouncement would not be removed except at the explicit request of the king (2 June).[52] The same day, the pope wrote letters to the archbishop of Reims, the bishop of Senlis, and the abbot of St Denis, allowing them to pronounce excommunication against the Flemings if the

---

[49] *Ibid.*, no. 1003.   [50] *Ibid.*, no. 6046.

[51] From 1309 Flemish affairs became, in Favier's terms, the 'veritable department' of Marigny: Favier, *Un conseiller de Philippe le Bel*, pp. 129–30, 134–5. On Guillaume de Plaisians, see A. Henry, 'Guillaume de Plaisians, ministre de Philippe le Bel', pp. 32–8. On Gilles Aycelin, see F. J. Pegues, *The Lawyers of the Last Capetians*, pp. 92–8.

[52] Clement explicitly declared that 'quibus omnibus sententiis supradictis ipsi vel eorum successores, terre et ville ipsorum aut pertinentie earundem non absolventur nec possint absolvi, nisi ad requisitionem regis Francie vel illius, qui super hoc speciale mandatum habuerit ab eodem': *Regestum Clementis Papae V*, no. 1680; *Codex Diplomaticus Flandriae*, vol. II, no. 203, pp. 24–7.

need arose. Although the letters were sealed, and they do appear in the papal registers, Clement did not send them, thus reserving to himself the right of application when and where he would find it necessary.[53] Still, the pope's public threat was effective enough. In a meeting held in Loches, the count and the representatives of the towns renewed their oath to comply with all clauses of Athis-sur-Orge while subordinating themselves to the penalties declared by the pope (5 June).

In a rather uncompromising manner, Clement seemingly bestowed apostolic blessing on Capetian policy in front of the count, the nobles, and the representatives of the towns. It soon became evident, however, that the fiscal clauses of Athis-sur-Orge were impossible to fulfil, since the count's whole income – let alone his motivation – was much less than the sums stipulated by the treaty.[54] Moreover, the towns, led by Bruges, were reluctant to submit to the extreme dictates of Philip the Fair:

> Wherefore the said commonalties, mostly in the towns and country districts of Flanders, conceived a deep hatred against the king and the count and his brothers and all the nobles and rich burgesses, who desired such a peace. For they feared that they might be reduced to slavery by the understanding between the nobles and the patricians, as had happened in some other lands, where the humble folk were all alike enslaved.[55]

These developments were carefully followed by the papal curia. In a letter to the archbishop of Reims, Clement mentioned the popular unrest and the gradual retreat from the peace treaty (31 December 1308). This letter suggests Clement's awareness of the problems that affected the county and that could seldom be solved by threats of excommunication and interdict, even less by their implementation, as required by Philip the Fair. Moreover, Clement's reluctance to publish the apostolic ban or to enlist ecclesiastical punishments in the service of Capetian interests indicates not only the pope's independent policy but also his more adequate perception of the crisis. Although Clement publicly gave Philip the Fair apostolic blessing, the pope's main tendency between 1307 and 1308 was to avoid the use of force – either ecclesiastical or secular – which, if implemented, could hardly procure an agreement in the long run.

The pope's adamant position was well known by both parties. When royal officials tried to enforce the treaty and threatened the count and the nobles with the implementation of ecclesiastical penalties – as they had

---

[53] *Regestum Clementis Papae V*, no. 1681; *Codex Diplomaticus Flandriae*, vol. II, no. 204, pp. 27–8; Funck-Brentano, *Philippe le Bel en Flandre*, pp. 511–12.

[54] Van Werveke emphasised the devastating influence of Capetian monetary policy, which raised the original payments stipulated in Athis six times. Philip's concessions were, therefore, just an adjustment dictated by financial reality: van Werveke, 'Les charges financières issues du traité d'Athis', pp. 81–92. [55] *Annales Gandenses*, p. 90.

been established in Athis-sur-Orge and affirmed in Poitiers – they were met with scorn. The Flemings argued that they knew from reliable sources that the pope had not yet sent the pertinent letters. This was the background to the mission of Pierre de Latilly, the bishop of Châlons-sur-Marne and one of Philip's chief financial agents who had succeeded Nogaret as keeper of the seals, to the papal court, in order to urge the pope to send the letters. But Clement did not hasten to fulfil Philip's requests. At first, the pope claimed that Pierre de Latilly was not properly empowered for his mission (31 December 1308). Eventually, Clement wrote to Philip that, after deliberating with many cardinals, all of them very attached to the king, about the best policy to be followed, they had decided to do whatever possible to help the king, inasmuch as it would not affect 'the honour of God and of the Holy Church'.[56] This was a rather ambiguous declaration with regard to the pope's and the cardinals' readiness to rescue Philip the Fair from the impasse.

Clement also wrote to the archbishop of Reims and the bishops of Tournai, Cambrai, and Thérouanne to enlist them in his efforts at mediation. The pope declared that he had learned from reliable sources that the people of Flanders were beginning to forget the many troubles of the last conflict. He had carefully read the confirmation of the treaty of Athis by Robert de Béthune and his subjects, whom the pope accused of acting against the peace and disregarding the disastrous results of a new military campaign. The irresponsible behaviour of the count and the towns of Flanders had adversely affected the projected expedition to the Holy Land, whose accomplishment the pope had envisaged for the near future. Following quite closely the precedent of the renowned decretal of Innocent III, *Novit ille qui nihil ignorat*,[57] Clement declared that his primary obligation was to foster peace among the faithful in a spirit of Christian charity. Furthermore, he was obliged to make all sides respect the oaths that they had exchanged, so that all obstacles to the implementation of the crusade would be removed.[58] Consequently, the prelates

---

[56] These letters were sent to Philip by the papal chaplain, the Dominican Guillaume de Peyre de Godin, in January 1309: *Collectio actorum veterum*, pp. 115–16. Notwithstanding the great confidence that the pope had in his chaplain, he did not disclose to him the content of the letter because of the delicacy of the issue: G. Mollat, 'La diplomatie pontificale au XIVe siècle', p. 508. About a dozen letters close, addressed to Philip IV, were written by the papal chamberlain, Bertrand de Bordes. One of them makes it clear that Bertrand had been entrusted with engrossing it because of the secrecy of its content. See Zutshi, 'The Political and Administrative Correspondence of the Avignon Popes', p. 379.

[57] Decretal. Gregor. IX, l. II, tit. I, c. 13, *CIC*, vol. II, cols. 242–4.

[58] Most fourteenth-century publicists who maintained that the pope could intervene in temporal affairs 'by reason of sin', often illustrated this claim by reference to papal power to arbitrate when questions of war and peace or the breaking of an oath were concerned. See Aegidius Romanus (Gilles Colonna), *De ecclesiastica potestate*, 3. 6, p. 177; Alvarus Pelagius (Alvarez Pelayo), *De Planctu*

were ordered to proceed to Flanders to promote the attainment of a peace treaty and to annul any pledges that might have been exchanged among the insurgent factions. The bottom line was a renewed threat of interdict, should the Flemings dare to disobey.[59]

Alongside the precedent of Innocent III – who also wrote to the clergy of France in his attempts to mediate between Philip August and John Lackland (1204) – Clement's attempt to mobilise the clergy of the province of Reims to stand in the vanguard of the peace treaty seems a more balanced policy, and perhaps also more useful, than the coercive approach supported by the Capetian court. Clement's moderate policy in Flanders becomes most evident when compared to papal methods in other areas of Christendom at the same time, especially in Italy. In 1309, Arnaud de Pellegrue launched a crusade against the Venetians, who had been excommunicated and had an interdict laid on their city. Christian rulers were urged to confiscate the goods and to arrest any representatives of Venice in their territory.[60] True, Flanders was not part of the Papal State as was Ferrara; still, the large gap between Clement's policy in Italy and that pursued in Flanders, where Capetian interests were at play – i.e., not the pope's – raises a question about Clement's supposed subservience to Philip the Fair.

As the situation in Flanders deteriorated, Philip's appeals to Clement became more urgent. On 19 January 1309, the king sent Guillaume de Plaisians to the curia in order to foster the excommunication of all Flemings who were obstructing the fulfilment of the treaty. Philip carefully mentioned in his petition that the absence of papal letters of interdict and excommunication had made a mockery of his threats, thus indirectly feeding unrest among the Flemings. In a rather suggestive tone, the king further declared that the deteriorating situation in Flanders had forced him to divert to the county his meagre resources, which he had originally collected for the recovery of the Holy Land. The conclusion was therefore clear: the conflict in Flanders and the lack of papal support were actually jeopardising Philip's plans to depart for overseas.[61]

Contemporary sources, however, suggest that the nominal threat of excommunication and interdict was quite powerful enough to bring the county to the verge of a civil war. The annalist of Ghent reflects this climate of opinion:

Ecclesiae, ch. 56, p. 159, in N. Iung, *Un franciscain théologien*; Giacomo da Viterbo, *De Regimine Christiano*, II, 8, p. 254; McCready, 'Papalists and Antipapalists', pp. 254–5.
[59] Letters of 31 December 1308 and 15 April 1309; Funck-Brentano, *Philippe le Bel en Flandre*, pp. 542–3. Neither letter was copied into the papal registers.   [60] See above, pp. 142–7.
[61] Funck-Brentano, 'Additions au *Codex Diplomaticus Flandriae*', pp. 532–5.

Also [they thought] that if any Fleming contravened anything in the letter, such excommunication would be inflicted upon him and could be removed by the pope alone, and not even by the pope, except at the king's request and desire. So they were quite unwilling to agree. Nay, rather, highly indignant with the others, the burgesses and tradesmen, they hastened to take up arms. Great fear and trembling arose in the town at this ferocious civil war.[62]

Before a papal response materialised, however, a new agreement was signed. The Flemings eventually succeeded in obtaining some concessions, such as leaving in place the fortifications of Ghent and Ypres.[63] In accordance with the new stipulations, Robert de Béthune wrote to the bishops of Thérouanne and Tournai and asked them to publish the sentences of excommunication and interdict against those who would dare infringe upon the peace.[64] A similar request was sent by Nicolas Delpierre, who acted as proctor of the towns. Consequently, the bishops of Thérouanne and Tournai pronounced the sentences *ad cautelam* on 11 and 30 July 1309. Bruges finally joined Ghent and Ypres and signed the renewed treaty with France (27 July), which had been approved by the pope two days earlier.[65] Philip, though, remained adamant in his opposition to any concessions to Bruges, whose castles were to be demolished and the perpetrators of the Matins to depart on pilgrimage.[66] About sixty pilgrims eventually left the city and came to Avignon to receive papal absolution, a rather formal gesture of goodwill towards the vindictive conscience of Philip the Fair.[67]

After both sides found a way to compromise, the scene was prepared for a papal blessing. On 13 June 1310, Clement once again received, in consistory, the count and the representatives of the towns, who required him to pronounce excommunication against the transgressors of the peace treaty. Clement confirmed the treaty of Athis in its new version, which had been signed in Paris in April 1309.[68] Soon afterwards, he renewed an old letter of Honorius III, who had ordered the archbishop of Reims and the bishop of Senlis to pronounce an interdict on Flanders, should the count or his subjects violate their obligations towards the king

---

[62] *Annales Gandenses*, p. 96.   [63] *Codex Diplomaticus Flandriae*, vol. II, no. 260, pp. 149–54.

[64] *Ibid.*, vol. I, no. 13, pp. 62–5.

[65] *Ibid.*, vol. I, nos. 5, 8, pp. 28–44; *Annales Gandenses*, pp. 93, 96–7; *Regestum Clementis Papae V*, nos. 10426–8.   [66] Jean de St Victor, *Prima Vita*, pp. 15–16.

[67] On 23 June 1308, Philip accepted 300,000 *livres de fors tournois* to exempt the Flemings, other than those from Bruges, from their obligation to send 3,000 people on pilgrimage. The king eventually also bestowed a royal pardon on Bruges: *Codex Diplomaticus Flandriae*, vol. II, nos. 233, 258, pp. 91, 147; *Chronicon Flandriae*, p. 312; Funck-Brentano, *Philippe le Bel en Flandre*, pp. 556–8.

[68] *Regestum Clementis Papae V*, nos. 6166–89. The papal letters specified the names of all Flemish cities that had requested Clement's intervention and had submitted *a priori* to the sentences of excommunication and interdict that would be delivered against those who infringed the peace treaty.

of France.[69] Clement specified that the excommunication would enter into effect if the treaty were violated, and those found guilty would not be absolved, except at the specific request of the king.[70] Soon afterwards, however, the pope retracted this exceptional concession (23 October 1310). During the negotiations over the trial of Boniface, Clement declared to Enguerrand de Marigny that his earlier engagement to ask for the king's consent to withdraw sentences of excommunication had been made thoughtlessly and was contrary to canon law.[71] Clement pointed out that both human and divine law bestowed on the pope full authority to absolve penitent sinners, a fact that no human being might or could prevent.[72] Though the pope promised to keep his retraction secret so that it would not encourage the Flemings with second thoughts, he gave clear indications that his decision was final, thus leaving Philip the Fair with no alternative. Once again, this episode provides convincing proof of the manipulative approach of Clement V towards Capetian interests. The claim of negligence cannot be taken seriously because of both the pope's legal training and the fact that the clause about the removal of excommunication on royal approval had been in effect for more than three years. Clement's devotion to canon law during the trial of Boniface VIII appears, rather, as lip-service, a rhetorical counter-weight to Philip's no less theoretical devotion to the crusade during the Flemish crisis. Both pope and king knew well the weaknesses of the other side and exploited them, without upsetting the basic equilibrium between them.

When the unrest in Flanders grew stronger, Philip again summoned Robert de Béthune and Louis de Nevers (Tournai, 14 October 1311). Though the count and his son did not come, the representatives of the towns provided a captive audience, before which Capetian officers preached the royal creed that the king was sovereign in his realm. The essence of this sovereignty was his right to judge all men and all cases in

---

69 The letter of Honorius III was sent to the archbishop of Narbonne, the archdeacon of Rouen, and an official of Paris.

70 The pope specifically stated that there would be no cancellation of this punishment 'nisi ad requisitionem regis Francie'. See n. 52 above. See also *Regestum Clementis Papae V*, nos. 10466–8.

71 Marigny enjoyed a unique position in the curia, a fact borne out by the considerable number of papal privileges. Favier estimated their number as being lower only than those received by the pope's nephew, Raimond de Got, but equalling those of another nephew, Arnaud de Pellegrue. Besides, many papal letters from 1307 onwards included the formula 'consideratione Ingerrani de Marigniaco': *Regestum Clementis Papae V*, nos. 1742, 1775, 4537–9, 4542–3, 4553, 7791–7809, etc.; Favier, *Un conseiller de Philippe le Bel*, pp. 130, 136, 186; Pegues, *The Lawyers of the Last Capetians*, p. 57. Little wonder that Marigny cried when the news of Clement's death reached him: *La chronique métrique attribuée à Geffroy de Paris*, p. 200.

72 'Nam iure divino vel humano illa clausula non fulcitur; quilibet excommunicatus sufficienti satisfactione premissa debet absolvi, etiam si adversarius contradicat, nec nos potestatem absolvendi a nobis abdicare possumus': *Histoire du differend d'entre le pape Boniface VIII et Philippes le Bel*, p. 294.

the last instance.[73] A new agreement was signed in Pontoise (11 June 1312), but both sides were still reluctant to fulfil it. One year later, Philip summoned his army to make a demonstration of force. Although the king's move directly affected the Flemings, it was also conducted against the tempo, if not the intentions, of papal policy, and it clearly manifested Philip's intention to end the Flemish conflict by whatever means necessary (22 July 1313).[74] Clement hastened to instruct his nuncio in France, Cardinal Nicolas de Fréauville, to apply all necessary means to prevent the outbreak of hostilities.[75] The *Chronographia* presents an accurate report of the papal perspective. It reports the genuine joy of the pope when he heard that Philip the Fair had taken the Cross together with his sons. But Clement's original joy was soon replaced by his concern for the absence of Robert de Béthune and Louis de Nevers from the ceremony and the fact that the count of Flanders and his son had no plans to sail overseas. The pope was well aware that, in such circumstances, Philip the Fair would be unlikely to leave the kingdom, thus jeopardising the implementation of the crusade.[76] The chronicle further points to Nicolas de Fréauville as the main party responsible for impeding a military expedition against Flanders.[77] Papal correspondence corroborates the difficult alternatives that faced Clement V at this point. In a letter to the nuncio, the pope severely criticised the seditious policy of the count of Flanders and his son, who had endangered the peace among Christians and, therefore, the renewal of the crusade, as well (20 June 1313).[78]

By accusing the Flemings of impeding the Christian enterprise *Outremer*, Clement faithfully adopted the Capetian position as it had been carefully elaborated by Enguerrand de Marigny. Though Marigny personally opposed the active participation of Philip the Fair in the crusade, he made good use of the Holy War in order to increase papal support in the Flemish crisis and to alleviate the chronic shortage of the royal treasury. The manipulative approach of the chief royal councillor became evident in 1313, when Clement asked for a provision of ships on behalf of the crusade. Against Philip's original intention to comply with the papal request, Marigny spun out a negative response. The vast expenses

---

[73] Funck-Brentano, *Philippe le Bel en Flandre*, pp. 602–4.

[74] *Codex Diplomaticus Flandriae*, vol. II, no. 293, pp. 236–9; Jean d'Hocsem, *Gesta Pontificum Leodiensium*, p. 366; *Continuationis chronici Guillelmi de Nangiaco*, p. 387; *Les grandes chroniques de France*, pp. 382–4.

[75] Some sources mentioned Jacques Duèse and Arnaud d'Aux as papal legates to Flanders; such a possibility is not confirmed by the papal registers, however: *Istore et croniques de Flandres*, p. 300; *Chronographia regum Francorum*, pp. 212–13.

[76] *Chronographia regum Francorum*, p. 211; *Anciennes chroniques de Flandre*, pp. 399–400; *Istore et croniques de Flandres*, p. 300.

[77] *Chronographia regum Francorum*, pp. 215–17; *Anciennes chroniques de Flandre*, pp. 400–1.

[78] *Collectio actorum veterum*, pp. 122–3.

in Flanders and, rather curiously, also in Gascony and the festivities for the knighthood of Philip's sons, he claimed, did not allow the king of France to support the papal demand. The refusal was, however, accompanied by touching declarations with regard to Philip's devotion to the Holy Land. These were persuasive enough to convince the papal camera to grant the royal treasury a loan of 160,000 florins.[79] Whether Clement was convinced by the Capetian – that is, Enguerrand de Marigny's – argumentation or whether this was a papal gesture of subservience to Philip the Fair is difficult to establish. It seems that Clement did believe in Philip's devotion to the crusade, and it was this belief that led the pope to invest large sums of the camera's income in support of his partner in the future enterprise *Outremer*. Still, papal generosity did not advance Capetian interests in Flanders. Once again, Philip had to content himself with new promises to observe the treaty of Athis (24 July).[80] The papal curia closely followed the new agreement and annulled the interdict that had been pronounced against the county *ad cautelam* (27 August). The fragility of the situation became evident just one year later, after Clement's death, when the sentences against the Flemings were renewed in Tournai, Paris, St Omer, Noyon, Arras, and Douai.[81] The Flemish crisis was also to characterise the reign of the last Capetians and of Philip VI of Valois, and it reached its zenith with the outbreak of the Hundred Years War.[82]

The degree to which Clement was responsible for the lack of a clear settlement in the Flemish crisis is still open to further analysis. Devious as it was, however, papal policy in Flanders reveals new aspects of Clement's personality, especially of his problematic relationship with Philip the Fair. During the endless negotiations between the king of France and the count of Flanders, Clement gave proof of political wisdom when, without rejecting the urgent requests of Philip the Fair, the pope did not actually fulfil them either. Besides evincing a consistent tendency to avoid extreme measures, Clement did his best to encourage both sides to reach a compromise. He published ecclesiastical punishments only after an agreement was actually reached, and hastened to annul them as soon as the chances for peace seemed to be real. The pope

---

[79] 'Primo quod circa recuperationem Terre Sancte est tota affectio et intentio sua': J. Schwalm, 'Beiträge zur Reichsgeschichte des 14. Jahrhunderts', pp. 562–4.

[80] See the summary record of the Flemings' obligations towards the court of France in Funck-Brentano, 'Additions au *Codex Diplomaticus Flandriae*', pp. 556–60; *Les grandes chroniques de France*, p. 290.   [81] *Chronique et annales de Gilles le Muisit*, p. 83.

[82] Guillemain saw in the outbreak of hostilities between France and England not only the failure of papal mediation, with its implicit consequences for the crusade, but also the end of papal arbitration in Christendom: Guillemain, 'Les tentatives pontificales de médiation dans le litige franco-anglais de Guyenne', p. 432.

appears to have been not only more moderate than Philip the Fair, but also more aware of circumstances. The religious zeal of Philip the Fair, whether in enforcing collective penance or in attempting to barricade himself behind ecclesiastical coercion, suggests a complete misunderstanding of the complex situation of Flanders with its highly organised and semi-independent system of local government. This misconception eventually caused the continuation of the conflict for generations to come. These aspects of papal policy, in open contradiction of Capetian interests, corroborate the diplomatic skills of Clement V, whom modern research has often deprecated as 'lacking in initiative'. Papal policy in Flanders further suggests the gap between Clement's and Philip's perceptions of the crisis, a gap that obviously did not advance royal interests. Clement saw in the unrest in Flanders a main impediment to the accomplishment of the crusade, which he defined in terms of *Gesta Dei per Francos*.[83] This evaluation exposed the pope to Capetian pressure, but not to surrender to Philip the Fair. On the other hand, whether consciously or not, Philip relied on papal support to solve the impasse in Flanders, support that was not assured by Clement V. The delicate balance between pope and king was further tested, and in a more challenging way, by the accusations of heresy levelled by the Capetian court against Pope Boniface VIII.

THE TRIAL OF BONIFACE

At the beginning of Clement's pontificate, Philip rejected a papal offer of compromise: absolution for the outrage at Anagni in return for revoking the accusations of heresy against Boniface VIII.[84] Although the king's refusal accorded with the inflexible policy that he followed against his own family and the Templars, there were, aside from Philip's religious zeal, no less important personal and political considerations. Guillaume de Nogaret and the Cardinals Colonna, looking for better conditions, opposed any possible compromise. A strict line was especially important for Nogaret, who was still under excommunication and had become a central voice in keeping alive the accusations against Boniface. The trial of Boniface was also a useful means of exercising pressure on the papal curia and consolidating Philip's position as the most powerful ruler in

---

[83] The same idea was expressed by Galvano da Levanto in his heart-rending appeal to Philip the Fair that 'proprias guerras suspendat', thus allowing him to go and free the Holy Land from the sacrilegious rule of Islam: 'Liber sancti passagii Christicolarum', p. 231.

[84] A papal letter had been prepared absolving Philip IV, Guillaume de Nogaret, and Rinalda da Supino for the outrage of Anagni. It was not, however, delivered because of the lack of a positive response from Philip: *Regestum Clementis Papae V*, no. 10381.

Christendom. Only when these goals were achieved would the way to an agreement be at hand.[85] From a theological point of view, the radical line followed by Philip and his advisors was partly justified by the Inquisition's claim that accusations of heresy were not extinguished with the culprit's death. Moreover, the charges against Boniface were not unprecedented in the annals of the medieval papacy. Canon law explicitly defined heresy as the only crime with which a pope could be charged.[86] John X and Benedict V had been subjected to trial and deposition, while Gregory VII, Gelasius II, and Alexander III had been exposed to powerful antipopes and to sustained personal invective.[87] Historical precedents, however, could not forecast the political implications of the trial of Boniface. By basing himself on his defence of the faith and powers directly conferred on him by Jesus, Philip was actually claiming the right not only to judge, but also to seize and punish a heretical pope.[88] The trial of Boniface thus reflects additional facets of the new challenges presented by the emerging national state *vis-à-vis* the traditional claims of papal monarchy.

On 12 August 1308 – that is, less than a year after the arrest of the Templars – Clement V apprised Christendom of a new trial, one also connected with suspicions of heresy, but this time involving his predecessor at the See of St Peter. The trial of Boniface was scheduled to begin in Avignon in February 1309.[89] Contemporary reactions hint at differences of opinion as to the gravity of the situation. Having been informed in advance of the pope's intentions, James II of Aragon wrote to Clement on behalf of Boniface and emphasised the scandalous nature of such a trial.[90] Arnaud de Villanova aspired to clear Clement of any initiative and carefully reported the pope's displeasure at the whole affair. He provided first-hand testimony of Clement's declaration that 'the affair of Pope Boniface gave us so much pain, that even the most close persons could not help us [to overcome it]'.[91] Though Bernard Gui and Jean de

---

[85] *La chronique métrique attribuée à Geffroy de Paris*, p. 152, vv. 3211–35. See the letter of Piero Colonna to Clement: Finke, *Papsttum und Untergang des Templerordens*, vol. II, no. 27, pp. 40–3. On Philip's messengers to the pope on the charges against Boniface, see *ibid.*, vol. II, no. 26, pp. 39–40.

[86] 'A nemine [papa] est judicandus, nisi deprehendatur a fide devius': 'Si papa', Gratian, prima pars, dist. XL, c. 6, *CIC*, vol. I, col. 146; Ullmann, *Medieval Papalism*, p. 156.

[87] Peters, *The Shadow King*, pp. 220–2.

[88] Wilks, *The Problem of Sovereignty in the Later Middle Ages*, p. 236.

[89] Finke, *Papsttum und Untergang des Templerordens*, vol. II, no. 92, p. 157. Lizerand links the Capetian pressure in the Boniface affair with Clement's refusal to promote Charles de Valois' candidacy to the Empire; see Lizerand, *Clément V et Philippe IV, le Bel*, p. 192. If such were the case, the pope's attempt to use the mediation of Charles de Valois to induce Philip to abandon the charges against Boniface seems rather inappropriate: *Histoire du différend d'entre le pape Boniface VIII et Philippes le Bel*, pp. 290–2; E. Caman, *Papes et antipapes à Avignon*, p. 11.

[90] 'Nos, qui ipsum vidimus ac novimus, hoc incredibilius suscepimus et orribile reputamos': *Acta Aragonensia*, vol. I, no. 102, p. 150.   [91] *Ibid.*, vol. II, no. 435, p. 693.

St Victor were aware of the pressure exerted by Philip the Fair on the papal curia, they justified the trial on the grounds that the king was obliged to protect the 'good of the realm' – a rather questionable justification of royal policy in Anagni and afterwards.[92] Conversely, chroniclers from England regarded the attack on Boniface's memory as scandalous.[93]

The repeated delays in the commencement of the trial hint at Clement's hesitation, which was unavoidable in the light of the serious implications of any judgement of the late pope.[94] Although Clement summoned the detractors of Boniface to Avignon for 13 September 1309, the trial was postponed for six additional months, to 22 March of the following year.[95] Clement sent a personal summons to the close advisors of Philip the Fair – Louis d'Evreux, the counts Gui de St Pol and Jean de Dreux, and Guillaume de Plaisians[96] – but carefully omitted Guillaume de Nogaret, who was still under excommunication. The pope further made it clear that the start of the trial did not reflect his agreement with the Capetian position. On the contrary, Clement used the occasion to defend his predecessor passionately: Boniface, he recalled, had been born to an acknowledged Catholic family and had spent most of his life in the Roman curia. Before he reached the See of St Peter, many popes had exploited his wisdom and diplomatic skills and entrusted him with important missions. Before and after his election to the papacy, Boniface surrounded himself with Catholic men; he wrote pious treatises and delivered fervent sermons. Bearing in mind all these proofs of genuine Catholic faith, Clement expressed full confidence that the lack of a basis for the accusations of heresy would be satisfactorily proved. The pope recognised, though, that the charges of heresy and the requests of Philip IV justified further investigation of the case.[97]

Although Philip the Fair did not come to the public consistory summoned in Avignon, the royal position was faithfully represented by one

---

[92] Johannes Quidort von Paris, *De potestate regia et papali*, c. xx, p. 178.

[93] *Annales Paulini*, pp. 265–6. Walsingham speaks of 'instantia importuna': *Historia Anglicana*, p. 111.

[94] See the apologetic letters of the pope to Philip, explaining the continuous delays: *Histoire du différend d'entre le pape Boniface VIII et Philippes le Bel*, pp. 292–5; *Collectio actorum veterum*, pp. 101–2.

[95] *Regestum Clementis Papae V*, no. 10364. 'Et en ce meismes an, le pape Climent fist publiquement afficher en son palais à Avignon une intimacion, en laquelle il estoit contenu que generalement il intimoit à touz ceulz qui vouldroient proceder en fait de l'appellacion contre le pape Boniface, tant pour lui comme contre li par quelque maniere qu'il fussent pourveuz, dedenz le dimenche que l'en chante "Oculi mei" [22 March] et devant le pape se presentassent, ou autrement sur ce, d'ore en avant il n'i seroient receuz; mais dès maintenant et dès ore en avant, il leur denioit toute audience et leur imposoit silence quant en ceste partie': *Les grandes chroniques de France*, p. 269.

[96] *Regestum Clementis Papae V*, nos. 6318, 10443–4; Schmidt, *Der Bonifaz-Prozess*, pp. 205ff.

[97] *Histoire du différend d'entre le pape Boniface VIII et Philippes le Bel*, pp. 368ff.; *Regestum Clementis Papae V*, no. 5068.

clergyman, Alain de Lamballe, archdeacon of Saint Brieuc, and four leading personages of the Capetian court: Guillaume de Nogaret, Guillaume de Plaisians, Pierre de Galart, master of the arbalesters, and Pierre de Broc, seneschal of Beaucaire. They were joined by a numerous army of followers, advisors, and sergeants, all of whom came to the papal curia.[98] Contemporary chroniclers stressed the 'very powerful entourage' that the royal court had mobilised for the Just War against the late pope.[99] The defence of Boniface relied on his nephews, Cardinal Francesco Caetani and Theobald d'Anagni, and also on Cardinal Giacomo Caetani Stefaneschi. Their stand on behalf of the late pope expressed, among others, their fear that a 'proven' charge of heresy would actually make Boniface's nominations to the Sacred College, theirs included, null and void.[100] They were joined in the defence by a large number of personages from the ecclesiastical and intellectual elite who lacked personal interests of this kind. Among the canonists who tried to exonerate Boniface were Gozio da Rimini and Baudry Biseth, the latter very active in the difficult discussions. Thomas de Morrovalle, Giacomo da Modena, Blasius da Priverno, Crescentius da Paliano, Nicolas da Veroli, Giacomo da Sermoneta, Conrad da Spoleto, and Ferdinand Velasquez also took part in the defence.[101] The outcome of the trial could not therefore be said to be dictated by a lack of balance, since the opposing sides sheltered themselves behind a strong battlement of advisors. On the other hand, the resulting equilibrium between the parties, fragile as it was, broadened the room for papal intervention while paving the way for a compromise. Once again, Clement's tendency to protect himself with endless delays proved effective against the religious zeal of the king of France.

In a public consistory held on 16 March 1310, Boniface's supporters and detractors employed much energy to prove the illegitimacy of the other faction, whether because of the impossibility of defending an heretical pope, as claimed by the *oppositores*, or because of the scandalous behaviour of Nogaret and his followers at Anagni, which, according to the *defensores*, nullified the testimony of the Capetian side.[102] The wide gap between the contenders caused Clement to rescind oral proceedings and to ask for written reports; these were expected by August, to be delivered to Cardinals Etienne de Suisy and Bérenger Frédol.[103] Besides the political advantage implied by such a method, it provides additional evidence of Clement's detour from oral practice. The pope's preference

---

[98] *Regestum Clementis Papae V*, no. 10460.

[99] *Les grandes chroniques de France*, p. 269; *Continuationis chronici Guillelmi de Nangiaco*, p. 374.

[100] Agnolo di Tura, *Cronaca Senese*, p. 299.   [101] Schmidt, *Der Bonifaz-Prozess*, pp. 156–78.

[102] *Regestum Clementis Papae V*, nos. 10452–3.

[103] *Histoire du différend d'entre le pape Boniface VIII et Philippes le Bel*, pp. 367–70; Schmidt, *Der Bonifaz-Prozess*, pp. 247–84.

for written proceedings was in keeping with his expertise in Roman law and was further manifested during the Council of Vienne. On 20 March, Boniface's supporters sent a first addendum to their former rejection of Capetian claims.[104] The French party presented three memoranda, two of which were former requests written by Guillaume de Nogaret and Guillaume de Plaisians in 1303.[105] The Capetian representatives also provided a list of eight cardinals, all of whom had been appointed by Boniface, whose testimony was suspected of being biased and, as such, should be rejected.[106] Between August and September 1310 and again between April and May of the following year, the Capetian representatives provided about thirty-seven depositions, all of which elaborated the different facets of Boniface's alleged heresy.[107] Though the formal trial reopened on 10 November 1310, Clement announced on 22 December a new delay of three months on the grounds of his illness. 'Papal illness' allowed secret negotiations, which eventually led to the desired compromise.[108]

In February 1311, Philip wrote the pope a letter reporting the Anagni events from a new, more suitable perspective. The king of France confessed that Boniface's misdeeds had forced him to intervene in Church affairs, his intervention being supported by the community of the realm, the masters of the university, and neighbouring countries, as well. The opposition to Boniface thus acquired a pan-Christian character while bestowing on Philip the Fair the natural role of *advocatus ecclesiae*, not only for his own kingdom but for the whole of Christendom. Yet Philip's request to proceed with a trial of Boniface did not suggest that the king had tried to act as judge or prosecutor against the Holy See. Rather, as a simple subordinate, the king argued, he had attempted to facilitate the summoning of a general council. The violence of Anagni had actually resulted from a personal vendetta, which Boniface's many and powerful enemies plotted against him. Guillaume de Nogaret, though, following Philip's instructions, had limited himself to transmitting to Boniface the royal summons to the forthcoming council. Having cleared his conscience, and also that of his main counsellor, as to

---

[104] *Histoire du differend d'entre le pape Boniface VIII et Philippes le Bel*, pp. 371–2.

[105] *Ibid.*, pp. 315–46. Analysis of Nogaret's declarations can be found in M. Melville, 'Guillaume de Nogaret et Philippe le Bel', pp. 60–5.

[106] The names of Leonard d'Albano, Pietro da Sabina, Lucas Fieschi, Giacomo Stefaneschi, and Francesco Caetani headed the list of those whose depositions were to be excluded. See *Histoire du differend d'entre le pape Boniface VIII et Philippes le Bel*, pp. 435ff.

[107] *Ibid.*, pp. 523–6; Hefele and Leclercq, *Histoire des conciles*, vol. VI-1, pp. 565–7; on the nature of the accusations, see Menache, 'Un peuple qui a sa demeure à part', pp. 193–208.

[108] On 29 August 1310, Clement sent the bishop of Avignon, Jacques Duèse, to Philip the Fair, 'de arduis quibusdam cum illo ecclesie Romanae negotiis agat': *Regestum Clementis Papae V*, no. 6334.

any misdeed against the former pope, Philip the Fair finally declared his complete submission to any final judgement that Clement would reach on the matter.[109]

Philip's letter provided an effective way out of the problematic affair of Anagni. After receiving several testimonies on behalf of his predecessor, when the trial was resumed, Clement published his formal decision in different documents, the most important of which was *Rex gloriae virtutum* (27 April 1311).[110] The pope stated that he recognised Philip's Christian zeal as 'fighter for the faith' and 'defender of the Church'. He justified the king's deeds, since they had been committed 'by the call of his conscience, urged by need, not because of hate, wrath, or malevolence, but because of his complete devotion to the faith'. Accordingly, Clement abrogated any apostolic decisions, laws, constitutions, or declarations pronounced after 1 November 1300 either by Boniface VIII or Benedict XI that had not been included in the *Sextus* and that could be detrimental to the kingdom of France and its king.[111] Guillaume de Nogaret was exonerated *ad cautelam* on account of his participation in the forthcoming crusade and pilgrimage to various shrines in France and the Iberian peninsula (Rocamadour, Le Puy, Boulogne-sur-Mer, Chartres, St-Gilles, Montmajour, and Compostella).[112] Still, if one considers the papal privileges bestowed on Nogaret the following year, including the right to hear mass in areas under interdict, it is difficult to believe that the penance imposed was taken seriously either by the repentant Nogaret or by the benevolent Clement himself. In a formal letter that awarded Nogaret the use of a movable altar (11 May 1312), allusion was made to his 'sincere devotion', a rather curious lapse by the papal chancery in regard to the perpetrator of the outrage of Anagni.[113] Clement's forgiveness also embraced the citizens of Anagni and their notorious leaders, Rinalda da Supino, Sciarra Colonna, and Pietro da Genazzano.[114] Only

---

[109] *Ibid.*, no. 10637; *Histoire du differend d'entre le pape Boniface VIII et Philippes le Bel*, pp. 296–300; Schmidt, *Der Bonifaz-Prozess*, p. 387. This version was accepted by Fawtier, who assumes that the outrage at Anagni was actually the result of the Colonnas' vendetta against Boniface. Conversely, Nogaret was in the town on a peaceful mission to summon the pope to a council and eventually saved Boniface's life: Fawtier, 'L'attentat d'Anagni', pp. 178–9. This possibility is convincingly refuted by Melville, 'Guillaume de Nogaret et Philippe le Bel', p. 66.

[110] *Regestum Clementis Papae V*, no. 7501; *Histoire du differend d'entre le pape Boniface VIII et Philippes le Bel*, pp. 590–602.   [111] *Continuationis chronici Guillelmi de Nangiaco*, pp. 382–3.

[112] *Histoire du differend d'entre le pape Boniface VIII et Philippes le Bel*, p. 601.

[113] The letter was indeed a regular formula employed by the papal chancery; rather obviously, it did not suit the case of Nogaret: *Regestum Clementis Papae V*, no. 7928. The same privilege was awarded to Guillaume de Plaisians and his wife the same day, probably owing to the intervention of Philip the Fair: *ibid.*, no. 7927. See Berger, 'Bulle de Clément V en faveur de Guillaume de Nogaret', pp. 268–70.

[114] *Regestum Clementis Papae V*, nos. 7502–3, 7505, 7507, 8248; *Les grandes chroniques de France*, pp. 280–1; *Continuationis chronici Guillelmi de Nangiaco*, pp. 384–5.

those implicated in 'misappropriating, retaining, and ensconcing the apostolic treasure' in Anagni were deprived of papal absolution.[115]

Clement's declarations on behalf of the Christian zeal of Philip the Fair in the Anagni affair may be regarded as a complete volte-face; actually, it was a rather similar move to that forced on Boniface VIII with regard to the taxation of the clergy in 1297. *Rex gloriae virtutum*, as generous as it was, however, remained a theoretical declaration that released the pope and the papacy from the Capetian threat of a trial of Boniface. One may question the expediency of such a move for the papal monarchy in the long term, especially in the light of the delicate balance between subservience to the king of France, on the one hand, and the claim that the pope should not be judged by any human instance, on the other. None the less, *Rex gloriae virtutum*, in the short term, not only freed Clement from Capetian pressure but also fostered the French–papal alliance in the forthcoming expedition *Outremer*.

The ambiguous combination of Clement's uncompromising declarations in favour of the religious zeal and pious devotion of Philip the Fair and his termination of the trial of Boniface caused papal policy to be seldom understood. Papal magnanimity, indeed, did not encounter much approbation among contemporary chroniclers. Amalric Auger stressed the many irregularities that typified the behaviour of the Capetian representatives during the trial, 'because of whom a great scandal was produced almost every day'.[116] Moreover, the extremism of Guillaume de Nogaret and Guillaume de Plaisians made Boniface seem a martyr even to chroniclers who were usually loyal to Capetian policy. The continuator of Guillaume de Nangis was echoed by the chronicler of St Denis in acclaiming the obstinacy of the defence in proving the orthodox faith of the late pope; they both supported Clement's decision to disqualify forged documents produced on behalf of the prosecution, and justified relegation of the trial to the final judgement of the pope.[117] Other writers went further, explaining the compromise reached by Clement as additional evidence of his faith in the orthodoxy of his predecessor.[118] Nor was the king of France completely cleared. An anonymous song depicted Philip the Fair as the antichrist, who together with the pope was busily plotting the fall of Christendom.[119] Only a few voices on the Ile-de-France treated Nogaret's absolution as a papal gesture of goodwill towards Philip the Fair.[120]

---

[115] *Regestum Clementis Papae V*, no. 7504; Schmidt, *Der Bonifaz-Prozess*, pp. 374–427.

[116] Amalric Auger, *Sexta Vita*, p. 100.

[117] *Continuationis chronici Guillelmi de Nangiaco*, pp. 373–5, 378–9; *Les grandes chroniques de France*, pp. 269–70.   [118] *Continuatio chronici Girardi de Fracheto*, pp. 32–4.

[119] Boutaric, *La France sous Philippe le Bel*, p. 435.

[120] They presented the papal decision as being done 'consideratione regis pro ipso supplicantis': *Continuatio chronici Girardi de Fracheto*, pp. 35–6; *Ex anonymo regum Franciae chronico*, p. 19.

Away from the sphere of influence of Philip the Fair, the chroniclers' criticism of papal policy only increased. Tolomeo da Lucca, for example, was not impressed by Clement's forgiving nature and termed bribery the payment of 100,000 florins by the Capetian treasury to the pope.[121] Though this suggestion hardly flattered Clement V, it does suggest a belief in the eventual defeat of Philip the Fair and his advisors. In the context of the many rumours about the causes and outcomes of the papal move, the continuator of Guillaume de Nangis argued that Guillaume de Nogaret had nominated Clement his legal heir.[122] This claim expressed a belief in Philip's defeat, as well as in the pope's basic greed and avarice, the main two factors that according to many contemporaries dictated Clement's policy. Without going so far, other authors, too, viewed Clement's absolution of Nogaret as pure simony.[123] Clement's refusal to take a clear stand on the question of Boniface's heresy was also justified by the principle of 'par in parem potestatem non habeat'.[124] Dante Alighieri considered the trial of Boniface to be yet another expression of the prostitution of the curia by the king of France (*fiordaliso*).[125] The Aragonese representative in the curia concluded that Philip was 'king, and pope, and emperor!', who obtained whatever he wanted from Clement V.[126] The *Flores historiarum* compared the co-operation between pope and king to the old alliance between Herod and Pilate, an alliance that would jeopardise the fate of the Church and Christendom.[127]

---

[121] Rather specifically, he claimed that 'pro quadam recompensatione laborum circa dictam causam': Tolomeo da Lucca, *Secunda Vita*, p. 39.

[122] *Continuationis chronici Guillelmi de Nangiaco*, p. 385.

[123] Biax sire Diex! qui vit trop voit.
Ainsi s'asolution prist
Du pape cil qui tant mesprist,
Si com l'en dist, et fu assolz,
Non pas por Dieu, mes por les solz.
La chronique métrique attribuée à Geffroy de Paris, p. 153, vv. 3236–40.

Renan joins in this approach, regarding papal policy as an expression of the French victory over the papacy. Lizerand, on the other hand, saw Nogaret as the real victim of the agreement between pope and king. See Renan, *Etudes sur la politique religieuse du règne de Philippe le Bel*, p. 342; Lizerand, *Clément V et Philippe IV, le Bel*, pp. 220–41.

[124] Tolomeo da Lucca, *Secunda Vita*, p. 36.

[125] Dante Alighieri, *Divina Commedia*, *Inferno*, c. XIX, vv. 79–81; *Purgatorio*, c. XX, vv. 82–90.

[126] Finke, *Papsttum und Untergang des Templerordens*, vol. II, no. 78, p. 123. Regarding the important political functions of these representatives during the reign of James II, see Berger, 'Jacques II d'Aragon, le Saint-Siège et la France', pp. 281–2.

[127] Ecclesiae navis titubat, regni quia clavis
Errat; rex, papa, facti sunt unica capa;
Haec faciunt do, des, Pilatus hic, alter Herodes.
Flores historiarum, app., p. 323.

A contemporary copy redacted in Chartres includes some minor variations:

The sharp criticism of Clement's policy during the trial of Boniface that characterises most sources is not supported in historical research. Georges Lizerand suggests that, within Clement's limited freedom of action, the pope's resistance to following Philip's designs was unexpectedly strong.[128] Jean Favier transfers the focus of analysis to the Capetian court and sees in the many changes throughout 1311 the rising influence of the pragmatic Marigny against the doctrinaire Nogaret. The invalidation of the charges against Boniface was, accordingly, part of a total reconsideration of royal policy in both the internal and external arenas; it included the activation of the Guelph league against Henry VII, the transfer of the trial of the Templars to Vienne, and an amicable solution to the trial of Guichard de Troyes.[129] Obviously, it is possible to connect Philip's late readiness to compromise in the case of Boniface and Clement's predisposition to retribution in regard to the Templars, since both cases actually proceeded in parallel. Such considerations, however, were completely foreign to the religious perspective of Philip the Fair. If the king was still convinced of Boniface's heresy, as he undoubtedly was in 1302–3, he would have deprecated any compromise. Favier's interpretation throws open the old question about the division of labour between Philip the Fair and his lawyers, while leaving the king in the dubious role of blindly following their conflicting dictates. Conversely, it is clear that Clement won an irrefutable victory. The only concession he was forced to make involved his generous praise of Philip's behaviour – but this was a theoretical concession that the pope often found very easy to make. The canonisation of Pietro da Morrone, the former pope Celestine V and predecessor of Boniface, provides another factor in the fragile balance between Clement V and Philip IV.

THE CANONISATION OF PIETRO DA MORRONE

Fourteenth-century sources saw in the canonisation of Pietro da Morrone additional proof of Clement's complaisance towards Philip the Fair. From the Capetian perspective, acknowledgement of the holiness of Celestine V, who had enjoyed in his own lifetime all the attributes of a hermit saint, rather obviously shadowed the memory of Boniface VIII.

Jam Petri navis titubat, racio quia clavis
Errat; Rex, Papa, facti sunt unica capa,
Dechirant, do, des, Pilatus et alter Herodes.

According to Jusselin, this copy suggests that clergymen were hostile to Philip but avoided direct criticism. See M. Jusselin, 'Une satire contre Philippe le Bel et Clément V', pp. 280–1.
[128] Lizerand, *Clément V et Philippe le Bel*, p. 220.
[129] Favier, 'Les légistes et le gouvernement de Philippe le Bel', p. 104.

Moreover, the canonisation of Celestine was expected to sharpen the contrast between the angelic pope, who had been compelled to relinquish the papacy, and his manipulative, aggressive, and arrogant successor.[130] Such an achievement would also weaken the aura of martyrdom that gradually surrounded Boniface during his trial.[131] André Vauchez views the case of Pietro da Morrone as the highest degree of political canonisation; he argues that 'Philip the Fair insistently urged Celestine's inscription in the catalogue of the saints and Clement V and the Council of Vienne acquiesced in order to avoid any pronouncement against the memory of Boniface VIII, which was also requested by the king of France.'[132] To support this claim, Vauchez calls attention to the fact that hermits, who enjoyed much prestige in Christian society, were not usually rewarded with sainthood throughout the thirteenth century. On the other hand, saints like Louis IX, Antonio da Padova (the celebrated preacher and first lector in theology in the Franciscan Order), and Pietro Martyr (the inquisitor murdered by the crowd in the suburbs of Milan in 1252) hint at the main concerns of the papacy at the time, namely, the propagation of the true faith in the fight against either the Infidel or sectarians and heretics.[133] Although the political meaning of Pietro's canonisation – not only for Philip the Fair, but also for the Colonnas and the Angevins – can hardly be contested, it cannot simply be regarded as a papal surrender to the pressure exercised by the Capetian court. The biographies of the saint and the many miracles attributed to him in his lifetime faithfully mirror his ethical values and charismatic personality, which encountered fervent support among his contemporaries.[134] Further, the political factor behind the Capetian position was largely neutralised by Clement's decision to vest sanctity in the private person, Pietro da Morrone, not in the pope, thus making any comparison between Celestine V and his successor more difficult.[135]

Pietro da Morrone was born in 1209 or 1210 to a humble family; his mother, Maria, led him to fervent religiosity from childhood. In 1231, on the road from Isernia to Rome, he made his profession at the Benedictine monastery of Faifoli, near Limosano.[136] In keeping with the

---

[130] F. Baethgen, *Der Engelpapst*, pp. 206ff.

[131] On the relationship between Celestine and Boniface, see Finke, *Aus den Tagen Bonifaz VIII*, pp. 24–43.   [132] A. Vauchez, *La sainteté en Occident aux derniers siècles du moyen âge*, p. 91.

[133] *Ibid.*, p. 454.

[134] *Annales Genuenses*, p. 79. On Celestine's *vitae*, see E. Pasztor, 'S. Celestino V', pp. 7–20. From the table provided by Vauchez, only Hugues de Bonnevaux, who died in 1194, surpassed the number of miracles performed by Pietro da Morrone in his lifetime. See Vauchez, *La sainteté en Occident aux derniers siècles du moyen âge*, p. 587.

[135] Wood, 'Celestine V, Boniface VIII, and the Authority of Parliament', p. 49.

[136] The most accurate biography is provided by P. Herde, *Cölestin V*, pp. 1–30.

rule of St Benedict, he became a hermit on Mount Palleno, near Castel di Sangrio in the Abruzzi.[137] He was ordained a priest in Rome at the age of twenty-four, and lived as a hermit on Mount Morrone near Sulmone for five years. In search of greater solitude, he later journeyed to Mount Majella, where he built a hermitage with the aid of two disciples. A growing number of followers joined him, attracted by his reputation for humility, penitence, and charity.[138] As time went by, Pietro built several new foundations, all of them dedicated to the Holy Spirit. Urban IV enrolled the Celestinian hermits under Benedictine rule (1 June 1263), and Gregory X gave apostolic blessing to their attempt to imitate the government of the Cistercians and the poverty of the Franciscans (22 March 1273). By the end of the thirteenth century, the Order embraced about 600 members and thirty-six houses in Italy, which often replaced old Benedictine foundations.[139] Elected pope in July 1294, Pietro, now Celestine V, renounced the papacy in December of the same year. According to the version provided by Ferreti, Pope Celestine justified his decision on the grounds of humility, a troubled conscience, his aspiration for a more humble life, and the salvation of his soul, which was endangered by the many honours of the Holy See.[140] He died soon afterwards, but not before he was arrested and made to suffer all kinds of mistreatment by Boniface, his successor to the Holy See. Immediately after Pietro's death in 1296, the Celestinians, under the leadership of Cardinal Thomas de Ste Cecilia, undertook an inquiry into his life and miracles that spawned two biographies and an autobiography.[141] The official biographies, written by his disciples, emphasise the many obstacles that stood in Pietro's way to perfection and the numerous disciples and crowds that intruded on his solitude. They further refer to Pietro's unwilling assumption of the papal tiara, and his detention by Boniface, who prohibited his return to eremitic life after he had abdicated the papacy.[142]

---

[137] P. Golinelli, 'Monachesimo e santità', pp. 45–66.   [138] M. Goodich, *Vita Perfecta*, pp. 137–8.

[139] The papal confirmations in the *Regesta Pontificum Romanorum*, nos. 18551, 21066; A. Trinci, 'Perfezione spirituale e fedeltà alla regola', pp. 239–55. In his last will of 1311, Philip left a large bequest of 4,000 *l.t.* to the Celestines: Brown, 'Royal Salvation and Needs of State', p. 371.

[140] On his abdication as seen from the perspective of *papa inutilis*, see Peters, *The Shadow King*, pp. 217–20, 225–32. On Celestine's election to the papacy and his brief pontificate, see Herde, *Cölestin V*, pp. 31–142.

[141] Written partially in the first person and ostensibly left by Pietro in his cell before his death, the autobiography contains elements of undoubted authenticity; nevertheless, its authorship is uncertain and its polemical purpose apparent. The work may have been composed by close associates of Pietro in an attempt to support his canonisation. See A. Frugoni, *Celestiniana*, pp. 25–67; Herde, *Cölestin V*, pp. 223–6.

[142] 'Vie et miracles de S. Pierre Célestin par deux de ses disciples', pp. 393–458; 'Die *Vita* Coelestini V des Petrus de Alliaco', and 'Die *Vita* Coelestini V des Matteus Vegius', pp. 147–208; Herde, *Cölestin V*, pp. 191–206.

Obviously, any attempt to bring about the canonisation of Celestine was doomed to failure during the pontificate of Boniface VIII. The election of Clement V introduced new possibilities in the light of both his good relationship with the Capetians and the Angevins and his readiness to open the trial of Boniface. In 1306, indeed, Clement ordered James, the archbishop of Naples, and Francis Raimond de Latto, the bishop of Valve, to proceed with an inquiry into the miracles and life of Pietro da Morrone 'according to the requests of Philip the Fair'.[143] To this end, 322 witnesses appeared, largely from the vicinity of Sulmona. Every local occupation was represented; and despite Pietro's strong efforts to avoid women, at least one-third of the witnesses were female.[144] Most of the inquiries focused on the most distant locations of the Abruzzi, where Pietro da Morrone had spent almost fifty years. Contemporaries bore witness to his many sacrifices and continuous suffering,[145] his tortured face moving people to tears.[146] Some testified that just looking at him and his tormented body made one realise that only divine grace could allow him to remain alive.[147] As to his religious fervour, many reported that Pietro read the Psalter and other passages of the Bible and the canonical hours daily, and made 500 genuflections (which increased to 1,000 during Lent).[148] All witnesses testified to Pietro's poor clothes, his walking barefooted – only in winter did he use wooden shoes – and his continuous flagellation with horse hair strengthened with many knots. He never ate beef, eggs, milk products, or oil, but fed himself on rootstock, bulbs, and herbs. During Lent, he fasted for two and even four days a week.[149]

Notwithstanding popular fervour and broad admiration for Pietro, the proceedings of the oral inquiry in Naples did not persuade Clement to arrive at an immediate decision; the pope opted to forward the documentation to four cardinals for their consideration. He later appointed an expanded commission of eight cardinals to review the whole matter. The candidacy of Pietro da Morrone for sainthood was brought to the Council of Vienne, where a new commission was appointed, its

---

[143] Schimmelpfennig, *Die Zeremonienbücher der römischen Kurie im Mittelalter*, pp. 167–8. The text appears also in L. H. Labande, 'Le cérémonial romain de Jacques Cajétan', p. 61; and 'Das *Opus metricum* des Kardinals Jacobus Gaietani Stefaneschi', pp. 1–146. See also V. Licitra, 'Considerazione sull' *Opus metricum* del Card. Jacopo Caetani Stefaneschi', pp. 185–201.

[144] Only 162 testimonies, however, survived. They have been published in 'Die Akten des Kanonisationsprozess in dem Codex zu Sulmona', pp. 209–331.

[145] See an analysis of the testimonies in A. Marini, 'Pietro del Morrone monaco negli Atti del Processo di canonizzazione', pp. 93–6. On Pietro's therapeutic powers, see G. P. Ferzoco, 'Historical and Hagiographical Aspects of the Religious World of Peter of Morrone', pp. 227–37.

[146] 'In solo aspectu faciei illius, quociens ostendebat se populo, nullus fere de astantibus abstinere poterat ex devocione concepta a compunctionis lacrimis cum singultu': 'Die Akten des Kanonisationsprozesses in dem Codex zu Sulmona', p. 211.   [147] *Ibid.*, pp. 329, 333.

[148] *Ibid.*, pp. 333–4.   [149] *Ibid.*, pp. 308, 328–30.

members being prelates from outside the papal curia.[150] Though Giacomo Stefaneschi justified the absence of a decision on the grounds of the many subjects that were on the agenda, it seems that the prelates were no more decisive than the pope and the cardinals in regard to the holiness of Pietro da Morrone.[151] Eventually, the matter returned to the papal curia.[152] After several more brief inquiries, Clement held two consistories, one secret and one open (2 May 1313), about which we have the faithful report of Giacomo Stefaneschi. Nineteen miracles were reported for the cardinals' consideration, the pope reserving his own judgement to the end of each session. Only fourteen miracles – most of them associated with the cure of illnesses that doctors found incurable or with raising people from the dead – were fully confirmed. Clement was not always supportive of the miraculous nature attributed to Celestine's deeds, and many cardinals were also hesitant.[153] Exceptions were the Cardinals Colonna, who found incontestable proof of the sanctity of each of Celestine's deeds. Against their dubious devotion, there consistently stood Cardinals Richard Petroni da Siena, Giacomo Stefaneschi, and sometimes Jacques Duèse, as well.[154] The long trial came to an end on Saturday, 5 May 1313, when Clement finally canonised Pietro da Morrone.[155] The pope based his sermon on Isaiah, 12:6, 'Cry out and shout, thou inhabitant of Zion: for great is the Holy One of Israel in the midst of thee.' Clement referred to Pietro's humble origins and lack of intellectual skills and experience, which made his holiness and virtues all the more remarkable.[156] The pope neither surrendered to the Capetian vendetta against Boniface nor vested sanctity in his predecessor, but on Pietro da Morrone.[157]

---

[150] Schimmelpfennig, *Die Zeremonienbücher der römischen Kurie im Mittelalter*, p. 170; L. H. Labande, 'Le cérémonial romain de Jacques Cajétan', pp. 61–2.

[151] 'Procès-verbal du dernier consistoire sécret préparatoire à la canonisation de S. Pierre de Morrone', pp. 391–2.

[152] In the reports to James of Aragon (7 March 1313), emphasis was laid on the fact that the canonisation process of Pietro was due to the *magna instancia* of the king of France: *Acta Aragonensia*, vol. III, no. 113, pp. 235–7.

[153] Schimmelpfennig, *Die Zeremonienbücher der römischen Kurie im Mittelalter*, pp. 170–2; L. H. Labande, 'Le cérémonial romain de Jacques Cajétan', pp. 64–5.

[154] The consistory referred to the miracles that Pietro da Morrone performed before, during, and after his pontificate, as well as before and after his death. See 'Procès-verbal du dernier consistoire sécret préparatoire à la canonisation de S. Pierre de Morrone', pp. 475–87.

[155] Finke, *Papsttum und Untergang des Templerordens*, vol. II, no. 120, pp. 225–6.

[156] 'Eum magnum fuisse, non generis nobilitate, non scientie magnitudine, non experientie, sed sanctitatis et virtutum et, dum papa fuit, dignitatis, et fuit prosecutus . . . Quod miracula fecerat ante papatum, in papatu, post papatum adhuc vivens, in vita et in morte': Schimmelpfennig, *Die Zeremonienbücher der römischen Kurie im Mittelalter*, p. 172; L. H. Labande, 'Le cérémonial romain de Jacques Cajétan', pp. 65–6.

[157] *Regestum Clementis Papae V*, no. 9668; Bernard Gui, in *Tertia Vita*, p. 57; Bernard Gui, in *Quarta Vita*, p. 75; Amalric Auger, *Sexta Vita*, p. 103.

The sagacity of Clement's decision did not escape his contemporaries; once again, though, there was no consensus as to the relationship between the pope and the king of France.[158] Jean de St Victor echoed the support that Pietro da Morrone had gained among wide sections of society. He referred to his canonisation as the result of the 'holiness of his life and the true of his miracles', which had been carefully investigated into and faithfully corroborated. To facilitate the work of his readers, Jean further provides the prayer to be said on Pietro da Morrone's day, 19 May.[159] In spite of the attempts to laud the holy life of the new saint, Walsingham and John of Burgundy expressed reservations at what they considered to be an additional submission to Philip the Fair by Clement V. Referring to the meeting between king and pope in Poitiers, when the canonisation of Celestine V had first been suggested by Philip, John of Burgundy added that 'consequently Pope Boniface will be damned'. Furthermore, John regarded the king's request for Celestine's canonisation to fall within the framework of excessive Capetian demands on the papal curia.[160] Dante Alighieri, on the other hand, criticised Celestine's renunciation of the papacy as a cowardly act.[161] Although the sanctity of Pietro da Morrone was well substantiated by popular belief, it is rather clear that contemporary authors reacted according to their expectations – one may say prejudices – regarding Clement V and his policy. The same may be said about the division of opinion among the cardinals, many of whom approached the sanctity of the late pope according to their political inclinations and personal interests. Still, the criticism of papal policy in this particular case hints at the mature approach of contemporary chroniclers, who did not fall easy prey to the arguments put forth on behalf of the saint by either the Capetian or the papal court. On the other hand, their criticism strengthened the stereotyped image of Pope Clement V.

Analysis of papal policy in France allows the conclusion that Clement V succeeded in advancing the papacy from the dead-end to which it had

---

[158] 'Per quod videtur dictus dominus Clemens ratificasse renuntiationem, quia noluit ipsum vocari Celestinum': Tolomeo da Lucca, *Secunda Vita*, p. 49; *Notae ad vitas*, vol. II, p. 90; *Annales Lubicenses*, pp. 422–3.   [159] Jean de St Victor, *Prima Vita*, p. 20.

[160] 'Dicitur tamen quod multa petit, de quibus quedam indecentia sunt ad petendum set et ad concedendum essent inde[cent]issima': Finke, *Papsttum und Untergang des Templeordens*, vol. II, no. 23, p. 35; cf. Walsingham, *Historia Anglicana*, p. 111.

[161] And some I knew among them; last of all
I recognised the shadow of that soul
who, in his cowardice, made the great denial.
Dante Alighieri, *Divina Commedia*, Inferno, c. III, vv. 55–7.

On Dante's reference to Celestine in the climate of opinion of the time, see G. Padoan, 'Colui che fece per viltà il gran rifiuto', pp. 75–103; D. J. Leclercq, 'La renonciation de Célestin V', pp. 183–92.

been pushed by the aggressive policy of Boniface VIII. The pope also succeeded in preventing an outbreak of hostilities between France and
England and between France and Flanders. These accomplishments
acquired maximum importance for the implementation of the crusade, the
most important goal of Clement's pontificate. In this respect, what many
contemporaries regarded as a complete papal surrender to the Capetian
king appears, upon closer analysis, as a coherent policy with clear goals.
True, Clement was ready to sacrifice theoretical principles and to make an
important contribution to the cult of monarchy during the reign of Philip
the Fair. For Clement, however, this was paying lip-service in order to
advance the recovery of the Holy Land. Whatever the successes or failures
of Clement's policy in France, however, the pope failed to achieve broad
support. Only a few chroniclers were ready to analyse the accomplishments of papal policy from a realistic point of view. More often than not,
contemporary authors voiced their expectations of a militant Church and
a more independent papacy, in complete disregard of the political circumstances of the early fourteenth century. The melancholic tone of their
approach created a very biased perspective of papal policy, which prepared
the ground for the 'Babylonian captivity' of Clement V's pontificate.

THE TRIAL OF THE TEMPLARS

The trial of the Templars constituted a crucial episode during the
pontificate of Clement V; no other subject in this period has been so
extensively documented. Supporters and critics have recorded their opinions of the respective roles and motives of pope and king, the two leading
dramatis personae during the long trial.[162] The fate of the Templars also
dominated the extensive correspondence between Clement V and Philip
IV for five years.[163] Notwithstanding this rich documentation and the
fecund research of the last 150 years, many issues still require further
investigation. To mention but a few: the motivations behind the arrest,
the vicissitudes of papal policy from 1307 to 1312, and the causes and outcomes of the abolition of the Order of the Temple; all these issues call
for more research.

The report by Jean de St Victor reflects the first stage of the drama and
the initial reactions to the arrest of the Templars on the Ile-de-France:

In the early hours of the morning, on Friday the 13th of October, a strange event
occurred, the likes of which have never been heard since ancient times. The

---

[162] See a historiographical survey up to the end of the nineteenth century by G. Salvemini,
'L'abolizione dell'Ordine dei Templari', pp. 230–56.
[163] *Collectio actorum veterum*, pp. 78–86, 90–4, 108–11, 115–16, 141–3, etc.

Grand Master of the Temple . . . was arrested in the Temple of Paris and, on the same day, all Templars in France were suddenly arrested and incarcerated in various prisons. Everybody was stunned by such action [but assumed that] it was ordered by the Roman curia, in consultation with the king, and carried out by the knights Guillaume de Nogaret and Reginald de Roy . . . On the following Sunday [15 October], a public preaching was held in the king's gardens. The reasons for the arrest were there explained to the people and the aforesaid matter was discussed, first by the Dominicans and then by the king's officers, so that the people might not be too violently shocked by the sudden arrest, since the Templars were most powerful, both in riches and renown.[164]

Some 15,000 persons – knights, chaplains, sergeants, *confratres*, retainers, even labourers on Templar farms – were seized on 13 October 1307. No more than 500 of them were probably full members of the Order, and fewer than 200 professed brethren.[165] The simultaneous arrests of Templars throughout France reflects the high level of efficiency attained by the Capetian court, which had undertaken similar actions against Jews and Lombards a few months earlier. 'No modern dictatorship', Joseph R. Strayer reminds us, 'could have done a better job.'[166] Only one or two dozen Templars managed to elude capture.[167] On the other hand, the testimony of Jean de St Victor exposes the weaknesses of the royal action. The arrest of the Templars stunned contemporaries, since there was no precedent for such an action against an exempt Order and since the Templars were wealthy and highly respected, a fact often emphasised by chroniclers.[168] The Capetian court sensed the mood of criticism and wished to dispel any reservations. The arrest warrants suggested a prior consultation 'with our most holy father in Christ, the pope'.[169] These words, by implicating the pope in the arrest, were intended to protect Philip from any charge of violating ecclesiastical immunity. Conversely, they corroborate the king's devotion to the Church and to the pope as its head. In a letter to James of Aragon, too, Philip explicitly referred to previous consultations with the pope at Lyons and Poitiers. The king further alleged that, if the Templars were found innocent, their wealth would be returned to them; otherwise it would be reserved on behalf of

---

[164] Jean de St Victor, *Prima Vita*, pp. 8–9; *Notae ad vitas*, pp. 52–5.

[165] These numbers, which seem rather low, are provided by D. Seward, 'The Dissolution of the Templars', p. 631. See the hesitations of A. Demurger on the subject, *Vie et mort de l'ordre du Temple*, p. 300.   [166] Strayer, *The Reign of Philip the Fair*, p. 286.

[167] *Le procès des Templiers*, vol. I, pp. 29–30, 509; vol. II, pp. 1, 33, 144, 147, 157, 159, etc.

[168] For the history of the Order, see M. Barber, *The New Knighthood*.

[169] Philip specifically declared that 'ad indagandum super premissis plene veritatis indaginem, prehabito super hoc cum sanctissimo patre in Domino C., divina providencia sacrosancte Romane et universalis ecclesie summo pontifice, colloquio et diligente tractatu ac cum prelatis et baronibus nostris deliberatione consilii plenioris': Lizerand, *Le dossier de l'affaire des Templiers*, no. 2, p. 20.

the Holy Land (16 October 1307).[170] Royal documentation thus reflects, from the outset, the official response to the main charge levelled against Philip the Fair during the trial, namely, of having conducted an independent policy against an exempt Order out of his designs to expropriate its wealth.

Although there are clear signs that the need to reform the Temple, and perhaps also the Hospital, had been discussed by Philip the Fair and Clement V, papal correspondence does not confirm any previous understanding as to the policy, let alone the drastic measures, that eventually were undertaken by Philip the Fair. Clement received the news of the arrests soon afterwards, when staying outside Poitiers. The pope hastened to the city and held a secret consistory (16 October). Two weeks later, he revealed his anger and wounded pride in a letter to Philip (27 October):

> You, our dear son . . . have, in our absence, violated every rule and laid hands on the persons and properties of the Templars. You have also imprisoned them and, what pains us even more, you have not treated them with due leniency . . . and have added to the discomfort of imprisonment yet another affliction . . . You have laid hands on persons and property that are under the direct protection of the Roman Church . . . Your hasty act is seen by all, and rightly so, as an act of contempt towards ourselves and the Roman Church.[171]

Without expressing any view regarding the truth of the charges against the Templars, Clement's concern thus focused on Philip's oversight in regard to ecclesiastical immunity. From the pope's perspective, the independent royal policy, albeit at the formal request of the inquisitor in France, could only be construed as a frontal assault on papal authority.[172] It was this attitude that dominated Clement's actions for the next five years and that provides some explanation of the otherwise arbitrary changes in papal policy. Furthermore, Clement's concern with protecting papal authority caused the prolongation of the trial and, ultimately, the dissolution of the Order 'by means of apostolic provision or command'.[173]

---

[170] Finke, *Papsttum und Untergang des Templerordens*, vol. II, no. 30, pp. 46–7.

[171] *Ad preclaras sapientie*. The pope stressed his feelings of betrayal: 'Dolori vero nostro admiratione et dolorose princeps inclite causam prestant quod nobis quos semper invenisti benevolos pre cunctis aliis Romanis pontificibus qui temporibus tuis Ecclesie Romane prefuerunt et honori tuo intentos in regno tuo pro tuis et ejusdem regni ac totius christianitatis utilitatibus in loco tibi vicino morantibus, postquam tue Serenitati per nostras innotuerat litteras quod nos in eodem negocio et ad diligenter investigandam veritatem illius procedere volebamus, et te per easdem duxeramus litteras requirendum, quod ea que de predictis factis inveneras nobis significare curares, et quod nos tibi significare curaremus ea que circa negocium inveniremus predictum' (*Notae ad vitas*, p. 54); Boutaric, 'Clément V, Philippe le Bel, et les Templiers', pp. 331–2.

[172] Guillaume de Paris had indeed ordered the inquisition of the Templars on 22 September 1307. See his order to the inquisitors of France: Finke, *Papsttum und Untergang des Templerordens*, vol. II, no. 29, pp. 44–6; Barber, *The Trial of the Templars*, pp. 72–3.

[173] *Conciliorum Oecumenicorum Decreta*, p. 342.

The pope's avoidance of the central matter, namely, the Templars' alleged heresy, gives credence to previous consultations that had been conducted between Clement V and Philip IV at Lyons and Poitiers.[174] In a letter of 24 August 1307 to the king of France – that is, almost two months before the arrests – the pope, indeed, had announced his resolution to open an inquiry into the Temple and to summon the leaders of the Order to Poitiers. Though Clement argued that his first reaction to the charges of heresy was one of complete scepticism, referring to them as 'incredible and impossible', second thoughts on the whole matter, he declared, led him to make some inquiries.[175] Some chroniclers point to Clement's summons of the masters of the Military Orders in 1306 as a move meant to prevent the arrest of the Templars by the king, notice of which the pope had heard from Philip himself.[176] Although this interpretation lumps together the project of a crusade – on behalf of which Clement had summoned the masters of the Temple and the Hospital to the curia[177] – and the pope's plan to carry out an investigation of the charges levelled against the Templars, it gives some insight into Clement's policy and the mutual confidence between the pope and the Order prior to the arrests. The summons of the Templars to Poitiers, indeed, suggests Clement's fear of a Capetian initiative and, consequently, his intention to preserve papal prerogatives over an exempt Order. Such an inquiry had actually been requested by the Templars themselves in order to exonerate their Order. In early October 1307, the visitor Hugues de Pairaud, accompanied by sixteen or seventeen brothers, came to Poitiers and waited for an audience with the pope. The meeting, however, did not materialise, since soon afterwards the Templars were arrested and their representatives transferred to Loches.[178] Apparently, rumours about charges against the Order were well known by both the pope and the Templars themselves. It is also clear that the knights relied on papal protection, which had been given unconditionally to the Order for the two hundred years of its existence. Clement V himself shared this point of view and, by summoning the Templars to Poitiers, hoped to free the Order from the religious zeal of Philip the Fair.

The pope's plan, however, was doomed to failure. Moreover, Philip's independent move put the alliance between pope and king to a most difficult test, since it brought about a reconsideration of the division of

---

[174] An anonymous chronicler argued that Philip, after being required by the pope to make further inquiries about the serious charges against the Templars, proceeded with maximum secrecy to the point that he did not share the matter with his own brothers: *Extraits d'une chronique . . . 1308*, p. 137; Finke, *Papsttum und Untergang des Templerordens*, vol. II, no. 88, p. 149.

[175] *Collectio actorum veterum*, p. 60.   [176] *Continuationis chronici Guillelmi de Nangiaco*, pp. 358–9.

[177] See above, p. 105.

[178] Finke, *Papsttum und Untergang des Templerordens*, vol. II, no. 39, p. 58.

labour between the Most Christian King and the Vicar of God on earth. This was the perspective shared by most contemporaries, thus indicating the challenge that faced the papal curia and Clement V at its head. In most cases, belief in the Templars' heresy went hand in hand with acceptance of the royal initiative *de jure* or *de facto*.[179] Consequently, most reactions to the arrest and subsequent trial did not focus on the question of heresy, but on royal power and the web of relations between the king and the pope. Some chroniclers, faithful to the king, voiced the Capetian version that the arrests had been made 'according to the order of the king of France, Philip the Fair, and the authorisation and consent of the sovereign pontiff, Pope Clement'.[180] Jean d'Hocsem referred to the king's full report to the pope in Poitiers as an irrefutable fact. Accordingly, Philip had acted out of a belief in the Templars' heresy, while Clement's later hesitations were dictated by his cupidity, since, according to Jean, the pope was 'greedy of gold and full of simony'.[181] An anonymous author referred to the arrest of the Templars in both France and England simultaneously as having taken place 'according to the authorisation and consent of pope Clement'.[182] The annalist of Ghent, too, echoed the Capetian version of a joint action by the curia and not only Philip but all Christian rulers as well. It assumed the simultaneous arrest of the Templars throughout Christendom while incorporating an additional charge, that of usury:

In this year, on one and the same day, fixed with the greatest precision for this purpose by the pope, the cardinals, and many Christian kings and princes, all the Templars in France, England, Spain, and many parts of Italy were seized and sent to prison, on suspicion of making outrageous and wicked profit, and also of idolatry and sodomy.[183]

The predisposition of some chroniclers to blur the royal initiative in France and, instead, to attribute *Pastoralis praeeminentiae* – i.e., the later papal legitimacy of the arrest – to the whole of Christendom, France included, suggests the unprecedented nature of the situation. Hence, the tendency of contemporaries to assume traditional patterns of behaviour, especially in regard to royal acceptance of the overall authority of the

---

[179] According to an anonymous chronicler, the Templars had been arrested 'du commandement le roy Phelippon de France': *Extraits d'une chronique . . . 1308*, p. 137; *Chronicon Guillelmi Scoti*, p. 205; *Continuatio chronici Girardi de Fracheto*, p. 29; *E chronici Rotomagensis continuatione*, p. 347; Amalric Auger, *Sexta Vita*, pp. 93–7; *Chronicon Angliae Petriburgense*, p. 159.

[180] *Les grandes chroniques de France*, p. 256; *Continuationis chronici Guillelmi de Nangiaco*, pp. 358–9, 362–3. [181] Jean d'Hocsem, *Gesta Pontificum Leodiensium*, p. 348.

[182] *Extraits d'une chronique . . . 1383*, p. 142.

[183] *Annales Gandenses*, p. 88. This basic position was also shared by the author of the *Chronographia*, who refers to the arrest of the Templars as being done 'auctoritate domini Clementis pape V': *Chronographia regum Francorum*, pp. 179–80.

papacy over an exempt Order.[184] Most chroniclers in France, though, were shocked by the arrest, which they described in terms of an 'incredible, extraordinary event'.[185] Some authors were fully aware that the arrests were an independent act of the king, an exercise of his initiative, and a display of his power.[186] Jean de St Victor and Bernard Gui dwelt on the consternation that Philip's hasty act caused the pope and the curia.[187] Even among chroniclers who believed the accusation of heresy, there were some who foresaw a second divine judgement and warned the pope of the implications of his acquiescent attitude.[188] On the other hand, there were also voices that welcomed royal policy against the Templars. The arrest was warmly supported by Guillaume le Maire and Gervais du Bus, who were usually very critical of Capetian policy in ecclesiastical matters. Gervais even regarded Philip's actions against the Templars to be in tune with the spiritual heritage of his grandfather, St Louis – a most flattering comparison with regard to Philip the Fair.[189]

In England, most chroniclers were receptive to the version circulated by the Capetian court; they considered Philip to be merely the executor of the pope's will, since the Templars' heresy was a matter for the pope to deal with, not for the king.[190] Besides the lack of reliable information, the discrepancy of approaches among different chroniclers does not reflect distinct attitudes to the charges levelled against the Templars,

---

[184] *Extraits d'une chronique . . . 1383*, p. 142.

[185] Bernard Gui, in *Quarta Vita*, p. 63; *Fragment d'une chronique . . . 1328*, p. 149.

[186] Amalric Auger, *Sexta Vita*, pp. 93–6; *Chronique normande du XIVe siècle*, p. 29.

[187] 'Dicebatur autem quod papa, captione Templariorum per totum regnum audita, primum turbatum est, quia rex hoc videbatur nimis festinanter et quasi precipitanter egisse. Ob hoc ei primo impetu displicebat. Sed postea placuit et captionem approbavit, ita tamen quod rex absque judicio pape et curie romane executioni non presumeret demandare': Jean de St Victor, *Prima Vita*, pp. 9–10; Bernard Gui, in *Quarta Vita*, p. 63; *Notae ad vitas*, p. 55.

[188] Mes garde soi bien, s'il fet mal,
Car, s'il le fet, il peche plus
Que ne fet tout l'autre surplus.
La chronique métrique attribuée à Geffroy de Paris, p. 159, vv. 3568–70.

The chronicle actually reproduces the Capetian version of the Templars' heresy: *ibid.*, pp. 156–67, vv. 3416–3565. And still the anonymous writer asks:

Ou sont il? Que sont devenu
Qui tant ont de plait maintenu
Que nul a elz ne s'ozoit prendre?
Ibid., p. 157, vv. 3488–90.

[189] Port, 'Le livre de Guillaume le Maire', p. 472; Gervais du Bus, *Le roman de Fauvel*, pp. 37–40, vv. 936–1019. For an analysis of different approaches to the Templars before and during the trial, see Mühlethaler, *Fauvel au pouvoir*, pp. 304–71.

[190] Philip was commonly reported as having acted *per papalem mandatum*: *Annales Hibernie*, p. 336; *Annales Londonienses*, p. 152; *Flores historiarum*, app., pp. 331–2; *Chronicon Henrici Knighton*, p. 407. This version was echoed by the *Chronique normande du XIVe siècle*, p. 29, a rather exceptional attitude among the records of the Capetian kingdom.

whose alleged heresy was readily accepted in large areas of France and England. It reflects, rather, a difference of opinion concerning the legitimacy of Philip's move. The chroniclers of France well knew their king's methods in ecclesiastical matters from the time of his prolonged struggle with Boniface VIII. Consequently, they were more prepared to accept the independent policy of Philip the Fair against an exempt Order, whether it was in accordance with recognised norms or not. The opposition to the arrest was particularly vehement in Germany and Italy, though more connected with the base designs ascribed to Philip and Clement than to a belief in the Templars' innocence. Some chroniclers explained Philip's action and the pope's silence as intended to swell the coffers of the king of France, who had acted out of envy and greed.[191] Villani coupled the king's design to dispossess the Templars with the pope's interest in removing the Capetian threat to renew the trial against Boniface. He, too, emphasised the immeasurable power and wealth of the Templars, which proved to be of no avail against the early commitments of the former archbishop of Bordeaux to the king of France and their consequent alliance.[192] Recognition of the power and wealth of the Templars thus appear to have played a central role in the shock of contemporaries and their resulting approach to the arrest as an unprecedented act. Some chroniclers stressed the violation of Church immunity, a course of action they found characteristic of Philip the Fair.[193] Others assumed that the arrest of the Templars was intended to pave the way for the crowning of a Capetian scion as king of Jerusalem.[194] A third version saw both Philip and Clement as beneficiaries of the arrest, since they were both going to benefit from the seized property. Both pope and king, for their base motives, were accused of bringing many innocents to a

---

[191] John of Viktring emphasises this view when mentioning the arrest of the Templars in the same passage with the confiscation of the Jews' wealth (pp. 352–3). Agnolo di Tura points at the use of torture against the Templars to foster their confessions: Agnolo di Tura, *Cronaca Senese*, pp. 299–300; Matthew of Nüwenburg, *Cronica*, p. 237.

[192] '[Il re] mosso da avarizia si fece promettere dal Papa secretamente di disfare la detta ordine de'Tempieri, opponendo contro a loro molti articoli di resia; ma più si dice, che fu per trarre di loro molta moneta . . . Il Papa per levarsi da dosso il Re di Francia per contentarlo per la richiesta del condennare Papa Bonifazio, della quale il menava per lunga, . . . o ragione o torto che fosse per piacere al Re li assentì di ciò fare . . . [i Tempieri] erano quasi innumerabili di podere e di ricchezza': Villani, *Istorie fiorentine*, l. viii, c. 92, pp. 184–5.

[193] Dino Compagni, *Cronica*, pp. 219–20; *Henrici Rebdorfensis Annales*, p. 552. Marco Battaglia mentioned in the same context Philip's confiscation of the Jews' wealth in 1306 *pro avaritia*: *Marcha di Marco Battagli da Rimini*, p. 65.

[194] This was the opinion of Geoffrey le Baker, who also refers to Philip's animosity against the Templars as stemming from his request for a loan, which was rejected by the Order: *Chronicon Galfridi le Baker de Swynebroke*, p. 5; Finke, *Papsttum und Untergang des Templerordens*, vol. II, no. 34, p. 51. The suspicion of Capetian interests in the kingdom of Jerusalem was in time corroborated by Guillaume de Nogaret and Guillaume de Plaisians, who advised such a move. See also the memoir of Pierre Dubois, written after 23 May 1308: *Collectio actorum veterum*, pp. 154–62.

certain death.[195] A few chroniclers went even further and completely denied the truth of the charges of heresy. Pipini, for example, wrote that the heresy ascribed to the Templars is 'not only extraordinary, but also difficult to believe'.[196] German sources pointed to the heroic past of the Order and its spirit of self-sacrifice, which would not have allowed it to sink to the disgraceful and sinful acts imputed to its members.[197]

The rulers of Christendom, too, did not support Philip's policy but reacted with restraint. James of Aragon and Albert of Habsburg expressed regret at the charges of heresy, but stipulated that any action against the Templars should follow the formal request of the pope.[198] The loyalty of both kings to the papacy was undoubtedly affected by political factors, such as James' need of financial support and Albert's hopes to be crowned emperor. On the other hand, at least in the case of Aragon, James' economic problems did not persuade him to co-operate with both the papal blockade in the Mediterranean and the crusade against Venice. Moreover, the accusations against the Templars had first been brought by Esquieu de Floyran to the king of Aragon, who did not give them credence.[199] Edward II, who at the time of the arrest had been in power for only four months, was perhaps the ruler most incensed by the policy of Philip the Fair. In a letter to the kings of Portugal, Castile, Aragon, and Sicily, he did not hold back in condemning his father-in-law's base motives for arresting the Templars.[200] The reluctance of the kings of Aragon, Germany, and England to co-operate with the king of France suggests a basic belief in the innocence of the Templars, an opinion shared by some of their subjects, both lay and ecclesiastical. It may also suggest the irrelevancy of the economic factor, at least at this early stage of the trial, when it was assumed that the property of the Templars, if found guilty, would be kept for the recovery of the Holy Land.[201] The basic belief of Christian princes in the innocence of the Templars and the prevailing uncertainty with regard to their wealth indicates the crucial weight of the pope in establishing the fate of the Order: whether the arrests would remain an isolated, perhaps also ephemeral, episode in France or whether the trial of the Templars would embrace the whole of Christendom.

---

[195] 'Unde, ut dicebatur, pape cupiditas et regis inordinata voluntas erant occasio, quod multi saltem innocentes perierunt, omnes enim ad condictum diem igne combusti sunt': *Gestorum abbatum monasterii Sancti Trudonis, pars 2*, p. 412; *Annales Colbazienses*, p. 717.

[196] *Chronicon fratris Francisci Pipini*, col. 750.

[197] *Gesta archiepiscoporum Magdeburgensium*, pp. 427–8.

[198] 'Non processimus . . . nec procedere poteramus, set . . . cum fuerimus per ecclesiam requisiti': Finke, *Papsttum und Untergang des Templerordens*, vol. II, no. 37, pp. 55–6.

[199] See Esquieu's letter to the king (21 January 1308): *ibid.*, vol. II, no. 57, pp. 83–5.

[200] Following the arrest in France, Philip sent a trusty clerk to urge a similar policy in England: *Foedera*, I-4, pp. 94–5, 101; Boutaric, 'Notices et extraits de documents inédits relatifs à l'histoire de France sous Philippe le Bel', no. 23, pp. 161–2.   [201] See n. 170 above.

Outside France, therefore, no voice in either political or ecclesiastical circles was ready to legitimise Capetian policy. The very charge of heresy, whether it was accepted or rejected according to personal predispositions, was not deemed sufficient to revoke the immunity of an exempt Order, let alone to justify an independent royal move against it. A pan-Christian consensus emerged concerning the exclusive right of the pope to decide the fate of the Order, a position obviously shared by Clement V. The difference of opinion between Clement V and his contemporaries did not focus on the goals of papal policy, namely, the protection of ecclesiastical immunity, which in practice meant the defence of the Templars. The controversy centred, rather, on the most suitable ways of achieving this goal within the limitations posed by Philip the Fair's initiative and constant pressure, on the one hand, and the intricacy of papal political interests, on the other.

The charges against the Templars ran to 127 articles, which can be summarised as follows:[202]

When a new brother was received into the Order, he was encouraged by his receptors to abjure Jesus Christ and sometimes also the Holy Virgin and the saints. The brother was told that Jesus was not the true God, but a false prophet who had been crucified, not for the redemption of humankind, but on account of his sins. Jesus' *passio* did not, therefore, provide any hope of salvation. Consequently, the brother was encouraged to spit, trample, or urinate upon a crucifix or an image of Jesus.

The Templars revered idols, Baphomet among them.[203] Specific mention was made of a cat and a three-headed figure that was worshipped as a saviour and a giver of life. The brothers supposedly encircled it with the small cords they wore around their waists.

The Templars did not believe in the sacraments, and their priests omitted the words of consecration during Mass.

The Templars maintained that the Grand Master and other leaders could hear their confessions and absolve them from sin, despite the fact that many leaders were laymen.

The receptors of new brothers kissed them on the mouth, the navel, the stomach, the buttocks, and the spine. Homosexuality was encouraged and, indeed, enjoined on them.

The Templars sought gain for the Order by whatever means came to hand, whether lawful or not. Donations made to the Order were not used in licit ways or apportioned to charity.

---

[202] This summary follows Malcolm Barber's categories in *The Trial of the Templars*, pp. 178–92. For the original charges, see *Le procès des Templiers*, vol. I, pp. 89–96. The Capetian version is faithfully voiced in *Les grandes chroniques de France*, pp. 274–6.

[203] S. Hutin, 'A propos du "Baphomet" des Templiers', pp. 278–86.

Chapter meetings and receptions were held in secret, at night, under heavy guard, and only Templars were present. Brothers who revealed to an outsider what had occurred were punished by imprisonment or death.[204]

To these serious allegations, Guillaume de Plaisians later added another fault, namely:[205]

The Templars had betrayed the Christian enterprise overseas while conducting secret negotiations with the Muslims, thus actually causing the loss of the Holy Land.[206]

These allegations, which found a receptive audience in lower social strata, were still to be proved. Joseph R. Strayer convincingly argued: 'Men who were intelligent enough to handle the complicated administrative work of the Temple, men who could run a banking business more extensive than that of any Italian firm, should have been able to produce a more coherent and appealing counter-religion, if they were foolish enough to try.'[207] Some charges, especially those concerning idolatry and sacrilege, were reminiscent of the allegations against Boniface VIII and, as such, clearly indicative of the propaganda genius of Guillaume de Nogaret and Guillaume de Plaisians.[208] On the other hand, the accusations of homosexual practices,[209] secret conventicles, and greed[210] seem quite in line with previous criticism levelled not only against the Templars,[211] but also against other Military Orders.[212] These charges, which often hinted at the rivalry between the Military Orders and other sectors of the ecclesiastical establishment, did not always remain in the

---

[204] On the interaction of magic, heresy, and conspiracy with regard to the Templars, see Partner, *The Murdered Magicians*, pp. 42, 53–5.

[205] On Plaisians' career, see Pegues, *The Lawyers of the Last Capetians*, pp. 102–3.

[206] 'Communionem et confederationem cum perfidis Sarracenis ultra mare contra christianos habebant, et quod ipsi, ut fertur, fuerunt causa perditionis civitatis Achon et totius terre sibi conjuncte, quam antea christiani crucesignati pro Christi fide et cum magna ipsorum sanguinis effusione acquisiverunt et eam longo tempore possederunt pacifice et quiete': Amalric Auger, *Sexta Vita*, p. 96. This charge was first pronounced by Guillaume de Plaisians at Poitiers: Finke, *Papsttum und Untergang des Templerordens*, vol. II, nos. 87–8, pp. 139, 145.

[207] Strayer, *The Reign of Philip the Fair*, p. 292.

[208] On Plaisians' many records on the Templars, see the list provided by Langlois, 'Les papiers de Guillaume de Nogaret et de Guillaume de Plaisians au trésor des Chartes', nos. 365, 446, 470, 488, 489, 510; Barber, 'Propaganda in the Middle Ages', p. 57; cf. Menache, 'Un peuple qui a sa demeure à part', pp. 193–208.

[209] M. L. Bulst-Thiele, *Sacrae Domus Militiae Templi Hierosolymitani Magistri*, pp. 350ff.

[210] William of Tyre accused them of transgressing their original ideology while aspiring to rival the wealth of monarchs: *Willelmi Tyronensis Archiepiscopi*, 12. 7, pp. 553–5. John of Würzburg, a German priest who travelled to the Holy Land between 1160 and 1170, speaks of their 'much property and countless revenues': *Description of the Holy Land by John of Würzburg*, p. 21.

[211] Menache, 'The Templar Order', pp. 2–15.

[212] H. Nicholson, *Templars, Hospitallers, and Teutonic Knights*, pp. 25–33, 41–8, 68–75.

domain of unfounded rumours. Only two years earlier, in 1305, a trial had begun against the Livonian branch of the Teutonic Knights. The charges included the imprisonment of the archbishop of Riga, infringement of ecclesiastical privileges, preventing missionary work, corruption in the Order's ranks, and the sale of castles and weapons to the Lithuanians.[213] Both the propaganda precedents of the Capetian court in the case of Boniface and Clement's readiness in 1313 to reach a compromise with the Teutonic Knights without discernible results justify turning the focus of analysis from the charges of heresy against the Templars to the political balance between Philip IV and Clement V.[214] This is not to say that Philip the Fair did not believe in the heresy of the Templars. He probably did. Conversely, the policy of Clement V suggests the pope's hesitations in this regard and his desire to find a suitable solution to the *fait accompli* with which the king of France had confronted him.

Between October 1307 and January 1308, the Capetian court concentrated its efforts in proving the heresy of the Templars. After being delivered to inquisitorial scrutiny, 134 of the 138 Templars arrested in Paris confessed the charges against them. Although all depositions carefully mention that the confession was not extorted by 'violence, or from fear of torture, or imprisonment, or any other reason', but had been given freely 'for the safety of the soul', there is clear evidence that the Templars had been subjected to both physical and psychological torture.[215] Moreover, the leaders of the Order, the master at their head, played a major role in the collapse of the Temple. During the very first stages of the trial, Jacques de Molai gave a full confession, one that in fact exceeded the most optimistic expectations of the Capetian court (24 October). The Grand Master, who might have been in his sixties by this time, gave the appearance of a confused and frightened man. He confessed that at the time of his reception into the Order forty-two years

---

[213] *Das Zeugenverhör des Franciscus de Moliano*, pp. 1–145; *Regestum Clementis Papae V*, nos. 5544, 6447, 7508. The inquiry was still going on in 1310, when Clement nominated the archbishop of Bremen and Albert of Milan, a papal chaplain, to deal with the charges. In 1311, Albert was replaced by Francis of Moliano, who supported the excommunication of the brethren: *Vetera Monumenta Poloniae et Lithuaniae gentiumque finitimarum historiam illustrantia*, nos. 204, 206, pp. 119–23; Housley, *The Avignon Papacy and the Crusades*, pp. 269–71.

[214] The charges against the Teutonic Knights, however, were quite different in kind from those in the Templar trial. Moreover, criticism of the Templars before the trial had little relevance at the trial itself, whereas there was a direct link in the case of the Teutonic Knights.

[215] The chronicles of Flanders refer to the inquisition of the Templars as a kind of friendly meeting between the knights and the king that led to their voluntary confession: 'tous furent amenez devers le roy, ilz furent amiablement questionnez . . . sans torture ne contrainte': *Anciennes chroniques de Flandre*, p. 398. Cf. Barber, *The Trial of the Templars*, pp. 58–71.

earlier, he had been required to deny Jesus Christ and to spit on his image.[216] Although Molai denied the charge of homosexuality, his alleged act of sacrilege cast a shadow over the orthodoxy of the entire Order.[217] Aware of the propaganda value of the Grand Master's confession, the Capetian court forced him to repeat his declaration the next day before the masters of the University of Paris. Speaking in general terms, Jacques de Molai fully described the Order's perversion of its original goals, which had been sanctioned by the Church and had earned the admiration and support of Christendom. He then announced his full repentance, asked for ecclesiastical absolution, and called on all other Templars to follow his example and to confess their crimes.[218] Similar confessions were obtained from other leaders, such as Gérard de Gauche, Gui Dauphin, Geoffroi de Charney, and Gautier de Liancourt, who were in France at the time of the arrest.[219]

On 17 November 1307, five weeks after the arrest and three weeks after Jacques de Molai's confession, Clement sent his chaplain, Arnaud de Falguières, to the Capetian court.[220] Five days later, the pope issued a letter, *Pastoralis praeeminentiae*, to all leaders of Christendom in order to create a common front with regard to the Templars. Without pronouncing any clear verdict, Clement required all Christian princes to 'prudently, discreetly, and secretly' arrest all Templars and to hold their property in safe custody. The pope used the occasion to praise the good faith of Philip the Fair and his pure religious motivations in the arrest.[221] The papal order led to the arrest of the Templars in England, Ireland, Castile, Aragon, Portugal, Germany, Italy, and Cyprus. *Pastoralis praeeminentiae* undoubtedly freed Philip from political isolation and conferred on him apostolic legitimacy. Still, Clement's praise of the king's actions, which the pope himself had strongly criticised less than one month earlier,[222] suggests a more complex situation than the description that is

---

[216] On the Master's career, his character, and weaknesses, see Barber, 'James of Molay, the Last Grand Master of the Order of the Temple', pp. 91–124.

[217] Lizerand, *Le dossier de l'affaire des Templiers*, no. 3, p. 34.

[218] *Continuationis chronici Guillelmi de Nangiaco*, pp. 361–2.

[219] *Regestum Clementis Papae V*, nos. 10587–8, 10591–5; Finke, *Papsttum und Untergang des Templerordens*, vol. II, nos. 32, 150, pp. 49, 310–12. Philip also hastened to send to the king of Aragon the confessions of the Order's leaders, who, according to the king of France, 'spontanee sunt confessi' (26 October 1307): Finke, *Papsttum und Untergang des Templerordens*, vol. II, no. 31, pp. 47–8.   [220] *Collectio actorum veterum*, pp. 90–1.

[221] *Acta Imperii Angliae et Franciae*, no. 181, pp. 120–2; *Foedera*, I-4, pp. 99–100. The pope reissued his letter to Henry VII on 7 August 1309: *Acta Henrici VII*, no. 3, pp. 6–8; *Constitutiones et acta publica imperatorum et regum*, vol. IV-1, no. 300, pp. 265–7. For the reactions to the papal letter in Italy, see Agnolo di Tura, *Cronaca Senese*, p. 300; Paolo di Tommaso Montauri, *Cronaca Senese*, p. 233; *Chronicon Parmense*, p. 113.   [222] See n. 171 above.

usually presented, of a weak, indecisive pope easily falling into a carefully laid trap set by a dominant king. In a letter to Philip of 1 December 1307, Clement expressed surprise at the king's recent claim that the papal lawyer, Geoffroi du Plessis, had transmitted to him apostolic letters asking for the arrest of the Templars; the pope, therefore, was again denying any role in the arrest of the Templars, which *Pastoralis praeeminentiae* had supported before the whole of Christendom only two weeks earlier.[223] The pope's basic attitude is confirmed by Tolomeo da Lucca; this chronicler emphasised Clement's adamant rejection of the royal claim that the arrest had been formally requested by Guillaume de Paris,[224] a request that the Capetian court saw as giving papal legitimacy to royal policy, 'since the high pontiff did not accept that without consulting the aforesaid See, [the king] could deal with such important matter'.[225]

Comparison of the two papal versions – that appearing in *Pastoralis praeeminentiae* and the other reserved to Philip and corroborated by Tolomeo da Lucca – shows a serious discrepancy. Clement never hid from Philip his opposition to the arrest or his scepticism at the charges of heresy. If one bears this basic position in mind, *Pastoralis praeeminentiae* may be seen in a new light. The pope's readiness to enlist all Christian kings in the trial of the Templars was not meant to strengthen Philip's position but, rather, Clement's. The creation of a common Christian front neutralised the former dominant status of the king of France and prevented him from maintaining his lead in the trial of the Templars. These considerations in fact lay behind the mission of Arnaud de Falguières to the Capetian court only five days before the publication of *Pastoralis praeeminentiae*. Given the limitations posed by medieval communication, this was a rather short period of time for serious negotiations, and merely enabled the transmission of information. If such was the case, we have here a convincing explanation of the pope's readiness to praise the motivations of Philip the Fair before Christendom, which was not as great a concession to royal pride as it might appear. As for the Templars, they could apparently do nothing to help their cause, especially following the public confession of their leaders. Clement's first move against the Order, indeed, came only after the full confession of Jacques de Molai.

On 24 December 1307, two months after his confession, however, the

---

[223] *Collectio actorum veterum*, pp. 91–2.

[224] A Dominican, prior of the convent of St Jacques, doctor in theology, and royal chaplain, he became the king's confessor in 1305 and remained in this charge until his death in 1312. During the trial of the Templars, he maintained close contacts with Nogaret. See Minois, *Le confesseur du roi*, pp. 196–8.   [225] Tolomeo da Lucca, *Secunda Vita*, p. 30.

Grand Master retracted his former declarations before Cardinals Bérenger Frédol, Landolfo Brancaccio, and Etienne de Suisy, who had been commissioned by the pope to verify the Templars' depositions.[226] The example of the Grand Master was soon followed by other members of the Order. Many Templars defended the innocence and integrity of their Order so fearlessly that the cardinals' doubts concerning the legitimacy of the arrests actually increased. This unexpected development encouraged Philip's declarations of good faith before the pope and the curia. On the same day as Molai's retraction, the king voiced his commitment to the Church. He reminded the pope that he had carried out the arrests 'according to the request of the inquisitor of heresy, who had been sent to our kingdom by apostolic authority'. Philip further assured the curia that his action was not meant to harm the Church, 'but to protect in their integrity both ours and the Church's rights', and that the Templars' wealth would be kept 'for the subsidy of the Holy Land'.[227] This assurance, however, did not mollify the pope or compensate for the delay in transferring the Templars and their property to his representatives. The consequences came rather soon. In February 1308, Clement stopped all inquisitorial activities in France – a move that could easily have jeopardised all royal achievements up to this date – thereby bringing the trial of the Templars to a dead-end. The pope later justified this move on the grounds that he had become suspicious of the great power wielded by the king and of the accuracy of the charges levelled against the Templars.[228]

Clement's change of policy was largely applauded by contemporaries, who had vociferously criticised what they judged to be the pope's complete surrender to Capetian interests. Arnaud de Baynuls had strongly attacked Clement V for being a 'worthless individual'; after all, 'everyone knows that the pope has no voice, and he [Philip] does as he pleases with the pope and the Church'.[229] Aragonese sources close to the curia had stressed the cardinals' opposition to papal policy, which they considered to be detrimental to the dignity of the Church.[230] The king of Aragon, more practical at this stage, initiated a long-range diplomacy intended to ensure papal blessing for his appropriation of Templar wealth. On 5 February 1308, James sent clear instructions to his representatives in the curia to prevent any possibility of transferring Templar property to

---

[226] *Regestum Clementis Papae V*, nos. 2291–3. On their mission, see the exchange of correspondence between Clement and Philip: *Collectio actorum veterum*, pp. 91–2, 98–100, 109.

[227] *Collectio actorum veterum*, pp. 92–4.

[228] Finke, *Papsttum und Untergang des Templerordens*, vol. II, no. 71, p. 110. The order does not appear in the papal registers.

[229] 'Car tot lo mon sap, quel papa no es negun et que el fa tot ço ques vol del papa et de la esglea': *ibid.*, vol. II, no. 78, p. 123.   [230] *Ibid.*, vol. II, no. 101, p. 183.

any private person, the Church of Rome, or another Order.[231] Philip himself, however, was beginning to have doubts about his ability to manipulate the pope according to his own designs. The suspension of the inquisition in France might put into question his initial achievements and bring the whole affair to an impasse. To avoid this contingency, the Capetian court launched a formidable propaganda campaign, often accompanied with intimidating tones against the pope himself. In late February 1308, the king asked the masters of theology in Paris about the most suitable action that should be taken against an Order charged with heresy. Should this charge be proved, the king further asked, what would be the most proper management of the property?[232] This appeal to the university in matters pertaining to orthodoxy indicates Philip's readiness to ignore the pope and, instead, to approach the masters as the highest spiritual authority in Christendom.[233] Further, the king's questions about Templar property stood in complete opposition to his former declarations, both before the pope and before the king of Aragon, that its integrity would be preserved for the recovery of the Holy Land.[234]

The theologians, however, did not provide Philip with a comfortable answer on which he might base further his policy against the Templars. Recognition of the immunity of the Church formed the basic principle underlying their response (25 March 1308). Placed in the difficult dilemma of opting between the *regnum* and the *sacerdotium*, they praised Philip's devotion to the faith, but stated that 'the king's rights do not supersede, or justify, the usurpation of others' rights'. Though the confessions of the Templars justified the resumption of the inquisition, this was not a matter for the king to decide. Philip could not initiate any action against heretics, but 'had to act at the request and demand of the Church'. The fact that the Templars were knights suspected of heresy, moreover, did not affect their religious profession. The theologians were equally uncompromising with regard to Templar property. It had not

---

[231] James declared 'que ell per nuyla re no sofferria, quels castells ni la terra, quels Templers han en son regne, fos assignada a neguna singular persona, maiorment que el papa enteses, que fos tenguda en feu per la esgleya de Roma o per altra esgleya . . . Encara mes noli plaura, que fos assignada a altre ordre antic, per ço çor los antecessors del senyor rey, qui dotaren lo Temple e Lospital els altres ordens de cavalleria en sa terra, ço que partiren entre molts, no volgren tot dar': *ibid.*, vol. II, no. 60, p. 89.

[232] Lizerand, *Le dossier de l'affaire des Templiers*, no. 5, pp. 56–62; Finke, *Papsttum und Untergang des Templerordens*, vol. II, no. 70, pp. 107–9.

[233] On Philip's tendency to incorporate the university into the political body and the masters' growing loyalty to the king, see Bernstein, '*Magisterium* and License', pp. 305–6; I. P. Wei, 'The Self-Image of the Masters of Theology at the University of Paris', pp. 426–30; Menache, 'La naissance d'une nouvelle source d'autorité', pp. 320–7. During the late Avignonese period, the monopoly of the University of Paris as arbiter of the faith was severely weakened. On the popes' support of this tendency, see Knoll, 'The Papacy at Avignon and University Foundations', p. 196.

[234] See nn. 170 and 227 above.

been given to the knights *ad personam*, but for the sake of the crusades and the Latin Kingdom of Jerusalem; it had to continue to serve these causes in the most effective way. There was, though, a grain of consolation for the king in this very disappointing document. In the closing paragraph, the masters expressed loyalty to Philip and grateful recognition of the spiritual and material benefits he imparted to the community of the realm.[235] Philip was not, therefore, thought competent to replace the pope in the struggle against heresy. On the contrary, the masters of Paris unequivocally recognised the pope's primacy in the Church and his complete freedom of action in spiritual matters. Similar arguments were voiced by Agostino Trionfo in a short treatise about the Templars.[236] Agostino stated that heresy was a spiritual matter and, as such, reserved to the Church. Although kings and princes in the days of the Old Testament were permitted to punish heretics on their own authority, 'since the time of the old law has reached its end, these precepts are over, too, and anyone attempting to follow them is committing a sin'.[237] Neither Templars nor heretics, he declared, could be arrested or judged by secular authority without the specific request of the Church. Secular rulers could arrest heretics only when they were unable to consult the Church properly and a real threat faced their kingdoms. Such action, however, was to remain provisional, since they had to restore these heretics to the Church as soon as possible. The authority of the Church, thus, was pre-eminent in spiritual matters. Agostino further maintained that it was not his purpose to pronounce a verdict regarding the Templars' innocence or guilt, but to establish the complete monopoly of the Church in matters of heresy.[238] The declarations of the University of Paris and Agostino Trionfo thus altered the focus of debate from the heresy ascribed to the Templars to the responsibilities of the pope and of the king, and the dividing line between their respective spheres of authority. On the other hand, a most touching defence of the Templars appears in a manuscript found in Corpus Christi College, Cambridge. The anonymous author of this open letter, apparently written after the royal appeal to the University of Paris and also addressed

---

[235] 'Regiam majestatem vestram, quam firmiter credimus non solum regimini temporali reipublice, verum eciam spirituali profectui ecclesie fructuosam': *Chartularium Universitatis Parisiensis*, pp. 125–30; Lizerand, *Le dossier de l'affaire des Templiers*, no. 5, pp. 62–70.

[236] It was probably written between 1307 and 1309. See Wilks, *The Problem of Sovereignty in the Later Middle Ages*, p. 9; and short biographical data on Agostino, *ibid.*, pp. 4–5.

[237] Accordingly, 'cessante statu illo [veteris legis], cessaverunt ille precepta': Agostino Trionfo, 'Brevis tractatus super facto Templariorum', p. 512.

[238] Agostino thus concluded that 'illos non possunt punire proprio iudicio reges et principes, qui non sunt de foro eorum, nisi postquam relinquntur eis ab ecclesia, sed tales sunt ipsi heretici': Agostino Trionfo, 'Brevis tractatus super facto Templariorum', pp. 180–3, 508–16; J. Rivière, *Le problème de l'Eglise et de l'état au temps de Philippe le Bel*, pp. 356–7.

to its masters, did not hesitate to praise the courage of the Templars, thirty-four of whom had already died in Capetian prisons as martyrs for the exoneration of their Order.[239] While mentioning the great 'pain, anguish, misery, cruelty, and all kind of torments' to which the Templars had unjustly been subjected, the author labelled as 'fatuity and insanity' the very attempt to impute heresy to the brothers, nobles, clerks, and all members of the Order.[240]

The negative reaction by leading intellectuals to the arrest of the Templars strengthened Philip's attempt to find another body that would show more readiness to co-operate. The Assembly, which had proved its efficacy in the struggle against Boniface VIII, was just such a body – loyal to the king, ready to serve his interests, and willing to legitimise his policy.[241] The Assembly of Tours was therefore meant to turn the *natio Gallicana* as a whole into the king's partner in the trial of the Templars. The goal is clearly reflected in contemporary documents. The summons to the Assembly appealed to the religious, national feelings of the nobility, the clergy, and the bourgeoisie alike (24–9 March 1308).[242] The king declared that following the precedents of his ancestors, he had acted against the Templars for no other cause but 'for the glory of God, for the salvation of our mother the Holy Church, and for the defence of the rights and liberties of the Church of France'. Philip further stressed his allegiance to the inheritance of his forefathers – a clear appeal to the glorious image of St Louis – which had dictated his zeal for the Catholic faith.[243] The heresy of the Templars, he thundered, was such that both heaven and earth had been annoyed; against such sinful plague, all laws and arms, all men, and all four elements would rise up. The Templars were thus presented as a threat to the symmetry of the Gothic world, their crimes striking at God, its supreme architect.[244] After bestowing on the Templars' heresy a cosmic dimension, the king called on his faithful subjects to join him and to imitate his devotion to the basic creed that

---

[239] 'Set ex ipsis plurimi, eligentes deo servire pocius quam Mammone, veritatem forcius amplectentes, tanquam athlete Christi per eadem tormenta numero .xxxvi. in domo Parisi solummodo . . . per palmam martirii migrantes ad dominum regna celestia sunt adepti': 'Lamentacio quedam pro Templariis', edited by C. R. Cheney, in Cheney, 'The Downfall of the Templars and a Letter in Their Defence', p. 323.   [240] *Ibid.*, pp. 325–6.

[241] G. Picot, *Histoire des Etats-généraux*, vol. I, pp. 19–26.

[242] Though the cities were requested to be represented by suitable proctors, nobles and prelates were expected to come in person, and only severe illness was accepted as justification for absence. Even in such cases, the illness had to be formally certified by the king's officers.

[243] 'Mandement adressé individuellement aux membres du clergé' (26 March 1308), in *Documents relatifs aux Etats Généraux et Assemblées*, no. 658, pp. 488–9. Note the connection between the king's goals and those of God.

[244] Barber, 'The World Picture of Philip the Fair', pp. 15–16. Barber recognises, however, Philip's failure to convince the Christian world of his right to defy conventional power relationships: *ibid.*, p. 26.

'Christus est nobis via, vita, et veritas.'[245] Royal devotion to Jesus Christ, which dictated the king's 'path, life, and truth', should guide all inhabitants of the realm. All France was to share the religious zeal of the royal house, thus becoming a 'most precious marguerite of the Catholic faith'.[246] As such, it was blessed with special divine grace to uphold justice and maintain the stability of the faith.[247]

The Assembly met at Tours from 5 to 15 May 1308. In the absence of official records, it is difficult to reconstruct the debates. Eventually, the king gained the support of the representatives of the bourgeoisie, 700 in all, who were easy prey for royal propaganda.[248] The conspicuously large number of absentees among prelates and nobles, on the other hand, indicates their reserve towards royal policy.[249] The clergy refrained from supporting the king in order to avoid a repetition of the dilemma with which it had been confronted during the pontificate of Boniface VIII. As for the nobles, the family links that many had with members of the Order could hardly have facilitated their belief in the heresy ascribed to the Templars. Moreover, they had good reason to fear that the dissolution of the Temple would lead to a greater concentration of power in the king's hands, to their detriment. The absence of nobles and prelates eventually enabled royal pressure to be exerted more effectively. A large majority of the Assembly, four-fifths of its members, supported the resumption of negotiations with the pope along the lines already adopted, while assuring complete royal control over the persons and property of the Temple. From now on, Philip could rely on a *consensus regni*, a contingency that was well known to his contemporaries. Jean de St Victor concluded, in a rather fatalistic mood, that 'the king has acted wisely; for he sought the support of all his people, and of all social classes, so that none could criticise his policy in the future'.[250]

The religious zeal and devotion of the people of France was expected to place Clement V in an uneasy position before the meeting with the king in Poitiers (26 May 1308). The 'great multitude'[251] that accompanied Philip the Fair acquired, in the words of Guillaume de Plaisians, a universal character, and was presented as such to the pope: 'And so, most

---

[245] 'Convocation adressée aux villes du royaume' (25 March 1308), in *Documents relatifs aux Etats Généraux et Assemblées*, no. 660, pp. 490–1; Boutaric, 'Notices et extraits de documents inédits relatifs à l'histoire de France sous Philippe le Bel', no. 25, pp. 164–5.

[246] *Documents relatifs aux Etats Généraux et Assemblées*, no. 660, p. 490.

[247] 'Lettres du roi au clergé' (24 March 1308): *ibid.*, no. 658, p. 487.   [248] *Ibid.*, p. lvi.

[249] *Ibid.*, pièces DCCXXI, DCCXXXV, DCCLXVI, and passim. Quite remarkable was the absence of the counts of Flanders, Brittany, Nevers, Périgord, Comminges, Auvergne, and Forez, and the viscounts of Narbonne, Turenne, and Polignac.

[250] Jean de St Victor, *Prima Vita*, p. 11; Tolomeo da Lucca, *Secunda Vita*, p. 29.

[251] *Continuatio chronici Girardi de Fracheto*, p. 30; *Continuationis chronici Guillelmi de Nangiaco*, p. 365.

holy father, appeal the king of France and all prelates, chapters, barons, and all peoples of the whole kingdom of France, who [come] before you, some in person, some through representation, namely through their proctors and syndics.'[252] Gradually, the issue under negotiation between pope and king was no longer the Templars' alleged heresy and Clement's desire to protect ecclesiastical immunity. Rather, it was the guilt of a pope, convicted by the people of France. Two anonymous pamphlets, probably written by Pierre Dubois, hint at the Capetian strategy. The author did not limit himself to a reiteration of the terrible crimes ascribed to the Templars, which largely justified the pope's immediate proceedings against them. He went further and, in unprecedented criticism, placed Clement V on the same level as Boniface VIII because of the nepotism of the former, which was said to surpass that of forty popes altogether.[253] Though the other memoir refrained from criticising Clement's failings in regard to his relatives, it implied the moral obligation of the king of France, 'not as censor or arbitrator but as minister of God and warrior of the Christian faith', to extirpate the heresy of the Templars; for the king had to give a full accounting of his deeds before divine justice. In an admirable use of rich symbolism, the author called on the pope, in his capacity as father and shepherd, to fulfil his duty towards his congregation before the Templar wolves could devour it, to follow the call of the Church of France and extinguish the fire of heresy before it was too late.[254] The speech by Guillaume de Plaisians also took a militant approach from its opening clause: 'Christus vincit, Christus regnat, Christus imperat!' Plaisians referred to Jesus' victories in the past and compared them to a similar victory in his own time – that of Philip the Fair against the Templars. He particularly stressed the religious zeal of the king, the nobles, the clergy, and all inhabitants of France, whose devotion to the Church he praised. Plaisians also cleared the king of any suspicion of coveting Templar property, since it would be held by the

---

[252] *Documents relatifs aux Etats Généraux et Assemblées*, no. 657, pp. 487–8; Finke, *Papsttum und Untergang des Templerordens*, vol. II, no. 88, pp. 145–6.

[253] 'Or voit le pueble [de France] que leur père espirituel, par l'affection de sanc, ha doné des bénéfices de sainte yglise Deus as prochains de luy, à son neveu le cardinal, plus que telx quarante papes y a il eu ne donnerent oncques à touz leurs lignages, et, plus que Boniface, ne nul autre, ne dona oncques à tout son lignage': Boutaric, 'Notices et extraits de documents inédits relatifs à l'histoire de France sous Philippe le Bel', nos. 27–8, pp. 176, 180–1.

[254] 'Pater ergo familias domus Dei scitis horam presentem qua fur venit diabolus ad perfodiendum domum vestram; jam vobis furto subtraxit oves Templariorum conversas in lupos, ceteras que remanserunt in grege furari nitens . . . Inciditis enim in grave status vestri periculum negocium solummodo diferendo . . . Clama tota Ecclesia Gallicana . . . "Ad ignem, ad ignem, securrite, securrite"!'; *ibid.*, no. 29, pp. 182–6. See also the list of papal letters concerning the Templars brought to the king from Poitiers by Guillaume de Plaisians (5 September 1308): *ibid.*, no. 33, pp. 191–4.

Church and dedicated to the glory of God and to the spread of the Catholic faith.[255] This praise of Philip had the effect of placing him above Clement, and Plaisians added insult to injury by reminding the pope of the duties of his office. As for the Templars, he not only attempted to substantiate the charge of heresy, but also added a further imputation – their responsibility for the loss of the Holy Land. Finally, Plaisians called upon Clement to acknowledge the guilt of the Templars without delay. If the pope would not do so, the inhabitants of France, as 'most zealous champions of the Christian faith', would execute God's judgement with their own hands.[256]

Royal rhetoric, however, did not persuade Clement to hand over his authority to Philip. The pope declared that he would not take any decision until the members and the property of the Order had been transferred to him. If the Templars were to be found innocent, he would set them free; if not, he would put them beyond the Church.[257] The fate of the Order's property was eventually left to the decision of the Council of Vienne.[258] Clement's speech at the closure of the meeting centred on the need to do justice following the call of Amos: 'Hate the evil, and love righteousness, and establish judgement in the gate' (5:15). The prophet's words referred to the pope's own difficult situation, for he saw himself in the position of God confronted with Abraham's challenging question: 'Wilt thou also destroy the righteous with the wicked?' (Gen. 18:23). Stressing the Order's prestige and its good relations with the papal curia, Clement expressed his determination to examine the whole matter very thoroughly.[259] The meeting in Poitiers, thus, apparently failed to fulfil the expectations of the Capetian court. Clement V was not impressed by the religious zeal of the people of France and retained his ultimate prerogative to decide the fate of the Temple. Furthermore, papal rhetoric did not fall short of that employed by royal speakers, both sides proving themselves most eloquent in their devotion to Catholic faith and to divine justice. Although public declarations suggest an impasse, subsequent developments hint at the possibility of secret negotiations that paved the way for a compromise between pope and king.

The first move was made by Philip, who sent to the papal curia

---

[255] None the less, after the Templars were arrested, Philip claimed that, since the Order was heavily indebted to him, a large part of its wealth was rightly his. He was, therefore, able to divert much of the regular income from Templar holdings to the royal treasury.

[256] Finke, *Papsttum und Untergang des Templerordens*, vol. II, nos. 87, 88, pp. 135–40, 146–7; Lizerand, *Le dossier de l'affaire des Templiers*, no. 8, pp. 110–37.

[257] L. Blancard, 'Documents relatifs au procès des Templiers en Angleterre', pp. 417–18.

[258] Tolomeo da Lucca, *Secunda Vita*, pp. 30–1; Jean de St Victor, *Prima Vita*, pp. 11–12; *Les grandes chroniques de France*, pp. 260–1; *Notae ad vitas*, pp. 56–7.

[259] Finke, *Papsttum und Untergang des Templerordens*, vol. II, no. 88, pp. 148–50.

seventy-two Templars who had been carefully selected. On 27 June, they confessed the crimes of their Order before Clement just as they had been forced to admit by royal officers, in patterns that scrupulously followed the designs of the Capetian court.[260] In parallel, royal propaganda continued its merciless campaign against the Templars. The degree to which it succeeded may be learned from a curious letter sent by the count of Foix and Rodez to James II. The count asked the king of Aragon about the accuracy of rumours in regard to plans by the king of Granada to invade Aragon with the help of Saracens, Jews, and Templars, who were in the process of converting to Islam.[261] Rumours of this sort were not unprecedented; whether directed against Templars, Jews, Muslims, or lepers, they actually served as a collective defence mechanism for or against the many fears plaguing medieval Christendom.[262] What was new, however, was the alleged participation by the former knights of Christ (i.e., the Templars) in such a sinister plot. More reliable sources referred to the fact that some Templars, after succeeding in escaping their confinement, found refuge among the Saracens, a feasible action that could have engendered rumours of a Saracen–Templar plot.[263]

Between July and August 1308, Clement contributed his share to the Capetian campaign against the Templars. The papal letter, *Ad omnium fere* (12 August 1308), recorded the different stages of the trial: Clement's original incredulity in regard to the heresy ascribed to the Templars and their confessions of serious crimes, which had forced the pope to reconsider his policy. This was a likely outcome of the secret negotiations in Poitiers, facilitated, again, by the Templars' declarations of heresy, this time made in the papal curia.[264] In a series of letters written in July and August, the pope allowed the inquisitor in France to proceed with the trial and ordered the clergy to prevent members of the Order from receiving any help; those prelates who dared disobey would incriminate themselves with charges of heresy.[265] Concomitantly, all princes of Christendom were urged to arrest any Templar still free in their territories.[266] Clement, further, restored the prerogatives of Guillaume de Paris, thus allowing the

---

[260] K. Schottmüller, *Der Untergang des Templer-Ordens*, vol. II, pp. 13–71. Sixty per cent of these Templars were either apostates from the Order or had been terrified by torture; see Barber, *The Trial of the Templars*, pp. 98–105.

[261] 'Quod rex Granate cum ingenti Sarracenorum, Iudeorum et Templariorum nunc ad legem Sarracenam conversorum multitudine cum armis regnum vestrum intrare et dampnificare proponuit' (5 May 1309): Finke, *Papsttum und Untergang des Templerordens*, vol. II, no. 105, p. 188.

[262] Barber, 'Lepers, Jews, and Moslems', pp. 1–17; Menache, 'Tartars, Jews, Saracens, and the Jewish–Mongol "Plot" of 1241', pp. 319–42.

[263] *La chronique métrique attribuée à Geffroy de Paris*, p. 177, vv. 4543–4.

[264] *Regestum Clementis Papae V*, no. 3400.

[265] *Ibid.*, nos. 3641–2, 5063–6, 5073–5, 5098–100, 5102.

[266] *Callidi serpentis*, *ibid.*, nos. 3643, 4637–52.

inquisition to continue in France.[267] The Templars themselves were to be handed over to Cardinal Pierre de la Chapelle, acting on behalf of the pope, who provided special curators for the administration of their property.[268] Eight papal commissioners were to be appointed to investigate the Order as a whole, while provincial councils would examine individual Templars.[269] Clement also laid down the procedure for the inquisition of the Templars by local bishops, two canons of the cathedral church, two Dominicans, and two Franciscans.[270] Still, the pope remained adamant against making any concessions regarding Templar wealth; should the heresy of the Templars be proved, a contingency that would justify the abolition of the Order, its wealth would then be devoted to the Holy Land.[271]

Aside from his clear position regarding the wealth of the Templars, it is difficult to establish what Clement's intentions actually were at this stage. The confessions of the Templars in the curia manifested all the characteristics of a well-prepared performance meant to justify a change in papal policy. It was also clear that the resumption of the diocesan inquisition in France gave Philip a free hand to bring about the collapse of the Order. Clement's new readiness to co-operate with the king of France was a move not only completely opposed to the pope's own policy up to 1308, but also to the climate of opinion outside France. Moreover, the pope's declarations in respect of Templar property would not have gained the support of other Christian princes, such as the king of Aragon, who showed little readiness to make concessions in this matter. The possibility of a *quid pro quo* at this stage – namely, papal concessions in the case of the Templars in exchange for Philip's withdrawing charges against Boniface – also seems questionable, since the compromise with regard to the late pope was reached only in 1311. Whether Clement was convinced of the genuineness of the confessions obtained under physical and

---

[267] *Ibid.*, no. 3401.

[268] *Collectio actorum veterum*, pp. 79–83. On the pope's intructions, see *Regestum Clementis Papae V*, no. 3515. Clement repeated his mandate on 5 January 1309 (*ibid.*, no. 5011), and on 12 May 1311 (*ibid.*, no. 6816). The repetition of papal commands corroborates, in fact, the neglect shown by Philip the Fair and his officers in fulfilling former pledges.

[269] *Faciens misericordiam, Regestum Clementis Papae V*, nos. 3402–3514, 3532–3; *Le procès des Templiers*, vol. I, pp. 2–7. On the wages paid to the inquisitors of the Templars, see *Regestum Clementis Papae V*, nos. 3516–31.

[270] See the instructions of the bishop of Paris (1309): Lizerand, *Le dossier de l'affaire des Templiers*, no. 9, pp. 138–44.

[271] *Collectio actorum veterum*, pp. 78–9. The pope's explanation two days later that he did not intend to cause any harm to the rights of the king, the nobles, or the clergy of France could not conceal the impact of his former declaration, which was actually put into practice at the Council of Vienne. See *Collectio actorum veterum*, p. 79. The pope repeated his basic position in a letter to the prelates of France (5 January 1309): *Regestum Clementis Papae V*, nos. 5011, 10421. For Castile and Leon, see *ibid.*, nos. 4653, 5069; for Aragon, *ibid.*, nos. 5012–14, 5016–18; for Sicily, *ibid.*, no. 5062.

psychological torture, it is impossible to ascertain. Contemporary chroniclers, for example, approached the use of torture and its effect on the
Templars according to their own prejudices. It seems, rather, that after
Clement was faced with a *fait accompli* – namely, not only the arrest but
also, and, perhaps first and foremost, the subsequent confessions of the
Templars – he chose a line of diplomacy that he preferred most, that of
endless delays. Although the pope, the traditional ally of the Order,
seldom did his best to help the Templars, their own confessions, especially those of their leaders, had severely reduced Clement's room for
manoeuvring *vis-à-vis* the king of France.

Philip the Fair opted for a contrary tactic, that of procuring a final
verdict against the Templars and their Order as soon as possible. Those
Templars who confessed to heresy were immediately set free, while those
who protested their innocence were sentenced to life imprisonment.
Audiences begun by the papal commission did not change this situation.
On 22 November 1309, eight commissioners appointed by the pope
began their sessions and soon encountered Templars from all over France
who were ready to testify on behalf of their Order.[272] This unexpected
development suggests, again, the Templars' confidence in the papacy,
their traditional protector in times of crisis. It was, however, wishful
thinking, not justified by Clement V, even less by his representatives. The
members of the commission had been selected carefully by the Capetian
court and most of them acted under its influence: Gilles Aycelin, archbishop of Narbonne, who was the chairman;[273] Guillaume Durant,
bishop of Mende; and Guillaume Bonet, bishop of Bayeux. All had
expressed their total antagonism to the Templars and publicly favoured
the immediate abolition of the Order. Philip, though, was very strict in
carrying out all formalities, and the commission continued its work for
eighteen months.[274] Against the scenario prepared by the Capetian court,
the Templars found it difficult to defend themselves suitably. Jacques de
Molai refused to be nominated chief advocate for the Order on the
grounds of his lack of knowledge and experience. Instead, Renaud de
Provins, preceptor of Orléans, and Pierre de Bologna, the procurator of
the Order at the curia, assumed the defence.[275] Even in such inferior

---

[272] *Le procès des Templiers*, vol. I, pp. 59–87.

[273] Being a close counsellor of Philip and his supporter during the conflict with Boniface, Gilles
Aycelin was entrusted with guarding the seals during Nogaret's absence. At Poitiers, he compared the Templars to the Midianites, who had perverted Israel: Finke, *Papsttum und Untergang
des Templerordens*, vol. II, no. 88, p. 147; J. A. McNamara, *Gilles Aycelin*, pp. vii, 160–4.

[274] This policy characterised the reign of Philip as a whole; see Fournier, 'Les conflits de juridiction
entre l'Eglise et le pouvoir séculier', p. 458.

[275] 'Dixit eciam quod ipse non erat ita sapiens sicut expediret sibi, nec tanti consilii quod posset defen-
dere dictum ordinem per se ipsum.' See Lizerand, *Le dossier de l'affaire des Templiers*, no. 10, p. 148.

circumstances, hundreds of Templars persisted in speaking in defence of their Order, an inconvenience that led the Capetian court to look for additional means of repression. It found an adequate response in Philippe de Marigny, archbishop of Sens and brother of the royal chamberlain, Enguerrand de Marigny, who was chosen to teach the Templars a lesson. Fifty-four Templars who had retracted their former confession of heresy before the commission, and thus became *relapsi*, were put to the stake outside Paris, near the convent of St Antoine (12 May 1310); nine others were burned in Senlis.[276]

Jean d'Hocsem offers an emotion-laden description of the Templar victims of the Capetian vendetta in their last moments. He mentions the many efforts of friends and relatives desperately trying to convince the brothers to confess to the crimes attributed to them, and the Templars' adamant refusal. Up to their last tortured moments, they proclaimed the innocence of their Order while commending themselves to God, the Virgin Mary, and the saints.[277] The overt use of brutal punishment against defenceless Templars who protested their innocence achieved its goal in the short term. It created an atmosphere of terror and fear, which led to the collapse of the Temple and broke any former readiness to defend the Order. Further, these punishments transformed the work of the papal commission into a fabrication, the main goal of which was no longer to verify the accusations levelled against the Templars but to satisfy the king's peculiar sense of justice. Still, the papal commission continued its work – now freed of having to listen to unnecessary testimonies of innocence – and heard the last depositions on 26 May 1311. The commission finished its work a while later, after hearing 231 witnesses.[278] The use of force in public planted the first seeds of antagonism towards royal policy, especially on the Ile-de-France, an area that up to this stage had showed only support. The fearless persistence with which many Templars at the stake declared the purity of their faith aroused wonder and admira-

---

[276] *Chronographia regum Francorum*, p. 181. Faithful to his basic belief in the Templars' heresy, the St Denis chronicler found reprehensible the lack of contrition of those sentenced to death, and admonished them with heavenly punishment: 'Mais yceus, tant eussent à souffrir de doleur, onques en leur destruction ne vouldrent aucune chose recognoistre; pour laquelle chose leurs âmes, si comme il estimoient, en porent avoir perpetuel dampnement, car il mistrent le menu peuple en très grant erreur': *Les grandes chroniques de France*, pp. 272–3. Still, an anonymous chronicler mentioned the fact that the Templars had asserted that their former confessions had been extracted by torture: *Fragment d'une chronique . . . 1328*, p. 150.

[277] 'Dum igitur talia paterentur eorum amici et consanguinei hortabantur eos, ut confiterentur tales eorum defectus, ne tam enormia paterentur tormenta. Sed illi nolentes ac prae dolore et nimio cruciatu clamantes, dicebant se sine causa talia pati: invocabant proinde Deum et Beatam virginem ac alios sanctos, et sic vitam inter tormenta finiebant': Jean d'Hocsem, *Gesta Pontificum Leodiensium*, p. 348. See also Agnolo di Tura, *Cronaca Senese*, p. 300; *Continuatio chronici Girardi de Fracheto*, pp. 33–4.   [278] McNamara, *Gilles Aycelin*, pp. 170–86.

tion.[279] Some chroniclers found it difficult to reconcile the diabolical image of the Temple voiced by royal propaganda since 1307 with the Templars' heroic martyrdom in 1310.[280]

The doubts concerning the Templars' heresy and the mistrust of Capetian policy were even more acute outside the Capetian kingdom. England offers a fitting case-study of the trial of the Templars removed from the direct sphere of influence of Philip the Fair. England, Scotland, and Ireland counted 144–230 knights of some 4,000 in the whole Order.[281] Their annual income from land property did not exceed 4,800 *l.* in England and 411 *l.*, 11 *s.*, 2 *d.* in Ireland – figures that would hardly give rise to strong feelings of jealousy. Though the Order sometimes abused its chartered rights, there is no evidence that such acts were frequent or flagrant enough to instil general dislike.[282] Still, the papal decree was duly executed, and on 9–11 January 1308 all Templars in England and Scotland were arrested and imprisoned, followed by those in Ireland on 3 February.[283] Chroniclers in England believed the charges of heresy and justified the pope's decree of arrest, which had required the king's co-operation.[284] Clement's sanction of the arrest thus gave credence to the Capetian accusations, which were faithfully repeated in every detail.[285] Quite different, however, were reactions outside the monastic Order. Edward II and the prelates were sceptical about both the alleged charges of heresy and the problematic co-operation between Clement V and Philip the Fair. The prevailing suspicions were reflected in the favourable treatment proffered the Templars after their arrest, especially the king's offer of a daily allowance, which ranged from 2 *s.* to 6 *d.* Edward, moreover, in the orders to the sheriffs, specifically instructed that a fitting place be found for the Templars, 'but not in a hard and vile

---

[279] Jean de Pouilli remained among the very few who saw in the Templars' obstinacy proof of their guilt. See N. Valois, 'Jean de Pouilli, théologien', p. 229.

[280] 'Qui tamen omnes, nullo excepto, nil omnino finaliter de impositis sibi criminibus cognoverunt, sed constanter et perseveranter in abnegatione communi perstiterunt, dicentes semper sine causa morti se traditos et injuste; quod quidem multi de populo non absque multa admiratione stuporeque vehementi conspicere nullatenus potuerunt': *Continuationis chronici Guillelmi de Nangiaco*, p. 378. [281] *Original Papal Letters in England*, no. 48, p. 25.

[282] *Foedera*, i-4, pp. 138–9, 156. Clement's letters to the king suggest his concern about the wealth of the Templars 'which may be used for the service of the Holy Land, should the brethren of the Order be found guilty': *Calendar of Entries in the Papal Registers*, p. 64; C. Perkins, 'The Knights Templar in the British Isles', pp. 223–9; Perkins, 'The Wealth of the Knights Templar in England', p. 254; Seward, 'The Dissolution of the Templars', p. 629.

[283] *Foedera*, i-4, pp. 101, 104, 105. On the arrest and the slight value of Templar property in Ireland, see J. F. Lydon, 'The Enrolled Accounts of Alexander Bicknor, Treasurer of Ireland', pp. 9–46.

[284] *Annales Londonienses*, p. 158; *Annales Paulini*, p. 265; *Chronicon Henrici Knighton*, p. 407; *Chroniques de London*, p. 34; Walsingham, *Historia Anglicana*, p. 120. 'De mandato domini papae Clementis ad instantiam domini regis Francorum': *Chronica Pontificum Eboracensis*, p. 413.

[285] *Flores historiarum*, p. 143; app., pp. 331–3; *Gesta Edwardi de Carnavan*, pp. 28–32; *Annales Londonienses*, pp. 179–98.

prison' (20 December 1307).[286] In most shires, the Templars were taken to royal castles, their imprisonment being far from strict. The grand preceptor of England, William de la More, and the preceptor of Yorkshire, William de Grafton, received special royal authorisation to be accompanied by some of their servants and came to prison with their own furniture and silver vessels.[287]

Clement tried to reverse the comfortable situation of the Templars in England, though initially with little success. On 12 August 1308, all prelates of England received careful instructions regarding the procedure to be followed against the Templars. The pope also enlisted the leading members of the Church to what by now had become a merciless campaign against the Order. The patriarch of Jerusalem and bishop of Durham, the archbishop of York, the bishops of Lincoln, Chichester, and Orléans, and the rector of Hayes in the diocese of London were appointed to manage the inquiry into the Templars in the provinces of York and Canterbury. The abbots of Lagny and St Germain des Près joined them later. The archbishops of St Andrews, Armagh, Dublin, and Tuam were directed to carry out in person or by deputy a similar inquiry in Scotland and Ireland.[288] The patriarch of Jerusalem was nominated together with the archbishops of Canterbury and York to administer Templar property.[289] On 13 September 1309, Dieudonné, abbot of Lagny, and Sicard de Vaur, canon of Agen and papal chaplain, came to England as papal inquisitors.[290] Two weeks later, the papal commission notified the clergy that all Templars were to be questioned,[291] and summoned all brethren to London.[292] After questioning forty-seven Templars (20 October–18 November 1309), the commission failed to obtain confessions consonant with those in France.[293] The lack of an effective outcome caused the Council of London (St Paul's, 24 November) to request special royal permission for the use of torture.[294] Edward II consented, and William of Dieu was appointed to the task.[295] The additional pressure,

---

[286] *Calendar of the Close Rolls (1307–1313)*, pp. 48–9; for Ireland, see *ibid.*, p. 179; *Gesta Edwardi de Carnavan*, p. 32; *Chronicle of Walter of Guisborough*, p. 386.

[287] *Foedera*, I-4, p. 120; Perkins, 'The Trial of the Knights Templar in England', p. 433.

[288] In Scotland, for example, only two Templars were arrested. They were carefully examined on 17 November 1309 by the bishop of St Andrews and a deputy of the papal inquisitors.

[289] *Foedera*, I-4, pp. 126–7; *Records of Antony Bek*, no. 110; *Registrum Roberti Winchelsey Cantuariensis archiepiscopi*, vol. II, pp. 1005–9, 1083–4.

[290] *Foedera*, I-4, p. 152; *Calendar of the Patent Rolls (1307–1313)*, pp. 190, 267, 289; *Calendar of Entries in the Papal Registers*, p. 82; *Registrum Simonis de Gandavo*, vol. I, pp. 351–5.

[291] For the inquisition of the Templars in Ireland and Scotland, see *Foedera*, I-4, pp. 156–8, 171.

[292] *Records of Antony Bek*, no. 145.   [293] *Concilia Magnae Britanniae et Hiberniae*, pp. 335–46.

[294] *Registrum Roberti Winchelsey Cantuariensis archiepiscopi*, vol. II, pp. 1004–5, 1010–12; *Registrum Simonis de Gandavo*, vol. I, pp. 375–7.

[295] According to the law of the realm, torture was not allowed to obtain a confession from prison-

however, did not produce results other than confessions about some irregularities in the administration of penance.[296] At the same time, the archbishop of York was summoned to meet the other commissioners for a preliminary deliberation in London (18 December).[297]

In their report to Clement (5 April 1310), the members of the papal commission referred to the main factors that had prevented them from accomplishing their mission and, in particular, to Edward's opposition to delivering the wealth of the Templars. First, the king had asked for time to deliberate, since the matter touched not only his own interests but also those of the nobles and the entire community of the realm. After further delays, the king finally answered that he could do nothing without consulting the earls and barons, for reasons the pope could understand. The commission was still awaiting the king's reply.[298] Rather obviously, Edward II, like his peers on the Continent, recognised the advantages implied in the arrest of the Templars, and thereafter displayed great diligence in assessing the value of their property as a preliminary to confiscation.[299] This policy gained him the vociferous support of the chroniclers. They expressed particular satisfaction with the king's willingness to share the Templars' possessions with the nobles, since the latter had been the original supporters of the Order and the main contributors of its property.[300] Clement's letters to Edward II reflect the pope's resolution to reverse this lamentable situation by every means. At first, the pope expressed perplexity at the discrepancy in the confessions extracted in England and in France.[301] By August, well aware of the causes of this discrepancy, Clement requested the king to employ torture, in complete disregard of the unprecedented character of its use in England.[302] At the same time, the pope ordered the archbishops of Canterbury and York and their suffragans to proceed with all severity against anyone who dared to help the Templars or to obstruct their inquisition.[303] Winchelsey decided to co-operate and displayed much energy in persecuting wandering

ers. The Angevin system regarded the common opinion of the country, shown by the jurors of the neighbourhood, as sufficient evidence of guilt. On the change of this policy in Canterbury, see *Foedera*, 1-4, pp. 154–5, 163, 165, 166; *Councils and Synods*, pp. 1240–3. Edward ordered the sheriffs to arrest all Templars who were wandering in secular habit in their bailiwicks and to send them to suitable places of confinement in London, Lincoln, and York (14 December 1309): *Calendar of the Close Rolls (1307–1313)*, p. 189.

[296] *Registrum Clementis Papae V*, nos. 6376, 6378. On the results of the inquisition in England, Ireland, and Scotland, see *Monumens [sic] historiques relatifs à la condamnation des chevaliers du Temple*, pp. 259–63.   [297] *Records of Antony Bek*, no. 147.   [298] *Ibid.*, no. 150.

[299] *Registrum Clementis Papae V*, nos. 3626–33; *Lettres de rois, reines, et autres personnages*, pp. 27–9, 37–8.   [300] *Chronicon Galfridi le Baker de Swynebroke*, p. 6.   [301] *Regestum Clementis Papae V*, no. 5061.

[302] 'Nec hoc poterat nec potest ex consuetudine vel lege aliqua impediri, cum in talibus omnis lex, omnis consuetudo, omneque privilegium cesset omnino': *ibid.*, no. 6378.

[303] *Regestum Clementis Papae V*, nos. 6376–7; *Calendar of Entries in the Papal Registers*, p. 78.

Templars, whom he delivered into ecclesiastical custody.[304] He further ordered his commissary to take a public notary with him to the parish of Ewell and to compel the vicar and three or four men of high repute in the neighbourhood to investigate the heresy of the Templars. The archbishop of Canterbury asked for a secret, detailed report to be sent to him before the next meeting of the provincial council, scheduled for 18 April 1312.[305] Still, Winchelsey's emissaries found it extremely difficult to elicit testimony from the laity against the Templars, a further indication of the relative support that the Order enjoyed in England.[306] Not satisfied with these meagre results, Clement promised Edward a general indulgence if he transferred the Templars to France in order to facilitate the work of the inquisitors.[307] Edward was inclined to comply, if not because of the divine forgiveness offered by the pope, at least because of his deteriorating political situation at home, which required papal support.[308] Still, the trial of the Templars in England followed its own course. Between June and July 1310, fifty-nine Templars either abjured certain heresies or admitted their guilt in general terms and were sent to monasteries to complete their penance. Only three fully confessed the crimes attributed to them.[309] On orders from the king, the Council of Canterbury decided to carry out a second inquisition, using torture short of causing death (22 September).[310] In utter contrast with the example of the Grand Master and the Templar leaders in France, William de la More, the grand preceptor of England, and Imbert Blanke, the preceptor of Auvergne, stood fast to the very end in defence of their Order. The former was left to the pope's mercy and finally died in the Tower (20 December 1312). Imbert, locked in double irons, also died in prison.[311]

The developments in the province of Canterbury do not indicate either a consensus regarding the Templars' heresy or a general willingness to co-operate with the pope in finding the necessary proof. On the contrary, the Council of York expressed considerable reluctance to go along with papal policy (May 1310).[312] Initially, the prelates avoided any binding decisions on account of the delay in the opening of the Council of

---

[304] *Registrum Roberti Winchelsey Cantuariensis archiepiscopi*, vol. II, pp. 1240–1. See also the royal orders on the matter: *Foedera*, I-4, p. 182.

[305] *Registrum Roberti Winchelsey Cantuariensis archiepiscopi*, vol. II, pp. 1241, 1247–8.

[306] Perkins, 'The Knights Templar in the British Isles', pp. 224–9.

[307] *Foedera*, I-4, pp. 174–8; *Registrum Clementis Papae V*, no. 6670.

[308] *Calendar of the Patent Rolls (1307–1313)*, p. 226.

[309] *Ibid*. (22 July 1311), p. 376; *Annales Paulini*, p. 270; *Annales Londonienses*, pp. 176–7. Murimuth, however, reflects the prevailing doubts about the heresy attributed to the Templars and the lack of convincing evidence for most charges: Adae Murimuth, *Continuatio chronicarum*, pp. 14–15.

[310] *Councils and Synods*, p. 1290.

[311] Perkins, 'The Trial of the Knights Templar in England', pp. 442–3.

[312] See the summons for the provincial council: *The Register of John de Halton*, vol. II, pp. 15–16.

Vienne.[313] They also justified their lack of initiative on the grounds of the discrepancy between the reports of the diocesan inquisition and those coming from France.[314] Walter of Guisborough mentioned the consternation of the clergy upon receiving the papal letter, *Ad omnium fere*, which repeated almost verbatim the charges of heresy levelled by the Capetian court.[315] He also questioned the pope's claim that the confessions obtained in France were given 'freely and spontaneously, without any coercion or [use of] force'.[316] The resulting opposition of the bishops in the province of York to allowing the use of torture reflects not only their doubts concerning the Templars' heresy – a discrediting of papal policy in itself – but also their awareness of the dangers of such a precedent. 'Torture', they declared, 'has never been used in the kingdom of England.'[317] After lengthy deliberations, they decided to compel all twenty-four Templars to take an oath of self-purification in which they declared their complete aversion to all heresies, especially those contained in the papal letter. The brothers further guaranteed their strict observance of the Catholic faith as defined and taught by the Holy Roman Church.[318] The version of the oath provided by the local chronicler is even more explicit, leaving no doubt about the reservations of the clergy of York in regard to papal accusations.[319] After they publicly pronounced the oath, the Templars were granted indulgence and sent to various monasteries to complete the penitential process (29 July 1311).[320]

The discrepancy between the councils of York and Canterbury–London do not reflect different attitudes towards the charges of heresy levelled against the Templars. The inquisition carried out in both

---

[313] *Councils and Synods*, pp. 1277–84. Powicke and Cheney emphasise the tolerant approach of Archbishop Greenfield, notwithstanding the fact that he himself and his suffragan, Antony Bek of Durham, were papal commissioners in the trial of the Templars in England: *ibid.*, pp. 1277–8.

[314] *Concilia Magnae Britanniae et Hiberniae*, pp. 371–3, 393–401. The Lanercost chronicler emphasises the unique stand of the Yorkshire Templars compared to those of London: 'Eodem anno fuerunt Templarii Angliae examinati de supradictis criminibus eis impositis per inquisitores a domino papa missos, qui apud Eboracum omnia negaverunt, sed tres eorum apud Londonias omnia concesserunt' (*Chronicon de Lanercost*, p. 215). For the trial of the Templars in Ireland and Scotland, see *Concilia Magnae Britanniae et Hiberniae*, pp. 373–83.

[315] 'Perlecta itaque bulla attoniti sunt multi audientes eam': *Chronicle of Walter of Guisborough*, p. 395.

[316] The papal letter in *Collectio actorum veterum*, pp. 108–11; *Chronicle of Walter of Guisborough*, pp. 387–90, 392–4.

[317] *Chronicle of Walter of Guisborough*, pp. 391–2; *Chronica Pontificum Eboracensis*, p. 414.

[318] 'Ego talis detestor et abiuro ad hec sancta quatuor evangelia omnes hereses, et precipue illas in bulla papali contentas, de quibus diffamatum sum; et promitto de cetero observare fidem catholicam atque ortodoxam, quam tenet, docet, et predicat sancta Romana ecclesia. Sic me deus adiuvet et hec sancta dei evangelia': *Councils and Synods*, p. 1338.

[319] *Chronicle of Walter of Guisborough*, p. 395.

[320] *The Register of William Greenfield*, vol. 1, pp. 58–9; *Councils and Synods*, p. 1339; *Regestum Clementis Papae V*, no. 10643. The local record emphasised the fact that Greenfield was moved by pity towards the Templars: *Chronica Pontificum Eboracensis*, p. 414.

provinces revealed certain irregularities in the administration of penance, but this could not really justify the implementation of extreme punishment. The readiness of the province of Canterbury to force the Templars to confess to heresy, thereby facilitating the task of the papal envoys, basically reflects a political attitude with regard to the king and, in the case of Winchelsey, with regard to the exempt Orders. Most prelates in the southern province, many of them from the ranks of royal clerks, were ready to co-operate with Edward II, who from 1310 onwards was interested in fulfilling the papal requests. Winchelsey himself, the defender of ecclesiastical liberty who could have acted otherwise, saw the Templars in their capacity as an exempt Order, for which he himself, like many other prelates in the Council of Vienne, had little sympathy. Though Winchelsey summoned the prelates to the councils at London and Canterbury (1308–9), he himself did not participate in the deliberations or in the inquisition of the Templars, which was directed by papal envoys. On the other hand, he actively contributed in eliciting testimonies against the Order, an action that suggests his belief in the Templars' heresy and/or his antagonism to them.[321]

In other countries of Christendom, the trial of the Templars did not meet the pope's expectations. After months of siege, the Aragonese Templars were eventually arrested and brought to trial.[322] Yet, the brothers and the Order were found innocent by the councils of Tarragona, Salamanca, and Lisbon, respectively.[323] Aimery of Cyprus allowed the Templars, his former political partners who had facilitated his usurpation, to surrender conditionally.[324] The return of Henry II of Lusignan to power, however, brought about a radical change in policy and the Templars were subjected to the full jurisdiction of the Inquisition.[325] One may conclude that, with few exceptions, the charges of heresy against the Templars were readily believed mostly among the lower clergy, monks (who voiced their opinions in contemporary chronicles),[326] and towns-

---

[321] See above, nn. 304–6.

[322] Clement's order to surrender to his representative, his chaplain Bertrand de Cassano, obviously fell on deaf ears (5 January 1309): *Regestum Clementis Papae V*, nos. 5015–17.

[323] Fernández Conde and Oliver, 'La corte pontificia de Aviñón', pp. 373–5.

[324] The Templars also had advanced Aimery a considerable loan of 50,000 byzantines: *Chronique d'Amadi*, pp. 248, 261. In a letter to the pope, Aimery advised a cautious policy towards the Templars because of the critical security situation in Cyprus: *Collectio actorum veterum*, pp. 84–6, 115–16.

[325] Before April 1306, Henry had required papal intervention against the Templars, whom the king accused of endangering the peace of the realm: Mas Latrie, *Histoire de l'Ile de Chypre*, vol. II, pp. 108–9.

[326] In an anonymous letter addressed to the University of Paris, the Friars were accused of having abused the use of torture against the Templars in order to appropriate their wealth; see Cheney, 'The Downfall of the Templars and a Letter in Their Defence', p. 324.

men. Beside their receptiveness to Capetian propaganda, these resented the privileged status of the Order, which had at times prejudiced their situation and affected their income.[327] Conversely, being more aware of the long-range implications of papal policy, princes and prelates were much more derogatory.[328] A consensus emerged, however, concerning the Templar wealth, whose transfer to papal representatives was universally condemned.[329]

The problematic nature of the trial of the Templars found full expression at the Council of Vienne. Ottobono Razzi, patriarch of Aquila, presided over the planning committee, which received the inquisitorial reports and was expected to make the work of the council more effective.[330] Fifty prelates, or about a third of all participants in the council, were selected, according to their country of origin, to reach a decision with regard to the fate of the Order and its members. This large number, as against ten or fifteen prelates on other commissions, raises new questions about Clement's intentions at this stage. After the pope had been accorded formal rule over the Templars and their property in Poitiers, he displayed great diligence in advancing their trial all over Christendom. Also, Clement had supported the use of torture in order to achieve a guilty verdict as quickly as possible. On the other hand, the nomination of fifty prelates to deal with the charges against the Templars suggests a more ambivalent policy and, perhaps, the pope's tendency to use the prelates in order to counteract Philip the Fair. The additional volte-face at this stage might be connected with the compromise reached between pope and king over the trial of Boniface (27 April 1311), which had freed the former of a very dangerous threat.

One month after the opening of the Council of Vienne, the Aragonese representative wrote to James II:

Concerning the Order of the Templars, the results of the investigations that have been carried out so far are being studied. On the basis of what we have heard

---

[327] Matthew Paris, *Chronica Majora*, vol. II, p. 145; Menache, 'Rewriting the History of the Templars According to Matthew Paris', pp. 185–214.

[328] In retrospect, their hesitations were well expressed by Langland:

Bothe riche and religious, bat Rode bei honoure,
hat in grotes is ygraue. and in golde nobles.
For coneityse of bat crosse. men of holykirke
shul tourne as templeres did. be tyme apporcheth faste.
The Vision of William Concerning Piers Plowman – Text B, p. 282.

[329] *Regestum Clementis Papae V*, nos. 6740, 7034, 7493–8.

[330] Müller, *Das Konzil von Vienne*, pp. 96–9; Finke, *Papsttum und Untergang des Templerordens*, vol. I, pp. 348–9; Ehrle, 'Ein Bruchstück der Akten des Konzils von Vienne', p. 434. On 18 June 1311, Clement urged all archbishops of France immediately to send detailed reports of the Templars' inquisition in their respective provinces. See *Regestum Clementis Papae V*, nos. 7517, 7524–8.

from cardinals and clergymen, it is not possible to condemn the Order as a whole, since there is no evidence of guilt on the part of the Order . . . However, since most of the members of the Order have been found guilty of serious transgressions, the pope will issue a decree for the dissolution of the Order . . . and the setting up of a new Order to be based overseas.[331]

This was the basic position of Guillaume le Maire and Jacques Duèse (the future John XXII), who recommended the dissolution of the Order *rigore juris* or *de plenitudine potestatis*.[332] According to Guillaume le Maire, the Order 'should be destroyed without delay, since grave scandal has arisen against it throughout Christendom . . . especially since many errors and heresies have clearly been proved against its members'. Though Jacques Duèse was less assertive, he also supported a similar policy on the grounds that the Templars had apostatised their vocation and that their arrogance and riches had provoked the hatred of Christendom. Both prelates suggested that the pope should suppress the Order *ex officio*. Jacques de Thérines, however, was less convinced of the justice inherent in a radical solution of this sort. He asked, rather rhetorically, how the alleged heresy could have polluted the Order, whose members were of noble birth and had devoted their life to the defence of the Holy Land. The Cistercian abbot called attention to the readiness of many Templars to retract their former confessions and to defend their Order, notwithstanding the risk of death. Ultimately, he mentioned the many contradictions found in the inquisitorial protocols.[333] Jacques de Thérines was not alone. Walter of Guisborough pointed out that 'most of the prelates stood by the Templars, except for the prelates from France who, it would seem, did not dare to act otherwise for fear of the king, the source of all this scandal'.[334] His report is supported by authors from Aragon and Italy, who emphasised the prelates' general opposition to a shameful submission to Capetian interests.[335]

In a letter to Philip, Clement expressed anxiety over the climate of opinion that was prevalent in the council and that supposedly accounted for 1,000 Templars who, if only allowed, were ready to defend their Order (November 1311).[336] At the beginning of December, the pope

---

[331] Finke, *Papsttum und Untergang des Templerordens*, vol. ii, no. 128, p. 251.

[332] *Concilia*, ed. Mansi, vol. xxv, cols. 418–26; Hefele and Leclercq, *Histoire des conciles*, vol. vi-2, pp. 648–9.

[333] *Contra impugnatores Exemptionum*, in Valois, 'Jacques de Thérines, cistercien', pp. 199–200.

[334] *Chronicle of Walter of Guisborough*, p. 396.

[335] Finke, *Papsttum und Untergang des Templerordens*, vol. ii, no. 132, p. 259; Tolomeo da Lucca, *Secunda Vita*, p. 43.

[336] Though the pope had officially invited the Templars to defend their Order (*Regestum Clementis Papae V*, nos. 3584–5), such attendance was rather unexpected. In late October 1311, seven Templars appeared in Vienne, and they were followed by many others. The pope's numbers seem, however, quite exaggerated.

summoned the members of the large commission to a secret meeting, at which he raised four main questions:

Should the council give the right of self-defence to those Templars who were ready to exonerate their Order?

If granted, will the right of self-defence concern only those Templars who attended the council one month earlier?

If not granted, should Templars from all over Christendom choose one proctor for the Order?

If such a design proved too difficult or even impossible to achieve, should the pope nominate an advocate for the Templars?[337]

The prelates were required to provide a written response and by a large majority opted for granting the Templars the right of self-defence.[338] In a letter to Edward II, his proctor in the curia informed the king of the great altercation between the pope and the prelates with regard to the defence of the Templars, all the prelates taking the side of the Order and only five or six, from the kingdom of France and close to the king, remaining adamant.[339] In any case, the proctor concluded, all sessions focused on the fate of the Templars, and no other topic received attention (27 December).[340]

The alarming benevolence showed by most prelates towards the Templars, at least from the perspective of Philip the Fair, lay behind the secret delegation that he sent to Vienne (17 February 1312). Over the course of twelve days, Louis of Navarre, the counts of Boulogne and St-Pol, Enguerrand de Marigny, Guillaume de Plaisians, and Guillaume de Nogaret deliberated with the pope and his closest advisors – Cardinals Arnaud de Pellegrue, Arnaud de Canteloup, Bérenger Frédol, Nicolas de Fréauville, and Arnaud Nouvel – on the best manner in which to bring the trial of the Templars to an end. In parallel, Philip chose the same means that had proved effective four years earlier. On 10–14 March, the king summoned an additional Assembly to Lyons, only a short distance up-river from Vienne.[341] Episcopal cities were apparently summoned to

---

[337] Finke, *Papsttum und Untergang des Templerordens*, vol. II, no. 132, pp. 258–9.

[338] Among those who opposed such a move were one Italian bishop, the archbishops of Sens, Rouen, and Reims, and Guillaume le Maire, bishop of Angers: Müller, *Das Konzil von Vienne*, pp. 691–3.

[339] This report was confirmed by Tolomeo da Lucca, who described the general consensus among the prelates, those of France included, excepting only the archbishops of Reims, Sens, and Rouen. See *Secunda Vita*, p. 42.

[340] Langlois, 'Notices et documents relatifs à l'histoire du XIIIe et XIVe siècles', pp. 75–6.

[341] Finke, *Papsttum und Untergang des Templerordens*, vol. II, no. 137, pp. 273–4. The original summons mentioned 10 February, but Philip did not arrive in Lyons on that date. The king declared his plan to use the Assembly 'ad informandum et Christi negocium ordinandum et disponendum': Lalou, 'Les assemblées générales sous Philippe le Bel', p. 16. Taylor contests this date and argues that there is no satisfactory evidence that the meeting did not begun on schedule, namely, on 10 February. See C. H. Taylor, 'The Assembly of 1312 at Lyons–Vienne', p. 339.

join the magnates and the king in the negotiations with the pope.[342] On 20 March, Philip himself came to Vienne with a large retinue.[343] It was in this atmosphere of fear and pressure that the council met to decide whether to allow the Templars to defend their Order or whether, by exercise of apostolic authority, to dissolve the Temple as a deterrent measure. The decision was taken on 3 April, with most prelates (four-fifths) voting for the immediate abolition of the Order. By this time, Clement had decided on the assignment of the Templar property to the Hospital,[344] an arrangement that he justified on the grounds of the Order's international nature in contrast to the national character of Calatrava, Uclès, and the Teutonic Knights.[345] Basing his sermon on Ps. 1:5, 'the ungodly shall not stand in the judgement, nor sinners in the congregation of the righteous', Clement V summarised the grave crimes imputed to the Templars without pronouncing a guilty verdict on the Order as a whole.[346] The constitution, *Vox in excelso*, published at the last meeting of the conciliar commission (22 March), bestowed apostolic legitimacy on the abolition of the Temple:

Considering therefore the infamy, suspicion, noisy insinuation, and the other things above which have been brought against the Order, and also the secret and clandestine reception of the brothers of this Order, and the difference of many of these brothers from the general custom, life, and habits of the others of Christ's faithful; . . . considering moreover the grave scandal which has arisen from these things against the Order, which it did not seem could be checked while this Order remained in being, and also the danger both to faith and souls; . . . not without bitterness and sadness of heart, not by way of judicial sentence, but *by way of provision or apostolic ordinance*, we abolish the aforesaid Order of the Temple and its constitution, habit, and name by an irrevocable and perpetually valid decree, and we subject it to perpetual prohibition with the approval of the Holy Council, strictly forbidding anyone to presume to enter the said Order in the future, or to receive or wear its habit, or to act as a Templar. Which if anyone acts against this, he will incur the sentence of excommunication *ipso facto*. Furthermore, we reserve the persons and goods of this Order to the ordinance and disposition of our apostolic see, which, by the grace of divine favour, we intend to make for the honour of God and the exaltation of the Christian faith and the prospering state of the Holy Land, before the present council is ended.[347]

---

[342] Taylor, 'The Assembly of 1312 at Lyons–Vienne', pp. 340–4.

[343] *Continuationis chronici Guillelmi de Nangiaco*, p. 389.

[344] In a secret interview in November 1310, Clement expressed his concern about Templar property in France, which had been dissipated and lost, a situation that may explain the pope's pressure to reach a binding decision: Langlois, 'Le procès des Templiers d'après des documents nouveaux', pp. 417–19.

[345] Finke, *Papsttum und Untergang des Templerordens*, vol. II, no. 139, pp. 280–4.

[346] *Ibid.*, vol. II, no. 144, pp. 292–3; *Continuationis chronici Guillelmi de Nangiaco*, pp. 390–1; *Les grandes chroniques de France*, p. 286. [347] *Conciliorum Oecumenicorum Decreta*, p. 342.

The constitution, *Considerantes dudum* (6 May), left to Clement's decision the fate of Templar leaders: the Grand Master Jacques de Molai; the visitor of France, Hugues de Pairaud; the pope's former chamberlain, Olivier de Penne; the preceptor of Normandy, Geoffroi de Charney; the preceptor of Aquitaine and Poitou, Geoffroi de Gonneville; and the preceptor of Cyprus, Raimbaud de Caron.[348] Calling for Christian charity towards those Templars who showed signs of sincere contrition, the pope appointed special commissioners to carry out the conciliar decisions throughout Christendom.[349] Provincial councils were to decide the fate of the Templars. Those who were found innocent or had submitted to the Church were to be given a pension, drawn on the property of the Order, in accordance with their respective status. They could reside either in former Templar houses or in other monasteries, although not in considerable numbers. Those who relapsed or remained impenitent were to be treated with the full rigour of canon law. All fugitives were ordered to appear before the relevant provincial council within one year, failing which they were to be declared heretics.[350]

All that remained now was the fate of Templar property, a subject towards which Clement V displayed great obstinacy: 'Finally the pope told the prelates that he would like best to have their consent to the transfer of the property to the Order of St John, but that he was determined to do this with or without their agreement.'[351] The constitution, *Ad providam* (2 May),[352] indeed, transferred the Templar property 'to those who are ever placing their lives in jeopardy for the defence of the faith beyond the seas'. The Order of St John was to inherit 'all that was in the possession of the Templars in the month of October 1307, when they were arrested in France'.[353] *Ad providam*, however, did not include the

---

[348] *Ibid.*, pp. 347–9; *Regestum Clementis Papae V*, no. 8784. The pope already had referred to this possibility on 22 May 1309. See *Regestum Clementis Papae V*, no. 5067.

[349] *Conciliorum Oecumenicorum Decreta*, pp. 348–9; *Regestum Clementis Papae V*, no. 7886.

[350] As late as March 1313, the trials of Templars throughout Christendom had not yet concluded, a situation clearly indicated by the papal letter to the bishop of Majorca: *Regestum Clementis Papae V*, no. 9170. See some data on the pensions granted to the Templars in Barber, *The Trial of the Templars*, pp. 238–40.

[351] Finke, *Papsttum und Untergang des Templerordens*, vol. II, no. 146, p. 299.

[352] The considerable interval between the two meetings, instead of the four days anticipated by Clement, may well point to the prelates' opposition to the papal plans because of the considerable property already possessed by the Hospital.

[353] *Conciliorum Oecumenicorum Decreta*, p. 345; *Regestum Clementis Papae V*, nos. 7885–6; *Calendar of Entries in the Papal Registers*, p. 95; *Foedera*, II-1, pp. 5–6. Although the continuator of Guillaume de Nangis recognised that the transfer of Templar wealth to the Hospital was meant 'ad ejusdem terrae recuperationem sive subsidium possent effici fortiores ex ipsis', he concluded, rather pessimistically, 'ut apparuit processu temporis, facti sunt deteriores'. See *Continuationis chronici Guillelmi de Nangiaco*, p. 392. Luttrell evaluates the opposition of the prelates in the framework of their general hostility to the exempt Orders. See Luttrell, 'Gli Ospitalieri e l'eredità dei Templari', pp. 76–8. The transfer of Templar wealth led to an ominous identification of the

Templars' property in Castile, Aragon, Portugal, and Majorca, the fate of which was left to the pope's later judgement.[354] Yet the principal instigator of the whole affair had not yet said his last word. In a letter to the pope, Philip the Fair eventually agreed to transfer the Templars' wealth to the Hospital, provided that the pope managed to undertake a complete reform of that Order 'both in its head and members' (24 August 1312).[355] The king further specified that the goods of the Templars would be transferred to the Order of St John only 'after the deduction of necessary expenses for the custody and administration of these goods' and without affecting the rights 'of the king, the prelates, barons, nobles, and all other persons of the kingdom who had a share in the aforesaid property'.[356] Both the stipulation of necessary reforms in the Hospital and the claim of legitimate royal rights to Templar property appear as a warning of Philip's designs.[357] Edward II went even further, admonishing the Hospitallers against any attempt to make use of the council decision to 'usurp' Templar wealth.[358] He also faithfully followed the example of his father-in-law in defence of the rights of the crown and the barons of England.[359]

The last event in the Templar tragedy came in 1314. In accordance with the decisions of the Council of Vienne, Clement V delegated the judgement of the Templar leaders to three cardinals – Nicolas de Fréauville, Arnaud d'Aux, and Arnaud Nouvel (22 December 1313).[360] Three months later, they sentenced the knights to life confinement (14 March 1314). Though Hugues de Pairaud and Geoffroi de Gonneville acquiesced in their fate, Jacques de Molai and Geoffroi de Charney protested, contending that their only crime had been to confess under torture the false charges against their Order. On 18 March, the two were burned to death as *relapsi* on the Ile des

---

Hospital with the Temple: 'Fratres Hospitales in illis commorantes adhuc apud vulgus Templarii nominantur' (*Chronica monasterii Sancti Bertini*, p. 796).

[354] *Conciliorum Oecumenicorum Decreta*, p. 345; *Regestum Clementis Papae V*, no. 7886; Finke, *Papsttum und Untergang des Templerordens*, vol. II, no. 146, pp. 298–302.

[355] Lizerand, *Le dossier de l'affaire des Templiers*, nos. 11–12, p. 200.

[356] *Ibid.*, p. 202. See the decision carried by the parliament of 1312: *Les olim ou registres des arrêts rendus par la cour du roi*, pp. 580–2.

[357] Philip still retained 260,000 *l.t.* from the Templars' resources: 200,000 *l.t.* as compensation for his and his ancestors' contributions to the Order, and 60,000 *l.t.* for the expenses generated during the trial (*Chronicon fratris Francisci Pipini*, col. 750; Causse, *Eglise, finance, et royauté*, vol. I, p. 249). The repetition of papal letters calling on other Christian kings to transfer the wealth of the Templars to the Hospitallers indicates that France was not the exception: *Regestum Clementis Papae V*, nos. 7952, 8862, 8961, 8973–4, 9383–6, 9496, 9618, 9984, 10166.

[358] *Foedera*, II-1, p. 10.

[359] *Calendar of the Patent Rolls (1313–1317)*, p. 52; *Calendar of the Close Rolls (1307–1313)*, p. 544; *Calendar of the Close Rolls (1313–1318)*, pp. 29–30, 88–9; *Chronicon Angliae Petriburgense*, p. 159. For Ireland, see *Annales Hibernie*, p. 343.   [360] *Regestum Clementis Papae V*, no. 10337.

Juifs.[361] Giovanni Boccaccio's father, who saw the morbid drama, was moved to compassion by their miserable fate, a feeling shared by other contemporaries as well.[362] The leaders of the Templars gone, the question remained as to the effects of the trial on Clement V and, particularly, on the image of the pope in Christendom.

All during the long trial, contemporary chroniclers were aware of the pernicious influence of Philip the Fair.[363] Even those who supported the papal decision to transfer Templar property to the Order of St John did not do so from a sense of identification with the Hospitallers 'and their self-sacrifice beyond the seas', but out of a desire to obstruct the greed and endless ambition of the king of France.[364] On the other hand, Jean d'Hocsem, faithful to the stereotyped image he held of Clement, referred to the papal decision on behalf of the Hospital as a sale for all intents and purposes, since, he argued, the Hospitallers had paid to the pope full price for the transfer. This approach was common to other chroniclers in Italy and Germany.[365] Especially in England, the chroniclers did not conceal their satisfaction with the failure of Philip's designs: 'For this king hoped

---

[361] An eyewitness of the execution wrote a reliable description with these touching lines:

> Le mestre, qui vi le feu prest,
> S'est dépoillié sans nul arrest;
>   . . . Tout nu se mist en sa chemise
> Liement et a bon semblant.
>   . . . Les mains li lient d'une corde
> Mès ains leur dist: 'Seignors, au moins,
> Lessez-moi joindre un po mes mains
> Et vers Dieu fère m'oraison, . . .
>   . . . mourir me convient brement
> Diex set qu'à tort et à pechié.
> S'en vendra en brief temps meschié
> Sus cels qui nous dampnent à tort;
> Diex en vengera nostre mort.'
> *Continuationis chronici Guillelmi de Nangiaco*, pp. 403–4.

Les grandes chroniques de France, p. 295; *La chronique métrique attribuée à Geffroy de Paris*, pp. 197–9, vv. 5623–5770; Jean d'Hocsem, *Gesta pontificum Leodiensium*, p. 349. Notwithstanding the fact that Ferreto de' Ferreti was completely hostile to the Order and endorsed the charges of heresy, he voiced Molai's curse against Clement and Philip and took care to record its fulfilment soon afterwards: Ferreto de' Ferreti, *Historia rerum in Italia gestarum*, pp. 184–7. On Molai's curse, see Beaune, 'Les rois maudits', pp. 9–13, 23–4.

[362] Giovanni Boccaccio, *De casibus virorum illustrium libri novem*, c. XXI, p. 262.

[363] Bernard Gui, in *Tertia Vita*, p. 57; Bernard Gui, in *Quarta Vita*, p. 71; Amalric Auger, *Sexta Vita*, p. 101; Finke, *Papsttum und Untergang des Templerordens*, vol. II, no. 140, p. 287.

[364] See Clement's letters of 16 May 1312 urging the archbishops, bishops, and nobles of England to help his envoys to transfer the Templar wealth to the Hospital, in *Original Papal Letters in England*, nos. 68–9, p. 34.

[365] 'Papa vero statim bona templi infinito thesauro fratribus vendidit hospitalis sancti Ioannis': Jean d'Hocsem, *Gesta Pontificum Leodiensium*, p. 349. Paolo di Tommaso Montauri also refers to an 'amount of money' that the pope had received from the Hospital in exchange for the transaction: *Cronaca Senese*, p. 233; *Annales Forolivienses*, p. 59.

to make one of his sons king of Jerusalem and that all the lands of the Templars should be granted to his son. This scheme was foiled, and justly so, and the pope has transferred the land and property of the Templars to the Hospitallers.'[366] When it came to implementing the papal decision in England, however, the chroniclers strongly criticised this same policy as infringing upon the rights of the king and the nobles, whose ancestors had contributed to the Templars' wealth. They rejoiced over the fiasco of papal envoys who attempted to transfer Templar property to the Hospital.[367]

The Catholic camp did not, therefore, celebrate any victory over heresy at the close of the Council of Vienne. By 1312, very few connected the papal decision to abolish the Temple with the charge of heresy levelled against the Order five years earlier.[368] A sense of consternation was evident even among chroniclers on the Ile-de-France on account of the manner in which an ancient Order had been abolished. Some authors tried to dispel doubts by citing the Templars' confessions before the University of Paris and the provincial councils of Reims and Sens. They attempted to neutralise the influence of torture by claiming that the Templars were brave men, who could not easily have been intimidated.[369] After recognising the high pedigree of the Templars and their being members of the nobility and legitimate sons of their parents – both facts apparently considered a warrant for their Catholic faith – the author of the *Chronographia* reached the unavoidable conclusion that their heresy must had been the work of the devil.[370] In England, only a few sources related the abolition of the Order to the charges of heresy.[371] Revealing an awareness of the drift of opinion in the council, the great majority openly expressed its disapproval of Philip's motives and the weight of his influence.[372] In those places where the influence of Capetian propaganda was weaker, reactions to the abolition of the Temple were even stronger. Chroniclers in Germany, Aragon, and Italy described the dissolution of

---

[366] This charge was repeated twice by Murimuth; see Adae Murimuth, *Continuatio chronicarum*, pp. 16–17; *Chronicon Galfridi le Baker de Swynebroke*, p. 6.

[367] Adae Murimuth, *Continuatio chronicarum*, p. 16. A number of nobles, the overlords of the Templars for certain estates, seized their lands and refused to surrender them to the Hospital. When called to ecclesiastical courts to answer for their contumacy, they brought writs of prohibition *de laico foedo*, which accused the Church courts of encroaching upon royal jurisdiction over lay fees and lay chattels. See W. R. Jones, 'Relations of the Two Jurisdictions', pp. 132–7; and above, pp. 76–80.   [368] *Chronographia regum Francorum*, pp. 205–10.

[369] 'Nec est verisimile quod viri tam nobiles, sicut multi inter eos erant, umquam tantam vilitatem recognoscerent nisi veraciter ita esset': Jean de St Victor, *Prima Vita*, p. 23.

[370] *Chronographia regum Francorum*, p. 209; *Notae ad vitas*, pp. 68–9.

[371] *Flores historiarum*, pp. 147–8.

[372] *Annales Paulini*, p. 271; Adae Murimuth, *Continuatio chronicarum*, p. 17; Walsingham, *Historia Anglicana*, p. 127; *Chronicon Galfridi le Baker de Swynebroke*, p. 5.

the Temple as an act of injustice calculated to serve the unbridled ambition of Philip the Fair.[373] *De laude novae militiae* of Bernard de Clairvaux inspired John of Viktring to confront Clement V with Abraham's challenging question: 'Wilt thou destroy the righteous with the wicked?' (Gen. 18:23).[374] Two anonymous chroniclers further referred to Clement's painful remorse in his last moments for his unjust decision against the Templars two years before.[375] According to Dante Alighieri, the dissolution of the Order was yet another act of the 'new Pilate' – i.e., Philip the Fair – to undermine Christendom.[376] The chronicler of Pistoia went even further, considering the abolition of the Temple as one of the three main causes of the Black Death.[377] In the course of time, resentment against the Templars abated and their memory was sanctified with a halo of martyrdom. The leaders' brave deaths at the stake increased the prestige of the Order, and their martyred bodies were treated as holy relics.[378] These reactions showed that Capetian propaganda had not succeeded in convincing most contemporaries of the Templars' heresy and, consequently, of the genuineness of Philip's commitment to the faith.[379] Contemporary sources did not refer to the Templars' trial as a Holy War; nor did the entire episode gain Clement V the image of a champion of orthodoxy – on the contrary, it strengthened suspicion of his pro-French bias.

Modern scholars who have written about the dissolution of the Order of the Temple have approached the event as an additional stage in the Capetian tendency to eliminate feudal barriers, the Templars being one of them.[380] The initiative of Philip the Fair against the Temple appears

[373] Finke, *Papsttum und Untergang des Templerordens*, vol. II, no. 126, p. 245; Agnolo di Tura, *Cronaca Senese*, p. 315. Trithemius used the occasion to indicate that Clement had in fact been elected to the papacy thanks to the intervention of Philip the Fair. He further stated that the Templars were arrested because Philip coveted their property, thus 'crimen eis haereseos falsum imposuit': Trithemius, *Chronicon Hirsaugiensi*, col. 408.   [374] John of Viktring, pp. 369–70.

[375] *Cronica S. Petri Erfordensis Moderna*, p. 446; *Cronica Reinhardsbrunnensis*, p. 651.

[376] I see another Pilate, so full of spite
not even that suffices: his swollen sails
enter the very Temple without right.
Dante Alighieri, *Divina Commedia*, Purgatorio, c. XX, vv. 91–3.

[377] *Storie Pistoresi*, ad a. 1346, p. 224.

[378] *Continuatio chronici Girardi de Fracheto*, p. 40; *Continuationis chronici Guillelmi de Nangiaco*, pp. 402–4; *Annales Hibernie*, p. 341; Agnolo di Tura, *Cronaca Senese*, p. 300; *Chronica S. Petri Erfodensis Moderna*, p. 446; *Chronica Reinhardsbrunnensis*, p. 65; Villani, *Istorie fiorentine*, l. viii, c. 92, pp. 187–8; Mühlethaler, *Fauvel au pouvoir*, pp. 341–4.

[379] Menache, 'Contemporary Attitudes Concerning the Templars' Affair', pp. 142–7.

[380] Hefele and Leclerq, *Histoire des conciles*, vol. VI, p. 517; Hillgarth, *Ramon Lull and Lullism in Fourteenth-Century France*, pp. 88, 94–5; Boutaric, *La France sous Philippe le Bel*, p. 145; Langlois, 'Philippe le Bel et Clément V', p. 177.

logical, if not justifiable, in the framework of similar policies that he had adopted against both Jews and Lombards in 1306. The financial needs of the Capetian monarchy and its tendency to replace 'foreign', intermediary groups with the rising *tiers état* provide an additional explanation for Philip's five-year battle against the Templars.[381] This view, however accurate it appears up to some point, focuses on the role of Philip the Fair but neglects that of the pope, who actually was the ultimate judge in the trial of the Templars. The abolition of the Temple should also be connected with the changes that affected Christendom in the early fourteenth century, which the Order, first and foremost its leaders, had proved completely unable to foresee.

The Order of the Temple had been based on the Christian ideals of knighthood and monastic life, the symbiosis of which was the most original outcome of the Crusader Kingdom. Twenty years after the fall of Acre, however, the emergence of 'national' monarchies brought about the deterioration of the former universal nature of Christendom, which was at the very core of the crusades. Other Military Orders found territorial substitutes for the Latin Kingdom, such as the Hospitallers in Rhodes or the Teutonic Knights in north-eastern Europe.[382] Not so the Templars, whose stubborn adherence to an international character only accentuated their anachronism. The financial activities of the Order, moreover, could seldom be justified, since the kingdom they were expected to serve no longer existed, and the Templars' devotion to the crusade was questioned, if not made null, by Capetian propaganda.[383] These facts alone, without any reference to the alleged heresy, may explain the royal move to abolish the Order. Yet, the enigma remains with regard to the motivations and goals of Clement V. The universal 'anachronism' of the Order of the Temple was in harmony with the tenets of the papal monarchy. Despite the fact that in the short term the abolition of the Temple freed the curia of the Capetian threat to renew the trial of Boniface, this *do ut des* does not provide a satisfactory explanation of the tortuous line of papal policy during the long trial. Initially, Clement V did not support the arrest or favour the brutal persecution of the Templars by Philip the Fair.[384] Once the Templars had been arrested and, especially, after they had openly confessed their crimes, the pope's room for manoeuvring, however, was considerably restricted. Under the circumstances dictated by the king of France, Clement perceived only

---

[381] Menache, 'The Templar Order', pp. 16–21.
[382] J. Prawer, 'Military Orders and Crusader Politics in the Second Half of the Thirteenth Century', pp. 227–8.
[383] D. M. Metcalf, 'The Templars as Bankers and Monetary Transfers Between West and East', p. 12.   [384] Boutaric, 'Clément V, Philippe le Bel, et les Templiers', p. 39.

one way to protect ecclesiastical immunity, particularly the papal monarchy: the abolition of the Order by apostolic decision. In this regard, the
question of whether Clement believed in the Templars' heresy or not
loses relevance. The pope's changing policy during the long trial should
be reviewed from the perspective dictated by papal interests and the problematic relationship between the curia and an exempt Order, on the one
hand, and between them both and the emerging national monarchy, on
the other.

During its two hundred years of existence, the Temple – the former
militia Christi, which the popes expected to turn into a *militia papae* – did
not fulfil the expectations of the papacy. A long series of papal letters provides testimony of the Templars' disregard of apostolic interests both
before and after the fall of Crusader Acre.[385] Jacques de Molai's opposition to the unification of the Temple with the Hospital closed the door
on finding a compromise between the Order, which was too jealous in
the protection of its interests and prerogatives, and papal needs and limitations in the early fourteenth century. These considerations affected the
Hospital and the Teutonic Knights as well. Indeed, there is clear evidence
of the pope's serious plans for a reform of both Orders soon after the
Council of Vienne.[386] Yet neither the arrest of the Templars nor the
abolition of the Order could be regarded as initiatives of Clement V, nor
were they in accordance with either his character or the policy evinced
during his nine-year pontificate. In the end, the responsibility for the
cruel and inexorable path of the trial of the Templars remains the dubious
privilege of Philip the Fair. On the other hand, although the initiative
for the arrest of the Templars undoubtedly came from Philip the Fair, he
did not dictate the final decision. Both the avoidance of a clear verdict
on the guilt of the Order and, even more important from the Capetian
perspective, the transfer of Templar wealth to the Hospital clearly contra-
dicted the expectations and interests of the king of France. Conversely,
these acts were in direct accord with the plans of Clement V, the main
promoter and supporter of the Hospitaller Crusade in 1310. In this
regard, Joseph R. Strayer recognises the fact that Clement's reasons for
suppressing the Order at the Council of Vienne were 'reasonably honest'.
The Templars were no longer very useful, and any further delay would
increase lay usurpation of their property.[387] Many questions, however,
still remain open to inquiry: why did Clement not exploit in a more positive manner the general consensus about his sole prerogative to decide
the fate of the Templars? Did Clement consider this support to be too

---

[385] See, for instance, Nicholas III's letter of 1278: *Les registres de Nicolas III*, no. 167.
[386] *Regestum Clementis Papae V*, nos. 8961–2, 8973–5; Luttrell, 'Gli Ospitalieri e l'eredità dei
Templari', pp. 76–8.   [387] Strayer, *The Reign of Philip the Fair*, p. 292.

unreliable to challenge the Capetian court? If the response lies in Clement's subservience to Philip the Fair, as has been often argued, how does one explain the pope's challenge in the Council of Vienne when he opted for the transfer of Templar wealth to the Hospital? Notwithstanding continuous and unremitting research on the Templars, the 'mystery' of which they were accused at the beginning of the fourteenth century still seems to obscure our understanding of the interplay among the *militia*, the Vicar of God on earth, and the Most Christian King.

Chapter 6

ENGLAND

The pro-French bias that is usually attributed to Clement V stems, to some degree, from the pope's family roots in Gascony and an alleged preference for his place of origin. Such an assumption, the origins of which go back to the fourteenth century, overlooks the fact that Gascony was dependent on England and that the former archbishop of Bordeaux was the senior prelate in the continental domain of Edward I. Further, analysis of Clement's pontificate clearly evinces the pope's strong support of the kings of England, notwithstanding the many inconveniences of such a policy. It eventually placed Clement not only against most barons and prelates of England, but also against the community of the Scottish realm in its fight for independence. In both cases, the pope's unconditional support of Edward I and Edward II was in open opposition to prevailing views among the nobility and the prelates, thus leaving Clement with a fragile alliance with the crown, the utility of which may be questioned. It seems, however, that, in the English context, political and economic considerations were of marginal importance for Clement V and papal policy was basically dictated by the pope's high regard for the kings of England. Whether Clement's esteem was reciprocated in actual practice by either Edward I or Edward II remains a question open to debate.

The correspondence between Clement V and Edward I is characterised by expressions of mutual confidence and appreciation that went beyond diplomatic gestures. During the first year of Clement's pontificate, Edward paid great deference to the former archbishop of Bordeaux, from whose personal integrity and rich experience, the king declared, he had long benefited.[1] Edward recognised, in warm terms, Bertrand's continuous devotion to the crown of England and, upon his

---

[1] 'Fecundae dilectionis integritas quam ad nos magna experientia vos habere, et habuisse probavimus a iam diu': *Foedera*, I-4, p. 60.

election to the papacy, his benign treatment of royal representatives.[2] When Edward heard rumours of the pope's illness, he immediately sent his yeoman, Bernard Ferrant, to the curia to be directly informed in the most reliable way about Clement's health.[3] Edward went even further, ordering John of Havering, the seneschal of Gascony, to convey to the pope-elect that all royal lands and property were at his disposal. This was a very generous declaration, but one with little if any practical value.[4] Besides his continuous correspondence with Clement, Edward also dispatched regular missions to the curia for advancing 'arduous affairs concerning him and his realm'.[5] These were clear symptoms of the precarious situation in England and of the king's designs to have the pope play a crucial role in the defence of royal prerogatives.

The affectionate relationship between the pope and the king of England was further manifested following the death of Edward I (Burgh-by-Sands, 7 July 1307).[6] The news reached the curia in Poitiers two weeks later, and Clement performed solemn obsequies for the king's memory. Quoting profusely from the Book of Maccabees, the pope exalted Edward's many merits, the strength of his rule, his sense of justice, his clemency, his crusading fervour, and his many successes against all enemies. This ceremony was an exceptional gesture on behalf of a secular prince, never recorded before in the annals of the medieval papacy.[7] The pope's sincere sorrow upon Edward's death was immortalised, in moving terms, in one of the earliest books of history written in the vernacular.[8]

---

[2] 'De ipso statu [sc. nostro] tam pie et tenere cogitare, atque disponere, quod utique ab iuncto sanguine et antiqua gratitudine novimus processisse': Zutshi, 'The Letters of the Avignon Popes', p. 264; *Calendar of the Close Rolls (1302–1307)*, p. 437. Edward accompanied his declarations with different gestures of goodwill towards the pope's relatives: *Calendar of the Patent Rolls (1301–1307)*, 9 March 1306, p. 420.   [3] 19 December 1305: *Calendar of the Close Rolls (1302–1307)*, p. 424.

[4] 6 April 1306: *ibid.*, p. 431.   [5] *Ibid.*, p. 437.

[6] It was common practice in the early fourteenth century for the king to regard himself as a 'persona mixta, laica et clerica', whose priestly kingship was indelible. Edward I was buried as both king and priest. See Wilks, *The Problem of Sovereignty in the Later Middle Ages*, p. 379.

[7] Edward I's exequies supplied the model for the ceremonial in the office for the dead laid down in the *Ordo Romanus XIV*, which was composed by Cardinal Giacomo Caetani Stefaneschi: Ullmann, 'The Curial Exequies for Edward I and Edward III', pp. 26, 33–5. On Edward I's image, see V. H. Galbraith, 'Good Kings and Bad Kings in Medieval English History', pp. 119–32.

[8] A Peiters a lapostoile;
Vne messager la mort li dist.
E la pape vesti lestole;
A dure lermes les lettres prist.
Alas ceo dist comment morist;
A qi dieu donna tant honur.
A lalme en face dieu mercist;
De seint eglise il fu la flour.
Lapostoile en sa chambre entra;
A pein se poeit sustenir.

Clement also shared with Edward II reminiscences of his father's generosity towards the future pope, when he was a poor, young Gascon clergyman.[9] The benevolence that characterised the policy of Clement V towards Edward I and, later, towards Edward II as well thus appears to be an additional stage in a long-term, friendly relationship that had developed long before Bertrand de Got reached the pontifical throne. Clement attested to this exceptional situation when he declared to Edward II that 'there has never been a High Pontiff. . . who was so devoted to your house as we have always been'.[10] Analysing the reasons for Clement's magnanimity towards both Edwards, W. E. Lunt wonders if the fundamental reason for papal concessions had to do with a trait in Clement's character 'which made it difficult for him to refuse a favour sought by a powerful king'.[11] One may question whether 'powerful' is an exact description of the status of Edward II and whether it also applied to the pope's relationships with the kings of Germany, Aragon, and even France. Obviously not. It is clear, though, that Clement found it difficult, if not impossible, to oppose the wishes of the kings of England; but this was a peculiar situation, well rooted in the pope's past and, especially, in the close relationship of his family with the kings of England, rather than a symptom of Clement's weak character and his supposed subservience to royalty as a whole.

PAPAL SUPPORT IN DOMESTIC AFFAIRS

On 4 October 1305, Edward I sent a letter to the pope-elect declining the invitation to attend the papal coronation ceremony with the prince of Wales because of the conflict in Scotland.[12] The king, though, sent an influential embassy to Lyons to conduct negotiations concerning the crusade, the peace with the king of France, 'and other matters concerning the salvation of the king's soul'.[13] The degree to which these goals

E les cardinals trestuz manda;
Durement commenca de plurir.
Les cardinals li funt teisir;
. . . Lapostoile meismes vint a la messe;
Oue mult grant sollempnite.
An Anonymous Short English Metrical Chronicle, pp. 106–7, vv. 578–95.

[9] 'Dum nos minor status haberet et assisteremus obsequiis dicti regis multis nos graciis et favoribus honoravit, nostrisque consiliis fiducialiter inherebat, ac de vassallis et terris suis utilis traximus nos et nostri': Zutshi, 'The Letters of the Avignon Popes', p. 264. On the relationship between Bertrand de Got and the king of England at this stage, see above, pp. 7–8.
[10] PRO, SC 7/11/16; *Foedera*, 1–4, p. 117.
[11] Lunt, *Financial Relations of the Papacy with England*, p. 417.
[12] *Calendar of the Close Rolls (1302–1307)*, p. 348.
[13] There were actually two delegations. The royal letters for the first embassy were issued on behalf of three men travelling to the curia, among them Roger la Warre (7 July 1305). The second embassy

were indeed achieved became evident soon afterwards. A long series of papal gestures of goodwill ensued and, more importantly, the pope displayed categorical support of Edward I in the domestic arena, particularly in regard to the barons.[14]

During the first two years of his pontificate, Clement reinforced the royal status while eradicating the effects of Boniface's legislation against taxation of the clergy.[15] In the first nomination to the College of Cardinals, the pope promoted Thomas Jorz – a Dominican and master of theology from Oxford, who served in Edward's court – to the rank of cardinal-priest of Santa Sabina.[16] The new cardinal, in a letter to the king, acknowledged that his nomination was due to 'the love and honour of you, sir, whom he [the pope] much cares about and loves'.[17] Antony Bek, bishop of Durham, won the nomination of patriarch of Jerusalem, with dispensation to hold the bishopric of Durham *in commenda*.[18] Clement awarded Edward I the privilege that no papal envoy was to pronounce excommunication, suspension, or interdict against his person or his chapels without the express authorisation of the Apostolic See.[19] In

included Walter, the treasurer and bishop of Coventry and Lichfield; William, bishop of Worcester; Henry de Lacy, earl of Lincoln and the king's kinsman; Hugh le Despenser; the knights Amaneus de Lebreto and Otto de Grandson; John de Benstede, chancellor of the Exchequer and canon of Salisbury; Robert de Pykering, canon of York; Bartholomew of Ferentino, canon of London; and Philip Martel, canon of Chichester (15 October 1305): *Calendar of the Patent Rolls (1301–1307)*, pp. 387–8; *Calendar of the Close Rolls (1302–1307)*, p. 351; Denton, *Robert Winchelsey and the Crown*, pp. 224ff.

[14] Edward wrote to the cardinals commending his ambassadors and requesting them to exert their influence to advance royal affairs (20 October 1305): *Calendar of the Close Rolls (1302–1307)*, p. 353.

[15] *Foedera*, I-4, pp. 45–6; *De immunitate ecclesiarum*, Clementinarum, l. III, tit. xvii, *CIC*, vol. II, col. 1178; Langlois, 'Documents relatifs à Bertrand de Got', p. 49. On the resulting resentment among the priesthood, which bore the brunt of papal generosity, see *Polychronicon Ranulphi Higden*, p. 7.

[16] Biographical data in 'Thomas de Jorz, Anglicus', in *Scriptores Ordinis Praedicatorum*, vol. II, pp. 508–10, nos. 3814–19. See also above, p. 42.

[17] Langlois, 'Notices et documents relatifs à l'histoire du XIIIe et du XIVe siècles', pp. 68–9.

[18] 26 February 1306: *Regestum Clementis Papae V*, nos. 305–6; *Calendar of Entries in the Papal Registers*, pp. 10, 12. The pope exempted Bek from personal obedience to the archbishop of York in his capacity of patriarch, but his officials and vicars remained bound to the archbishop, the chapter, and the church of York: *Records of Antony Bek*, no. 115. One month earlier, Antony Bek had taken the Cross, a deed that obviously gained him Clement's esteem: *Records of Antony Bek*, no. 110. A long list of privileges on behalf of Bek indicates the high appreciation he enjoyed in the curia: *Regestum Clementis Papae V*, nos. 441–3, 721–2, 821–2, 925–8. Walter of Guisborough, however, suggests a simoniacal nomination, 'Et hoc qui erat dives episcopus et papa pauper': *Chronicle of Walter of Guisborough*, pp. 364–5. Whatever the reasons, this nomination cannot be regarded as a gesture of papal goodwill towards Edward I. Edward resented Bek's policy in the peace agreement with the barons (1297) and supported Richard de Hoton's claims for independence against episcopal rights of visitation. The Parliament of Carlisle seized all lands held by the bishop in lay fee on the grounds that Bek had supported Robert Bruce: *Records of Antony Bek*, nos. 119, 121, app. B-a, pp. 191–204; Richardson and Sayles, 'The Parliament of Carlisle', p. 436. Edward II eventually restored Bek to royal favour (4 September 1307): *Foedera*, I-4, p. 91.

[19] *Foedera*, I-4, pp. 45–6, 58; *Original Papal Letters in England*, no. 12, p. 8. The same privilege was accorded to the Prince of Wales on 1 January 1306: *ibid.*, nos. 17–18, pp. 10–11. Edward II asked for its confirmation on 21 May 1309, during the conflict with the barons: *ibid.*, no. 58, p. 29.

addition, the pope authorised the prelates of England to absolve the king's subjects from sentences of excommunication and to grant dispensation for irregularities that they might have incurred during past wars. Under the clause, 'the custom of enemy against enemy', the pope referred to the possibility that certain of the king's subjects, in pursuing royal enemies and rebels, had slain many of them by sword or otherwise, had beaten and mutilated others, had set fire to churches and ecclesiastical places, and had committed spoliation and rapine. The Vicar of God on earth thus enlisted his treasure of merits to alleviate the consciences of the loyal subjects of the king of England.[20] Queen Margaret, as well, enjoyed papal generosity, and a long list of privileges was accorded her.[21]

Besides spiritual benefices, the initial contacts between Clement V and Edward I were critically affected by the political situation in England and the king's pursuit of papal blessing to revoke his former pledge to the nobles (*Confirmatio cartarum*, 5 November 1297).[22] The barons' demands, as expressed in *De Tallagio non concedendo*, essentially consisted of a reissue of the Magna Carta. The nobility expected the king to cease arbitrary exactions, both financial and military, and to submit his policy to the consent of the community of the realm in parliament.[23] Edward was forced to confirm this undertaking in the *Articuli super cartas* (6 March 1300).[24] Following his own concessions that were meant to avoid any infringement of the Charters, though, the king carefully added a concluding passage that maintained the rights and prerogatives of the crown above any other pledge.[25] The result was a rather vague political situation, for which Edward I tried to enlist papal support in order to free himself from baronial pressure. The king was not seeking to overthrow

---

[20] *Calendar of the Close Rolls (1302–1307)*, p. 435.

[21] *Regestum Clementis Papae V*, nos. 620–4, 1612–13; *Calendar of Entries in the Papal Registers*, pp. 9, 23.

[22] *The Statutes of the Realm*, vol. I, pp. 114–24; B. Wilkinson, *Studies in the Constitutional History of Thirteenth and Fourteenth Centuries*, pp. 61–6; J. G. Edwards, '*Confirmatio Cartarum* and Baronial Grievances in 1297', pp. 147–69, 273–300.

[23] The discrepancy between king and barons in this regard was quite serious. In demanding taxation, the king interpreted common profit as common peril. Conversely, the barons judged the effects of taxation in terms of common welfare. Taxation for the profit of the realm should not impoverish it, for it was the mark of a tyrant to impoverish and enslave his subjects. This message was common to the *Confirmatio* and the Ordinances of 1311. In the first case, the barons had questioned the wisdom of Edward's aggressive policy in Flanders; in the second, the Ordainers were critical of his son's defence of the northern border: G. L. Harris, 'War and the Emergence of the English Parliament', pp. 37–43.   [24] *The Statutes of the Realm*, vol. I, pp. 136–41.

[25] '[And notwithstanding] all these things before mentioned, or any point of them, both the king and his council, and all they that were present at the making of this Ordinance, will and intend that the right and prerogative of his crown shall be saved to him in all things': *ibid.*, vol. I, p. 141; M. Prestwich, *War, Politics, and Finance Under Edward I*, pp. 248–65.

the Magna Carta, but to assert his rights and to satisfy his resentment at having been taken advantage of while in an awkward position.[26]

The papal letter, *Regalis devotionis integritas* (Lyons, 29 December 1305), fulfilled Edward's wishes and released him from any obligation towards the *Confirmatio cartarum*. Clement V, in clear language that did not leave room for doubt regarding his political stand, faithfully echoed the royal version of past political events: in 1297, while the king was absent in Flanders, some of his magnates, nobles, and others had formed a conspiracy and incited the people against royal authority. Edward, consequently, had been coerced into making unjust concessions concerning the Forest and other legitimate royal rights. These considerations justified Clement's decision to absolve the king of his former pledges to the barons:

Accordingly, now that this apostolic see, *which esteems the aforesaid realm highly amongst all the kingdoms of the world, and holds both you and it in the closest affection*, has learned of these concessions, assumed and granted at the expense of your honour and to the detriment of the royal excellence, we quash and annul and from the plenitude of our power we revoke these concessions and their force, and whatever has arisen from them in any manner, and also the sentences of excommunication which were perhaps promulgated in those churches or elsewhere to ensure their observance.[27] We pronounce them worthless, null and void ... We determine that you and your successors, kings of England, are not bound in future to observe them, even if you may have taken an oath to do so; especially since, when you performed the ceremony of your coronation, you took an oath, as it is claimed on your behalf, to preserve the honour and rights of the crown.[28] Or if you have bound yourself on that account to any penalty [if you break your oath], from this and from the guilt of perjury, if you have incurred this, we absolve you also [emphasis added].

Clement further prohibited any enforcement of the Great Charter and the Forest Charter in the future without special sanction by the Holy See.[29] The papal document, however, did not clarify the precise clauses

---

[26] Powicke, *The Thirteenth Century*, pp. 215–18; H. Rothwell, 'Edward I and the Struggle for the Charters', p. 331.

[27] In the *Confirmatio*, the king agreed to deposit sealed copies of the Charters in cathedral churches – so that they could be read to the people twice a year – and to pronounce excommunication on all those infringing the Charters: *Statutes of the Realm*, vol. I, p. 123, arts. 3 and 4; translation by Wilkinson, *The Constitutional History of England*, vol. I, pp. 227–8.

[28] The pope was actually changing the fundamental purpose of the coronation oath to protect the kingdom while restricting the king's freedom of action. Clement clearly stated that Edward I did take the non-alienation oath, as Henry III had before him. It was the papal legate in England who probably introduced the idea of inalienability: Richardson, 'The English Coronation Oath', p. 44; Kantorowicz, 'Inalienability', pp. 488–9.

[29] *Foedera*, I-4, pp. 45, 46. The papal letter reached Edward at Canford in Dorset on 11 February 1306: *Original Papal Letters in England*, nos. 16, 18, pp. 10–11; translation by Wilkinson, *The*

to which he referred. It certainly annulled the *Confirmatio cartarum* of 1297 but it did not specifically mention the *Articuli super cartas* of 1300.[30]

The arguments voiced by Clement in 1305 had appeared in the papal releases given to King John in connection with the Magna Carta (1215) and to Henry III with regard to the Charters of Bromholm (1232) and the Provisions of Oxford (1258). Thirteenth-century popes, indeed, had continuously backed their liege-vassals against the Great Charter and the belligerent nobility who stood behind its claims.[31] From a papal perspective, the Magna Carta appeared to be the barons' attempt to usurp royal rights that were inherent in the king's *ministerium*. Furthermore, the Christian order, as it had been established by God and interpreted by generations of canonists and theologians, was one in which kings ruled by divine grace, which had been delegated to them by the pope. According to the Christian scheme, *gratia Dei* bestowed on kings the complete submission of their subjects, 'for there is no power but of God; and the powers that be are ordained of God. Therefore he that resisteth the power, withstandeth the ordinance of God' (Rom. 13:1–2). The king's position and rights were to be determined solely by God or His Vicar, the pope. This was a one-way relationship that did not leave room for partners. The barons' attempt to nullify royal rights, therefore, had to be interpreted as a bold affront to the designs of providence and to their effective implementation by the pope as well.[32] This conservative attitude, which was common to popes and kings, regarded past political conditions as a fixed legal situation on the level of a private contract. The only new concept in Clement's declaration was that the oath taken by Edward I was invalid because it was made with a mental reservation that it would not be honoured. The undertaking of the oath was never truly consented to, and because of this, the pope declared, it was void or non-existent.[33] Clement thus clearly reiterated Edward's opposition to the spirit and methods of the barons and gave the king the justification he sought. Backed by papal support, Edward issued in 1306 a new Forest Statute revoking all disafforestments that severely reduced the boundaries of the royal forest and that he had sworn to observe. Still, in a gesture of

Constitutional History of England, vol. 1, pp. 230–2. The archbishop of York, who was commissioned with its execution, sent copies to the prelates: *The Register of John de Halton*, vol. 1, pp. 264–7.

[30] The London annalist, however, recorded the papal letter as absolving the king from both his oath regarding the Forest and the terms of perambulation: *Annales Londonienses*, p. 146; *Flores historiarum*, p. 130; Denton, *Robert Winchelsey and the Crown*, pp. 229–31, 237–8.

[31] See, for instance, *Etsi carissimus* (24 August 1215): *Foedera*, 1-1, pp. 67–8.

[32] Ullmann, *Principles of Government and Politics in the Middle Ages*, pp. 53–74.

[33] W. H. Bryson, 'Papal Releases from Royal Oaths', p. 29. Bryson's claim that papal releases were confined to the thirteenth century seems rather inaccurate as do the reasons he adduced to justify such a contingency.

goodwill, the king remitted all penalties for forest offences committed in disafforested lands.[34] Clement's absolution did not affect royal policy in other respects.

Though papal support of the king of England against restless barons was hardly unprecedented, the continuous drift of papal policy did not avoid criticism. An anonymous pamphlet, probably written soon after Clement's invalidation of the *Confirmatio cartarum*, stressed the arbitrariness of 'Roman' legislation (a lapse or, perhaps, a manifestation of past traditions?), which stigmatised the Church. Papal sanction of infringements of vows, the abrogation of the *Confirmatio*, the king's inconsistencies, and the arbitrariness of the pope – all these were said to be leading the kingdom, its laws, and its institutions to the ways of the devil:

> Rome can do and undo, she acts thus full often;
> that is neither good nor becoming;
> for this Holy Church is put to shame.
> Merewell who agrees to such counsel is Vicar of God . . .
> The provision is made of wax . . .
> and it has been held too near the fire
> and has all melted away.
> I no longer know what to say,
> but all goes out of joint,
> court and law,
> hundred and shire,
> it all goes the way of the devil.[35]

Notwithstanding Clement's assertions in favour of Edward's good faith, both king and pope were accused of perjury, a crime that until the sixteenth century was considered an offence against religion. The Malmesbury chronicler suggests the negative implications of papal policy for the deteriorating image of the English crown in both the internal and the external arena, not only in Edward's reign but during his son's as well. He refers to such a lamentable outcome when considering the factors that seemingly had caused Robert Bruce to reject the peace offer of Edward II in 1312. The king of Scotland had justified his refusal with the rhetorical question:

---

[34] Note the king's affirmation, besides his concern for the welfare of his people, that 'we do resume our power', a clear indication of his antagonism towards his former concessions: *The Statutes of the Realm*, vol. I, pp. 147–9; L. F. Salzman, *Edward I*, p. 170.

[35] *English Historical Documents*, p. 921. The occasion of this poem is uncertain. Version J, reproduced here, which appears to be the earliest, has the title 'On the Provision of Oxford'. On the other hand, its reference to 'Merewell', presumably Henry of Woodlock of Marwell, bishop of Winchester between 1305 and 1316, suggests that the poem had been written in this period. Clement's letter of 29 December 1305 absolving Edward from his constitutional concessions of 1297–1301, followed in 1306 by the king's Forest Ordinance, would have provided a sufficient occasion for this composition.

'How shall the king of England keep faith with me, since he does not observe the sworn promises made to his liege men, whose homage and fealty
he has received, and with whom he is bound in reciprocity to keep faith?'[36]

The anointment of Edward II brought about a closer relationship
between the royal court and the papal curia, a situation that cannot be
explained in terms of political expedience. Edward's fragile situation at
home, his injudicious links with Gaveston, his futile struggle against
Scotland – each of them could have justified a more balanced papal
policy. The difficult heritage left by his father, especially but not only on
the fiscal level, encouraged Edward II to ask for papal support, which was
generously given by Clement V, notwithstanding the growing price the
papacy was forced to pay.[37] Queen Isabella, as well, shared Clement's
affection, and upon her marriage and coronation was provided with a
long list of papal privileges.[38] This was not, however, a two-way relationship, and Edward II felt free to oppose papal claims in the ecclesiastical
domain, and thereby to win the support of magnates in parliament.[39]

In order to encourage papal benevolence, Edward II found useful
mediation in the many branches of the de Got family. The Gascon Rolls
provide clear evidence of the care taken by Edward II to enlist Clement's
family in support of royal interests. Bertrand de Sauviac, Arnaud Garsie
de Got, Bertrand de Bordes, Guillaume de Bordes, and Forcius d'Aux
were among the many members of the pope's family who enjoyed the
generosity of the king of England.[40] And, indeed, the expectations of
Edward II were satisfactorily fulfilled. Bertrand de Sauviac became an
active partner in the king's attempts to solve his critical financial situation
by means of a papal loan.[41] In May 1313, the papal nuncio in England,

---

[36] *Vita Edwardi Secundi*, p. 22; H. Silving, 'The Oath, I', p. 1329.

[37] 'Probably no medieval king left his finances in a more hopeless confusion than did the great
Edward. Certainly none of them ever handed to his successor so heavy a task with such inadequate means to discharge it': Tout, *The Place of the Reign of Edward II in English History*, p. 35. Cf.
Prestwich, *War, Politics, and Finance Under Edward I*, p. 272. At Edward I's death, he was in debt by
about 200,000 pounds. Still, Maddicott refuses to see in the reign of Edward II an unavoidable
sequel to his father's and emphasises, instead, the relatively good position that Edward II enjoyed
upon his accession to the throne. See J. R. Maddicott, *Thomas of Lancaster*, pp. 69–70. Cf.
J. Conway Davies, *The Baronial Opposition to Edward II*, p. 57. The Lanercost chronicler compared
the succession of Edward II to that of Rehoboam to Solomon: *Chronicon de Lanercost*, p. 209. The
Malmesbury chronicler uses the same pattern to suggest the danger implied in the respect that
Edward II had for young, inexperienced advisors, and concludes that he 'might through impru-
dence be deprived of his throne and his kingdom': *Vita Edwardi Secundi*, pp. 18, 36.

[38] *Regestum Clementis Papae V*, nos. 3014–20, 3068–9, 4092–4101, 4105–8, 8207–8, 8210–13;
Calendar of Entries in the Papal Registers, pp. 44, 47.   [39] See above, pp. 76–81.

[40] *Gascon Rolls*, nos. 1, 780, 40–1, 140; Renouard, 'Edouard II et Clément V d'après les Rôles
gascons', pp. 119–41.

[41] See the special royal protection and safe-conduct given to him on 14 February 1312: *Calendar of
the Patent Rolls (1307–1313)*, p. 430. For the payment of his expenses, see *Foedera*, II-I, pp. 21, 34;
royal grants on his behalf are *ibid.*, II-I, pp. 44–5.

Guillaume Testa, loaned Edward 2,000 marks. This was a provisional advance during the long negotiations conducted by the king's representatives for more credit from the papal camera. On 28 October 1313, Edward was granted a loan of 160,000 florins from the pope 'as a private person, out of friendship and without any gain'. Although the loan was defined *ex causa gratuiti et amicalis*, Clement was to be repaid by direct control of the bulk of royal revenues in Gascony.[42] The loan was finally confirmed in the king's chamber at Westminster on 20 January 1314, and the 160,000 florins, which amounted to 25,000 pounds, were received by Anthony Pessagno on the king's behalf the following March.[43] The loan to the king of England by Clement 'as a private person' again demonstrates the lack of differentiation between the papal camera and the pope's own funds, if any. It also corroborates Clement's partiality towards his relatives and his native land, both of which expected to receive benefit from papal direct control of royal revenues in Gascony. The attempt to avoid the involvement of the papacy in the loan, however, might have been connected with Clement's tendency to maintain the neutrality of the papacy and, especially, essential room for manoeuvring with respect to both the barons and the Scots. Eventually, when papal money reached the royal treasury, the negotiations with the barons were quite advanced and the loan was used to subsidise the war in Scotland. In either case, though, it is rather doubtful whether Clement's readiness to bear the expense of a bloodthirsty conflict among Christians could have been justified.

THE GAVESTON AFFAIR

During the initial years of the reign of Edward II, most abuses of royal policy were identified with the pernicious influence of the king's favourite, Piers Gaveston.[44] Whether Gaveston was cause or symptom of the serious political contest, Clement V displayed active concern at all stages of the long confrontation between Edward II and the barons. From

---

[42] The king gave authority to the papal representatives so that 'percipiant, levent et recolligant omnes redditus, exitus et proventus ad nos spectantes, quomodolibet et in quibuslibet rebus consistant, nostri ducatus Aquitaniae et terre Vasconie et generaliter omnium aliorum locorum in regno Francie ad nos spectancium, comitatu Pontivi dumtaxat excepto, quousque de totali summa predicta ex ipsis fructibus et proventibus vel alias per nos fuerit plenarie satisfactum': *Gascon Rolls*, nos. 1131, 1130, 1132; Tout, *The Place of the Reign of Edward II in English History*, pp. 196–8.

[43] The rate was 3 *s.*, 1 1/2 *d.* sterling for each florin: *Gascon Rolls*, no. 1133; *Calendar of the Patent Rolls (1313–1317)*, p. 205. Pessagno was active in Edward's service between 1312 and 1320: N. Fryde, 'Antonio Pessagno of Genoa, King's Merchant of Edward II of England', pp. 159–78.

[44] On conflicting perspectives of the Gaveston crisis, see J. S. Hamilton, *Piers Gaveston, Earl of Cornwall*, p. 11. Cf. Conway Davies, *The Baronial Opposition to Edward II*, pp. 358, 369.

1307 to 1312, Clement consistently supported the king and his favourite while confronting not only the barons but also some of the prelates, particularly the primate of England, Robert Winchelsey.

Piers Gaveston was a Gascon knight, born probably in the early 1280s. He joined the army of Edward I in Flanders (1297) and Scotland (1300), where he demonstrated military skills and courteous behaviour.[45] By the end of 1300, he had become foster-brother and playmate of the prince of Wales in the royal household.[46] The chroniclers were unanimous in depicting Edward's love for Piers Gaveston from their first encounter: 'Upon looking on him, the son of the king immediately felt such love for him that he entered into a covenant of constancy, and bound himself with him before all other mortals with a bond of indissoluble love, firmly drawn up and fastened with a knot.'[47] The almost unanimous criticism by contemporaries of what they considered Edward's low taste – idling, applying himself to making ditches, and digging – also assumed that it must carry a preference for low company, and Gaveston received a place of preference in this regard.[48] In the first stages, however, the peculiar relationship between the prince of Wales and his Gascon partner, with or without homosexual undertones, did not arouse noticeable antagonism.[49] On the other hand, Piers became the main victim of the rather tense relationship between the old, irascible Edward I and his son. On 18 October 1306, during the campaign in Scotland, Edward I instructed the sheriffs to arrest and seize the lands of twenty-two knights and other men-at-arms who 'have crossed to foreign parts for a tournament . . . without licence, before the war was ended, deserting the king and his son in those parts in contempt of the king and to the retarding of the king's business there'.[50] Piers Gaveston was among them. Although Edward I pardoned all deserters by 23 January 1307, he ordered the exile of Piers Gaveston to Gascony one month later. The king also forced the prince of Wales and his favourite

[45] *Chronicon Galfridi le Baker de Swynebroke*, p. 4. On Gaveston's childhood, see P. Chaplais, *Piers Gaveston*, p. 4.
[46] *Vita Edwardi Secundi*, p. 14. At this stage, the positive attitude of Edward I towards Gaveston is also suggested by the grants he bequeathed him at the request of the prince of Wales: *Calendar of the Patent Rolls (1301–1307)*, p. 244.
[47] This chronicle is part of a series of letters and other documents entitled 'Fragmenta de bellis et causis bellorum civilium tempore Edwardi II', British Museum, MS, Cotton Cleopatra D. IX, fols. 83r–85r, edited by G. L. Haskins, 'A Chronicle of the Civil Wars of Edward II', p. 75.
[48] *Chronicon de Lanercost*, p. 234; H. Johnstone, 'The Eccentricities of Edward II', pp. 264–7.
[49] See the claim advanced by Pierre Chaplais that Edward II contracted an arrangement of adoptive brotherhood, be it brotherhood-in-arms or some other kind of fraternity, with Piers Gaveston, as opposed to the homosexual relationship commonly ascribed to them: Chaplais, *Piers Gaveston*, pp. 20–2, 109–14. [50] *Calendar of the Fine Rolls (1272–1307)*, pp. 543–4.

to swear upon a consecrated Host and various relics that they would submit to the royal ordinance.[51]

Piers' banishment from England, however, ended that summer with the death of Edward I (7 July 1307). The first act of the heir to the throne was to call Piers back, only three months after he had begun a rather comfortable exile in Ponthieu (6 August).[52] Upon his return to England, Piers enjoyed royal favour in a most ostentatious manner. Edward II nominated him earl of Cornwall, a position that Edward I had reserved to his sons from his second wife, Margaret of France.[53] Gaveston also became keeper of the realm while Edward went to France to fetch his bride, Isabella (20 December).[54] The increasing power of the king's favourite fomented unrest among the barons,[55] who threatened to impede Edward's coronation, scheduled for February 1308.[56] They did not limit themselves to threats. Following the so-called Declaration of 1308,[57] the Parliament of Westminster formally sanctioned Gaveston's second exile (28 April–18 May).[58] By the terms of the agreement between king and barons, Piers was to leave England by 25 June at the latest, and the lands he held as earl of Cornwall were to revert to the crown although Piers retained the title. This accord received religious sanction, and Winchelsey threatened Gaveston with excommunication should he either fail to obey or attempt to return to England (18 May).[59]

In clear contrast to his previous pledges, Edward's actions from June

---

[51] *Foedera*, I-4, p. 70. Murimuth argues that Gaveston's first exile resulted from his bad advice to the Prince of Wales: Adae Murimuth, *Continuatio chronicarum*, p. 9. Cf. *Chronicon Galfridi le Baker de Swynebroke*, p. 3; Johnstone, *Edward of Carnarvon*, pp. 122–3.   [52] *Foedera*, I-4, pp. 88–9.

[53] *Calendar of the Close Rolls (1307–1313)*, p. 12; *Calendar of the Patent Rolls (1307–1313)*, pp. 9, 187. The Malmesbury chronicler emphasised the arbitrariness of this appointment by which Edward 'was trying to promote the unknown over the known, the stranger over his brother, and the foreigner over the native': *Vita Edwardi Secundi*, pp. 15–16. The author further mentioned that 'there was a doubt whether the king could lawfully alienate the said earldom, which he held with the crown': *Vita Edwardi Secundi*, p. 1. Yet seven earls affixed their seals to Gaveston's charter of enfeoffment, thus suggesting the absence of friction between them and the king at this early stage.

[54] *Calendar of the Patent Rolls (1307–1312)*, pp. 43, 46; *Foedera*, I-4, pp. 95–6; *Vita Edwardi Secundi*, p. 3.

[55] *Annales Paulini*, pp. 258–9; *Annales Londonienses*, p. 151; Adae Murimuth, *Continuatio chronicarum*, p. 11; *Gesta Edwardi de Carnavan*, p. 32. Cf. Maddicott, *Thomas of Lancaster*, p. 72.

[56] J. R. S. Phillips, *Aymer de Valence, Earl of Pembroke*, pp. 26–9, 316–17.

[57] On its constitutional importance and, especially, the differentiation between king and crown, see Wilkinson, *The Constitutional History of England*, vol. II, pp. 100–1.

[58] At this stage, the opposition against Edward included, besides the barons, his wife, Isabella, her father, Philip the Fair, and her aunt, the dowager queen, Margaret. A curious letter from the Lincoln archives refers to Clement's summoning of Piers Gaveston; but if this audience ever took place, no record of it has survived: Maddicott, *Thomas of Lancaster*, p. 79.

[59] *Calendar of the Patent Rolls (1307–1313)*, pp. 71, 80; *Vita Edwardi Secundi*, p. 5; *Annales Londonienses*, pp. 154–5; *Annales Paulini*, p. 263. The events that culminated in Gaveston's forced exile suggest that, within a year, Edward II had alienated from his court the earls of Lincoln and Pembroke, his father's most faithful servants, and the earls of Warwick, Hereford, Warenne, and Gloucester, who had been his companions from youth.

1308 to August 1309 were calculated to assure Gaveston's return. The king acted on three main fronts, namely, at home, with the barons,[60] and abroad by appealing to both Clement V and Philip the Fair. On 16 June 1308, Edward sent a long letter to the pope that gave his rather dubious version of the Gaveston affair. The king referred, in emotional terms, to his friend's appointment as earl of Cornwall by the will and consent of the magnates, a claim that Edward justified by the seals of seven earls that had accompanied the charter of enfeoffment. Edward further claimed that the earldom had been granted at the barons' request and without Gaveston's prior knowledge. The inexplicable reversal of the barons, he continued, had forced the king to send Gaveston into exile, an unlawful and unjust measure that required the pope's immediate intervention. A second letter dealt more specifically with the crucial issue of Gaveston's conditional excommunication, which the king asked the pope to revoke.[61] Edward's requests to the pope were accompanied by important gestures of goodwill, such as royal collaboration in the trial of the Templars and the release, 'by the authority of the supreme pontiff', of Walter Langton, bishop of Coventry and Lichfield, the king's enemy from youth, whose release Edward had recently refused (9 November). The Scottish Bishops Lamberton of St Andrews and Wishart of Glasgow – for whose freedom the pope had been pressing since April – also benefited from Edward's new spirit of collaboration and were released.[62] Edward addressed the cardinals, too, in an effort to enlist their support; and his personal representative in the curia, Otto de Grandson, was urged to act on Gaveston's behalf.[63] The king's offensive in the curia was accompanied by generous gifts to the pope's relatives as well as to Clement himself. Several hundred pounds, indeed, were spent on jewels for the pope (January 1309). On 16 June 1308, the same day on which he wrote to Clement on behalf of Gaveston, Edward granted the castle of Blanquefort in Gascony to Bertrand de Got, the pope's nephew. The king attributed his gift to 'the love which we bear towards the supreme pontiff',[64] an attitude that soon earned him the pope's effusive gratitude.[65]

On 11 August 1308, Clement announced his decision to send special

---

[60] The Malmesbury chronicler describes in a rather derogatory tone the political volte-face of the barons within one year: 'See how often and abruptly great men change sides. Those whom we regard as faithless in the north we find just the opposite in the south. The love of magnates is as a game of dice, and the desires of the rich like feathers' (*Vita Edwardi Secundi*, pp. 7–8).

[61] *Foedera*, I-4, pp. 122–3.

[62] *Ibid.*, I-4, pp. 126, 129–30. See the safe-conduct for Arnaud, bishop of Poitiers, who conducted Robert of Glasgow, 'the king's enemy', to the pope (1 December 1308): *Calendar of the Patent Rolls (1307–1313)*, p. 94; *Annales Londonienses*, p. 111; Hamilton, *Piers Gaveston, Earl of Cornwall*, p. 70.   [63] *Foedera*, I-4, pp. 122–3, 182–3.

[64] *Calendar of the Patent Rolls (1307–1313)*, p. 83; *Foedera*, I-4, pp. 123–4.   [65] *Foedera*, I-4, p. 129.

envoys to England in order to foster peace between the king and the barons.[66] Concomitantly, Clement shared with Philip the Fair his great concern about the fragile political situation of Edward II.[67] Being aware of the pope's fears, Edward sent an impressive embassy to the papal curia (4 March 1309). The bishops of Norwich and Worcester and the earls of Pembroke and Richmond were expected to persuade Clement V that the English magnates, both lay and ecclesiastical, were now on good terms with the king and had consequently accepted Gaveston's return.[68] Clement, in response, urged the king to reach a stable agreement with the barons and sent his own nuncios to England to negotiate between the conflicting sides. Peter, cardinal-bishop of Sabina, Arnaud, bishop of Poitiers (later to be nominated cardinal-bishop of Albano), and Bertrand Caillan, a nephew of Piers Gaveston, represented the pope in this difficult task.[69]

Edward obtained his precious reward on 25 April, when Clement agreed to nullify Winchelsey's threat of excommunication, thus clearing the way for Gaveston's return.[70] With special satisfaction, the pope used the occasion to expose the many shortcomings of the procedure followed by the archbishop of Canterbury to pass sentence on Gaveston without giving him either previous admonition or the chance to confess. Although Clement had originally decided not to intervene in the dispute between the king and the barons and, instead, to refer the matter to Hugh Gerald, cantor of Périgord, the pope was compelled to change his stand. Clement took care to point out that he had abandoned his neutral attitude, not because of Gaveston's claim that the excommunication was invalid nor because of Edward's supplications, but because the king had assured him that the dispute with the magnates had been settled and that the latter were ready to accept Gaveston's recall.[71] To what degree the

---

[66] *Original Papal Letters in England*, no. 54, pp. 27–8.

[67] *Collectio actorum veterum*, pp. 86–90. See also Edward II's letter to Philip (16 June 1308): *ibid.*, pp. 96–7.

[68] The embassy also included Otto de Grandson; Boniface de Saluciis, archdeacon of Buckingham; Amanieu VII, lord of Albret; and Robert Fitz Payn: *Foedera*, I-4, pp. 136–7; *Calendar of the Patent Rolls (1307–1313)*, pp. 102–3. See the papal letter concerning this embassy in *Original Papal Letters in England*, no. 61, pp. 30–1: Chaplais, *Piers Gaveston*, pp. 54–8.

[69] *Foedera*, I-4, p. 142; *Calendar of the Patent Rolls (1307–1313)*, pp. 16, 94. In 1312, the pope ordered his nuncio, Arnaud of St Prisca, to defend from any injury or interference 'Bertrand Caillan, citizen of Bordeaux, sent by the king to the pope on the business of the peace between him and the nobles': *Regestum Clementis Papae V*, no. 8822; *Calendar of Entries in the Papal Registers*, p. 107. On Gascon bankers during the reign of Edward II, see Tout, *The Place of the Reign of Edward II in English History*, p. 75.

[70] Pierre Chaplais, however, adduces a later date, c. 21 May, which better suits later developments, especially Edward's summons of Winchelsey on 9 June, when the papal letter of absolution was read to him: Chaplais, *Piers Gaveston*, pp. 58–9.

[71] 'Non monitum, non citatum, non confessum, nec super aliqua fraude convictum': *Registrum Simonis de Gandavo*, vol. I, pp. 314–16; *Registrum Ricardi de Swinfield*, pp. 451–2; *Chronicon de Lanercost*, p. 213.

pope's conviction was sincere may be learned from his confirmation of Edward's privilege, by which the king of England was exempted from any excommunication or interdict on his person or his chapels without the express authorisation and consent of the Holy See.[72] Perhaps we have here another symptom of Clement's vindictive character – as reflected in his acts against Gauthier de Bourges, bishop of Poitiers, and Gilles Colonna, archbishop of Bordeaux;[73] this time it was against Robert Winchelsey, whose return to England had been requested by Edward II against the pope's advice.[74]

Whatever factors might have influenced the pope, the sentence of excommunication was annulled, and Gaveston was free to return from Ireland without fear of being arrested by the barons as an excommunicate. The papal absolution, however, was given *ad cautelam* for procedural reasons, not because the sentence had been unjust. The appeal judges were to decide this last point, and Bertrand Caillau, the proctor of Gaveston in the curia, had sworn in advance to observe the court's decision in his name.[75] If the appeal failed and if the grounds on which the sentence of excommunication had been passed were found just, then Gaveston ran the risk of being excommunicated once again.[76] In this rather unambiguous way, Clement interfered in the most critical issue presented to Edward II by the barons, who had but recently confirmed their refusal to allow Gaveston's return (Parliament of Westminster, 27 April–13 May).[77] At this stage, the king could rely on the loyalty of at most only five earls – Pembroke and Richmond (then in Avignon), Gloucester, Hereford, and Lincoln – in addition to a number of barons, led by Despenser and Henry Percy. In this regard, Clement's reference to the barons' approval appears to be but lip-service to the community of the realm and the constitutional patterns that had developed in the last century. The king, however, obtained his wish. On 11 June, Edward read the papal letter of absolution before the archbishop of Canterbury and the bishops of London, Winchester, and Chichester. Although Winchelsey tried to enlist his suffragans in counteracting the papal move, he did not encounter much support.[78] Piers Gaveston returned to

---

[72] *Serenitatis tue precelsa* (21 May 1309): *Original Papal Letters in England*, no. 60, p. 30; *Foedera*, 1-4, p. 141.   [73] See above, pp. 10–11, 88.   [74] See above, p. 63.

[75] *Registrum Simonis de Gandavo*, vol. I, p. 316.

[76] Edward begged the pope to release Gaveston from the oath that Caillau had taken in his name (4 September 1309). See below, n. 81; Chaplais, *Piers Gaveston*, pp. 59–60.

[77] The eleven articles presented in parliament represent a half-way stage between the *Articuli super cartas* of 1300 and the more developed reform plan in the Ordinances of 1311.

[78] Winchelsey asked his suffragans to deliberate on the papal revocation of Gaveston's excommunication and to report the results to him (16 June 1309): *Registrum Simonis de Gandavo*, vol. I, pp. 313–14. The evasive response of the bishop of Salisbury reflects the prevailing mood: 'Certum

England by 27 June and the next month was reinstated as earl of Cornwall in the Parliament of Stamford.[79] In a rather clear *quid pro quo*, Edward then accepted the eleven articles submitted by the barons on behalf of the *Communalté*, and that constituted for the most part a repetition of the *Articuli super cartas* of 1300.[80] The king was well aware of the crucial weight of papal intervention in reaching this accord. He thanked Clement for absolving his favourite and requested that both Gaveston and his proctor, Bertrand Caillan, be absolved from their undertaking to stand against those who wished to confront the favourite with the charges for which he had originally been excommunicated (4 September).[81]

Clement's intervention, with its compulsory undertones, in the English political scene, however, could only have ephemeral influence; it could not eradicate the many contentious issues that existed between the king and the magnates. Throughout 1310, the growing dissatisfaction brought about the election of twenty-one Ordainers, who redacted the forty-one articles of the Ordinances.[82] The twentieth clause sanctioned the favourite's exile, and Gaveston was again threatened by Winchelsey with excommunication should he dare to disobey.[83] On 27 September 1311, the Ordinances were made public at St Paul's, and on

---

non possumus respondere . . . Nos igitur super hiis habere dignetur vestra paternitas reverenda solita si placet clemencia quesumus excusatos' (28 June; *ibid.*, vol. I, pp. 316–17). To encourage the absence of prelates from the Parliament of Stamford, Winchelsey arranged for the consecration of John Droxford to Bath and Wells on 10 August, a fortnight after the date set for the opening of parliament: *ibid.*, vol. I, pp. 322–4; *Registrum Roberti Winchelsey Cantuariensis archiepiscopi*, vol. II, pp. 1113–14. Edward saw in Winchelsey's behaviour a personal affront to him and the crown.   [79] *Calendar of the Patent Rolls (1307–1313)*, p. 187.

[80] *The Statutes of the Realm*, vol. I, pp. 154–6. Some chroniclers made it clear that royal concessions were exchanged for Gaveston's stay in England: *Chronicle of Walter of Guisborough*, p. 384; H. F. Hutchison, *Edward II, the Pliant King*, pp. 63–4.   [81] *Foedera*, I-4, p. 152.

[82] *The Statutes of the Realm*, vol. I, pp. 157–67; *Vita Edwardi Secundi*, p. 10. The Malmesbury chronicler emphasised that the appointment of the Ordainers actually put the principle of consent into practice since 'Quod enim omnes tangit ab omnibus debet approbari': *Vita Edwardi Secundi*, p. 16.

[83] 'Since it is well known and has been found by the examination of prelates, earls, barons, knights, and other good people of the realm, that Peter of Gaveston has misled and ill-advised our lord the king, and enticed him to do evil in various deceitful ways . . . we ordain, by virtue of the commission our lord the king has granted us, that Peter of Gaveston, as an open enemy of the king and his people, shall be altogether exiled from England, Scotland, Ireland, and Wales, and from all the dominion of our lord the king, both on this and on the other side of the sea; and that he shall avoid the realm of England and all the above lands, and all the dominion of our lord the king, between now and All Saints' day next': *The Statutes of the Realm*, vol. I, p. 162; translation by Johnstone, *A Hundred Years of History*, pp. 210–11. It is symptomatic that, in his account of the Ordinances, the author of the *Vita* transcribed in full only the article that referred to Gaveston: *Vita Edwardi Secundi*, pp. 18–22; *Annales Londonienses*, pp. 169–70; *Chronicle of Walter of Guisborough*, p. 386; J. H. Trueman, 'The Statute of York and the Ordinances of 1311', pp. 64–81. On an early draft of the Ordinances, see Prestwich, 'A New Version of the Ordinances of 1311', pp. 189–203.

5 October they were sealed and formally issued under royal authority. Edward opposed the implementation of the Ordinances from the outset.[84] On 12 October – i.e., only a few days after their publication – the king sent Robert de Newenton and William de Lughtebergh to Clement, who was at the time leading the Council of Vienne. The king's representatives were ordered to deliver a formal protest, asking the pope to invalidate the Ordinances if they proved prejudicial to the crown.[85] An additional letter requested Clement to absolve Edward II from his oath to uphold the Ordinances and, also, to send special legates to England.[86] The king was attempting, rather obviously, to make Clement his shield against baronial opposition and, through the pope, to break the bilateral character of the political interplay. Though Gaveston left England on 3 November, probably for Flanders, he returned before the end of the year.[87] On 18 January 1312, Edward declared Gaveston to be a good and loyal subject who had been exiled contrary to the laws and customs of the realm. A few days later, all lands were restored to the favourite.[88] The royal designs were not, however, supported by the community of the realm or, more precisely, by those who acted in its name. Archbishop Winchelsey, in a joint front with the barons, immediately reacted against the king's overt slight to the Ordinances, a situation that caused Edward to seek, once again, the help of his most loyal partner against his restless subjects: Pope Clement V.

An additional royal embassy was dispatched to the curia in February. It was still in Avignon the following May, when Clement appointed Cardinals Arnaud of St Prisca and Arnaud of Albano as his special nuncios to England 'to preserve the peace of the realm', and granted them special power to annul the Ordinances.[89] The Lanercost chronicler suggests the many difficulties that stood in the way of the papal peace mission, which arrived in England in September 1312 and negotiated

---

[84] By asking the pope for an absolution from his promise to observe the Ordinances, Edward attempted to follow his father's precedent of 1305: Keen, *England in the Later Middle Ages*, p. 85. On the influence of the Ordinances on political practice, see Conway Davies, *The Baronial Opposition to Edward II*, p. 393.

[85] The English representatives were the archbishop of York, the bishops of London, Winchester, and Carlisle, and Otto de Grandson, Amanieu d'Albret, and Adam de Orleton.

[86] *Liber Epistolaris of Richard of Bury*, p. 104. Edward got his wish only in 1320, when John XXII absolved him of any obligation towards the Ordinances.

[87] See the commission to H. Curteny and W. Martyn to search for Piers Gaveston, who was supposed to be wandering in the counties of Cornwall, Devon, Somerset, and Dorset 'contrary to the Ordinance made by the prelates, earls, and barons for his expulsion from the realm': *Foedera*, I-4, pp. 201–2; *Calendar of the Patent Rolls (1307–1313)*, p. 405.

[88] *Foedera*, I-4, pp. 195, 203; *Calendar of the Patent Rolls (1307–1313)*, p. 429.

[89] *Regestum Clementis Papae V*, nos. 8786–8825, 9911–14, 9937–40; *Calendar of Entries in the Papal Registers*, pp. 104–7, 117. They sent to the pope the *Rationes Baronum*, a report of the negotiations between Edward and the nobles from 1312 to 1313.

with the king and the barons until October 1313.[90] Notwithstanding papal efforts, indeed, the political process followed its own, violent course. Piers Gaveston was captured on 19 May 1312, and executed in June.[91] The series of events reflected the complete failure of the papal policy that had consistently been sustained on behalf of the king of England and his favourite since 1307.[92] The price of the pope's unfortunate intervention became clear soon enough as the barons consolidated renewed opposition to papal arbitration.

The papal nuncios, Cardinals Arnaud of St Prisca and Arnaud of Albano, together with Louis d'Evreux, the earl of Gloucester, and several bishops, employed the services of local clergymen in trying to mediate between the conflicting parties.[93] Since evidence of the deliberations with the clergy is lacking,[94] the nuncios' efforts at mediation may be studied through the negotiations with the barons.[95] After fixing their residence in St Albans (from 3 to 28 September), the nuncios sent monks to Wheathampstead to deliver the papal letters to the barons, with the following results:

Even though the barons had heard of letters delivered by foreigners, they received the [messengers of the] papal legates peacefully. But they refused to accept the letters, with the excuse that they were not learned men, only such who had been taught arms and fighting. They therefore did not even trouble to read the letters. Then the barons were asked if they were willing to talk with the lords [of the monks], legates of the Holy See, who had come to England to make peace. To this the barons replied that there were many bishops in the realm, both

---

90 *Chronicon de Lanercost*, p. 220; *Annales Paulini*, pp. 271–2; *Vita Edwardi Secundi*, pp. 33–6; *Calendar of the Patent Rolls (1307–1313)*, p. 557. The presence of Louis d'Evreux, Philip the Fair's half-brother, attested to the tendency of the king of France to take an active part in the political crisis affecting his son-in-law and, through him, his daughter, the queen.

91 Edward secured a posthumous papal absolution for Gaveston only in 1314, thus allowing his burial in Langley. Arnaud-Guillaume de Marsan, Piers' brother, was sent to the curia for this purpose in November 1311. See Edward's letters to the pope requesting a favourable reception for his envoys: *Foedera*, 1-4, pp. 196, 202; *Vita Edwardi Secundi*, pp. 28, 58–9; *Annales Paulini*, p. 273; *Flores historiarum*, p. 153; Trokelowe, *Annales*, p. 77; *Chronicon Henrici Knighton*, p. 409.

92 The Malmesbury chronicler refers to Edward's hopes in 1312 of winning the support of Philip the Fair and Clement V 'because the king of England would have given them Gascony in fee': *Vita Edwardi Secundi*, p. 24. Edward, in a letter of 11 June, thanked Philip for his concern and agreed to desist from making new moves until the arrival of the papal and French envoys: *Foedera*, II-1, p. 7; *Treaty Rolls*, pp. 202–3.

93 Edward II took advantage of the presence of the cardinal of St Prisca to have him officiate at the baptism of his first-born and successor, the future Edward III (12 November 1312). The godfathers were Arnaud, bishop of Poitiers; John of Droxford, bishop of Bath and Wells; Walter Reynolds, bishop of Worcester; Louis d'Evreux, Hugh le Despenser; John de Britannia, earl of Richmond; and Aymer de Valence, earl of Pembroke: *Calendar of the Close Rolls (1307–1313)*, p. 558. The event was widely reported in contemporary chronicles: *Chroniques de London*, p. 37; *Flores historiarum*, p. 154; *Chronicon Angliae Petriburgense*, p. 160.   94 *Councils and Synods*, p. 1377.

95 See the extremely well-documented report that the nuncios submitted to the pope: *Edward II, the Lords Ordainers, and Piers Gaveston's Jewels and Horses*, pp. 1–26.

learned and honest, whose advice they were willing to accept, though not that of foreigners, who know nothing of the causes of their struggle . . . [Further,] they would never permit a stranger from a foreign country to interfere in their affairs or in any business of theirs within the boundaries of the kingdom.[96]

The nuncios were apparently so frightened by the vehemence of this negative response that they immediately left St Albans and retreated to London, from where they conducted future negotiations. The barons were not alone in their opposition to the legates. Murimuth, for instance, depicted Arnaud, bishop of Poitiers, as a 'dishonest, vulgar, and ignorant [prelate], who did not deserve the office of cardinal-bishop of Albano to which he was appointed later on'.[97] Such a vicious character, however, did not prevent the cardinal from fulfilling his mission. After long, difficult bargaining, a new treaty between the king and the barons was sealed in London, in the presence of the cardinals, Louis d'Evreux, and the earls of Gloucester and Richmond (20 December).[98] However, Lancaster's opposition to restoring Gaveston's valuables to Edward led to further delays.[99] Finally, on 14 October 1313, the barons made their submission to the king in Westminster Hall, apologised for their deeds, and received royal pardon for Gaveston's murder.[100] The settlement contained no reference to the Ordinances, but by acknowledging their guilt for Gaveston's death, the barons had implicitly accepted that the Ordinances were not in force when he was killed.[101] The nuncios remained in England during the summer, and at least one of them was present at the Michaelmas parliament.[102]

---

[96] Trokelowe, *Annales*, p. 78; Walsingham, *Historia Anglicana*, pp. 133–4.

[97] Adae Murimuth, *Continuatio chronicarum*, p. 16.

[98] *Foedera*, II-1, pp. 21–2; a detailed report in the *Annales Londonienses*, pp. 210–25; *Annales Paulini*, pp. 271–2; *Flores historiarum*, app., p. 337; *Vita Edwardi Secundi*, p. 33.

[99] *Edward II, the Lords Ordainers, and Piers Gaveston's Jewels and Horses*, p. 14; *Calendar of the Patent Rolls (1307–1313)*, pp. 525, 553; Maddicott, *Thomas of Lancaster*, pp. 139–45; Chaplais, *Piers Gaveston*, pp. 90–108.

[100] *The Statutes of the Realm*, vol. I, pp. 169–70; *Calendar of the Close Rolls (1307–1313)*, p. 574; *Foedera*, II-1, pp. 51–2. On the reception of Gaveston's jewels, see *Foedera*, II-1, pp. 30–2; *Vita Edwardi Secundi*, pp. 43–4. On the aftermath of Gaveston's assassination, see Wilkinson, *The Later Middle Ages in England*, pp. 121–31.

[101] When reviewing the first six years of Edward's reign, the *Vita* claims that Edward 'had achieved nothing praiseworthy or memorable': *Vita Edwardi Secundi*, p. 39. Charles T. Wood laid emphasis on the restraint with which the magnates had acted during Edward II's reign, given the hatred engendered by Piers Gaveston: Wood, 'Personality, Politics, and Constitutional Progress', pp. 532–3.

[102] *Vita Edwardi Secundi*, p. 43. On 28 August 1313, Edward requested Philip the Fair to send Louis d'Evreux and Enguerrand de Marigny to the parliament to be held in London, both because of his brother's previous experience in the negotiations and because of the peace-loving nature of both men: *Foedera*, II-1, p. 48; *Treaty Rolls*, pp. 208–9. French chroniclers emphasised the high esteem for Louis d'Evreux in England: *La chronique métrique attribuée à Geffroy de Paris*, pp. 179–80, vv. 4667–74.

It is difficult to evaluate the influence of the papal nuncios in comparison with that of the king of France in reaching the final accord. Whatever the influence of the former, it did not favour the leadership of Clement V or the status of his delegates in England. True, opposition to papal intervention, described as that of a foreigner, was hardly new.[103] Yet it became more resolute during the pontificate of Clement V. Seven years after Clement became pope, the earlier support for the former archbishop of Bordeaux completely disappeared, to be replaced by suspicion and mistrust. The papal stay in the Comtat-Venaissin did nothing to facilitate good relations with the barons, who, long before the outbreak of the Hundred Years War, referred to the pope as 'a stranger from a foreign country, who knows nothing of the causes of their struggle'. The barons opposed not only what they considered papal oppression of the Church of England – a position clearly enunciated in parliament[104] – but also the pope's feudal approach to England and its king. Although the many economic and political benefits they obtained from the curia led both Edward I and Edward II to tolerate, in exchange, some of Clement's claims for the Church, royal sufferance was not shared by the nobility, who had to pay the political price of the alliance between pope and king.[105] Similar resentment and suspicion were to be found among chroniclers who reported the conflict between Edward II and the nobility. This correlation between the barons' political behaviour and the chroniclers' attitude suggests the growth of opposition to Clement. Those who approved of papal policy were, mainly, former royal clerks who had been promoted by the king and represented his interests.[106] Yet they could hardly counterbalance the weight of Clement's intervention in the English domestic scene, which contributed an additional element of friction between the pope and the community of the realm, the prelates at its forefront. One may argue that Clement's alliance with the kings of England was in tune with his support of Philip the Fair. From this perspective, Clement's letter *Regalis devotionis integritas* to Edward I in 1305 sets a precedent for *Rex gloriae virtutum* to Philip the Fair in 1311. England and France were important for the crusade and both the conflict between the two countries and/or domestic political crises presented a major impediment against its renewal. Yet the relative power of Philip the Fair, in contrast to the many weaknesses of Edward II, constituted a determining factor in the failure of papal policy in England. Clement himself was aware of this difference, and therefore did not exercise towards Edward II the same caution as he did towards Philip the

---

[103] For precedents, see Matthew Paris, *Chronica Majora*, ad a. 1216, p. 645; ad a. 1255, p. 514.
[104] See above, pp. 76–81.   [105] Fryde, *The Tyranny and Fall of Edward II*, pp. 13–26.
[106] *Chronicon de Lanercost*, pp. 216, 220.

Fair. By pandering to Edward's desires, however, Clement did little to help the king and, in the long term, even less to sustain papal authority in England.

Much more effective was papal intervention in the negotiations between England and France. The engagement of Isabella of France, the only daughter of Philip the Fair,[107] to the prince of Wales formed an integral part of the truce reached through the mediation of Boniface VIII. The Treaty of Montreuil (19 June 1299) had clarified the conditions of the royal marriage, which was expected to hasten the French evacuation of Gascony.[108] Clement also counted on it to favour the renewal of the crusade.[109] The papal nuncio, Peter the Spaniard, cardinal-bishop of Sabina,[110] equipped with a draft of the treaty that was acceptable to both Philip the Fair and the pope, appeared before the Parliament of Carlisle and stressed the many advantages of peace (15 March 1307).[111] The next day or the day after, William Greenfield, the archbishop of York, announced to the assembly that Edward I, the prince of Wales, the arch-bishops and bishops, abbots and priors, earls and barons, all the king's council, and the commonalty of the land agreed to the marriage, 'since the king of France had granted to the prince and his daughter all the lands that once pertained to the crown of England, reserving to himself only the homage due from these lands'.[112] Clement bestowed apostolic

---

[107] On Philip's deep affection for his sole daughter and her diplomatic success in advancing Edward II's interests at the court of France, see Brown, 'Diplomacy, Adultery, and Domestic Politics at the Court of Philip the Fair', pp. 53–83.

[108] *Foedera*, 1-2, pp. 208–9; G. P. Cuttino, *English Diplomatic Administration*, pp. 62–87. On Clement's concern for the peace process between the two countries, see also the papal letter to Edward I in 1306: *Calendar of the Close Rolls (1302–1307)*, p. 447; *Annales prioratus de Wigornia*, p. 538; *Gesta Edwardi de Carnavan*, p. 32.

[109] See the papal letter from Bordeaux (25 August 1305), in which Clement specifically referred to the marriage in terms of 'ad solidandam pacem inter reges Anglie et Francie': *Original Papal Letters in England*, no. 13, pp. 8–9. To foster this purpose, the pope sent to England his nuncio, Raimond, bishop of Lescar, who was joined by Guillaume Testa: *ibid.*, nos. 35–6, pp. 19–20 (28 November 1306).

[110] Cardinal Peter, also called the Spaniard, was Castilian by birth and an experienced member of the papal curia. Bishop of Burgos and papal referendary, he was raised to the cardinalate by Boniface VIII, to whom he remained loyal to the very end. In 1302–3, Prince Edward sent him a cope embroidered with pearls that cost 60 pounds. On his nomination as nuncio, see *Regestum Clementis Papae V*, nos. 2246–54. In the safe conduct he wrote for the nuncio, Edward I refers to him as 'amicus noster karissimus': *Foedera*, 1-4, pp. 67, 69.

[111] *Chronicle of Walter of Guisborough*, pp. 370–1. On Boniface's mediation, see *ibid.*, pp. 317–22.

[112] Richardson and Sayles, 'The Parliament of Carlisle', pp. 436, 430–1. On the long negotiations before and after the royal wedding for the fulfilment of this clause, see Brown, 'The Political Repercussions of Family Ties in the Early Fourteenth Century', pp. 573–95; Brown, 'The Marriage of Edward II of England and Isabella of France: A Postscript', pp. 373–9.

blessing on the marriage, though the bride was no more than twelve years old (27 November 1307).[113]

The marriage of Edward II and Isabella (Boulogne, 25 January 1308) drew much attention, both for the magnificence displayed by Philip the Fair 'for the love of his daughter' and for the massive presence of notable figures from all areas of Europe.[114] The chroniclers emphasised in a positive manner the influence of the curia in facilitating the marriage, which was expected to foster the peace process between France and England.[115] The negative reaction of Amalric Auger, who bitterly complained that 'because of this matrimony many scandals and endless adversities came to the kingdom of France', appears rather exceptional.[116] It does, though, represent an omen of the future, especially the claim of Edward III to the throne of France and the onset of the Hundred Years War. Amalric's criticism, however, does not reflect the prevailing climate of opinion in the early fourteenth century, when the royal wedding was welcomed as auguring just the opposite, namely, the end of a lasting conflict among Christians.[117]

The positive reactions to Clement's diplomacy in fostering the marriage between Isabella and Edward acquire the utmost importance in the political climate of the times, which was characterised by growing reservations over papal interference in international matters. In practice, Clement succeeded in warding off the renewal of hostilities between England and France, an important achievement that may be explained, at least in part, by the excellent relations of the former archbishop of Bordeaux with both courts.[118] Clement was aware of the need to maintain a balance, however fragile, between his two closest allies in order to keep his position as arbitrator. Thus, the pope refused to support Edward II during the difficult negotiations over the future of Gascony (Périgueux, 1311–12).[119] Although Clement requested that he be informed of the progress of the negotiations, he refused to be actively involved or to take a clear stand,

---

[113] P. C. Doherty, 'The Date of the Birth of Isabella', pp. 246–8. Twelve years old was the canonical age for a royal bride to assume her marital duties.

[114] *Anciennes chroniques de Flandre*, pp. 397–8; *Chronicon Galfridi le Baker de Swynebroke*, p. 3; *Chronicon de Lanercost*, p. 211; *La chronique métrique attribuée à Geffroy de Paris*, p. 153, vv. 3251–68; *Flores historiarum*, pp. 140–2; *Chronographia regum Francorum*, pp. 177–9.

[115] 'Romana curia consulente et procurante propter bonum pacis': Jean de St Victor, *Prima Vita*, p. 10. On Isabella's biography and political career, see Menache, 'Isabelle of France, Queen of England', pp. 107–24. [116] Amalric Augerii, *Sexta Vita*, p. 93.

[117] Upon the royal couple's arrival in England, its inhabitants displayed great joy, an attitude particularly noticeable in London. The city was decorated to become 'like a new Jerusalem', and the crowd assisted in the coronation ceremony: *Annales Londonienses*, p. 152; *Flores historiarum*, p. 141.

[118] Clement tried to avoid the remote causes of the conflict while focusing on practical ways to solve it: Gaudemet, 'Le rôle de la papauté dans le réglement des conflits entre états', pp. 98–9.

[119] Cuttino, *English Diplomatic Administration*, pp. 87–100. See the letters of credence of the king's representatives: *Treaty Rolls*, p. 197.

and the matter was not discussed in the Council of Vienne.[120] If one considers the pope's complaisance towards both Edward I and Edward II in very difficult issues, his neutrality in the negotiations with France clearly manifests Clement's careful approach towards achieving a tenuous balance between the leading monarchies of Christendom which the pope considered the key to the renewal of the crusade.

SCOTLAND

The neutrality characteristic of papal diplomacy in the negotiations between England and France disappeared as if it had never been in the case of Scotland. Notwithstanding the fact that Scotland's fight for independence was supported by Philip the Fair, the northern kingdom was completely abandoned by Clement V on behalf of the aggressive policy of Edward I and Edward II. When Clement was elected to the papacy, the conflict between England and Scotland seemed to have been resolved to the entire satisfaction of Edward I. Since the great *chevauchée* of 1303–4, a crushed Scotland had not bothered the king of England overmuch.[121] Yet, military victories proved short-lived, and the Scottish conflict was to remain unsettled until the end of Clement's pontificate. The wide gap between Scottish and English positions made compromise a very difficult, if not an impossible, mission. Most Scots viewed Scotland as an independent country, over which only the pope might claim some form of lordship. Theirs was therefore a just war of self-defence, led from 1306 by a rightful king, Robert Bruce.[122] The position taken by Edward I and many of his nobles was quite different. After the death of Margaret of Norway (1290), the granddaughter and only descendant of Alexander III (d. 1286), the king of England claimed feudal lordship over Scotland.[123]

---

[120] See Edward II's letter to his representatives, who dealt with the peace treaty with France (2 August 1310): *Gascon Rolls*, no. 393.

[121] On the execution of William Wallace after being charged with treason (1305), see *Annales Londonienses*, pp. 139–42; *Chronicon Galfridi le Baker de Swynebroke*, p. 2. On Edward I's 'establishment of our realm of Scotland' at a full assembly of parliament (28 February–21 March 1305), see *Anglo-Scottish Relations*, pp. 120–9. On the contribution of the Irish army on the battlefield, especially during the decisive siege of Stirling castle, see Lydon, 'Edward I, Ireland, and the War in Scotland', pp. 43–61.

[122] This basic claim was clearly voiced by the Declaration of Arbroath in 1320. See *The Declaration of Arbroath*, pp. 6–8; Wilkinson, *The Later Middle Ages in England*, p. 123.

[123] The English claims to overlordship of Scotland, set forth in the Treaty of Norham (1212), were never abrogated. When Alexander III did liege homage to Edward I, though homage for Scotland had not been specifically mentioned, it may be argued that it had been implied. From the rich documentation and literature on the subject, see especially *Edward I and the Throne of Scotland*; *Anglo-Scottish Relations*; *Documents and Records Illustrating the History of Scotland*, p. 69; *Documents Illustrative of the History of Scotland*, vol. II, nos. 377, 569, pp. 59–77, 377; A. Tuck, *Crown and Nobility*, p. 30; Prestwich, 'England and Scotland During the Wars of Independence', pp. 181–4.

On the other hand, Robert Bruce VIII, who was the grandson of Robert the Competitor, one of the claimants to the throne in 1296, gained considerable support, including that of leading ecclesiastical persons, the bishops of Glasgow and St Andrews at their head.

In order to fortify his position while avoiding potential competition, Bruce tried to reach an accord with Red Comyn. Having received a negative reply[124] and perhaps being accused of his former treason, Bruce brutally murdered Comyn in the Franciscan church at Dumfries in the diocese of Glasgow (10 February 1306). Far from excommunicating Bruce, Bishop Robert Wishart exhorted his flock to fight for Bruce's just war. He produced the royal standard from its hiding place and at Scone Abbey crowned Bruce the new king of Scotland (25 March).[125] From then on, Bruce succeeded in mobilising all the vital forces of Scotland in his struggle.[126] Walter of Guisborough, a hostile witness, frankly reports Bruce's coronation as a great public event, 'attended and consented to by four bishops, five earls, and the people of the land'.[127] There is, indeed, historical evidence for the large assistance, which meant widespread support for the new king. Robert Wishart and William Lamberton, who had been Bruce's old partners and former guardians, and David Murray, bishop of Moray, whose family was deeply identified with the Scottish war of independence, led the list of prelates who stood by Bruce's side.[128]

Robert Bruce's assumption of the crown did not change Edward's basic belief in his legitimate rights over Scotland. On the contrary, Bruce was considered a traitor to his feudal lord and an enemy. This attitude clearly appeared in the protocol employed by royal chancery during the reigns of Edward I and Edward II, which at best addressed the actual ruler and Scotland as 'Sir Robert de Bruce and the Scottish people', with no reference to any king or independent kingdom.[129] The developments in Scotland faced Edward I with a *fait accompli* and made a mockery of his former achievements, at both the military and propaganda levels. Edward looked for papal help, a move encouraged by Clement's supportive attitude

---

[124] Having surrendered to Edward in 1304, Red Comyn might had been reluctant to join Bruce in another uprising, which could result in the latter's usurping the Scottish throne.

[125] *Documents and Records Illustrating the History of Scotland*, vol. II, p. 348. On the pope's severe reaction, see nn. 142–4 below.

[126] G. W. S. Barrow, *Robert Bruce and the Community of the Realm of Scotland*, pp. 142–51.

[127] *Chronicle of Walter of Guisborough*, p. 367. The Lanercost chronicler, as well, emphasised that after Bruce's coronation, 'adhaeserunt ei multi majores et minores de terra': *Chronicon de Lanercost*, p. 203.   [128] Barrow, *Robert Bruce and the Community of the Realm of Scotland*, p. 263.

[129] This approach was also followed by the papal curia, thus justifying Bruce's later allegation that 'if his father [the pope] and his mother [the Church] did not wish to harm the other side by recognising him as king, he does not deem it to have been necessary to cause him harm by denying him the title of king, so long as the matter has not been settled' (7 December 1317): *Foedera*, II-1, p. 134.

towards him, on the one hand, and the broad support that Robert Bruce enjoyed among the leading churchmen in Scotland, on the other. Edward's appeal to the pope hints at the strong feelings of an already old, irascible, and perhaps exhausted king. In a letter to Clement and the cardinals, Edward asked to transfer the abbey of Scone from its present site 'in the midst of a perverse nation' (10 November 1306).[130] The pope took Edward's request seriously, and informed him that he had already requested the archbishop of York and the bishop of Ely to inquire into the relics, the rights of patronage, and the founder of the abbey. Finally, Clement conveyed to Edward his concern about the matter.[131] The report of the archbishop of York, however, was inconclusive.[132] Although the royal request did not materialise in this particular case, Edward I succeeded within a year in changing the fragile political balance once again so that, among many others, the bishops of St Andrews and Glasgow were at his mercy.

Clement V gave unconditional support to the aggressive policy of the kings of England, thus sacrificing Scotland to the exigencies of his alliance with Edward I and Edward II. On 5 June 1306, a papal letter denouncing the murder, in a church, of John the Red Comyn of Badenoch was publicly read at St Paul's Cross.[133] Emphasising the sacrilege, Clement excommunicated Robert Bruce. In fact, the pope repeated the arguments of Edward I, thereby bestowing apostolic legitimacy on royal policy.[134] A year later, during the Parliament of Carlisle, William of Geinsborough, bishop of Worcester, reported Edward's version of the murder of John Comyn and asked Cardinal Peter of Sabina for indulgence for Comyn's soul and excommunication for his murderers. The papal nuncio readily granted an indulgence of one year to anyone who would pray for Comyn's soul during his stay in England and for a hundred days thereafter. Afterwards, the cardinal and the bishops assumed their pontificals and, with due ceremony, pronounced the excommunication against Bruce and his supporters (19 March 1307).[135] It is little wonder that such a collaborationist policy removed Edward's former opposition to papal intervention 'in the temporal affairs of England', for which Boniface VIII had been criticised vociferously in the Parliament of Lincoln (1301).[136]

[130] *Ibid.*, 1–4, p. 65.

[131] *Ibid.*, 1–4, p. 53; *Regestum Clementis Papae V*, no. 1048; *Original Papal Letters in England*, nos. 27, 28, 31, 44, pp. 15–17, 23.   [132] *The Register of William Greenfield*, vol. v, no. 2493, pp. 60–1.

[133] On this occasion, the papal letter revoking the king's oath to observe the Forest Charter was also read.   [134] *Foedera*, vol. 1–4, pp. 49, 52–3.

[135] *Chronicle de Lanercost*, p. 206; *Chronicle of Walter of Guisborough*, p. 370; *Annales Londonienses*, pp. 146–7; *Annales Hibernie*, p. 334. On the historical context, see Tout, *The History of England*, pp. 225–35.

[136] *Foedera*, vol. 1–4, pp. 5–6; *Annales Londonienses*, pp. 121–4; Rishanger, *Chronica*, pp. 200–10; Walsingham, *Ypodigma Neustriae*, pp. 230–2; Walsingham, *Historia Anglicana*, pp. 81–2, 87–97.

Clement's support of Edward I in the conflict with Scotland appears in stark contrast to papal policy in Flanders. During the equally long conflict between Philip the Fair and the county of Flanders, Clement succeeded in maintaining a more balanced attitude, one that obviated the renewal of hostilities and allowed both sides to reach a compromise. The completely different papal stand in Scotland, where Clement unconditionally supported the aggressive line of Edward I, disqualified the pope from a similar mediating role. Clement's policy in Scotland, moreover, acquires a problematic character both because of the close links between the prelates of Scotland and the papacy[137] and their active participation in the war of independence. Indeed, although the Scottish bishops had been subject to the archbishop of York, they were exempted by Celestine III (1192), Innocent III (c. 1200), and Honorius III (1218).[138] At least nine bishops – Aberdeen, Brechin, Caithness, Dunblane, Dunkeld, Glasgow, Moray, Ross, and St Andrews – were immediately subject to the pope. Partly because of the pro-Scottish policy of Boniface VIII, the Scots had been able to secure the consecration of bishops favourable to their patriotic cause. William Lamberton, bishop of St Andrews (1273–1328), and Robert Wishart, bishop of Glasgow (1272–1316), in particular, played a dominant role in the rebellion against England and had been closely associated with Robert Bruce since 1306.[139] After the military campaign of 1306, however, both bishops were imprisoned by the English. Although Edward I could not and did not, order the death penalty for them – as he did for most of the Scottish lay leaders – he had the two bishops and the abbot of Scone kept in irons in the castles of Winchester and Portchester.[140] They were imprisoned in the keeps, which were locked and the drawbridges raised.[141]

The arrest of bishops was not an unprecedented measure in the early fourteenth century, when ecclesiastical immunity could seldom stand against the royal policy of centralisation. Quite surprisingly and regardless of his acquiescent response in the case of Guichard de Troyes,[142] Clement tried to defend the immunity of the Scottish prelates; but this was a losing battle *vis-à-vis* Edward I. In May–June 1306, the pope ordered William Greenfield, archbishop of York, to summon the bishop of Glasgow to the papal curia 'because of his nefarious and presumptu-

---

[137] Clement maintained close links with the church in Scotland; at least eleven pertinent letters written by the pope between 1307 and 1308 are extant: *Vetera Monumenta Hibernorum et Scotorum Historiam Illustrantia*, nos. 377–403; P. C. Ferguson, 'Clement V to Scone Abbey', pp. 69–72.

[138] *Anglo-Scottish Relations*, pp. xxi–xxii.   [139] Barrow, *The Kingdom of the Scots*, pp. 233–54.

[140] On the death penalty for convictions of treason during the reigns of Edward I and Edward II, see R. W. Kaeuper, *War, Justice, and Public Order*, pp. 230–1.

[141] *Foedera*, I-4, p. 59. See also Edward's letter to the cardinals on the matter: *ibid.*, p. 63.

[142] See above, pp. 84–6.

ous deeds'.[143] This was a rather devious reference to Robert Wishart's role in the coronation of Bruce, which had brought about his immediate suspension. The archbishop of York wrote to the bishops of Carlisle and Withorn, as well as to Sir William de Bevercotes and Sir John de Sandale, the chancellor and chamberlain of Scotland, that they were to summon Robert Wishart. Before the archbishop's letters arrived, so the recipients argued, the bishop of Glasgow had been taken prisoner, along with others of the king's enemies, and brought to the castle of Cupar in the county of Fife. Thus William Greenfield was unable to serve the papal summons without the king's licence, which was denied. Edward declared that he would send messengers to the pope to explain his reasons for refusing.[144] In this regard, the version of the London chronicler, suggesting the king's readiness to loyally obey the pope's request concerning the fate of the prelates, seems rather dubious.[145]

The accession of Edward II to the throne brought about a considerable change of policy. Moved by his pressing need for papal support over Gaveston, Edward ordered the release of William Lamberton, bishop of St Andrews, admittedly under severe financial terms and with the proviso that he was to remain within the bounds of the diocese of Durham (1308).[146] By the end of the year, however, the bishop was playing an active role in the negotiations with Scotland, France, and England. Absolved by Edward, probably because of the intervention of the earl of Pembroke on his behalf, Lamberton was allowed to stay in Scotland from 1311 onwards. Conversely, the bishop of Glasgow was handed over to the pope to answer the serious charges against him (1308),[147] and Edward II tried to bring about his removal and the nomination of Stephen Segrave instead (1311).[148] Clement did not suspend or deprive Wishart of his rank, but neither did he restore the old bishop to his see.[149] It was only after the Battle of Bannockburn that Robert Wishart, much aged and going blind, was finally able to make his way back to Scotland, in

[143] *Regestum Clementis Papae V*, nos. 421–2; *Calendar of Entries in the Papal Registers*, pp. 6–7.

[144] *The Register of William Greenfield*, vol. v, no. 2490, pp. 55–7.

[145] 'Mès il [le roi] ne voleit eux mettre à juyse pur çeo q'ils estoyent prelat; mès les fit garder touz armez taunqe le roy eust maundement de apostoile quei serreit à faire de eux': *Chroniques de London*, pp. 32–3. Cf. *Chronicon de Lanercost*, pp. 204–5.

[146] *Calendar of Documents Relating to Scotland*, vol. III, no. 50.

[147] Since the accession of Edward II to the throne, Clement had intensively fostered the release of both bishops and of Walter Langton, as well. See the papal letters to the king on 9 August and 4 October 1308: *Original Papal Letters in England*, nos. 51–2, 56–7, pp. 26–9.

[148] *Calendar of Documents Relating to Scotland*, vol. III, no. 207; M. Prestwich, 'England and Scotland During the Wars of Independence', pp. 194–5.

[149] Edward II ordered the prior and convent of Ely to provide a suitable place in their priory for the bishop 'until Scotland should be recovered and good peace restored there' (20 November 1313). They were instructed to guard him 'so that he may not leave the priory except to walk and take air', and always have him accompanied: *Calendar of the Close Rolls (1313–1318)*, p. 83.

exchange for the earl of Hereford.[150] The vicissitudes of the Scottish prelates hint at the risks to which the pro-English policy of Clement V was exposed, and its pernicious influence on the web of relations between the pope and the clergy of Scotland. Clement's support of the kings of England neither changed the political balance nor reversed the growing power of Robert Bruce and the wide support he enjoyed in the community of the Scottish realm, first and foremost among the prelates. During the quarrel between Edward II and the barons, in fact, Robert Bruce succeeded in consolidating his position and even carried his war against the English far into the northern shires. Papal and French mediation, however, brought about a provisional truce from 12 February to 1 November 1308.[151]

On 16–17 March 1309, Robert Bruce held his first parliament at St Andrews. The Scottish magnates and prelates swore him fealty as king, affirmed his right to the throne, and declared their firm belief in the independence of Scotland. They further suggested a sensitivity to history no less developed than that of Edward I eighteen years earlier,[152] and voiced their own version of political developments. They claimed that John Balliol had been made king by Edward I in defiance of the universal belief among the Scots that Robert Bruce the Competitor possessed a better right to the title. After asserting the claims of the younger Bruce to the throne, the parliament proceeded to enumerate the many evils and disasters that had befallen Scotland as a result of the English invasion. Through the inspiration of divine providence, according to the parliament, the people had eventually, and rightly, chosen Robert Bruce to be king. He had through Christ's mercy recovered and restored the kingdom, following the example of many kings of Scotland who had won and held their country's independence 'as is fully related in the ancient and magnificent chronicles of the Scots'.[153] At the same time, the parliament promised to aid Philip the Fair in the forthcoming crusade as soon as Scotland recovered its liberty and was at peace.[154] Thus, in defiance of Clement's contention that the war in Scotland was an obstacle to the implementation of the crusade, the Scots provided arguments against both their spiritual leader and their political enemy, while addressing Philip the Fair in an attempt to gain reciprocal support.[155] In a

---

[150] *Vita Edwardi Secundi*, p. 58; Barrow, *Robert Bruce and the Community of the Realm in Scotland*, pp. 263–4.   [151] *Chronicon de Lanercost*, p. 213; *Chronicle of Walter of Guisborough*, p. 384.

[152] *Anglo-Scottish Relations*, pp. 96–109; E. L. G. Stones, 'The Appeal to History in Anglo-Scottish Relations', pp. 11–21.

[153] Barrow, *Robert Bruce and the Community of the Realm in Scotland*, p. 187.

[154] *Scottish Historical Documents*, pp. 48–50.

[155] On the political poems and the elaboration of national stereotypes, see Menache, 'Les Hébreux du XIVe siècle', pp. 55–65.

manifesto that E. L. G. Stones tentatively dates to 1310, the prelates of Scotland further emphasised their complete support for Robert Bruce:

He might reform the defects of the realm, correct what had to be corrected, and direct what was without guidance. By their authorship [i.e., of the whole people of the realm of Scotland] he was set over the realm, and formally established as king of Scots, and with him the faithful people of the realm wish to live and die, as with one who, by right of birth and by endowment with [sic] other cardinal virtues, is fit to rule, and worthy of the name of king and of the honour of the realm . . . If anyone, however, defends his claim to the realm by producing sealed letters from the past, which record the consent of the whole people, be it known that this entire business was in fact carried through by force and violence which nobody could then resist, and by intimidation and many tortures of the body, and by various threats which were able to pervert the senses and the minds of even the best of men.[156]

The English counteroffensive was limited, rather pitifully, to a mere repetition of the papal excommunication against Bruce and all those who dared to offer him 'assistance, advice, or [any] benefit' (Parliament of Northampton).[157] Bruce, not satisfied with diplomatic invective alone, exerted full pressure on the battlefield. His ravage of Northumberland, Westmorland, and Cumberland weakened the English and increased their insecurity and unrest. It also provided him with a large income from plunder and redemption money paid by the cities, which were forced to buy their safety at full price.[158] The Battle of Bannockburn (24–5 June 1314) marked a turning point in the balance of power between Scotland and England.[159] For Edward II, it represented a major disaster. For the first time, the king of England had to flee from his enemy and lose a battle.[160] For the Scots, it proved the success of the alliance between Robert Bruce and the community of the realm. Tentative proposals for peace came to nothing, and the English were expelled from the whole of Scotland except for Berwick. The Scots now expanded the war into northern England and opened a second front in Ireland. For Clement V, it represented an additional failure in his alliance with the kings of England, especially his unconditional support of Edward II.

THE CANONISATION OF THOMAS DE CANTILUPE

Like Philip the Fair, Edward I and Edward II tried to exploit their harmonious relationship with Clement V in order to bring about the

---

[156] *Anglo-Scottish Relations*, pp. 141–2.   [157] *Chronicon de Lanercost*, p. 213.
[158] *Vita Edwardi Secundi*, p. 48.
[159] For the battle and the many losses on the English side, see *Chronicon Galfridi le Baker de Swynebroke*, pp. 7–8; *Chronicon Angliae Petriburgense*, p. 160.
[160] N. Fryde, *The Tyranny and Fall of Edward II*, pp. 119, 122, 124.

canonisation of a candidate of their own, Thomas de Cantilupe. Thomas' candidacy did not face the pope with the embarrassment inherent in the canonisation of Pietro da Morrone, Boniface's predecessor in the Holy See. Thomas had been regarded popularly as a saint soon after his death, his shrine becoming second only to that of St Thomas of Canterbury. Clement, however, was most meticulous in his scrutiny and did not finalise the canonisation process. It was eventually left to John XXII to inscribe the name of Thomas de Cantilupe in the Christian calendar (17 April 1320); he thus became the last Englishman to be canonised in the Middle Ages.[161]

Born in Buckinghamshire c. 1218, Thomas was a member of an illustrious and influential family; his uncle, Walter of Cantilupe, bishop of Worcester, supported his studies at Oxford and Paris. In 1262, Thomas was elected chancellor of Oxford, and as such supported the barons' political position in Amiens. After the defeat of Henry III in the Battle of Lewes, Simon de Montfort brought about Thomas' nomination as chancellor (22 February 1265). Although he gained wide renown for his judicial wisdom and fairness, he was deprived of his charge only six months later, upon his protector's death.[162] In the years to follow, Thomas taught theology at Paris and Oxford, until he was appointed bishop of Hereford in June 1275. He administered the diocese most zealously, appointing responsible vicars, visiting them regularly, and showing himself a model pastor through his holiness and charity. At the council of Reading, Thomas led episcopal resistance against Archbishop Pecham and was eventually excommunicated (1282). He appealed to Rome and was benevolently received by Martin IV, but died shortly afterwards (Orvieto, 25 August 1282).[163]

Upon Clement's election to the papacy, Edward I found the time propitious for the canonisation of an English saint. To that end, the king wrote to the bishop and clergy of Hereford to ask for a detailed list of the miracles performed by their former bishop, to be sent to the pope (12 August 1305).[164] Three months later, the king wrote to Clement on Thomas' behalf, declaring that 'he perceives that he and his people are daily helped by his suffrages, and more especially in order that he may merit to have as propitious a patron in heaven as he had as a familiar on earth'.[165] There is no indication that Winchelsey supported the royal petition. Although Thomas had been a man of considerable learning and

[161] On his life and miracles, see *Acta Sanctorum*, 1 October, pp. 599–705.

[162] N. D. S. Martin, 'The Life of St Thomas of Hereford', pp. 15–19; D. Carpenter, 'St Thomas Cantilupe', pp. 57–72.

[163] R. C. Finucane, 'The Cantilupe–Pecham Controversy', pp. 103–23.

[164] *Registrum Ricardi de Swinfield*, pp. 440–1. The bishop accordingly reported to the king the apostolic life and many miracles performed by his predecessor (8 September 1305): *ibid.*, pp. 420–1.

[165] 2 November 1305: *Concilia Magnae Britanniae et Hiberniae*, p. 283.

had shown concern for his pastoral duties, he had also been an advisor of the king and a bitter opponent of Archbishop Pecham. Notwithstanding his support of the barons, his candidacy could find but little sympathy with the archbishop of Canterbury.[166] Following the king's appeal, Clement nominated a special commission and charged its members – the bishops of Mende and London and the papal nuncio, Guillaume Testa – to inquire into the life and miracles attributed to the former bishop of Hereford.[167] The pope was especially concerned with the excommunication of Thomas, whether it was still in effect at the time of his death or not.[168] A first stage was accomplished in 1307, when the papal commission found Thomas innocent and thus proceeded with the canonisation inquiry.[169] Edward tried to hasten the process and asked for the good services of the cardinal-bishop of Porto.[170] Additionally, the dean and chapter of Hereford appointed proctors to survey the parishioners about the many miracles performed by Thomas de Cantilupe.[171] Edward II, as well, wrote to Clement in an attempt to expedite the inquiry (12 December 1307).[172] In a rare act of political solidarity with his son-in-law, Philip the Fair supported Thomas' candidacy and interceded with the pope on his behalf at the Council of Vienne.[173] Yet in this particular case, Clement did not meet the request of either the English or the French kings, and Thomas de Cantilupe was not to join the ranks of Catholic saints until the pontificate of John XXII. The case of Thomas de Cantilupe leaves many questions open to further inquiry. To mention but a few: the pressure of the kings of England to bring about his canonisation notwithstanding Thomas' pro-baronial stand, Clement's reluctance to comply in a matter that could only benefit papal popularity in England, and the intervention of Philip the Fair are all factors meriting further consideration. Furthermore, the pope's hesitations throughout the process of Thomas' canonisation is at odds with Clement's benevolence towards Edward I and Edward II in all other areas.

---

[166] Denton, *Robert Winchelsey and the Crown*, pp. 227–8.

[167] *Letanter nuper* (23 August 1305): *Registrum Simonis de Gandavo*, vol. i, pp. 247–8; *Annales Londonienses*, p. 150. See also their letter to the prelates of England containing special instructions about the miracles attributed to Thomas: *Registrum Simonis de Gandavo*, vol. i, pp. 249–52.

[168] 1 September 1305: *Registrum Simonis de Gandavo*, vol. i, pp. 248–9.

[169] E. M. Jancey, *St Thomas of Hereford*, pp. 5–19.

[170] 23 April 1306: *Calendar of the Close Rolls (1302–1307)*, p. 436; *Foedera*, i-4, p. 51. In May 1307, Edward also raised the canonisation of Robert Grosseteste, bishop of Lincoln, but he did not exert much pressure on this matter: *Foedera*, i-4, pp. 73, 74.

[171] 15 September 1306: *Registrum Ricardi de Swinfield*, p. 430. The long inquiry caused heavy expenses to the diocesan treasury; see *ibid.*, pp. 490–1.

[172] *Foedera*, i-4, p. 103. See also Edward's letters to the cardinals (5 April 1308): *Foedera*, i-4, p. 117.

[173] Edward warmly thanked his father-in-law for his intervention (15 September 1312): *Treaty Rolls*, vol. i, p. 203. The same day, Edward repeated his request before the pope: *Foedera*, ii-1, p. 14.

Clement, indeed, was very devoted to royal interests, despite the unpopularity and even the futility of such a policy, during the troubled reigns of Edward I and Edward II. This policy was harmful not only to papal leadership and finances but, also, and perhaps primarily, to the constitutional development of England. By mobilising the tenth for the royal treasury, the pope allowed the kings of England to finance their wars without recourse to parliament. Thanks to papal support, both Edward I and Edward II could advance their policy in open contravention of the *Confirmatio cartarum*, without asking for consent. Edward I and Edward II were each able to replace the uneasy appeal to parliament with a facile appeal to the pope, who generously supplied their needs. It is rather dubious whether the achievements of papal diplomacy in the short term – such as the acceptability of papal mediation – were worth the high price that the papacy had to pay in terms of its authority and leadership in the kingdom of England. Clement's subservient policy in both the domestic and foreign affairs of England involved the papacy in difficult, if not impossible, situations in relation to the baronage, a large proportion of the prelates of England, and the community of the realm of Scotland as a whole. In contrast to the consensus in regard to the 'Babylonian Captivity' of the Avignon papacy, with Philip the Fair being its main promoter and the kings of France as a whole its main beneficiary, the pontificate of Clement V thus displayed no concurrent captivity with the location of the papacy in southern France. It was the pope's own option to co-operate with and even make papal interests subservient to the kings of England rather than to the king of France. As indicated by Froissart: 'The pope . . . was a Gascon from Bordeaux and all his ancestors had been subject to the kings of England. In his status and actions he was an Englishman who would never harm the king of England.'[174] One may conclude that Clement's benevolence towards the kings of England expressed both the sympathies and the essential weakness of the former archbishop of Bordeaux towards his feudal lords of earlier times but, also, and perhaps first and foremost, towards his family and protégés.

---

[174] Jean Froissart, *Chroniques*, p. 52; Tout, *The Place of the Reign of Edward II in English History*, p. 195.

Chapter 7

THE COUNCIL OF VIENNE AND THE
CLEMENTINAE

W. A. Pantin has called attention to the fact that 'the fourteenth century saw a remarkable combination of the centralisation of the Church on the one hand, with well-developed nationalism, on the other'.[1] One of the most significant aspects of Clement's pontificate was the pope's genuine attempt to find a *via media* between different and often opposing interests. Clement was well aware of the limitations on the Church posed by the emergence of the national state. He tried – succeeding to a significant degree – to pave the road that the Church should take in a world undergoing an accelerated process of change that jeopardised ecclesiastical immunity. From this perspective, the legislation of Clement V should be appreciated as a very positive outcome only a few years after the outrage of Anagni. Although Clement V has often been criticised for his lack of initiative – John XXII being credited with the consolidation of the papal monarchy in the Avignon period[2] – there was hardly an issue concerning the Church that escaped his attention. Clement analysed in depth the Church's fragile balance with the rulers of Christendom as well as the different facets of ecclesiastical life, both in the secular and monastic orders, and the ties between the exempt Orders and the secular clergy, the Spirituals and the Conventuals. The result in the form of a juridical document, the *Clementinae*, gives ample proof of the pope's legal skills.[3] As the seventh book of the Decretals, the *Clementinae* complemented the legislative process that had begun in the thirteenth century, the classical era of canon law.[4]

One important subject that called for papal attention was the proper

---

[1] Pantin, 'The Fourteenth Century', p. 159.
[2] Guillemain, 'Punti di vista sul papato avignonese', pp. 194–202.
[3] Cardinal Giacomo Caetani Stefaneschi, who was not among Clement's supporters, declared that one main factor in the election of Bertrand de Got to the papacy was his well-known expertise in canon law.
[4] G. le Bras, *Histoire du droit et des institutions de l'Eglise en Occident*, vol. I, pp. 162–3.

operation of the College of Cardinals in times of interregnum, particularly the need to elect a new pope in as short a time as possible. In order to avoid a long interregnum, Clement's constitution, *Ne Romani*, clarified the conditions for convening the conclave.[5] It established the cardinals' duty to meet within ten days following the pope's death in the same city or diocese where the pope had passed away.[6] This constitution was duly put into practice following Clement's death, when the conclave met in Carpentras.[7] Yet, the legal apparatus proved of no avail. Two and a half years were to pass before Jacques Duèse, cardinal-bishop of Porto, was elected to the papacy, and not without external intervention.[8] In August 1316 – i.e., twenty-six months after Clement's death – Philip, count of Poitiers and future king of France, summoned the cardinals to the Dominican convent in Lyons and then announced that no one would be allowed to leave until they nominated a new pope. The threat had the desired effect and brought the prolonged interregnum to its end (7 August 1316).[9]

Clement V was more successful in organising other aspects of ecclesiastical life, such as canonisation procedures, over which he strengthened papal control.[10] The pope's attempt to counterbalance the increasing pressure of western kings in advancing their candidates is faithfully illustrated by the cases of Pietro da Morrone and Thomas de Cantilupe. Although in both instances the kings of France and England finally obtained their wishes, and the Christian calendar was enriched with two new saints, Clement did not relinquish his plenary authority in the canonisation process, and detailed scrutinies were carried out.[11] On a more earthly level, and in response to strongly felt needs, the constitution, *Saepe contingit*, established a special summary procedure for use in litigations involving benefices and the scope of the clergy's spiritual authority (1306).[12] The core of Clement's legislation, however, undoubt-

---

[5] The Second Council of Lyons, as well, dealt with the subject; see *Conciliorum Oecumenicorum Decreta*, [2], pp. 314–18; Elze, 'Sic transit gloria mundi', pp. 36–8.

[6] *De electione et electi potestate, Clementinarum*, l. 1, tit. iii, c. 2, *CIC*, vol. 11, cols. 1135–6.

[7] G. Mollat, 'L'élection du pape Jean XXII', pp. 34–49, 147–66.

[8] There were persistent rumours that it was actually Bertrand de Got, the pope's nephew, who was responsible for the fire that caused the violent interruption of the conclave. See *Continuationis chronici Guillelmi de Nanagiaco*, p. 406; *E chronici Rotomagensis continuatione*, p. 348. On the strong criticism of the cardinals' negligence in the election of a new pope, see *Flores historiarum*, p. 175; *La chronique métrique attribuée à Geffroy de Paris*, pp. 201–2, vv. 5815–67; A. Pezard, 'Dante et l'apocalypse de Carpentras', pp. 61–100. Edward II accused the cardinals of political opportunism, and Philip the Fair threatened to transfer the nomination to a conciliar framework. See *Foedera*, II-1, p. 87; *Collectio actorum veterum*, p. 243.

[9] *Fragment d'une chronique anonyme . . . 1328*, p. 151; *E chronico anonymi Cadomensis*, p. 26.

[10] L. Ferrier, 'Aspects du rôle de la curie dans le déroulement des procès de canonisation', p. 269.

[11] See above, pp. 199–204, 275–7.

[12] *De verborum significatione, Clementinarum*, l. v, tit. xi, c. 2, *CIC*, vol. 11, col. 1200; Williman, 'Summary Justice in the Avignonese Camera', pp. 438–9, 449.

edly was concerned with the Council of Vienne, where the representatives of Christendom provided a suitable, though not always supportive, framework for advancing the papal monarchy.

THE COUNCIL OF VIENNE

The encyclical, *Regnans in caelis* (Poitiers, 12 August 1308),[13] summoned the prelates to a council to be held in Vienne[14] on 1 October 1310.[15] Clement carefully defined the three main topics on the agenda, namely, the fate of the Temple, the renewal of the crusade, and the reform of the Church.[16] The prelates were requested to prepare written reports on the actual situation of the Church in their respective areas, while mentioning all matters 'that require the immediate intervention of the Holy See for their correction and reform'.[17] The encyclical focused on the Temple, which was the centre of curial attention at the time. It praised the devotion of Philip the Fair to the Church and cleared him of any suspicion of coveting the property of the Order.[18] Clement also summoned to the council those Templars who wished to defend their Order and appointed Pierre de la Chapelle, cardinal-bishop of Palestrina, as counsellor to their leaders.[19] *Regnans in caelis* was sent to 253 prelates: 4 patriarchs, 75 archbishops, 151 bishops, 13 abbots, 7 masters of monastic Orders, and 3 priors.[20] Clement took into account that some prelates would delegate full power to 'appropriate proctors'.[21] The formal use of proctors was in

---

[13] *Regestum Clementis Papae V*, nos. 3628–33. The fact that 483 papal letters were dated this day – the last consistory in Poitiers – suggests that the register includes letters that were actually written in August and September. See J. Lecler, *Vienne*, p. 24. The papal summons was renewed on 22 November 1310: *Regestum Clementis Papae V*, no. 7479.

[14] Vienne was part of the kingdom of Arles and, as such, under the rule of Henry VII. During the council, the archbishop and lord of the city, Briand de Lagnieu, conveyed to the pope temporal rule over the location.

[15] The original date was postponed by one year to allow for the end of the Templars' inquisition (4 April 1310): *Regestum Clementis Papae V*, no. 6293–5; *Calendar of Entries in the Papal Registers*, pp. 49, 78; *Acta Henrici VII*, no. 5, pp. 8–9; *Registrum Simonis de Gandavo*, vol. I, pp. 385–6; *The Register of John de Halton*, vol. II, pp. 21–2; *Records of Antony Bek*, no. 129; *Continuationis chronici Guillelmi de Nangiaco*, p. 377. [16] *Les grandes chroniques de France*, pp. 261–2.

[17] *Regestum Clementis Papae V*, nos. 3628–33. Written reports were introduced by the Second Council of Lyons. This practice hints at the growing importance of written reports, a process that the laity found more difficult and, consequently, was slower to execute. See H. J. Graff, 'The Legacies of Literacy', pp. 71–5; W. A. Graham, *Beyond the Written Word*, pp. 36–9.

[18] 'Non tipo avaritie . . . sed fidei orthodoxe fervore, tuorum progenitorum vestigia clara sequens': *Regestum Clementis Papae V*, no. 3626; Paulin, bishop of Pozzuoli, *Quinta Vita*, p. 81.

[19] *Regestum Clementis Papae V*, nos. 3584–5.

[20] The numbers are based on the list of participants provided by Müller, *Das Konzil von Vienne*, pp. 663–70; *Regestum Clementis Papae V*, no. 3628–33.

[21] A proctor or *procurator* was an individual formally empowered, within certain limits, to transact business on behalf of another. His powers were wider and his duties less ceremonial than those of an envoy or an ambassador in the fourteenth and fifteenth centuries: M. Kaser, *Das römische*

keeping with the development of representative patterns in parliaments and assemblies.[22] It further took into consideration the many problems caused by the vicissitudes of medieval geography and old age, and was meant to assure maximal participation.[23] Clement, indeed, was anxious to assure the attendance of most prelates. At the end of the council, the pope praised those who had come to Vienne, whose obedience to the Holy See had made them worthy of apostolic favour; he rewarded them with a long list of privileges that would provide reimbursement for their expenses.[24] On the other hand, Clement was quite severe towards those prelates who did not come for frivolous reasons. In the letter, *Illius vices*, the pope forbade the absentees from entering their churches 'in order that they would not take pride of their contumacy'.[25]

The pope also called for the participation of Christian rulers: Philip IV of France, Henry VII of Luxemburg, Louis of Navarre, Charles II of Naples, Edward II of England, James II of Aragon, Ferdinand IV of Castile, James II of Majorca, Denis of Portugal, John I of Bohemia, Carobert of Hungary, Henry II of Cyprus, Frederick III of Trinacria, and Jean II of Vienne headed the list of lay personages invited.[26] Christian princes, however, stayed away.[27] Only the dauphin of Vienne attended the opening session. Still, there were impressive delegations from Aragon, England, Sicily, Portugal, Castile, Cyprus, and France.[28] There is no convincing evidence of the participation of Henry VII or his representatives, perhaps because the emperor-elect was fighting in Italy at the time for his political survival. Nor was the participation of prelates impressive.

Privatrecht, vol. I, pp. 263–7. On the use of proctors in the papal curia, see Zutshi, 'Proctors Acting for English Petitioners in the Chancery of the Avignon Popes', pp. 15–29. On the election of proctors in the Church, see P. C. Timbal, 'La vie juridique des personnes morales ecclésiastiques en France', pp. 1431–41.

[22] Bisson, 'The General Assemblies of Philip the Fair', pp. 550–6; R. Villers, 'Réfléxions sur les premiers Etats Généraux de France', pp. 93–7; T. F. Ruiz, 'Oligarchy and Royal Power', pp. 95–101; Marongiù, *Medieval Parliaments*, pp. 8–73.

[23] See, for instance, the letters to the bishops of Worcester and Durham in which Clement, at Edward II's request, excused them from assistance to the council but required them to send their proctors: *Regestum Clementis Papae V*, nos. 7609, 7627; *Calendar of Entries in the Papal Registers*, p. 93; *Foedera*, I-4, pp. 194, 197. A curious case is provided by the bishop of Lincoln, who received papal dispensation because of his age. It was asserted that he could ride about in England, and so his not coming to the council was contumacy; he incurred ecclesiastical sentences, from which he was eventually absolved by Clement: *Regestum Clementis Papae V*, no. 8742; *Calendar of Entries in the Papal Registers*, p. 104. For other cases, see *Regestum Clementis Papae V*, no. 7610.

[24] *Regestum Clementis Papae V*, nos. 8719–23. A year later, Pierre, bishop of Auxerre, received additional concessions on the grounds of the many expenses that he had incurred during the council (19 July 1313): *ibid.*, no. 9475.   [25] *Ibid.*, nos. 8843, 8850.

[26] *Ibid.*, nos. 3626–7; *Calendar of Entries in the Papal Registers*, p. 49.

[27] Finke, *Papsttum und Untergang des Templerordens*, vol. II, no. 126, p. 239.

[28] Philip IV was represented by Guillaume de Plaisians, one chaplain, and two secretaries: *ibid.*, vol. II, no. 127, p. 248. For Edward II's instructions to Otto de Grandson, see *Treaty Rolls*, p. 197; *Foedera*, I-4, p. 191.

Only between 144 and 170 'prelates with mitres' attended the formal opening (16 October 1311).[29] Even if the higher figure is accepted, it was a relatively small number in comparison with the average ecclesiastical participation in thirteenth-century councils. A main cause of the small numbers was the pope's selective summons to bishops, generally only two from each province. The archbishop of Reims, for example, was accompanied by the bishops of Soissons and Châlons-sur-Marne; the archbishop of Rouen, by the bishops of Bayeux and Coutances; and the archbishop of Tours, by the bishops of Le Mans and Angers.[30] Contemporary chronicles, however, mention additional factors accounting for the relatively small assistance, in particular the fear of fiscal demands from the curia. This possibility was suggested by the chronicle attributed to Geffroy de Paris,[31] whose suspicions acquired the weight of fact in the writings of Jean de St Victor.[32]

At the opening of the council, Clement V based his sermon on the psalm 'I will praise the Lord with my whole heart, in the assembly of the upright, and in the congregation. The works of the Lord are great, sought out of all them that have pleasure therein' (Ps. 111:1–2).[33] The pope reported the different stages in the prosecution of the Templars and announced the appointment of two committees to review the inquisitorial protocols.[34] He alluded in general terms to the project of the crusade, and then referred in more detail to the difficult situation of the Church, which called for immediate reform. After giving his blessing to all participants, Clement dismissed the assembly without announcing a date for the ensuing meeting. The pope's silence about the council's schedule was not fortuitous. It actually indicates the transition from former patterns of large assemblies, 'viva voce', to more professional

---

[29] *Les grandes chroniques de France*, p. 285. The Lanercost chronicler mentions only 130 archbishops and bishops in Vienne: *Chronicon de Lanercost*, p. 217. Different sources give different numbers at the opening. E. Müller identifies twenty cardinals, four patriarchs, twenty-nine archbishops, seventy-nine bishops, and thirty-eight abbots. About half of the prelates came from the kingdom of France. See the complete list in Müller, *Das Konzil von Vienne*, pp. 73–8. I have found only one source that refers to the assistance of prelates, abbots, and masters of Military Orders 'in numero copioso': *Annales Osterhovenses*, p. 557.

[30] L. Wetzel, *Le concile de Vienne*, p. 22. Since the book was written in the early 1920s but published only after the author's death in 1993, it is very out of date, and some serious errors escaped the editor's attention. [31] *La chronique métrique attribuée à Geffroy de Paris*, p. 177, vv. 4523–4.

[32] Jean de St Victor, *Prima Vita*, p. 19.

[33] Though the papal sermon has not been preserved, its contents are known from the reports of Giacomo Stefaneschi and the Aragonese representatives: Finke, *Papsttum und Untergang des Templerordens*, vol. II, no. 126, pp. 239–40; Ehrle, 'Zur Geschichte des päpstlichen Hofceremoniells im 14. Jahrhundert', p. 575. On the liturgical ceremonial of the opening session, see H. Jedin, *Ecumenical Councils of the Catholic Church*, pp. 96–8.

[34] As late as August 1311, Clement was still demanding that the prelates of Castile, Aragon, Portugal, Tuscany, Lombardy, Cyprus, and Latin Greece send their reports concerning the inquisition of the Templars. See *Regestum Clementis Papae V*, nos. 7524–8, 7595–7600, 7604–8, 7611–12.

commissions.[35] Against the thirteenth-century tradition of periodic assemblies every eight to twenty days, the committee system in Vienne reduced the general sessions to three, those on 16 October 1311, 3 April 1312,[36] and 4 May 1312. The commissions relied on written reports, which for the most part were carefully redacted before presentation to the council. The new system made the work of the council more efficient and, concomitantly, assured the pope's more effective control of the different commissions and, through them, of the decisions. Clement V was an active participant in all commissions, though he delegated the preparatory work to the cardinals. The pope also introduced *nationes*, namely, prelates grouped according to geographical criteria, as a legitimate group of reference. He consulted with the prelates according to their country of origin, and their reports were classified accordingly; national categories also dictated participation on the different commissions. All these new practices turn Clement V into a pioneer in modernising ecumenical councils.

CHURCH REFORM

Reference to the need for Church reform in Vienne was hardly a new phenomenon in the annals of medieval councils. Rather, it was in harmony with ecclesiastical norms of the previous two centuries, which had turned the need for reform into an integral subject of conciliar deliberations. Still, new problems and new points of conflict called for new approaches, a challenge that faced the prelates in Vienne and the pope at their head. Following Clement's invitation to submit reports on the reform of the Church, a large number of documents reached the council. Some bishops had called on local councils, the better to prepare *schemata*; some drew up personal memoranda, as did Guillaume Durant the Younger, bishop of Mende,[37] and Guillaume le Maire, bishop of Angers. Certain dioceses and provinces prepared more general schemes, and at times regional and national councils were conducted to discuss the reports to be delivered. Clement appointed Cardinals Nicolas de Fréauville, Napoleone Orsini, and Jacques Duèse to read the reports of the prelates and, accordingly, to define the most pressing matters requiring amelioration in ecclesiastical life.[38] Most of the preliminary work was

---

[35] The constitution *Vox in excelso* hints at this procedure, which prevailed in later councils. See *Conciliorum Oecumenicorum Decreta*, pp. 340–1.

[36] In contrast to the lone participation of the dauphin of Vienne at the opening, Philip IV, Charles de Valois, Louis of Navarre, the count of St Pol, and the son of the count of Brittany attended the second meeting.

[37] The best survey of Guillaume's ideas and influence appears in Fasolt, *Council and Hierarchy*.

[38] Müller, *Das Konzil von Vienne*, pp. 117–20.

in fact done by Jacques Duèse, as he attested in a letter to Edward II.[39] Clement himself was active in the deliberations of the three-cardinal commission from mid-January 1312, as is suggested in the protocol by sentences like 'it was commanded', 'it was proscribed by our lord', 'it was heard that the highest pontiff . . . ordered'.[40] The *gravamina* or solicitations presented to the council – most of which have not survived, with the exception of those from Sens and Auch[41] – were classified according to the country of origin into thirty *rotuli*, and these were arranged into *rubricae*. Each *rubrica* was further divided into six points.[42] Every *gravamen* received full attention and was enclosed with its respective *remedium* or solution. The fourteen ecclesiastical provinces of France comprised ten rolls;[43] Italy and Sicily nine; the Iberian peninsula five; England, Ireland, and Scotland two; and Denmark one.[44]

Among the most important subjects in need of immediate amelioration were 'inflictions caused by temporal lords'. These included serious complaints against usurpations of ecclesiastical lands and infringement of the Church's jurisdiction over tenths, wills, and contracts. Additional protests were raised against the many impediments to the spiritual disciplining of criminal priests and lay appeals to ecclesiastical courts. The prelates also objected to the infringement of Church privileges by royal agents, the continuous damage they caused to Church members and property, and their readiness to exonerate crimes committed against the Church.[45] Paradoxically, the French clergy, which had solicited royal sanction for its contribution to the crusade, now called for the council's (i.e., Clement's) assistance against royal policy, which harmed its privileges and income. Well aware of the curia's limited freedom of action, Gilles Colonna advised that a joint commission of ecclesiastical and royal

---

[39] L. E. Boyle, 'A Committee Stage at the Council of Vienne', pp. 25–6.

[40] Müller, *Das Konzil von Vienne*, p. 119, nn. 180, 183.

[41] G. Mollat, 'Les doléances du clergé de la province de Sens au Concile de Vienne', pp. 319–26. Ehrle had published the grievances of Auch, which emphasised the aggressive methods pursued by the king in Gascony, especially against the abbot of Saint-Pé. See Ehrle, 'Ein Bruchstück der Akten des Konzils von Vienne', pp. 368, 374. On secular lords who seized ecclesiastical benefices, see *ibid.*, p. 370; Duffour, 'Doléances des évêques gascons au Concile de Vienne', pp. 244–59.

[42] Ehrle, 'Zur Vorgeschichte des Konzils von Vienne' (1887), p. 185; Ehrle, 'Ein Bruchstück der Akten des Konzils von Vienne', pp. 366–99.

[43] The province of Narbonne was among the very few that did not present any complaints, either because of the successful policy of its archbishop, Gilles Aycelin, in restraining royal officers – as claimed by McNamara – or, conversely, because of the archbishop's pro-royal stand, which restrained the freedom of action of his suffragans: McNamara, *Gilles Aycelin*, p. 187.

[44] Boyle, 'A Committee Stage at the Council of Vienne', pp. 27–35.

[45] Philip the Fair and his officers were very active in this field. For the Toulouse area, see *Lettres inédits de Philippe le Bel*, pp. 62–84; for Languedoc, see 'Gravamina que inferuntur per curiam ecclesiasticam', in Boutaric, 'Notices et extraits de documents inédits relatifs à l'histoire de France sous Philippe le Bel', no. 10, pp. 132–5.

officers examine the scope and exercise of Church jurisdiction and co-operate in punishing violators. He also warned against the overuse of excommunication and interdict, which would nullify their effect.[46] Even Gilles, though, failed to focus on the core of the problem – the fact that Philip the Fair no longer recognised the principle of ecclesiastical immunity in practice. The royal view had been clearly proclaimed a few years earlier, during the struggle with Boniface VIII, when Philip established his supreme jurisdiction over both the members and the property of the Church.[47] As the knight declared in the *Disputatio inter clericum et militem*:

Just as everything within the boundaries of the Empire is known to be subject to the Empire, so everything within the boundaries of the realm is subject to the king. And just as the Emperor may establish, amend or withdraw laws for his whole Empire, so the French King can reject all imperial laws, or change them as he pleases, or proscribe and abolish them from his whole realm, and make new ones if he wishes . . . By his royal power, the king is supreme over the laws, customs, privileges, and liberties which have been granted.[48]

Declarations of this kind, even if they reflect political goals to be achieved and not the actual situation, indicate the ever-growing gap between traditional patterns – on which the immunity of the Church rested – and the national state, with a king who was most zealous of his prerogatives at its head.

Most prominent along the broad spectrum of internal problems affecting the Church were the exempt Orders.[49] They were accused of infringing the rights of the secular clergy and of a long list of particular offences. The accusations included permitting Christian burial to excommunicated criminals who had not shown full repentance, bestowing sacraments on the laity, extending their many privileges to the *confratres*, and encouraging their peasants to elude due payment of the tenth. Although the charges levelled against the Templars were of a completely different nature, their worsened situation did not make the status, let

---

[46] Ehrle, 'Ein Bruchstück der Akten des Konzils von Vienne', pp. 415–17.

[47] 'Item certum est, notorium et indubitatum quod de hereditatibus et juribus et rebus immobilibus ad jus temporale spectantibus qui, sive petitorio agatur sive possessorio, sive pertineant ad Ecclesias et Ecclesiasticas personas, sive ad dominos temporales, agendo et defendendo, cognitio pertinet ad curiam temporalem; specialiter autem domini Regis ipsius': *Scriptum contra Bonifacium*, in *Triatez des droits et libertéz de l'Eglise gallicane*, vol. II, p. 113. On the problematic relationship between state and Church during the reign of Philip the Fair, see Fournier, 'Les conflits de juridiction entre l'Eglise et le pouvoir séculier', pp. 449–58.

[48] *Disputatio inter clericum et militem*, in N. N. Erickson, 'A Dispute Between a Priest and a Knight', p. 308.

[49] See the reports of Gilles Colonna, who opposed their many privileges and, contrariwise, their enthusiastic defence by Jacques de Thérines, abbot of Chaalis: Müller, *Das Konzil von Vienne*, pp. 495–6, 503–14; Valois, 'Jacques de Thérines, cistercien', pp. 193–211.

alone the image, of other exempt Orders any more acceptable.[50] The prelates eventually succeeded in re-establishing the constitution, *Super cathedram*, of Boniface VIII, thus significantly restricting the prerogatives of the exempt Orders. The final version published in the *Clementinae*, however, was much less effective, thereby hinting at Clement's own hesitations with regard to the policy of his predecessor.[51]

The Council of Vienne further dealt with the clergy's conduct and mutual relations between papal delegates and the secular hierarchy. Recognising the many vices that affected the Church, Guillaume Durant was a leading voice calling for reform of the Church 'in both its head and members'. He challenged papal primacy and tried to transfer the core of ecclesiastical power to the council. The pope, he argued, should not reverse conciliar decisions, and the council's sanction was necessary whenever the pope legislated for the whole Church. In order to allow the exercise of such a division of labour, Durant advised assembling the prelates every ten years, thus making councils an organic part of Church government.[52] These suggestions, though, did not receive much support at this stage.[53] Although the papal practice of reservation and taxation aroused much criticism, no clear decision against Clement's policy of centralisation is noticeable during the council's deliberations.[54] Those few prelates, as well as the many chroniclers, who called for reform of the papacy thus remained isolated voices. Furthermore, John XXII contin-ued Clement's policy and, in fact, brought about the full implementation of papal provisions.[55] More effective were the council discussions with regard to heretical and heterodox groups – such as the Free Spirit, the Beghards, and the Beguines – and Muslims living in Christendom.

---

[50] *La chronique métrique attribuée à Geffroy de Paris*, pp. 176–7, vv. 4471–4522.

[51] Müller, *Das Konzil von Vienne*, pp. 553–9, 686–7, nos. 9, 10, 20.

[52] *Tractatus de modo celebrandi concilii*, in Viollet, 'Guillaume Durant, le jeune, évêque de Mende', pp. 79–86. Cf. Port, 'Le livre de Guillaume le Maire', pp. 471–99. Constantin Fasolt sees Guillaume's proposals as 'radically new'; it was this radical quality that brought about Durant's trou-bles with Clement V and his later retraction in the *Tractatus Minor*. In the long term, Durant's ideas received full consideration in the Council of Constance. See Fasolt, *Council and Hierarchy*, pp. 4–5.

[53] Johannes Quidort von Paris went further, seeing in the prelates' collegial rule the best govern-ment for the Church: 'Sic certe esset optimum regimen ecclesiae, si sub uno papa eligerentur plures ab omni provincia et de omni provincia, ut sic in regimine ecclesiae omnes aliquo modo haberent partem suam' (*De potestate regia et papali*, 19, ad 35um, p. 175). See also J. Rivière, *Le problème de l'Eglise et de l'Etat au temps de Philippe le Bel*, pp. 299ff. H. Arquillière contends that, at the beginning of the fourteenth century, there was no criticism of papal supremacy over the council; the pope's pre-eminence was also recognised by Philip the Fair in 1311. Only the possibil-ity of a heretical pope could have transferred the source of power to the representatives of Christendom. See H. X. Arquillière, 'L'appel au concile sous Philippe le Bel et la genèse des théories conciliares', pp. 23–55.   [54] Lecler, *Vienne*, pp. 126–33.

[55] Of a total of 55,420 *lettres communes*, 31,555 letters of John XXII concerned papal provisions; of these, 16,773, or more than half, dealt with the Church of France: L. Caillet, *La papauté d'Avignon et l'Eglise de France*, p. 20.

Inquisitorial procedures were reviewed, and the scope of usury and its consequences vehemently condemned.

Basing his closing sermon on the words of the prophet, 'I have set watchmen upon thy walls, O Jerusalem' (Isa. 62:6), Clement summarised the main aims of the Council of Vienne and its many decrees. The pope announced his intention to mitigate some punishments but to consider all constitutions, including those that had not yet been read, as published.[56] All decrees, however, would be formally implemented only after their official reading and delivery to the universities.[57] This policy led an anonymous chronicler to charge that, except for the conciliar decisions with regard to the Templars and the Franciscans, the pope actually 'had abrogated and destroyed all [other] acts of the Council of Vienne'.[58] This view was also shared by Walter of Guisborough, who claimed: 'And so ended the deliberations of the council, if it may be called a council, since the pope made all the decisions himself, without seeking the approval of the holy council or even consulting anyone.'[59] The outright condemnation expressed by Walter of Guisborough hints at the new balance between the pope and the representatives of the universal Church. At Vienne, Clement succeeded in advancing his policy with or without the support of most prelates. The decrees regarding the Templars, the exempt Orders, and the Beguines, to mention the most outstanding examples, indicate the large extent of the pope's authority in the Church.

THE *CLEMENTINAE*

Of the 106 canons of the *Clementinae*, only thirty-eight ever mention in different versions the formula 'with the approbation of the holy council', and were therefore regarded in some sense as the work of the Council of Vienne – more exactly, its third session (6 May 1312).[60] However, pronouncements hinting at the council's consent should not necessarily be

---

[56] 'Nunquam tamen in dicto concilio [constitutiones] fuerunt publice promulgata, sed penitus judicio apostolico libere fuerunt reservata, et ad plenum dimissa': *Continuationis chronici Guillelmi de Nangiaco*, p. 392.

[57] 'Volumus . . . quod constitutiones non lecte haberentur publicate, et publicande non obligent seu adstringant, quousque misse essent ad studia, et infra tempus, quod ordinabit, ut legerunt, post misse erunt': from the ceremonial of Cardinal Giacomo Caetani Stefaneschi, in Müller, *Das Konzil von Vienne*, p. 678. On the cardinal's life and the manuscripts of his work, see E. Condello, 'I Codici Stefaneschi', pp. 21–61.   [58] *Continuatio Pontificum Anglica Brevis*, p. 715.

[59] He also stressed the pope's domineering behaviour during the few general sessions of the council: '[papa] inhibuit sub pena excommunicacionis maioris ne aliquis loqueretur verbum in concilio nisi licenciatus vel requisitus a papa' (*Chronicle of Walter of Guisborough*, p. 396). Cf. Ullmann, *A Short History of the Papacy*, p. 281.

[60] Hefele and Leclercq, *Histoire des conciles*, vol. VI-2, pp. 666–99; J. Tarrant, 'The Manuscripts of the *Constitutiones Clementinae*', 101–70 (1984), p. 68. See also M. Mollat and P. Tombeur, *Le concile de Vienne*.

288

regarded as indicators of the prelates' participation in the redaction of the decrees, let alone the sanction of the final version. Guillaume Mollat accurately pointed out that the council may have issued a decree, but its Clementine form may not faithfully reproduce the statements actually passed.[61] Moreover, according to Johannes Andreae, who finished his *apparatus* in 1322, which quickly attained general recognition as the *glossa ordinaria*,[62] at least three constitutions – *Dudum a Bonifacio*, *Quoniam ex constitutione*, and *Ex frequentibus prelatorum* – were written before the Council of Vienne. The dictum, 'Clement in the Council of Vienne', found in *Pastoralis cura* and *Romani principes* is also misleading, since both constitutions were written and published almost two years after the closure of the assembly.[63]

The codification of the *Clementinae* was probably assigned to Guillaume de Mandagout, who had edited the *Liber Sextus* of Boniface VIII. Clement wanted his compilation to be named *Septimus* as a continuation of the *Liber Sextus*, and his contemporaries indeed refer to it thus.[64] It was, however, quickly replaced by the more personal appellation of *Clementinae*.[65] On 21 March 1314, Clement convened a consistory at Monteux, near Avignon, in order to promulgate his new collection of canon law. Consequent to the pope's death a few weeks later, however, the circulation of the text was suspended for more than three years.[66] Though the *Clementinae* were accepted as binding in 1314, they were officially sanctioned only one year after the election of John XXII. The new pope sent the pertinent letters to the universities of Bologna, Paris, and Avignon in October–November 1317.[67] The postponement was explained by Johannes Andreae as being due to the modifications that John XXII introduced in the text. Andreae's assertion hints, therefore, at three stages in the complex development of the

---

[61] G. Mollat, 'Les Clémentines', col. 635.

[62] S. Kuttner, 'The *Apostillae* of Johannes Andreae on the Clementines', p. 196.

[63] Lizerand, 'Les constitutions *Romani principes* et *Pastoralis cura*', p. 756; Della Piana, 'Intorno ad una bolla papale', pp. 23–50.

[64] *Chronicon fratris Francisci Pipini*, col. 750; *Excerpta ex expositione Hugonis de Rutlingen*, p. 132; *Martini continuatio Brabantina*, p. 262; *Notae ad vitas*, pp. 169–70.

[65] Amalric Auger hints at this change when he emphasises that papal legislation '*hodie* Clementine vocantur'. See Amalric Auger, *Sexta Vita*, p. 104.

[66] Paulin, bishop of Pozzuoli, *Quinta Vita*, p. 82; Bernard Gui, in *Tertia Vita*, p. 57; Bernard Gui, in *Quarta Vita*, p. 76.

[67] *Gesta archiepiscoporum Magdeburgensium*, pp. 428, 430. John XXII used the occasion to praise his predecessor, 'quin etiam ante et post ipsum concilium constitutiones plurimas edidit': *Clementinarum* 119r., Cambridge University Library, MS Ii iii 7 (Letter of John XXII to the University of Paris, 1 November 1317, and the reception of the papal letter by the masters of Toulouse, 22 December 1317). On the extant manuscripts of the *Clementinae*, see the detailed list in Tarrant, 'The Manuscripts of the *Constitutiones Clementinae*'. See also *Chartularium Universitatis Parisiensis*, nos. 754–5, pp. 211–12.

Clementinae. They originated just before and during the Council of Vienne though they excluded from its statutes the suppression of the Temple and the call for a crusade. A post-conciliar commission headed by Clement V revised the decrees to be included in canon law. Finally, John XXII made further revisions. The discussion which follows does not attempt to summarise all sections of papal legislation, but to indicate its main trends and to provide a better understanding of the goals and achievements of Clement V, particularly the pope's relations with all members of the ecclesiastical order.

One main aim of the *Clementinae* was to safeguard the remnants of ecclesiastical immunity, which was adversely affected by the emerging states.[68] *Si quis suadente diabolo* set forth excommunication, interdict, and severe punishments for anyone, as well as his advisors and partners, who dared to blaspheme, harm, or imprison bishops or other members of the clergy.[69] *Multorum ad nos* referred in negative terms to those who imprisoned ecclesiastics in order to compel them to renounce their benefices or to prevent them from attending an apostolic summons.[70] Special punishment was envisaged for those who forced the clergy to celebrate Mass and other Christian rites in areas under interdict.[71] Bishops who had been unlawfully removed from their see were allowed to excommunicate their aggressors and, under certain limitations, to exercise their ordinary jurisdiction 'in a foreign diocese'.[72] They could apply to three bishops, who would receive special papal letters (*litterae conservatoriae*) empowering them to summon the culprits within an area of a four-day journey.[73]

If one bears in mind the many grievances presented against royal officials and their continuous infringement of ecclesiastical immunity, the scope of the *Clementinae* in this regard seems wholly inadequate.[74] The arrest and long imprisonment of Bernard Saisset, bishop of Poitiers,[75] Guichard, bishop of Troyes,[76] Walter Langton, bishop of Coventry and Lichfield, William Lamberton, bishop of St Andrews, and Robert

---

[68] On the anti-clerical trends, see G. Lagarde, *Bilan du XIIIe siècle*, pp. 157–71. For France, see G. de Llobet, 'Varieté des croyances populaires au comté de Foix', pp. 115–18.

[69] *De poenis, Clementinarum*, l. v, tit. viii, c. 1, *CIC*, vol. II, cols. 1187–8; *Conciliorum Oecumenicorum Decreta*, [33], pp. 388–9.

[70] *De poenis, Clementinarum*, l. v, tit. viii, c. 2, *CIC*, vol. II, cols. 1188–9; *Conciliorum Oecumenicorum Decreta*, [34], pp. 390–1.

[71] *De sententia excommunicationis, suspensionis, et interdicti, Clementinarum*, l. v, tit. x, c. 2, *CIC*, vol. II, cols. 1191–2; *Conciliorum Oecumenicorum Decreta*, [36], p. 391.

[72] *De foro competenti, Clementinarum*, l. II, tit. ii, c. un., *CIC*, vol. II, cols. 1144–5; *Conciliorum Oecumenicorum Decreta*, [7], pp. 363–4. [73] Müller, *Das Konzil von Vienne*, p. 687, no. 21.

[74] Wetzel, *Le concile de Vienne*, pp. 219–20.

[75] Saisset was imprisoned on 24 October 1301 and returned to royal grace only in 1308: Boutaric, 'Notices et extraits de documents inédits relatifs à l'histoire de France sous Philippe le Bel', no. 35, pp. 195–7. [76] See above, pp. 84–7.

Wishart, bishop of Glasgow[77] – to cite but the most outstanding examples – reflect the ambiguous dividing line between ecclesiastical immunity and royal jurisdiction that was to be found in Christendom at the beginning of the fourteenth century. Indeed, the active participation of prelates in royal administration and their resulting involvement in politics threatened to obliterate the principle of *libertas ecclesiae*, the justification of which had been formulated more than two hundred years earlier. Papal provisions did not make the situation any easier, since they paved the way for royal clerks to attain leading ecclesiastical positions, thus making even more vague the borders between *sacerdotium* and *regnum*. The need for a new concordat between kings and the ecclesiastical order, however, was not a challenge that any one particular pope could meet, either at this time or in the next centuries. In this regard, the *Clementinae* are symptomatic of both Clement's efforts to preserve some harmony between the secular and ecclesiastical arms and the pope's awareness of the limitations posed by the emerging national state.

The decree *Dudum a Bonifacio* sanctioned and renewed the effect of Boniface's constitution *Super cathedram*,[78] which had been abrogated by Benedict XI on 17 February 1304.[79] *Dudum a Bonifacio* defined the division of labour between the Friars and the secular clergy, whose privileges had been critically affected in terms of preaching, administration of sacraments,[80] and obsequies.[81] The many grievances presented by the secular clergy against the exempt Orders were meant to gain the former papal protection against their rivals.[82] In this particular case, the dictum, 'by the request and with the approbation of the holy council', suggests the prelates' pressure on Clement V to change Benedict's and his own policy in favour of the Friars. According to Jean de St Victor, indeed, 'it was a great altercation with regard to the exempt, since the prelates requested that the exempt Orders, both religious and secular, would be submitted to their rule. But the pope was reluctant to acquiesce.'[83] In the Clementine version, *Dudum a Bonifacio* moderated the views of the prelates while echoing the pope's own interpretation of a suitable division of labour between both members of the Church. Clement

---

[77] See above, pp. 259, 271–4.

[78] *De sepulturis, Extravagantes Communes*, l. III, tit. vi, c. 2, *CIC*, vol. II, col. 1273; Müller, *Das Konzil von Vienne*, pp. 678–9.

[79] *De privilegiis, Extravagantes Communes*, l. v, tit. vii, c. 1, *CIC*, vol. II, cols. 1296–1300.

[80] *De privilegiis et excessibus privilegiatorum, Clementinarum*, l. v, tit. vii, c. 1, *CIC*, vol. II, cols. 1186–7; *Conciliorum Oecumenicorum Decreta*, [31], pp. 387–8.

[81] *De sepulturis, Clementinarum*, l. III, tit. vii, c. 2, *CIC*, vol. II, cols. 1161–4; *Conciliorum Oecumenicorum Decreta*, [10], pp. 365–9.

[82] *Ex chronico pontificum et imperatorum Ratisponensi*, p. 288; C. Erickson, 'The Fourteenth-Century Franciscans and Their Critics', 13 (1975), pp. 107–35; 14 (1976), pp. 108–47.

[83] Jean de St Victor, *Prima Vita*, p. 19.

attempted to create a more stable equilibrium within the ranks of the Church, while calling on both sides to reconsider their respective behaviour.

Religiosi quicunque envisaged severe punishment against those Friars who dared to administer sacraments without obtaining due sanction from the local clergy or who intruded in the collection of the tenth.[84] The Friars were further exhorted by *Cupientes eos* to refrain from criticising the sermons of the secular clergy and from interfering in their ordinary jurisdiction.[85] They were called, instead, to display great concern for the duties of the faithful towards the clergy and local churches.[86] The Franciscans, in particular, but also the Dominicans, were strictly prohibited under threat of excommunication to receive the Tertiaries in their churches or to provide the sacrament of penance in areas under interdict.[87] *Ut professores* reduced the Friars' freedom of movement while regulating their transfer to other Orders.[88] In order to limit the extent of the Friars' itinerancy, without entirely abrogating former privileges, any brother who left his original institution was deprived of the right of participation in the general chapter of his new destination; further, he would not be considered for honorary appointments.[89]

Alongside these measures restricting the Friars, Clement also tried to limit the interference with and sometimes also the damage that the secular clergy caused them. The *Clementinae* explicitly refer to the offences committed by some prelates against the exempt Orders, a subject that received full attention in the report submitted by the Cistercian abbot, Jacques de Thérines.[90] *Frequens et assidua* exhorted the prelates to

---

[84] *De decimis, primitiis, et oblationibus, Clementinarum,* l. III, tit. viii, c. 1, *CIC*, vol. II, cols. 1164–5; *Conciliorum Oecumenicorum Decreta,* [11], p. 369; Müller, *Das Konzil von Vienne,* p. 686, nos. 9–10.

[85] *De poenis, Clementinarum,* l. V, tit. viii, c. 3, *CIC*, vol. II, cols. 1189–90; *Conciliorum Oecumenicorum Decreta,* [35], pp. 390–1. On the fascination engendered by the Friars' sermons compared with those of the local clergy, see Moorman, *Church Life in England in the Thirteenth Century,* pp. 79ff.; on the prelates' neglect of their preaching, see P. Adam, *La vie paroissiale en France,* pp. 208–9.

[86] On the *exempla* of the secular clergy and their shameful behaviour, see J. Horowitz and S. Menache, *L'humour en chaire,* pp. 79–106.

[87] *De sententia excommunicationis, suspensionis, et interdicti, Clementinarum,* l. V, tit. x, c. 3, *CIC*, vol. II, col. 1192; *Conciliorum Oecumenicorum Decreta,* [37], p. 391.

[88] Opposition to geographical mobility lay at the very heart of ecclesiastical legislation from the early middle ages. To this the Friars were rather alien, both in their settlement among urban populations and in their nomadic life style. The *Clementinae* did not deal with this problem in depth, but tried to limit the Friars' freedom of movement: Menache, *The Vox Dei,* pp. 250 ff.; J. Le Goff, 'Au moyen âge', pp. 417–33.

[89] *De regularibus et transeuntibus ad religionem, Clementinarum,* l. III, tit. ix, c. 1, *CIC*, vol. II, col. 1165; *Conciliorum Oecumenicorum Decreta,* [13], p. 370.

[90] In contradicting the charges levelled by Gilles Colonna in his *Contra Exemptos,* Jacques de Thérines wrote four different treatises: *Contra impugnatores exemptionum, Compendium contra impugnatores exemptionum, Quaestio de exemptionibus,* and *Responsio ad quaedam quae petebant praelati in praejudicium exemptorum.* He emphasised the discipline of the exempt Orders, the Cistercians in

'charitably treat and defend' the Friars and other members of exempt Orders, to respect their privileges, and to refrain from preventing abbots and priors from attending the chapters of their Order. In a rather paternalistic manner, the pope reminded both prelates and monks that they were members of the same body and, as such, were obliged to show mutual understanding and co-operation.[91] *Cum sit naturae consonum*[92] and *Ad nostrum*[93] referred to the painful subject of the prelates' rights of visitation, namely, their receiving suitable hospitality in exempt institutions, a subject that had enjoyed detailed legislation. In 1200, for example, the synod of London–Westminster, presided over by Archbishop Walter Hubert, had endorsed the legislation of the Third Council of Lateran (1179), which limited the retinue of an archbishop to forty to fifty persons and established a maximum escort of twenty to thirty for bishops and of five to seven for archdeacons.[94] The synod of Oxford (1222) complemented this legislation while restricting the economic burden that the summons to chapters and synods implied for local churches and monasteries.[95] Notwithstanding the many, detailed enactments in this regard, the visitations of prelates continued to constitute a serious source of economic loss and, therefore, of resentment, not only for the exempt Orders but for the local clergy as well. There were complaints against prelates who, being dissatisfied with the hospitality they received, had actually plundered sacred utensils from churches.[96] Clement tried to find a compromise between the prelates' excessive demands for victuals and accommodation and the reluctance of monks and local clergy to satisfy their demands.

The pope also attempted to find a *via media* and to leave a positive mark on the long internal struggle among the heirs of St Francis, especially with regard to the dissident Spiritual wing.[97] The critical ideas of the Spirituals were based on two important influences: the survival,

---

particular, their charity, and their scrupulous accomplishment of the rule. Conversely, he resolutely criticised the way of life of some prelates and their arbitrary demands during visitations. See Valois, 'Jacques de Thérines, cistercien', pp. 193–211.

[91] 'Decet ut omnes, qui eiusdem sunt corporis, unius etiam sint voluntatis et sicut fratres adinvicem vinculo caritatis sint adstricti': *De excessibus praelatorum, Clementinarum*, l. v, tit. vi, c. un., *CIC*, vol. II, cols. 1185–6; *Conciliorum Oecumenicorum Decreta*, [30], pp. 385–6.

[92] *De censibus, exactionibus, et procurationibus, Clementinarum*, l. III, tit. xiii, c. 1, *CIC*, vol. II, col. 1172; *Conciliorum Oecumenicorum Decreta*, [19], pp. 376–7.

[93] *De censibus, exactionibus, et procurationibus, Clementinarum*, l. III, tit. xiii, c. 2, *CIC*, vol. II, cols. 1172–3; *Conciliorum Oecumenicorum Decreta*, [20], pp. 377–8.

[94] *Conciliorum Oecumenicorum Decreta*, [4], pp. 213–14; *Concilia*, ed. Mansi, vol. XXII, cols. 455–6; *Councils and Synods*, vol. I, pp. 1062–3.   [95] *Councils and Synods*, vol. II, [27], p. 114.

[96] See the legislation of the synod of Narsiac, in *Concilia*, ed. Mansi, vol. XXV, col. 790; Adam, *La vie paroissiale en France*, pp. 213–15.

[97] On the historical background, see D. Nimmo, *Reform and Division in the Medieval Franciscan Order*, pp. 51–108; J. Paul, 'Les franciscains et la pauvreté aux XIIIe et XIVe siècles', pp. 33–7.

especially in small rural centres in Umbria and the March of Ancona, of primitive Franciscan attitudes towards poverty, and the adoption of a philosophy of history derived from the writings of Joachim of Fiore. During the pontificate of Boniface VIII and the first years of Clement V, the Conventuals had gained papal recognition, their position regarding the *usus pauper* being the sole one heard in the curia.[98] This balance was broken by Arnaud de Villanova, Clement's physician and a close friend of Ubertino da Casale, who called the pope's attention to the desperate situation of the Spirituals.[99] Yet, the Conventuals' strong counteroffensive, led by Raymond de Fronsac and Bonagrazia da Bergamo, succeeded in establishing a full investigation of Olieu's writings, as well.[100] After hearing the testimonies of both sides — the Conventuals represented by the minister-general, Gonzalve de Valbonne, and the Spirituals by Ubertino da Casale, their leader in Tuscany — Clement appointed a commission of cardinals, all of them theologians, to deal with the matter. The pope asked Guillaume de Peyre de Godin (Dominican), Gérard de Bologna (Carmelite), and Arnaud de Toulouse (Hermits of St Augustine) to investigate four main questions:

the execution of the Franciscan rule;

the relationship, if any, between the Spirituals and the heretical sect of the Free Spirit;[101]

the doctrinal orthodoxy of Pierre Jean Olieu, the indisputable past leader of the Spirituals in Provence;[102] and

the persecution of the Spirituals by the superiors of the Order.[103]

In a rather exceptional sentence, Clement exempted the Spirituals' leaders 'from the jurisdiction of and all obedience' to their superiors; they were to be subject, instead, to a commission of cardinals nominated by the pope.[104] The minister-general or his procurator were ordained to pro-

---

[98] D. Burr, *Olivi and Franciscan Poverty*, pp. 124–8.

[99] Manselli, 'Arnaldo da Villanova e i papi del suo tempo', p. 154. In 1299, Arnaud resigned his chair of medicine at Montpellier to devote himself to his mystical calling and to the service of the crown of Aragon. He facilitated the settlement of a large group of Spirituals in Sicily, an area that underwent a mystical revival during the reign of Frederick III: Backman, *The Decline and Fall of Medieval Sicily*, pp. 216–21.

[100] Ehrle, 'Zur Vorgeschichte des Konzils von Vienne', pp. 33–48.

[101] On the problematic relationship between the Franciscans and heretical sects, especially the Waldenses, see B. Marthaler, 'Forerunners of the Franciscans', pp. 133–42. On the heresy of the Free Spirit and its different branches, see R. E. Lerner, *Heresy of the Free Spirit*.

[102] G. Barone, 'L'oeuvre eschatologique de Pierre Jean-Olieu et son influence', pp. 56–9.

[103] See the reports presented to the pope: Ehrle, 'Zur Vorgeschichte des Konzils von Vienne', pp. 48–195.

[104] *Dudum ad apostolatum* (14 April 1310), *Regestum Clementis Papae V*, no. 6272; see also 'Relatio commissionis in concilio Viennensi institutae ad decretalem "Exivi de paradiso" praeparandam', ed. G. Fussenegger, pp. 145–77.

mulgate the papal command, so that there would be no pleas of ignorance.[105] Clement further envisaged that the Franciscan affair would be fully discussed in the Council of Vienne.[106]

The cardinals appointed by the pope were joined in Vienne by two commissions, which dealt with the *usus pauper* issue and the doctrines of Pierre Jean Olieu, respectively. The new members of these commissions were Bérenger de Landorra (Dominican), Jacques de Thérines (Cistercian),[107] Gilles Colonna, archbishop of Bourges,[108] Raymond Concoreggi, archbishop of Ravenna, Guillaume de Mandagout, archbishop of Aix en Provence, Guidoctus de Tabiatis, bishop of Messina, Guillaume Durant, bishop of Mende, Raymond Despont, bishop of Valence, and G. Pellicioni, bishop of Parma. These prelates were joined by Jean de Pouilly, Geranselmus Joannis, a master of Roman law, another master of Paris, and one layman. Some prelates participated in both commissions, which received for their consideration the *Arbor vitae crucifixae* and the *Rotulus* of Ubertino da Casale;[109] the Conventual doctrine was represented by the essays *Postilla in Joannem* and *Religiosi viri*.[110] The laborious scrutiny by both commissions was formally sanctioned in the decrees *Exivi de paradiso* and *Fidei Catholicae fundamenta*.

Exivi de paradiso (6 May 1312)[111] defined a compromise level of Franciscan observance, while forbidding the advocates of opposing views to implicate their adversaries in heresy.[112] On the crucial question of whether an obligation to poverty was contained in the Franciscan vow of profession, the *Clementinae* chose a middle course: 'We declare that the lesser brothers by profession of their rule are specially obliged to the poor or restricted uses contained in the rule [itself] in the form in which they are there expressed.' The decree did not define a specific standard of use, thus leaving vital decisions to individual interpretation. Still, it made a

[105] *Bullarium Franciscanum*, vol. v, pp. 65b–68a. [106] *Ibid.*, vol. v, pp. 38–9.

[107] For biographical data, see Valois, 'Jacques de Thérines, cistercien', pp. 180–93.

[108] 'Aegidii Romani impugnatio doctrinae Petri Ioannis Olivi an. 1311–1312, nunc primum in lucem edita', ed. L. Amorós, pp. 399–451.

[109] Though the general structure of the *Arbor* was influenced by Bonaventure's *Lignum Vitae*, it reflected also the double influence of Italian local pietism and of sophisticated theological reactions to the theology of Joachim of Fiore.

[110] Ehrle, 'Zur Vorgeschichte des Konzils von Vienne', pp. 33–195.

[111] *Regestum Clementis Papae V*, no. 8873. This is the date provided by the register, which is also mentioned by Jean de St Victor and Bernard Gui (*Vitae*, pp. 19, 73), and accepted by G. Mollat. Many manuscripts of the *Clementinae*, however, do not mention this decretal at all. This lapse is explained by Jacqueline Tarrant as indicating awareness of the interdiction of Nicholas III in the decretal *Exiit qui seminat* against re-examining the question of Franciscan poverty: *Sexti Decretal.* l. v, tit. xii, c. 3, *CIC*, vol. II, cols. 1109–21; Tarrant, 'The Manuscripts of the *Constitutiones Clementinae*', 101–70 (1984), pp. 68–71.

[112] *De verborum significatione, Clementinarum*, l. v, tit. xi, c. 1, *CIC*, vol. II, cols. 1193–1200; *Conciliorum Oecumenicorum Decreta*, [38], pp. 392–401; A. Volpato, 'Gli Spirituali e l'*intentio* di S. Francesco', pp. 118–53.

clear differentiation between commands and regulations, the accomplishment of which was compulsory and, as such, had to be consummated, and recommendations or no-precepts, as they were called in medieval times, the fulfilment of which was reserved to individual discretion. Notwithstanding the influence of *Exivi de paradiso* in the realm of ideas throughout the middle ages, it did not restore peace in the Franciscan ranks.[113] Clement limited himself to the punishment of those Conventuals who persecuted the Spirituals and of those Spirituals who did not submit to papal canons; they were eventually handed over to the Inquisition.[114] Although Clement did his best to assure the unity of the Order while giving deference to both extreme conceptions of Franciscan ideals, the internal schism was too deep.[115] Clement's death and the Spirituals' open revolt called for more extreme solutions, which were put into practice during the pontificate of John XXII.[116]

Fidei Catholicae fundamenta condemned some errors found in the tenets of Pierre Jean Olieu.[117] The decretal opens with a clear definition of the incarnation of the Son, who subsists with the Father for eternity in the unity of divine nature.[118] It also clarifies other issues in Olieu's doctrine, such as the death of Jesus. Calling Olieu's distinction between the rational or intellectual soul and the body 'erroneous and opposing the integrity of the Catholic faith', the decretal emphasises the complete unity of soul and body in the human nature of Jesus and, consequently, in humankind. It also refers to the effects of baptism on both adults and children, on whom it bestowed divine grace.[119] Though some prelates tried to assure the orthodoxy of Olieu's faith, even Ubertino da Casale, his most enthusiastic supporter, recognised that his master's intentions, though all orthodox, were sometimes obscure in expression and, therefore, questionable.[120]

Clement's interest in the Friars was not exceptional, but reflected the pope's genuine interest in the monastic Orders as a whole. Having been a pupil of the former prior, Pierre de Caussac, in the retreat of Deffez at

---

[113] M. Erburo, 'Clemente V en la historia de la moral', pp. 651–701.

[114] On 23 July 1312, the pope summoned to the curia the Franciscan leaders of Provence, under threat of excommunication, to discuss the future of their Order: *Regestum Clementis Papae V*, no. 8851. A year later, Clement enlisted the bishops of Lucca, Pistoia, and Arezzo to bring about the obedience of the Spirituals of Tuscany: *ibid.*, no. 9494.

[115] Tabacco, 'Il papato avignonese nella crisi del Francescanesimo', pp. 328–9.

[116] M. D. Lambert, 'The Franciscan Crisis Under John XXII', pp. 123–43.

[117] *De Summa Trinitate et Fide Catholica, Clementinarum*, l. I, tit. i, c. un., *CIC*, vol. II, cols. 1133–4; *Conciliorum Oecumenicorum Decreta*, [1], pp. 360–1.

[118] 'Fidei catholicae fundamento . . . firmiter inhaerentes . . . unigenitum Dei Filium in his omnibus, in quibus Deus Pater exsistit, una cum Patre aeternaliter subsistentem: *Conciliorum Oecumenicorum Decreta*, [1], p. 360.   [119] Hefele and Leclercq, *Histoire des conciles*, vol. VI-2, pp. 667–73.

[120] J. Koch, 'Die Verurteilung Olivis auf dem Konzil von Vienne und ihre Vorgeschichte', pp. 489–522; C. Partee, 'Peter John Olivi', pp. 215–60.

St Férreol, Clement did not hide his admiration for the Order of Grandmont. In 1305, the pope visited the monastery, where he spent five days. Clement also formulated a series of revised statutes for the Order (20 April 1310), and three years later supervised the elections for a new abbot.[121] During the deliberations in Vienne, the Benedictines received attention in the decree, *Ne in agro dominico*,[122] which established in detail their garments (*flocus, cuculla*),[123] their discipline, and their duties regarding confession, the celebration of Eucharist, and the reading of the rule. The decree strictly forbade the participation of monks in hunting or leaving the monastery without the permission of the abbot. *Attendentes quod*[124] concerned the nuns, 'who had promised themselves to Christ in a formal vow'. They were placed under the control of the diocesan bishop and exhorted to accomplish their oath of poverty and chastity, and to avoid any frivolous fashion that suited the secular world.[125] The nuns' participation in the amusements of the laity was also strictly prohibited.

Rather obviously, monks and nuns were not the only members of the Church who were exposed to the harmful influence of the temporal world. *Quoniam*[126] defined in detail the proper garments of the clergy while strongly forbidding any imitation of the laity's fashion, 'which makes them inapt to profess the prerogatives of their Order'.[127] *Gravi nimirum turbatione*[128] focused on the celebration of Mass and other forms of divine office, and defined the many irregularities found among both secular and monastic Orders.[129] The superiors were called upon to

---

[121] *Regestum Clementis Papae V*, nos. 5366, 9114. On the history of the Order, see D. J. Dubois, 'Grandmontains et Chartreux, ordres nouveaux du XIIe siècle', pp. 3–22. On Clement's attitude to the Order and his contribution to its rule, see C. Hutchison, *The Hermit Monks of Grandmont*, pp. 137–43.

[122] *De statu monachorum vel canonicorum regularium, Clementinarum*, l. III, tit. x, c. 1, *CIC*, vol. II, cols. 1166–8; *Conciliorum Oecumenicorum Decreta*, [14], pp. 370–3.

[123] On abbots' and monks' pursuit of the latest in fashion, see the previous criticism of Caesarius of Heisterbach and of the *Alphabetum narracionum*, which urged, rather hopefully, that 'abbas debet esse conformis subditis in vestibus et victualibus': Caesarius von Heisterbach, *Dialogus Miraculorum*, IV.12, IV.13; *Alphabetum narracionum*, no. 5; E. R. Curtius, *La littérature européenne et le moyen âge latin*, p. 214.

[124] *De statu monachorum vel canonicorum regularium, Clementinarum*, l. III, tit. x, c. 2, *CIC*, vol. II, cols. 1168–9; *Conciliorum Oecumenicorum Decreta*, [15], pp. 373–4.

[125] On the pomp and excesses of contemporary fashion, see F. Piponnier, *Coutume et vie sociale*, pp. 83–126, 301–2; R. Pernoud, *La femme au temps des cathédrales*, pp. 100–1.

[126] *De vita et honestate clericorum, Clementinarum*, l. III, tit. i, c. 2, *CIC*, vol. II, cols. 1157–8; *Conciliorum Oecumenicorum Decreta*, [9], p. 365.

[127] On the sharp criticism by contemporary preachers of the frivolous fashion of the clergy, see Horowitz and Menache, *L'humour en chaire*, pp. 82–99.

[128] *De celebratione missarum, et aliis divinis officiis, Clementinarum*, l. III, tit. xiv, c. 1, *CIC*, vol. II, cols. 1173–4; *Conciliorum Oecumenicorum Decreta*, [22], pp. 378–9.

[129] Irregularities in the celebration of Mass was actually the only subject on which a charge was proved against the Templars in York and in other countries outside France: *Councils and Synods*, pp. 1338–9.

exercise full authority and to see to the due fulfilment of the Church's canons. They were strongly requested to prevent dances and theatre presentations in churches and cemeteries, as these were performed 'in offence of divine majesty and to the commotion of the people present'.[130] *Diocesanis locorum* demanded that prelates be more aware of their responsibility towards the clergy and strictly prohibit any members or candidates for ordination from becoming butchers or from working in taverns. Both were considered shameful occupations that some clergymen, none the less, dared to exercise 'in person and in public'.[131]

The *Clementinae* inquired into other aspects of ecclesiastical life as well. Vacant benefices of the regular clergy over a period of six months were conferred by *Quia regulares* on the diocesan bishop, who would bestow them on the secular clergy or on exempt monks.[132] In addition to these guidelines, Clement also tried to simplify procedures in ecclesiastical tribunals, which, especially in the papal court, often appeared to go on endlessly.[133] The decree, *Dispendiosam prorogationem litium*, following the lines established in 1306 by *Saepe contingit*, focused on benefices, canonries, the tenth, and marriages, with the intention to have them proceed 'straightaway and in a simple manner' without unnecessary delays.[134] As a further manifestation of papal monarchy, the decree, *Dignum prorsus*, exempted the clergy and monks serving in the curia from the regulations of their original diocese; they had to submit, instead, to the ritual of the papal curia.[135]

Being a man of letters, Clement was mindful of the 'pernicious ignorance' of part of the clergy, especially those in the lower orders, and of many monks.[136] The pope approached illiteracy as a regrettable vice

---

[130] On the scope of these practices, see Horowitz, 'Les danses cléricales dans les églises au moyen âge', pp. 279–92.

[131] *De vita et honestate clericorum, Clementinarum,* l. III, tit. i., c. 1, *CIC,* vol. II, col. 1157; *Conciliorum Oecumenicorum Decreta,* [8], pp. 364–5. See also *English Synodalia of the Thirteenth Century,* ed. C. R. Cheney, pp. 17–33; *Veterum scriptorum et monumentorum historicorum,* vol. VII, col. 1367.

[132] *De iure patronatus, Clementinarum,* l. I, tit. v, c. un., *CIC,* vol. II, col. 1139; *Conciliorum Oecumenicorum Decreta,* [4], pp. 362–3. Concerning benefices, see also *Ut ii, qui divinis* and *Ut constitutio: Clementinarum,* l. I, tit. vi, c. 2, *CIC,* vol. II, cols. 1139–40; *Conciliorum Oecumenicorum Decreta,* [5], p. 363; *Clementinarum,* l. III, tit. xii, c.1, *CIC,* vol. II, col. 1171; *Conciliorum Oecumenicorum Decreta,* [18], p. 376.

[133] This was the claim of Guillaume Durant, 'Tractatus de modo celebrandi concilii', pt III, tit. 27, in Viollet, 'Guillaume Durant, le jeune, évêque de Mende', p. 107. Pierre Jame, as well, complained of the length and arbitrary costs of papal justice and called for St Peter's help to alter this unfortunate state of affairs. See Fournier, 'Pierre Jame (Petrus Jacobi) d'Aurillac, jurisconsulte', p. 509.

[134] *De iudiciis, Clementinarum,* l. II, tit. i, c. 2, *CIC,* vol. II, col. 1143; *Conciliorum Oecumenicorum Decreta,* [6], p. 363.

[135] *De celebratione missarum, et aliis divinis officiis, Clementinarum,* l. III, tit. xiv, c. 2, *CIC,* vol. II, col. 1174; *Conciliorum Oecumenicorum Decreta,* [23], p. 379.

[136] Although by the fourteenth century the monastic Orders had abandoned the attitude of scorn with regard to literacy that was characteristic of early monks, much improvement in this area was

that affected not only the image of the Church as a whole but also the exercise of ecclesiastical duties in a proper form.[137] Clement's approach received further stimulus in two projects presented to the council by Guillaume Durant and Guillaume le Maire. The two prelates placed special emphasis on the fact that 'ignorance is the step-mother of all errors in the Church of God'. The unavoidable conclusion was that 'ignorant persons . . . should not be accepted for ecclesiastical positions'. Durant, furthermore, complained of the lack of a real education programme and produced substantial proposals to rectify the matter.[138] *Ne in agro dominico* reflects Clement's positive attitude to these proposals, which received support from Ramon Lull, though from a missionary perspective. The decree stipulated that in each monastery there 'must be placed a suitable master, who diligently would teach them elementary science'.[139] *Inter sollicitudines* promoted chairs of Oriental languages in the leading universities of the day.[140] 'Two Catholic men' were to teach Hebrew, Arabic, and 'Chaldean' at the Universities of Paris, Bologna, Oxford, and Salamanca and in the papal curia. They were further expected to translate important treatises from these languages into Latin, while their pupils would become missionaries. The king of France was to finance the chairs in Paris;[141] the prelates and monasteries of England, those at Oxford; the bishops and monasteries of Italy, those at Bologna; the Church of Spain, the chairs at Salamanca; and the papacy was to be responsible for the chairs at the curia.[142] These instructions were another manifestation of Clement's allegiance to the crusade, the knowledge of Oriental languages being an integral requisite for its implementation. Pierre Dubois, as well, advocated the study of Oriental languages to secure the permanent settlement of Christians in the Levant, after the Holy Land was

---

still necessary. See the statutes of Malmesbury and Gloucester in this regard: *Registrum Malmesburiense*, vol. I, p. 376; *Historia et cartularium Monasterii Gloucestriae*, vol. I, p. lxxxiv. For early monasticism, see J. Lacarrière, *Les hommes ivres de Dieu*, pp. 176–80.

[137] On the scope of illiteracy among contemporary clergy, including the bishops' ignorance of Latin, see F. Rapp, *L'Eglise et la vie religieuse en Occident à la fin du moyen âge*, pp. 122–6; G. G. Coulton, *Life in the Middle Ages*, vol. I, pp. 86–7.

[138] Bellone, 'Cultura e studi nei progetti di riforma presentati al concilio di Vienne', pp. 97–108; T. N. Tentler, 'The *Summa* for Confessors as an Instrument of Social Control', pp. 103–13.

[139] *De statu monachorum vel canonicorum regularium*, *Clementinarum*, l. III, tit. x, c. 1, *CIC*, vol. II, cols. 1166–8; *Conciliorum Oecumenicorum Decreta*, [14], pp. 372–3. Ramon Lull, in his *De locutione angelorum*, tells of his efforts to foster the study of Oriental languages in the Council of Vienne. On Lull's missionary efforts, see Hillgarth, *Ramon Lull and Lullism in Fourteenth-Century France*, pp. 25–7, 47–52, 132–4.

[140] *De magistris, et ne aliquid exigatur pro licentia docendi*, *Clementinarum*, l. v, tit. i, c. 1, *CIC*, vol. II, col. 1179; *Conciliorum Oecumenicorum Decreta*, [24], pp. 379–80.

[141] See the papal letter to the University of Paris on 6 May 1312: *Chartularium Universitatis Parisiensis*, no. 695, pp. 154–5.   [142] Hefele and Leclercq, *Histoire des conciles*, vol. VI-2, pp. 688ff.

recovered.[143] Until 1320, however, very little was done to comply with papal instructions. At the Universities of Oxford and Paris, Hebrew was the only Oriental language taught. Although the tax to provide for the teaching posts had been levied in England since 1321, the Oxford curriculum did not include Arabic and Persian until the sixteenth century.[144] This state of affairs suggests a lack of interest in Oriental languages, the knowledge of which was related to missionary purposes and, as such, left solely to the Friars. Until the end of the thirteenth century, indeed, the Dominicans ran at least five language schools that focused on the teaching of Arabic.[145]

Quia contingit interdum refers to the many complaints presented at the council against hospitals and leper-houses that did not belong to the Church. It was argued that these establishments were not properly maintained, and their furniture and possessions were often expropriated by untrustworthy guardians, 'who refuse to change their inhuman behaviour and damagingly convert the revenues for their own use'. The *Clementinae* conferred the administration of such organisations on reliable laymen, who would depend on the supervision of the diocesan bishop.[146] This decision heralded a new stage in the growing readiness of the Church to promote the more active participation of the laity in charitable tasks, thus reducing the clergy's former monopoly in this area.[147]

More problematic was the case of the Beguines, who received full attention in the constitutions *Cum de quibusdam*[148] and *Ad nostrum qui*.[149] Having formally condemned the heresy of the Free Spirit and its advocates, the Beghards, the Council of Vienne emphasised the irregular status of the Beguines while re-asserting the legislation of the Second

---

[143] Pierre Dubois, *De recuperatione Terrae Sanctae*, XXXVI.59, XXXVII.60–1, pp. 151–64, LI. 83, pp. 166–7. On the linguistic problems raised by the crusade, see Menache, 'The Communication Challenge of the Early Crusades', pp. 294–5.

[144] R. Weiss, 'England and the Decree of the Council of Vienne on the Teaching of Greek, Arabic, Hebrew, and Syriac', pp. 3–7.

[145] R. I. Burns, 'Christian–Islamic Confrontation in the West', pp. 1402–12. The Dominican master, Bérenger de Landorra, in an encyclical of 1312, requested that all brothers who volunteered for missionary efforts should have a fair knowledge of Oriental languages: Richard, *La papauté et les missions d'Orient*, pp. 126–8.

[146] *De religiosis domibus, ut episcopo sint subiectae*, Clementinarum, l. III, tit. xi, c. 2, *CIC*, vol. II, cols. 1170–1; *Conciliorum Oecumenicorum Decreta*, [17], pp. 374–6.

[147] This development was in keeping with the Church's support, during the thirteenth century, of confraternities of laymen dedicated to charity and other pious works. See G. Meeserman, 'Etudes sur les anciennes confréries dominicaines', 20 (1950), pp. 5–113; 21 (1951), pp. 51–196; 22 (1952), pp. 5–176; 23 (1953), pp. 275–308.

[148] *De religiosis domibus, ut episcopo sint subiectae*, Clementinarum, l. III, tit. xi. c. 1, *CIC*, vol. II, col. 1169; *Conciliorum Oecumenicorum Decreta*, [16], p. 374.

[149] *De haereticis*, Clementinarum, l. v, tit. iii, c. 3, *CIC*, vol. II, cols. 1183–4; *Conciliorum Oecumenicorum Decreta*, [28], pp. 383–4.

Council of Lyons against new Orders.[150] In his revision of council decrees, Clement clarified the distinction between three different groups of women. *Cum de quibusdam* condemned the way of life of certain Beguines although the decree was intended to protect orthodox Beguines, whose lifestyle was otherwise not referred to in the council. Conversely, the Beguines of *Ad nostrum qui* were part of a group of women and men in Germany whose error centred on the nature of human perfection and its achievement in this life. The *Clementinae* ordered the diocesan authorities and inquisitors to proceed with a full investigation of the lives and opinions of this 'abominable sect of unfaithful women'.[151] Thus, in contrast to the obedient, devout Beguines and other lay women who deserved encouragement, Clement pointed to another category, the allies of the Beghards, who shared their condemnation. The pope ordered those ignorant women, whom he accused of confounding both themselves and others by their unlawful preaching, to desist from this practice.[152] Clement's distinction of three different categories of Beguines was eventually overlooked, however, perhaps because of Johannes Andreae's commentary, which regarded all three as a united threat to orthodoxy.[153]

The decrees *Multorum querela* and *Nolentes* referred to inquisitorial procedures and the irregularities found by a commission of cardinals nominated by the pope.[154] Though heresy was not very widespread during Clement's pontificate, there were still some foci in Italy and France. The most popular movement was that of Dolcino in Lombardy, who enlisted from 200 to 3,000 followers, according to different sources.[155] Dolcino was arrested by the bishop of Vercelli in early 1307 and sentenced to death together with his followers.[156] Another heresy was put forward by Margareta Porette, whom Bernard Gui considered 'not so much

---

[150] This exposition follows the convincing thesis of Jacqueline Tarrant, 'The Clementine Decrees on the Beguines', pp. 300–8. Joseph Lecler regards these decrees as 'les plus importants du concile de Vienne sur la vie religieuse': Lecler, *Vienne*, p. 159.

[151] The papal decision was recorded in contemporary sources to justify the persecution of Beguines and Beghards of both sexes in Germany; see *Gesta archiepiscoporum Magdeburgensium*, p. 441.

[152] On the scope of female preaching, see J. Dalarun, 'Regards de clercs', pp. 31–54; C. Casagrande, 'La femme gardée', pp. 83–116.

[153] Some chroniclers refer to the pope's deep remorse when on the verge of death at having caused them harm: *Cronica S. Petri Erfordensis Moderna*, p. 446; *Cronica Reinhardsbrunnensis*, p. 651.

[154] *De haereticis, Clementinarum*, l. v, tit. iii, c. 1, 2, *CIC*, vol. ii, cols. 1181–3; *Conciliorum Oecumenicorum Decreta*, [26, 27], pp. 380–3.

[155] Villani, *Istorie fiorentine*, l. viii, c. 84, pp. 171–2; *Continuationis chronici Guillelmi de Nangiaco*, pp. 357–8; *Les grandes chroniques de France*, pp. 254–5; Bernard Gui, in *Quarta Vita*, p. 63.

[156] *Collectio actorum veterum*, pp. 52–3. The pope recognised the importance of the bishop's achievement and conferred on him a long list of privileges to balance his budget, which have been severely harmed by his unconditional war against heresy: *Regestum Clementis Papae V*, nos. 1848, 1854, 2411.

maleficent as heretical', probably hinting at her considerably smaller influence but also at her more extreme tenets.[157] Margareta, indeed, was a 'Free Spirit'; she taught a daring version of the doctrine that the individual soul can become united with God this side of paradise and thereby reach a state of extreme 'annihilation' or passivity.[158] The Inquisition had questioned Margareta, who refused to renounce her erroneous ways, and she was ultimately handed over to the secular arm to be put to death.[159] Guiard de Cressonessart, who called himself 'the angel of Philadelphia' (Rev. 3:7–13), having been sent by the Lord to console the faithful, repented and was sentenced to perpetual imprisonment.[160]

Besides its focused treatment of heretical manifestations, the Council of Vienne dealt in more detail with the function of the Inquisition. To avoid regrettable transgressions, the *Clementinae* clearly established that the use of torture, the pronouncement of a definitive sentence, and the management of houses of detention would be the common responsibility of the bishop and the inquisitors acting in his diocese. The *Clementinae* thus restricted the former freedom of action of papal inquisitors, who were normally chosen from among the Friars and who had neutralised diocesan judges. Though each party maintained its right to imprison those suspected of heresy without consulting the other, both sides were obliged to commence joint action soon afterwards. Both the inquisitors and the diocesan judges, moreover, were prevented from speaking with prisoners, except in the presence of representatives from the other side; and both were vigorously forbidden to prevent relatives from bringing victuals, to extort money from prisoners or their relatives, or to use weapons excessively. A short period of eight days was allowed for mutual consultation. Should there be any impediment, this period was expected to enable the nomination of suitable representatives or to provide both parties with the necessary interval to send a written response. The minimum age established for inquisitors was forty because of the heavy responsibility delegated to them.

The regulation of inquisitorial activities and the pope's attempt to create an internal system of checks and balances reflect, *inter alia*, the painful experience of the trial of the Templars and the fact that the papal inquisitor in France had actually become a tool in the hands of Philip the Fair. Clement was also aware of the restless situation in Languedoc, espe-

---

[157] Bernard Gui, in *Quarta Vita*, p. 64.
[158] Langlois, 'Marguerite Porete', pp. 295–9; Lerner, *Heresy of the Free Spirit*, pp. 68–77, 200–8.
[159] *Continuationis chronici Guillelmi de Nangiaco*, pp. 379–80; *Les grandes chroniques de France*, p. 273.
[160] *Continuationis chronici Guillelmi de Nangiaco*, vol. I, p. 380; Lerner, 'An "Angel of Philadelphia" in the Reign of Philip the Fair', pp. 343–64.

cially in Albi, Cordes, and Carcassonne, whose inhabitants had almost reached the point of open insurrection against the Dominicans in 1291, 1296, and 1303. The fragile political situation of the crown in the area had caused Philip the Fair to restrict the power of the inquisitors, forcing them to consult with the bishops prior to enjoying royal assistance.[161] Early in Clement's pontificate, the inhabitants of Albi had appealed to the pope to take action against local inquisitors. In 1308, Clement denounced the Inquisition process against the vidame of Amiens, Jean de Picquigny, who died at the curia when appealing against an excommunication that had been placed on him for transferring convicted heretics to a royal jail. On 6 June 1309, following further complaints by local inhabitants, the pope nominated Cardinals Pierre de Chapelle and Bérenger Frédol to investigate the activities of the Inquisition in Carcassonne.[162] Several months later, the pope commissioned the bishop of Albi to investigate inquisitorial activities in Albi and Carcassonne (8 February 1310).[163] The *Clementinae* thus show the close connection between papal legislation and actual needs, to which Clement was most attentive, even if it meant acting against his own representatives.

In a more general field affecting Christendom, *Ex gravi ad nos* paid attention to Christian morals or, rather, their neglect under prevalent financial pressures. The decree focused on the scope of usury,[164] which it censured on the grounds that it was practised 'in offence of God and, in the same manner, against both divine and human law'.[165] Clement tightened the restrictions established by the Third Lateran Council and the Second Council of Lyons,[166] thus voicing a prevailing opinion among theologians. Both Gilles Colonna and John of Paris condemned the iniquity of usury, since 'money should not become [the last] goal'. Gilles asserted that usury ought not to be practised by anyone. If monarchs and rulers wished to govern according to nature, he stated, they had to forbid usury without further consideration. Usury was sinful because it involved a sale of time, which was common to all temporal creatures.[167] On the other hand, the extent to which these claims remained in the realm of pure theory may be learned from the letter of forty-eight communities of Quercy, which appealed to Clement against the punishment inflicted

---

[161] *Ordonnances des roys de France de la troisième race*, vol. I, pp. 330–1; Boutaric, *La France sous Philippe le Bel*, pp. 84–7.   [162] *Regestum Clementis Papae V*, no. 4754.   [163] *Ibid.*, no. 5238.

[164] *De usuris*, Clementinarum, l. v, tit. v, c. un., *CIC*, vol. II, col. 1184; *Conciliorum Oecumenicorum Decreta*, [29], pp. 384–5.

[165] This attitude was shared by Philip the Fair, who sanctioned various statutes against usury and usurers. See *Ordonnances des roys de France de la troisième race*, pp. 484–7, 489–91, 494–6, 508–9; *Lettres inédites de Philippe le Bel*, no. 180.   [166] B. Nelson, *The Idea of Usury*, pp. 3–23.

[167] O. Langholm, *Economics in the Medieval Schools*, pp. 45–52, 386–90, 395–6.

by the bishop of Cahors on those who violated the laws against usury (March 1311).[168]

Cedit quidem[169] exhorted Christian princes whose territories contained Muslim inhabitants to limit public manifestations of Islamic rituals, which were 'in offence of the divine name and cast opprobrium on the Christian faith'. Besides sacrilege, those rites might provide an aberrant example for the faithful.[170] To complete the patterns of behaviour expected of Christian princes, *Quum Iudaei*[171] urged them to limit the freedom of action of both Muslims and Jews. These decisions accorded with the xenophobia prevailing in Christendom, which a few years earlier had brought about the expulsion of Jews from England and Gascony in 1290, to be followed by that from France in 1306.[172]

The Council of Vienne and the *Clementinae* thus reflect, in a rather clear manner, the main dilemmas that affected the Church, both within its own ranks and in its dealings with royal authority and religious minorities at the beginning of the fourteenth century. They provide additional proof of Clement's skills as the head of the Church, and his attempts to deal in detail with its spiritual and its material aspects. On the other hand, the Council of Vienne and the reactions to it provide further evidence of the gap between the pope and many of his contemporaries. Clement's new practices in the Council of Vienne were criticised by some chroniclers as symptoms of arbitrariness without any attempt to reconsider former patterns of behaviour in the light of the new needs. This gap in conceptions was not unique to the relationship between the pope and the chroniclers; it also characterised the relationship of Clement V with large sectors of the clergy. Although the principle of papal monarchy was not seriously condemned in the council, the policy to be adopted with regard to the exempt Orders in general and the Temple in particular provides clear evidence of the increasing controversy in the ranks of the Church. Ultimately, however, Clement succeeded in advancing his policy with or without the approval of the council. On the other hand, Clement V, and the Council of Vienne under his leadership, remained faithful to former concepts regarding a crucial subject like usury, notwithstanding the increasing demands of the economic market. The same may be said about the futile attempts to prevent the participation of the clergy in the process

---

[168] The letter, however, was not sent. See the original text in Brown, *Customary Aids and Royal Finance in Capetian France*, pp. 275–7.

[169] *De iudaeis et Sarracenis, Clementinarum*, l. v, tit. ii, c. un., *CIC*, vol. II, cols. 1180–1; *Conciliorum Oecumenicorum Decreta*, [25], p. 380. [170] B. Z. Kedar, '*De Iudeis et Sarracenis*', p. 213.

[171] *De testibus, Clementinarum*, l. II, tit. viii, c. I., *CIC*, vol. II, col. 1147.

[172] Menache, 'Faith, Myth, and Politics', pp. 351–74.

of change that affected contemporary society as a whole. One may further argue that, in very difficult cases, such as papal elections, infringement of ecclesiastical privileges, and the conflict between Spirituals and Conventuals, Clement's legislation proved of no avail and failed to prevent crises in the near future. Moreover, Clement himself, and the curia under his leadership, hardly set a good example for a reformed Church, at least with regard to visitations and the many tolls that the papal curia levied on the local clergy. Though we lack conclusive evidence of Clement's way of life, many of his cardinals were strongly criticised for their ostentatious behaviour. Neither revolutionary nor conservative, the Council of Vienne maintained, on the whole, the doctrinaire path established by former councils. One may therefore conclude that the main contribution of the *Clementinae* lay in providing a systematic attempt to pave a path of compromise not only among the ranks of the Church but also with the emerging national state, the only road available to the papacy on the eve of the modern era.

AFTERWORD

Clement V's important achievement, the *Clementinae*, faithfully reflects his awareness of the dilemmas facing the Christian polity and body, and the pope's attempt to find a compromise between opposing tendencies both inside and outside the Church. Clement learned the lessons of the pontificate of Boniface VIII and, instead of fighting a hopeless battle against secular princes without being assured of the clergy's support, joined forces with the western kings in an attempt to safeguard the papal monarchy. This tendency became most evident in England and France, where Clement's policy reveals itself as a logical reaction to the limitations posed by the emergence of the national state. In this regard, Clement V paved the way for the papacy in the modern era, when ecclesiastical prerogatives became the subject of ever more painful bargaining between the king and the clergy, and between them both and the pope. From an ecclesiastical perspective, however, the consequences of Clement's alliance with the kings of France and England were hardly satisfactory. Papal taxation covered the growing needs of royal treasuries while papal provisions became a convenient compensation for royal clerks. The curia thus lost both income from and influence in the national Churches. Moreover, the growing resentment of the kings' policies of centralisation was easily diverted towards the pope, who offered a convenient target for royal propaganda.

Clement's notorious nepotism, as well, offered a ready target, easily manipulated by his opponents. The constant feeling of being on the verge of death – with cancer affecting the pope's proper functioning throughout his nine-year pontificate – encouraged Clement to favour his relatives, friends, and the whole area of Gascony, where he was born, educated, and schooled in the first stages of a successful ecclesiastical career. The papal registers clearly evince Clement's favouritism, which found ample expression in ecclesiastical appointments. On the other hand, the nomination of relatives to high Church positions was hardly a policy unique to the de Got family; in most cases, furthermore, the pope's relatives justified their nomination, whether in the curia or on difficult diplomatic missions. Ultimately, it was Clement's complete lack of differentiation between the papacy as an institution and himself as the *indignus heres* of St Peter that exposed the pope and the papacy to criticism. Thus, Clement's will, with its generous bequests to his family, friends, and servants, as well as to the treasuries of England and France, put into question the probity of papal policy and its scale of priorities on all fronts.

Beyond the narrow, nepotistic level, Clement's concessions to the western kings, considerable as they were, gained the pope the co-operation of Philip the Fair, Edward I, and Edward II. The advantages of the papal–royal alliance became evident with the transformation of the European political arena. Clement succeeded in avoiding the outbreak of hostilities between England and France, in bringing about the pacification of Flanders, and by 1313 in creating a united Christendom ready to depart *Outremer*. Clement's death in 1314 seemingly proved the ephemeral nature of these achievements: the crusade did not materialise, the unrest in Flanders grew, and in a few years England and France were involved in the Hundred Years War. Furthermore, the endless conflict between the two leading monarchies of Christendom put an end not only to the hopes for an immediate recovery of the Holy Land but also to papal arbitration between Christians. These developments in themselves do not, however, blur the successes of Clement V or the wisdom of his policy. On the contrary, the pope's moderation, as much as it was criticised by his contemporaries, was the only feasible path in fourteenth-century Christendom. One can further point to Clement's achievements in the long term, such as the Hospitaller conquest of Rhodes, the advance of papal authority in Cilician Armenia, Cyprus, and Hungary, and the growing influence of the Catholic Church among both the orthodox Serbians and the pagan Mongols.

Notwithstanding the achievements of his nine-year pontificate, Clement failed entirely to gain the support of his contemporaries. The pope's image, as designed by fourteenth-century authors and often echoed in historical research, was isolated from the historical background and the many limitations imposed on the curia. This is not to say that Clement V was an exemplary pope; it is to assert that he was a true reflection of his age, with political and legal skills above the average. Neither an exemplary pope nor a weak subject of Philip the Fair, Clement V, or more accurately his image, was often sacrificed on the altar of unhistorical judgements, of longings for a more militant papacy that could no longer exist. Dreaming of what Georges Duby has characterised as a perfectly ordained, immutable world, with God being its supreme architect, fourteenth-century chroniclers found it difficult to follow, let alone to justify, the accelerated process of change, which implicated the See of St Peter as well. They looked at the pope and his policy from a conservative point of view, one legitimated by generations, though no longer acceptable. Submission to Philip the Fair, betrayal of Rome and the crusade, the endless list of weaknesses ascribed to Clement V – all hint at the growing gap between the papacy in a process of modernisation and the normative character of most chroniclers. More than papal policy itself, it was this irreconcilable difference in perspective that ultimately condemned Clement V, and his successors after him, to the 'Babylonian captivity' of the papacy.

BIBLIOGRAPHY

PRIMARY SOURCES

Acta Aragonensia: Quellen zur deutschen, italienischen, französischen, spanischen, Kirchen-, und Kulturgeschichte aus der diplomatischen Korrespondenz Jaymes II (1291–1327), ed. Heinrich Finke, 3 vols. (Münster and Berlin, 1908–22)

Acta Clementis PP V (1303–1314) e Regestis Vaticanis aliisque fontibus, ed. F. M. Delorme and A. L. Tâutu, Fontes, ser. 3, vol. VII-1 (Vatican, 1955)

Acta Henrici VII Romanorum Imperatoris et monumenta quaedam alia suorum temporum historiam illustrantia, ed. Francesco Bonaini and Petrus Berti, 2 vols. in 1 (Florence, 1877)

Acta Imperii Angliae et Franciae ab anno 1267 ad annum 1313, ed. Fritz Kern (Tübingen, 1911)

Acta Inter Bonifacium VIII, Benedictum XI, Clementem V PPP et Philippum Pulchrum Regem Christianissimus, ed. S. Vigor and F. Pithou (Paris and Troyes, 1614)

Acta Sanctorum, ed. Socii Bollandiani, new edn, 66 vols. (Paris, 1863–1940)

Actes du Parlement de Paris, ed. E. Boutaric, 2 vols., Inventaires et documents publiés par l'ordre de l'Empereur, ed. Comte de Laborde, 1st ser. (Paris, 1863–7)

Adae Murimuth, *Continuatio chronicarum*, ed. Edward M. Thompson, RS (London, 1889)

Aegidius Romanus, *De ecclesiastica potestate*, ed. R. Scholz (Leipzig, 1929)

'Aegidii Romani impugnatio doctrinae Petri Ioannis Olivi an. 1311–12, nunc primum in lucem edita', ed. Leo Amorós, *Archivum Franciscanum Historium* 27 (1934), pp. 399–451

Agnolo di Tura del Grasso, see *Cronaca Senese attribuita ad*

Agostino Trionfo, *Summa de potestate ecclesiastica edita AD 1320* (Rome, 1584)

'Brevis tractatus super facto Templariorum', in Scholz, *Die Publizistik zur Zeit Philipps des Schönen und Bonifaz VIII*

'Akten des Kanonisationsprozess in dem Codex zu Sulmona, Die', ed. Franz X. Seppelt, in *Monumenta Coelestiniana*, pp. 209–331

Albertini Mussati Paduani . . . Heinrici VII Caesaris Historia Augusta XVI Libris comprehensa, Muratori, *RIS*, vol. x (Milan, 1727), pt 2

Alphabetum narracionum, see Arnold de Liège

Amalric Auger, see *Sexta Vita* and *Septima Vita*

Anciennes chroniques de Flandre, see *Extraits d'une chronique anonyme intitulée Anciennes chroniques de Flandre*

Anglo-Scottish Relations, 1174–1328: Some Selected Documents, ed. E. L. G. Stones (London, 1965)

Bibliography

Annales Austriae, ed. D. Wilhelmus Wattenbach, *MGH, SS*, vol. IX

Annales Cistercensium in Heinrichow, ed. Wilhelmo Arndt, *MGH, SS*, vol. XIX

Annales Colbazienses, ed. Wilhelmo Arndt, *MGH, SS*, vol. XIX

Annales ecclesiastici, ed. G. D. Mansi, 34 vols. (Lucca, 1738–59)

Annales ecclesiastici ab anno 1198 ubi desinit Cardinal Baronius auctore Odorico Raynaldus, 24 vols. (Lucca, 1738–50), vol. XXIII (Lucca, 1749), vol. XXIV (Lucca, 1750)

Annales Forolivienses, ed. Giuseppe Mazzatinti, *RIS*, n.s., vol. XXII-2 (Città di Castello, 1903)

Annales Gandenses, ed. Hilda Johnstone (London, 1951)

Annales Genuenses, see Georgii et Iohannis Stellae

Annales Halesbrunnenses Maiores, ed. G. Waitz, *MGH, SS*, vol. XXIV

Annales Hibernie [Annals of Ireland], in *Chartulaires of St Mary's Abbey – Dublin*, ed. J. Gilbert, 2 vols., *RS* (London, 1884), vol. II

Annales Londonienses, in *Chronicles of the Reigns of Edward I and Edward II*, vol. I

Annales Lubicenses, ed. I. Lappenberg, *MGH, SS*, vol. XVI

Annales monasterii de Oseneia, in *Annales Monastici*, vol. IV

Annales Monastici, ed. H. R. Luard, 5 vols., *RS* (London, 1864–9)

Annales Osterhovenses, ed. W. Wattenbach, *MGH, SS*, vol. XVII

Annales Parmenses Maiores, ed. Philippo Jaffé, *MGH, SS*, vol. XVIII

Annales Paulini, in *Chronicles of the Reigns of Edward I and Edward II*, vol. I

Annales prioratus de Wigornia, in *Annales Monastici*, vol. IV

Annales Tielenses, ed. G. Waitz, *MGH, SS*, vol. XXIV

Annales Urbevetani, ed. L. C. Bethmann, *MGH, SS*, vol. XIX

Annales Zwetlenses, in *Annales Austriae*

Anonymous Short English Metrical Chronicle, An, ed. Ewald Zettl, Early English Text Society 196 (London, 1935)

Arnold de Liège, *Alphabetum narracionum*, ed. Colette Ribaucourt (Ph.D diss., Ecole des Hautes Etudes, 1985)

Bernard Gui, see *Tertia Vita* and *Quarta Vita*

Branche des royaux lignages: Chronique métrique de Guillaume Guiart, ed. J. A. Buchon, Collection des chroniques nationales écrites en langue vulgaire du XIIIe au XVe siècle (Paris, 1828)

Bullarium Franciscanum, ed. K. Eubel, 5 vols. (Rome, 1898–1904)

Caesarius von Heisterbach, *Dialogus Miraculorum*, ed. J. Strange (Cologne, 1856)

Calendar of Documents Relating to Scotland, ed. J. Bain, et al., 5 vols. (London, 1881–8; Edinburgh, 1986)

Calendar of Entries in the Papal Registers Relating to Great Britain and Ireland: Papal Letters, 1305–1342, ed. W. H. Bliss (London, 1895)

Calendar of the Close Rolls Preserved in the Public Record Office (1302–1307) (London, 1908)

Calendar of the Close Rolls Preserved in the Public Record Office (1307–1313) (London, 1892)

Calendar of the Close Rolls Preserved in the Public Record Office (1313–1318) (London, 1893)

Calendar of the Fine Rolls Preserved in the Public Record Office (1272–1307) (London, 1911)

Calendar of the Fine Rolls Preserved in the Public Record Office (1307–1319) (London, 1912)

Calendar of the Patent Rolls Preserved in the Public Record Office (1292–1301) (London, 1895)

Calendar of the Patent Rolls Preserved in the Public Record Office (1301–1307) (London, 1898)

Calendar of the Patent Rolls Preserved in the Public Record Office (1307–1313) (London, 1894)

Calendar of the Patent Rolls Preserved in the Public Record Office (1313–1317) (London, 1898)

Bibliography

Calendar of the Register of John of Drokensford, Bishop of Bath and Wells (1309–1329), ed. Bishop Hobhouse, Somerset Record Society (London, 1887)

Cartulaire général de l'ordre des Hospitaliers de St Jean de Jérusalem, ed. J. Delaville Le Roulx, Bibliothèque des écoles françaises d'Athènes et de Rome, 4 vols. (Paris, 1894–1906)

Chartularium Universitatis Parisiensis, ed. Henricus Denifle and Aemilio Chatelain, 4 vols. (Paris, 1891–9), vol. II

Chronica Monasterii de Melsa a fundatione usque ad annum 1396 auctore Thoma de Burton Abbate, ed. Edward A. Bond, 3 vols., *RS* (London, 1866–8)

Chronica Monasterii S. Albani, ed. H. T. Riley, 7 vols., *RS* (London, 1863–76)

Chronica Monasterii Sancti Bertini auctore Johanne Longo, ed. O. Holder-Egger, *MGH, SS*, vol. XXV

Chronica Pontificum Ecclesiae Eboracensis partes 3, in *The Historians of the Church of York and Its Archbishops*, ed. J. Raine, 3 vols., *RS* (London, 1879–94), vol. II (1886)

Chronicle of Walter of Guisborough Previously Edited as the Chronicle of Walter of Hemingford or Hemingburgh, The, Royal Historical Society, Camden Series 89 (London, 1957)

Chronicles of the Reigns of Edward I and Edward II, ed. William Stubbs, 2 vols., *RS* (London, 1882)

Chronicon Angliae Petriburgense, ed. J. A. Giles, Caxton Society (London, 1845)

Chronicon comitum Flandrensium, in *Recueil des chroniques de Flandre*, vol. I

Chronicon de Lanercost, 1201–1346, ed. Joseph Stevenson (Edinburgh, 1839)

Chronicon Elwacense, ed. D. Otto Abel, *MGH, SS*, vol. X

Chronicon Estense, Muratori, *RIS*, vol. XV (Milan, 1729)

Chronicon Flandriae, in *Recueil des chroniques de Flandre*, vol. I

Chronicon fratris Francisci Pipini Bononiensis Ordinis Praedicatorum (1176–1314), Muratori, *RIS*, vol. IX (Milan, 1726)

Chronicon Galfridi le Baker de Swynebroke, ed. Edward Maunde Thompson (Oxford, 1889)

Chronicon Guillelmi Scoti, *RHGF*, vol. XXI

Chronicon Henrici Knighton vel Cnitthon, Monachi Leycestrensis, ed. Joseph Rawson Lumby, *RS* (London, 1889)

Chronicon Mutinense (1002–1383) auctore Johanne de Bazano, Muratori, *RIS*, vol. XV (Milan, 1729)

Chronicon Parmense ab anno 1038 usque ad annum 1338, ed. Giuliano Bonazzi, *RIS*, n.s., vol. IX-9 (Città di Castello, 1902)

Chronicon Parmense (de Rubeis), in *Acta Imperii Angliae et Franciae*

Chronique artésienne et chronique tournaisienne (1296–1314), ed. Frantz Funck-Brentano, Collection de textes pour servir à l'étude et à l'enseignement de l'histoire (Paris, 1899)

Chronique d'Amadi, in *Chroniques d'Amadi et de Strambaldi*, ed. René de Mas Latrie, Collection de documents inédits sur l'histoire de France, 2 vols. in 1 (Paris, 1891–3), pt 1

Chronique de Ramon Muntaner, ed. J. A. Buchon, Collection des chroniques nationales françaises écrites en langue vulgaire du XIIIe au XVe siècle (Paris, 1827)

Chronique de Strambaldi, in *Chroniques d'Amadi et de Strambaldi*, ed. René de Mas Latrie, Collection de documents inédits sur l'histoire de France, 2 vols. in 1 (Paris, 1891–3), pt 2

Chronique et annales de Gilles le Muisit, abbé de Saint-Martin de Tournai (1272–1352), ed. Henri Lemaître, Société de l'histoire de France (Paris, 1906)

Chronique métrique attribuée à Geffroy de Paris, La, ed. Armel Divèrres (Strasburg, 1956)

Bibliography

Chronique normande du XIVe siècle, ed. Auguste Molinier and Emile Molinier (Paris, 1882)

Chroniques de London, ed. George James Augier, Camden Society (London, 1844)

Chroniques de Sempringham, in *Le livere de reis de Brittanie e le livere de reis de Engleterre*, ed. J. Glover, *RS* (London, 1865)

Chronographia regum Francorum, ed. H. Moranvillé, Société de l'histoire de France, 3 vols. (Paris, 1891–7), vol. I

Clementinarum, 119r, Cambridge University Library, MS Ii iii 7

Clementis Papae V, Monitorum, et declaratio excommunicationis, interdicti, et aliarum poenarum ecclesiasticarum contra Venetos, qui civitatem Ferrariensem et ejus comitatum hostiliter invaserant et occupaverant. Et absolutio a predicta excommunicatione et aliis censuris, per praefatum pontificem Venetis concessa (Rome, 1606)

Codex Diplomaticus Dominii Temporalis S. Sedis, ed. Augustin Theiner, 3 vols. (Rome, 1861–2), vol. I

Codex Diplomaticus Flandriae (1296–1325) ou Recueil de documents relatifs aux guerres et dissensions suscitées par Philippe le Bel, roi de France contre Gui de Dampierre, comte de Flandre, ed. Comte Thierry de Limbourg-Stirum, 2 vols. (Bruges, 1879–89)

Codice diplomatico dantesco, ed. Renato Piattoli (Florence, 1940)

Collectio actorum veterum, in *Vitae*, vol. III

Concilia Magnae Britanniae et Hiberniae, a Synodo Verolamiensi AD 446 ad Londinensem AD 1717, ed. David Wilkins, 4 vols. (London, 1737), vol. II

Conciliorum Oecumenicorum Decreta, ed. Josepho Alberigo, et al., 3rd edn (Bologna, 1973)

Constitutiones et acta publica imperatorum et regum, *MGH, Legum sectio IV*, vols. IV-1, IV-2, ed. Iacobus Schwalm (Hanover, 1906–11)

Continuatio chronici Girardi de Fracheto, *RHGF*, vol. XXI

Continuatio Florianensis, ed. Wilhelmus Wattenbach, *MGH, SS*, vol. IX

Continuatio Mellicensis, in *Annales Austriae*

Continuatio Pontificum Anglica Brevis, ed. O. Holder-Egger, *MGH, SS*, vol. XXX-1

Continuatio Zwetlensis tertia, in *Annales Austriae*

Continuationis chronici Guillelmi de Nangiaco pars prima, in *Chronique latine de Guillaume de Nangis de 1113 à 1300 avec les continuations de cette chronique de 1300 à 1368*, ed. H. Géraud, 2 vols. (Paris, 1843), vol. I

Corpus chronicorum Bononiensium, ed. Albano Sorbelli, *RIS*, n.s., vol. XVIII-1, 3 vols. (Città di Castello, 1911), vol. I

Corpus Iuris Canonici, ed. A. Friedberg, 2 vols. (Leipzig, 1897; cited as *CIC*)

Corpus Iuris Civilis editio stereotypa quinta, ed. Paul Krueger and Theodor Mommsen, 2 vols. (Berolini, 1888–9)

Councils and Synods with Other Documents Relating to the English Church, ed. F. M. Powicke and C. R. Cheney, 2 vols. (Oxford, 1964), vol. II

Cronaca Senese attribuita ad Agnolo di Tura del Grasso detta la Cronaca Maggiore, in *Cronache Senesi*, vols. I and II

Cronaca Senese conosciuta sotto il nome di Paolo di Tommaso Montauri, in *Cronache Senesi*, vol. I

Cronaca Senese di autore anonimo del secolo XIV, in *Cronache Senesi*, vol. I

Cronache Senesi, ed. Alessandro Lisini and Fabio Iacometti, *RIS*, n.s., vol. XV-6, 2 vols. (Bologna, 1934)

Cronica di Dino Compagni delle cose occorrenti ne'tempi suoi, La, ed. Isidoro del Lungo, *RIS*, n.s., vol. IX-2 (Città di Castello, 1913)

Cronica Reinhardsbrunnensis, ed. O. Holder-Egger, *MGH, SS*, vol. XXX-1

Bibliography

Cronica S. Petri Erfordensis Moderna, ed. O. Holder-Egger, *MGH, SS*, vol. xxx-1

Dante Alighieri, *Divina Commedia*, The John Ciardi Translation (New York, 1954)

    Dantis Alagherii Epistolae, ed. Paget Toynbee, 2nd edn (Oxford, 1966)

    Il Convito, translation by Christopher Ryan, Stanford French and Italian Studies (Saratoga, 1989)

    De Monarchia, translation by Prue Shaw, Cambridge Texts in the History of Political Thought (Cambridge, 1996)

Declaration of Arbroath, The, ed. J. Fergusson (Edinburgh, 1970)

Description of the Holy Land by John of Würzburg (AD 1160–1170), Palestine Pilgrims' Text Society 5, pt 2, ed. Aubrey Stewart and C. W. Wilson (London, 1890)

Dino Compagni, see *La cronica di*

Documents and Records Illustrating the History of Scotland, ed. Sir Francis Palgrave (London, 1837)

Documents historiques inédits tirés des collections manuscrites de la bibliothèque royale, ed. Jacques Joseph Champollion-Figeac, 4 vols. (Paris, 1841–8)

Documents Illustrative of the History of Scotland from the Death of King Alexander III to the Accession of Robert Bruce, ed. Joseph Stevenson, 2 vols. (Edinburgh, 1870), vol. II

Documents relatifs aux Etats Généraux et Assemblées réunis sous Philippe le Bel, ed. Georges Picot, Collection de documents inédits sur l'histoire de France, vol. XI (Paris, 1901)

Durandi Episc. Mimatensis, G., *Speculum juris* or *judiciale*, cum Ioan. Andreae, Baldi, ed. Alexandro de Nevo, 2 vols. (Frankfurt, 1592)

E chronici Rotomagensis continuatione, RHGF, vol. XXIII

E chronico Aimerici de Peyraco, Abbatis Moissiacensis, RHGF, vol. XXIII

E chronico anonymi Cadomensis ad annum 1343 perducto, RHGF, vol. XXII

Edward I and the Throne of Scotland, 1290–1296: An Edition of the Record Sources for the Great Cause, ed. E. L. G. Stones and Grant G. Simpson, 2 vols. (Oxford, 1978)

Edward II, the Lords Ordainers, and Piers Gaveston's Jewels and Horses (1312–1313), ed. R. A. Roberts, Camden Miscellany 15 (1929)

English Historical Documents, gen. ed. D. Douglas, 10 vols. (London, 1955–77), vol. III, ed. Harry Rothwell (London, 1975)

English Synodalia of the Thirteenth Century, ed. C. R. Cheney (London, 1940)

Ex altera chronici Rotomagensis continuatione, RHGF, vol. XXIII

Ex anonymo regum Franciae chronico circa annum 1342 scripto, RHGF, vol. XXII

Ex chronico pontificum et imperatorum Ratisponensi, ed. L. Weiland, *MGH, SS*, vol. XXIV

Ex libro memoriarum S. Blasii Brunsuicensis, ed. G. Waitz, *MGH, SS*, vol. XXIV

Excerpta ex expositione Hugonis de Rutlingen in chronicam metricam: 1218–1348, FRG, vol. IV

Extraits d'une chronique anonyme finissant en 1380, RHGF, vol. XXI

Extraits d'une chronique anonyme finissant en 1383, RHGF, vol. XXI

Extraits d'une chronique anonyme française finissant en 1308, RHGF, vol. XXI

Extraits d'une chronique anonyme intitulée Anciennes chroniques de Flandre, RHGF, vol. XXII

Ferreto de' Ferreti, *Historia rerum in Italia gestarum ab anno 1250 ad annum usque 1318*, ed. Carlo Cipolla, Fonti per la Storia di Italia, Istituto Storico Italiano, 2 vols. (Rome, 1908–14), vol. I

Flores historiarum, ed. R. H. Luard, 3 vols., RS (London, 1890), vol. III

Foedera, conventiones, literae . . . inter reges Angliae . . . ab ineunte saeculo duodecimo . . . ad nostra usque tempora, ed. T. Rymer, 10 vols. (The Hague 1739–45), vols. I and II

Fontes Rerum Germanicarum, ed. J. Böhmer, 4 vols. (Stuttgart, 1843–68; cited as FRG)

Bibliography

Fragment d'une chronique anonyme finissant en 1328, et continuée jusqu'en 1340, puis jusqu'en 1383, RHGF, vol. xxi

Fürstenfeld, see *Monachi Fürstenfeldensis*

Gallia Christiana, in provincias ecclesiasticas distributa, ed. D. Sammarthani, et al., 17 vols. (Paris, 1715–86, 1856–65)

Galvano da Levanto, 'Liber sancti passagii Christicolarum contra Saracenos pro recuperatione Terrae Sanctae', in *Mélanges pour servir à l'histoire de l'Orient latin et des croisades*, ed. C. Kohler, 2 vols. (Paris, 1900–6), vol. i, pp. 228–40

Gascon Rolls Preserved in the Public Record Office, 1307–1317, ed. Yves Renouard and Robert Fawtier (London, 1962)

Geffroy de Paris, see *La chronique métrique attribuée à*

Geffroy des Nés, 'La desputaison de l'église de Romme et de l'église de France', in 'Un débat inédit du quatorzième siècle', ed. William P. Shepard, in *Mélanges de linguistique et de littérature offerts à A. Jeanroy par ses élèves et ses amis* (Paris, 1928)

Georgii et Iohannis Stellae, *Annales Genuenses*, ed. Giovanna Petti Balbi, RIS, n.s., vol. xvii-2 (Bologna, 1975)

Gervais du Bus, *Le roman de Fauvel*, ed. Arthur Langfors, Société des anciens textes français (Paris, 1914–19)

Gesta archiepiscoporum Magdeburgensium – Continuatio prima, ed. Guillel. Schum, MGH, SS, vol. xiv

Gesta Edwardi de Carnavan auctore canonico Bridlingtoniensi, in *Chronicles of the Reigns of Edward I and Edward II*, vol. ii

Gesta Regum Continuata, in *The Historical Works of Gervase of Canterbury*, ed. W. Stubbs, 2 vols., RS (London, 1880), vol. ii

Gestorum abbatum monasterii Sancti Trudonis, pars 2, ed. Rudolf Koepke, MGH, SS, vol. x

Giacomo Capocci Viterbese, *De Regimine Christiano*, ed. H. Arquillière, *Le plus ancien traité de l'Eglise: Etude des sources et édition critique* (Paris, 1926)

Giacomo da Viterbo, see Giacomo Capocci Viterbese

Gilles li Muisis, 'Li estas des papes', ed. A. Coville, in *Histoire littéraire de la France* 37 (1938), pp. 250–324

Giovanni Boccaccio, *De casibus virorum illustrium libri novem*, ed. H. Ziegleri (Augsburg, 1544)

Giovanni Villani, *Istorie fiorentine*, Società Tipografica de' Classici Italiani, 8 vols. (Milan, 1802–3)

    Cronica di Giovanni Villani a miglior lezione ridotta, ed. Franc. Gherardi Dragomanni, 4 vols. (Florence, 1845), vol. ii

Grandes chroniques de France, Les, ed. Jules Viard, Société de l'histoire de France, 10 vols. (Paris, 1920–53), vol. viii (Paris, 1934)

Guillaume Durant, see Durandi

Heinrici Rebdorfensis Annales imperatorum et paparum, FRG, vol. iv

Higden, see *Polychronicon Ranulphi Higden*

Histoire du differend d'entre le pape Boniface VIII et Philippes le Bel Roy de France, ed. Pierre Dupuy (Paris, 1655)

Historia diplomatica Friderici Secundi, ed. Jean Louis-Huillard-Bréholles, 11 vols. in 6 (Paris, 1852–61)

Historia et cartularium Monasterii Gloucestriae, ed. W. H. Hart, 3 vols., RS (London, 1876)

Historia Gulielmi et Albrigeti Cortusiorum, De novitatibus Paduae et Lombardiae, Muratori, RIS, vol. xii (Milan, 1728)

Bibliography

Historiae Dunelmensis Scriptores Tres: Gaufridus de Coldingham, Robertus de Graystanes, et Willielmus de Chambre, ed. J. Raines, Surtees Society 9 (Durham, 1839)

Historical Poems of the Fourteenth and Fifteenth Centuries, ed. Rossell Hope Robbins (New York, 1959)

Hugo de Rutlingen, see *Excerpta ex expositione Hugonis de Rutlingen*

Inventaire d'anciens comptes royaux dressés par Robert Mignon sous le règne de Philippe de Valois, ed. Charles V. Langlois (Paris, 1899)

Iohannes Victoriensis [John of Viktring], *1211–1343, FRG*, vol. I

Istore et croniques de Flandres, d'après les textes de divers manuscrits, ed. Kervyn de Lettenhove, in *Recueil des chroniques de Flandre*, vol. I

Italienische Analekten zur Reichsgeschichte des XIV Jahrhunderts (1310–1378), ed. T. E. Mommsen, *Schriften der MGH*, vol. XI (Stuttgart, 1952)

Jean de Jandun, 'Tractatus de laudibus Parisius', in *Histoire générale de Paris: Paris et ses historiens aux XIVe et XVe siècles*, ed. A. le Roux de Lincy, Documents inédits sur l'histoire de France (Paris, 1867)

Jean de St Victor, see *Prima Vita*

Jean d'Hocsem, *Gesta Pontificum Leodiensium*, in *Gesta Pontificum Tungrensium, Traiectensium, et Leodiensium scripserunt auctores praecipui . . .*, ed. Jean Chapeaville, 3 vols. (Liège), 1612–16), vol. II

Jean Froissart, *Chroniques*, ed. G. Diller (Paris, 1972)

Johannes de Trokelowe, *Annales*, in *Chronica Monasterii S. Albani*, vol. IV

Johannes Quidort von Paris, *De potestate regia et papali*, ed. F. Bleienstein (Stuttgart, 1969)

John of Viktring, see *Iohannes Victoriensis*

Knighton, see *Chronicon Henrici Knighton*

Laie Bible, La, ed. J. Clarke (New York, 1923)

Lettres de rois, reines, et autres personnages des cours de France et d'Angleterre depuis Louis VII jusqu'à Henri IV, ed. Jacques Joseph Champollion-Figeac, vol. IX-2, Collection de documents inédits sur l'histoire de France, 2 vols. (Paris, 1839)

Lettres inédites de Philippe le Bel, ed. Adolphe Baudouin (Paris, 1887)

Lettres secrètes et curiales du pape Jean XXII relatives à la France, ed. A. Coulon and S. Clemencet, 4 vols. (Paris, 1900–60)

Liber Epistolaris of Richard of Bury, ed. Noël Denholm-Young, Roxburghe Club (Oxford, 1950)

Livre des coutumes, ed. H. Barckhausen (Bordeaux, 1890)

Livre des privilèges, Archives municipales de Bordeaux 2 (Bordeaux, 1878)

Livres des bouillons, Archives municipales de Bordeaux 1 (Bordeaux, 1867)

Luccheser Fortsetzung derselben Chronik, in *Acta Imperii Angliae et Franciae*

Marcha di Marco Battagli da Rimini (1212–1354), ed. Aldo Francesco Massèra, *RIS*, n.s., vol. XVI-3 (Città di Castello, 1912)

Marino Sanudo Torsello, 'Liber secretorum fidelium crucis', in *Gesta Dei per Francos*, ed. Jacques de Bongars, 2 vols. (Hanau, 1611), vol. II

Martini continuatio Brabantina, ed. L. Weiland, *MGH, SS*, vol. XXIV

Martini continuationes Anglicae Fratrum Minorum, ed. L. Weiland, *MGH, SS*, vol. XXIV

Matthew of Nüwenburg, see *Matthiae Nuewenburgensis*

Matthew Paris, *Chronica Majora*, ed. H. Luard, 7 vols., *RS* (London, 1872–83)

Matthiae Nuewenburgensis [Matthew of Nüwenburg], *Cronica 1273–1350, FRG*, vol. IV

Monachi Fürstenfeldensis (vulgo Volcmari) [Fürstenfeld], *Chronica de gestis principum a tempore Ruldolfi regis usque ad tempora Ludwici imperatoris. 1273–1326, FRG*, vol. I

Bibliography

Monumens [sic] historiques relatifs à la condamnation des chevaliers du Temple et à l'abolition de leur ordre, ed. M. Raynouard (Paris, 1813)

Monumenta Coelestiniana, Quellen zur Geschichte des Papstes Coelestin V, ed. Franz X. Seppelt (Paderborn, 1921)

Monumenta Germaniae Historica: Scriptores, ed. G. H. Pertz, et al. (Hanover, Weimar, Berlin, Stuttgart, and Cologne, 1826–34; cited as *MGH, SS*)

Murimuth, see Adae Murimuth

Nicolai episcopi Botrontinensis Relatio de itinere italico Henrici VII imperatoris ad Clementem V papam, in *Collectio actorum veterum*

Notae ad vitas paparum Avenionensium, in *Vitae*, vol. II

Olim ou registres des arrêts rendus par la cour du roi sous les règnes de St Louis . . . (1254–1318), Les, Documents inédits sur l'histoire de France, 4 vols. (Paris, 1839–48), vol. II

'*Opus metricum des Kardinals Jacobus Gaietani Stefaneschi, Das*', ed. Franz X. Seppelt, in *Monumenta Coelestiniana*, pp. 1–146

Ordonnances des roys de France de la troisième race, ed. M. de Laurière, 21 vols. (Paris, 1723–34), vol. I

Original Papal Letters in England, 1305–1415, ed. Patrick N. R. Zutshi (Vatican, 1990)

Paolo di Tommaso Montauri, see *Cronaca Senese conosciuta sotto il nome di*

Patrologiae cursus completus Series Latina, ed. J. P. Migne (Paris, 1844–64; cited as *PL*)

Paulin, bishop of Pozzuoli, see *Quinta Vita*

Petri Azarii, *Liber Gestorum in Lombardia*, ed. Francesco Cognasso, *RIS*, n.s., vol. XVI-4 (Bologna, 1939)

Petri Cantinelli, *Chronicon (1228–1306)*, ed. Francesco Torraca, *RIS*, n.s., vol. XXVIII-2 (Città di Castello, 1902)

Pierre Dubois, *Summaria brevis et compendiosa doctrina felicis expedicionis et abreviacionis guerrarum ac litium regni Francorum*, ed. Hellmut Kämpf (Leipzig and Berlin, 1936)

   De recuperatione Terrae Sanctae, ed. Angelo Diotti (Florence, 1977)

Piers Plowman, see *The Vision of*

Pisaner Chronik, in *Acta Imperii Angliae et Franciae*

Polychronicon Ranulphi Higden Monachi Cestrensis, ed. Rev. Joseph Rawson Lumby, 9 vols., *RS* (London, 1865–86)

Prima Vita Clementis V auctore Joanne canonico Sancti Victoris Parisiensis, in *Vitae*, vol. I

Privilèges accordés à la couronne de France par le Saint Siège, ed. A. Tardif, Collection des documents inédits sur l'histoire de France 4 (Paris, 1855)

PRO, Ancient Correspondence, 15/87, 20/77

PRO, Chancery Diplomatic Documents (C47), 29/1/16

PRO, Liber B, fol. 256r

PRO, SC 1/14/144

PRO, SC 7/11/13

PRO, SC 7/11/16

PRO, SC 7/11/24

PRO, SC 7/11/33

PRO, SC 7/12/14

Procès des Templiers, Le, ed. M. Michelet, 2 vols., Collection de documents inédits sur l'histoire de France, vol. XXIX-1 (Paris, 1841–51)

'Procès-verbal du dernier consistoire sécret préparatoire à la canonisation de S. Pierre de Morrone', *Analecta Bollendiana* 16 (1897), pp. 389–92, 475–87

Quarta Vita Clementis V (excerpta ex chronicis quae nuncupantur *Flores chronicorum* seu

Bibliography

Cathalogus pontificum romanorum) auctore Bernardo Guidonis episcopo Lodovensi, in *Vitae*, vol. I

Quinta Vita Clementis V, Paulino veneto ordinis fratrum minorum, episcopo Puteolano, in *Vitae*, vol. I

Records of Antony Bek, Bishop and Patriarch, 1283–1311, ed. C. M. Fraser, Surtees Society 162 (London, 1953)

Records of the Trial of Walter Langton, ed. Alice Beardwood, Camden 4th ser. (London, 1969)

Recueil des chroniques de Flandre, ed. J. J. de Smet, 4 vols. (Brussels, 1837–65)

Recueil des historiens des Gaules et de la France, ed. M. Bouquet, et al. (Paris, 1737–1904; cited as *RHGF*)

Regesta Pontificum Romanorum ad 1304, ed. A. Potthast (Berlin, 1874–5)

Regestum Clementis Papae V ex Vaticanis archetypis . . . nunc primum editum cura et studio monachorum ordinis sancti Benedicti, 8 vols., Bibliothèque des écoles françaises d'Athènes et de Rome (Rome, 1884–94)

Register of John de Halton, Bishop of Carlisle, 1292–1324, The, ed. W. N. Thompson, 2 vols., Canterbury and York Society 12–13 (London, 1913)

Register of William Greenfield, Lord Archbishop of York (1306–1315), The, ed. William Brown and A. Hamilton Thompson, 5 vols., Surtees Society 145–53 (Durham, 1931–8)

Registres de Boniface VIII, Les, ed. G. Digard, et al., 4 vols., Bibliothèque des écoles françaises d'Athènes et de Rome (Paris, 1884–1931)

Registres de Nicolas III (1277–1280), Les, ed. Jules Gay, Bibliothèque des écoles françaises d'Athènes et de Rome (Paris, 1898–1932)

Registres de Nicolas IV, Les, ed. Ernest Langlois, 2 vols., Bibliothèque des écoles françaises d'Athènes et de Rome (Paris, 1886–91)

Registres du Trésor des Chartes: Règne de Philippe le Bel – Inventaire analytique, ed. Robert Fawtier (Paris, 1958), vol. I

Registrum Henrici Woodlock, diocesis Wintoniensis, ed. A. W. Goodman, 2 vols., Canterbury and York Society 43–4 (Oxford, 1940–1)

Registrum Malmesburiense, ed. J. Brewer, 2 vols., *RS* (London, 1879–80)

Registrum Palatinum Dunelmense, the Register of Richard de Kellawe, Lord Palatine and Bishop of Durham, 1311–1316, ed. Thomas Duffus Hardy, 4 vols., *RS* (London, 1873)

Registrum Ricardi de Swinfield episcopi Heresfordensis, 1283–1317, ed. William W. Capes, Canterbury and York Society 6 (London, 1909)

Registrum Roberti Winchelsey Cantuariensis archiepiscopi (1294–1313), ed. Rose Graham, 2 vols., Canterbury and York Society 51–2 (Oxford, 1952–6)

Registrum Simonis de Gandavo diocesis Saresbiriensis, AD 1297–1315, 3 pts, ed. C. T. Flower and M. C. B. Dawes, 2 vols., Canterbury and York Society 41 (Oxford, 1914–34)

'Relatio commissionis in concilio Viennensi institutae ad decretalem "Exivi de paradiso" praeparandam', ed. G. Fussenegger, *Archivum Franciscanum historicum* 50 (1957), pp. 145–77

Répertoire des sources historiques du moyen âge, ed. U. Chevalier, 2 vols. (Paris, 1905–7)

Rerum Britannicarum Medii Aevi Scriptores (Rolls Series) (London, 1858–96; cited as *RS*)

Rerum Italicarum Scriptores, ed. L. A. Muratori (Milan, 1723–38; cited as *RIS*)

Rerum Italicarum Scriptores, n.s., ed. G. Carducci, et al. (Città di Castello and Bologna, 1900–; cited as *RIS*, n.s.)

Rishanger, see *Willelmi Rishanger . . . Chronica*

Bibliography

Rôles gascons, Collection des documents inédits sur l'histoire de France, 3 vols. (Paris, 1885–1962), vol. II, ed. Charles Bémont (Paris, 1900)

Rotuli Parliamentorum, ut et petitiones, et placita in Parliamento (1278–1503), ed. J. Topham, P. Morant, and T. Astle, 6 vols. (London, 1783)

Sacrorum Conciliorum Nova et Amplissima Collectio, ed. G. Mansi, 59 vols. (Florence and Venice, 1759–98; cited as *Concilia*)

Scottish Historical Documents, ed. G. Donaldson (Edinburgh, 1974)

Scriptores Ordinis Praedicatorum, ed. Jacobus Quétif and Jacobus Echard, 2 vols. (Paris, 1719–21)

Secunda Vita Clementis V auctore Ptolemaeo Lucensi ordinis praedicatorum (excerpta ex *Historia ecclesiastica*), in *Vitae*, vol. I

Septima Vita Joannis XXII auctore Amalrico Augerii, priore Beate Marie de Aspirano Elnensis dioecesis (excerpta e chronicis quae dicuntur *Actus Romanorum Pontificum*), in *Vitae*, vol. I

Sexta Vita Clementis V auctore Amalrico Augerii de Biterris priore Sanctae Mariae de Aspirano in dioecesi Elnensi (excerpta e chronicis quae dicuntur *Actus Romanorum Pontificum*), in *Vitae*, vol. I

Sifridi de Balnhusin Compendium Historiarum, ed. O. Holder-Egger, *MGH, SS*, vol. XXV

Statutes of the Realm, The, vol. I (London, 1810)

Storia dal principio del secolo XIII fino al 1341 di un anonimo fiorentino con annotazioni di un anonimo lucchese, in *Miscellanea Novo Ordine Digesta*, ed. E. Baluze and J. D. Mansi, 4 vols. (Lucca 1761–4), vol. IV

Storie Pistoresi (1300–1348), ed. Silvio Adrasto Barbi, *RIS*, n.s., vol. XI-I (Città di Castello, 1927)

Tables des Registres de Clément V, ed. Yvonne Lanhers and Cyrille Vogel, Robert Fawtier and Guillaume Mollat, 2 vols. (Paris, 1948–57)

Tertia Vita Clementis V auctore Bernardo Guidonis episcopo Lodovensis (excerpta e *Cathalogo Brevi Romanorum Pontificum*), in *Vitae*, vol. I

Thomae Walsingham, *Historia Anglicana*, in *Chronica monasterii S. Albani*, vols. I and II (London, 1863–4)

> *Ypodigma Neustriae a Thoma Walsingham*, in *Chronica monasterii S. Albani*, vol. VII (London, 1876)

Tolomeo da Lucca, see *Secunda Vita*

Tractatus contra articulos inventos ad diffamandum sanctissimum patrem dominum Bonifacium papam sancte memorie et de commendacione eiusdem, in Heinrich Finke, *Aus den Tagen Bonifaz VIII, Quellen*

Treaty Rolls Preserved in the Public Record Office (1234–1325), vol. I, ed. Pierre Chaplais (London, 1955)

Triatez des droits et libertéz de l'Eglise gallicane, ed. Pierre Dubois, 2 vols. (Rouen, 1639)

Trithemius, *Chronicon Hirsaugiensi*, in *Concilia*, ed. Mansi, vol. XXV

Trokelowe, see Johannes de Trokelowe

Vetera Monumenta Hibernorum et Scotorum Historiam Illustrantia (1216–1547), ed. Augustinus Theiner (Rome, 1864)

Vetera Monumenta Historica Hungariam Sacram Illustrantia (1216–1352), ed. Augustinus Theiner, 2 vols. (Rome, 1859–60)

Vetera Monumenta Poloniae et Lithuaniae gentiumque finitimarum historiam illustrantia (1217–1409), ed. Augustinus Theiner, 2 vols. (Rome, 1860–4)

Bibliography

Vetera Monumenta Slavorum Meridionalicum Historiam Illustrantia (1198–1549), ed. Augustinus Theiner, 2 vols. (Rome, 1863–4)

Veterum scriptorum et monumentorum historicorum, dogmaticorum, moralium amplissima collectio, ed. Edmond Martène and U. Durand, 9 vols. (Paris, 1724–33)

'Vie et miracles de S. Pierre Célestin par deux de ses disciples', *Analecta Bollandiana* 16 (1897), pp. 393–458

Villani, see Giovanni Villani

Vision of William Concerning Piers Plowman – Text B, The, ed. W. Skeat, Early English Text Society (Oxford, 1869)

'*Vita* Coelestini V des Petrus de Alliaco, Die' and 'Die *Vita* Coelestini V des Matteus Vegius', ed. Franz X. Seppelt, in *Monumenta Coelestiniana*, pp. 147–208

Vita Edwardi Secundi Monachi Cuiusdam Malmesberiensis, ed. Noël Denholm-Young (London, 1957)

Vitae Paparum Avenionensium hoc est historia pontificum romanorum . . . ab anno Christi 1305 usque ad annum 1394, ed. Etienne Baluze, new edn, Guillaume Mollat, 4 vols. (Paris 1916–28)

Walsingham, see Thomae Walsingham

Walter of Guisborough, see *The Chronicle of*

Willelmi Rishanger quondam monachi S. Albani Chronica, in *Chronica monasterii S. Albani*, vol. III (London, 1865), pp. 1–230

Willelmi Tyronensis Archiepiscopi, ed. R. B. C. Huygens, 2 vols., Corpus Christianorum 63 (Turnhout, 1986)

Zeugenverhör des Franciscus de Moliano (1312), Das, ed. A. Seraphim (Königsberg, 1912)

SECONDARY SOURCES

Abulafia, David, *A Mediterranean Emporium: The Catalan Kingdom of Majorca* (Cambridge, 1994)

Adam, Paul, *La vie paroissiale en France au XIVe siècle* (Paris, 1964)

Andrat, L., 'L'entrevue de Bertrand de Got et de Philippe le Bel à Saint Jean d'Angély', *Bulletin de la Société des archives historiques de la Saintonge et de l'Aunis* 5 (1885), pp. 230–2

Aratò, Paulus, 'Bibliographia Historiae Pontificae', *Archivum Historiae Pontificae* 17 (1979), pp. 481–678

Arnaldi, Girolamo, 'Le origini del Patrimonio di S. Pietro', in *Comuni e signorie nell' Italia nordorientale e centrale*, ed. G. Galasso, *Storia d'Italia*, vol. VII (Turin, 1987), pp. 105–47

Arquillière, H. X., 'L'appel au concile sous Philippe le Bel et la genèse des théories conciliaires', *Revue des questions historiques* 45 (1911), pp. 23–55

Ashtor, Eliahu, 'Investments in Levant Trade in the Period of the Crusades', *Journal of European Economic History* 14 (1985), pp. 427–41

Atiya, A. S., *The Crusade in the Later Middle Ages* (London, 1938)

Aux origines de l'état moderne: Le fonctionnement administratif de la papauté d'Avignon (Rome, 1990)

Backman, Clifford R., 'The Papacy, the Sicilian Church, and King Frederick III (1302–1321)', *Viator* 22 (1991), pp. 229–49

  The Decline and Fall of Medieval Sicily: Politics, Religion, and Economy in the Reign of Frederick III, 1296–1337 (Cambridge, 1995)

Baethgen, F., *Der Engelpapst: Idee und Wirklichkeit* (Leipzig, 1943)

Barber, Malcolm, 'James of Molay, the Last Grand Master of the Order of the Temple', *Studia monastica* 14–1 (1972), pp. 91–124

'Propaganda in the Middle Ages: The Charges Against the Templars', *Nottingham Mediaeval Studies* 17 (1973), pp. 42–57

The Trial of the Templars (London, 1978)

'Lepers, Jews, and Moslems: The Plot to Overthrow Christendom in 1321', *History* 66 (1981), pp. 1–17

'The World Picture of Philip the Fair', *Journal of Medieval History* 8 (1982), pp. 13–27

The New Knighthood: A History of the Order of the Temple (Cambridge, 1994)

Barbiche, Bernard, *Les actes pontificaux originaux des Archives nationales de Paris*, vol. III (Vatican, 1982)

'Les procureurs des rois de France à la cour pontificale d'Avignon', in *Aux origines de l'état moderne*, pp. 81–112

Barone, Giulia, 'L'oeuvre eschatologique de Pierre Jean-Olieu et son influence: Un bilan historiographique', *Cahiers de Fanjeaux* 27 (1992), pp. 49–61

Barraclough, Geoffrey, *Public Notaries and the Papal Curia* (London, 1934)

Papal Provisions: Aspects of Church History, Constitutional, Legal, and Administrative in the Later Middle Ages (Oxford, 1935)

Barrow, G. W. S., *The Kingdom of the Scots: Government, Church, and Society from the Eleventh to the Fourteenth Century* (London, 1973)

Robert Bruce and the Community of the Realm of Scotland, 3rd edn (Edinburgh, 1988)

Bautier, Robert-Henri, 'Diplomatique et histoire politique: Ce que la critique diplomatique nous apprend sur la personnalité de Philippe le Bel', *Revue historique* 259 (1978), pp. 1–27

Beardwood, Alice, 'The Trial of Walter Langton, Bishop of Lichfield, 1307–1312', *Transactions of the American Philosophical Society*, n.s., 54 (1964), pt 3, pp. 5–42

Beaune, Colette, 'Les rois maudits', *Razo: Cahiers du centre d'études médiévales de Nice* 12 (1992), pp. 2–24

Bellone, Ernesto, 'Cultura e studi nei progetti di riforma presentati al concilio di Vienne (1311–1312)', *Annuarium Historiae Conciliorum* 9 (1977), pp. 67–111

Berger, Elie, 'Jacques II d'Aragon, le Saint-Siège, et la France', *Journal des Savants*, n.s., 6 (1908), pp. 281–94, 348–59

'Bulle de Clément V en faveur de Guillaume de Nogaret', in *Mélanges offerts à Emile Chatelain par ses élèves et ses amis* (Paris, 1910), pp. 268–70

Bernard, J., 'Le népotisme de Clément V et ses complaisances pour la Gascogne', *Annales du Midi* 61 (1949), pp. 369–411

Bernstein, Alan B., '*Magisterium* and License: Corporate Autonomy Against Papal Authority in the Medieval University of Paris', *Viator* 9 (1978), pp. 291–307

Bingham, Caroline, *The Life and Times of Edward II* (London, 1973)

Bishop, M., *Petrarch and His World* (Bloomington, Ind., 1963)

Bisson, Thomas N., 'The General Assemblies of Philip the Fair: Their Character Reconsidered', *Studia Gratiana* 15 (1972), pp. 537–64

Black, J. G., 'Edward I and Gascony in 1300', *English Historical Review* 17 (1902), pp. 518–27

Blancard, L., 'Documents relatifs au procès des Templiers en Angleterre', *Revue des sociétés savantes*, 4th ser., 6 (1867)

Boase, T., *Boniface VIII* (London, 1933)

Bibliography

Boase, T. S. R., 'The History of the Kingdom', in *The Cilician Kingdom of Armenia*, pp. 1–33

Bordeaux sous les rois d'Angleterre, ed. Yves Renouard (Bordeaux, 1965)

Bordonove, Georges, *Philippe le Bel: Roi de fer* (Paris, 1984)

Boucherie, J., 'Inventaire des titres qui se trouvent au trésor de l'archevêché de Bordeaux', *Archives historiques de la Gironde* 23 (1893)

Bourgain, L., 'Contribution du clergé à l'impôt sous la monarchie française', *Revue des questions historiques*, n.s., 48 (1890), pp. 62–132

Bousquet, Péroline, 'Papal Provisions in Hungary, 1305–1370', (MA thesis), *Annual of Medieval Studies at the Central European University* (1994–5), pp. 101–11

Boutaric, Edgard, *La France sous Philippe le Bel: Etude sur les institutions politiques et administratives du moyen âge* (Paris, 1861)

'Notices et extraits de documents inédits relatifs à l'histoire de France sous Philippe le Bel', *Notices et extraits des manuscrits de la Bibliothèque impériale* 20–2 (1865), pp. 83–237

'Clément V, Philippe le Bel, et les Templiers', *Revue des questions historiques* 10 (1871), pp. 301–42; 11 (1872), pp. 5–42

Bowsky, William, 'Clement V and the Emperor-elect', *Medievalia et Humanistica* 12 (1958), pp. 52–69

'Dante's Italy: A Political Dissection', *Historian* 21 (1958), pp. 82–100

'Florence and Henry of Luxemburg, King of the Romans: The Rebirth of Guelfism', *Speculum* 33 (1958), pp. 177–203

Henry VII in Italy: The Conflict of Empire and City-State, 1310–1313 (Lincoln, 1960)

A Medieval Italian Commune: Siena Under the Nine, 1287–1355 (Berkeley, 1981)

Boyle, Leonard E., 'A Committee Stage at the Council of Vienne', in *Studia in Honorem Eminentissimi Cardinalis Alphonsi M. Stickler*, pp. 25–35

Brandt, Walter I., 'Pierre Dubois, Modern or Medieval?', *American Historical Review* 35 (1930), pp. 507–21

Bréhier, Louis, *L'Eglise et l'Orient au moyen âge*, 5th edn (Paris, 1928)

Brejon de Lavergnée, J., 'Le serment de fidélité des clercs au roi de France pour le temporel relevant de la couronne', in *Mélanges offerts à Jean Dauvillier* (Toulouse, 1979), pp. 127–33

Brel-Bordaz, Odile, 'Broderies d'*Opus Anglicanum* à Saint-Bertrand-de-Comminges', *Monuments historiques de la France* 115 (1981), pp. 65–7

Brentano, Robert, *Rome Before Avignon: A Social History of Thirteenth-Century Rome* (London, 1991)

Brett James, Norman G., 'John of Drokensford, Bishop of Bath and Wells', *Transactions of the London and Middlesex Archaeological Society*, n.s., 10 (1951), pp. 281–301

Brown, Elizabeth A. R., '*Cessante causa* and the Taxes of the Last Capetians: The Political Applications of a Philosophical Maxim', *Studia Gratiana* 15 (1972), pp. 565–87

'Taxation and Morality in the Thirteenth and Fourteenth Centuries: Conscience and Political Power and the Kings of France', *French Historical Studies* 8–1 (1973), pp. 1–28

'Royal Salvation and Needs of State in Late Capetian France', in *Order and Innovation in the Middle Ages: Essays in Honor of Joseph R. Strayer*, ed. William C. Jordan, Bruce McNab, and Teófilo Ruiz (Princeton, 1976), pp. 365–83

'The Prince Is Father of the King: The Character and Childhood of Philip the Fair of France', *Medieval Studies* 49 (1987), pp. 282–334

Bibliography

'The Political Repercussions of Family Ties in the Early Fourteenth Century: The Marriage of Edward II of England and Isabelle of France', *Speculum* 63 (1988), pp. 573–95

'Diplomacy, Adultery, and Domestic Politics at the Court of Philip the Fair: Queen Isabelle's Mission to France in 1314', in *Documenting the Past*, pp. 53–83

'The Marriage of Edward II of England and Isabelle of France: A Postscript', *Speculum* 64 (1989), pp. 373–9

Customary Aids and Royal Finance in Capetian France: The Marriage Aid of Philip the Fair (Cambridge, Mass., 1992)

Bryson, William Hamilton, 'Papal Releases from Royal Oaths', *Journal of Ecclesiastical History* 22 (1971), pp. 19–33

Buck, Mark, *Politics, Finance, and the Church in the Reign of Edward II: Walter Stapeldon, Treasurer of England* (Cambridge, 1983)

Bulst-Thiele, M. L., *Sacrae Domus Militiae Templi Hierosolymitani Magistri: Untersuchungen zur Geschichte des Templerordens 1118/19–1314* (Göttingen, 1974)

Burns, Alfred, *The Power of the Written Word: The Role of Literacy in the History of Western Civilization* (Cambridge, 1987)

Burns, Charles, 'Vatican Sources and the Honorary Papal Chaplains of the Fourteenth Century', in *Römische Kurie. Kirchliche Finanzen. Vatikanisches Archiv. Studien zu Ehren von Hermann Hoberg*, Miscellanea Historiae Pontificiae 45 (Rome, 1979), pp. 65–95

Burns, Robert I., 'The Catalan Company and the European Powers, 1305–1311', *Speculum* 29 (1954), pp. 751–71

'Christian–Islamic Confrontation in the West: The Thirteenth-Century Dream of Conversion', *American Historical Review* 76 (1971), pp. 1386–1434

Burr, David, *Olivi and Franciscan Poverty: The Origins of the Usus Pauper Controversy* (Philadelphia, 1989)

Caggese, R., *Roberto d'Angiò e i suoi tempi*, 2 vols. (Florence, 1921–30)

Caillet, L., *La papauté d'Avignon et l'Eglise de France* (Paris, 1975)

Callebant, André, 'Une soi-disant bulle de Clément V contre Saint Gautier de Bruges, évêque de Poitiers, OFM', *Archivum Franciscanum Historicum* 8 (1915), pp. 667–72

'Une bulle du temps de Frédéric II exploitée sous Clément V contre Saint Gautier, évêque de Poitiers', *Archivum Franciscanum Historicum* 16 (1923), pp. 34–56

Caman, Emile, *Papes et antipapes à Avignon* (Avignon, 1931)

Campbell, G., 'The Attitude of Monarchy Toward the Use of Ecclesiastical Censures in the Reign of St Louis', *Speculum* 35 (1960), pp. 535–55

Carpenter, David, 'St Thomas Cantilupe: His Political Career', in *St Thomas of Cantilupe, Bishop of Hereford*, pp. 57–72

Casagrande, Carla, 'La femme gardée', in *Histoire des femmes en Occident*, pp. 83–116

Caselli, Fausto Piola, 'L'espansione delle fonti finanziarie della Chiesa nel XIV secolo', *Archivio della Società romana di storia patria* 110 (1987), pp. 63–97

'L'evoluzione della contabilità camerale nel periodo avignonese', in *Aux origines de l'état moderne*, pp. 411–37

Causse, Bernard, *Eglise, finance, et royauté: La floraison des décimes dans la France du moyen âge*, 2 vols. (Lille and Paris, 1988)

Cavalcabò, A., *Le ultime lotte del comune di Cremona per l'autonomia* (Cremona, 1937)

Chaplais, Pierre, 'Some Private Letters of Edward I', *English Historical Review* 77 (1962), pp. 79–86

Piers Gaveston: Edward II's Adoptive Brother (Oxford, 1994)

Bibliography

Cheney, C. R., *Notaries Public in England in the Thirteenth and Fourteenth Centuries* (Oxford, 1972)

'The Downfall of the Templars and a Letter in Their Defence', (1965), 2nd edn in *Medieval Texts and Studies*, ed. C. R. Cheney (Oxford, 1973), pp. 314–27

Chevalier, U., *Répertoire des sources historiques du moyen âge*, 2 vols. (1894–9, repr. New York, 1959)

Chiappini, Luciano, *Gli Estensi* (Oglio, 1967)

Christophe, Jean-Baptiste, *Histoire de la papauté pendant le XIVe siècle*, 3 vols. (Paris, 1853)

Cilician Kingdom of Armenia, The, ed. T. S. R. Boase, et al. (Edinburgh, 1978)

Cipolla, Carlo M., 'Une crise ignorée: Comment s'est perdue la propriété ecclésiastique dans l'Italie du nord entre le XIe et le XVIe siècle', *Annales ESC* 2 (1947), pp. 317–27

Clergeac, A., 'Les concessions d'indulgences de Clément V aux églises de Gascogne', *Revue de Gascogne*, n.s., 22 (1927), pp. 104–12

Cognasso, Francesco, 'L'unificazione della Lombardia sotto Milano', in *Storia di Milano*, Fondazione G. Treccani degli Alfieri per la Storia di Milano, 17 vols. (Milan, 1953–66), vol. v (Milan, 1955), pp. 1–567

Condello, Emma, 'I Codici Stefaneschi: Uno scriptorium cardinalizio del trecento tra Roma e Avignone?', *Archivio della Società romana di storia patria* 110 (1988), pp. 21–61

Constable, Olivia R., *Trade and Traders in Muslim Spain* (Cambridge, 1994)

Conway Davies, James, *The Baronial Opposition to Edward II: Its Character and Policy – A Study in Administrative History*, 2nd edn (Cambridge, 1918)

Coste, Jean, 'Les lettres collectives des papes d'Avignon à la noblesse romaine', in *Aux origines de l'état moderne*, pp. 151–70

Coulton, George Gordon, *Life in the Middle Ages*, 4 vols. (Cambridge, 1928–30)

Cox Russell, Josiah, 'The Canonization of Opposition to the King in Angevin England', in *Anniversary Essays in Medieval History by Students of Charles Homer Haskins* (New York and Boston, 1929), pp. 279–90

Curley, M., 'An Episode in the Conflict Between Boniface VIII and Philip the Fair', *Catholic Historical Review*, n.s., 7 (1927), pp. 194–226

Curtius, E. R., *La littérature européenne et le moyen âge latin* (Paris, 1956)

Cuttino, G. P., *English Diplomatic Administration, 1259–1339*, 2nd edn (Oxford, 1971)

Dalarun, Jacques, 'Regards de clercs', in *Histoire des femmes en Occident*, pp. 31–54

Davidsohn, R., *Forschungen zur Geschichte von Florenz*, 4 vols. (Berlin, 1896–1908)
Geschichte von Florenz, 4 vols. (Berlin, 1896–1927)

Day, John, *The Medieval Market Economy* (Oxford, 1987)

De Flamere, L., 'Le pape Clément V à Nevers', *Bulletin historique et philologique du comité des travaux historiques* (1890), pp. 13–22

De Vic, Claude, and J. Vaissête, *Histoire générale du Languedoc*, 10 vols. (Toulouse, 1872–)

Dean, Trevor, *Land and Power in Late Medieval Ferrara: The Rule of the Este, 1350–1450* (Cambridge, 1988)

Deeley, Ann, 'Papal Provision and Royal Rights of Patronage in the Early Fourteenth Century', *English Historical Review* 43 (1928), pp. 497–527

Della Piana, M., 'Intorno a una bolla papale: La *Pastoralis cura* di Clemente V', *Rivista storica del diritto italiano* 31 (1958), pp. 23–50

Demurger, Alain, *Vie et mort de l'ordre du Temple* (Paris, 1993)

Denifle, H., *Die Universitäten des Mittelalters bis 1400* (Berlin, 1885)

Denton, Jeffrey H., 'Pope Clement V's Early Career as a Royal Clerk', *English Historical Review* 83 (1968), pp. 303–14

Bibliography

'Canterbury Archiepiscopal Appointments: The Case of Walter Reynolds', *Journal of Medieval History* 1 (1975), pp. 317–27

'Walter Reynolds and Ecclesiastical Politics, 1313–1316: A Postscript to "Councils and Synods, II"', in *Church and Government in the Middle Ages: Essays Presented to C. R. Cheney*, ed. C. N. L. Brooke, et al. (Cambridge, 1976), pp. 247–75

Robert Winchelsey and the Crown, 1294–1313: A Study in the Defence of Ecclesiastical Liberty (Cambridge, 1980)

'The Clergy and Parliament in the Thirteenth and Fourteenth Centuries', in *The English Parliament in the Middle Ages*, ed. R. G. Davies and J. H. Denton (Manchester, 1981), pp. 88–108

'Complaints to the Apostolic See in an Early Fourteenth-Century Memorandum from England', *Archivum Historiae Pontificiae* 20 (1982), pp. 389–402

Documenting the Past: Essays in Medieval History Presented to George Peddy Cuttino, ed. J. S. Hamilton and Patricia J. Bradley (Woodbridge, 1989)

Doherty, Paul Charles, 'The Date of the Birth of Isabella, Queen of England (1308–1358)', *Bulletin of the Institute of Historical Research* 48 (1975), pp. 246–8

Dubois, Jacques OSB, 'Grandmontains et Chartreux, ordres nouveaux du XIIe siècle', in *L'ordre de Grandmont: Art et histoire*, Actes des journées d'études de Montpellier, 7–8 octobre 1989, ed. Geneviève Durand and Jean Nougaret (Montpellier, 1992), pp. 3–22

Duchesne, François, *Histoire de tous les cardinaux français de naissance*, 2 vols. (Paris, 1690)

Duffour, J., 'Doléances des évêques gascons au Concile de Vienne (1311)', *Revue de Gascogne*, n.s., 5 (1905), pp. 244–59

'Le lieu de naissance de Clément V', *Revue de Gascogne*, n.s., 5 (1905), p. 371

Dupré-Theseider, Eugenio, *Roma dal comune di popolo alla signoria pontificia (1252–1377)*, in *Storia di Roma*, vol. XI (Bologna, 1952)

Problemi del papato avignonese (Bologna, 1961)

Edbury, Peter W., *The Kingdom of Cyprus and the Crusades, 1191–1374* (Cambridge, 1991)

Edwards, J. G., '*Confirmatio Cartarum* and Baronial Grievances in 1297', *English Historical Review* 58 (1943), pp. 147–71, 273–300

Edwards, Kathleen, 'The Political Importance of the English Bishops During the Reign of Edward II', *English Historical Review* 49 (1944), pp. 311–47

'The Social Origins and Provenance of the English Bishops During the Reign of Edward II', *TRHS*, 5th ser., 9 (1959), pp. 51–79

Ehrle, Franz, 'Zur Geschichte des Schatzes, der Bibliothek, und des Archivs der Päpste im vierzehnten Jahrhundert', *Archiv für Literatur und Kirchengeschichte des Mittelalters* 1 (1885), pp. 1–305

'Die Spiritualen, ihr Verhältnis zum Franziskanerorden und zu den Fraticellen', *Archiv für Literatur und Kirchengeschichte des Mittelalters* 1 (1885), pp. 509–69; 2 (1886), pp. 108–65, 353–416; 3 (1887), pp. 553–623; 4 (1888), pp. 1–200

'Zur Vorgeschichte des Konzils von Vienne', *Archiv für Literatur und Kirchengeschichte des Mittelalters* 3 (1887), pp. 1–195; 2 (1886), pp. 353–416

'Ein Bruchstück der Akten des Konzils von Vienne', *Archiv für Literatur und Kirchengeschichte des Mittelalters* 4 (1888), pp. 361–602

'Der Nachlass Clemens V und der in Betreff desselben von Johann XXII (1318–1321) geführte Prozess', *Archiv für Literatur und Kirchengeschichte des Mittelalters* 5 (1889), pp. 1–166

Bibliography

'Zur Geschichte des päpstlichen Hofceremoniells im 14. Jahrhundert', *Archiv für Literatur und Kirchengeschichte des Mittelalters* 5 (1889), pp. 565–603

Eitel, Anton, *Der Kirchenstaat unter Klemens V* (Berlin and Leipzig, 1907)

Elze, Reinhard, '*Sic transit gloria mundi*: La morte del papa nel medioevo', *Annali dell'Istituto storico italo-germanico in Trento* 3 (1978), pp. 23–41

Emden, A. B., *A Biographical Register of the University of Oxford to AD 1500*, 3 vols. (Oxford, 1975)

England and Her Neighbours, 1066–1453: Essays in Honour of Pierre Chaplais, ed. M. Jones and M. Vale (London, 1989)

Entrèves, A. P. d', *Dante as a Political Thinker* (Oxford, 1952)

Erburo, Miguel, 'Clemente V en la historia de la moral', *Apollinaris* 43 (1970), pp. 651–701

Erickson, C., 'The Fourteenth-Century Franciscans and Their Critics', *Franciscan Studies* 13 (1975), pp. 107–35; 14 (1976), pp. 108–47

Erickson, Norman N., 'A Dispute Between a Priest and a Knight', *Proceedings of the American Philosophical Society* 111 (1967), pp. 288–309

Fasolt, Constantin, *Council and Hierarchy: The Political Thought of William Durant the Younger* (Cambridge, 1991)

Favier, Jean, *Un conseiller de Philippe le Bel: Enguerran de Marigny* (Paris, 1963)

'Temporels ecclésiastiques et taxation fiscale: Le poids de la fiscalité pontificale au XIVe siècle', *Journal des Savants* (1964), pp. 102–27

'Les légistes et le gouvernement de Philippe le Bel', *Journal des Savants* (1969), pp. 92–108

Philippe le Bel (Paris, 1978)

Fawtier, Robert, *L'Europe occidentale de 1270 à 1328*, in *Histoire générale*, ed. G. Glotz, *Histoire du moyen âge*, vol. VI-1 (Paris, 1940)

'L'attentat d'Anagni', *Mélanges d'archéologie et d'histoire* 60 (1948), pp. 153–79

'Comment le roi de France au début du XIVe siècle pouvait-il se représenter son royaume?', in *Mélanges offerts à M. Paul E. Martin par ses amis, ses collègues, ses élèves* (Genève, 1961), pp. 65–77

Fédou, René, *Les papes du moyen âge à Lyon* (Lyons, 1988)

Fei, R., 'Il Cardinale Niccolò da Prato (1250–1321)', *Mémoire dominicaine* 39 (1922), pp. 467–83

Ferguson, Paul C., 'Clement V to Scone Abbey: An Unprinted Letter from the Abbey Cartularies', *Innes Review* 40-1 (1989), pp. 69–72

Fernández Conde, J., and A. Oliver, 'La corte pontificia de Aviñón y la Iglesia española', in *La Iglesia en la España de los siglos VIII al XIV*, vol. II of *Historia de la Iglesia en España*, ed. Ricardo García-Villoslada, 7 vols. (Madrid, 1982), pp. 365–415

Ferrier, Luc, 'Aspects du rôle de la curie dans le déroulement des procès de canonisation', in *Aux origines de l'état moderne*, pp. 269–91

Ferzoco, George Pietro, 'Historical and Hagiographical Aspects of the Religious World of Peter of Morrone', in *S. Pietro del Morrone*, pp. 227–37

Finke, Heinrich, *Aus den Tagen Bonifaz VIII: Funde und Forschungen* (Münster, 1902)

Papsttum und Untergang des Templerordens, 2 vols. (Munich, 1907)

Finucane, R. C., 'The Cantilupe–Pecham Controversy', in *St Thomas of Cantilupe, Bishop of Hereford*, pp. 103–23

Folz, Robert, *L'idée d'Empire en Occident du Ve au XIVe siècle* (Paris, 1953)

Fornaseri, Giovanni, 'Il conclave perugino del 1304–1305', *Rivista di storia della Chiesa in Italia* 10 (1956), pp. 321–44

Bibliography

Fournier, Paul, 'Les conflits de juridiction entre l'Eglise et le pouvoir séculier de 1180 à 1328', *Revue des questions historiques* 27 (1880), pp. 432–64

'Jesselin de Cassagnes, canoniste', *Histoire littéraire de la France*, vol. XXXV (1921), pp. 348–61

'Pierre Jame (Petrus Jacobi) d'Aurillac, jurisconsulte', *Histoire littéraire de la France* 36 (1927), pp. 481–521

'France anglaise' au moyen âge, La, Actes du 111e congrès national des sociétés savantes, Poitiers 1986 (Paris, 1988)

Fraser, C. M., *A History of Antony Bek, Bishop of Durham, 1283–1311* (Oxford, 1957)

Frugoni, Arsenio, *Celestiniana*, in *Istituto storico italiano per il medio evo: Studi storici*, fasc. 6–7 (Rome, 1954)

Fryde, E. B., 'The Financial Policies of the Royal Governments and Popular Resistance to Them in France and England, c. 1270–c. 1420', *Revue belge de philologie et d'histoire* 57 (1979), pp. 824–60

Fryde, Natalie, 'Antonio Pessagno of Genoa, King's Merchant of Edward II of England', in *Studia in memoria di Federigo Melis*, 5 vols. (Naples, 1978), vol. II, pp. 159–78

The Tyranny and Fall of Edward II, 1321–1326 (Cambridge, 1979)

Funck-Brentano, Frantz, 'Additions au *Codex Diplomaticus Flandriae*', *Bibliothèque de l'Ecole des Chartes* 57 (1896), pp. 373–417, 529–72

Les origines de la Guerre de Cent Ans: Philippe le Bel en Flandre (Paris, 1896)

Gaignard, Romain, 'Le gouvernement pontifical au travail: L'exemple des dernières années du règne de Clément V, 1er août 1311–20 avril 1314', *Annales du Midi* 72 (1960), pp. 169–214

Galbraith, V. H., 'Good Kings and Bad Kings in Medieval English History', *History* 30 (1945), pp. 119–32

Gardelles, J., 'Le tombeau de Clément V', *Bulletin archéologique du comité des travaux historiques et scientifiques. Fasc. a: antiquités nationales* (1957), pp. 81–6

'La reconstruction de la cathédrale', in *Bordeaux sous les rois d'Angleterre*, pp. 325–42

Gasnault, Pierre, 'L'élaboration des lettres secrètes des papes d'Avignon: Chambre et chancellerie', in *Aux origines de l'état moderne*, pp. 209–22

Gatto, Ludovico, 'I problemi della guerra e della pace nel pensiero politico di Pierre Dubois', *Bollettino dell'Istituto storico italiano per il medio evo e Archivio Muratoriano* 71 (1959), pp. 141–79

Gaudemet, Jean, 'Le rôle de la papauté dans le règlement des conflits entre états aux XIIIe et XIVe siècles', *Recueils de la société Jean Bodin* 15 (1961), pp. 79–106

'Aspects de la primauté romaine du Ve au XVe siècle', *Ius Canonicum* 11 (1971), pp. 93–133

Gauthier, Marie-Madeleine, 'Uzeste: L'église Notre Dame, ancienne collégiale, et le tombeau de Bertrand de Got, pape sous le nom de Clément V (1305–1314)', *Congrès archéologique de France, Bordelais et Bazadais* [Gironde] 145 (1987), *Société française d'archéologie* (Paris, 1990), pp. 271–324

Golinelli, Paolo, 'Monachesimo e santità: I modelli di vita di Celestino V', in *S. Pietro del Morrone*, pp. 45–66

Goodich, Michael, *Vita Perfecta: The Ideal of Sainthood in the Thirteenth Century*, Monographien zur Geschichte des Mittelalters 25 (Stuttgart, 1982)

Gorra, Egidio, 'Dante e Clemente V', *Giornale storico della letteratura italiana* 69 (1917), pp. 193–216

Gouron, André, 'Enseignement du droit, légistes, et canonistes dans le Midi de la France à

Bibliography

la fin du XIIIe et au début du XIVe siècle', *Recueil de mémoires et travaux publiés par la société d'histoire du droit et des institutions des anciens pays de droit écrit* 5 (1966), pp. 1–33

Gouron, M., 'Le premier séjour de Clément V en Guyenne (29/7–3/9/1305)', *Revue historique de Bordeaux* 16 (1923), pp. 257–65

Graff, Harvey J., 'The Legacies of Literacy: Continuities and Contradictions in Western Society and Culture', in *Literacy, Society, and Schooling*, ed. Suzanne de Castell, et al. (Cambridge, 1986), pp. 61–86

Graham, William A., *Beyond the Written Word: Oral Aspects of Scripture in the History of Religion* (Cambridge, 1987)

Gransden, Antonia, 'The Continuations of the *Flores Historiarum* from 1265 to 1327', *Mediaeval Studies* 36 (1974), pp. 472–92

Green, Louis, 'The Image of Tyranny in Early Fourteenth-Century Italian Historical Writing', *Renaissance Studies* 7–4 (1993), pp. 335–51

Guenée, Bernard, 'Etat et nation en France au moyen âge', *Revue historique* 237 (1967), pp. 17–30

'Espace et état dans la France du bas moyen âge', *Annales ESC* 23 (1968), pp. 744–58

Histoire et culture historique dans l'Occident médiéval (Paris, 1980)

Guérard, Louis, 'La succession de Clément V et le procès de Bertrand de Got, vicomte de Lomagne (1318–1321)', *Revue de Gascogne* 32 (1891), pp. 5–20

Guillemain, Bernard, 'Le personnel de la cour de Clément V', *Mélanges d'archéologie et d'histoire* 63 (1951), pp. 139–81

'Punti di vista sul papato avignonese', *Archivio storico italiano* 111 (1953), pp. 181–206

'Les tentatives pontificales de médiation dans le litige franco-anglais de Guyenne au XIVe siècle', *Bulletin philologique et historique du comité des travaux historiques et scientifiques* (Paris, 1957–8), pp. 423–32

'L'apogée religieux', in *Bordeaux sous les rois d'Angleterre*, pp. 293–325

La cour pontificale d'Avignon (1309–1376): Etude d'une société (Paris, 1962)

'L'essor religieux', in *Bordeaux sous les rois d'Angleterre*, pp. 127–72

'Les Français du Midi à la cour pontificale d'Avignon', *Annales du Midi* 74 (1962), pp. 29–38

Le diocèse de Bordeaux, in *Histoire des diocèses de France*, ed. J. R. Palanque and B. Plougeron, vol. II (Paris, 1974)

Les recettes et les dépenses de la chambre apostolique pour la quatrième année du pontificat de Clément V (Introitus et Exitus 75), Collection de l'Ecole française de Rome 39 (Rome, 1978)

'Les papes d'Avignon, les indulgences, et les pèlerinages', *Cahiers de Fanjeaux* 15 (1980), pp. 257–68

Gutsche, F., *Die Beziehungen zwischen Reich und Kurie vom Tode Bonifaz VIII bis zur Wahl Heinrichs VII (1303–1308)* (Marburg, 1913)

Haines, Roy M., *The Administration of the Diocese of Worcester in the First Half of the Fourteenth Century* (London, 1965)

The Church and Politics in Fourteenth-Century England: The Career of Adam Orleton, c. 1275–1345 (Cambridge, 1978)

Hamilton, J. S., *Piers Gaveston, Earl of Cornwall, 1307–1312: Politics and Patronage in the Reign of Edward II* (Detroit and London, 1988)

Harris, Gerald L., 'War and the Emergence of the English Parliament, 1297–1360', *Journal of Medieval History* 2 (1976), pp. 35–56

Haskins, George L., 'A Chronicle of the Civil Wars of Edward II', *Speculum* 14 (1939), pp. 73–81

Hauréau, Barthélemy, 'Arnaud de Villeneuve, médecin et chimiste', *Histoire littéraire de la France* 28 (1881), pp. 26–126

Heath, Peter, *Church and Realm, 1272–1461: Conflict and Collaboration in an Age of Crises* (London, 1988)

Hefele, Charles J., and Dom H. Leclercq, *Histoire des conciles d'après les documents originaux*, 8 vols. (Paris, 1909–17)

Heidelberger, F., *Kreuzzugsversuche um die Wende des 13. Jahrhunderts* (Berlin and Leipzig, 1911)

Henry, A., 'Guillaume de Plaisians, ministre de Philippe le Bel', *Le moyen âge* 5 (1892), pp. 32–8

Herde, Peter, *Cölestin V (1294) (Peter vom Morrone) Der Engelpapst*, Päpste und Papsttum 16 (Stuttgart, 1981)

    'Celestino V e Bonifacio VIII di fronte all'eremitismo francescano', in *Eremitismo nel francescanesimo medievale*, Atti del XVII convegno internazionale Assisi, 12–14 ottobre 1989, pp. 97–127

Hillgarth, J. N., *Ramon Lull and Lullism in Fourteenth-Century France* (Oxford, 1971)

    The Problem of a Catalan Mediterranean Empire, 1229–1327, English Historical Review, suppl. 8 (London, 1975)

    'El problema del Imperio Catalano-Aragonés (1229–1327)', *Anuario de estudios medievales* 10 (1980), pp. 145–59

Histoire des femmes en Occident, 5 vols., vol. II, ed. G. Duby and M. Perrot (Paris, 1991)

Hodgson, F. C., *Venice in the Thirteenth and Fourteenth Century: A Sketch of Venetian History from the Conquest of Constantinople to the Accession of Michele Steno, AD 1204–1400* (London, 1910)

Holmes, George, 'Dante and the Popes: His Attitudes to Boniface VIII and Clement V and to Emperor Henry VII', in *The World of Dante: Essays on Dante and His Times*, ed. Cecil Grayson (Oxford, 1980), pp. 18–43

    Florence, Rome, and the Origins of the Renaissance (Oxford, 1986)

Horn, E., 'La mission diplomatique d'un franciscain', *Etudes franciscaines* 37 (1925), pp. 405–18

Horowitz, Jeannine, 'Les danses cléricales dans les églises au moyen âge', *Le moyen âge* 95–2 (1989), pp. 279–92

Horowitz, Jeannine, and Sophia Menache, *L'humour en chaire: Le rire dans l'Eglise médiévale* (Genève, 1994)

Housley, Norman, *The Italian Crusades: The Papal–Angevin Alliance and the Crusades Against Christian Lay Powers, 1254–1343* (Oxford, 1982)

    'Pope Clement V and the Crusades of 1309–1310', *Journal of Medieval History* 8 (1982), pp. 29–43

    The Avignon Papacy and the Crusades, 1305–1378 (Oxford, 1986)

    The Later Crusades, 1274–1580: From Lyons to Alcazar (Oxford, 1992)

Hughes, Jill, 'Walter Langton, Bishop of Coventry and Lichfield, 1296–1321: His Family Background', *Nottingham Medieval Studies* 35 (1991), pp. 70–6

Huizinga, J., *The Waning of the Middle Ages* (1924; New York, 1949)

Hutchison, Carole, *The Hermit Monks of Grandmont* (Kalamazoo, Mich., 1989)

Hutchison, Harold F., *Edward II, the Pliant King* (London, 1971)

Bibliography

Hutin, Serge, 'A propos du "Baphomet" des Templiers', *Atlantis* 344 (1986), pp. 278–86

Huyskens, A., 'Das Kapitel von St Peter in Rom unter dem Einfluss der Orsini (1276–1342)', *Historisches Jahrbuch* 27 (1906), pp. 266–90

Hyde, J. K., 'Contemporary Views on Faction and Civil Strife in Thirteenth- and Fourteenth-Century Italy', in *Violence and Civil Disorder in Italian Cities, 1200–1500*, ed. Lauro Martines (Berkeley, 1972), pp. 273–307

Iung, N., *Un franciscain théologien du pouvoir pontifical au XIVe siècle: Alvaro Pelayo* (Paris, 1931)

Jancey, E. M., *St Thomas of Hereford* (Hereford, 1978)

Jeanroy, A., 'La poésie provençale dans le sud-ouest de la France et en Catalogne du début au milieu du XIVe siècle', *Histoire littéraire de la France* 38 (1949), pp. 1–138

Jedin, Hubert, *Ecumenical Councils of the Catholic Church: An Historical Outline* (Freiburg, 1959), translation by Ernest Graf (Edinburgh, 1960)

Johnstone, Hilda, *A Hundred Years of History* (London, 1912)

'The Eccentricities of Edward II', *English Historical Review* 48 (1933), pp. 264–7

Edward of Carnarvon, 1284–1307, Manchester Historical Series 83 (Manchester, 1946)

Jones, P. J., 'Communes and Despots: The City State in Late Medieval Italy', *TRHS*, 5th ser., 15 (1965), pp. 71–96

The Malatesta of Rimini and the Papal State: A Political History (Cambridge, 1974)

Jones, W. R., 'Relations of the Two Jurisdictions: Conflict and Cooperation in England During the Thirteenth and the Fourteenth Centuries', *Studies in Medieval and Renaissance History* 7 (1970), pp. 77–210

Jordan, E., *Les origines de la domination angevine en Italie* (Paris, 1909)

Jordan, William C., *The French Monarchy and the Jews* (Philadelphia, 1989)

Jugie, Pierre, 'Les *familiae* cardinalices et leur organisation au temps de la papauté d'Avignon: Esquisse d'un bilan', in *Aux origines de l'état moderne*, pp. 41–59

Jullien de Pommerol, Marie-Hemiette, and Jacques Monfrin, 'La bibliothèque pontificale à Avignon au XIVe siècle', in *Histoire des bibliothèques françaises*, 4 vols. (Paris, 1989), vol. I, pp. 147–69

Jusselin, Maurice, 'Une satire contre Philippe le Bel et Clément V', *Bibliothèque de l'Ecole des Chartes* 69 (1908), pp. 280–1

Kaeuper, Richard W., *War, Justice, and Public Order: England and France in the Later Middle Ages* (Oxford, 1988)

Kantorowicz, Ernst H., '*Pro patria mori* in Medieval Political Thought', *American Historical Review* 56 (1951), pp. 472–92

'Inalienability: A Note on Canonical Practice and the English Coronation Oath in the Thirteenth Century', *Speculum* 29 (1954), pp. 488–502

The King's Two Bodies: A Study in Medieval Political Theology (Princeton, 1957)

Kaser, M., *Das römische Privatrecht*, 2nd edn, 2 vols. (Munich, 1971–5)

Kedar, Benjamin Z., and Sylvia Schein, 'Un projet de passage particulier proposé par l'Ordre de l'Hôpital, 1306–1307', *Bibliothèque de l'Ecole des Chartes* 137 (1979), pp. 211–26

'*De Iudeis et Sarracenis*: On the Categorization of Muslims in Medieval Canon Law', in *Studia in Honorem Eminentissimi Cardinalis Alphonsi M. Stickler*, pp. 207–13

Keen, M. H., *England in the Later Middle Ages: A Political History* (London, 1973)

Kennedy, Edward Donald, *Chronicles and Other Historical Writing*, in *Manual of the Writings in Middle English*, ed. Albert E. Hatung, vol. VIII (New Haven, 1989)

Bibliography

Kicklighter, Joseph A., 'La carrière de Béraud de Got', *Annales du Midi* 85 (1973), pp. 327–34

'An Unknown Brother of Pope Clement V', *Medieval Studies* 38 (1976), pp. 492–5

'English Bordeaux in Conflict: The Execution of Pierre Vigier de la Rousselle and Its Aftermath, 1312–1324', *Journal of Medieval History* 9 (1983), pp. 1–14

'English Gascony and the Parlement of Paris: A Study of Anglo-Gascon Legal Representatives, 1259–1337', in *Documenting the Past*, pp. 119–36

Kirsch, J. P., 'Die Annatenbulle Klemens V für England, Schottland, und Irland vom 1. Febr. 1306', *Römische Quartalschrift* 27 (1913), pp. 202–7

Knoll, Paul W., 'The Papacy at Avignon and University Foundations', *Kirkohistorik Årsskrift* 41 (1977), pp. 191–6

Koch, Joseph, 'Die Verurteilung Olivis auf dem Konzil von Vienne und ihre Vorgeschichte', *Scholastik* 5 (1930), pp. 489–522

Kohler, C., 'Documents chypriotes du début du XIVe siècle', *Revue de l'Orient latin* 11 (1905–8), pp. 440–52

Kraack, Elisabeth, *Rom oder Avignon?: Die römische Frage unter den Päpsten Clemens V und Johann XXII*, Marburger Studien zur älteren deutschen Geschichte, 2–2 (Marburg, 1929)

Kuttner, Stephan, 'The *Apostillae* of Johannes Andreae on the Clementines', in *Etudes d'histoire du droit canonique dédiées à Gabriel Le Bras*, 2 vols., (Paris, 1965), vol. I, pp. 195–201

Kyer, Clifford Ian, '*Legatus* and *Nuntius* as Used to Denote Papal Envoys: 1245–1378', *Mediaeval Studies* 40 (1978), pp. 473–7

Labande, Edmond René, 'Clément V et le Poitou', *Bulletin de la société des antiquaires de l'Ouest*, 4th ser., 4 (1957), pp. 11–33, 83–109

'Les idées politiques de Dante', *Bulletin de la société d'études dantesques* 13 (1963–4), pp. 21–35

Labande, L. H., 'Le cérémonial romain de Jacques Cajétan: Les données historiques qu'il renferme', *Bibliothèque de l'Ecole des Chartes* 54 (1893), pp. 45–74

Lacarrière, Jacques, *Les hommes ivres de Dieu* (Paris, 1975)

Lagarde, Georges, *Bilan du XIIIe siècle*, in *La naissance de l'esprit laïque au déclin du moyen âge*, 5 vols. (Louvain and Paris, 1956), vol. I

Laiou, Angeliki E., *Constantinople and the Latins: The Foreign Policy of Andronicus II (1282–1328)* (Cambridge, Mass., 1972)

Lalou, Elisabeth, 'Les assemblées générales sous Philippe le Bel', in *Recherches sur les Etats Généraux et les Etats Provinciaux de la France médiévale*, 110e congrès des sociétés savantes, Montpellier 1985 (Paris, 1986), pp. 7–29

'Les négotiations diplomatiques avec l'Angleterre sous le règne de Philippe le Bel', in *La 'France anglaise' au moyen âge*, pp. 325–55

'Les révoltes contre le pouvoir à la fin du XIIIe et au début du XIVe siècle', in *Violence et contestation au moyen âge: Actes du 114e congrès national des sociétés savantes* (Paris, 1990), pp. 159–83

'Les questions militaires sous le règne de Philippe le Bel', in *Guerre et société en France, en Angleterre, et en Bourgogne, XIVe–XVe siècle* (Lille, 1991), pp. 37–62

Lambert, M. D., 'The Franciscan Crisis Under John XXII', *Franciscan Studies* 32 (1972), pp. 123–43

Langholm, Odd, *Economics in the Medieval Schools:Wealth, Exchange, Value, Money, and Usury According to the Paris Theological Tradition, 1200–1350* (Leiden, 1992)

Bibliography

Langlois, Charles Victor, 'Documents relatifs à Bertrand de Got, Clément V', *Revue historique* 40 (1889), pp. 48–54

'Le procès des Templiers d'après des documents nouveaux', *Revue des deux mondes* 103 (1891), pp. 382–421

'Satire cléricale du temps de Philippe le Bel', *Le moyen âge* 5 (1892), pp. 146–8

'Marguerite Porete', *Revue historique* 54 (1894), pp. 295–9

'Notices et documents relatifs à l'histoire de France au temps de Philippe le Bel: Documents italiens', *Revue historique* 60 (1896), pp. 307–28

'Notices et documents relatifs à l'histoire de France à la fin du XIIIe et au commencement du XIVe siècle: Geffroy du Plessis, protonotaire apostolique de France', *Revue historique* 67 (1898), pp. 70–83

'Philippe le Bel et Clément V: L'affaire des Templiers', in *Histoire de France*, ed. E. Lavisse, vol. III-2 (Paris, 1901), pp. 174–200

'Notices et documents relatifs à l'histoire du XIIIe et du XIVe siècle: Nova Curie', *Revue historique* 87 (1905), pp. 55–79

'Les papiers de Guillaume de Nogaret et de Guillaume de Plaisians au trésor des Chartes', *Notices et extraits des manuscrits de la Bibliothèque nationale* 39 (1909), pp. 211–54

Larner, John, *The Lords of Romagna: Romagnol Society and the Origins of the Signorie* (New York, 1965)

Laurent, Jane K., 'The Signory and Its Supporters: The Este of Ferrara', *Journal of Medieval History* 3 (1977), pp. 39–51

Laurière, J. de, and E. Muentz, 'Le tombeau de Clément V à Uzeste', *Mémoires de la société des antiquaires de France* 8 (1887–8), pp. 275–92

Le Bras, Gabriel, *Histoire du droit et des institutions de l'Eglise en Occident*, 2 vols. (Paris, 1955)

Le Goff, Jacques, 'Au moyen âge: Temps de l'Eglise et temps du marchand', *Annales ESC* 15 (1960), pp. 417–33

Lecler, Joseph, *Vienne*, in *Histoire des conciles oecuméniques*, vol. VIII, ed. Gervais Dumeige (Paris, 1964)

Leclercq, Dom Jean, 'La renonciation de Célestin V et l'opinion théologique en France du vivant de Boniface VIII', *Revue d'histoire de l'Eglise de France* 25 (1939), pp. 183–92

'Un sermon prononcé pendant la guerre de Flandre sous Philippe le Bel', *Revue du moyen âge latin* 1 (1945), pp. 165–72

Leclerq, H., 'Roi très chrétien', *Dictionnaire d'archéologie chrétienne et de liturgie*, 15 vols. in 29 (Paris, 1920–53), vol. XIV-2, cols. 2462–4

Lerner, Robert E., *Heresy of the Free Spirit in the Later Middle Ages* (Berkeley, 1972)

'An "Angel of Philadelphia" in the Reign of Philip the Fair: The Case of Guiard of Cressonessart', in *Order and Innovation in the Middle Ages: Essays in Honor of Joseph R. Strayer*, ed. William C. Jordan, Bruce McNab, and Teófilo F. Ruiz (Princeton, 1976), pp. 343–64

Leroux, Alfred, 'Les portails commémoratifs de Bordeaux: Essai d'interprétation par l'histoire locale', *Annales du Midi* 28 (1916), pp. 306–53, 413–61

Levillain, L., 'A propos d'un texte inédit relatif au séjour du pape Clément V à Poitiers en 1307', *Le moyen âge* 10 (1897), pp. 73–86

Licitra, Vicenzo, 'Considerazione sull' *Opus metricum* del Card. Jacopo Caetani Stefaneschi', in *S. Pietro del Morrone*, pp. 185–201

Bibliography

Lizerand, Georges, *Clément V et Philippe IV, le Bel* (Paris, 1910)

    Clément V et Philippe le Bel (Paris, 1911)

    'Les constitutions *Romani principes* et *Pastoralis cura* et leurs sources', *Nouvelle revue historique de droit français et étranger* 37 (1913), pp. 725–57

    Le dossier de l'affaire des Templiers, Les classiques de l'histoire de France au moyen âge 2 (Paris, 1923)

Llobet, Gabriel de, 'Variété des croyances populaires au comté de Foix au début du XIVe siècle, d'après les enquêtes de Jacques Fournier', *Cahiers de Fanjeaux* 11 (1976), pp. 109–26

Lunt, William E., 'The First Levy of Papal Annates', *American Historical Review* 18 (1912–13), pp. 48–64

    'The Account of a Papal Collector in England in 1304', *English Historical Review* 28 (1913), pp. 313–21

    'Papal Taxation in England in the Reign of Edward I', *English Historical Review* 30 (1915), pp. 398–417

    'William Testa and the Parliament of Carlisle', *English Historical Review* 41 (1926), pp. 332–51

    'Clerical Tenths Levied in England by Papal Authority During the Reign of Edward II', in *Anniversary Essays in Medieval History by Students of Charles Homer Haskins*, ed. C. Taylor and J. La Monte (New York and Boston, 1929), pp. 157–82

    Papal Revenues in the Middle Ages, 2 vols. (New York, 1934)

    Financial Relations of the Papacy with England to 1327, 2 vols. (Cambridge, Mass., 1939)

Luttrell, Anthony T., 'The Aragonese Crown and the Knights Hospitallers of Rhodes: 1291–1350', *English Historical Review* 76 (1961), pp. 1–19

    'The Crusades in the Fourteenth Century', in *Europe in the Late Middle Ages*, ed. J. R. Hale, J. R. L. Highfield, and B. Smalley (London, 1965), pp. 122–54

    'The Latins of Argos and Nauplia (1311–1394)', *Papers of the British School at Rome*, n.s., 21 (1966), pp. 34–55

    'Feudal Tenure and Latin Colonization at Rhodes: 1306–1415', *English Historical Review* 85 (1970), pp. 755–75

    'The Hospitallers' Interventions in Cilician Armenia', in *The Cilician Kingdom of Armenia*, pp. 118–44

    'The Hospitallers of Rhodes: Prospectives, Problems, Possibilities', in *Die geistlichen Ritterorden Europas* (Sigmaringen, 1980), pp. 243–66

    'Notes on Foulques de Villaret, Master of the Hospital, 1305–1319', in *Guillaume de Villaret Ier Recteur du Comtat-Venaissin 1274, Grand Maître de l'Ordre des Hospitaliers de Saint Jean de Jérusalem, Chypre 1296* (Paris, 1985), pp. 73–90

    'Gli Ospitalieri e l'eredità dei Templari, 1305–1378', in *I Templari: Mito e storia*, ed. G. Minnucci and F. Sardi (Siena, 1989), pp. 67–86

Lydon, James F., 'Edward I, Ireland, and the War in Scotland, 1303–1304', in *England and Ireland in the Later Middle Ages: Essays in Honour of Jocelyn Otway-Ruthven*, ed. James Lydon (Naas, 1981), pp. 43–61

    'The Enrolled Accounts of Alexander Bicknor, Treasurer of Ireland, 1308–1314', *Analecta Hibernica* 30 (1982), pp. 9–46

McCready, William D., 'The Problem of the Empire in Augustinus Triumphus and Late Medieval Papal Hierocratic Theory', *Traditio* 30 (1974), pp. 325–49

    'Papalists and Antipapalists: Aspects of the Church/State Controversy in the Later Middle Ages', *Viator* 6 (1975), pp. 241–73

McCurry, C., '*Utilia Metensia*: Local Benefices for the Papal Curia, 1212–c. 1370', in *Law,*

Bibliography

Church, and Society: Essays in Honor of Stephen Kuttner, ed. K. Pennington and R. Somerville (Philadelphia, 1977), pp. 311–23

McNamara, Jo Ann, *Gilles Aycelin: The Servant of Two Masters* (Syracuse, 1973)

Maddicott, J. R., *Thomas of Lancaster, 1307–1322: A Study in the Reign of Edward II* (Oxford, 1970)

Mancusi-Ungaro, Donna, *Dante and the Empire* (New York, 1987)

Manselli, Raoul, 'Arnaldo da Villanova e i papi del suo tempo: Tra religione e politica', *Studi romani* 7 (1959), pp. 146–61

'La Repubblica di Lucca', in *Comuni e signorie nell' Italia nordorientale e centrale*, ed. G. Galasso, *Storia d'Italia*, vol. VII (Turin, 1987), pp. 610–743

Marchal, Georges, 'Autour du pape Clément V: Voyage de Poitiers, aller et retour', *Revue historique de Bordeaux* 19 (1926), pp. 201–5; 20 (1927), pp. 232–7

'Autour de Clément V, le pape en Toulousain', *Revue historique de Bordeaux* 20 (1927), pp. 227–32

Marini, Alfonso, 'Pietro del Morrone monaco negli Atti del Processo di canonizzazione', in *S. Pietro del Morrone*, pp. 67–96

Marongiù, Antonio, 'Il principio della democrazia e del consenso (*Quod omnes tangit ab omnibus approbari debet*) nel XIV secolo', *Studia Gratiana* 8 (1962), pp. 555–75

Medieval Parliaments, translation by S. J. Woolf (London, 1968)

'Le "corts" catalane e la conquista della Sardegna nel XIV secolo', *Anuario de estudios medievales* 10 (1980), pp. 871–81

Marthaler, Berard, OFM Conven., 'Forerunners of the Franciscans: The Waldenses', *Franciscan Studies* 18 (1958), pp. 133–42

Martin, Nona D. S., 'The Life of St Thomas of Hereford', in *St Thomas of Cantilupe, Bishop of Hereford*, pp. 15–19

Mas Latrie, M. L. de, *Histoire de l'Ile de Chypre sous le règne des princes de la maison de Lusignan*, 3 vols. (Paris, 1852–61)

'Traité des Vénitiens avec l'émir d'Acre en 1304', *Archives de l'Orient latin* 1 (1881), pp. 406–8

Meeserman, G., 'Etudes sur les anciennes confréries dominicaines', *Archivum Fratrum Praedicatorum* 20 (1950), pp. 5–113; 21 (1951), pp. 51–196; 22 (1952), pp. 5–176; 23 (1953), pp. 275–308

Melville, Marion, 'Guillaume de Nogaret et Philippe le Bel', *Revue d'histoire de l'Eglise de France* 36 (1950), pp. 56–66

Menache, Sophia, 'Les Hébreux du XIVe siècle: La formation des stéréotypes nationaux en France et en Angleterre', *Ethnopsychologie* 35 (1980), pp. 55–65

'Contemporary Attitudes Concerning the Templars' Affair: A Propaganda Fiasco?', *Journal of Medieval History* 8 (1982), pp. 135–47

'La naissance d'une nouvelle source d'autorité: L'université de Paris', *Revue historique* 268–2 (1982), pp. 305–27

'Vers une conscience nationale: Mythe et symbolisme au début de la Guerre de Cent Ans', *Le moyen âge* 89 (1983), pp. 85–97

'Isabelle of France, Queen of England: A Reconsideration', *Journal of Medieval History* 12 (1984), pp. 107–24

'Philippe le Bel: Genèse d'une image', *Revue belge de philologie et d'histoire* 62 (1984), pp. 689–702

'Faith, Myth, and Politics: The Stereotype of the Jews and Their Expulsion from England and France', *Jewish Quarterly Review* 75 (1985), pp. 351–74

Bibliography

'Un peuple qui a sa demeure à part: Boniface VIII et le sentiment national français', *Francia* 12 (1985), pp. 193–208

'Réflexions sur quelques papes français du bas moyen âge: Un problème d'origine', *Revue d'histoire ecclésiastique* 81 (1986), pp. 117–30

'A Juridical Chapter in the History of the Order of Calatrava: The Election of Don Alonso de Aragón', *Journal of Legal History* 55 (1987), pp. 321–34

'The King, the Church, and the Jews: Some Considerations on the Expulsions from France and England', *Journal of Medieval History* 13 (1987), pp. 223–36

'Religious Symbols and Royal Propaganda in the Late Middle Ages: The Crusades', in *Propaganda and Symbolism in France*, ed. Myriam Yardeni (Paris, 1987), pp. 55–61

'A Propaganda Campaign in the Reign of Philip the Fair: 1302–1303', *French History* 4 (1990), pp. 427–54

The Vox Dei: Communication in the Middle Ages (New York, 1990)

'The Templar Order: A Failed Ideal?', *Catholic Historical Review* 79 (1993), pp. 1–21

'Communication Changes in the Crusader Period: Transmission of News Between Europe and the Levant', in *Kommunikation zwischen Orient und Okzident: Veröffentlichungen des Instituts für Realienkunde des Mittelalters und der frühen Neuzeit*, vol. XVII (Vienna, 1994), pp. 69–90

'The Communication Challenge of the Early Crusades, 1099–1187', in *Autour de la première croisade*, ed. Michel Balard (Paris, 1996), pp. 293–314

'Communication in the Jewish Diaspora: A Survey', in *Communication in the Jewish Diaspora: The Pre-Modern World*, ed. S. Menache (Leiden, 1996), pp. 15–57

'Rewriting the History of the Templars According to Matthew Paris', in *Cultural Convergences in the Crusader Period: Festschrift in Honor of Aryeh Grabois* (New York, 1996), pp. 185–214

'Tartars, Jews, Saracens and the Jewish–Mongol "Plot" of 1241', *History* 81 (1996), pp. 319–42

'The Hospitallers in the Pontificate of Clement V: The Spoiled Sons of the Papacy?' (forthcoming)

Menache, Sophia, and Jeannine Horowitz, 'Rhetoric and Its Practice in Medieval Sermons', *Historical Reflections* 22–2 (1996), pp. 321–50

Metcalf, D. M., 'The Templars as Bankers and Monetary Transfers Between West and East in the Twelfth Century', in *Coinage in the Latin East: The Fourth Oxford Symposium on Coinage and Monetary History*, ed. P. W. Edbury and D. M. Metcalf (Oxford, 1980), pp. 1–17

Michelet, Jules, *Histoire de France*, 17 vols. (Paris, 1837–40)

Migne, J. P., *Dictionnaire des cardinaux* (Paris, 1857)

Miller, E., 'War, Taxation, and the English Economy in the Late Thirteenth and Early Fourteenth Century', in *War and Economic Development: Essays in Memory of David Joslin*, ed. J. M. Winter (Cambridge, 1975), pp. 11–31

Minois, Georges, *Le confesseur du roi: Les directeurs de conscience sous la monarchie française* (Paris, 1988)

Miserey, A., *A l'âge d'or d'Avignon, Jean XXII* (Paris, 1966)

Miskimin, Harry A., *Money, Prices, and Foreign Exchange in Fourteenth-Century France* (New Haven and London, 1963)

Mollat, Guillaume, 'Les doléances du clergé de la province de Sens au Concile de Vienne (1311–1312)', *Revue d'histoire ecclésiastique* 6 (1905), pp. 319–26

Bibliography

'L'élection du pape Jean XXII', *Revue d'histoire de l'Eglise de France* 1 (1910), pp. 34–49, 147–66

Les papes d'Avignon (1305–1378) (Paris, 1912)

Etude critique sur les Vitae Paparum Avenionensium d'Etienne Baluze (Paris, 1917)

La collation des bénéfices ecclésiastiques par les papes d'Avignon, in Mollat, *Lettres communes de Jean XXII (1316–1334)* (Paris, 1921–47), vol. I

'Papes d'Avignon', *Dictionnaire apologétique de la foi catholique*, 4 vols. (Paris, 1926), vol. III, cols. 1534–63

'Les Clémentines', in *Dictionnaire de droit canonique*, 7 vols. (Paris, 1924–65), vol. IV (Paris, 1949), cols. 635–40

'Contribution à l'histoire du Sacré-Collège de Clément V à Eugène IV', *Revue d'histoire ecclésiastique* 46 (1951), pp. 22–112, 566–94

'La diplomatie pontificale au XIVe siècle', in *Mélanges d'histoire du moyen âge dédiés à la mémoire de Louis Halphen*, pref. Charles-Edmond Perrin (Paris, 1951), pp. 507–12

'Clément V', *Dictionnaire d'histoire et de géographie ecclésiastiques* (Paris, 1953), vol. XII, cols. 1115–29

Mollat, Michel, and Paul Tombeur, *Le concile de Vienne: Concordance, Index, listes de fréquence, tables comparatives* (Louvain, 1978)

Moorman, John R. H., *Church Life in England in the Thirteenth Century* (Cambridge, 1955)

Morerod, Jean Daniel, 'Taxation décimale et frontières politiques en France aux XIIIe et XIVe siècles', in *Aux origines de l'état moderne*, pp. 329–50

Morghen, Raffaello, 'La lettera di Dante ai cardinali italiani', *Bollettino dell' Istituto storico italiano per il medio evo e Archivio Muratoriano* 68 (1956), pp. 1–31; 70 (1958), pp. 513–19

Dante, profeta tra la storia e l'eterno (Milan, 1983)

Mühlethaler, Jean-Claude, *Fauvel au pouvoir: Lire la satire médiévale* (Paris, 1994)

Muldoon, James, 'The Avignon Papacy and the Frontiers of Christendom: The Evidence of Vatican Register 62', *Archivum Historiae Pontificiae* 17 (1979), pp. 125–95

Müller, Ewald, *Das Konzil von Vienne (1311–1312), seine Quellen und seine Geschichte*, Vorreformationsgeschichtliche Forschungen 12 (Münster, 1934)

Mundill, R. R., 'Medieval Anglo-Jewry: Expulsion and Exodus' (forthcoming)

Nelson, B., *The Idea of Usury: From Tribal Brotherhood to Universal Otherhood* (Princeton, 1949)

Nicholson, Helen, *Templars, Hospitallers, and Teutonic Knights: Images of the Military Orders, 1128–1291* (Leicester, 1993)

Nimmo, Duncan, *Reform and Division in the Medieval Franciscan Order: From St Francis to the Foundation of the Capuchins* (Rome, 1987)

O'Callaghan, Joseph F., 'Las definiciones medievales de la Orden de Montesa, 1326–1468', *Miscelanea de textos medievales* 1 (Barcelona, 1972), pp. 213–51

Otte, W., 'Der historische Wert der alten Biographieen des Papstes Clemens V', in *Kirchengeschichtliche Abhandlungen*, ed. Max Sdralek (Breslau, 1902), vol. I, pp. 3–73

Padoan, Giorgio, 'Colui che fece per viltà il gran rifiuto', *Studi Danteschi* 38 (1961), pp. 75–128

Pantin, William Abel, *The English Church in the Fourteenth Century* (Cambridge, 1955)

'The Fourteenth Century', in *The English Church and the Papacy in the Middle Ages*, ed. C. H. Lawrence (New York, 1965), pp. 157–94

Paravicini Bagliani, Agostino, 'Der Papst auf Reisen im Mittelalter', in *Feste und Ferien im Mittelalter*, ed. D. Altenburg, et al. (Sigmaringen, 1991), pp. 501–14

Bibliography

Parisset, Georges, 'L'établissement de la primatie de Bourges', *Annales du Midi* 14 (1902), pp. 145–84, 289–328

Partee, Carter, OFM, 'Peter John Olivi: An Historical and Doctrinal Study', *Franciscan Studies* 20 (1960), pp. 215–60

Partner, Peter, 'Florence and the Papacy, 1300–1375', in *Europe in the Late Middle Ages*, ed. J. R. Hale, J. R. L. Highfield, and B. Smalley (London, 1965), pp. 76–121

'Guelf and Ghibelline in Italy', *History Today* 21 (1971), pp. 575–84

The Lands of St Peter: The Papal State in the Middle Ages and the Early Renaissance (London, 1972)

The Murdered Magicians: The Templars and Their Myth (New York, 1982)

Pasdermadjian, H., *Histoire de l'Arménie*, 3rd edn (Paris, 1971)

Pasztor, Edith, 'S. Celestino V. Elezione e rinuncia al pontificato: Esegesi di una fonte', in *S. Pietro del Morrone*, pp. 7–20

Paul, Jacques, 'Les franciscains et la pauvreté aux XIIIe et XIVe siècles', *Revue d'histoire de l'Eglise de France* 52 (1966), pp. 33–7

Pegues, Franklin J., *The Lawyers of the Last Capetians* (Princeton, 1962)

Perkins, Clarence, 'The Trial of the Knights Templar in England', *English Historical Review* 24 (1909), pp. 432–47

'The Knights Templar in the British Isles', *English Historical Review* 25 (1910), pp. 209–30

'The Wealth of the Knights Templar in England and the Disposition of It After Their Dissolution', *American Historical Review* 15 (1910), pp. 252–63

Pernoud, Régine, *La femme au temps des cathédrales* (Paris, 1980)

Perrat, C., 'Un diplomate gascon au XIVe siècle, Raymond de Piis, nonce de Clément V en Orient', *Mélanges d'archéologie et d'histoire* 44 (1927), pp. 35–90

Peters, Edward, *The Shadow King: Rex Inutilis in Medieval Law and Literature* (New Haven and London, 1970)

'The Failure of Church and Empire: Paradiso 30', *Medieval Studies* 34 (1972), pp. 326–35

Pézard, André, 'Dante et l'apocalypse de Carpentras (Ep. xi: 25), 1314–1316', *Archives d'histoire doctrinale et littéraire du moyen âge* 50 (1984), pp. 61–100

Pflugk-Harttung, J. von, *Iter Italicum* (Stuttgart, 1883)

Phillips, J. R. S., *Aymer de Valence, Earl of Pembroke, 1307–1324: Baronial Politics in the Reign of Edward II* (Oxford, 1972)

Picot, G., *Histoire des Etats-généraux, considerés au point de vue de leur influence sur le gouvernement de la France de 1355 à 1614*, 4 vols. (Paris 1872)

Piponnier, Françoise, *Coutume et vie sociale: La cour d'Anjou XIVe–XVe siècles* (Paris, 1970)

Port, Célestin, 'Le livre de Guillaume le Maire', Collection des documents inédits sur l'histoire de France, *Mélanges historiques* 2 (Paris, 1877), pp. 471–99

Post, Gaines, 'A Romano-Canonical Maxim, *Quod omnes tangit*, in Bracton', *Traditio* 4 (1940), pp. 197–251

Power, Eilen E., 'Pierre Du Bois and the Domination of France', in *The Social and Political Ideas of Some Great Medieval Thinkers: A Series of Lectures Delivered at King's College University of London*, ed. F. J. C. Hearnshaw (London, 1923), pp. 139–66

Powicke, Frederick Maurice, 'Pierre Dubois: A Medieval Radical', in *Historical Essays by Members of the Owens College, Manchester*, ed. T. F. Tout and James Tait (London, 1902), pp. 169–91

'Pope Boniface VIII', in F. M. Powicke, *The Christian Life in the Middle Ages and Other Essays* (Oxford, 1935), pp. 48–73

The Thirteenth Century, 2nd edn (Oxford, 1962)

Bibliography

Prawer, Joshua, 'Military Orders and Crusader Politics in the Second Half of the Thirteenth Century', in *Die geistlichen Ritterorden Europas*, ed. Josef Fleckenstein and Manfred Hellman (Sigmaringen, 1980), pp. 217–29

Prestwich, Michael, 'A New Version of the Ordinances of 1311', *Bulletin of the Institute of Historical Research* 57 (1984), pp. 189–203

Edward I (London, 1988)

'England and Scotland During the Wars of Independence', in *England and Her Neighbours*, pp. 181–97

War, Politics, and Finance Under Edward I, 2nd edn (Aldershot, 1991)

Quaglioni, Diego, '*Fidelitas habet duas habenas*: Il fondamento dell' obbligazione politica nella glosse di Bartolo alle costituzioni pisane di Enrico VII', in *Origini dello stato: Processi di formazione statale in Italia fra medioevo ed età moderna*, Annali dell'Istituto storico italo-germanico 39, ed. Giorgio Chittolini, Anthony Molho, and Pierangelo Schiera (Bologna, 1994), pp. 381–96

Rabanis, M., *Clément V et Philippe le Bel: Lettre à M. Charles Daremberg sur l'entrevue de Philippe le Bel et de Bertrand de Got à Saint Jean d'Angély* (Paris, 1858)

Rabikauskas, Paulius, 'La parte sostenuta dalla cancelleria nelle concessioni papali delle grazie', in *Aux origines de l'état moderne*, pp. 223–36

Rapp, Francis, *L'Eglise et la vie religieuse en Occident à la fin du moyen âge* (Paris, 1971)

Reeves, M., 'Some Popular Prophecies from the Fourteenth to the Seventeenth Centuries', *Studies in Church History* 8 (1972), pp. 107–34

'History and Prophecy in Medieval Thought', *Medievalia et Humanistica*, n.s., 5 (1974), pp. 51–75

Regibus, A. de, 'Le contese degli Angioini di Napoli per il trono di Ungheria (1290–1310)', *Rivista di storia del diritto italiano* (1934), pp. 38–85, 264–305

Renan, Ernest, 'De diverses pièces relatives aux différends de Philippe le Bel avec la papauté', *Histoire littéraire de la France* 27 (1877), pp. 371–81

'Guillaume de Nogaret', *Histoire littéraire de la France* 27 (1877), pp. 233–371

'Bertrand de Got, pape sous le nom de Clément V', *Histoire littéraire de la France* 28 (1881), pp. 272–314

Etudes sur la politique religieuse du règne de Philippe le Bel (Paris, 1899)

Renouard, Yves, 'Les papes et le conflit franco-anglais en Aquitaine de 1259 à 1337', *Mélanges d'archéologie et d'histoire publiés par l'école française de Rome* 51 (1934), pp. 258–92

Les rélations des papes d'Avignon et des compagnies commerciales et bancaires (Paris, 1941)

'Edouard II et Clément V d'après les Rôles gascons', *Annales du Midi* 67 (1955), pp. 119–41

'Bordeaux dans le monde au XIVe siècle', in *Bordeaux sous les rois d'Angleterre*, pp. 215–21

The Avignon Papacy, 1305–1403, translation by Denis Bethell (London, 1970)

Rey, R., 'L'énigme du portail nord de la cathédrale de Bordeaux', *Annales du Midi* 63 (1951), pp. 97–104

Reydellet-Guttinger, Chantal, *L'administration pontificale dans le Duché de Spolète (1305–1352)* (Florence, 1975)

Richard, Jean, *La papauté et les missions d'Orient au moyen âge (XIIIe–XVe siècles)* (Rome, 1977)

Bibliography

Richardson, H. G., 'Clement V and the See of Canterbury', *English Historical Review* 56 (1941), pp. 97–103

'The English Coronation Oath', *Speculum* 24 (1949), pp. 44–75

Richardson, H. G., and G. O. Sayles, 'The Parliament of Carlisle, 1307: Some New Documents', in *The English Parliament in the Middle Ages*, ed. H. G. Richardson and G. O. Sayles (London, 1981), pp. 425–37

Rieder, K., *Römische Quellen zur Konstanzer Bistumsgeschichte zur Zeit der Päpste in Avignon (1305–1378)* (Innsbruck, 1908)

Rigault, E., *Le procès de Guichard, évêque de Troyes* (Paris, 1896)

Rivière, Jean, *Le problème de l'Eglise et de l'état au temps de Philippe le Bel* (Louvain and Paris, 1926)

Rothwell, Harry, 'Edward I and the Struggle for the Charters, 1297–1305' in *Studies in Medieval History Presented to Frederick Maurice Powicke*, ed. R. W. Hunt, W. A. Pantin, and R. W. Southern (Oxford, 1948), pp. 319–32

Ruiz, Teófilo F., 'Oligarchy and Royal Power: The Castilian Cortes and the Castilian Crises, 1248–1350', *Parliaments, Estates, and Representation* 2 (1982), pp. 95–101

S. Pietro del Morrone: Celestino V nel medioevo monastico, ed. Walter Capezzali, Centro Celestiniano, Convegni Celestiniani 3 (L'Aquila, 1989)

Sachs, A., 'Religious Despair in Medieval Literature and Art', *Medieval Studies* 26 (1964), pp. 231–56

Salavert y Roca, Vicente, *Cerdeña y la expansión mediterranea de la corona de Aragón*, 2 vols. (Madrid, 1956)

'Notas sobre la política italiana de Clemente V y sus repercusiones en Aragón', in *Miscellanea in onore di Roberto Cessi*, 3 vols., *Storia e Letteratura*, vols. LXXI–LXXIII (Rome, 1958), vol. I, pp. 255–98

Salvemini, Gaetano, 'L'abolizione dell'Ordine dei Templari', *Archivio storico italiano*, 5th ser., 15 (1895), pp. 225–64

Salzman, L. F., *Edward I* (London, 1968)

Samaran, C., and G. Mollat, *La fiscalité pontificale en France au XIVe siècle* (Paris, 1905)

Schein, Sylvia, 'Philip IV and the Crusade: A Reconsideration', in *Crusade and Settlement*, ed. Peter W. Edbury (Cardiff, 1985), pp. 121–6

Fideles Crucis: The Papacy, the West, and the Recovery of the Holy Land (1274–1314) (Oxford, 1991)

Schimmelpfennig, Bernhard, *Die Zeremonienbücher der römischen Kurie im Mittelalter* (Tübingen, 1973)

'Papal Coronations in Avignon', in *Coronations: Medieval and Early Modern Monarchic Ritual*, ed. János M. Bak (Berkeley, 1990), pp. 179–96

Schmidt, Tilmann, *Der Bonifaz-Prozess: Verfahren der Papstanklage in der Zeit Bonifaz VIII und Clemens V*, Forschungen zur kirchlichen Rechtsgeschichte und zum Kirchenrecht 19 (Cologne and Vienna, 1989)

'Zwei neue Konstitutionen Papst Clemens V zur Restitution der Colonna (1306)', in *Papsttum, Kirche, und Recht im Mittelalter: Festschrift für Horst Fuhrmann zum 65. Geburstag*, ed. Hubert Mordek (Tübingen, 1991), pp. 335–45

Scholz, Richard, *Die Publizistik zur Zeit Philipps des Schönen und Bonifaz VIII* (Stuttgart, 1903)

Schottmüller, Konrad, *Der Untergang des Templer-Ordens*, 2 vols. (Berlin, 1887)

Schwalm, Jakob, 'Beiträge zur Reichsgeschichte des 14. Jahrhunderts: Aus dem vatikanis-

Bibliography

chen Archiv', *Neues Archiv der Gesellschaft für ältere deutsche Geschichtskunde* 25 (1900), pp. 559–84

Schwarz, B., *Die Organisation Kurialer Schreiberkollegien* (Tübingen, 1972)

Sclafert, T., 'Les routes du Dauphiné et de la Provence sous l'influence du séjour des papes à Avignon', *Annales d'histoire économique et sociale* 1 (1929), pp. 183–92

Seward, Desmond, 'The Dissolution of the Templars', *History Today* 21 (1971), pp. 628–35

Sharwood Smith, E., 'Dante and the World Empire', in *The Social and Political Ideas of Some Great Medieval Thinkers: A Series of Lectures Delivered at King's College University of London* (London, 1923), pp. 107–38

Sicard, Germain, 'Les Etats Généraux de la France capétienne', in *Las Cortes de Castilla y León, 1188–1988*, 2 vols. (Valladolid, 1990), vol. II, pp. 57–100

Silving, H., 'The Oath, I', *Yale Law Journal* 68 (1959), pp. 1329–90

Small, Carola M., 'An Episode at Sutri in the Patrimony of St Peter: Louis of Savoy and the Constitutional Position of the Pope in Rome (1311)', *Archivum Historiae Pontificae* 19 (1981), pp. 309–15

Smith, A., *Church and State in the Middle Ages* (Oxford, 1913)

Smith, Waldo E. L., *Episcopal Appointments and Patronage in the Reign of Edward II: A Study in the Relations of Church and State* (Chicago, 1938)

Soranzo, G., *La guerra fra Venezia e la Santa Sede per il dominio di Ferrara (1308–1313)* (Città di Castello, 1905)

Southern, R., 'Aspects of the European Tradition of Historical Writing: The Classical Tradition from Einhard to Geoffrey of Monmouth', *TRHS*, 5th ser., 20 (1970), pp. 73–96

Spiegel, Gabriela M., 'Political Utility in Medieval Historiography: A Sketch', *History and Theory* 14 (1975), pp. 314–25

'"Defense of the Realm": Evolution of a Capetian Propaganda Slogan', *Journal of Medieval History* 3 (1977), pp. 115–33

St Thomas of Cantilupe, Bishop of Hereford: Essays in His Honour, ed. Meryl Jancey (Hereford, 1982)

Stengel, E. E., *Avignon und Rhens: Forschungen zur Geschichte des Kampfes um das Recht in der ersten Hälfte des XIV. Jahrhunderts* (Weimar, 1930)

Stones, E. L. G., 'The Appeal to History in Anglo-Scottish Relations Between 1291 and 1401', *Archives* 9 (1969), pp. 11–21, 80–3

Storey, R. L., 'Papal Provisions to English Monasteries', *Nottingham Medieval Studies* 35 (1991), pp. 77–91

Strayer, Joseph R., 'Consent to Taxation Under Philip the Fair', in Joseph R. Strayer and Charles H. Taylor, in *Studies in Early French Taxation* (Cambridge, Mass., 1939), pp. 3–105

'Philip the Fair: A "Constitutional King"', *American Historical Review* 62 (1956), pp. 18–32

'Defense of the Realm and Royal Power in France' (first published in 1949), in Strayer (ed.), *Medieval Statecraft and the Perspectives of History* (Princeton, 1971), pp. 291–9

'France: The Holy Land, the Chosen People, and the Most Christian King' (first published in 1969), in Strayer (ed.), *Medieval Statecraft and the Perspectives of History* (Princeton, 1971), pp. 300–14

'The Costs and Profits of War: The Anglo-French Conflict of 1294–1303', in *The Medieval City*, ed. H. A. Miskimin, et al. (Yale, 1977), pp. 277–91

Bibliography

'The Case of Bishop Guichard of Troyes: Relations Between Church and State Under Philip IV and Comparisons with the Byzantine Empire', in *Charanis Studies: Essays in Honor of Peter Charanis*, ed. Angeliki E. Laiou-Thomadakis (New Brunswick, N. J., 1980), pp. 248–60

The Reign of Philip the Fair (Princeton, 1980)

Studia in Honorem Eminentissimi Cardinalis Alphonsi M. Stickler, ed. Rosalio Iosepho (Rome, 1992)

Sulkowska-Kuraś, Irena, and Stanisław Kuraś, 'La Pologne et la papauté d'Avignon', in *Aux origines de l'état moderne*, pp. 113–33

Swanson, R. N., *Church and Society in Late Medieval England* (Oxford, 1993)

Tabacco, Giovanni, *The Struggle for Power in Medieval Italy: Structures of Political Rule*, transl. by Rosalin Brown Jensen (Cambridge, 1989)

'Il papato avignonese nella crisi del Francescanesimo', *Rivista storica italiana* 101 (1989), pp. 317–45

Tamburini, Filippo, 'La penitenzieria apostolica durante il papato avignonese', in *Aux origines de l'état moderne*, pp. 251–68

Tarrant, Jacqueline, 'The Clementine Decrees on the Beguines: Conciliar and Papal Versions', *Archivum Historiae Pontificae* 12 (1974), pp. 300–8

'The Manuscripts of the *Constitutiones Clementinae*, Part I: Admont to München; Part II: Napoli to Zwetti', *Zeitschrift der Savigny-Stiftung für Rechtsgeschichte/Kanonistiche Abteilung* 101–70 (1984), pp. 67–133; 102–71 (1985), pp. 76–146

Tauzin, M. l'abbé, 'Les sénéchaux anglais en Guyenne, 1137–1453', *Revue de Gascogne* 32 (1891), pp. 149–66, 197–212

Taylor, Charles H., 'The Assembly of 1312 at Lyons–Vienne', in *Etudes d'histoire dédiées à la mémoire de Henri Pirenne par ses anciens élèves* (Brussels, 1937), pp. 337–49

Tentler, Thomas N., 'The *Summa* for Confessors as an Instrument of Social Control', in *The Pursuit of Holiness in Late Medieval and Renaissance Religion*, Papers of the University of Michigan Conference, ed. Charles Trinkaus and Heiko A. Oberman (Leiden, 1974), pp. 103–30

Thier, Ludger, *Kreuzzugsbemühungen unter Papst Clemens V (1305–1314)*, Franziskanische Forschungen 24 (Werl-Westf., 1973)

Thomas, William, *A Survey of the Cathedral Church of Worcester With an Account of the Bishops Thereof, from the Foundation of the See to the Year 1660* (London, 1736)

Thompson, A. Hamilton, *The English Clergy and Their Organization in the Later Middle Ages* (Oxford, 1947)

Thompson, B., '*Habendum et tenendum*: Lay and Ecclesiastical Attitudes to the Property of the Church', in *Religious Belief and Ecclesiastical Careers in Late Medieval England*, ed. C. Harper Bill (Woodbridge, 1991), pp. 197–238

Thompson, E. Margaret, 'The Petition of 1307 Against Papal Collectors', *English Historical Review* 35 (1920), pp. 419–20

Tierney, Brian, *Origins of Papal Infallibility – 1150–1350: A Study on the Concepts of Infalliblity, Sovereignty, and Tradition in the Middle Ages* (Leiden, 1972)

Timbal, P. C., 'La vie juridique des personnes morales ecclésiastiques en France aux XIIIe et XIVe siècles', in *Etudes d'histoire du droit canonique dédiées à Gabriel Le Bras*, 2 vols. (Paris, 1965), vol. II, pp. 1425–45

Tout, T. F., *The History of England from the Accession of Henry III to the Death of Edward III (1216–1317)* (1905; repr. New York, 1969)

Bibliography

The Place of the Reign of Edward II in English History, ed. Hilda Johnstone, 2nd edn (Westport, 1976)

Trabut-Cussac, Jean-Paul, 'L'occupation française (1294–1303)', in *Bordeaux sous les rois d'Angleterre*, pp. 197–212

L'administration anglaise en Gascogne sous Henri III et Edouard I de 1254 à 1307 (Paris, 1972)

Trenchs Odena, José, 'Las tasas apostólicas y el "gratis" papal en la primera mitad del siglo XIV', *Anuario de estudios medievales* 7 (1970–1), pp. 313–35

'*De Alexandrinis*: El comercio prohibido con los musulmanes y el papado de Aviñón durante la primera mitad del siglo XIV', *Anuario de estudios medievales* 10 (1980), pp. 237–320

Trinci, Annalaura, 'Perfezione spirituale e fedeltà alla regola: Monachesimo celestiniano e francescanesimo spirituale', in *S. Pietro del Morrone*, pp. 239–55

Trueman, John H., 'The Statute of York and the Ordinances of 1311', *Medievalia et Humanistica* 10 (1956), pp. 64–81

Tuck, Anthony, *Crown and Nobility, 1272–1461: Political Conflict in Late Medieval England*, 2nd edn (Oxford, 1986)

Tyerman, J. C., 'Marino Sanudo Torsello and the Lost Crusade: Lobbying in the Fourteenth Century', *TRHS*, 5th ser., 32 (1982), pp. 57–73

Ullmann, Walter, *Medieval Papalism: The Political Theories of the Medieval Canonists* (London, 1949)

'The Curial Exequies for Edward I and Edward III', *Journal of Ecclesiastical History* 6 (1955), pp. 26–36

Principles of Government and Politics in the Middle Ages, 2nd edn (London, 1966)

The Growth of Papal Government in the Middle Ages (London, 1970)

A Short History of the Papacy in the Middle Ages (London, 1972)

Vaini, Mario, *Dal comune alla signoria: Mantova dal 1200 al 1328* (Milan, 1986)

Vale, Malcolm G. A., 'The Gascon Nobility and Crisis of Loyalty (1294–1337)', in *La 'France anglaise' au moyen âge*, pp. 207–16

'The Anglo-French Wars, 1294–1340: Allies and Alliances', in *Guerre et société en France, en Angleterre, et en Bourgogne, XIVe–XVe siècle* (Lille, 1991), pp. 15–35

Valois, Noël, 'Jacques de Thérines, cistercien', *Histoire littéraire de la France* 34 (1914), pp. 179–219

'Jean de Pouilli, théologien', *Histoire littéraire de la France* 34 (1914), pp. 220–81

Van Werveke, H., 'Les charges financières issues du traité d'Athis (1305)', *Revue du Nord* 32 (1950), pp. 81–93

Vasina, Augusto, 'Il papato avignonese e il governo dello Stato della Chiesa', in *Aux origines de l'état moderne*, pp. 135–50

Vauchez, André, *La sainteté en Occident aux derniers siècles du moyen âge d'après les procès de canonisation et les documents hagiographiques* (Paris and Rome, 1981)

Vercauteren, F., 'Henri de Jodoigne, légiste, clerc, et conseiller des princes (d. 1352)', *Bulletin de l'Institut historique belge de Rome* 27 (1952), pp. 451–505

Villers, Robert, 'Réflexions sur les premiers Etats Généraux de France au début du XIVe siècle', *Parliaments, Estates, and Representation* 4 (1984), pp. 93–7

Viollet, Paul, 'Guillaume Durant, le jeune, évêque de Mende', *Histoire littéraire de la France* 35 (1921), pp. 1–139

Volpato, A., 'Gli spirituali e l'*intentio* di S. Francesco', *Rivista di storia della Chiesa in Italia* 33 (1979), pp. 118–53

Volpi, G., *Movimenti religiosi e sette ereticali nella società medievale italiana secoli XI–XIV* (Florence, 1926)

Waley, Daniel, *Mediaeval Orvieto: The Political History of an Italian City State, 1157–1334* (Cambridge, 1952)

'An Account Book of the Patrimony of St Peter in Tuscany, 1304–1306', *Journal of Ecclesiastical History* 6 (1955), pp. 18–25

The Papal State in the Thirteenth Century (London, 1961)

'Opinions of the Avignon Papacy: A Historiographical Sketch', in *Storiografia e storia: Studi in onore di Eugenio Dupré-Theseider* (Rome, 1974), pp. 175–88

'Lo Stato Papale dal periodo feudale a Martino V', in *Comuni e signorie nell' Italia nord-orientale e centrale*, in *Storia d'Italia*, ed. G. Galasso, vol. VII (Turin, 1987), pp. 231–320

Wattenbach, W., 'Fausse correspondence du sultan avec Clément V', *Archives de l'Orient latin* 2 (1884), pp. 299–303

Wei, Ian P., 'The Self-Image of the Masters of Theology at the University of Paris in the Late Thirteenth and Early Fourteenth Century', *Journal of Ecclesiastical History* 46 (1995), pp. 398–431

Weiss, Robert, 'England and the Decree of the Council of Vienne on the Teaching of Greek, Arabic, Hebrew, and Syriac', *Bibliothèque d'humanisme et renaissance* 14 (1952), pp. 1–9

Wenck, Karl, *Clemens V und Heinrich VII: Die Anfänge des französischen Papsttums* (Halle, 1882)

'Aus den Tagen der Zusammenkunft Papst Klemens V und König Philipps des Schönen zu Lyon: November 1305 bis Januar 1306', *Zeitschrift für Kirchengeschichte* 27 (1906), pp. 189–203

Wetzel, Lilian, *Le concile de Vienne, 1311–1312, et l'abolition de l'Ordre du Temple* (Paris, 1993)

Wieruszowski, Helene, *Vom Imperium zum nationalen Königtum: Vergleichende Studien über die publizistischen Kämpfe Kaiser Friedrichs II und König Philipps des Schönen mit der Kurie* (Munich, 1933)

Wilkinson, Bertie, *Studies in the Constitutional History of Thirteenth and Fourteenth Centuries* (Manchester, 1937)

The Constitutional History of England, 1216–1399, With Select Documents, 3 vols. (Toronto, 1948–58)

The Later Middle Ages in England, 1216–1485 (London, 1969)

Wilks, Michael, *The Problem of Sovereignty in the Later Middle Ages: The Papal Monarchy with Augustinus Triumphus and the Publicists* (Cambridge, 1963)

Willemsen, C. A., *Kardinal Napoleon Orsini (1263–1342)* (Berlin, 1927)

Williman, Daniel, *Bibliothèques ecclésiastiques au temps de la papauté d'Avignon*, Centre National de la Recherche Scientifique 43 (Paris, 1980)

'Summary Justice in the Avignonese Camera', in *Proceedings of the Sixth International Congress of Medieval Canon Law*, ed. Stephan Kuttner and Kenneth Pennington (Vatican, 1985), pp. 437–49

Wood, Charles T., 'Regnum Francie: A Problem in Capetian Administrative Usage', *Traditio* 23 (1967), pp. 117–47

'Personality, Politics, and Constitutional Progress: The Lessons of Edward II', *Studia Gratiana* 15 (1972), pp. 519–36

'Celestine V, Boniface VIII, and the Authority of Parliament', *Journal of Medieval History* 8 (1982), pp. 45–62

Bibliography

Wright, J. R., 'The Supposed Illiteracy of Archbishop Walter Reynolds', *Studies in Church History* 5 (1969), pp. 58–68

The Church and the English Crown, 1305–1334: A Study Based on the Register of Archbishop Walter Reynolds (Toronto, 1980)

Yunck, John A., 'Economic Conservatism, Papal Finance, and the Medieval Satires on Rome', *Medieval Studies* 23 (1961), pp. 334–51

Yver, G., *Le commerce et les marchands dans l'Italie méridionale au XIIIe et au XIVe siècles* (Paris, 1903)

Zutshi, Patrick N. R., 'Proctors Acting for English Petitioners in the Chancery of the Avignon Popes (1305–1378)', *Journal of Ecclesiastical History* 35 (1984), pp. 15–29

'Some Early Letters of Pope Clement V (1305–1314) in the Public Record Office', *Archiv für Diplomatik* 33 (1987), pp. 323–35

'The Letters of the Avignon Popes (1305–1378): A Source for the Study of Anglo-Papal Relations and of English Ecclesiastical History', in *England and Her Neighbours*, pp. 259–75

'The Political and Administrative Correspondence of the Avignon Popes, 1305–1378: A Contribution to Papal Diplomacy', in *Aux origines de l'état moderne*, pp. 371–84

INDEX

Ad nostrum, 293
Ad nostrum qui, 300–1
Ad omnium fere, 225, 233
Ad providam, 239
Adam de Orleton, 263 n. 85
advocatus ecclesiae, 1, 61, 81, 91, 99, 195
advowson, 76–7 n. 252, 79
Aegidius Romanus, *see* Gilles Colonna
Agostino Trionfo (Triumphus), 28, 88 n. 305, 169–70, 180, 220
Aimery of Cyprus, 102–3, 234
Aimery of Tyre, *see* Aimery of Cyprus
Alain de Lamballe, 194
Albert I of Habsburg, 105, 152–3, 212
Albert of Milan, 215 n. 213
Aldevrandino d'Este, 142–3
Alexander III, 192
Alexander III, king of Scotland, 269
Alfonso XI, 124
Alvarez Pelayo, 29, 185 n. 58
Amadeus de Savoy, 162, 181
Amaneus de Lebreto, 250
Amanieu d'Albret, 139, 260, 263 n. 85
Amanieu de Fargues, 49
Anagni, 14–15, 18, 36, 86, 180, 193–7, 279
Ancona, March of, 132, 134, 139, 148, 293
André Frédol, 50
Andronicus II, 109, 119–21, 124, 152
annates, 54, 71, 74, 76–7, 92, 113, 156
Anthony Pessagno, 256
antichrist, 15, 47, 197
anti-papalists, 3
Antonio da Padova, 200
Antony Bek, 55–6 n. 140, 233 n. 313, 250
Arbroath, Declaration of, 269
Arezzo, 141
Armenia, 101–5, 108, 110, 118, 120, 127, 307
Arnaud Bernard de Pressac, 148
Arnaud d'Aux, 45, 63, 78–9, 80, 189, 240, 260, 263–5

Arnaud de Canteloup, 41, 48, 68, 237
Arnaud de Falguières, 44, 158, 167, 216–17
Arnaud de Pellegrue, 40–1, 144–7, 158, 186, 188 n. 71, 237
Arnaud de St Astier, 143–5
Arnaud de Toulouse, 294
Arnaud de Villanova, 121 n. 114, 192, 294
Arnaud Garsie de Got, 12, 40 n. 27, 49, 148, 255
Arnaud-Guillaume de Marsan, 264 n. 91
Arnaud Nouvel, 44, 63, 78–9, 237, 240, 263–5
Arnaud of Albano, *see* Arnaud d'Aux
Arnaud of St Prisca, *see* Arnaud Nouvel
Articuli super cartas, 251, 253, 262
assembly, 5, 39, 92–3, 175, 282
Athens, Duchy of, 111–12, 124
Athis-sur-Orge, Treaty of, 181–5, 187, 190
Attendentes quod, 297
auditor, 93
Avignon, 23, 26, 29, 31 n. 127, 45 n. 66, 63 n. 175, 117–19, 137, 149, 154, 161, 187, 192, 195, 263
  period, 2–3, 30, 62, 87, 138, 149, 153, 179, 279
Avignon, University of, 26, 289
Aymer de Valence, 258 n. 56, 260–1, 264 n. 93
Azzo VIII d'Este, 142–3 n. 57

Babylonian captivity, 2, 13, 26, 35 n. 2, 205, 278, 307
Bajamonte Tiepolo, 131
Bannockburn, Battle of, 55–6 n. 140, 273, 275
Bardi, 53
Bartholomew of Ferentino, 70, 249–50 n. 13
Baudry Biseth, 194
Beghards, 287, 300–1
Beguines, 287, 300–1
Benedict V, 192
Benedict XI, 9, 13, 23, 70, 75 n. 247, 91–2, 133, 196, 291

Benedictines, 41 n. 31, 45 n. 63, 55 n. 132, 200–1, 297
benefices, ecclesiastical, 38, 67–9, 78–9, 81–2, 84, 90, 298
Benevento, 148
  Battle of (1266), 129, 155
Béraud de Got, 6, 8
Bérenger de Landorra, 295, 300
Bérenger Frédol (the elder), 41–2, 47 n. 79, 50, 150, 194, 218, 237, 303
Bérenger Frédol (the younger), 45, 50
Bernard de Clairvaux, 243
Bernard de Coucy, 139
Bernard de Fargues, 48, 89
Bernard de Garves, 44
Bernard de Montepulciano, 172
Bernard Délicieux, 45 n. 68
Bernard Ferrant, 248
Bernard Saisset, 60, 86, 291
Bertinoro, 156
Bertrand Caillan, 260–2
Bertrand de Bordes, 44, 54, 185 n. 56, 255
Bertrand de Cassano, 234 n. 322
Bertrand de Got (Clement's uncle), 6, 49
Bertrand de Got (Clement's nephew), 115–16, 148, 259, 280 n. 8
Bertrand de Sauviac, 49, 148, 255
Blanche of Artois, 84
Blasius da Priverno, 194
blockades, 106–7, 110, 122, 127, 212
Bologna, 130, 133–4, 140–1, 143, 145–6, 150, 155–6, 161, 164, 166
Bologna, University of, 7, 31, 289, 299
Bonagrazia da Bergamo, 294
Bonaventure, 295 n. 109
Boniface VIII, 8–10, 13 n. 39, 14, 19, 23, 26, 36, 43, 70 n. 220, 74, 77, 86–7, 89, 91, 97, 99, 122 n. 116, 130, 135, 180, 223, 250, 267, 271–2, 286–7, 289, 291, 294, 306
  trial of, 188, 191–9, 226, 244
Boniface de Saluciis, 260 n. 68
Bordeaux, 9–11, 52, 58, 86 n. 298, 88–9, 109, 145, 247, 278
bourgeoisie, 1, 175, 184, 187, 222–3
Brescia, 163
Briand de Lagnieu, 281
bribery, 65, 149, 198
Bruges, 181–4, 187
  Matins of, 180–1, 187
bulls, 5, 74

Caetani, 130, 132, 138
Calatrava, Order of, 125, 238
Caltabellota, Treaty of, 121 n. 114
Cambridge, University of, 64

camera, papal, 39, 41, 53–4, 71–2, 104, 107–8, 112, 133, 190, 256
Campagna-Marittima, 132
canon law, 7, 13, 26, 45, 55 n. 136, 83, 86, 142, 188, 192, 239, 279 n. 3, 289–90
canonisation, 63 n. 173, 70 n. 219, 199–204, 277, 280
Canterbury, Council of, 232–4
Carlisle, Parliament of, 75–7, 79, 98, 250 n. 18, 267, 271
Carobert, 125–6, 282
Castello, 156
Catalan Grand Company, 112, 121, 124
Catalonia, 106, 118–20
Catherine of Courtenay, 119
Cedit quidem, 304
Celestine III, 272
Celestine V, 8, 23, 47, 200–1
census, 54, 71, 77, 155
Cerchi family, 53
chamberlain, 41, 54, 75, 185
chancellor, 42 n. 39, 45 n. 66, 55 n. 133, 65 n. 192, 69, 83
chancery, 5, 41, 53, 55 n. 133, 196 n. 113
Charlemagne, 176
Charles I of Anjou, king of Sicily, 129, 155
Charles II, king of Naples, 14, 19, 26, 104, 122, 139, 178 n. 23, 282
Charles IV, 116
Charles de Valois, 17, 85, 119–21, 152, 154, 159, 178 n. 23, 192 n. 89, 284 n. 36
Charles Martel, 175
Charles of Anjou, *see* Charles II
Clement IV, 22 n. 89, 37
Clementinae, 279, 288–306
Clericis laicos, 58, 97, 113, 179
collectors, 70, 75, 96
College of Cardinals, *see* Sacred College
Colonna family, 13 n. 39, 18–19, 43, 89, 130, 132, 137–8, 141, 165–7, 177, 191, 200, 203
  see also individual family members
Comtat-Venaissin, 25, 27, 30, 134, 136–7, 266
conclave, 15, 18, 280
confessors, 42 n. 38, 42 n. 40
Confirmatio cartarum, 251–4, 278
Conrad da Spoleto, 194
Considerantes dudum, 239
consistory, 65 n. 191, 154, 187, 194, 203, 207, 281
Constance, Peace of, 160
Conventuals, 294–5, 305
conversion, 114
Corsica, 111, 122
council, 36, 92, 195, 239, 287
  see also Lateran; Lyons; Rome; Vienne

Courtrai, Battle of, 180

Cremona, 162–3

crusade, 17, 36, 39, 42, 51, 58, 71–2, 91, 93, 97, 101–10, 140–1, 144, 156, 186, 188–91, 196, 208, 220, 249, 269, 274, 307–8
 at the Council of Vienne, 112–16, 283, 285
 of the Poor, 117–19

Cum de quibusdam, 300–1

Cum sit naturae consonum, 293

Cupientes eos, 292

curator, 226

Cyprus, 101–5, 108, 110–11, 114, 118, 127, 307

Dante Alighieri, 20, 25 n. 96, 45–6, 116, 136, 141, 158–9, 169, 171–2, 198, 204, 243

David Murray, 270

Denis of Portugal, 282

Dieudonné, 230

Dignum prorsus, 298

Diocesanis locorum, 298

Dispendiosam prorogationem litium, 298

Disputatio inter clericum et militem, 286

Dolcino, 301

Domenico d'Anguillara, 135–6

Dominicans, 226, 250, 292, 303

Donation of Constantine, 151, 168

Dublin, University of, 31

Dudum a Bonifacio, 289, 291

ecclesiastical courts, 11, 79

Edward I, 17, 32, 42 n. 40, 49, 105, 137, 151 n. 106, 257–8, 275–8, 307
 intervention in the Church of England, 55 nn. 134–5, 55 nn. 137–8, 56–60, 70–2, 98–9
 policy in Scotland, 269–73
 relations with Clement, 7–8, 247–54

Edward II, 42 n. 38, 49, 115, 127, 275–8, 280 n. 8, 282, 307
 Gaveston affair, 256–66
 intervention in the Church of England, 55 nn. 133–8, 55 n. 140, 60–9, 72–80, 98–9
 marriage to Isabella, 78, 101, 179, 258, 267–8
 policy in Scotland, 273–5
 policy in the trial of the Templars, 212, 229–34
 relations with Clement, 255–6

Edward III, 264 n. 93, 268

encyclicals, 17, 101, 154, 157, 281, 300

Enguerrand de Marigny, 83, 86, 177, 183 n. 41, 188–90, 199, 228, 237, 265 n. 102

envoys, papal, 5, 78, 130, 134, 138–9, 148–50, 159, 234, 260, 281 n. 21

Esquieu de Floyran, 212

Estates, 5

Etienne de Suisy, 42, 194, 218

Ex frequentibus prelatorum, 289

Ex gravi ad nos, 303

Exchequer, 62, 70 n. 220

excommunication, 10, 74, 79–80, 93, 106–7, 109, 111, 119–20, 123, 132, 139, 143, 172, 181–4, 186–8, 191, 193, 250–2, 258–62, 270–1, 275–7, 286, 290, 292, 296 n. 114

exempt Order, 234, 286, 304

Exivi de paradiso, 295–6

Ferdinand IV, 121–4, 282

Ferdinand Velasquez, 194

Ferrara, 130, 142–50, 155

Fidei Catholicae fundamenta, 295–6

Flanders, 19, 93, 97, 176, 272, 307
 conflict with Philip the Fair, 180–91

Florence, 129–30, 136–7, 139–41, 144–6, 157
 conflict with Henry VII, 160–1, 164–6, 171–2

Folco d'Este, 142

Forcius d'Aux, 255

Forest Charter, 252–4

Francesco Caetani, 13, 15, 68, 194

Françesco d'Este, 142–3, 147

Francis of Moliano, 215

Franciscans, 126, 200–1, 226, 292, 293–6

Frederick I Barbarossa, 155 n. 125

Frederick II Hohenstaufen, 144, 161, 168

Frederick III of Trinacria, 36 n. 7, 112, 121 n. 114, 122, 124, 165, 282, 294

Free Spirit, 287, 294, 300, 302

Frequens et assidua, 292

Fresco d'Este, 142–3, 147

Friars, 33, 234 n. 326, 292–3

Fulk of Villaret, 102–3, 105, 108–10

G. Pellicioni, 295

Gailhard de Faugères, 139

Gallicanisation, 27, 43, 99

Galvano da Levanto, 176, 191 n. 83

Gaucher II, duke of Athens, 112

Gauthier de Bourges, 11, 45, 261

Gautier de Liancourt, 216

Geffroy de Plessis, 14, 96

Gelasius I, 154

Gelasius II, 192

Genoa, 103, 106–7, 109–11, 116, 128, 164–5, 171

Gentile da Montefiore, 125

Gentile Orsini, 165

Geoffroi de Charney, 216, 239–40

Geoffroi de Gonneville, 239–40

Geranselmus Joannis, 295

Gérard Albuini, 126

Gérard de Bologna, 294
Gérard de Gauche, 216
Gérard de Moor, 181
Gérard de Pecorara, 75 n. 247
Gérard de Sotteghem, 181
Ghazan, 102
Ghibellines, 3, 129–32, 134, 139, 140–2, 144,
    146, 150, 155, 157 n. 132, 160–73
Giacomo Caetani Stefaneschi, 194, 203, 248,
    279 n. 3, 283 n. 33, 288 n. 57
Giacomo da Modena, 194
Giacomo da Sermoneta, 194
Giacomo da Viterbo, 185–6 n. 58
Gilbert Segrave, 66
Gilles Aycelin, 51, 181, 183, 227, 285 n. 43
Gilles Colonna, 10–11, 88, 90, 183, 185 n. 58,
    261, 285–6, 292 n. 90, 295, 303
Gilles de Rome, *see* Gilles Colonna
Giovanni Colonna, 43
Giovanni da Ignano, 135
Giovanni da Montecorvino, 126
Gonzalve de Valbonne, 294
Gozio da Rimini, 194
Grandmont, Order of, 297
gravamina, see grievances
Gravi nimirum turbatione, 297
Gregorian Reform, 46, 99
Gregory VII, 2, 142, 192
Gregory IX, 23, 142 n. 57
Gregory X, 23, 150, 201
grievances, 78, 92, 285, 291
Guelphs, 3, 129–32, 134, 139–42, 144, 146–50,
    155 n. 126, 157–8, 160–3, 171, 173
    league, 136, 164–9, 199
Guglielmo da S. Marcello, 138
Gui Dauphin, 216
Gui de St Pol, 193, 284 n. 36
Guiard de Cressonessart, 302
Guichard of Troyes, 60, 83–7, 199, 272, 290
Guido della Torre, 162
Guidoctus de Tabiatis, 295
Guilhem Ruffat, 41
Guillaume Bonnet, 81, 227
Guillaume de Bordes, 255
Guillaume de Bruniquel, 147
Guillaume de Mandagout, 44, 289, 295
Guillaume de Nogaret, 14–15, 114, 177, 185,
    191, 193–9, 206, 211 n. 194, 214, 217 n.
    224, 237
Guillaume de Paris, 217, 225
Guillaume de Peyre de Godin, 45, 185 n. 56,
    294
Guillaume de Plaisians, 177, 183, 186, 193–7,
    211 n. 194, 214, 222–4, 237, 282 n. 28
Guillaume de Trie, 84
Guillaume de Villanova, 126

Guillaume Durant, 4, 50, 113, 115 n. 81, 134,
    139, 227, 284, 287, 295, 298–9
Guillaume Frédol, 50
Guillaume Géraud de Sore, 75
Guillaume le Maire, 35, 114, 210, 236, 237 n.
    338, 284, 299
Guillaume Seguin de Got, 7–8
Guillaume Testa, 45, 75, 78, 256, 267 n. 109,
    277
Guitto Farnese, 138
Gundisalvo of Toledo, 123

Hagenau, 156
hearth-tax, 133
Henry II of Lusignan, 102–3, 114, 234, 282
Henry III, 252 n. 28, 253, 276
Henry VII of Luxemburg, 17, 111, 113, 130,
    132, 151 n. 103, 153, 281 n. 14, 282
    election of, 154–9
    imperial coronation of, 166–70
    journey to Italy of, 136, 160–5
Henry de Lacy, 249–50 n. 13
Henry of Woodlock, 55, 81 n. 270, 254 n. 35
Henry Percy, 261
heresy, 36, 142, 192–5, 199, 208–15, 218–29,
    232–4, 241 n. 361, 242, 245, 301–2
Hetoum II, 102
Honorius III, 187, 272
Hospital (Order of St John), 102–3, 105–10,
    112, 116, 118, 123, 127, 207, 239–45, 307
hospitality, 16, 293
Hugh Gerald, 260
Hugh le Despenser, 249–50 n. 13, 261, 264 n.
    93
Hugues de Bonnevaux, 200 n. 134
Hugues de Pairaud, 208, 239–40
Hundred Years War, 266, 268, 307
Hungary, 36 n. 7, 307

Imbert Blanke, 232
immunity, ecclesiastical, 60, 207, 209, 211, 213,
    219, 223, 286, 290–1
inalienability, 252 n. 28
indulgence, 52, 76, 87, 108–10, 120, 122 n.
    121, 126, 233
Innocent III, 61, 106, 165, 185–6, 272
Inquisition, 192, 207, 215, 218–19, 225–6,
    230–5, 281 n. 15, 283, 302–3
Inter sollicitudines, 299
interdict, 67, 130, 132, 141, 145 n. 66, 150, 163
    n. 166, 181–4, 187, 190, 196, 261, 286,
    290, 292
Isabella of France, 56, 78, 179, 255, 258, 267–8

Jacopo Colonna, 31 n. 126
Jacques Arlotti, 138

Jacques de Molai, 102, 105 n. 25, 114, 215–18, 227, 239, 240, 245
Jacques de Thérines, 89, 236, 286 n. 49, 292, 295
Jacques Duèse, 27, 45, 189 n. 75, 195 n. 108, 203, 236, 280, 284–5
  see also John XXII
James I of Aragon, 122
James II of Aragon, 25, 97, 105, 111, 121–4, 127, 145 n. 66, 192, 198 n. 126, 206, 212, 218, 282
James II of Majorca, 122, 282
Jean II of Brittany, 17
Jean II of Vienne, 282
Jean de Calais, 85
Jean de Cuyk, 181
Jean de Dreux, 181, 193
Jean de Gravina, 165
Jean de Jandun, 176
Jean de Marigny, 83
Jean de Picquigny, 303
Jean de Pouilly, 295
Jean de Schoorisse, 181
Jean le Moine, 29
Jeanne de Navarre, 84–5
Jesselin de Cassagnes, 29
Joachim of Fiore, 294
Johannes Andreae, 5, 289, 301
Johannes Quidort von Paris, 287 n. 53, 303
John I of Bohemia, 282
John X, 192
John XXII, 31 n. 127, 54, 64 n. 181, 68 n. 206, 70 n. 219, 86, 125, 171, 179, 276–7, 279, 287, 289–90, 296
John Balliol, 274
John Dalderby, 70
John de Benstede, 249–50 n. 13
John de Sandale, 273
John Lackland, 61, 186, 253
John of Droxford, 55–6, 81 n. 270, 264
John of Havering, 16, 67, 248
John of Würzburg, 214 n. 210
John Pecham, 64, 276–7
John Salmon, 81 n. 270

Kharbanda, 102

Landolfo Brancaccio, 218
Lateran, Church of, 30, 136 n. 24
  Third Council of, 106, 293, 303
  Fourth Council of, 106
Lausanne, 156
legates, 5, 31, 74, 78, 104, 110, 123, 139–46, 149, 158, 164, 166–7, 189, 252 n. 28, 263
Leo IV, king of Cilician Armenia, 102
Lewes, Battle of, 276

libertas ecclesiae, 81, 99, 291
Lincoln, Parliament of, 271
Lisbon, Council of, 234
Lodi, 162 n. 165, 163
London, Council of, 80, 230, 234
London–Westminster, synod of, 293
Louis IX, *see* St Louis
Louis X, 85, 96, 116, 237, 282, 284 n. 36
Louis de Nevers, 188–9
Louis de Villard, 89
Louis d'Evreux, 17, 181, 193, 264–5
Louis of Navarre, *see* Louis X
Louis of Savoy, 135–6, 155, 165–6
Luca Fieschi, 167
Lucca, 139–41, 145–6, 161, 166
Lyons, 16–17, 21, 51, 89, 151, 164 n. 177, 177–8, 208, 249, 252, 280
  Assembly of, 237
  Second Council of, 38, 280 n. 5, 281 n. 17, 301, 303

Magna Carta, 251–3
Majorca, 122 n. 116
Manfred Hohenstaufen, 129, 155
Mantua, 142–3 n. 57, 146
Margaret, queen of England, 67, 71, 251, 258
Margaret of Norway, 269
Margareta Porette, 301–2
Mario Querini, 131
Martin IV, 8, 22 n. 89, 23, 276
Matteo Rosso Orsini, 13–14
Matthew Paris, 4, 77 n. 255, 98, 235 n. 327, 266
Meruit, 179
Michael Palaeologus, 109, 119
Michel du Bec, 45
Milan, 146, 160, 162–3, 200
mission, 126–7, 299–300
Modena, 150
Mongols, 126–7
Mons-en-Pévèle, Battle of, 180
Montesa, Order of, 125
Montpellier, University of, 31
Montreuil, Treaty of, 267
Mouchet, *see* Musciatto Franzesi
Multorum ad nos, 290
Multorum querela, 301
Musciatto Franzesi, 14

Napoleone Orsini, 14–16, 18, 25, 140–1, 146, 149, 284
Ne in agro dominico, 297, 299
Ne Romani, 280
nepotism, 21, 25, 30, 35, 46, 49–51, 83, 89, 138, 140, 149, 223, 306–7
Niccolò Alberti da Prato, 19, 154, 167

Index

Nicholas III, 23, 155, 245, 295 n. 111
Nicholas IV, 23, 51, 106
Nicholas of Thebes, 103
Nicolas da Veroli, 194
Nicolas de Fréauville, 42, 83, 115, 189, 237, 240, 284
Nicolas de Lusarches, 81–2
Nicolas Delpierre, 187
Noffo Dei, 85
Nolentes, 301
Northampton, Parliament of, 275
nuncios, 5, 63, 68, 79, 80, 115, 143–4, 189, 255, 260, 265–7, 271, 277

Olivier de Penne, 239
Onofrio de Trevi, 143
Ordinances, 251 n. 23, 261 n. 77, 262–5
Orléans, University of, 7, 31, 41 n. 36, 44 n. 56
Orsini family, 137–8
  see also individual family members
Orvieto, 130, 133, 138–9, 156, 160
Oshin, king of Cilician Armenia, 102–4
Otto de Grandson, 70, 82, 111, 250, 259, 260 n. 68, 263 n. 85, 282 n. 28
Ottobono Razzi, 235
Oxford, Provisions of, 253
  synod of, 293
Oxford, University of, 42 n. 40, 55 n. 135, 55 n. 138, 61 n. 163, 64, 65 n. 192, 70 n. 219, 250, 276, 299–300

Padua, 145–6, 161, 171
papalists, 3
Paris, Assembly of, 11–12
Paris, University of, 10, 42, 45 n. 67, 64, 65 n. 192, 195, 216, 219–20, 234 n. 326, 242, 276, 289, 299–300
parliament, 39, 56, 63 n. 173, 99, 251, 255, 265–6, 274, 278, 282
  see also specific parliaments by name
Parma, 163, 165, 171
Pastoralis cura, 170, 289
Pastoralis praeeminentiae, 209, 216–17
Patrimony of St Peter in Tuscany, 130, 132–3, 136, 139, 156
patronage, 61, 69
Pelfort de Rabastens, 134, 139
penitentiary, 29, 41, 53, 138
Peregrino da Castello, 126
Perugia, 13–14, 137, 156, 160, 164, 166
Perugia, University of, 31
Peter, cardinal-bishop of Sabina, 78, 260, 267, 271
Peter Hispanus (or the Spaniard), *see* Peter, cardinal-bishop of Sabina

Peter of Savoy, 61
Peter's pence, 76
Petrarch, 2
Philip II, August, 186
Philip III, 150, 151 n. 103
Philip IV, the Fair, 43, 46, 49, 107–8, 113–15, 119–21, 130, 145–6, 151–4, 155 n. 126, 160 n. 151, 164 n. 177, 174–8, 204–5, 258, 260, 266–9, 275, 277, 280–2, 284 n. 36, 285 n. 45, 286, 303, 307–8
  conflict with Boniface VIII, 36, 191–9, 226, 244, 286
  meeting with the pope at Poitiers, 26, 178–80, 208, 222–5, 227 n. 273, 235
  monetary policy, 53
  participation in the crusade, 104–6, 110, 127, 274
  policy in Flanders, 180–91
  policy in the Church of France, 60, 67, 81–99
  relations with Bertrand de Got, 11–12, 19
  and trial of the Templars, 205–29, 237–8, 240–6
Philip V, 116
Philip VI, of Valois, 190
Philip Martel, 249–50 n. 13
Philip of Taranto, 178 n. 23
Philippe de Marigny, 83–4, 228
Piero Colonna, 43, 192 n. 85
Pierre de Belleperche, 81, 92, 282 n. 24
Pierre de Bologna, 227
Pierre de Broc, 194
Pierre de Galart, 194
Pierre de Grès, 83, 85, 96
Pierre de la Chapelle, 41, 43 n. 43, 226, 281, 303
Pierre de Laon, 84
Pierre de Latilly, 185
Pierre de Mirepoix, 84 n. 288
Pierre de Mornay, 181
Pierre de Pleine Chassagne, 104, 110
Pierre Dubois, 29–30, 46–7, 150–2, 169, 176, 211 n. 194, 223, 299
Pierre Jame, 298
Pierre Jean Olieu, 45 n. 68, 294–6
Pierre of Rodez, *see* Pierre de Pleine Chassagne
Piers Gaveston, 60, 72, 80–1, 255–65
Pietro da Genazzano, 196
Pietro da Morrone, 199–204, 280
  see also Celestine V
Pietro Martyr, 200
pilgrimages, 28, 52, 108, 136, 181, 187, 196
Pisa, 171
Pistoia, 139–40, 146

349

plena potestas, 37
Poitiers, 26 n. 99, 45 n. 65, 109, 126, 179, 185,
    207–8, 222–5, 227, 248, 281
Poncello Orsini, 165
prebend, 69, 74
proctors, 63 n. 175, 177 n. 14, 182, 187, 221,
    237, 261–2, 281
procuration, 64 n. 185, 90
propaganda, 1, 84, 87, 110, 118, 175, 214–16,
    219, 222, 225, 228, 235, 242–4, 270
protégés, 40, 81–2, 89 n. 314, 90, 99, 175, 278
provision, papal, 36–8, 54 n. 131, 61–2, 64 n.
    185, 66–9, 75, 89, 99, 207, 254, 287, 291,
    306

Quia contingit interdum, 300
Quia regulares, 298
Quoniam, 297
Quoniam ex constitutione, 289
Quum Iudaei, 304

Raimbaud de Caron, 239
Raimond d'Aspello, 145
Raimond de Got, 40–1, 69 n. 213, 145, 152,
    188
Raimond de Lescar, 267 n. 109
Raimond de Piis, 103–4
Raimond de Saint-Séver, 45
Raimond-Guilhem de Budos, 49, 148
Raimond-Guilhem de Fargues, 44
Ralph Baldock, 70
Ramon Lull, 114, 176, 299
Raoul Grosparmi, 83, 85
Rationes Baronum, 263 n. 89
Raymond Athon d'Aspet, 148, 150
Raymond Concoreggi, 295
Raymond de Fronsac, 294
Raymond Despont, 295
Reconquista, 121–3
rectors, 133, 145, 148, 150, 155, 158, 162
Red Comyn, 270–1
regalia, 69
Regalis devotionis integritas, 252, 266
Reggio, 150, 163, 165
Reginald de Roy, 206
Regnans in caelis, 281
Reims, Council of, 242
Religiosi quicunque, 292
Renaud de Provins, 227
reservation, 37, 61–4, 68, 82, 89, 287
Rex gloriae virtutum, 175, 196–7, 266
Rhodes, 109–11, 116, 127–8, 244, 307
Riccardi family, 53
Richard de Kellaw, 55–6
Richard Petroni da Siena, 203
Richard Swinfield, 58

Rimini, 146
Rinalda da Supino, 191 n. 84, 196
Robert Bruce VIII, 72, 254, 269–75
Robert d'Auberives, 148
Robert de Béthune, 181–9
Robert de Bourgogne, 181
Robert de Brus, *see* Robert Bruce
Robert de Newenton, 263
Robert de Pykering, 249–50 n. 13
Robert Fitz Payn, 260 n. 68
Robert Grosseteste, 277 n. 170
Robert Kilwardby, 64
Robert of Anjou, *see* Robert of Naples
Robert of Naples, 121, 122, 130, 136, 139,
    147, 153, 155, 161, 163 n. 169, 164–71
Robert the Competitor, 270, 274
Robert Winchelsey, 56, 58–60, 63–7, 72, 80–1,
    98, 231–2, 234, 257–63, 276
Robert Wishart, 259, 270–3, 291
Roger de Flor, 124
Roger la Warre, 249 n. 13
Romagna, 130, 132, 134, 141, 145, 148, 150,
    155–6, 171
Roman law, 7, 13, 41 n. 36, 44 n. 54, 45, 55 n.
    136, 83, 195
Romani principes, 170, 289
Rome, 23–5, 27–30, 89, 130, 134–8, 140–1,
    153, 156–8, 160, 165–8, 200–1, 254, 276
    Council of, 12

Sacred College, 8, 13, 16, 40, 43–51, 75, 83,
    178, 194, 280
Saepe contingit, 280, 298
Salamanca, Council of, 234
Salamanca, University of, 299
Sanche Grasie de Manas, 148
Sardinia, 111, 122
Sciarra Colonna, 165, 196
Scone Abbey, 270–1
Scotland, 73, 75, 78, 255–6
    conflict with England, 269–75
Sens, Council of, 242
Sextus, 42 n. 37, 196, 289
Si quis suadente diabolo, 290
Sicard de Vauro, 230
Sicilian Vespers, 12, 129, 147
Sicily, 36 n. 7, 121 n. 114, 122 n. 116, 165
Siena, 145, 161, 166
signoria, 134–5, 155, 160, 162
Simon de Montfort, 276
simony, 21, 43, 46, 65, 97, 198, 209, 250 n. 18
Spini family, 53
Spirituals, 14, 293–6, 305
Spoleto, Duchy of, 132–3, 148
St Bertrand de Comminges, 8–9, 30, 52, 75
St Jean d'Angély, 19, 43, 154, 179

Index

St John, Order of, *see* Hospital
St Louis, 93, 151, 176–7, 200, 210, 221
St Thomas of Canterbury, 276
Stamford, Parliament of, 79–80, 98, 262
Stefano Colonna, 138
Sutri, 135–6

tallia militum, 133
Tarragona, Council of, 234
taxation, 40, 70–81, 89–100, 134, 251 n. 23, 287, 306
Templars, 41–2 n. 36, 42 n. 37, 42 n. 39, 44 n. 52, 44 n. 54, 51, 69, 70 n. 219, 86, 93, 101–2, 105, 112, 127
  at the Council of Vienne, 235–46, 281, 283
  trial of, 199, 205–35, 297 n. 129, 302
  wealth of, 114, 124–5, 238–40
tenth, 39, 53–4, 71–2, 91–3, 99, 106, 112–13, 116, 120, 122–3, 125, 127, 156, 285–6, 292
Tertiaries, 292
Teutonic Knights, 107, 127, 215, 238, 244–5
Theobald d'Anagni, 194
Thomas Cobham, 63–4
Thomas de Cantilupe, 61–2 n. 168
  canonisation of, 275–7, 280
Thomas de Morrovalle, 194
Thomas de Ste Cecilia, 201
Thomas Jorz, 42, 51 n. 104, 250
Thomas of Lancaster, 265
torture, 227, 231, 235, 302
Toulouse, University of, 31, 44 n. 54, 289 n. 67
Tours, Assembly of, 221–2
Tuscany, League of, 160

Ubertino da Casale, 294–6
Uclés, Order of, 238
Ulrich vom Seyfriestorf, 126
Unam sanctam, 179
university, 47, 65, 288, 299
  see also individual universities
Urban II, 22 n. 89
Urban IV, 22 n. 89, 201
Urban V, 51 n. 104
Urban VI, 100
Uros II, Milutin, 126–7
usury, 288, 303–4
Ut professores, 292

vacancy, 62 n. 169, 69, 75
Venice, 106–7, 111, 118, 120, 124, 128, 131, 160, 212
  war in Ferrara, 132, 142–7, 147–8 n. 84, 150, 186
Verona, 142–3 n. 57, 146
Vicenza, 145
Vidal de Villanova, 32
Vidal du Four, 45
Vienne, Council of, 72, 78, 93, 147, 154, 195, 200, 202, 224, 226 n. 271, 232–3, 263, 269, 277
  Church reform, 284–8
  crusade, 112–16, 281, 299
  legislation, 288–305
  summons and organisation, 281–4
  Templars, 235–42, 283
Visconti family, 146, 162 n. 165
visitation, 90, 250 n. 18
Viterbo, 133, 136
Vox in excelso, 238, 284 n. 35

Waldenses, 294
Walter Hubert, 293
Walter Jorz, 56
Walter Langton, 60, 70, 80–1, 249–50 n. 13, 259, 290
Walter of Cantilupe, 276
Walter Reynolds, 55, 60–6, 81 n. 270, 264 n. 93
Walter Stapeldon, 67
Wenceslas II, 125
Wenceslas III, 125
Westminster, Parliament of, 258, 261
William de Bevercotes, 273
William de Grafton, 230
William de la More, 230, 232
William de Lughtebergh, 263
William Greenfield, 55, 233 n. 313, 267, 272–3
William Lamberton, 259, 270–3, 290
William of Dieu, 230
William of Geinsborough, 61, 249–50 n. 13, 271
William of Tyre, 214 n. 210
William Wallace, 269 n. 121
wills, 51, 76, 142, 285

York, Council of, 232–3

Cambridge Studies in Medieval Life and Thought
Fourth series

Titles in series

1 The Beaumont Twins: The Roots and Branches of Power in the Twelfth Century
   D. B. CROUCH

2 The Thought of Gregory the Great★
   G. R. EVANS

3 The Government of England Under Henry I★
   JUDITH A. GREEN

4 Charity and Community in Medieval Cambridge
   MIRI RUBIN

5 Autonomy and Community: The Royal Manor of Havering, 1200–1500
   MARJORIE KENISTON MCINTOSH

6 The Political Thought of Baldus de Ubaldis
   JOSEPH CANNING

7 Land and Power in Late Medieval Ferrara: The Rule of the Este, 1350–1450
   TREVOR DEAN

8 William of Tyre: Historian of the Latin East★
   PETER W. EDBURY AND JOHN GORDON ROWE

9 The Royal Saints of Anglo-Saxon England: A Study of West Saxon and East Anglian Cults
   SUSAN J. RIDYARD

10 John of Wales: A Study of the Works and Ideas of a Thirteenth-Century Friar
   JENNY SWANSON

11 Richard III: A Study of Service★
   ROSEMARY HORROX

12 A Marginal Economy? East Anglian Breckland in the Later Middle Ages
   MARK BAILEY

13 Clement VI: The Pontificate and Ideas of an Avignon Pope
   DIANA WOOD

14 Hagiography and the Cult of Saints: The Diocese of Orléans, 800–1200
   THOMAS HEAD

15 Kings and Lords in Conquest England
   ROBIN FLEMING

16 Council and Hierarchy: The Political Thought of William Durant the Younger
   CONSTANTIN FASOLT

17 Warfare in the Latin East, 1192–1291★
   CHRISTOPHER MARSHALL

18 Province and Empire: Brittany and the Carolingians
   JULIA M. H. SMITH

19 A Gentry Community: Leicestershire in the Fifteenth Century, *c.* 1422–*c.* 1485
   ERIC ACHESON

20 Baptism and Change in the Early Middle Ages, *c.* 200–1150
   PETER CRAMER
21 Itinerant Kingship and Royal Monasteries in Early Medieval Germany, *c.* 936–1075
   JOHN W. BERNHARDT
22 Caesarius of Arles: The Making of a Christian Community in Late Antique Gaul
   WILLIAM E. KLINGSHIRN
23 Bishop and Chapter in Twelfth-Century England: A Study of the *Mensa Episcopalis*
   EVERETT U. CROSBY
24 Trade and Traders in Muslim Spain: The Commercial Realignment of the Iberian
   Peninsula, 900–1500*
   OLIVIA REMIE CONSTABLE
25 Lithuania Ascending: A Pagan Empire Within East-Central Europe, 1295–1345
   S. C. ROWELL
26 Barcelona and Its Rulers, 1100–1291
   STEPHEN P. BENSCH
27 Conquest, Anarchy and Lordship: Yorkshire, 1066–1154
   PAUL DALTON
28 Preaching the Crusades: Mendicant Friars and the Cross in the Thirteenth Century*
   CHRISTOPH T. MAIER
29 Family Power in Southern Italy: The Duchy of Gaeta and Its Neighbours, 850–1139
   PATRICIA SKINNER
30 The Papacy, Scotland and Northern England, 1342–1378
   A. D. M. BARRELL
31 Peter des Roches: An Alien in English Politics, 1205–1238
   NICHOLAS VINCENT
32 Runaway Religious in Medieval England, *c.* 1240–1540
   F. DONALD LOGAN
33 People and Identity in Ostrogothic Italy, 489–554
   PATRICK AMORY
34 The Aristocracy in Twelfth-Century León and Castile
   SIMON BARTON
35 Economy and Nature in the Fourteenth Century: Money, Market Exchange and the
   Emergence of Scientific Thought
   JOEL KAYE
36 Clement V
   SOPHIA MENACHE

* Title available in paperback